THE FIRST JESUITS

The
First Jesuits

John W. O'Malley

Harvard University Press
Cambridge, Massachusetts
London, England

Library of Congress Cataloging-in-Publication Data
O'Malley, John W.
    The first Jesuits / John W. O'Malley.
        p.   cm.
    Includes bibliographical references and index.
    ISBN 0-674-30312-1 (cloth)
    ISBN 0-674-30313-X (pbk.)
    1. Jesuits—History—16th century.   I. Title.
    BX3706.2.O43   1993
    271'.53'009031—dc20
    92-39813
        CIP

Fratribus carissimis in Societate Jesu

Acknowledgments

LIKE SO MANY projects, this book seemed relatively easy to write and quick to complete when I first conceived it. The process proved long and arduous and made me contract debts of gratitude that I can never adequately repay. I must at least list the debts, not as if they were weights upon my conscience but to acknowledge what I really take them to be—signs of friendship and of commitment to our common enterprise of trying to understand the past.

The American Council of Learned Societies granted me a research fellowship for 1988–89 that allowed me to do the basic research and begin to sketch the first draft, and shortly thereafter the Jesuit Conference provided funds for a research assistant. The administration of the Weston School of Theology meantime devised strategems to lighten my teaching and other responsibilities, for which I am especially grateful to the then president, Edward M. O'Flaherty.

Almost every part of the book deals with highly technical matters, and I would like to thank colleagues who read sections or chapters where their specialized knowledge saved me from egregious mistakes—Wietse de Boer, Paul Grendler, Margaret Guider, James Keenan, and Thomas Tentler. I of course appreciate the generosity (and admire the constancy) of those who, at one stage or another, read the whole manuscript and still had energy left to offer me their comments and suggestions—Brian Daley, Howard Gray, John Padberg, Philip Rule, and Thomas Worcester. The extensive and sometimes detailed comments from William Bouwsma, Mark Edwards, George Ganss, and John Headley were particularly helpful. Michael Buckley read the manuscript with extraordinary care and—with equally extraordinary generosity—shared with me his insights into the Jesuit materials, correcting and enriching my treatment of them. I can hardly convey how much help Benjamin Westervelt, my research assistant at Weston, has been to me. He performed with finesse the usual bibliographical runs and similar tasks, but, much more important, he engaged me in conversation over some three years, leading me to reshape questions and ways to answer them, inducing me to clarify my thought and interpretation.

Elizabeth Antébi, Andreas Falkner, and Thomas Lucas helped me choose and locate the illustrations. Andrew Cameron-Mowatt undertook for me some complicated maneuvers on word processing equipment. I am grateful to my Portuguese friends—Nuno Tovar de Lemos and Herminio Rico—for help with the language and with obtaining materials. James Dunkly, head of the library at the Weston School of Theology, went out of his way to make my way as easy as possible, as did members of his staff. Hopkins's untitled poem from which I have quoted at the beginning of the book can be found in *Gerard Manley Hopkins,* ed. Catherine Phillips (Oxford and New York: Oxford University Press, 1986), p. 129.

While I held the Gasson Professorship at Boston College, I received many kindnesses from James Cronin, chair of the History Department, and from Lois Dunn Bilsky, secretary to the department, that helped me in the last stages of preparation of copy. I especially want to thank Mary Frances Smith, my research assistant at Boston College, who has been unfailingly generous and perceptive in proofreading, in helping to construct the index, and in all those other tasks that a book like this requires as it is about to see the light of day. At Harvard University Press I am grateful to Lindsay Waters and Christine Thorsteinsson.

John W. O'Malley, S.J.
Weston School of Theology
Cambridge, Massachusetts

Contents

Illustrations

~ THE FIRST JESUITS

As kingfishers catch fire, dragonflies draw flame;
  As tumbled over rim in roundy wells
  Stones ring; like each tucked string tells, each hung bell's
Bow swung finds tongue to fling out broad its name;
Each mortal thing does one thing and the same:
  Deals out that being indoors each one dwells;
  Selves—goes itself; *myself* it speaks and spells,
Crying *What I do is me: for that I came.*

Gerard Manley Hopkins

Introduction

"SEVEN SPANISH DEVILS" entered Italy after the year 1530. Thus wrote the English historian and litterateur John Addington Symonds in *The Catholic Reaction*, published a little over a century ago. Among Symonds's devils was "Jesuistry, with its sham learning, shameless lying, and casuistical economy of sins."[1] That particular devil in fact arrived in Italy at Venice in 1535 in the person of Ignatius of Loyola. Ignatius was soon joined by nine other men, not all of them Spaniards, who had known each other at the University of Paris and banded together to become the nucleus of the future Society of Jesus.

In 1622, less than a century after the arrival of the group in Italy, Pope Gregory XV canonized two of them—Ignatius and Francis Xavier—and thereby held them up for emulation as models of piety and probity. By simple association the remaining eight somewhat shared the same glory, and one of them, Pierre Favre, was in fact declared a "blessed" by Pope Pius IX in 1872. Also canonized as saints from the first generation of Jesuits were Francisco de Borja (or Borgia, 1671) and Peter Canisius (1925).

Reviled as devils, revered as saints—the Jesuits have evoked these extremes of characterization throughout the 450 years the Society of Jesus has existed. In the course of the centuries more balanced appreciations of the Society have sometimes appeared, but always conditioned by the national, cultural, and religious assumptions of those evaluating it. The story of the Jesuits is, of course, inseparable from the so-called Counter Reformation, and the Jesuits have often been regarded as emblematic of all that was bad or all that was good in that phenomenon.

The past several decades have seen a renewed interest in sixteenth-century Catholicism, inspired in part by the massive scholarship of Hubert Jedin and his disciples on all aspects of the Council of Trent and in part by the quite different approach of practitioners from the *Annales* school of the Ecole Pratique des Hautes Etudes. Grounded in better methods of research and less animated by unexamined prejudices than previous scholars, these and other historians are gradually helping us see with new eyes the complexity of the Catholic situation in that religiously troubled era. Accompanying the mass of new information presented in these studies have been reinterpretations of old information and even complete turnarounds in evaluating it.[2] Our understanding of the Reformation has likewise changed, as scholarship has moved from major figures such as Luther and Calvin to the impact they and their movements had as they were interpreted and put into action at the grass roots.[3]

Where do the Jesuits fit into this new configuration? We still await an adequate answer. Most popular writing on the Society of Jesus, whether favorable or unfavorable, has been woefully inadequate. Scholarly articles and monographs of reliable quality appear each year, although perhaps not in the quantity one might expect.[4] Until relatively recently practically all the scholarship came from Jesuits. Generally characterized by technical accuracy, it tended to take up familiar and even familial issues and was relatively unaffected by the new historiography. Even today this scholarship is not always free of hagiographical vestiges, especially when dealing with Ignatius, for whom we still await a biography that satisfies sophisticated canons of scholarship.[5]

There are many exceptions to these generalizations, as for instance Mario Scaduto's two-volume study of the Jesuits in Italy during the generalate of Diego Laínez, early companion of Ignatius and his successor as head of the Society.[6] The standards of scholarship in the *Archivum Historicum Societatis Iesu*, the journal of the Jesuits' Historical Institute in Rome, are high, as are those of the monographs published by the same Institute. No book exists in any language, however, that treats the ministries and culture of the first Jesuits in the comprehensive way that I attempt here.

The difficulties of such an undertaking daunt all but the most foolhardy. The amount of documentation is overwhelming. By 1565 the Society numbered about thirty-five hundred members, who were exhorted or obliged to maintain regular correspondence with each other and especially with the Jesuit leadership in Rome. A large number of these letters have survived and been edited in the more than 125 volumes of the *Monumenta Historica Societatis Iesu* and elsewhere. The letters of Saint Ignatius alone fill 12 volumes in the *Monumenta,* constituting the largest correspondence extant of any sixteenth-century figure, none excepted.[7] To all this correspondence must be added the numerous other documents, official and unofficial, that the early Jesuits produced to use as instruments of ministry, to guide them in their way, and to explain to friends and enemies what they were about. The responses of both friends and enemies are many, scattered in various sources.

A second difficulty comes from the great range of activities in which the early Jesuits engaged. They dealt with kings and paupers, with the devout and with public sinners, with popes and prelates, with lowly pastors and with convents of nuns. They excluded no category of the laity from their ministry. By 1565 they were active in many countries of Western Europe, but also in Brazil, India, Japan, and elsewhere. They preached, taught catechism, proposed new sacramental practices, and sought to help orphans, prostitutes, and prisoners in jail. They developed patterns of piety that were peculiarly their own, no matter how traditional the elements upon which they drew. They appropriated both scholastic and humanistic learning and tried to relate these two cultures to one another. They wrote plays and were present at the Council of Trent. They engaged in polemics with Protestants and, to their dismay, found themselves caught in controversies among Catholics. They supported various Inquisitions, yet sometimes found themselves the object of inquisitorial scrutiny and censures. They taught in universities. Within seven or eight years of their papal approval, they founded and operated schools.

Every one of the areas of activity treated in this book has led me into technical and often controversial areas of scholarship. Moreover, the way the Jesuits engaged in even the same activities differed from place to place— Brazil was not Germany, Italy was not France. In such a predicament both author and reader must be guided by clear aims and have secure points of reference.

My first aim in this book is to understand the early Jesuits as they understood themselves. This is pursued by studying what they said about themselves to each other and to outsiders and especially by looking at how they translated that understanding into action in their many ministries and in the style of life they adopted. Exposition of the consistencies and inconsistencies in that translation fall under the same aim.

I also try to discover the origins of the Jesuits' self-understanding and to take account of the contexts into which they inserted themselves that furthered their process of self-definition. That is my second aim. The Jesuits did not think, feel, or act in a vacuum or in the timeless arena of eternal verities. In a panoramic study like this one, it is impossible to develop these points with the amplitude they deserve. Once a reliable overview is achieved, however, such development can be left to other scholars.

By taking account of so many contexts, the book accomplishes a task that falls outside my formally stated aims. It acts as a series of windows through which we catch glimpses of almost every conceivable aspect of Roman Catholicism in the mid-sixteenth century. These glances are perforce fleeting and originate from a special perspective, but they are richly instructive.

This book spans the first quarter century of the existence of the Society of Jesus, officially founded in 1540 with Pope Paul III's bull *Regimini militantis ecclesiae.* The terminal date of 1565 is somewhat arbitrary. It carries us to the death of Diego Laínez, the second superior general and the only one of Ignatius's companions from the early days to hold that office. It also takes us beyond the end of the Council of Trent in 1563, as well as beyond the death of Calvin in 1564. Concluding with the death of Ignatius in 1556 would have been easier, but the longer viewpoint makes clearer the directions the Society was taking. Although the Society would face many challenges after 1565 and undergo further changes, some of them significant, its design had by that time been set and the most fundamental elements of its "way of proceeding" established.

Among the basic points of reference to hold us on course are, as might be expected, five documents that came exclusively or in large measure from Ignatius. The importance traditionally ascribed to the *Spiritual Exercises,* which he began to compose at Manresa shortly after his conversion in 1521 and which were published in their practically final form in Rome in 1548, emerges from the following pages fully vindicated. The *Exercises* will be discussed at some length under two different aspects in chapters 1 and 3.

That document encapsulated the essence of Ignatius's own spiritual turnaround and presented it in a form meant to guide others to analogous changes of vision and motivation. Ignatius used the *Exercises* as the primary means of motivating his first disciples and prescribed it as an experience for all who later entered the Society. Although at no point intended exclusively for Jesuits, the *Exercises* remained the document that told Jesuits on the most profound level what they were and what they were supposed to be. Furthermore, the *Exercises* set the pattern and goals of all the ministries in which the Society engaged, even though it was not always explicitly recognized as doing so. There is no understanding the Jesuits without reference to that book.

The second document is much less well known and, hence, requires more description. It is generally referred to as the *Formula of the Institute* and was the result of deliberations in Rome in 1539 by the original companions and a few others. The object of the deliberations was to construct for papal approval the basic elements of the new association they by then hoped to found. At this stage the *Formula* consisted of "Five Chapters" *(Quinque Capitula),* each of which was not much more than a paragraph long. After some changes, the chapters were incorporated into *Regimini militantis ecclesiae* of the next year. They were meant to be and have remained the fundamental charter of the order, of which all subsequent official documents were elaborations and to which they had to conform. The *Formula* is to the Jesuits what the Rule is to other religious orders.[8] It was composed by a committee, but Ignatius's role in its articulation was of course pivotal.

In the light of experience, the *Formula* was somewhat revised in 1550 and incorporated into a second bull, *Exposcit debitum,* which was issued by Pope Julius III and served to confirm the Society. Further changes were considered after the death of Ignatius, but none were ever made.[9] Most variations in the second version were clarifications or specifications of the earlier one, or they took account of changes in actual practice introduced since 1540. For instance, the *Formula* of 1540 indicated the purpose of the Society as "the propagation of the faith and the progress of souls in Christian life and doctrine." In the version of 1550, the first phrase was significantly expanded to read "the defense and propagation of the faith."

With some discrepancy in wording, both versions listed the ministries by which this purpose was to be accomplished. The latter version was more complete:

> public preaching, lectures, and any other ministrations whatsoever of the Word of God, and further by means of the *Spiritual Exercises,* the education of children and unlettered persons in Christianity, and the spiritual consolation of Christ's faithful through hearing confessions and administering the other sacraments. Moreover, the Society should show itself no less useful in reconciling the estranged, in holily assisting and serving those who are found in prisons and hospitals, and indeed in performing any other works of charity, according to what will seem expedient for the glory of God and the common good.[10]

Unexceptional though this list might seem upon first reading, it gave the first generation of Jesuits a sense that in their ministries they were different from diocesan priests and from members of religious orders already in existence. They often referred to this list—to these "customary ministries" *(con-*

sueta ministeria) of the Society—and commented upon it. The list provides the outline for the first part of this book. We need to note that schools were not mentioned in either version. Besides the ministries, the *Formula* also listed the categories of persons to whom the ministries were to be addressed: "the Turks or any other infidels, even those who live in the region called the Indies, or . . . any heretics whatever, or schismatics, or any of the faithful."[11]

Moreover, the *Formula* established that, unlike other religious orders, the Society did not oblige its members to recite or chant in common the liturgical Hours such as matins, lauds, or vespers. Circumstances often forced the early Jesuits to defend this feature of their life, and they did so vigorously, for they saw it as emblematic of what was distinctive in them and their ministry. Related to this provision was another stipulating that they were to pronounce a special vow to God that would bind them to be on journey anywhere in the world to do ministry, when so ordered by the pope. They believed that these two provisions in their charter helped distinguish them from their predecessors in the mendicant orders of the Middle Ages, which they otherwise so closely resembled. Like them the Jesuits were to pronounce, for instance, the usual three vows of poverty, chastity, and obedience, but with special provisions concerning particularly how poverty was to be observed.

The Society was to have no obligatory penances or fasts, and in regard to food, clothing, and similar matters the members were to conform to the style of reputable priests in the regions where they found themselves. The Society could admit novices and provide for the training of its younger members. The second version of the *Formula* provided for graduated degrees of final membership in the Society by allowing the admission of "coadjutors," either priests or laymen who would not attain to the full incorporation reserved for the solemnly professed members. Both versions provided that, with the consultation of his confreres, the superior to be elected by the members would have the authority to construct constitutions that would make specific these more general provisions of the *Formula*.

The third document is the Jesuit *Constitutions*. Within about six months after the ratification of the original *Formula* by its substantial incorporation into *Regimini militantis ecclesiae*, Ignatius was elected superior, with none dissenting but himself. Among his many tasks few were more important than the construction of the constitutions that the papal bull enjoined. Despite the importance of this work, Ignatius did not set about it in a systematic way until about 1547, after he had secured the capable assistance of Juan Alfonso de Polanco as his secretary.

Polanco's role was crucial. Although the traditional interpretation that Ignatius himself was the principal inspiration behind the *Constitutions* and related documents still stands, much of the wording and arrangement and many of the details must be attributed to the secretary. In the long process of composition, Polanco made suggestions, raised questions, undertook research to help answer them, and drafted responses.[12] Everything was submitted to Ignatius for approval and revision, but, as in any case of such close collaboration, the problem of authorship cannot be solved by facilely attributing the contents to Ignatius and the form to Polanco. Polanco was also almost single-handedly responsible for the official Latin translation from the Spanish autograph.

A preliminary version was ready for promulgation by 1552, an office Ignatius entrusted to another highly capable assistant, a Majorcan named Jerónimo Nadal. Ignatius continued to modify the *Constitutions* until he died. The First General Congregation of the Society, convened to elect his successor, approved the text after minor changes and committed it to print in its Latin version for the first time in 1558–59. Its style and organization unmistakably distinguished it from earlier documents of the same genre, both religious and secular.

The *Constitutions* articulated the broad principles according to which the Society was to achieve its goals and reduced the generalities of the *Formula* to concrete structures and procedures. They did this first and foremost, however, by focusing on the quality of person essential for the successful functioning of such a voluntary association. They move, therefore, in a loosely chronological fashion, following the Jesuit from the moment he applied to be a member of the Society, through his training, up to the ministries in which he would engage, and they conclude with considerations concerning the qualities of the superior general and of the body of the Society as a whole. They are thus structured to a large extent on developmental principles—on the idea that the Jesuit would grow spiritually and that different provisions would therefore be appropriate at different times and stages.

Following this basic design, the *Constitutions* are divided into ten parts. In their structure and language, as well as in some of the basic insights that underlie them, one can detect the influence of both the scholastic and humanistic cultures that from the beginning helped form the outlook of these first Jesuits. More basic, however, would be the religious and pastoral experiences that the Jesuits themselves had undergone and that they postulated for every member of the order.

The term *Constitutions* refers first and foremost to this body of legislation and ideals, but is generally extended to include the *General Examen,* a conspectus composed by Ignatius, probably about 1546, to give somebody contemplating entrance into the Society essential information about the organization he was considering joining.[13]

The Jesuits sometimes spoke of their "Institute," by which they meant the way they lived and worked, and they thus included in the term all the official documents of the order, but especially the *Formula* and the *Constitutions.* Their favorite, most inclusive, and pregnant expression for their style of life and ministry, however, was "our way of proceeding" (*noster modus procedendi, nuestro modo de proceder*). According to Nadal, the expression originated with Ignatius.[14] While it of course indicated official documentation, it transcended it by suggesting more spontaneous and actualized ideals and attitudes that distinguished Jesuit life and ministry from that of others.

Another document from Ignatius particularly relevant to those ideals and attitudes is his *Autobiography,* dictated in three relatively short periods of time to Luís Gonçalves da Câmara in Rome in 1553 and 1555.[15] In it Ignatius succinctly narrated the story of his life up to 1538, the eve of the decision of the companions to bind themselves together in a permanent association. Polanco and Nadal importuned the narration from him as a kind of "testament" that would show his followers how and to what God had called him. It remains our most reliable source for the essential facts of the early life of Ignatius, sometimes called "the pilgrim years" because he consistently referred to himself in the *Autobiography* as "the pilgrim."

The *Autobiography* abounds, nonetheless, with critical problems. The text as we have it begins abruptly in 1521 at the great turning point in Ignatius's life, when he was wounded in the battle of Pamplona, which led to the long convalescence that was the beginning of his religious conversion. We know, however, that Ignatius began his story with his earliest years, when he was given over to "the vanities of the world," yet no trace has ever been found of that part, probably because da Câmara never communicated it.[16] Ignatius's account of his many mystical experiences raises problems of interpretation particular to such phenomena.

Moreover, as Ignatius narrated in Spanish to his Portuguese confidant, da Câmara listened attentively, but only afterward in his room did he jot down some notes about what he had heard. Sometime later he elaborated upon them and in turn dictated them to a Spanish scribe, who recorded his words verbatim. That was the procedure for the narration done in the first two periods. We know that for the third period a month elapsed between the narration and the time da Câmara found to dictate his notes, in this case to an Italian scribe. In the original document, therefore, the first two parts of the text are in Spanish, the last in Italian. Even granted that da Câmara had the superb memory with which his contemporaries credited him, the text we possess had filtered through several minds and languages before it reached the written page.

Other critical problems are endemic to any such personal memoir. Autobiography, especially such a brief one as this, includes and excludes according to motivations of which even the author is often unaware. Retrospective distortion is inevitable. The genre is at its best when the author's candor breaks through some of its conventions. Unlike Luther, to whom he is often considered the Catholic counterpart, Ignatius had few gifts in this regard; the person behind the stylized narrative is never fully revealed.

Nonetheless, the *Autobiography* is important because Nadal had clearly in mind that through it Ignatius would provide an incarnation of the meaning of the Society that could be held up for emulation and appropriation. Nadal in fact later utilized Ignatius's story in this way. "Our way of proceeding" could be no better exemplified. But Nadal also attributed a quasi-mystical force to what he called "the grace of the founder."[17] For our purposes, therefore, the *Autobiography* assumes an importance beyond simply supplying information about Ignatius's physical and spiritual journeys during his "pilgrim years."

The final Ignatian document of major importance is, of course, the correspondence.[18] It contains theory and ideals but interprets them against daily reality. Of the almost 7000 letters that survive, all but about 175 date from after Polanco's appointment as secretary, and a large number were explicitly written by him "on commission" from Ignatius. Much of the correspondence has, therefore, the same problems of attribution as the *Constitutions*.

Certainly important for the aims of this book are the writings of the nine companions who bonded together at Paris, principally under Ignatius's inspiration, between 1528 and 1536—Xavier, Laínez, Favre, Alfonso Salmerón, Simão Rodrigues, Nicolás Bobadilla, Claude Jay, Paschase Broët, and Jean Codure. Xavier of course went to India in 1540, spent two years in Japan, and died on the outskirts of Imperial China in 1552. He was the only one of the original band to leave Europe and thus provides a special perspective. Among the remaining eight, Laínez was the most accomplished and, ultimately, the most influential because of his election to the generalship in 1558. Besides their correspondence published in the *Monumenta*, these men produced a number of other texts that have come down to us.[19]

The same is true of others who joined after 1540, such as Peter Canisius, "the apostle of Germany,"[20] and Francisco de Borja, the duke of Gandía and great-grandson of Pope Alexander VI.[21] Borja succeeded Laínez as general in 1565. The writings of less well known figures, such as Gaspar de Loarte, Cristóforo de Madrid, and Diego de Ledesma, provide further data. For our purposes, however, two among these latter recruits—Polanco and Nadal— eclipse by far all others. They understood and presented themselves as mere transmitters and promulgators of "our way of proceeding." But, given the important offices Polanco and Nadal held and the way they fulfilled them, none of their counterparts had a wider, more immediate, or more profound impact on their generation of Jesuits and on the future. Along with Ignatius, therefore, they are the major figures guiding this book.

Polanco was born of a rich and influential family in Burgos in 1516.[22] Some of his forebears were probably "New Christians," that is, Jews converted to Catholicism, but this has never been proved. At age thirteen Juan began to study the humanities and philosophy at the University of Paris, where his uncle would later be rector. He remained at Paris for eight years. By 1541 he was employed as a *scriptor apostolicus* in the papal curia in Rome. That year he made the *Spiritual Exercises* under the guidance of Laínez and entered the Society. Ignatius sent him almost immediately to study theology for four years at the University of Padua. Soon thereafter he summoned him to Rome as secretary to the general of the order, a post Polanco held until a few years before his death in 1576. Far more than an amanuensis, he was a trusted consultant and guide not only to Ignatius but also to the other generals—Laínez and Borja—whom he served from 1547 until 1572.

Besides his role in writing the *Constitutions* and much of the generals' correspondence, Polanco drafted and composed many other official or semi-official documents on a wide variety of topics, including education.[23] In 1553–54, in consultation with other Jesuits, he compiled and published at Ignatius's behest a short work on confessors and penitents, one of the first books in print by a Jesuit.[24] In 1575 he published for the use of Jesuits a short treatise on ministry to the dying.[25]

As secretary of the Society he soon began the practice of writing a circular letter to all the members several times a year, in which he summarized the more important activities of Jesuits around the world as these were reported in the huge correspondence received from them in Rome. Although meant to edify, Polanco's circular letters are filled with concrete details about what the Jesuits were doing, how they were received, how they dealt with problems they faced. More important, they powerfully conveyed to all who read or heard them—and we must assume that was most members of the Society—what it meant to be a Jesuit and how "our way of proceeding" was put into practice around the globe. The impact had to be great.

By far the longest work to come from Polanco and the one most extensively utilized in this book follows the same plan as the circular letter—his *Chronicon Societatis Jesu,* dictated to one or more scribes at the end of his life, 1573–74.[26] Filling six huge volumes of the *Monumenta,* the work is what the title indicates, a detailed chronicle of the activities of members of the Society, house by house, province by province, country by country, year by year, from 1537 until the death of Ignatius in 1556. It was undertaken at the request of Everard Mercurian, the new general elected in 1572, to guide him in his governance. In the chronicle Polanco told, when he could, the number of Jesuits in any given house, their successes and failures in their ministries, and their relationships with high and low in society. He seasoned his account with anecdotes that reveal much about the mentality of both author and audience and that give life to the flat format of the chronicle.

The *Chronicon* destroys the stereotype of a religious order under strict military discipline, with each member a pawn acting only under orders from his superior. It replaces this image with a picture of a vast network of enterprising individuals who, while keeping in close communication with those in authority and receiving guidance and "consolation" from them, adapted to local needs and tried to seize opportunities as they presented themselves. The *Chronicon* provides the data from this period for answering the question about the degree to which the Jesuits had a clearly formulated strategy for their ministry in any given area.

Polanco ransacked the archives of the incoming correspondence for his information, which he knew better than anyone else. The *Chronicon* contains the imperfections of all such documents. Moreover, it favors victories over defeats. It often fails to deliver behind-the-scenes information that we would love to know. For such information, when it survives, we must have recourse to the correspondence itself and other documentation. Nonetheless, Polanco is a sober, frank, and even-handed reporter, never suppressing bad news simply because it is bad.

Whereas Polanco practically never left Rome after he became secretary, Jerónimo Nadal's life as a Jesuit was marked by long and frequent journeys throughout Europe on official business of the order.[27] During his travels he almost single-handedly negotiated the financial foundations for twenty Jesuit schools. In the intervals between his great trips, he held important offices in Rome.

The frequency and character of Nadal's travels meant that practically all the Jesuits in Europe met him and heard him speak, and many would have spent an hour or so with him privately at least once in their lives. Nadal thus knew and influenced more members of the Society more immediately than even Ignatius—and for a longer period of time. He continued to be engaged in these journeys under the next two generals until 1572, eight years before his death in 1580. More than any other individual, he instilled in the first two generations their *esprit de corps* and taught them what it meant to be a Jesuit.

Born of a prosperous family at Palma de Majorca in 1507, Nadal studied for about five years at the University of Alcalá. He then went to Paris, where at the university he knew Ignatius and his companions, but rejected their invitations to join them. In 1538 at Avignon he was ordained a priest and received a doctorate in theology from the university. Some years later in his native Majorca, after an intense spiritual conversion and after reading a letter then circulating of Xavier from India, he began to reconsider and traveled to Rome, principally to examine the new Society firsthand. There, in 1545, he was urged by Ignatius and others to make the *Exercises* for a month, which he did with the help of Jerónimo Doménech. In the course of this retreat Nadal was able, after much difficulty, to resolve his hesitations, and he decided to join the order. From that time onward his conviction that God had called him to the Society never seems to have wavered.

From the first Ignatius recognized his talents. Nadal just three years later was elected superior for the nine other Jesuits who founded in Messina, Sicily, what was in effect the first school of the Society of Jesus. Ignatius's confidence in Nadal continued to grow and led him in 1552 to send him back to Sicily and the next year to Spain and Portugal for the first promulgation of the *Constitutions*. On the latter occasion Polanco wrote of him: "He knows our father, Master Ignatius, well because he has had many dealings with him, and he seems to have understood his spirit and comprehended our Institute as well as anyone I know in the Society."[28] Ignatius himself at about the same time established Nadal's authority for the promulgation by writing that "he altogether knows my mind and enjoys [for this task] the same authority as myself."[29]

The journey to Spain and Portugal, emblematic of the many that followed, lasted two years. Nadal visited each community, stayed with it for weeks or longer depending on its size, delivered exhortations and commentaries on the Institute, and tried to meet privately with each Jesuit he encountered, including the novices. He then left behind recommendations and prescriptions, often in the form of "rules," about what needed to be done to adapt the Institute to local circumstances.

Besides promulgating and explaining the *Constitutions,* seeing to the establishment of schools, and tending to other important tasks, Nadal had to help restore peace and order in the wake of the first major crisis in the Society, which had just occurred in the province of Portugal. He acquitted himself well on this occasion and on similar ones thereafter, even though his dealings with Borja, Laínez, Rodrigues, and especially Bobadilla, as well as with others, sometimes ruffled their sensibilities. Nadal, with characteristic self-effacement, attributed these skirmishes to his own brusque and sometimes impetuous manner. No doubt he felt deeply and expressed himself strongly, but he was, in fact, not always the principal culprit.

In any case, he mediated the ideals of the Society to all those in Europe who had never met Ignatius, many of whom entertained confused and even erroneous ideas about the organization they had joined. Until the printing of the *Constitutions* in 1558–59, the only true Jesuit document they could easily obtain was (after 1548) the *Spiritual Exercises,* by definition an instrument directed to all serious Christians, not only to members of the Society.

Of the inner circle of first Jesuits, Nadal was the most profoundly influenced by the humanist movement, and his importance for the foundations of the Jesuit tradition of education can hardly be overestimated. Gifted with organizational abilities and with a fine eye for detail (too fine, in the opinion of some), he was also a thinker and a rhetorician, able to conceive and project a broad vision of the role and mission of the new Society. His understanding of Bonaventure, Aquinas, and other medieval thinkers enabled him to provide a more explicitly theological base for some of Ignatius's ideas.[30]

Like others among these early Jesuits, Nadal was an indefatigable writer, and he committed his ideas to paper in the form of exhortations, commentaries, instructions, meditations, dialogues, apologies, "rules," and letters, as well as in personal reflections intended only for himself. Many of these documents circulated in manuscript among his contemporaries and have been published in modern editions.[31] With only a few exceptions, they were intended for a Jesuit audience.

Modern studies vindicate for Nadal the reputation he enjoyed in his own lifetime as a faithful interpreter of Ignatius and the Institute.[32] He was, however, an interpreter. This means that there are features in his writings that we do not find elsewhere, even if they are nothing more than developments of ideas stated more succinctly in other sources. Here, as always, style and content are inextricably intertwined. Nadal's style is fuller, less reserved, and more rhetorically effective than Ignatius's. These qualities are especially verified in his exhortations. His only works with literary pretensions are the two long dialogues, or colloquies, he composed between 1562 and 1565 that purport to be a three-way conversation among a Lutheran, a disciple of the Jesuits, and another Catholic suspicious of them.[33] He was also capable of sober and technical commentary, as in his *scholia* on the *Constitutions*.[34]

UP TO THIS POINT I have tried to present my aims, describe the most important sources, and introduce the two Jesuits besides Ignatius most important for the formation of the Society of Jesus. There are, however, some other considerations that will be helpful for understanding what follows. The book falls into two somewhat overlapping parts. The first part (chapters 2 through 6) deals with the Jesuits' ministries. The second (chapters 6 through 9) deals with their culture. The Jesuits' "way of proceeding" is a theme that runs through the entire book.

I chose this topical format because, unlike narrative, it allows treatment in some depth of the technical issues with which the book often must be concerned. Throughout the book and in many particulars, however, I have attempted to indicate chronological developments, for one of my theses is that the Society in 1565 was different in important respects from what it was in 1540. This is hardly a surprising thesis, but we need to know what it meant in the concrete. The Society conformed to the inevitable laws of sociology affecting any group that grows rapidly from an informal bonding among friends to a worldwide organization numbering its members in the thousands. I take that for granted and try to illustrate, especially in the last chapter, how it happened—through deliberate choices and through influences over which nobody had much control. The Jesuits of this generation left behind the documentation to provide a superb case study of transition to institution from charismatic fellowship.

But the contexts into which the Society was born account in an intensified degree for some important changes that otherwise would surely not have occurred and that marked the Society so deeply as to become in the minds of many people almost definitions of it. With hindsight we can see that the potential for these changes was present from the beginning, but they would not have been actualized had the situation been different.

The humanist movement, for instance, had a palpable effect on the Society after it was founded. Even the members of the original band of ten had in varying degrees experienced its influence well before they entered Italy in 1537. Although they and many of their first recruits were more deeply imbued with the scholastic tradition of the Middle Ages, they had all learned how to speak and write Latin in a humanist style and were not unaffected by humanist criticism of scholastic theology and its practitioners. Deeper influences or congruences can be detected in the rhetorical or "accommodating" style that marked their ministries.

From an institutional viewpoint, however, the relatively belated decision that gained virtually irresistible momentum by about 1550 to undertake the founding and staffing of schools according to the humanist model challenged many features of an earlier vision. At the beginning the members conceived of themselves primarily as "pilgrims," as "apostles" who, like Paul, moved from place to place under the urgency of spreading the Gospel. They were primarily itinerant preachers, like Jesus and his disciples, and they were engaged in a holiness ministry.

They soon began to see the advantages of labors sustained in the same place over a longer period of time. Indeed, from the very beginning the Jesuits intended to establish some permanent residences, supported only by alms. Nonetheless, they assumed that for the most part their members would not reside for very long in what came to be called "professed houses," but would have to be ready at a moment's notice to move to other places and even to spend most of their lives in journeyings or pilgrimages of ministry, living on the voluntary offerings that might come their way. This ideal remained central in the Jesuit heritage,[35] but it now had to be reconciled with the maintenance of permanent institutions and, just as important, with the necessity of continuity in their personnel.

The schools brought about other important changes in the Society—in its relationship to culture, in a pattern of living off endowment rather than alms, and to some extent even in the classes of society to whom the Jesuits would minister. Although the Jesuits' most official documents never baldly stated it, the schools became a part of the Jesuits' self-definition. They symbolized and powerfully helped effect changes that set off from the first eight or twelve years of Jesuit history all that followed. The chapter that deals with the schools indicates, therefore, a chronological as well as cultural landmark. It belongs to the first part of the book because it deals with one of the Jesuits' ministries. It belongs to the second part, as well, because the schools so significantly influenced the Jesuits' culture.

The Jesuits were the first religious order in the Catholic Church to undertake formal education as a major ministry. They became a "teaching order." The boldness of the decision for its day is difficult for us to recapture. Its importance for the culture of early modern Catholicism was incalculable. By the time the Society was suppressed by papal edict in 1773, it was operating more than eight hundred universities, seminaries, and especially secondary schools almost around the globe. The world had never seen before nor has it seen since such an immense network of educational institutions operating on an international basis. The schools were often at the center of the culture of the towns and cities where they were located. They might produce several plays or even ballets per year, and some maintained important astronomical observatories.

At about the same time that the schools began to be founded the Jesuits became engaged more aggressively and in greater numbers with the Reformation in Germany. There is no need to insist that the Reformation influenced the image of the Society of Jesus, which in fact is often described as having been founded precisely in order to oppose Protestantism. That description of course misses the mark. In Paris the companions witnessed the incursions of "Lutheranism" into the French capital, and they had no use for what they understood to be the tenets of the new movement. Aware as they were of the Reformation, however, it played no palpable role in the future they then designed for themselves, and they make few references to it when they describe their years in Paris. When, in 1534, they took a vow to spend some time in ministry in a distant place, they set their eyes on Jerusalem, not Wittenberg.

Jerusalem dominated their imagination until the impracticability of passage forced upon them the alternative of going to Rome to find guidance from the wider vision of pastoral need that the pope presumably entertained. With that alternative came the likelihood, almost the inevitability, of enlisting in the battle against Protestantism. Favre was already in Germany in late 1540, but not because of Jesuit initiative. By 1550, however, "defense of the faith" had moved to its privileged place in the *Formula,* for the Jesuits had come to realize that the Reformation indicated for them a pastoral obligation of the highest urgency.

They in fact tended to understand the Reformation as primarily a pastoral problem. They saw its fundamental causes and cures as related not so much to doctrinal issues as to the spiritual condition of the persons concerned, and they helped perpetuate this interpretation, which correlated with their own understanding of what was most important in life. Some Jesuits began to read their own origins retrospectively as a providential response to the Reformation. As we today look back at those origins, we may be struck almost as much by the similarities between these two phenomena as by their admittedly profound differences.

In any case, although the Society of Jesus would have had a much different history, it would have come into being even if the Reformation had not happened, and it cannot be defined primarily in relationship to it. In many parts of the world, the direct impact of the Reformation on the Jesuits ranged from minimal to non-existent.

The indirect impact is another question altogether and much more complex. This brings us to the phenomenon sometimes designated the Counter Reformation or, more generally acceptable today, the Catholic Reform. Whatever term or combination of terms one adopts in this regard, one must face the thesis that measures taken to counter the Reformation effected or promoted some across-the-board changes in the "old church," operative even when and where Protestantism as such was unknown and even in institutions of long establishment.[36]

The truth of that thesis cannot, in my opinion, be denied. It of course has immense implications for the Society of Jesus, whose birth coincided with the beginnings of those changes. As we follow the evolution of the Society of Jesus during its first decades, we perforce follow the beginnings of significant shifts in religious mood and sensibilities within Catholicism. The changes in assumptions and procedures in catechesis are a case in point, as we shall see. To take a more palpable example—though the most extreme aspects of Pope Paul IV's efforts to enforce a rigid ecclesiastical discipline were repudiated soon after his death in 1559, they nonetheless signified a new alacrity in repression and confessional single-mindedness. Moreover, the implementation of the Council of Trent (1545–1563) began just as the period covered by this book comes to a close.

To apply this thesis to the Society of Jesus requires a careful examination of just how those changes operated in this particular case. Therefore, I look at how the Jesuits related to Roman Catholic institutions, including the papacy and the Council of Trent. Not all the characteristics we associate with "Tridentine Catholicism" find verification in the Society of Jesus. More specifically, despite the involvement of a few leading Jesuits in the Council of Trent and the unquestioned support of the Council by the Society, the Jesuits as a body had significantly different ways of meeting the generically common goals they shared with the Council. In other words, we must not take the decrees of Trent and their direct implementation as indicative of all that happened in Catholicism, nor, for all the impact the Council had on the Society, must we view the Jesuits primarily as agents of the agenda of the Council. They had an agenda of their own.

What was that agenda? Was it not "reform of the church"? That is, after all, the agenda commonly attributed to them in both popular and scholarly literature. One of the surprising features of early Jesuit sources, however, is how rarely that expression occurs; it is virtually never used to describe the agenda of the Society itself. It does not, in fact, capture what they thought they were about.[37]

When the simple term "reform" *(reformatio)* appears in Jesuit documentation, as it often does, it sometimes refers to the reform of specific institutions like a monastery or a convent. It more usually and characteristically refers to an individual and is the equivalent of conversion. That brings us much closer to the main item of the Jesuit agenda.

The Society was founded for "the defense and propagation of the faith" and for "the progress of souls in Christian life and doctrine." It was founded "for the greater glory of God"—*ad majorem Dei gloriam,* a phrase or idea found over a hundred times in the *Constitutions* and in time unofficially adopted by the Jesuits as their motto. They saw themselves as teachers of "Christianity" *(Christianitas* or *Christianismum),* that is, of basic beliefs and practices.

But of such expressions none occurs more frequently in Jesuit documentation—on practically every page—than "to help souls." In the *Autobiography, Constitutions,* and his correspondence, Ignatius used it again and again to describe what motivated him and was to motivate the Society. His disciples seized upon it and tirelessly repeated it as the best and most succinct description of what they were trying to do.

They helped souls through their ministries, and that is why the ministries of the Society play such a large role in this book. Their ministries and how they went about them were quintessential to the Jesuits' self-definition. This book has fewer theses that run through it more consistently. What the Jesuits did will tell us what they were.

This thesis needs to be stressed because, for the Jesuits as well as for other religious groups and institutions in the sixteenth century, scholars have directed their investigations to other issues—to politics, organization, doctrine and theology, ethics, spiritual teachings, social composition and setting. Important though these issues are, they are not ministry, the activity by which the Jesuits largely defined themselves.

"To help souls." By "soul" Jesuits meant the whole person. Thus they could help souls in a number of ways, for instance, by providing food for the body or learning for the mind. That is why their list of ministries was so long, why at first glance it seems to be without limits. No doubt, however, the Jesuits primarily wanted to help the person achieve an ever better relationship with God. They sought to be mediators of an immediate experience of God that would lead to an inner change of heart or a deepening of religious sensibilities already present. With varying degrees of clarity, that purpose shines through all they wrote and said as the ultimate goal they had in mind when they spoke of helping souls, whether through the simple *Christianitas* of their catechesis or through something more profound.

The religious and cultural framework in which the Jesuits lived meant that they believed that acceptance of the basic Christian dogmas was a necessary precondition for such an experience to be complete and fully genuine. They therefore studied that dogma and inculcated it, but not always in ways we might expect. Moreover, they hoped and intended to help others beyond an intellectual assent to orthodox truths to an acceptance of the lived reality of God's action in their lives. The necessity and desirability of this acceptance was their basic premise. Their paradigm for the turning of one's life and will over to the care of God was the conversion of Ignatius and, more closely, the change of heart that they themselves had presumably undergone through the *Spiritual Exercises.*

A sign that one was living open to God's action was "consolation," a word that appears prominently in the section of the *Formula* listing the ministries of the Society and then recurs insistently in other Jesuit documents. The Jesuits to a large extent conceived of themselves as engaging in a ministry of consolation. The word had for them a fairly precise meaning that was not the easy equivalent of feeling good. Ignatius described it several times in the *Exercises,* recognizing that it had different manifestations depending upon the spiritual state of the person experiencing it. It brought peace but might at the same time entail sorrow and grief:

> By consolation I mean what occurs when some interior motion is caused within the soul through which it comes to be inflamed with love of its Creator and Lord. As a result it can love no created thing on the face of the earth in itself, but only in the Creator of them all. Similarly, this consolation is experienced when the soul sheds tears that move it to love for its Lord—whether they are tears of grief for its own sins, or about the Passion of our Lord, or about other matters directly ordered to his service and praise. Finally, under the word consolation I include every increase in faith, hope and charity, and every interior joy that calls and attracts one to heavenly things and to the salvation of one's soul, by bringing it tranquility and peace in its Creator and Lord.[38]

Ignatius was later in life reported by Pedro de Ribadeneira as having described it in a more generic way when he said that he believed he could not live "without consolation, that is, without finding within himself something that neither was nor could be from himself but came purely from God."[39] Other Jesuits used different words to indicate and describe the same reality, often paraphrasing the *Exercises*. "Devotion" was one such synonym. But the Jesuits always meant a movement of the heart that came from God and brought one closer to God.

Some recent studies examining the religious feeling of the sixteenth century have continued to document the thesis that it was characterized by guilt and anxiety, and they have more than suggested that this state of disquiet continued and was even intensified in Catholicism as it tried to come to terms with the Reformation. Not everybody agrees with this thesis.[40] Nonetheless, scholars advancing it often attribute the guilt and anxiety directly to the practice and teaching surrounding the sacrament of Penance, a sacrament that in some ways is the centerpiece of Jesuit ministry. Hence, Jesuit insistence on the consolatory aspect of that sacrament and of the Christian life in general assumes particular significance.

The way the Jesuits approached the sacrament of Penance and their insistence on its consolatory features are symptomatic of the way they dealt with many traditional institutions. The Jesuits were, on the one hand, quite conventional, and they accepted the institutions and much of the practice surrounding them. On the other hand, they employed and interpreted them within a framework that to some extent refashioned them, even when they were not fully aware that they were doing so. Whether this refashioning was in every instance sufficient to overcome the problems inherent in the institutions that they so unquestioningly accepted is quite another matter.

They accepted, for instance, the various ecclesiastical tribunals known as Inquisitions. Mostly because of the Reformation these tribunals took on a new vigor and a new agenda by the middle of the sixteenth century and were operating in a different mode.[41] This development meant that the anxiety of which scholars speak was not confined to the private realm of one's conscience but found expression in the institutions of society at large.

In certain sectors, Catholicism in the early modern period was beset and bedeviled from within. Ugly suspicions of fellow Catholics and public vituperation and persecution of them were the order of the day. While Catholics rejoiced over the internecine feuds among Protestants, they often were guilty of the same.[42]

In other sectors a quite different reality appears. The Jesuits often touched a religious enthusiasm in those among whom they lived that was innocent of the great battles raging around them. When the Jesuits worked with confraternities, when they taught children to teach along with them in their catechesis, and when they looked for benefactors for their schools and other works, they reveal to us a prior engagement with religion by the Catholic population that was not the product of fear, hatred, or elitist campaigns.

The first Jesuits manifest their age because they were part of it. They soon came to be recognized also as among its leaders. They were, however, leaders who belonged to a voluntary association that had no direct power, ecclesiastical or civil, to coerce. They were sometimes able to force their ministrations upon the reluctant and recalcitrant by having powerful friends apply pressure. But, generally speaking, whatever authority they enjoyed derived from their own ability to persuade others and to present to their "clientele" options more attractive than the alternatives. By definition they had to rise above some of the conventions of the various situations in which they found themselves, dedicated though they were to promoting only what they believed was secure and tested by time. Especially as the years moved on, for instance, they accepted many of the accoutrements of the older religious orders, yet they, with considerable justification, thought of themselves all along as constituting a considerable change in the tradition of such orders.

From the very beginning, therefore, we note a certain cumulative character in how the Jesuits established their way of proceeding. Their vocation as itinerant preachers suffered the overlay of resident schoolmasters. Their ministry of internal consolation suffered the overlay of defense of a confessional orthodoxy. Their insistence on the direct action of God on the human person had to adjust to the concern for order and discipline that marks every institution. Their desire to do ministry without recompense soon accommodated itself to the necessity of reliable sources of income for the lasting institutions they hoped to establish. They wanted to be independent in their ministries, yet to accomplish their goals they found themselves beholden to benefactors and dependent upon the good will of prelates and lay magnates.

Their story is thus not without its ironies. We find in the origins of the Society of Jesus features that seem inconsistent or compromised. This helps account for some of the widely diverging reactions the Jesuits evoked in their earliest years and continued to evoke through subsequent centuries. What features like these really represent must be determined in each instance, but they point at least to polarities; they point also to paradoxes, some of which are almost endemic to the Christian religion.

The polarities and paradoxes as found in the story of the Society of Jesus may be simply indications of the richness of the tradition and of a vibrant and responsive organization, or in other instances expressions of a cultural and religious logic almost impossible for us to fathom, so different is it from our own. In any case, along with polarities and paradoxes existed certain assumptions about God, the world, human beings, and the interrelationship among them that were about as constant as anybody might hope to find in a sprawling and complex institution. These assumptions were the more important aspect of the Society of Jesus. They manifested themselves in a number of ways, but perhaps nowhere more clearly than in the Jesuits' ministries, in their attempts to "help souls." It is therefore with their ministries, after the *mise-en-scène* of the following chapter, that this book begins.

Foundations before the Founding

THE STORY OF THE first Jesuits does not begin, properly speaking, until the Society of Jesus officially came into existence with the papal bull of 27 September 1540. The history of the order is unintelligible, however, when viewed apart from the life of Ignatius up to that point and apart from the *Spiritual Exercises*, substantially completed by him years earlier.

Ignatius and the First Companions

Iñigo López de Loyola was born, the last of his father's many children, most probably in 1491 at the castle of Loyola in the Basque territory of northern Spain, near Azpetia in the province of Guipuzcoa.[1] He received the chivalric and academically sparse education of his class. When he was about thirteen, he was sent by his father to the household at Arévalo of Juan Velázquez de Cuéllar, chief treasurer of King Ferdinand of Aragon, where he was trained in the manners and the skills appropriate for a courtier. He remained at Arévalo for a number of years. In a visit to Loyola in 1515, Iñigo was cited in court for brawling; at that time he claimed he had been tonsured and hence had benefit of clergy. This incident and his admission much later in life that he had been indiscreet in his relationships with women—"satis liber in mulierum amore"—indicate that his clerical status, acquired we know not when, functioned for him only as a legal convenience.[2]

When Velázquez died in 1517, Iñigo entered military service under Don Antonio Marique de Lara, duke of Nájera and viceroy of Navarre. In 1521 King Francis I of France opened the first phase of his long contest with the newly elected emperor, Charles of Habsburg, who since 1516 had also been king of Spain. When French troops entered Spain and advanced on Pamplona, Iñigo was there to defend it, and on 20 May he suffered a blow from a cannonball that shattered his right leg and badly wounded his left. Despite several painful operations, the doctors were unable to save him from a life-long limp.

While recuperating at the castle of Loyola, he found none of the tales of chivalry that he loved to read. In some desperation he turned to the only literature at hand—the lives of the saints in *The Golden Legend* by Jacopo da Voragine and the *Life of Christ* by Ludolph of Saxony, both translated into Castilian. The former led him to speculate about the possibility of fashioning his own life after the saints and of imitating their deeds, cast by him into the mode of the chivalric heroes with whom he was so familiar. It was thus that Iñigo's conversion began.

In his imagination, however, he debated for a long time the alternatives of continuing according to his former path, even with his limp, or of turning completely from it to the patterns exemplified especially by Saint Francis of Assisi and Saint Dominic. He found that when he entertained the first alternative he was afterward left dry and agitated in spirit, whereas the second brought him serenity and comfort. By thus consulting his inner experience, he gradually came to the conviction that God was speaking to him through it, and he resolved to begin an entirely new life. This process by which he arrived at his decision became a distinctive feature of the way he would continue to govern himself and became a paradigm of what he would teach others.

Once his physical strength was sufficiently restored, he set out from Loyola for the Benedictine monastery of Montserrat in Catalonia, which he planned as the first step in a pilgrimage to Jerusalem. At Montserrat, after spending an entire night in vigil before the famous statue there of the Black Madonna, he laid down his sword and dagger and took up in their stead a pilgrim's staff and beggar's clothing. Early in the century Abbot García Jiménez de Cisneros had reformed the monastery and introduced, among other things, the practice of having the novices, prior to their investiture with the Benedictine habit, spend ten or more days preparing for a confession of their sins up to that time.[3] Iñigo, under the direction of the master of novices, followed a modified version of that practice by taking three days to write down his own sins before making a similar confession. These actions at Montserrat ritualized the definitive closing of the door on his past.

The precise direction that his new life would take, however, remained unclear, except that for the moment Jerusalem was his goal. When he left

Montserrat, he planned to spend a few days at the small town of Manresa, near Barcelona, in order to reflect upon his experience up to that point. For various reasons, including originally an outbreak of the plague, he prolonged his sojourn there to almost a year. According to Pedro de Ribadeneira, he later designated this period his "primitive church," probably meaning to suggest the simplicity and evangelical authenticity that the term had connoted to reformers since the eleventh century.[4]

At Manresa, Iñigo meditated on the life of Christ and discovered *The Imitation of Christ*, a book to which he remained devoted all his life. At the same time he gave himself up to a regimen of prayer, fasting, self-flagellation, and other austerities that were extreme even for the sixteenth century. He surrendered all care for his appearance and, in defiance of convention, let his hair and fingernails grow. Shortly after his arrival at Manresa, moreover, he began to experience an excruciating aridity of soul, obsessive doubts about the integrity of his sacramental confessions, and even temptations of suicide. He sought remedy for these afflictions by consulting priests whom he knew, but to no avail.

By attending once again to his inner inspiration, he began to find guidance. He greatly tempered his austerities, resolved his doubts about his confessions, and gradually experienced a return of serenity along with some great internal enlightenments, which sometimes took the form of visions that he believed were from God. He later described one of these enlightenments as being so powerful that he would believe what it contained "even if there were no Scriptures" that taught the same thing.[5] This description indicates his own conviction, as he forcefully expressed it, that he was directly "taught by God."[6]

During this time he began to use his religious experiences to help others, and he made notes with that end in view. After a certain point, scholars are now agreed, the essential elements of the *Spiritual Exercises* emerged and began to take form.[7] The book was a kind of simplified distillation of his own experience framed in such a way as to be useful to others. Although Iñigo continued to revise the book over the next twenty years, he had much of it fundamentally in hand when he left Manresa to complete his pilgrimage to Jerusalem.

After many frustrations he finally arrived there from Venice in the autumn of 1523. He enjoyed a fortnight visiting the places revered by Christians, where he began to hope to spend the rest of his days. Given the situation with their Turkish overlords, the Franciscans who looked after pilgrims in the Holy Land knew that they could not underwrite such a plan, and their

Posthumous portrait of Ignatius of Loyola, by Jacopino del Conte, 1556. The painting is in the Curia Generalizia of the Society of Jesus, Borgo Santo Spirito 5, Rome.

superior told Iñigo that he would have to leave. His reluctance was so great that the Franciscan threatened to levy an excommunication against him unless he obeyed promptly, which he did.

Iñigo did not reveal to the Franciscans that one of his reasons for wanting to stay in the Holy Land was to "help souls," whatever that meant to him at the time. Once he realized that his plan was at least for the moment not attainable and that he had to return to Europe, he tells us that he "felt inclined toward spending some time in studies" as a means to that same end.[8] Just how he came to see a relationship between learning and the ministry in which he now hoped to engage he does not tell, nor does he say here or elsewhere in his *Autobiography* that he saw these studies as leading to ordination to the priesthood, but the decision to study would in any case determine his future course.

By the autumn of 1524 he found himself in classes at Barcelona, trying to learn Latin grammar with children less than half his age. In the meantime he begged for his food and then in the evenings shared what he had acquired with vagrants he sought out on the streets. After two years he felt himself sufficiently grounded to venture into the lecture halls of the recently founded University of Alcalá, where the program of studies was strongly influenced by both the University of Paris and certain aspects of the humanist movement of Renaissance Italy. At this time Alcalá was also a center in Spain of enthusiasm for the writings of Erasmus, and Iñigo was befriended there by Miguel de Eguía, printer of the original Latin of Erasmus's *Handbook of the Christian Soldier* (1525) and of its translation into Castilian (1526).

Still wearing his pilgrim's garb, Iñigo attended, without much guidance or plan, lectures on dialectics, Aristotle's *Physics,* and Peter Lombard's *Sentences.* In his free hours he continued to beg for his sustenance and also began to guide a few people with the *Exercises* and to teach catechism to "the great number of people" who assembled, presumably in the streets, to hear him.[9] He was joined by several other men who dressed similarly and followed the same style of life, which included the suspect practice of receiving Communion every week.

Rumors soon spread that these "sack wearers" were in fact *alumbrados.* The "enlightened ones," adherents to a movement especially widespread in Castile that extolled the seeking of spiritual perfection through internal illumination, were pursued by fearful authorities as pseudo-mystics who belittled more traditional expressions of piety.[10] The rumors about Iñigo and his friends thus brought them several times to the attention of the Inquisition of Toledo, which eventually led to Iñigo's spending forty-two days in prison while he awaited a verdict. Although they were found innocent, he and his companions were admonished to dress like the other students and not to speak in public on religious matters until they had completed four more years of study.

The verdict on Iñigo was correct, for he was not an *alumbrado.* He had friendly relationships, however, with persons associated with the movement, and in a few important respects his teaching resembled theirs.[11] He and the early Jesuits had to spend much time and effort trying to clarify how they differed from the *alumbrados,* especially when "Lutherans," "Erasmians," and "enlightened ones" were sometimes thought to be simply different names for the same contemptible group.

Somewhat bewildered as to where the restrictions on his pastoral activities left him, Iñigo was soon confirmed by the friendly counsel of Alfonso de Fonseca y Acebedo, archbishop of Toledo, in his inclination to discontinue his studies in Alcalá and go to the most distinguished of the older Spanish universities, Salamanca. He and four companions had hardly arrived there in midsummer of 1527, however, when they fell under the suspicion of the Dominicans at the prestigious convent of San Esteban, at least some of whom saw the world as filled with the errors of Erasmus and misbelievers. Within two weeks Iñigo was again in prison. This time four judges interrogated him, all of whom had examined a manuscript copy of the *Spiritual Exercises* and paid special attention to the part dealing with "discernment of spirits," in which the movements in the soul of consolation and desolation and their role in finding and following the will of God are discussed.

The judges again acquitted him, this time allowing him to continue teaching catechism, but with the stricture that in so doing he not discuss the difference between mortal and venial sins until he had completed more years of study. Despite Iñigo's acquittal, the experience convinced him that he should not stay in Salamanca. He determined to pursue in Paris the studies that now seemed imperative, even though friends warned him that the political and military designs of the French king made the city dangerous for subjects of Charles of Habsburg. After a journey of almost seven hundred miles, on 2 February 1528 he arrived alone in Paris, where he was destined to stay, with brief interruptions, for seven years—until April 1535.

The brevity of the account of the Parisian years in his *Autobiography* belies their importance for the future Society of Jesus, and those few pages are remarkable more for what they do not recount than for what they do. They for the most part deal with Iñigo's attempts to beg for his living in Paris and elsewhere, which carried him for short visits to Flanders and England; they also provide some details about his communication with his former companions in Spain and give only the barest hints about the program of studies that led to his Master of Arts degree in 1535. They do not tell us, for instance, that while in Paris he attended lectures on Aquinas by the Dominicans at the convent of Saint-Jacques, or that he also probably studied under the Franciscans nearby. They say nothing about the tense political situation concerning which his friends had warned him and, more surprising, they do not mention a word about Lutheranism in Paris, even though in 1533–34 the university and the kingdom were thrown into a panic both by the Lutheranizing sermon of Nicolas Cop, rector of the university, on which Calvin almost certainly collaborated, and by the subsequent affair of the *Placards* on the night of 17 October 1534, which revealed the frightful extent of Lutheran infiltration into Paris and other places.

The *Autobiography* does indicate that while in Paris Iñigo curtailed his ministries in the interest of better pursuing his course at the university, but that he nonetheless continued to engage in devout conversation with others who felt the inclination for it. Toward the end, the book almost casually informs us that Iñigo and a new set of companions made the decision to go to Jerusalem to "spend their lives there helping souls" or, if that plan should fail, to go to Rome to offer themselves to the pope for whatever he would judge to be "for the greater glory of God and the good of souls."[12] Only two of the companions are mentioned by name—Francis Xavier and Pierre Favre. Practically everything else that we know or conjecture about these years is based on other sources.

Enrolled for his first year at the Collège de Montaigu, where earlier both Erasmus and John Calvin had been students, Iñigo strove to improve his still uncertain command of Latin.[13] He then joined the Collège Sainte-Barbe and began to refer to himself as Ignacio as well as Iñigo because he mistakenly thought the former was a variant of the latter.[14] At Sainte-Barbe Ignatius, as I shall henceforth call him, first met and shared quarters with two other students much younger than he—Favre and Xavier, a Basque cleric and nobleman like himself. They were his first permanent recruits for what would become the Society of Jesus.

Of the two, Favre fell more easily under Ignatius's influence.[15] Despite his humble origins as a shepherd boy in a small village of Savoy, he had had good training in the Latin and Greek classics under a tutor named Pierre Velliard, as had a friend of his, Claude Jay. Quite early in life Favre made a vow of chastity and decided to become a priest. When he arrived in Paris at the age of nineteen, however, he felt doubts about his future course and was tortured by religious scruples. The *Spiritual Exercises* made under Ignatius's guidance put these troubles to rest.

Between 1540 and his death in 1546 at the age of forty, Favre spent most of his time in Germany on two pastoral missions from Paul III. He was present at the famous Diet of Regensburg, 1541, the last and most promising of the efforts at reconciliation between Lutherans and Catholics before the Council of Trent. From Germany Favre alerted his brethren in Rome about the successes of the Lutherans, but he had minimal personal contact with them and seems to have read little, if anything, that they wrote. He more emphatically reported from his firsthand experience the shocking conditions in which he found Catholics, especially the clergy.

During these years Favre intermittently composed for his own use his *Memoriale,* a spiritual journal cast in the form of a conversation with himself and with God, vaguely reminiscent of Augustine's *Confessions.*[16] The document reveals Favre's eclectic theological formation, not untouched by Occamism and other Franciscan influences and much indebted to Rheno-Flemish mystics such as Tauler and Herp; it also reveals his conviction that inner conversion along the lines delineated in the *Exercises* was the only ultimately efficacious remedy for the troubles that afflicted the German church. This conviction helps account for the small interest he showed in strictly doctrinal issues and programs for institutional reform. Favre's most lasting contribution to German Catholicism was the decision made in 1543 by the young Dutch student of theology Peter Canisius to join the Society after making the *Exercises* under Favre's direction.

Xavier, a more robust and dashing personality than Favre, at first resisted Ignatius's importunities to examine his life and motivations. By early 1533, however, he had done so, with a resulting conversion as firm as Favre's but more dramatic because his life to that point had shown signs of more worldly ambitions.[17] Missioned to India in 1540 by Ignatius, who was acting upon a request from King John III of Portugal, Xavier sent letters back to Europe that electrified his brethren and everyone else who read them with the extent of his travels and news of the strange places in which he labored. This gave rise to a popular image of him as the prototypical missioner, zealous and unreflective—an image that was belied by his growing awareness of the problems facing Europeans who wanted to introduce Christianity into non-Western cultures, especially into one as proud and ancient as that of the Japanese. Xavier was the leader, inspiration, and official superior of the forty or so Jesuits who by the time of his death found themselves in "the Indies."

In the same year, 1533, Ignatius encountered on the streets of Paris two young Spaniards who had just entered the capital—Diego Laínez and Alfonso Salmerón, ages twenty and seventeen respectively. The pair latched onto him immediately because they knew no French and surely also because, like Ignatius, they had studied at Alcalá, although they arrived there just after Ignatius had left. At Alcalá, where they remained for five years before departing for Paris, they became lifelong friends. Laínez had heard about Ignatius Loyola and wanted to meet him, which must have invested the chance encounter in Paris with a special significance. In the winter of 1534 both Laínez and Salmerón made the *Spiritual Exercises* under the direction of Ignatius and therewith saw their lives take a radical turn.

Among these early companions in Paris, Laínez would enjoy the most respect for his grasp of scholastic philosophy and theology, as his academic success at Alcalá and Paris early indicated and his later assignments would testify.[18] He came from a wealthy family of Castile, still considered "New Christians" even though it was Laínez's great-grandfather who had converted from Judaism to Christianity. His easy election in 1558 to succeed Ignatius as superior of the Society, complicated though it was by the difficult relations with Pope Paul IV, manifested that his colleagues recognized his leadership qualities.

Salmerón remains less clearly defined, because he was overshadowed by his more gifted friend.[19] Since little is known of his family except that his parents came from small villages near Toledo, we infer that his origins were relatively humble. Despite his great interest in Scripture and his early exposure to the humanist tradition at Alcalá and Paris, he had almost unlimited confidence in the powers of scholastic learning. Once he had arrived in Italy as still a very young man, he showed himself particularly zealous in detecting and denouncing what he believed was Lutheranism, no matter in what quarter—a zeal that sometimes caused him and Ignatius embarrassment and that he later seems to have tempered. Although he never held positions of higher responsibility in the central government of the Society, he acquitted himself more than satisfactorily in other posts and in the *consueta ministeria* almost until his death in 1585. His sixteen volumes of commentary on the New Testament, published posthumously, are the single most extensive literary monument produced by Jesuits of this first hour.[20]

Sometime early in 1534 these five were joined by two other students—Nicolás de Bobadilla, who, after receiving a degree in philosophy at Alcalá and then teaching logic and studying theology at Valladolid, arrived in Paris in 1533, and a Portuguese who had studied in Paris since 1527, Simão Rodrigues. With temperaments more volatile than those of the others, they figure most prominently in the early story of the Society not so much because of their accomplishments, which for Rodrigues were considerable, but because first he and then Bobadilla stood at the center of the two major crises that shook the new order between 1552 and 1557.

Rodrigues was held responsible for the dangerous disarray of the Jesuit province of Portugal, a judgment he bore ill.[21] Bobadilla provoked the crisis between the Society and Pope Paul IV that followed the death of Ignatius, a crisis which set Nadal into a veritable rage against him and brought him under a cloud that subsequent historiography is only beginning to dispel.[22] Of course these later problems appeared nowhere on the horizon in the spring and summer of 1534, when the seven students spent their free hours together in devout conversation and in trying to imagine where their futures might lead. At this time they were simply "friends in the Lord."

Favre was ordained a priest in July, and by this time the others had decided to follow that same path. Surely under the leadership of Ignatius, they made the decision about going to Jerusalem and about offering themselves to the pope to be employed in whatever ministries he thought best. On the feast of the Assumption of Mary, 15 August 1534, they bound themselves by vow to this course of action, as well as to a life of poverty. The intention to live in celibate chastity was implicit in becoming priests. Despite these vows and the decision regarding ordination, they all insisted in later accounts of this crucial turning point in their lives that they had no intention of founding a new religious order. For Ignatius, however, a later letter to his brother indicates that at this time or shortly thereafter an idea along this line had already germinated.[23]

Hindsight surely allows us to see in the event of that August day the cornerstone of the future Society of Jesus. Those who laid it came from different nations and different social classes, and their ages ranged from nineteen to about forty-three. They were bound together by the leadership of Ignatius, by bonds of friendship that in some instances were of only a fragile few months, by their study at the same *alma mater,* and most deeply by the religious experience of the *Exercises,* in which each of them had been guided for a month or so by their author.

In the spring of 1535 Ignatius left Paris to make, as it turned out, his final visit to his homeland, after which he would join the others in Venice, where they would try to secure passage to Jerusalem. Before those six themselves departed from Paris about a year and a half later, they were joined in the same resolve by three Frenchmen—Claude Jay (the boyhood friend of Favre, from Savoy), Paschase Broët (from Picardy), and Jean Codure (from Provence), all of whom, like their new confreres, held the Master of Arts degree from the university.[24] Favre recruited these three new colleagues and guided them through the *Exercises.*

On their long and precarious journey on foot to Venice, the nine companions wore the dress of university students and, besides some clothing, carried with them in their leather rucksacks only their Bibles and personal papers. On 8 January 1537 they arrived in Venice, where Ignatius had been awaiting them for just over a year. He had spent his time there studying theology privately, having another brush with the Inquisition and a first and fateful brush with Cardinal Giampietro Carafa (the future Pope Paul IV), guiding some people through the *Exercises,* and, as a result, attracting to the group another recruit, an Andalusian priest named Diego Hoces, who died unexpectedly less than two years later.

Since ships did not sail to Palestine in the winter months, the companions divided themselves into two groups of five in order to work gratis in the Ospedale degli Incurabili, principally with victims of syphilis, and in the Ospedale Santi Giovanni e Paolo. They nursed patients, scrubbed floors, emptied slop pails, dug graves, and prepared corpses for burial and buried them. From Rodrigues's later account, they often felt half-dead themselves from hunger, fatigue, revulsion, and dread of contagion.[25] The two priests— Favre and Hoces—heard the confessions of the sick.

They interrupted this regimen in the spring for a visit to Rome to obtain Pope Paul III's blessing for their trip. Ignatius, the only one who had not worked in the hospitals, remained behind because he feared an unpleasant reception for himself from two figures influential at the papal court—Cardinal Carafa and Doctor Pedro Ortiz, who had denounced him in Paris to the Inquisitors for possible heresy. To the companions' surprise, Ortiz, now Catherine of Aragon's counsel at the Holy See for the defense of her marriage, had in the meantime formed an altogether favorable opinion of them that led to an invitation to conduct a theological disputation for the pleasure of the pope. On this occasion Paul III blessed their expedition, provided them with some unsolicited funds to help them buy passage, and gave them permission to be ordained by any bishop of their choice.

When they returned to Venice, they resumed their old employment, and on 24 June 1537, six of them, including Ignatius, were ordained to the priesthood. They soon thereafter left Venice and dispersed in groups of twos and threes to Verona, Vicenza, Monselice, Bassano, and Treviso, where they first spent forty days in seclusion and prayer and then engaged principally in street preaching, all the time living on alms they begged and lodging wherever a free room was offered. As winter approached and the political situation precluded any possibility of the trip to Palestine, the companions reassembled at Vicenza, whence they once again eventually dispersed to other cities.

Before they did so, however, they determined that to anyone asking them who they were they would reply that they were of the "Company of Jesus" (Compagnia di Gesù), since they had no other superior but him.[26] The Italian word *compagnia* in such a context meant nothing more than an association and was in widespread use in Italy at the time to designate various kinds of religious confraternities or brotherhoods. Its Latin equivalent was *societas*—thus, "Society of Jesus." There is no reason to believe that for the companions at this time *compagnia* had any of the military connotations that even otherwise well informed interpreters such as Nadal and Polanco sometimes attached to it.[27] It was chosen as perhaps not much more than a term of convenience, for they surely were not ready to designate themselves members of a religious order.

In dispersing from Vicenza the companions looked especially to cities where there might be hope of finding university students who wanted to join the compagnia—Padua, Siena, Bologna, and Ferrara. In this last city Vittoria Colonna, the reform-minded friend of Michelangelo, Reginald Pole, and Gasparo Contarini, eventually took in Jay and Rodrigues to rescue them from the shrew at the hospice where they were staying, who insisted on inspecting them stark naked for vermin before they got into bed at night.[28] This contact with Vittoria Colonna was the companions' first with the group known as Italian Evangelicals, or *spirituali*. It was also their first contact with the ruler of Ferrara, Duke Ercole d'Este, upon whom they made a favorable impression that would later stand them in good stead.

Ignatius, Favre, and Laínez, however, headed for Rome in order to offer their services to Paul III. The now ten companions had therefore decided to go with the alternative to the trip to Jerusalem, at least as a temporary measure. Their determining on a name for themselves and their concern to seek out others who might want to join them also indicate that they were by this time entertaining the possibility of some more lasting form of association.

At the little hamlet of La Storta on the outskirts of Rome, Ignatius experienced in prayer one of his best-known illuminations. Versions of the event differ in details, but in essence it was a vision of Jesus carrying the cross with God the Father at his side. "I wish you to serve us," said Jesus. The Father added, "I will be propitious to you in Rome," and Ignatius was placed by Jesus' side. What this meant Ignatius did not know, but he conjectured that he and his companions might suffer a virtual crucifixion in Rome. He also took the visitation as a confirmation of the name of Jesus upon which they had earlier decided, a point on which he would never yield, despite objections that the name seemed haughty or that all Christians were by definition members of the society of Jesus.

The three travelers entered Rome at the end of November and experienced another gracious reception from Ortiz, who soon made the *Exercises* for forty days under Ignatius's direction at the monastery of Monte Casino, south of Rome. He also gained them access once again to Paul III, who unexpectedly appointed Laínez and Favre lecturers of theology at the University of Rome and showed the trio other favors. Ignatius continued guiding persons through the *Exercises.* Among those guided, probably by Ignatius, was Cardinal Gasparo Contarini, who just a short while later would be the key figure in winning approval of the nascent Society of Jesus from the pope. They all began to preach and teach catechism in Spanish or in their faulty Italian and soon were joined by their confreres in these and other ministries as they drifted into Rome, without recruits, from the other cities where they had been preaching.

Rumors again spread among the powerful Spanish community in Rome that Ignatius and the others were *alumbrados* or Lutherans in disguise, but in late 1538 Ignatius obtained from the governor of the city a declaration of innocence. It is approximately at this point that he ends his *Autobiography* with the words "And Master Nadal can tell you the rest." Ignatius's pilgrim years had indeed ended, for he would spend the rest of his days in Rome.

Even into 1539, however, the members of the Compagnia di Gesù still nursed the hope of gaining passage to Jerusalem. According to a much later account by Bobadilla, Paul III, during a theological disputation some of the companions were holding for him, reproached them for this wish by saying that they could just as well help souls where they were—Rome could be their Jerusalem.[29] In any case, the matter of their future was once again becoming pivotal and led to a series of meetings among themselves that stretched from the middle of March until 24 June and issued in the "Five Chapters," that is, the substantial draft of the *Formula of the Institute.*

Through Contarini, Ignatius conveyed the document to Paul III. Although strong objections were raised in the papal curia concerning matters such as the abolition of choir and the precise meaning of the vow to obey the pope "concerning missions," as well as objections that the church already had too many religious orders and new ones had been forbidden as long ago as the Fourth Lateran Council (1215), Contarini defended the integrity of the "Chapters." Ignatius and his brethren took to prayer, but also enlisted in their cause some of the powerful friends they had by this time made in central Italy. Fifteen months after the "Chapters" had first been submitted to him, Paul III confirmed them by making them the substance of *Regimini militantis ecclesiae,* 27 September 1540.

Even before the deliberations in 1539 that produced the "Chapters," the Compagnia had added new members and would continue to do so throughout the subsequent months until the publication of the papal bull. At first these new members were mostly expatriate Iberians who for various reasons found themselves in Rome. Among them was Antonio de Araoz, a relative of Ignatius by marriage. Gifted and headstrong, he became in 1547 the first provincial of the Spanish province of the Society, which by then had approximately forty members. Diego and Esteban de Eguía, brothers of the printer, joined about this time. Diego, who had known and become friends with Ignatius in Alcalá and now soon his confessor, was a priest, Esteban a widower.

Jerónimo Doménech, a wealthy twenty-three-year-old canon from Valencia who was in Rome on family business at the papal court, had studied at Paris, where he knew some of the companions. Influenced especially by Xavier, he made the *Exercises* under Laínez in September 1539 and, despite great objections from his family, cast his lot with the Compagnia, in which he would hold a number of important offices until his death in 1592.

Pedro de Ribadeneira, a page in the service of Cardinal Alessandro Farnese, one day played truant from his duties and, afraid to return, sought refuge at the house where the companions were staying. He liked what he saw, and in August 1540 Ignatius received him into the Society. Ribadeneira was fourteen years old. Of lively disposition and intelligence, he had an especially close relationship with Ignatius and wrote his first biography, 1572.

About this time a few Italians began to join. One of them was Pietro Codacio, chamberlain at the papal court, who helped effect the transfer to the Compagnia of the church of Santa Maria della Strada, the first church ever held by the Jesuits and the site of the future Gesù in the center of Rome. The church was small and uncomfortable, but the location was ideal for men whose commitment to preaching and other ministries led them consistently to place their churches and houses as near as possible to the hub of the cities in which they found themselves.[30]

Only the ten companions of Paris were mentioned in the papal bull, and only they had the prerogative of voting in 1541 for their first superior. But even before the bull was published, the Society had grown substantially beyond them and already numbered twenty members or more—international in their origins, varied in their social backgrounds, but drawn almost exclusively from an academic elite. This profile of membership presaged the future.

The Spiritual Exercises

After 1540 few further changes were made in the *Exercises* before their printing, with papal approval, in 1548.[31] They were already, along with the *Formula,* the foundational document of the new order. Following their full course would be prescribed for all novices who joined the order. They would help the individual tap his inner resources for the motivation that lifelong commitment entailed, and they provided clear yet flexible principles for his own spiritual journey and the journey of those he wanted "to help." No previous religious order had a document like it.

One of the world's most famous books, the *Exercises* are in that category one of the least read and least well understood.[32] Reasons for this reality are not difficult to find. In the first place, the *Exercises* were never meant to be read, as somebody might read Luther's "Freedom of the Christian" or Erasmus's *Handbook of the Christian Soldier.* They were by and large not meant even to be in the hands of the person engaged in following their course, although the text itself often suggests so. They were, instead, a set of materials, directives, and suggestions for the person helping another through that course. They are in that regard more like a teacher's manual than a student's textbook.

There is another reason the book fails to entice. It consists of interspersed pieces from different literary genres—directives, meditations, prayers, declarations, procedures, sage observations, and rules. Although even a casual perusal reveals that all these elements are somehow meant to relate to a central structure of four "Weeks," the very diversity of genres at first glance suggests a scissors-and-paste composition. The book is not laid out in continuous discourse and lacks literary grace. Points critical for understanding it sometimes appear in what seem to be subordinate or supplementary sections. These qualities are surely due in part to limitations of the author and to the conditions in which the *Exercises* came into being, but are also due to the kind of book they are and what they hope to accomplish.

The *Exercises'* purpose is stated in the opening paragraph as "preparing and disposing our soul to rid itself of all its disordered affections and then, after their removal, of seeking and finding God's will in the ordering of our life for the salvation of our soul."[33] This statement requires two immediate comments. First, the wording in itself can sound Pelagian or semi-Pelagian, as if one sought and found God's will on one's own, apart from the action of grace. Some early commentaries on the *Exercises* by Polanco and others, though they generally insist on the necessity of grace in every stage of the process, at times sound the same way.[34] However, the most basic premises of the book taken in its entirety, other writings in the Ignatian *corpus*, as well as other commentaries on the *Exercises*, especially those by Nadal, indicate an orthodox meaning. Indeed, the fundamental premise of the *Exercises* is the continuous action of God in the whole process, or "retreat," as the practice of the *Exercises* came to be known.[35]

Second, although the statement of purpose seems generic and applicable at any moment in a person's life, subsequent parts of the book make clear that Ignatius had in mind in the first instance somebody in a position to make a determinative choice about the future, for example, to marry, to choose a certain profession, or to live henceforth in a notably different style. The *Exercises* were designed to enable one to make that choice with objectivity and freedom of spirit and under the most immediate inspiration of God. The process leading up to the choice comes to a climax at the end of the Second Week in a long series of considerations that generally concern this "election."[36] It is obvious from the text that the decision, or election, lies at the heart of the *Exercises* when they are made in their full integrity, which was foreseen as taking approximately a month in a situation in which one could devote oneself exclusively to the purpose at hand, removed from usual occupations.

The text allows, however, that not everybody would, for various reasons, be capable of that long course or be in a position to make a radical change in the external circumstances of his life, yet it indicates that much of what the *Exercises* hoped to accomplish could be of use to such persons. It provides, therefore, that only certain parts, especially those pertaining to the First Week, be presented to some people and in general that they "be adapted to the disposition of the persons who desire to make them, that is, to their age, education, and ability."[37] For those who could not disengage themselves from their affairs to devote an entire week or month exclusively to the *Exercises*, the text also provides for simply setting aside an hour and a half daily for a number of days or weeks.[38] The range of persons and situations the *Exercises* could accommodate was wide.

A glance at the *Exercises* shows, however, that they presuppose both good will on the part of persons entering upon them and that these persons are believing Catholics. Their flexibility surely cannot compromise, it would seem, on either of these points. Nonetheless, in 1553 Nadal in his *Apologia* for them against their detractors advanced his "personal" opinion that at least up to a certain point they could be adapted to heretics and even to pagans. His ultimate justification for this viewpoint was that the *Exercises* essentially taught nothing more than that human beings were "to love God above all things, with all their heart, all their mind, all their soul, and all their strength."[39] In the early days of the Society, a few Protestants did in fact make the *Exercises*.[40]

Among the many stumbling blocks that would deter heretics, infidels, and pagans from entering upon the full *Exercises,* the sacramental confession of the sins of one's past life, recommended for the end of the First Week, looms especially large. The "Principle and Foundation" before that Week presents considerations about the ultimate purpose of life and about the created universe as ordered to the praise, reverence, and service of God.[41] The First Week follows with considerations about the heinousness of sin and the havoc it wreaks in the individual and in society, about God's constant love, and about the necessity and sweetness of turning from one's old ways and attitudes to gratitude and love. The word "conversion" does not appear in the *Exercises,* yet it is a dynamic that underlies the First Week—meaning a turning from a sinful life or, probably more often, a turning to a more devout life.

Hence the significance of the "general" confession. The *Exercises* do not propose it as a ritual obligation required in order to be shriven from one's sins, for they presuppose that at least in most cases that has already been done, perhaps many times. This confession is something different. It is the climax of the program of the First Week, which has consisted of essentially two parts: first, a review, or moral inventory, of one's life up to that point and, second, a deepening awareness of the mercy and love of God, operative at every moment along the way, despite one's sins and failings. In this special context the confession is a dramatized statement to oneself, to God, and to another human being who here represents God that an important change in one's past patterns of thinking, feeling, and behaving is now desired with all one's heart and is in fact under way.

Obviously, such a statement does not in itself require a Catholic sacrament to achieve its end, but the sacrament was the mode Ignatius had learned and himself practiced at Montserrat and here transmitted to others. No evidence indicates, however, that it was particularly at Montserrat that he appropriated the other components of the First Week, most certainly not in the form in which he presented them.

Ignatius believed and inculcated that the *Exercises* could be expanded and contracted according to the situation and needs of various individuals to the extent that they might not be much more than an intensified form of late-medieval catechesis.[42] But he did not envision the possibility of omitting the basic elements of the First Week for anybody who wanted to continue beyond it. If the purpose of that Week was successfully achieved, the individuals had found a new and happier orientation at the very core of their being and were thus set more firmly than before on the path to salvation. When, for whatever reason, an individual could not continue with the rest of the *Exercises,* the better ordering of his life with which the *Exercises* were concerned had been essentially set in motion. To assure continuation of the movement, certain practices, including daily examination of conscience, are proposed and explained.

That continuing movement in fact constitutes the precondition for engaging in the next three Weeks. Those Weeks were constructed with a view to confirming the First, while moving the person along to further issues. Was some other change, especially in the external framework of one's life or the kind of future one envisioned for oneself, possible, desirable, and now to be made? Such a change would not only deepen the original experience but would make one's life even more conformable to the life and teachings of Jesus, accepted by Ignatius without question as the best to which human beings could aspire. More simply put, these Weeks were designed especially for a consideration of one's "vocation," or station in life, and for making an election concerning it by those who were still free to do so. Polanco and others echoed the *Exercises* when they pointed out, however, that the election could conceivably deal with any issue of great moment in one's life.[43]

The structure of the last three Weeks conforms basically to the story of Jesus in the New Testament. The Second Week, accordingly, presents contemplations on the life of Jesus until the Last Supper. It is preceded by a more synoptic contemplation on "The Kingdom of Christ,"[44] which later in the same Week is complemented by a similar meditation on "The Two Standards," or two banners, namely, those of Christ and of Satan.[45] This Week presumably would be the longest of the three—for the designation "Week" was actually an indeterminate period to be expanded or contracted according to the needs of the individual and the matter under consideration, so long as in their entirety the four Weeks did not exceed about thirty days.[46]

The Third Week begins with the Last Supper and ends with Jesus' death and burial. The Fourth, presumably the shortest Week, proposes for prayer Jesus' resurrection and everything thereafter. The *Exercises* end with the presentation of a "Contemplation to Attain the Love of God."[47]

Supplementary materials follow the "Contemplation." Some of these materials, such as the "Rules for the Ministry of Distributing Alms" and

"Notes toward Perceiving and Understanding Scruples," relate only indirectly to the substance of the text.[48] They develop issues that experience had taught Ignatius sometimes arose during the course of the *Exercises,* but they are peripheral to the essence of the book. The same cannot be said of the two sets of "Rules" about "discerning spirits."[49] As reflective codifications of how Ignatius believed his own conversion had happened at the castle of Loyola and continued at Manresa, and of his pastoral experience since then, they are at the very core of the *Spiritual Exercises.*[50]

These "Rules" deal with the inner movements of consolation and desolation that might be felt at different moments in the retreat, especially as the individual faced the challenge of the new beginning of the First Week and of the election in the Second. In a few pages they come as close as anything does to revealing the most basic assumptions Ignatius entertained about the dynamics of an individual's relationship to God, heightened in the individual's awareness and intensity during this period of seclusion, review, contemplation, and, if all went well, profound changes.

The description of the *Exercises* up to this point has dealt with their formal aspects, which might generate the impression that they are, within the context of a religious faith, a combination or series of passionless, almost stoic, techniques for taking oneself in hand. The "Rules for Discernment," however, unmistakably indicate that Ignatius thought God and the Devil were active in the whole process. Perhaps just as important, they reveal how seriously feelings like sadness, confusion, happiness, and serenity are to be taken. These rules are a critical introduction to the meaning of the whole book.

Indeed, as the text of the *Exercises* is scrutinized with that clue in mind, it manifests that the engaging of powerful emotions like grief, fear, horror, compunction, compassion, contentment, admiration, gratitude, wonder, joy, and especially love is the final and foreseen outcome of its various meditations and contemplations, especially the more climactic ones. The individual should feel bestirred "by great feeling"[51]—and at appropriate moments moved even to tears.[52]

The "Rules for Discernment" inculcate, as the term suggests, that impulsive acting on feelings is inappropriate, just as the "Rules for Scruples" inculcate the inappropriateness of acting on the compulsive feelings denoted by that term. It is true, moreover, that especially in the First Week the individual engages in a dialogical reasoning process with the inner self. Questions are posed for which answers are expected. These answers are often, however, not so much to be confirmed by one's affective reactions to them as affective responses are to be reviewed and tested by more objective criteria. The reasons of the heart have primacy.

The clearest and most important instance in the text of this confidence in affective response, under the right conditions, occurs when the *Exercises* describe three ways in which one arrives at a good election.[53] The first two are not by a reasoning process but by a special and peremptory inspiration or by attending to one's feelings of consolation or desolation when confronted with the alternatives of a choice. The third way, which consists to a large extent in weighing the pros and cons of one's alternatives, is to be used in conjunction with the second or when the second has not led to a clear choice.

Polanco later made explicit what is clearly implied in the text itself when he observed that the second way, that of consolation and desolation, is superior to the third, for in it the person is guided "by a better light than human reason."[54] That light of course is the direct action of God upon the individual, registered especially by appropriate feelings and desires. For a good decision even according to the third way (pondering pros and cons), serenity and composure are the preconditions. Attending to one's feelings is, then, crucial for the conversion of heart that is central to the *Exercises*—one completes the *Exercises* with "heart changed," as Polanco observed.[55]

Although it is of course important to examine the text of the *Exercises* to understand the presuppositions that undergird it, in itself it was not meant to convey any special theological viewpoint. Its origins lay not in a scholar's study, an academic disputation, an inquisitorial courtroom, or an ecclesiastical council. It was not a counterstatement to Luther, Erasmus, or the *alumbrados*. It originated in religious experience, first the author's and then others'. Its basic elements were well in place before the author had any theological education. It is not, therefore, a book of dogma, but a dogmatic book—that is, it assumes that its basic message is the common Christian heritage and that that message, therefore, need not be argued. What was needed was personal appropriation, a clinging to the message with all one's heart and then a translation of it with all one's heart into one's life.

Underlying the "Discernment of Spirits" is the basic assumption that a battle for the heart is being waged by forces of good and evil—by God and the Devil, who is "the enemy of human nature."[56] The heart registers the battle in its experience of consolation and desolation, and one's task is to discern in any given situation the origins of the movements the heart feels by trying to see where those movements are leading. The purpose of the *Exercises* and the precondition for their successful outcome at every stage is to find oneself under the inspiration of God, the "good spirit." The process of "discerning" within oneself various movements of consolation and desolation affected the way some of the first Jesuits interpreted their lives; its impact is clearly manifested in the few portions of the spiritual journal of Ignatius that survive, 1544–45, and in two longer but similar documents from disciples—Favre's *Memoriale* and Nadal's *Orationis observationes*.[57]

As was Ignatius himself at Manresa, the person making the retreat was to be "taught by God." It was surely for this reason that the individual was to have at hand only a few books, such as the Gospels, *The Imitation of Christ*, and the lives of the saints, and even those not until after the First Week.[58] Ignatius makes this crucial point more explicitly, but once again in an unprepossessing place, in number fifteen of the "Introductory Explanations." In it he warns the person guiding another in the *Exercises* that at the time of the election he should not try to influence the outcome one way or another, for "it is more appropriate and far better that the Creator and Lord himself communicate himself to the devout soul, embracing it with love, inciting it to praise of himself, and disposing it for the way that will most enable the soul to serve him in the future." He should "allow the Creator to deal immediately with the creature, and the creature with its Creator and Lord."[59] This immediate action of God on the individual is the fundamental premise of the *Exercises*.

The preceding "Explanation," number fourteen, is related in that it warns against allowing the individual in the rarefied atmosphere of the retreat to make any hasty promises or vows, especially a vow to enter a religious order.[60] The critical importance of these two "Explanations" is highlighted by the eagerness with which enemies attacked them and even friends questioned them once the *Exercises* began to be known.

The Dominican theologian Tomás de Pedroche, who in 1553 was urged on to the attack by the archbishop of Toledo, Juan Martínez Guijeño (known as Silíceo), linked the "Explanations" to the second way of making an election, that is, according to motions of consolation and desolation. For him these parts of the *Exercises* were "scandalous and heretical," the teaching of the *alumbrados*. At Trent as early as 1546–47, Cardinal Marcello Cervini, one of the three papal legates to the Council, had heard complaints about the teaching on election and interviewed Laínez and Salmerón about it. Others raised similar issues in friendly or unfriendly manner, with the specter of the *alumbrados* generally hovering on the horizon.[61]

The objections of the critics can be reduced to two points. The first was reliance, or too exclusive reliance, upon inner inspiration—just like the *alumbrados.* In the *Exercises* Ignatius in fact provided remedies for excesses in this regard, and, paradoxically, the fourteenth "Explanation" was one of them. The second point was the refusal to urge a life of poverty, chastity, and obedience as obviously a better election. Critics said that one should not hold oneself "indifferent," as the *Exercises* indicated, for that denied that poverty, chastity, and obedience were spiritually better choices. This objection echoed bitter controversies in which, besides Luther and other Reformers, the storm center was Erasmus, whose teaching on the matter, unlike that of the Reformers, was in its substance, although not in its emphasis and context, similar to that of Ignatius.[62]

In any case, the reasons Ignatius forbade the person directing the retreat to urge one way of life over another are fundamental in understanding the *Exercises,* and it should be obvious by now why he did so. As Polanco later stated in this regard, "Leave to God the whole matter of calling the one making the election to this or that state of life, in which God is the only one who can sustain the individual and provide the necessary help along the way."[63] Nonetheless, at many points the *Exercises* explicitly propose that a life of poverty is in some objective way the better course, for it more closely conforms to how Ignatius imagined that Jesus lived. The meditations on the "Kingdom of Christ" and the "Two Standards" evince this persuasion clearly.

In the "Kingdom of Christ," the individual imagines Christ to be a king calling disciples to follow him in labor, suffering, and poverty, and in the "Two Standards" he imagines him to be "the sovereign and true Commander" inviting disciples to enlist under his banner in order to be sent "throughout the whole world to spread his doctrine among people of every state or condition."[64] The emphasis is on poverty, which Ignatius himself practiced "in the world" for years before the Society was founded. He elsewhere stated clearly that one need not enter a religious order to lead one's life in poverty—or in chastity, or even in obedience.[65] Nonetheless, like his contemporaries, Ignatius saw joining an order as an especially commendable way to lead such a life. The attractive presentation of worldwide evangelization in the "Two Standards," furthermore, obviously favors a life devoted to ministry over a more contemplative one.

The *Exercises* helped Ignatius recruit the first members of the Compagnia, and his disciples would see them as a way of attracting more members to it. Despite the many warnings about respecting the freedom of the person making the election, the temptation to interfere with the process must have been great. Ignatius later especially denounced any manipulation toward entrance into the Society "because it is against the rule in the *Exercises* and against the purity of spirit of the Society, which does not seek members except those who come to it freely and according to the guidance and good pleasure of God."[66]

Nadal saw in the meditations on the "Kingdom" and the "Two Standards" special images of the Jesuit vocation.[67] He said in an exhortation to the Jesuits at Alcalá in 1576: "I want to know my Institute and to see what the Society is. In our *Exercises* there are two meditations from which much consolation and strength can be drawn, because they help us understand what the Society is—the 'Kingdom' and the 'Two Standards.' "[68]

Because these meditations employ military imagery they have helped advance the interpretation that the Society of Jesus was conceived along the lines of an army. In that same exhortation, as well as in other places, Nadal provided support for such a viewpoint when he asked, for instance, "Do you not see that we are at war, we are on campaign?"[69] He did so even more emphatically when he called the Society a "squadron."[70] In other Jesuit documents such imagery recurred and even had a certain prominence. It does not, however, dominate them as a leitmotif.

The *Formula* opens by describing a member of the Society "as a soldier of God beneath the banner of the cross"—"militare Deo sub vexillo crucis." *Militare Deo* was a medieval synonym for a member of a religious order.[71] Such imagery was thus common heritage, as the title of Erasmus's *Handbook of the Christian Soldier* also indicates. Some scholars have even tried to show that Ignatius was dependent upon the *Handbook* for that imagery in the *Exercises.* Their efforts were unsuccessful, but they pointed out striking parallels. The Jesuits more generally made use of other metaphors to describe what they were about, and, although they often thought of themselves as doing battle (and in a more intensified way than perhaps most other "Christian soldiers"), their references to the Society as a squadron or an army are exceedingly rare. Contrary to another popular misapprehension, the superior in Rome is "general" only in the sense of the adjective, that is, he is the "overall" superior. *Praepositus generalis* is the technical Latin term.

Despite the correlation between certain aspects of the *Exercises* and certain aspects of the Society of Jesus, as in the two meditations just discussed, the *Exercises* were always intended for a broader audience. The contemplation most emblematic of that reality is perhaps the final one, "The Contemplation to Attain Divine Love."[72] The basic idea of the meditation is that God is active in all life's circumstances, which are expressions of his love and care. The appropriate response is to commit oneself utterly to that love and care, expressed in the prayer included in the meditation. It is with this sentiment that the person ends the *Exercises*. Implicitly contained in the meditation is the ideal of "finding God in all things," as the correlative section of the *Constitutions* enjoined members of the Society.[73] This ideal surely had to be one of the inspirations for Nadal's repeated and bold statement that for him and his Jesuit confreres "the world is our house."[74]

The foregoing description of the *Exercises* indicates their essential elements. Whence did these elements derive? Some early Jesuits attributed the *Exercises* to divine inspiration.[75] We need not subscribe to that interpretation to agree with the modern consensus that they in some sense represent the "quintessence of the process of Ignatius's own conversion and purposeful change of life."[76]

It is possible to move beyond that generalization, but not very far. Ludolph of Saxony's *Vita Jesu Christi* had an extensive impact on the structure of the *Exercises*, on the style and content of methods of prayer, such as the contemplations and the "application of the senses," and on a number of particulars. Of the identifiable sources influencing the *Exercises*, Ludolph was without doubt the most important.[77] Ludolph was himself so dependent on the *Meditationes vitae Christi* that it is sometimes difficult to distinguish this text from his own. The *Meditationes*, once attributed to Saint Bonaventure and surely influenced by him, were composed by an Italian Franciscan in the late thirteenth or early fourteenth century and were the principal vehicle through which Franciscan piety first entered the Jesuit tradition.[78]

Alonso de Madrid's *Arte para servir a Dios*, published in 1521, may have influenced the formulation of the "Principle and Foundation."[79] Jean Gerson's *Monotessaron* possibly did the same for the meditation on the "Kingdom of Christ."[80] The *Exercises*, including their very title, were probably influenced by Abbot Cisneros's *Ejercitatorio de la vida espiritual*, which Ignatius may have seen in compendium form during his stay at Montserrat or Manresa, but the two books are very different.[81]

In fact, the very commonplace nature of the ideas in the *Exercises* has rendered frustrating the search for their sources.[82] Moreover, although the *Exercises* derived from medieval piety, they modified and in many ways transcended it. While they provided meditations on the suffering and death of Jesus, for instance, they did not dwell on them or make them the center of the Christian's prayer.[83]

What made the *Exercises* special was not particular themes or their mode of articulation. It was, rather, the coordination of the parts into an integral and novel totality. Although the practice of spending a period of time alone in contemplation is older than Christianity itself, no effective codification of a way of doing so existed until the *Exercises*—surely, none that had such clear design and movement. The book in effect created the institution known as the "retreat," and in that creation lay its primary originality.[84] Besides its many other influences on the first Jesuits, it handed them an instrument of ministry that was new and peculiar to them. It was thereby a keystone of their pastoral identity—in ways, as we shall see, that extended far beyond retreats. In an age of books, moreover, the Jesuits had a book of their own.

On a more pedestrian level, the *Exercises* recommended particular practices that the first Jesuits adopted, adapted, and promoted in a manner that would set them off from other ministers and that would have great impact. One of the most innovative features of the *Exercises* was the role played by the person who helped another engage in them.[85] If such guidance was helpful during the retreat, it might be helpful throughout one's life, either in confession or outside it. This kind of consultation of course antedates the *Exercises,* but, in great part because of Ignatius's book, "spiritual direction," or counseling, began to emerge with a new prominence in Catholicism as a formal and continuing relationship between the two persons involved.[86]

The practice of the "general" confession, daily examination of conscience, and other particulars of Jesuit ministry found their earliest expression among Jesuit documents in the book of the *Exercises*. Even when the promotion of some of these practices was not exactly new, the emphasis, the definition of purpose, and the way they figured in a general design for an individual's religious life often imbued them with special characteristics. Among these, the practice of prayer in the form of meditation or contemplation, as distinct from the recitation of set formulas, would be especially significant.

No doubt, the influence of the *Devotio Moderna* and other late-medieval traditions on Ignatius's teaching about prayer is palpable, but he gathered, reformulated, and transmitted that heritage in a way and to a degree that others did not. Despite many similarities between him and Erasmus concerning how the Christian message was to be lived, the latter has nothing to say about this kind of prayer even in his *De modo orandi Deum.* It was so central to the *Exercises,* however, that Nadal sometimes described their purpose simply as a response to the plea of Jesus' disciples "Lord, teach us how to pray" (Lk. 11:1).[87]

Teaching people how to pray played a large role in early Jesuit ministry not only because of its presumed perennial value but because it responded to what the Jesuits believed their age particularly required. When Nadal in his *Apologia* for the *Exercises* reviewed the "calamities" at present afflicting "the Christian world," he numbered ignorance of how to pray among the chief adversities. He affirmed that God called the Society into being to renew this "ancient and perpetual grace," which Catholics neglected and of which the heretics thought they had no need because of their doctrine of faith alone. The Jesuits had first to appropriate this grace themselves and then to be the occasion for renewing it for "everybody," because "God shows no partiality" (Gal. 2:6).[88]

For Nadal, every novice who entered the Society had to follow the full course of the *Exercises* precisely in order to learn "our way of proceeding" in prayer.[89] The *Exercises* have a special appendix on "Three Methods of Prayer,"[90] often taken as the substance of their teaching on the matter even though the body of the text provides many other ways of going about it, including the use of set formulas. The *Exercises* presume to introduce to meditation and contemplation those who previously seldom practiced it. As Doménech correctly observed in 1569, in the *Exercises* no single method is prescribed—different methods helped different people.[91]

Ignatius's most fundamental teaching was that individuals had to find the way that suited them best, but he and the other first Jesuits saw that all methods should lead to "familiar conversation" with God.[92] The conversation was to be intimate, conducted in the "language of the heart."[93] As we shall see, not all their Catholic contemporaries believed this an unsuspect teaching.

The general movement of the *Exercises* from the abjuration of sin and one's old ways in the First Week, through the contemplations on the life, death, and resurrection of Christ, to the culmination in the "Contemplation" at the end led almost immediately to understanding that movement as corresponding to the "three ways," or stages, in spiritual growth—purgative, illuminative, and unitive—that entered the Christian tradition through Dionysius the Pseudo-Areopagite in the sixth century. The text of the *Exercises* itself suggests this correlation.[94] Almost all the early Jesuits accepted the traditional belief that "Dionysius" was the person he claimed to be, that is, the person to whom Paul preached in Athens on the Areopagus (Acts 17:34), and they rejected the impious (but correct) speculations of their contemporaries that he was of much later vintage.

Nadal believed that Dionysius drew his threefold design from the Gospel[95] and affirmed as well that "the order and plan of development in the *Exercises* is purgation, illumination, union."[96] The correlation of the *Exercises* with the "ways" of Dionysius served, therefore, two purposes: it further validated the evangelical origins of the *Exercises,* and it broadened their scope beyond the month of retreat to a more general design for a person's spiritual journey throughout life.

For persons otherwise unfamiliar with the *Exercises,* the most famous section in them is among the supplementary materials found toward the end of the book, the "Rules for Thinking with the Church."[97] They were surely not composed until toward the end of Ignatius's student days in Paris, about 1534–35, and some of them probably not until shortly after his arrival in Rome.[98] They are thus the last part of any substance to be added to the book. This fact corroborates the impression that they correlate only indirectly with what preceded them in the text. They are not for that reason unimportant; they remind us of the general framework of Catholic belief and practice in which one engaged in the *Exercises,* and they place that belief and practice firmly in the context of the sixteenth century. They are among the few indications that the religious situation in Paris made an impression on Ignatius.

These rules are in their essence statements of attitudes that bear on both pastoral practice and interiorized appropriation of some religious values. Their specific origins, like those of so much of the text of the *Exercises,* are obscure. In certain details they bear a resemblance to some of the decrees of the Council of Sens, held in 1528, just after Ignatius had arrived in Paris.[99] Some of them are to be interpreted, in any case, as countering dangerous ideas then circulating, whereas others simply lay down a course of action that Ignatius considered prudent.

Against precisely whom they are directed is not clear, although "the Lutherans" are among them. Some of the earlier rules in the list clearly take positions contrary to ideas held by the *alumbrados* or attributed to them. With their emphasis on the more institutionalized aspects of religion, the rules can be interpreted as balancing the rest of the text, where these aspects are taken so little into account. They are thus a manifesto of Ignatius's own orthodoxy, frequently impugned precisely on this score. Polanco and others, however, saw them as an "antidote" to the heretics of the day, and that is what the wording of some of them most obviously suggests.[100]

Although that wording sometimes seems particularly emphatic, the doctrinal implications they contain do not differ from those to which Catholics of the sixteenth century would have subscribed. Even the thirteenth rule about believing what seems to me white to be in fact black, if so defined by the church, is no exception. Definitions of the church, in the technical sense in which we must assume Ignatius used it, were conceded by all to contradict in certain cases the evidence of the senses, as when the real body and blood of Christ are defined as present in the Eucharist in what appear to be bread and wine. No Catholic in the sixteenth century attacked or criticized this rule, which in fact does not run counter to a statement by Erasmus using similar wording with which it has often been contrasted.[101]

The only rule dealing with doctrinal matters that aroused controversy in the sixteenth century was rule fourteen, which advised caution in preaching about predestination. The Latin translation, done at Ignatius's behest by André des Freux, unwittingly seemed to favor an interpretation of predestination proposed by Ambrogio Politi (Catarino), a contemporary Dominican theologian with whom many of his Dominican confreres disagreed.[102] Sixteenth-century Catholics had more to criticize in the rules regarding religious practice, especially the advocacy in the second rule of weekly reception of the Eucharist.

Nonetheless, the relatively little comment and controversy aroused in the sixteenth century by the "Rules for Thinking with the Church" indicate that they should not be invested with the exaggerated orthodoxy they were often later made to represent. Moreover, important though they are in many ways, they were not seen to be integral to the *Exercises*. Polanco equivalently stated this in his "Directory" for the *Exercises* (1573–75) when he lumped them with three other sets of "Rules"—those for almsgiving, scruples, and use of food: "About these four the following can be said in general. They should be proposed not to everybody, but only to persons who seem to need them and for whom it is worth the effort."[103] The other commentators said practically the same thing.[104] The official *Directory*, not published until 1599, repeated this in only slightly stronger terms.[105] These "Rules" are not, therefore, the culmination or raison d'être of the *Exercises*, as if everything else was aimed at firing up the individual to accept them. They are, in fact, quite the opposite—among the few parts that under certain circumstances could be omitted even by somebody following the full thirty days.

Because many of the "Rules" dealt directly with pastoral practice, Jesuits themselves were surely expected to know them and, of course, abide by them. Sometime around 1562 Nadal composed a brief instruction that was, in effect, a loose commentary on how they bore on such practice.[106] But neither the "Rules" nor Nadal's instruction resolved or even attempted to resolve on a theoretical level any of the great doctrinal controversies of the day. The "Rules" for the most part simply urged a circumspect approach to what one said, preached, and did in ministry. Within that cautious framework, Jesuit pastoral practice often showed considerable creativity.

⌁ 2

Taking Shape for Ministry

BEFORE EXAMINING Jesuit ministries in detail in the next four chapters, I need to provide an overview of their general contours and of the broader norms and ideals that were supposed to guide them. The *Exercises* and the experience of Ignatius and his companions up to 1540 adumbrated what was to come. The *Formula* succinctly codified some norms and ideals, which the *Constitutions* later developed in detail and the *Autobiography* held up for emulation. Experience meanwhile led to new decisions and directions, which sometimes rendered aspects of these documents inadequate or anachronistic even as they were being formulated. Behind the patterns of ministry, however, lay more general patterns of organization, membership, and self-definition that are crucial for understanding the Jesuits' pastoral vision and enterprise.

The Theatines, an order founded in 1524 and similar in some ways to the Jesuits, had by mid-century about thirty members, all of whom lived in Italy. The Barnabites and Somascans, two other orders founded at roughly the same time, also had comparably small membership and were located also in Italy. By 1565 the Society of Jesus had well over three thousand members, dispersed in many countries of Western Europe as well as in India, Japan, Brazil, and other exotic places. Guiding this process were Ignatius and then Laínez, assisted by their confreres but primarily responsible for assuring that the original inspiration be safeguarded and promoted. In the heat of trial and experience they hoped to channel that inspiration into forms that would render stable the ever-expanding, increasingly complex, and geographically sprawling organization that was taking shape before their eyes.

The Basic Framework

Within the first decade, provinces had developed as the basic administrative unit of the Society, a pattern borrowed from the Dominicans, Franciscans, and other orders. Three were in operation by 1550—Portugal, Spain, and India. Each had its own superior, or "provincial," responsible directly to Ignatius—Simão Rodrigues, Antonio de Araoz, and Francis Xavier respectively. Ignatius directly governed everywhere else (Italy, Sicily, Germany, and France). On the local scene the houses established by the Society had a superior, or rector, who answered to the provincial or, if a provincial were lacking, to the general. Local communities sometimes had a "collateral," an assistant to the rector who was directly responsible to the provincial; this idea did not work well, however, and was soon abandoned.[1]

This was the basic design of the government of the Society. Simple in the extreme, it was sometimes complicated in these early years by the appointment of "commissaries," officials deputed for several provinces whose authority could override the provincials' or overlap with it. The commissary was an extremely important office in the Society as exercised by Nadal and others, but the sometimes fuzzy delimitations of the commissaries' authority generated confusion and bad feelings. In Spain, for instance, Nadal often found himself treading on the sensitive toes of Araoz and Borja and subsequently felt the sting of their resentment. For these reasons the office was officially abolished in 1565.

In the structure of its government, the Society departed most radically from the monastic and mendicant traditions by eliminating "chapters," assemblies of membership held at regular and specified intervals. These chapters elected superiors. They also set and reviewed policy for the local community, province, or whole order and made other decisions about membership and specific issues of governance.

Although before the *Constitutions* were ready Ignatius occasionally allowed superiors to be elected, he intended thereafter that provincials be appointed by the general and local superiors by the provincial or general. Policy for the whole Society was indeed set by General Congregations, the Jesuit equivalent of the General Chapters of the mendicant orders, but these were to meet rarely—upon the death of the general to elect his successor and for other serious reasons.[2] Ignatius died in 1556, but the First Congregation could not be assembled for two years because of peculiar circumstances. The Second was held within a short time after Laínez's death in January 1565. Only thirty-one have taken place since then.

The reason given in the *Constitutions* for the lack of regular Congregations was simply that "the superior general, through the communication he has with the whole Society and through the help he gets from those near him, can spare the Society as a whole from that work and distraction as far as possible."[3] The same reason applied to the provincial and local communities. It was consonant with the reason for eliminating communal recitation of the liturgical Hours: the chapters were time-consuming and would require regularly calling Jesuits back to their communities from their ministries.

Although the elimination of chapters helped perpetuate the image of the Society as a religious army whose members acted only upon orders from their commanders, it was consistent with the primacy of ministry in an organization originally conceived as operating to a large extent in conditions of diaspora. That is not to deny that other factors—temperamental, cultural, and ecclesiastical—played a role in the decision.

Like the pope and like abbots in monastic communities, but unlike the highest superior in the mendicant orders, the general of the Society was elected for life. Insofar as the analogy with papal government of the church is valid, however, the *Constitutions* clearly opted for a position more in accord with conciliarist theory, for they unambiguously placed the general of the Society under the General Congregation and obliged him to act as faithful executor of its decrees. Rectors and provincials had areas of discretion; although they received their authority from above, they were not simply deputies of the next highest superior. As administrative units, nonetheless, Jesuit provinces had less power of self-determination than did those of the mendicant orders because the General Congregations of the Society had more authority than the mendicants' chapters.

This structure of Jesuit government evolved rapidly under the press of numerical and geographical expansion. According to Polanco's figures, in 1549 Jesuits lived in twenty-two cities and towns, but had houses of their own *(proprium domicilium)* in only seven—Goa, Lisbon, Coimbra, Gandía, Rome, Padua, and Messina.[4] A number of houses were added by the next year, especially in Spain, and Jesuits had by then entered both Japan and Brazil.[5] In 1552 alone, eleven new schools were opened, including one north of the Alps, in Vienna.[6]

By the middle of 1553 six provinces were in full operation—India, Portugal, Castile, Aragon, Brazil, and Italy. Ignatius continued to govern directly the houses in Rome itself as well as those Jesuits whose ministries carried them beyond the boundaries of the established provinces.[7] When

Ignatius died in 1556 there were twelve provinces—Italy (except for Rome), Sicily, Upper Germany, Lower Germany, France, Aragon, Castile, Andalusia, Portugal, Brazil, India, and Ethiopia.[8]

The distribution of personnel among the provinces was always uneven. For most of the first two decades, 10 to 15 percent or more of all Jesuits lived in Rome itself. By 1555, for instance, there were 180 or more in the three major institutions there—112 in the Collegio Romano (faculty and students), a few in the Collegio Germanico, and the rest in the *casa professa*, of whom a large number were novices who had just entered the order.[9] By 1565 there were close to 300—about 143 in the Romano, 30 in the Germanico, 94 in the *casa* (including 30 novices), and 14 in the newly founded Seminario Romano. This disproportion reflected not so much that Rome was the Jesuits' headquarters as that it had become the principal training center for members of the order. Only about 25 percent of these Jesuits, therefore, were priests.[10]

Despite the large proportion of Spaniards in the Society by the time of the bull of approbation, growth in Spain itself was initially slower than in Portugal, the single most flourishing province until well beyond the first decade. Expansion in Spain picked up momentum by the mid-1550's. Italians entered the order at a steadily increasing pace from the very beginning because of the concentrated energy the Jesuits expended in Italy.

By contrast, in 1549 only thirteen Jesuits were in Paris and thirty in India.[11] By 1555 there were about fifty-five in Goa—twenty priests and thirty-five others, of whom seven were novices.[12] In the same year, twenty-five Jesuits were in Brazil, most of whom were not priests. The Ethiopian province had fifteen Jesuits assigned to it, but it existed only on paper. Wherever schools were established and flourished, a proportionately large Jesuit community inevitably resulted. At Messina in 1550, just two years after the college opened, the original nucleus of ten Jesuits had expanded to thirty, of whom ten were novices.[13]

The Society obviously recruited new members at a rapid pace. The Jesuits wanted to grow and harbored no misgivings about the speed with which growth was occurring. The *Exercises* early on proved a helpful instrument to dispose individuals to consider joining.[14] After the Jesuits opened their first school in 1548, they began to recruit over 50 percent of their novices from their students, but they also gained them in other ways, sometimes through the most casual encounters.[15]

A few Jesuit communities accounted for a disproportionately large number of recruits. Close to a fourth of the Spanish Jesuits in the order in

1562 had entered through the community at Alcalá. Although we can only speculate on the causes of this phenomenon, we know that at Alcalá the Jesuits were especially assiduous in promoting the *Exercises*.[16] Moreover, there seems to have been some correlation between the size of the communities and the numbers wanting to join the order. The community at Alcalá was large, as were those at Salamanca and Valencia, and they were all university cities; the three together produced almost 50 percent of those who joined the order in Spain. In 1562 the college at Cologne had forty-five Jesuits. It was the largest community north of the Alps, and it had by far the largest number in that region entering the Society through it.[17]

The Jesuits did not passively wait for young men to knock on their doors. By 1562 Nadal rather expected each community to have a *promotor* who would be especially charged with keeping his eyes open for likely candidates and guiding those who came seeking. He stressed that every Jesuit needed to do his part to see that "as many as possible of the very best" entered the Society—"quamplurimi et quam aptissimi." Although Jesuits were to respect the freedom of the inquirer, Nadal provided a program of prayer, reading, conversation, and reflection to be used to nurture a call if it was there.[18]

Why did you enter? In 1561–62 Nadal constructed and administered a remarkable thirty-point questionnaire to Jesuits in Spain and Portugal in which this was among the questions. He administered revised forms in other visitations in other parts of Europe until 1568.[19] Some 1250 replies are still extant. They provide a remarkable index of how a broad spectrum of Jesuits thought and felt about themselves, and they have been carefully analyzed.[20]

Those who had entered during the first decade often said they wanted to save their souls by fleeing the dangers of the world and rarely indicated the desire to be sent out to convert heathen or heretic as a motive for joining. Although those who entered later were somewhat more inspired by missionary and pastoral ideals, the other motivation continued to predominate. In Nadal's questionnaire and the autobiographical accounts that survive, Jesuits mentioned being attracted specifically to the Society over other orders by the Jesuits' cheerfulness, refinement, and graciousness—*hilaritas, elegantia morum, suavitas*. They sometimes also mentioned being impressed by the purposefulness of the Jesuit community and by the affection the Jesuits seemed to feel for one another.[21]

The Jesuits did not accept all who applied for admittance. They sometimes had to turn away prospective novices because the Society did not have enough money to support them, and they refused to resort to dowries.[22] In 1549 Salmerón accepted two young men into the Society at Belluno but had to tell others to wait because the Jesuits could not provide room and board, yet at that very moment he conformed to Jesuit practice by declining a large sum of money that some of the citizens offered him as direct recompense for his ministry.[23]

The Jesuits refused entry on other general grounds. In 1551 three priests from Burgos wanted to be admitted, but they were judged too ignorant.[24] Although in Portugal in 1547 the Jesuits turned away some candidates for the same reason, they accepted a few others because they seemed to have talent for learning.[25] At Cologne in 1554 Leonard Kessel discovered that a young man who had made the *Exercises* and wanted to become a Jesuit had sometime earlier seduced a girl and had a son by her. Kessel told him to provide for his son—and marry the girl.[26]

The Jesuits were especially concerned about the character and emotional maturity of those who wanted to join them. In 1556 a young Venetian asked to be admitted, but he was refused because he seemed "unstable."[27] They turned some boys away simply because they were too young, although the minimum age in general was low, given the lifetime commitment implied.[28]

Particularly during the first decade they occasionally accepted boys as young as thirteen.[29] In 1551 a boy who was only twelve was admitted by Diego Miró at Salamanca because of his extraordinary piety, intelligence, eloquence, and command of Latin, all of which he displayed when the Jesuits of the community twice invited him to preach to them in their dining room on the Gospel passage from the liturgy of the day.[30] The ages of some of the novices admitted in Rome in 1549 provide an example of what the typical spread was—one thirteen and one fourteen, eight between ages seventeen and twenty-nine, one forty.[31] Some years later Nadal instructed Jesuits who examined candidates for the Society not to accept anybody under fourteen.[32] In the 1560's the median age of those admitted was nineteen—with Germany admitting over 30 percent under sixteen, and Spain not quite 10 percent.[33]

Of those admitted, how many later left? The records, though often fragmentary and inexact, reveal across Europe a fairly consistent picture.[34] For Italy between 1540 and 1565 there is reliable indication that about 35 percent of the candidates either left or were dismissed, but the percentage may well be higher. Of those who departed for whom the evidence is clear, 22 percent left or were dismissed as novices (within two years), 46 percent during the next seven years, and 29 percent after being in the Society ten years or more. Of those who joined before they were eighteen, 44 percent eventually left.[35] These percentages seem to be about the same for the other larger provinces.[36]

Ignatius dismissed Jesuits from the Roman houses without previous warning and for seemingly minor offenses.[37] When in 1552 Xavier returned to India briefly after his sojourn in Japan, he dismissed six members for "reasons more than sufficient."[38] Peremptory dismissal after a Jesuit had pronounced his first vows following his training as a novice was, however, relatively rare. If things did not seem to be working out well, other measures were first employed, including moving the person from one community to another, an expedient that had only limited success.[39]

The best-known person told to leave the Society in these early years was the brilliant eccentric Guillaume Postel. He entered in Rome in 1544 already recognized for his talents, but Ignatius dismissed him the following year because of "opinions and judgments" that were deemed incompatible with the Society.[40] Only in 1549 did Ignatius reveal that the opinions and judgments were Postel's outlandish predictions and prophecies.[41] Although both parties in this affair thereafter regarded each other with some misgiving, neither bore the other any ill will. In 1562 Postel unsuccessfully petitioned Laínez to readmit him.[42]

In the documentation that has survived, reasons for departure or dismissal tend to be given in vague terms, if at all, but a growing sense of incompatibility on one side or the other, or both, is of course what is indicated.[43] In Florence in 1553 Laínez dismissed a Jesuit for "certain sins intolerable in the Society," a circumlocution probably indicating sexual misdeeds.[44] A few years later in Palermo the Inquisition accused a young man of being a heretic and placed him in the Jesuit community under a kind of house arrest. The man reconciled his differences with the Inquisition and then entered the Society. Sometime later he realized he could not "observe continency" and asked to be released from his vows, a request which was granted him. Polanco observed that he remained grateful to the Jesuits for everything they had done for him.[45]

In 1556 a German-speaking Jesuit who had just received his doctorate at the Collegio Romano began to hear confessions in Rome. He shortly thereafter was sent to Germany, where he defected to Lutheranism and married a Lutheran woman—the first such fall from orthodoxy of which Polanco was aware.[46] Others followed. In 1567, for instance, two scholastics and a young priest one after the other left the Jesuit college at Dillingen to become Lutherans.[47]

We should not infer that the only reason for dismissal or voluntary departure was a problem with the vow of chastity. The Jesuits' "way of proceeding" imposed other burdens that not all wanted or were able to shoulder. Ill health was the reason perhaps most often adduced for departures. The Jesuits were not unwilling to care for their sick; rather, there was mutual agreement that the ill could better recover and care for their health outside the order.[48] Chronic headaches, vertigo, insomnia, "melancholy," and "weakness of the stomach" were frequently mentioned symptoms that suggest psychosomatic or psychopathological origins, which helps explain departure from the order as a solution recognized by both sides as proper even if its implications were not fully understood.[49]

There were other reasons. At Venice in 1555 a young man was dismissed when the Jesuits learned that he intended to stay only long enough to get an education.[50] In 1556 Ignatius threatened Antonio Soldevilla with dismissal because of his consistently refractory conduct.[51] At Bologna in 1555 the rector, "moved by pity," admitted as a temporal coadjutor an ill-clad and otherwise needy man from Flanders. Shortly thereafter, while the rest of the community was in church, the man found his way to the community strongbox, stole everything he found, and fled.[52]

A more serious incident had occurred in Florence in 1553. A young Neapolitan novice, "unstable" *(inquietus),* had been sent to Florence, where Laínez was superior. He made his way into Laínez's room and stole letters in which Salmerón had written "freely" about some leading citizens of Naples who were ill-disposed toward the Jesuits. The novice went back to his native Naples, where he tried to blackmail Salmerón by threatening to show the letters to the bishop and others. Although Salmerón could have prosecuted him in court, Polanco reported, he instead sent another Jesuit to persuade the man to burn the letters. The Jesuit seemed to succeed in his mission, but he was not altogether sure everything was destroyed as promised. "I mention this incident," said Polanco, "so that we might realize how cautious we must be about what we put in writing."[53]

Incidents like these, as well as the large number of departures, led to directives to be more careful about admitting candidates, which probably had some effect.[54] As we have seen, by 1546 Ignatius had constructed the *General Examen* to give prospective Jesuits a fairly detailed description of the order and the kind of commitment required of them. He came to believe toward the end of his life that he had been too easy in granting admission.[55] The Jesuits slowly began to learn one lesson well from their sad experience: that they should not readmit persons who had left. Too often they walked out the door a second time.[56]

Jesuits resented departures when they suspected they had been exploited or when scandal ensued.[57] Their attitude toward those who departed under other circumstances seems to have been resigned or even benign.[58] The *Constitutions* urged gentleness, compassion, and consideration for those dismissed and suggested specific ways Jesuits might help them make the transition.[59]

In 1570 Bobadilla wrote to Jerónimo Doménech about the situation in Sicily, where a large number of Jesuits were either dismissed by a particularly rigid provincial or simply left because they could not handle the discipline he imposed. In a passage passionately indignant against the provincial, Bobadilla exclaimed that many who left the Society or were dismissed from it would go to heaven, whereas some of those who remained members would end up in hell.[60]

From Nadal's questionnaire, a reliable profile of the socioeconomic origins of Jesuits who entered the order between 1540 and 1568 has been constructed.[61] The parents of most of the priests and student members came from either the merchant or the professional class—doctors, lawyers, notaries. The professionals tended to be persons held in high esteem in their field, and the merchants were those from a prestigious trade. A few Jesuits came from the nobility, but they were more than counterbalanced by the number that had quite modest origins, like those who entered from the college at Bibona in Sicily.[62] In general, Jesuits came from urban families and from social categories that prized (and needed) literary and intellectual skills.

Patterns varied somewhat from region to region. In Portugal and northern Italy more Jesuits came from noble, wealthy, or aristocratic families than was true in other parts of Europe, and in those regions practically none except the lay brothers came from the lower social ranks. In northern Europe and central Italy the Society drew heavily from the sons of professionals, *rentiers,* and prosperous merchants. In Spain the pattern was thoroughly heterogeneous, with no single class predominating.

The Jesuits were proud that they drew their members from so many social strata.[63] They were also proud that persons from different European nations could live and work together in their common cause, even though national and ethnic prejudices sometimes caused friction.[64] Social, national, and racial egalitarianism and harmony were the ideals they held up for themselves, for that was what they read about the first Christian communities of the New Testament. Ignatius justified the admission into the Society of "New Christians" precisely by alluding to the Epistle to the Romans (10:12)—"en la Compañía non est distinctio judaei et graeci, etc."[65] This policy would cause the Jesuits great problems.

In Lisbon, Abbot Pedro Doménech, founder in 1549 of the royal orphanage and great friend of the Jesuits, saw to it that at least some of the boys, presumably all of whom were illegitimate, were trained in a way that would enable them later to enter the Society if they desired.[66] Beginning in 1550, some of the orphans went to Brazil to help the Jesuits teach catechism; a few of them were later accepted into the Society and held important positions in it.[67]

The Jesuits in India and Brazil soon came to oppose admitting native Indians and Brazilians to the Society, and for all practical purposes their policy prevailed, even though Ignatius and then Laínez urged mitigation of it. The Jesuits were somewhat more lenient toward sons of Portuguese fathers and native mothers, but they said experience taught them to be extremely cautious. In Brazil the overwhelming concern was without doubt for the vow of chastity. Although this was also a major concern in India, there considerations arising from the caste system and, indeed, the racial prejudices strong in some of the Jesuits played a determining role.[68] Outside Europe only among the Japanese did they eventually begin to recruit members, where by the turn of the century there were some seventy native Jesuits.[69]

It was in the wake of this policy that the Jesuits suffered their most tragic losses of life in the sixteenth century. Ignácio de Azevedo recruited in Portugal a large number of Jesuits for the mission in Brazil. In 1570 a fleet under the command of the Huguenot corsair Jacques Sore intercepted a ship headed for Brazil carrying forty of them, including Azevedo. Once Sore and his men learned who the passengers were, they slaughtered them and threw their bodies into the sea. This was by far the largest single contingent of Jesuits yet gathered to be sent to one place. The next year twelve more Jesuits on their way to Brazil were killed on the high seas under almost identical circumstances.

Class distinction was not altogether eliminated, even for actual members of the Society. The "temporal coadjutors" (or lay brothers) came from respectable and stable social origins—sons of artisans (40 percent); peasants who owned their land (25 percent); or small merchants (12 percent). Practically none were from families of day laborers, stevedores, and the like. They came to the Society, therefore, either with some practical skill or with the intention of learning one. They for the most part functioned as cooks, tailors, gardeners, buyers, masons, carpenters, even architects, and in other ways helped in "temporalities," ever more essential as communities grew larger. In the sixteenth century they constituted about 25 percent of the Society's total membership.[70]

These coadjutors were set off from other members of the Society by their lack of formal (or at least humanistic) education, and the *Constitutions* denied them the opportunity to acquire one.[71] If they were illiterate when they entered, so they would remain. Moreover, they could not become superiors. "Spiritual coadjutors" (who were priests), also suffered from the clash between assertions of brotherhood and socio-juridical realities.

With all those who entered, the Jesuits inculcated the importance of "indifference" as to where and how the new members might be employed in ministry, but they at the same time insisted that their superiors employ them according to their talents and "natural inclinations."[72] Perhaps even more important, they encouraged their student members to develop their gifts to the utmost. Nadal put it clearly in an exhortation at Alcalá in 1561:

> The Society wants men who are as accomplished as possible in every discipline that helps it in its purpose. Can you become a good logician? Then become one! A good theologian? Then become one! The same for being a good humanist [*humanista*], and for all the other disciplines that can serve our Institute . . . and do not be satisfied with doing it half-way![73]

The accomplishments of the first and second generation of Jesuits confirm that advice like this was taken to heart. In fact, the accomplishments were so formidable for such a relatively small number of men that they can create the impression that all those who remained in the Society gave full satisfaction. This was not true. The demands that their ministries, especially the schools, made upon the Jesuits were considerable, and many quickly revealed lack of talent and weaknesses of character and spirit.

Jesuit communities by and large functioned well, but some were disasters. Twelve Jesuits were sent to open the new school in Prague in 1556. Of those twelve, according to Polanco, one so misbehaved that he had to be dismissed from the Society; another gave so little satisfaction that he had to be sent to a different community; yet another suffered from headaches; three more were difficult to deal with; and the rector was incompetent.[74]

Late in life Nadal complained about the number in the Society who were inept, those to whom one could not confide a ministry of any substance, and about the number of others in poor health or psychologically debilitated—*defessi*. Among Nadal's recommendations were more careful examination of those who wanted to enter, more thorough testing of those admitted as novices, prompter dismissal of those found unsuitable, and a moratorium on opening new schools, whose needs for ever more Jesuits had led to laxer standards for admittance and less vigorous action on dismissal.[75]

It was not just Jesuits among the rank and file who, while remaining in the Society, in effect carved out for themselves or fell into patterns of life incompatible with what the order professed. Francisco Estrada, who joined Ignatius and his companions in Rome in 1538, became in a few years one of the most energetic and applauded preachers in the Society—in Parma, Louvain, Salamanca, and elsewhere. But after the death of Ignatius he showed increasing signs of alienation from the Society, living for long periods outside Jesuit houses and refusing invitations to preach or do any other work. As his contemporaries realized, he was not well and probably suffered as much from depression or other psychological maladies as from physical problems. His fellow Jesuits treated him gently, but they were alternately puzzled and scandalized by his deportment.

Even more serious was the case of Antonio de Araoz, who had held the highest positions in the Society in Spain. Especially after about 1565, he played his entrée to the Spanish court to the hilt, gave up pretense of performing any ministry, and successfully insisted on having two Jesuit temporal coadjutors as his servants. Because he had the full support of Count Rui Gómez, the most powerful person in the kingdom after Philip II himself, his Jesuit contemporaries were forced to write him off as a lost cause.[76]

The Campaign for Self-Understanding

If recruits were to be gained and members retained, they had to be instructed in what the Society was about and how it "proceeded," and then they had to be inspired to persevere in their commitment. Ignatius and his closest associates were keenly aware that communication of the ideals, goals, and style of the Society did not occur automatically and that it had to be sustained on a consistent and ongoing basis.

They were hampered in achieving such communication by the lack of any body of literature about the Society to which Jesuits and prospective Jesuits could be referred, except for the *Spiritual Exercises* (not printed until 1548) and the *Constitutions* (not printed until 1559). Moreover, as the Society expanded, fewer Jesuits had direct contact with Ignatius or with any others from the original nucleus.

This situation accounts for the extraordinary emphasis the *Constitutions* placed on correspondence as a means of achieving "union of hearts." When practicable, rectors were to write to the provincial and provincials write to the general as often as once a week; the general should respond to the provincials at least once a month, and the provincials respond just as often to the local rectors.[77] These provisions were too exacting ever to have been observed except in special cases, as during the crucial first months of the opening of a new school.[78] They set, nonetheless, an ideal of frequent and frank communication. Whenever they could, Jesuits carried on their official and unofficial correspondence with each other not in Latin but in the vernacular, which means that most of the letters from this period are in Spanish, Portuguese, or Italian.

There were obvious problems with correspondence as a means of communication. Although letters from Rome to certain Italian cities generally took no longer to arrive than they would today, four years might be required for a letter and response between Rome and India.[79] As late as February 1555, the Jesuits in Rome had no definite information about Xavier's death just outside mainland China in December 1552.[80] They also had to worry about deliberate interception of letters by enemies, as well as loss of letters through shipwreck and other natural disasters.

Besides conveying information and seeking or giving advice, some letters or parts of letters were meant by deliberate design to do something more. They had a professedly edifying purpose either for Jesuits themselves or for others, and were to that extent expurgated at their very source.[81] Jesuits especially looked forward to letters from their brethren in "the Indies" and read them at table in the Jesuit houses.[82] In September 1553, for instance, Nadal enthusiastically informed Ignatius that four ships had arrived in Lisbon carrying letters from those parts and that they were now being copied for distribution—"They are very edifying."[83] The Jesuits circulated letters of this kind to silence enemies, win friends, attract recruits, and fan their own enthusiasm for their vocation.[84]

Most important, both Jesuits and others learned who Jesuits were by reading about what they did, which is what made Polanco's circular letter sent two or three times a year "to the whole Society" so significant. Polanco's importance for Jesuit self-definition of course did not stop there. Partly on his own initiative, partly "upon commission" from respective generals over the course of twenty-six years, he produced a series of documents that taken as a whole projected an "image of the Jesuit," as a modern editor aptly designated them.[85]

For approximately the same number of years, Nadal, acting as commissary and empowered with sweeping authority, did *viva voce* what Polanco did in writing. After that first major visitation to Portugal and Spain in 1553–54 he returned to Rome. The next year he headed for Germany and Austria and then visited the thirteen Jesuit schools already established in northern

Italy. Later that year he departed for the Iberian peninsula for another visitation, which included begging money for the financially faltering Collegio Romano. Upon Ignatius's death on 31 July 1556, Nadal returned to Rome, where he remained during the turbulent period of transition until late 1560, when he again set out under Laínez's orders for Portugal and Spain. This trip, troubled and impeded in Spain by suspicions that had fallen on Francisco de Borja from the Inquisition and the royal court, lasted until April 1562. Nadal left Spain for visitations to France, the Low Countries, and Germany, which lasted about a year and a half. He did not return to Rome until 12 February 1564. In 1566 under the new general, Borja, he traveled to Austria, Germany, the Low Countries, and France for two years, and in 1571–72 he acted in Rome as vicar-general of the Society during Borja's absence, his last major assignment.[86]

Nadal often had the solution of specific problems assigned him for his visitation, but in his mind the overriding and consistent purpose of his trips was to expound to Jesuits the meaning of their Institute and to kindle their enthusiasm for it.[87] For the latter task he proved himself a genius. His creation of occasions for indoctrination and his bold rhetoric about the origins and meaning of the Jesuit vocation were the products of his own intelligence and imagination. Ignatius had told him what to do but not how to do it. The very survival of the Society owed a great deal to how effectively he accomplished the task.

On these visitations Nadal carried with him a collection of documents, including the *Constitutions*. Until that document was finally printed, he used handwritten copies and left extracts with superiors upon his departure, along with a number of "rules." His most immediate impact on the Society lay, however, in the exhortations he delivered to communities and in the formal and informal conversations he held with individual Jesuits.

During a visitation, Nadal might deliver on alternate days twenty or more instructions to the community, in which he would typically discourse on how the Society was founded, on certain aspects of the *Exercises,* on the admission of novices and their training, on the vows and the different grades in the Society, on the *consueta ministeria,* and on prayer. Meanwhile, he conducted private interviews with each individual; during meals he invited different members of the community in turn to his table, set up in a room apart from the refectory, and he sought other occasions to converse with them informally, especially to tell them what Jesuits elsewhere were doing.[88] Communities consistently registered satisfaction—indeed, great satisfaction—with this instructional, exhortatory, and even consolatory aspect of his visits. He brought "joy," "much joy and consolation," "great happiness and good spirits," "great *esprit de corps* and peace."[89]

Who are we? What are we? Whence did we come? These were the questions Jesuits asked. The last was perhaps the easiest to answer, but considerable effort had to be expended to put together accounts of the events that led up to the papal approval of 1540. Polanco saw the importance of gathering information immediately upon being appointed secretary in 1547, and within a few months he obtained from Laínez a long letter containing the first narration of what had happened, written for "our edification."[90] The next year, complementing Laínez's narrative with information he obtained elsewhere, Polanco composed a "summary" of the basic story, never published but circulated in manuscript.[91]

What was missing, of course, was an account from Ignatius, who was slow in self-disclosure. In 1552 Polanco and Nadal approached him with a request to put in writing how God had guided him from the time of his conversion to the present. This work would be a "testament" for members of the Society. They argued that founders of other religious orders had done so and that it behooved him to do the same. A year later Ignatius began dictating "the pilgrim's story," his *Autobiography*.

From the beginning, therefore, that story was meant to be, at least as Polanco and especially Nadal conceived it, something more than a recounting of the facts. For Nadal, answering the question of whence the Society came—that is, from Ignatius—put the Jesuits well on the road to answering who and what they were. Ignatius's story was a key element in the mythmaking required to give the order its sense of location in the grander scheme of things. In an exhortation at Alcalá in 1561, Nadal put the matter succinctly: in Ignatius one saw "the first form and grace" God gave to the Society.[92] At Cologne in 1567 he said practically the same thing: "The whole life of the Society is contained in germ and expressed in Ignatius's story."[93]

For Nadal, then, Ignatius's story was somehow the story of every Jesuit and, hence, revelatory of the deepest meaning of the Society as a whole. The story was basically one of the inner life of the soul. It moved in this sequence: a conversion to God from a previously unsatisfying or disordered life; visitations from God in the form of consolations, clarification of vision, dispositions to give oneself in God's service that resulted in an "election" to follow these dispositions; a period of probation and trial like that Ignatius experienced at Manresa; and a life thenceforth inspired by the desire "to help souls." Just as God had guided and aided Ignatius in this course, so God guided and aided every Jesuit.

In guiding Ignatius God had meant, therefore, to raise up the Society. Nadal provided no support in his writings and exhortations for the idea that the founding of the Society was a collaborative venture of the original companions. His interpretation was surely influenced by the great crises of 1553 and 1556–57, when Rodrigues and Bobadilla advanced that argument.

Early Jesuits such as Nadal, Polanco, and Laínez did not doubt that the Society was somehow of divine inspiration, as the *Constitutions* themselves indicated.[94] They sometimes spoke of its true founder as God, who used Ignatius as his instrument.[95] They believed, of course, that God had earlier done the same through Benedict, Dominic, Francis, and other founders of religious orders. The Jesuits were simply the latest in this ongoing series of divine interventions.

Nadal often reviewed these initiatives for his brethren. According to him, the essence of the life of a member of a religious order was seeking the highest spiritual good. This premise allowed Nadal to assert that in persons such as Adam before the Fall and Abel and Seth after the Fall religious life predated the coming of Jesus.[96] "There have been religious since the beginning of time."[97]

When Jesus came, he gave specification to the pursuit of holiness, especially in his words to the rich young man "If you would be perfect, go, sell what you possess and give to the poor, and you will have treasure in heaven; and come, follow me" (Matt. 19:21).[98] Central to this invitation was divesting oneself of earthly possessions, done either in actuality or "in spirit." The emphasis on poverty in the *Exercises* in fact echoed this and similar passages from the New Testament.

Nadal believed that Jesus extended to all the invitation to perfection and that "evangelical perfection" was attainable in a variety of circumstances and conditions of life and did not require membership in a religious order.[99] However, the circumstances and conditions included preeminently the Society and religious orders in general, in which poverty was "actual" rather than "spiritual" and to which celibate chastity and obedience under a superior were conjoined.[100]

What Jesus counseled the young man, the twelve special disciples, or Apostles, had already put into practice.[101] This led Nadal to the conclusion that the Christian specification of religious life antedated Jesus' creation of Christian priesthood and the ecclesiastical hierarchy, which did not take place until the Last Supper and after Jesus' resurrection from the dead respectively.

In considerations like these emerged the fundamental meaning that Nadal attached to the designation "apostolic" for the Jesuit vocation. That vocation was an imitation and revivification of the lifestyle of the first disciples of Jesus. Religious reformers and enthusiasts had since the eleventh century invoked the *vita apostolica* as warrant for their programs, and they meant different things by the expression. For Nadal, however, it meant essentially abandonment of worldly attachments and acceptance of Jesus' commission to preach and to heal—"and all this before there were either priests or bishops."[102]

If Nadal saw Jesuits following the path trod by Ignatius, he also saw them following a much older path: "Our vocation is similar to the vocation and training of the Apostles: first, we come to know the Society, and then we follow; we are instructed; we receive our commission to be sent [on ministry]; we are sent; we exercise our ministry; we are prepared to die for Christ in fulfilling those ministries."[103]

For Nadal, therefore, the way to understand the Society was to correlate two realities: on the one hand, the Old and New Testaments; on the other, the *Exercises*, the *Constitutions*, the living tradition of the life and ministries of Ignatius and other members of the Society.[104] The latter were authentic translations into the present of the fundamental message and patterns of the former.

Up to this point Nadal's characterization of the Society still lacked differentiation from many other religious orders in the history of Christianity. He often cursorily reviewed their founding and saw in them a rich variety of ways in which holiness could be pursued. "In one and the same Spirit" there were diverse gifts.[105]

Nadal knew that in significant ways the mendicants of the Middle Ages were different from monks. He nonetheless classified them and other orders as monastic insofar as they retained choir and monastic garb. They trained their novices in "choir and other ceremonies" and admitted members to profession before they were tried in ministry. This is where the Society differed from them, for even its novices did ministry, and its members were not admitted to solemn profession until after many years of experience in the ministries of the Society.[106]

In other orders the members lived in monasteries or convents. Jesuits lived in "houses" or "colleges," but they differed from the others most pointedly in that their "best house" was their "pilgrimages" and their "missions," that is, their journeying for ministry.[107] In these various ways Jesuits followed more closely the lifestyle of the early preachers of the Gospel—"The Apostles did not wear a monastic habit . . . They did not spend their time [in choir] chanting psalms and hymns."[108]

"We are not monks!" Nadal proclaimed continually.[109] If flight from the dangers of the world was the reason so many joined the Society, he needed to disabuse them of the mistaken notions about the character of the Society that this motivation seemed to imply. He needed to instill in them a new way of thinking about life in a religious order. For Nadal, in fact, the essence of the monk was "to flee the company of other human beings." But the essence of the Jesuit was to *seek* their company "in order to help them."[110]

"The world is our house." Again and again Nadal reiterated this point.[111] Ignatius never said it so boldly. Nadal's expression caught the reality at a depth that went beyond the immediate context of his words. He referred this statement to the geographical scope of the Jesuits' ministry, but, as we shall see, it had deeper resonances—as with his reconciliatory theology of nature and grace, the systemic relationship of the Jesuits to the *studia humanitatis* through their schools, and the "Contemplation to Obtain Divine Love" of the *Exercises.*

"We are not monks . . . The world is our house." The message sounds simple enough. But it was not always grasped to Nadal's satisfaction, nor was it always clear what it meant in detail. Nadal nursed suspicions that even somebody as influential as Borja, who had had little sustained contact with Ignatius, did not fully comprehend it. Symptomatic of the problem of working out what this expression meant in practice was the ongoing debate among Jesuits about how much and what kind of prayer was appropriate, a debate that began almost at the first hour and continued for decades.

The Jesuits' efforts to understand and explain themselves and how they fitted into the Christian tradition of ministry and religious life had a counterpart in the labels that others attached to them. Officially, of course, Jesuits were "members of the Society of Jesus," but that designation was too long-winded for quick reference. It also lacked any familiar specification.

Especially in Italy, people early began to call them simply "reformed priests" or "holy Roman priests," appellations they took in good part even though they obscured how many were not yet, or would never be, ordained.[112] These titles correlated, however, with the stipulation in the *Formula* that in externals the Jesuits' manner of life conform to the usages of "upright priests."[113]

In some localities, especially in Portugal, they were known as "apostles."[114] This designation, too, was not unpleasing, but Nadal warned that the term properly applied only to those disciples whom Jesus himself had chosen and sent to preach the Gospel. Jesuits imitated the Apostles and were sent "to do apostolic tasks," but were not themselves apostles.[115]

The Jesuits were not happy to be called "Theatines," a name they found hard to shake, especially in central Italy.[116] They were sometimes hard-pressed to explain just how they differed from that order founded by Gaetano Thiene and Giampietro Carafa, the future Pope Paul IV, with whom they had so much trouble.[117] When in 1562 Martin Chemnitz in his attack on the Society—the first major notice taken of the Jesuits by a Protestant theologian—made the mistake of asserting that Carafa was its founder, Nadal and others felt obliged to refute the error.[118]

In parts of Spain, Jesuits were called "Ignatians"—*ignistae* or *ignatiani*.[119] Sometimes used derisively, the name might have stuck—as had "Dominicans" for the Order of Preachers and "Franciscans" for the Friars Minor—had not it and all its rivals soon been driven from the field by "Jesuit." As early as 1544 Peter Canisius reported to Pierre Favre that that was what members of the Society were sometimes called in Cologne.

The Latin term *Jesuita* appeared in fifteenth-century texts in northern Europe in a positive sense to mean a good Christian, a follower of Jesus. Ludolph, in his *Vita Jesu Christi,* with which many Jesuits were familiar, said, "and in heaven we shall by Jesus himself be called Jesuits [*Jesuitae*], that is, saved by the Savior."[120] By the early sixteenth century the designation was also used pejoratively to mean a religious hypocrite, and surely in that sense it was sometimes applied to members of the Society. The Jesuits made the best of the situation by adopting it themselves as a shorthand for the official name of their organization, a name about which Ignatius was so insistent.[121]

Ignatius's doggedness concerned, of course, the use of "Jesus," which is what "Jesuit" captured. "Society" was probably just a term of convenience, but Nadal reappropriated its original meaning when he said that the members were bound together by brotherhood—*hermandad*.[122] Once the term "Compagnia" was officially adopted, however, it could be made to echo ideas found in the meditations on the "Kingdom" and the "Two Standards" in the *Exercises* and to relate to the vision at La Storta in 1537, after which Ignatius would not tolerate further discussion of the name of the Society. When Nadal described the event at La Storta for his brethren, he affirmed their common belief that God had inspired the name of their organization. In that name, Nadal found the essence of his message to his brethren about who and what they were: being members of the "Company of Jesus" meant being "companions of Christ Jesus"—*socii Christi Jesu*.[123]

Pastoral Ideals and Practice

We have seen how, after stating that the Society was founded for "the progress of souls in Christian life and doctrine and for the propagation of the faith," the original version of the *Formula* continued immediately with the list of ministries by which the twofold goal was to be accomplished. The first part of the goal corresponded to the actual experience of the Jesuits up to that time, whereas the second expressed a hope to work for the conversion of unbelievers that they had not been able to realize for Jerusalem, even though that hope had first banded them together. Once Xavier was sent to India in 1540 the hope took substance. During the period I am considering, however, most Jesuits were not engaged in converting unbelievers to the faith, or even heretics to orthodoxy, but were laboring with Catholics for their "progress in Christian life and doctrine" in the three countries from which the vast majority of Jesuits originated—Portugal, Spain, and Italy.

The pattern of denser distribution in these areas did not correspond to preconceived priorities but was the result of some obvious contingencies. Nadal came to see the ministry of the Jesuits in "the Indies" and in Germany as the "two wings" of the Society.[124] Precisely what he meant by this metaphor is not clear, but he surely intended to indicate the importance of these two areas. Favre, Jay, Canisius, and others would also insist on the special urgency of the German situation.

Jesuits did not refute such assessments or argue against sending as many men as possible to "the Indies." However, the practical problems of learning foreign languages and living in foreign lands, the threat of war, imprisonment, and death, the lack of support and even the opposition from prelates and princes, and, above all, the claims and opportunities of the local situation into which most of the Jesuits were born were reasons for the concentration in Italy and the Iberian peninsula. Moreover, because of the similarities in language and culture, the first Jesuits could in those regions move back and forth relatively easily.

The conditions under which the Jesuits labored when they were among heretics and pagans of course affected the style and content of their ministries. Preaching and similar ministries took on a more apologetic and aggressive cast in Protestant territories, and analogous changes had to be made for the indigenous peoples overseas. We must remember, however, that even in these situations Jesuits dealt, sometimes principally, with Catholics. Much in the general pattern of their ministries remained the same no matter what part of the world they were active in.

Conversion to Christianity or reconversion to Catholicism may seem far removed from the conversion of heart of the *Exercises*. The first Jesuits saw them as clearly related, however, with the former an almost ineluctable consequence of the latter. Their epistemology led them to believe that once the heart had been changed the veil of blindness would fall from the eyes of the mind and truth would be embraced. They surely did not want for that reason to be without credible answers to questions that may be raised, but they generally did not believe that argumentation and reasoning would in themselves accomplish their desired end.

This persuasion caused them to take less seriously some of the scriptural and theological arguments of the Protestants than we might otherwise have expected. Like other Christian thinkers, the Jesuits believed that heresy was essentially the result of some moral lapse. Despite their skills in theological controversy, therefore, the Jesuits manifested some ambivalence about their efficacy. They tended, especially in the first years, to see themselves as essentially peacemakers and promoters of reconciliation in all sectors of society, as the *Formula* suggested.[125] Ignatius, never soft on heresy, counseled moderation and restraint in dealing with misbelievers and especially urged the Jesuits not to become involved in controversies among Catholics, as his instructions in 1546 to Laínez, Jay, and Salmerón at Trent show.[126] Forces in society, in the church, and in other aspects of the Jesuits' heritage and understanding of themselves, however, often rendered such neutrality practically impossible. Nonetheless, not in controversy did the Jesuits see themselves making their primary contribution to "helping souls," but in their *consueta ministeria* and the way they went about them.

For those *ministeria* some evidence suggests that the Jesuits had their eyes primarily on persons in high places. As we have seen, they early had access to influential persons in Rome such as Ortiz, Contarini, and Paul III himself. In Rome in 1539 Codure became the confessor to Margaret of Austria, the emperor's daughter, who was married to Ottavio Farnese, the pope's grandson. The Jesuits almost immediately developed good relationships with King John III of Portugal and a few years later with King Ferdinand of Habsburg, the emperor's brother and future emperor himself. They had a cordial relationship with the Wittelsbach dukes of Bavaria. These names are but the tip of the iceberg, as a mere scanning of the list of addressees of Ignatius's correspondence reveals. They are, however, grossly misleading if they are interpreted to mean that the Jesuits directed their ministries primarily to the social and cultural elite. Almost the opposite is true, most certainly until the schools were founded in some number.

The social class of a few of them, including Ignatius and Xavier, the prestige deriving from their Parisian degrees, the attention that their manifest disinterest in personal comfort and advancement called to them, and rumors about something called the *Spiritual Exercises* were among the factors that first elicited the curiosity, the forbearance, and then often the support of the powerful. The first Jesuits sought that support, for they saw in it the indispensable means of accomplishing their goals.

The Jesuits in fact most palpably prospered in two territories where they had the warmest and most consistent support from the rulers—in Portugal from King John and Queen Catherine and in Sicily from the viceroy Juan de Vega and his consort Leonor Osorio.[127] They sometimes did well, however, in places where support from the highest authorities was grudging, indifferent, inconstant, or absent—or where the relationship was at least intermittently hostile, as in Spain under Philip II or Rome under Paul IV.

The ruling elite stood for order and stability, and the Jesuits came from social backgrounds that made it easy for them to identify with such values. The *Constitutions* taught, moreover, that greater good was achieved by influencing those in a position to influence others.[128] The Jesuits struck alliances. They did not always see how such alliances might in the short or long run compromise them. Nadal seems, for instance, to have been blind to how much the Spanish viceroy was hated by the Sicilians and to have taken no account of the troubles the Jesuits' deference to him would cause them. In Paris, as well as elsewhere, Jesuits learned that friendship with one magnate rendered them suspect to others.

More lowly motivations were also at work. Some documents almost purr with satisfaction at favors received from those in high places. Antonio de Araoz and Simão Rodrigues were criticized by their Jesuit brethren and by others for their seemingly easy accommodation to life at the Spanish and Portuguese courts. While Ignatius was general he occasionally treated his closest collaborators, such as Polanco and Nadal, with surprising harshness, but never, despite aggravations, Francisco de Borja, the former duke of Gandía, who shortly after the death of his wife in 1546 entered the order to Ignatius's great delight.[129] In 1550, moreover, he greeted with enthusiasm Borja's never-executed project to enhance the church that eventually became the Gesù with the body of his great-grandfather, Pope Alexander VI.[130] In Spain the Jesuits were accused of parading Borja around "like a trophy."[131] (They were of course embarrassed when murder and other violent crimes were with seeming justification imputed to members of his family.)[132]

Nonetheless, one of the most striking features of the early Jesuits is the wide variety of people to whom they ministered, including many of the poor and outcast. Some of the most impassioned lines issued from Nadal's pen were about Jesuit ministry as directed to persons "in need," to those who had no one to care for them or to minister to them. In so writing he believed he was simply echoing the *Constitutions* and elaborating on the deepest meaning of the vow to be on journey when so ordered by the pope, but his words are more forceful.[133] Shortly after Ignatius's death, for instance, he wrote in his personal journal: "The Society has the care of those souls for whom either there is nobody to care or, if somebody ought to care, the care is negligent. This is the reason for the founding of the Society. This is its strength. This is its dignity in the Church."[134] For him the Jesuit task par excellence was to search for the "lost sheep"—whether pagan, Muslim, heretic, or Catholic.[135]

It was easier for the Jesuits to yearn for lost sheep than to define who they were and to rank their need, which helps account for the Jesuits' lack of discrimination when choosing persons among whom they would work. The most urgent call was to those who were not Christians or to those who might abandon Catholicism through heresy. Thus, like the evangelizing Paul and the early disciples of Jesus who were models more powerfully operative in the Jesuits' self-image than the Christian soldier, their vocation, as the *Constitutions* put it, was "to travel through the world and to live in any part of it whatsoever where there is hope of greater service to God and of help of souls."[136] Nadal said more succinctly, "Paul signifies for us our ministry."[137]

On a more practical level, however, the Jesuits found needs of either soul or body wherever they happened to be, and they were loath not to respond. Their superiors occasionally urged restraint, but more often they supplied encouragement. The principles on the matter in the *Constitutions* were abstract and general, even if they explicitly entered into consideration, and thus allowed for broad interpretation.[138] The ministries listed in the *Formula* seem all-inclusive, but the wording in fact suggests that the list has not exhausted every possibility.

Was there nowhere to draw the line? On one important count the documents were clear. The *Constitutions* firmly enjoined that Jesuits were not to take up any beneficed "curacy of souls" *(cura animarum)* in the technical and canonical sense of the term.[139] This provision precluded, among other things, their becoming pastors of parishes. Innocent though it sounds, this stipulation marked a crucial line of demarcation.

At the time the Society was founded, Catholics to a large degree still sought their devotion in a wide variety of institutions, including shrines, manor chapels, itinerant preaching, collegiate churches, and confraternities. Nonetheless, the parish was, at least in theory, the primary and normative institution for the ministry of the church, and the legislation of the Council of Trent attempted to enhance and promote even further this status and the status of the pastor. Trent's concern over these institutions and the Jesuits' self-imposed exclusion from them is but one indication of how the Council and the Society were like two often intersecting and interlocking, but independent, vectors or trajectories.

The Jesuits forswore the parish for a variety of reasons. They believed it belonged more properly to the diocesan clergy than to members of an order. The benefice, or "living," attached to it conflicted with their version of the vow of poverty. Its fixity, generally as a lifetime appointment, restricted the mobility that was so intrinsic to their theory about their calling. It implied, finally, a ministry to those who already had pastors, a ministry to those who already had somebody to care for them.[140]

Pastors of parishes cared for their flocks principally through ritual and the administration of the sacraments. Especially since the famous decree *Omnis utriusque sexus* of the Fourth Lateran Council, 1215, pastors by virtue of their office had been increasingly invested with the power to invoke canonical penalties upon the faithful who, for instance, did not receive the sacraments of Penance and the Eucharist at least once a year in the parish church according to the stipulations of the decree. Trent strengthened pastoral prerogatives like these.

Because the Jesuits were not pastors, they could not by virtue of office or jurisdictional status oblige anybody to accept any of their ministrations. Those who came to them, therefore, came of their own free will. They would come only if they were convinced they were being better served by the Jesuits than by other ministers—including their pastors. The Jesuits, in other words, did not have a ready-made clientele of the "people in the pews," and they had to persuade people to take advantage of what they offered. This feature of the Jesuits' ministries is fundamentally important for understanding them and also for situating them in so-called Tridentine Catholicism.

Who were the people who came to the Jesuits? Polanco observed that in Messina in 1548 the Jesuits attracted "two extremes"—persons more than ordinarily intent upon deepening their spiritual lives and others whose lives up to that point had been notably bad.[141] His observation applied more broadly, for among Catholics it does seem to have been these "extremes" who especially sought the Jesuits and whom they themselves especially sought. On the basis of this reality, Polanco in another document generalized that on "simple and good" people Jesuits should not expend much attention, because little more could be hoped for than offering them consolations already available to them from other ministers.[142] They would presumably find such ministers in their parish church, if not elsewhere.

Jesuits admitted only males to their schools. As time went on they began to lay down for themselves some restrictions on hearing the confessions of women. With these two exceptions, they made no distinction in their ministries between the sexes. Without hesitation they enlisted women to help them and entrusted them with responsible positions, including guiding other women into a deeper spiritual life.[143] As with men, they led them in the *Exercises,* and outside the *Exercises* they taught them how to meditate.[144] In 1551 they proudly and typically reported a thriving ministry in Florence to widows, matrons, and young unmarried women.[145] They had a similar ministry in Bologna.[146] Occasionally they preached against customs that discriminated against women's freedom in religious practice and succeeded in having them changed, as in 1565 at Huelva, in Spain, where local practice forbade young girls from entering church until they were married and forbade the same to widows for a year or two after their husbands' deaths.[147]

This does not mean that they were free of the standard prejudices against the "weaker sex," as Laínez's treatise on women's use of cosmetics and jewelry betrays.[148] The treatise is also an example of the moral severity Laínez manifested on certain issues. In general, the Jesuits' practice in dealing with women was much better than their talk about it. As was often the case, the vocabulary they inherited was inadequate for the reality they lived, or at least wanted to live.

Ignatius corresponded with many women, mostly those in the upper strata of the social hierarchy.[149] Although he used these occasions to offer them spiritual counsel, he also often tried to enlist or confirm their support for the pastoral enterprises of the order.[150] In 1545 under pressure from Paul III, moreover, he accepted a few "devout women" to live in obedience to him, in effect as members of the Society, but the venture ended unsuccessfully within two years. Ignatius thereupon elicited from the pope a decree eliminating the possibility of a female branch of the Society.[151] He probably could imagine such a branch only according to the fully cloistered models of the existing "Second Orders" of women Dominicans and Franciscans; a woman's division of the Society would, among other things, require Jesuit priests as regular and fixed chaplains and be governed by the male branch.

In 1554, however, Juana of Austria, the talented and willful daughter of Charles V, sister of Philip II, and sometimes regent of Spain, managed to bring such strong pressure to bear that Ignatius took counsel with Nadal, Polanco, and several other Jesuits in Rome. This committee recommended the acceptance into the Society under certain carefully stated stipulations of "Mateo Sánchez," the code name for the Infanta. Juana therefore became a

Jesuit and remained one until her death in 1573—a secret known only to herself and a few members of the Society. The discomfort those Jesuits, including Ignatius, felt with this anomalous situation and with the possibility of the recriminations it might provoke from Juana's brother should he learn the secret was balanced by the hope that she might provide the Society with help and protection. She in fact threw her support behind the Jesuits in some important matters, but she also caused them much anxiety.[152] The experiment was never repeated.

Toward whomever they ministered, the Jesuits were urged to take a positive approach, to keep in mind their good qualities, and, if they seemed to have few, to remember that they were created in the image of God and redeemed by Christ. Laínez repeated a traditional theme when, during a "sacred lecture" in Rome in 1557, he told his congregation that infidels and Jews put Christians to shame by their fervor in their beliefs and that, if converted, they would make better Christians than themselves.[153] Although the Jesuits could not contain their anger toward "heresiarchs" like Luther, they tried their best to excuse more lowly heretics as persons misled.

The Jesuits also tried to be positive in their assessments of the indigenous peoples of India, Japan, and Brazil, but, as with recruitment from them for membership in the Society, they could not altogether overcome racial prejudice or blink at the difficulties of the situation. Although few Jesuits from this first generation labored outside Europe, those who did fulfilled the evangelizing aspirations of the first companions, and they set a powerful example for the generations to come. Xavier arrived in India on 6 May 1542.[154] For two years he catechized poor pearl fishers on the eastern coast of Cape Comorin with basic Christian prayers he had had translated into Tamil. As more Jesuits gradually joined him, he established Goa as the principal center for Jesuit ministry. For the next four years he reconnoitered widely, eventually traveling as far as the Molucca Islands, four thousand miles beyond India.

By 1548 he was back in Goa, where for a year he concentrated on organizing the activities of his several dozen confreres there and elsewhere. By 15 August 1549 he and two other Jesuits had landed at Kagoshima, a city in southern Kyushu.[155] Two months later Xavier's enthusiasm was still high: "We shall never find among heathens another race equal to the Japanese. They are a people of excellent morals—good in general and not malicious."[156] For two and a half years he remained in Japan, where he won permission to proselytize, impressing high-placed Japanese with gifts of clocks, spectacles, music boxes, and wine. He hoped to create liaisons between the learned class of Japan and the great universities of Europe, especially his alma mater, Paris. When he heard from the Japanese that the most erudite people in the world were the Chinese, he determined to enter the Celestial Empire. After many frustrations and hardships, he died on the island of Sancian, 3 December 1552, within a few miles of his goal.

By the time Xavier left Japan in late 1551, he could boast some thousand converts to Christianity. Under the capable leadership of Cosme de Torres, Xavier's successor as head of the mission, the number increased to about thirty thousand within the next twenty years. Since there were never more than nine Jesuits in Japan until 1563, the increment was encouraging. Jesuits came to believe that Japan was their most promising mission field in the East.

Among the Jesuits working in Japan in these early years, few were more important and none had a more unusual background than Luis de Almeida. He was by birth Jewish, then a convert to Catholicism from Protestantism. He came to Japan as a merchant in 1552 and entered the Society shortly thereafter as a temporal coadjutor. Among the Jesuits he had the reputation of best understanding the Japanese and was esteemed by them for his other skills, which were manifested in many ways, including the establishment of several medical clinics and orphanages.[157]

Five months before the Jesuits arrived in Japan in 1549, six Portuguese Jesuits landed at Bahía do todos os Santos in Brazil.[158] Their superior was the talented and energetic nobleman Manuel da Nóbrega, who within two weeks had organized children of the Portuguese colonists and natives into catechism classes that included singing and learning to read and write. Nóbrega then began scouting the settlements up and down the coastline, and by 1553 he had climbed the mountains behind Sâo Vincente to establish contact with the Tupi Indians of the forests. There he marked a site that would be the city of Sâo Paolo.

Four more Jesuits had meanwhile arrived in 1550, but in 1553 came the sickly and badly crippled José de Anchieta, a nineteen-year-old Basque. Despite his physical disabilities, Anchieta became, along with Nóbrega, the energy center for Jesuit work with the natives of Brazil, with whom he labored until his death forty-four years later. Within six months of his arrival he had composed a rough draft of a grammar in Latin characters of the Tupi language. His skill in rhyme and verse enabled him to set Christian beliefs to native tunes and to capitalize on the Indians' marvelous musical talent.

The talent of many of the natives in India, Japan, and Brazil elicited praise from the Jesuits who worked with them, as well as comparisons unflattering to their European counterparts.[159] As we have seen, Xavier eulogized the virtues and intelligence of the Japanese,[160] and his successors in Japan would continue to recognize that to win converts they would have to emphasize how Christianity was consonant with "reason."[161]

For boys and girls in India and Brazil the Jesuits provided a catechesis, education in reading and writing, and training in basic skills equivalent to what they provided in Europe. Once they established formal schools, they accepted native boys into classrooms with the sons of European parents.[162] When they taught catechism to the Brazilian children, they also taught them Portuguese, while the children taught them their language.[163]

Although these efforts smack of paternalism and a misguided sense of European cultural superiority, with all their attendant evils, they were not engaged in by the Jesuits without some feeling of mutuality, and they contrast with the attitudes and practices of many other Europeans who had settled in these places. In Brazil Jesuits took courageous stands against the abuses of the slave raids and evoked great wonderment from the natives as word sped through the jungles that among the Portuguese there were some who defended them.[164]

The Jesuits criticized European priests for their scandalous conduct and the way they evangelized.[165] Polanco wrote in 1550 that when Ignatius learned about the "military mode" *(militarem in modum)* in which other priests in India were baptizing persons without previous instruction, he determined that colleges and houses of catechesis be instituted there.[166] Nadal judged that one of the great benefits of Jesuit ministries in India and Japan was that they established the church "our way" *(a nostro modo),* that is, in orderly fashion, with special care for catechesis, and by inspiring an inner relish for spiritual things.[167]

The Jesuits did not lose their common sense. In Brazil in 1556 Bishop Pedro Fernandes Sardinha insisted that the natives stop violating "natural law" by going around totally naked, and he reproached the Jesuits for not abolishing the custom. In the Jesuits' report on the matter to their own superiors in Europe, they made clear that it was an unreasonable demand, for the natives were simply too poor to clothe themselves and the Jesuits too poor to help them.[168]

Native customs like this, along with other problems of working in these strange and difficult situations, soon revealed that the Jesuits themselves needed special strength of character if they were to survive and succeed. In their letters home they made this point and voiced the suspicion that Jesuits for whom useful employment could not be found in their own province were sometimes sent overseas.[169]

Some areas in which the Jesuits labored required especially strong stomachs. Although they were at first gratified to learn that idolatry was unknown among the Brazilians, they were dismayed to find that this meant they had no concept of God whatsoever.[170] In certain parts of the country the inveterate drunkenness of the men (established long before the arrival of the Europeans) and especially their cannibalism profoundly repelled the Jesuits and began to seem to at least some of them ineradicable except by force. This led to expressions of hope that the gold and gems found in those regions would attract Portuguese in sufficient numbers to enable these adventurers to bring the natives under their domination.[171]

Few things disconcerted the Jesuits more than the fact that the Brazilians seemed to have no idea of marriage as a stable and monogamous union. Because both men and women changed partners frequently and capriciously, they also had no conception of fornication or adultery. As Anchieta saw it, the result was a sort of compromise between polygamy and promiscuity. This situation left the Jesuits much perplexed as to how to deal with Brazilians who wanted to be baptized but who seemed utterly incapable of changing their sexual practices. Consequently, the Jesuits were extremely cautious about admitting adult Brazilians to Baptism and, as we have seen, practically adamant about not admitting them to the Society.[172]

As we begin to focus more on the ministers, we must note a fact that has rarely elicited comment. By the time the Society was approved in 1540, all ten of the first members had been ordained to the priesthood. We tend to assume, therefore, that the ministry in which the first generation of Jesuits engaged was all done by priests. This assumption seems confirmed by the prominent role in their ministry of sacramental confession, which of course could be administered only by the ordained. In fact, however, a great deal of their ministry was done by "scholastics," that is, members who were still awaiting ordination. Some ministering was even done by those who would never be ordained, the temporal coadjutors.

Precise figures cannot be retrieved, but we know that of the thousand members of the order when Ignatius died in 1556, the majority were not priests. The following cases chosen at random are representative of the Society as a whole: at the college in Venice in 1550, of twelve Jesuits only three were priests, and by 1554 the only priest was the rector; at Alcalá in that same year only six of the thirty Jesuits were ordained; at the college in Goa there were five priests out of a total of thirty; at Padua in 1555 there were three priests out of eleven; and at the Jesuit college in Vienna in 1556, five priests out of thirty-three.[173] Although in many of the houses some of the non-ordained members were pursuing their own studies, even they were expected to help in the ministry of the community.

The ministry of the Jesuits falls into four major categories, suggested by the *Formula* and made explicit in other documents.[174] The categories are: (1) various forms of ministry of the Word; (2) administration of sacraments such as the Eucharist and confession; (3) certain works of mercy; and (4) outside the *Formula* itself, the schools. Although it is obvious that ordination was not a prerequisite for the last two categories, it may come as a surprise to learn that preaching, even during mass, was done indiscriminately by priests and scholastics.

As early as 1545 Pope Paul III had granted permission to any member of the Society to preach anywhere in the world on any occasion, provided that he was approved for it by his superiors.[175] The Jesuit documents are replete with instances of such preaching by scholastics, sometimes done in solemn settings, as in the cathedral in the presence of the local bishop and magistrates of the city.[176] Occasionally scholastics guided persons in the *Spiritual Exercises*,[177] and they were especially active in catechesis and the works of mercy. They of course did much of the teaching in the colleges. There is at least one clear instance of a scholastic's being appointed in Spain in 1551 as superior of a small community in which there were also priests.[178]

The temporal coadjutors, generally of humbler background and education, were also expected to engage in the ministries of the Society, but according to the occasions that offered themselves commensurate with their competence. This was usually interpreted to mean finding or creating opportunities for devout conversation, not considered an insignificant ministry by the early Jesuits. The coadjutors sometimes also taught catechism, visited prisons and hospitals, and so forth.[179] The extensive ministry in the Society by the non-ordained is surely one of the factors that induced the Jesuits so often to entice laypersons to work with them side by side.

Thus, although most Jesuits would eventually be ordained, all of them were deeply involved in the ministries of the Society almost from the moment they entered it. In 1572 Nadal made precisely this point about Jesuit novices in an important memorandum to Carlo Borromeo intended for the eyes of Pope Gregory XIII. According to Nadal, what makes Jesuit novices different from those of other orders is that they are trained not for "choir and other ceremonies" but for ministry, and their actual practice of it begins in the novitiate.[180]

In accepting novices, therefore, the Jesuits were much concerned with the character, talents, and health of the candidate, what his interests were, and how well suited he was to the style of life in the Society and the character of its ministries—to "our manner of proceeding." The Ninth Part of the *Constitutions* lists the personal qualities that the superior general should possess.[181] The list can be taken as an idealized profile of what Ignatius hoped every Jesuit would be—prayerful, virtuous, compassionate but firm, magnanimous and courageous, not without learning, unswervingly committed to the Society and its goals, a person of sound judgment.

This last quality was recognized as especially necessary in the Jesuit, who almost by definition would often find himself on his own, far removed from his brethren and his superiors, and in new, strange, and difficult situations. It also conformed to what was required by one of the principles characteristic of Jesuit ministry: that it accommodate to circumstances and to the particular needs and situation of the persons to whom the Jesuit ministered. The principle was of course not new or peculiar to the Jesuits by any means. But Jesuits learned it explicitly from the *Exercises;* they saw it as essential in light of their ideal of ministering to almost every category of person, Catholic and other, and they recurred to it with distinctive insistency. It was inculcated in the Ignatian and other documents. In practice, of course, it might be separated by only a hair's breadth, or less, from opportunism.

Perhaps partly for that reason, Jesuits insisted that accommodation be monitored by prudence, which did not mean caution but good judgment.[182] Prudence implied learning from one's mistakes. This was a virtue that these sons of lawyers and merchants had surely heard praised long before they became Jesuits. In any case, reflection on what one had done, on how it had succeeded or failed, on how one was being led by God in one's ministry and in one's general "way of proceeding" was consistently enjoined upon them as members of the Society.[183] The most obvious occasion for such reflection was the examination of his conscience that the Jesuit scholastic was to make twice daily.

What prudence and good judgment meant concretely was that the Jesuit should be "flexible," "not rigid."[184] Xavier wrote from India asking for Jesuits who knew how to deal with others in "tender fashion" *(amabilem)* and not be "rigid, wanting to control others by instilling a servile fear," to which he added his ideal of the Society of Jesus itself as a "Society of love and union of hearts, not of a rigid and servile fear."[185] In this regard a somewhat self-serving but illuminating comparison between the Jesuits and the Theatines, with whom they were sometimes confused, appears in Polanco's *Chronicon:* the Theatines were recognized by the fear they aroused, which was quite different from the Jesuits' friendlier and more approachable style—*familiariter*.[186]

In 1545, in an impressive passage in his *Memoriale,* Favre commented sadly on the self-righteous spirit that animated some prelates and civil magistrates as they tried to obliterate abuses. They had forgotten that Paul had said "charity is kind, charity is patient" (1 Cor. 13:4). "In both church and secular society a lot of people would utterly suppress abuses, but they are moved more by a glacial impatience and a bitter zeal for justice than by the tender zeal that comes from love."[187]

No doubt Jesuits fell short of the ideal that Favre commended, but the ideal was, nonetheless, implicitly and explicitly communicated to them in a number of ways. Nadal expressed it many times, including when he said, "For the virtues and good deeds of others, let there be sweet rejoicing; for the opposite, if they be known for sure, let there be only compassion, no judgment."[188]

Around 1550 Polanco composed a list of sixteen qualities desired in candidates for the Society. The third was flexibility *(flexibilidad),* which he insisted they possess in both speculative and practical judgment, for "hard heads" *(duros de cabeça)* were not suited to the Jesuit life.[189] In an incident involving Carlo Borromeo, Polanco showed a similar attitude. In 1563 in Rome, the young Cardinal Borromeo began to undergo his famous conversion, which led him to adopt an extraordinarily austere style of life and therewith, in the opinion of his uncle, Pope Pius IV, to neglect his duties in the papal curia. The pope blamed the Jesuits for this unwelcome change, and in his annoyance he forbade them to have any contact whatsoever with his nephew. In a private letter to a fellow Jesuit, Polanco expressed dismay at the embarrassment the prohibition was causing the Jesuits in Rome. At the same time he deplored "these extremes" of Carlo, who was depriving himself even of "honest recreation," and went on to say they were the result of contact not with the Jesuits but with others "stricter and more rigid."[190]

Intransigence, bigotry, a narrow moralism, and a sometimes obsessive concern for conventions of behavior and rules to enforce them are much present in the pastoral practice of the first Jesuits, but the ideal, within the sixteenth-century context, followed a gentler and more flexible orientation. The sources for the ideal were many, but most important was the emphasis in the *Exercises* on the inner consolation that marked the person who has turned from sin and surrendered to God's will.

"Consolation"—few terms appear more often in early Jesuit documents. Sometimes it is simply a conventional greeting and means not much more than "blessings." It was a word, however, that had special resonances for the Jesuits even when it was not employed in the more technical senses of the "Rules for Discernment," because it almost perforce suggested that source and others which reiterated and paraphrased it, as Nadal did when he described consolation as "an inner joy, a serenity in judgment, a relish, a light, a reassuring step forward, a clarification of insight."[191] Desolation was the opposite of this.

The Jesuits wanted to live according to such consolation themselves and to help others do the same. This was in fact the goal of the *Exercises* stated in its most generic terms. If this meant at the beginning threatening with fire and brimstone, so be it. It was not the Jesuits' intention, if they were true to their spiritual tradition, to leave it at that. In the *Exercises* even the meditations of the First Week on sin and hell were constructed to elicit gratitude and hope, not fear.

In a passage in his *Memoriale,* Favre gave simple expression to the pastoral ideal consonant with this tradition:

> With great devotion and new depth of feeling, I also hoped and begged for this [from God], that it finally be given me to be the servant and minister of Christ the consoler, the minister of Christ the helper, the minister of Christ the redeemer, the minister of Christ the healer, the liberator, the enricher, the strengthener. Thus it would happen that even I might be able through him to help many—to console, liberate, and give them courage; to bring them light not only for their spirit but also (if one may presume in the Lord) for their bodies, and bring as well other helps to the soul and body of each and every one of my neighbors whomsoever.[192]

Ignatius probably first derived the category of consolation from the *Imitation of Christ,* where it is almost a leitmotif. But the idea was abroad. The consolatory aspects of sacramental confession were stressed by scholastic theologians in the late Middle Ages, at least in part to counter the anxiety and stress sometimes associated with that sacrament.[193] Consolation was a governing idea in the theology of the influential Jean Gerson in his latter years.[194] Under quite different formalities it was found in humanist literature.[195] In none of these instances, however, does it correspond exactly to the descriptions Ignatius and his Jesuit interpreters gave it.

The Jesuits, in any case, extended the application of the category far beyond confession to a theme that was especially and insistently characteristic of their pastoral ideal. They expected the manifestation of God's presence within the soul to be accessible, in some degree, to all human beings.

According to the *Constitutions*, the Jesuit minister was himself nothing more than "an instrument" united with God, in God's hand.[196]

Underlying the Jesuits' pastoral ideals and practice, therefore, were certain assumptions about God and about how the universe was governed. At least some of the more influential Jesuits shared an appreciation of the intimate immediacy and power of God's presence in the world and in the human soul, an appreciation undoubtedly related to what they learned from the "Contemplation to Obtain the Love of God."

This appreciation led to conclusions about the efficacious power of that divine presence to conduct an individual in the way of salvation and peace. The Jesuits by and large believed in a world in which God's grace was abundant. God willed all to be saved and had embraced the world with even greater love because of the life, death, and resurrection of Jesus.[197] When Nadal commented on the passage concerning how few are saved because of the narrowness of the gate and the straightness of the way leading to salvation (Matt. 7:14), he conceded its truth if one looks at "the effect," that is, the few saved; however, the way is wide indeed "because of the abundance of God's grace."[198]

The early Jesuits were free to espouse different theological explanations of predestination.[199] Even so, they rarely ventured opinions on how few or how many were among the elect, possibly because the "Rules for Thinking with the Church" warned against such speculation.[200] They never forgot that damnation was a real possibility even for themselves, but they generally emphasized the accessibility of the alternative. In so doing, they echoed the *Exercises* by speaking of "preparing" oneself, of "disposing oneself," for the grace that was always available. Such expressions unambiguously indicated a measure of human responsibility in the great enterprise of salvation.[201]

The stakes in ministry, therefore, were high and the possibility of failure real. Both the Jesuit ministers and those to whom they ministered bore some responsibility for the outcome, yet they all were to recognize that divine help was always present in greater measure than they could possibly imagine. The impact of considerations like these surely account for the earnestness, energy, and even buoyancy with which the Jesuits went about their many ministries and reported on them.

Programs of Ministry

The sheer number and variety of the ministries listed, especially in the second version of the *Formula,* suggest the complexity of Jesuit pastoral engagement; they also read like a grocery list, as if the individual elements had no relationship to one another. In this regard, it is essential to keep in mind that the Jesuits believed that in their ministries they were following the "apostolic" pattern; that is, they were imitating and reproducing for their own times the essential features of the ministries exemplified by Jesus' disciples in the New Testament. Their meditations on the Second Week of the *Exercises* gave them ample opportunity to reflect on the pertinent texts.

The fundamental pattern was laid down in a few passages, including Jesus' commissioning of the Twelve in the tenth chapter of Matthew and the ninth chapter of Luke. In such texts the Jesuits saw four points key to their self-understanding. First, like the Twelve, they too were "sent," that is, they were instructed to seek out persons in need, commissioned at least in some general way by their superiors. Second, they were "to preach the Gospel," that is, to engage in various ministries of the Word of God. Third, they were "to heal the sick," which meant healing from sin through confession and other means, but also alleviating physical ills whenever possible. Fourth, they were to do all these things without seeking financial recompense—they interpreted their vow of poverty especially in that sense.

The Jesuits translated these generalities into the pastoral institutions that they found already in place or that they established and adapted. They inherited many of the particulars of these institutions from the mendicant orders of the Middle Ages. Some of the institutions that they incorporated into their ministry—schools, for example—seem far removed indeed from the New Testament, but the Jesuits dealt with that problem only by conceding that everything, of course, had to be adapted to the needs of time, place, and other circumstances.

If we take a closer look at the institutions they employed, we can distinguish three programs among the Jesuit ministries. We must keep in mind, however, that these programs had an impact on one another and that their distinctions are sometimes clearer in theory than in actuality. The first of the programs consisted in the ministries of the *Formula*, including the *Exercises* according to the eighteenth "Preliminary Observation," that is, as an intensified catechesis. The second was the *Exercises* insofar as they constituted full-fledged "retreats." Both of these programs clearly harked back to the life of Ignatius and his companions before the official founding of the Society. The third program was the schools, undertaken later.

The first program was constituted by a triad—ministries of the Word, of the sacraments, and of works of mercy. The triadic structure is important. It was according to this that the *Formula* more or less grouped Jesuit minis-

Ministries at Santa Maria della Strada, Rome. In the foreground, Ignatius preaching and another Jesuit teaching catechism; in the background, Jesuits hearing confession and distributing Holy Communion. The engraving is from *Vita beati patris Ignatii,* Rome, 1609.

tries; it was how the first Jesuits understood them, as is especially clear in Nadal's commentaries on the *Formula,* and it is how they will be presented in the following chapters. The correlation between Word and sacrament was one of the fundamental premises of the Christian theological tradition. It is not surprising, therefore, to find these two kinds of ministries so closely juxtaposed.

Given the context into which the Society was born, the works of mercy may seem to be an early counter-statement to Luther on "good works," for Catholics mistakenly understood Luther to have denied such works any place in the Christian scheme of things. Although the works of mercy would sometimes be interpreted in an anti-Lutheran sense by the Jesuits themselves, they originated from a quite different, altogether traditional source.

As the *Autobiography* suggests, that source was Ignatius's earliest pastoral experience, while he was still a layman. He engaged in devout conversation, he guided individuals in the *Exercises,* and he taught "Christian Doctrine," that is, catechism. These three activities differed only slightly from one another, and the relationship between the *Exercises* and catechism was especially close.

What Ignatius taught in "Christian Doctrine" can be deduced from a number of clues. First, it can be inferred that for the most part he correlated catechism with the First Week, which deals with issues such as human origins, sin, and conversion. Second, his trouble with critics often revolved around the distinction between mortal and venial sin. Third, the subjects to be taught when the *Exercises* were given according to the eighteenth "Preliminary Observation" were the Commandments and Capital Sins, the uses of the five senses, the precepts of the church, and the works of mercy—all of which are the traditional subjects of late-medieval catechisms.[202] These same subjects, along with basic prayers such as the "Our Father," reappear in the *Exercises* in the considerations entitled "Methods of Prayer."[203]

The final clue, serving as confirmation of the others, is Ignatius's one extant lesson on "Christian Doctrine."[204] The lesson dealt, therefore, with what the late Middle Ages also meant by "Christianity"—*Christianitas* or *Christianismum*—synonyms for "Christian Doctrine" that appear in the Jesuit documents.[205] It dealt, therefore, not so much with abstract "doctrines" as with how life was to be led as a Christian. *Christianitas* was about the formation of the good Christian, not about ideas as such.

Late-medieval catechesis retained the traditional connection between catechesis and sacrament, but, whereas in the patristic church the sacrament had been Baptism, in the late-medieval church it was Penance, that is, confession. The teaching of "Christian Doctrine" thus became to a large extent an instruction on how to examine one's conscience in preparation for confession and, consequently, a "mirror" of the elements that constituted a good Christian.[206] Although in the late Middle Ages and the Renaissance the distinction between preaching and catechetical instruction was for the most part clear, in practice the two forms of discourse influenced each other and sometimes overlapped. According to a certain mentality, therefore, catechism became a form of ministry of the Word of God.

The examinations of conscience emphasized, sometimes to a seemingly pathological degree, the ways a Christian might deviate from the true path. The sacrament of Penance required confession of one's *sins.* Hence, "Christian Doctrine" in the late Middle Ages contained an exposition of the Seven Capital Sins, which gradually were displaced by the Decalogue or appeared along with it.[207] The negative wording of many commandments in the Decalogue—"thou shalt *not*"—provided warrant for preoccupation with deviations from the ideal.[208] But basic prayers, the Apostles' Creed, and sometimes other materials were also taught. There was, thus, another side to *Christianitas.*

What about the teaching of "Christian Doctrine" in Spain before Ignatius left for Paris? Such teaching had already become a serious concern, had a general but not exclusive orientation toward confession, was in some places being taught in dialogue form and even set to tunes, and contained the usual elements of the Decalogue, the Creed, and basic prayers. It might also contain teaching on the sacraments, the virtues, the Beatitudes, and the spiritual and corporal works of mercy.[209] This catechesis is the most obvious source for the "works" indicated in the *Formula.*

Spanish catechisms seem almost invariably to have provided a space for the seven spiritual and the seven corporal works of mercy, crucially important parts of the positive side of the "mirror." Whatever *Christianitas* might otherwise have encompassed, it surely included those works. There can be no doubt that this was the aspect of late-medieval catechesis that found most vivid expression in perhaps the liveliest religious institution of Spanish (as well as Italian) society, the confraternity.[210] Those works of mercy enjoy a correspondingly important role in Ignatius's "lesson on Christian Doctrine," and they are mentioned specifically in the eighteenth "Observation" in the *Exercises.*

The works are important for understanding the context and development of Jesuit ministry and thus bear listing. The corporal works, obviously directly related to chapter 25 of Matthew's Gospel, were: feed the hungry, give drink to the thirsty, clothe the naked, house the homeless, visit the sick, visit the imprisoned, bury the dead. The spiritual works: give good counsel, teach the ignorant, admonish sinners, console the afflicted, pardon offenses and injuries, bear offenses patiently, and pray for the living and the dead.

Giving good counsel, teaching the ignorant, admonishing sinners, and consoling the afflicted constituted, in fact, the most important goals of the

Jesuit ministry of the Word, whether the Jesuits exercised that ministry themselves or encouraged others to engage in it. They understood practically all seven of the corporal works of mercy to be aspects of their "apostolic" call to "heal the sick."

Contained in basic catechetical instruction, therefore, were the three prongs of the Jesuits' first program of ministry—word, sacrament, and works—a pastoral triad widely recognized and practiced in the epoch.[211] That instruction also provided a partial explanation of why, for the Jesuits, Penance enjoyed such preeminence among the seven sacraments; Ignatius's "sermon" begins, in fact, with an instruction on how to make one's confession.

All three prongs of this first program were undergoing profound changes during the period I am considering. The changes were in some measure due to the Jesuits' initiatives but more generally to other influences that affected the ways Jesuits went about these traditional ministries and dealt with the Christian ideals and practices they implied. The changes sometimes occurred ostensibly independent of one another but were generally the result of the same great shifts in religious and cultural sensibilities that occurred across western Europe in the sixteenth century.

The *Exercises*, when taken further than the minimum indicated in the eighteenth "Observation," represent a different program of ministry, a program which originated with the Jesuits and was distinctive of them—the "retreat." When the *Exercises* entailed a period of seclusion of some duration under a spiritual guide, they stood as an entity independent of other ministries. Although the early Jesuits did not cultivate and promote this ministry as assiduously as we might expect, especially after the first decade or so, they knew at least theoretically how important it was to them.

The *Exercises* not only created in the retreat a unique program of ministry, but they also had an impact on all the other ministries the Jesuit exercised. No other group had a book that so clearly and in such detail indicated what they were about in ministry. In other words, the *Exercises* were for the Jesuits not merely one program of ministry among several. They supplied the design for the basic course or movement the Jesuits wanted to make operative in whatever they did—a movement that in its first instance entailed turning to God in a new and more profound way, which brought with it a process of spiritual growth and an increasing recognition of God's activity in everything in the world. Concommitant with this movement and a test of its authenticity was the inner experience of consolation or, as Nadal said, "a relish for spiritual things." Insofar as the Jesuits correlated catechesis with the First Week of the *Exercises,* for instance, they were trying to change it from the so-called moral arithmetic that characterized much of the Catholic piety of the day to a process of inward appropriation of values.[212]

With the schools the Jesuits undertook a radically different program of ministry. They tried their best to relate that program to the other two, but the differences between them overshadow the similarities. Here they stepped outside ministry and piety as those realities had traditionally been understood and into a world of culture that in its humanistic component was to some extent a self-conscious break with them.

It is true, of course, that the Jesuits imbued their humanistic schools with features peculiarly their own, but they also accepted the basic premises shared by their contemporaries about the purpose and scope of such schools. The most fundamental of those premises was that the schools were directed toward *pietas,* that is, toward the development of character through the study of classical literature in preparation for a life of public service. Formation of character through a long process of formal schooling, moral inspiration from pagan sources, attainment of stylistic elegance from study of those same sources, promotion of the common weal through stable institutions of instruction—these goals, though not incompatible with the other two programs of ministry, signified a profound change.

These objectives indicated a reshaping of the Jesuits' self-understanding and a moving away from their more evangelical and charismatic orientation to an institutional commitment that invited or forced them to deal with broader cultural issues. They signified acceptance of a new kind of social responsibility. Nonetheless, the inculcation of *pietas* that the humanists saw as the goal of education had decided affinities with the *Christianitas* of the Jesuits' catechesis and other ministries, and the schools provided the Jesuits with a unique base from which to engage in those ministries.

~ 3

Ministries of the Word of God

THE JESUITS' MOST basic pastoral program consisted in the triad word-sacrament-works. They conceived of "word" broadly, so that it denoted for them much more than preaching or lecturing; indeed, after those two designations, the *Formula* spoke of "any other ministry whatsoever of the Word of God." The *Exercises* were special in a number of ways, but Nadal expressed an essential aspect of how Jesuits understood them when he said that in them "the Word of God is declared."[1] The particular emphasis the Jesuits gave to "teaching Christianity," that is, teaching catechism, and its close relationship to both preaching and the *Exercises* allow it to be considered in the same context.[2]

Each of these ministries had its own objective, more or less clearly recognized by the Jesuits, but they also much influenced one another, sometimes to the extent that one blended almost imperceptibly into another. Moreover, they all achieved their end through some form of discourse. Indeed, discourse was a hallmark of almost all the Jesuits' ministries, not just those considered in this chapter. It was, in fact, a hallmark of the way they understood themselves. The Jesuits were, in that sense, as well as in the theological sense of the term, first and foremost ministers of the *word*.

Preaching

The prominence the Protestant Reformers accorded to preaching and the attention scholars subsequently paid to their claims engendered the impression that, in the division of the spoils from the religious controversies of the sixteenth century, Protestants got the pulpit and Catholics the altar. This does little justice to either party on either issue. As far as preaching is concerned, both Protestants and Catholics were heirs to the revival that began with the mendicant orders in the thirteenth century, to the criticisms of the style and content of that preaching that swelled to a crescendo by the end of the fifteenth century, and to alternatives advocated and practiced in certain circles even before 1517.[3]

In both versions of the Jesuit *Formula*, preaching was the first ministry listed. This prominent location was not accidental. To "preach the Gospel" was the Jesuits' "apostolic" mandate. They understood the content of that mandate and the forms it might take differently than did many of their contemporaries, especially their Protestant contemporaries, but no group was more convinced of its primacy than they. The *Constitutions* rank preaching and lecturing as, generally speaking, more important than hearing confessions and giving the *Spiritual Exercises*.[4]

Nonetheless, the early Jesuits left behind no prescriptive or official statement telling us precisely how they understood the directive to preach. What they wanted to do by means of their preaching, what they thought they were doing, and what they in fact did can be recovered only by recourse to a wide variety of sources.

Perhaps the most striking thing those sources reveal is the immense amount of preaching the Jesuits did—even after the first decade, when the schools had begun to absorb more of their time and concern. They sometimes preached two or three times a day. Polanco commended brevity except for the most skilled preachers, but sermons lasting two, three, and even four hours were reported.[5] This led Jesuits in Italy and probably elsewhere to adopt the Italian custom of providing an intermission.[6] Because preaching was physically draining, Ignatius counseled some Jesuits to forgo it for a while, lest it injure their health.[7] He also allowed them to curtail or omit preaching during the summer heat.[8]

The frequency with which sermons were preached at the beginning of the sixteenth century varied widely in different parts of Europe. While Jesuits often conformed to local patterns in this regard, they tended to expand them whenever they could. The best-known example was their introduction into Rome, shortly after their arrival, of preaching in church on Sundays other than those of advent and lent, as had been the custom.[9] Within those two sacred seasons they almost everywhere followed the widespread custom of urban centers in the late Middle Ages of preaching daily, or at least three times a week.[10] They of course preached on the many feast days that the liturgical calendar offered, and they sought or created other occasions to speak.

The *Quarant' ore,* for instance, had been introduced into some churches in Italy in the 1520's. The Jesuits supported this practice of once or twice a year setting aside forty consecutive hours during which the faithful took turns on an hourly basis keeping vigil in a church for some impetratory or expiatory cause. Although the *Quarant' ore* was developing into a set formula of forty hours of silent prayer before the Eucharist exposed on the altar in a monstrance, with a sermon or two interspersed each day, the Jesuits used it for more preaching. In Perugia in 1554, two Jesuit scholastics preached every hour for three days to the rotating groups of people.[11] This was not a unique instance.[12]

The preaching described thus far took place in churches. These sermons were not usually preached during mass, but before or after it, or at some other time of day. In the first decade of the order, when the Jesuits had few churches of their own, such preaching occurred by invitation on an occasional basis either as single preachments or as a series, for example, during the lenten season. The Jesuits then often moved on to another church or city, as befitted their itinerant style. In Portugal in 1548 a Jesuit preached a sermon in a different village or hamlet every day of the week as he moved through the countryside. To summon people to hear the preacher, the men of the locality built bonfires on the hills.[13] Once the Society acquired more churches of its own, especially when the founding of a school meant a church would be attached, a more stable pattern emerged alongside this earlier one without ever completely displacing it.

When in 1537 the companions of Paris first began to preach in the Veneto, however, they did so in the open air and in the streets—a practice that continued throughout the period I am considering and that accounts for a great amount of the preaching in which the Jesuits engaged. They believed they were thereby imitating the practice of Jesus, his disciples, and Paul. The practice also conformed to their understanding of their own vocation of seeking out those in need, not waiting for them at the steps of the church.

They preached, therefore, in the streets, in public squares and markets, in hospitals, in prisons, aboard ships in dock, in fortresses, on playing fields, in hospices or hostels, in confraternities.[14] As Polanco reported it, in 1547 Father Silvestro Landini preached "wherever men and women gather and also in the churches."[15] When the Jesuits preached in sites like these, they were imitating their predecessors, the friars of the mendicant orders, but they also introduced the practice into localities where it had not been known and, as they saw it, imbued it with a new zest.

Their open-air preaching did not please everyone. In Naples in 1552, for instance, the Jesuits desisted from it because some of their lay friends told them it was inappropriate.[16] They aroused criticism in Medina del Campo in 1553 because the practice was alleged not to be customary in Spain.[17]

Where they did engage in open-air preaching, they reported some vivid scenes, especially in the early years. In Coimbra on the feast of Mary Magdalen in 1545, Jesuits marched through the streets at night shouting at sinners to do penance, and, when a crowd had gathered in the marketplace, Francisco Estrada preached on repentance and on loving Jesus the way Magdalen had. People hung out of windows and stood on benches to see and hear "this new and wonderful spectacle."[18]

At Valencia during Carnival in 1552, an even more dramatic scene occurred when six Jesuits walked through the streets barefooted, carrying crucifixes, with ropes hanging from their necks. They stopped at certain locations to preach about "death, judgment, the vanity of the world, and the good fruit of repentance."[19] In central Italy in 1549, a sermon by Landini incited a group of women to throw into the streets their "vanities"—perfumes, cosmetics, and similar items.[20]

Polanco reported a rumor circulating in 1550 that in Rome some Jesuits went through the streets "naked," carrying skulls, and preaching "childish things." Polanco had not verified the rumor, but, in any case, Ignatius let it be known that he disapproved of such displays when undertaken without consulting superiors and that open-air preaching should be done only by those qualified for it.[21]

In such displays the Jesuits were, again, imitating Franciscans, Carmelites, and members of other medieval orders. In general their preaching practice reveals the impact upon them of medieval traditions. The ninth chapter of the Second Rule of Saint Francis instructed the friars to preach "vice and virtue, punishment and glory."[22] That chapter encapsulated an earlier tradition and transmitted it with extraordinary success to succeeding generations reaching far beyond Franciscan confines, leading in 1546 to the incorporation of a paraphrase, without acknowledgment of source, into the only decree of the Council of Trent that dealt with the content of preaching.[23]

Although some Jesuits may have been influenced by the decree, their persuasion that preaching should deal to a large extent with "vice and virtue" was part of the late-medieval heritage antedating the Tridentine decree. This persuasion also indicates the close relationship, sometimes explicit, that their preaching bore to their catechesis.[24] When Ignatius allowed in the eighteenth "Observation" of the *Exercises* a wider application for the materials indicated there,[25] he provided grounds for taking them as topics for sermons to a more general audience, as was early done by Landini and then many others. In 1550, in fact, Landini was commissioned by an Italian bishop to teach the pastors in his diocese how to preach precisely the considerations from the First Week, which besides meditations stressing life's purpose, the destructiveness of sin, the unfailing love and forbearance of God, included standard catechetical topics such as the Commandments and the works of mercy, as we have seen.[26]

Ignatius himself believed sermons should to a large extent deal with vices and virtues.[27] When about 1550 Polanco drew up some advice for Jesuits in their ministries, he too suggested that for preaching they have at hand a list of commonplaces concerning vices and virtues, sins and their remedies, and the Decalogue and works of charity or mercy.[28] The next year he composed a list of fifty-one topics appropriate for preaching by young Jesuits as they practiced the art within their Jesuit communities, a list which was simply an expansion of his earlier advice.[29] The *Constitutions,* on which he and Ignatius were working at the same time, had a similar emphasis.[30]

Vices and the remedies for sin loomed large, therefore, in Jesuit talk about preaching, and it must be assumed that such prescriptive statements reflected the Jesuits' actual practice. Virtues and the consolation of an upright life, however, received equal or greater attention in Jesuit sources. Just how these two emphases were in fact balanced and just what motivations were adduced for the one or the other must rest upon conjecture, because even the relatively few sermons that survive from this generation have never been studied.

No sermon from Ignatius has come down to us.[31] Once he became general, he seems to have given up preaching almost altogether. What little we know about his preaching before then comes from others' recollections, as when Ribadeneira said that it was "always an exhortation to good morals and to enter into oneself, and to arrive at a knowledge and love of God and of prayer."[32]

Moreover, while the Jesuits might for a variety of reasons have found the First Week of the *Exercises* especially enticing for their preaching, they had presumably learned that the other three Weeks led to a more profound reality. All Christians were, according to their place in society, to "follow Christ" in his inner sentiments and in the healing he performed for others. The Beatitudes (Matt. 5:3–11; Lk. 6:20–26), as echoed and expanded in the traditional spiritual and corporal works of mercy, thus found a place in their sermons.

Ignatius enjoined upon Jesuits that they were not to preach on "doubtful matters."[33] In so doing he indirectly sanctioned topics from the Christian tradition that transcended the controversies of the "schools" of scholastic theology. When he urged Jesuits in Prague not to enter into polemics with the Protestants in the pulpit, a directive with little chance of being observed, he indirectly commended a positive presentation of Catholic belief and practice.[34]

In places where Protestantism was a danger, Jesuit presentation of "Catholic belief" obviously stressed points under contention. In other places, "Catholic belief" probably meant simply the articles of the Apostles' Creed. This is, however, surmise, based on the established role the Creed played in the teaching of *Christianitas*.

What is altogether clear is that the Jesuits, like their Catholic colleagues, did not single out any specific doctrine or teaching as capturing the essence of "the Gospel" and as therefore being the message that centered their preaching. In this regard they differed most markedly from their Lutheran contemporaries, for whom the proclamation of justification by faith alone and of the consequent relationship between Law and Gospel were the very definition of preaching.[35]

With such a definition, preaching tended almost perforce to have a primarily instructional aim. This was another way in which Lutheran understanding differed from that of the Jesuits'. The Jesuits of course believed that instruction was integral to any good sermon, but of the three traditional aims of preaching—to teach, to move, to please—the early Jesuits saw the second as most proper to it.

It is not surprising, therefore, that the Jesuits wanted to "move" people at times to quite specific actions. In 1549 near Foligno, Landini preached against superstitions and "magical incantations," and in 1550 in the diocese of Trani, Cristóforo de Madrid got eleven priests to give up their concubines, to stop wearing military uniforms, and to adopt garb befitting their status.[36] In Bologna in 1552 Francesco Palmio preached on contributing food and clothing to the poor who suffered from the severity of the winter.[37] In Genoa in 1554, as a result of Laínez's preaching, the city had contracts examined in order to eliminate excessive or usurious profits by the party issuing them.[38]

Reports about similar results from their preaching abound in Jesuit correspondence from the period, indicating how they liked to assess it by the change in conduct it effected. They especially wanted their sermons to bring people to the sacraments of Penance and the Eucharist, or to persuade them to receive them on a more frequent basis. If their sermons were meant to "move," the Jesuits' effectiveness could be judged by the emotional responses their audience manifested. Jesuit preachers welcomed an occasional swoon and found consolation and confirmation in sighs, moans, and especially tears, whether of sadness or joy.[39] They were sometimes so overcome that they wept themselves.[40]

In 1550 Canisius complained that even on feast days Catholics in Germany heard "frigid" preaching,[41] but in 1555 Nicolaus de Lanoy reported to Ignatius from Vienna that Canisius's own sermons did not stir the emotions powerfully enough.[42] All Jesuits, surely, could not arouse their listeners to a perceptible show of emotions; some of them probably had no desire to do so, and others recognized that such a display was considered odd in certain localities. Nonetheless, they subscribed seemingly without exception to the assumption that a sermon that did not somehow touch the feelings was no sermon at all.

In 1576–78 Gregory Martin, the English recusant and translator of the Rheims-Douay version of the Bible, visited Rome and described the preaching he heard there. Although his account dates somewhat later than our period and deals with the preaching of other orders as well as that of the Jesuits, it indicates how practice corresponded to theory:

> And to heare the maner of the Italian preacher, with what a spirit he toucheth the hart, and moveth to compunction (for to that end they employ their talke and not in disputinge matters of controversie which, god be thanked, there needeth not) that is a singular joy and a merveilous edifying to a good Christian man . . . what shal a man heare but rebuking of vice, and exhorting to vertue, the feare of gods Justice, the hope of his mercie, the love of his benefites? These things are so handled with such a grace coming from the preachers mouth, that it calleth of al sortes great multitudes, and worketh in their hartes marvelous effectes.[43]

He also left an account of Jesuit street preaching that manifests the same purposes and emphasis:

> And these be commonly Jesuites, which desire leave of their superiours so to be occupied, and then going every one with his felow, and deviding them selves into these forsaid assembles, make the verie stal or bulke of some window their pulpet, and without al other ceremonies, only a Crucifixe in their hand or ready aboute them, they beginne some good matter of edification, agreable to their audience, with ful streame of the plainest scriptures, and pike sentences of auncient fathers, and notable examples of former time, most sweetly exhorting to good life, and most

terribly dehorting from al sinne and wickednesse, often setting before them the paines of hel, and the joyes of Heaven. As sone as they either heare his voice, or see him in the place, as many as are within that compasse and vew, gather rounde about him with great silence and attention, and (I doubte not, for it must needes be so) with great fruite.[44]

How did the Jesuits construct their sermons to achieve this "great fruite"? How did they utilize the principles of classical rhetoric and patristic homiletics in the style and structure of their preaching? These were lively issues in their day. In the *Constitutions* only a single line addressed the issue: when Jesuits preached or delivered "sacred lectures," they were not to do so in "the scholastic manner."[45] This prescription was an outright repudiation of the scholastic *Artes praedicandi* of the Middle Ages and an indirect commendation of new theories being advanced, especially by humanists like Erasmus.

Polanco was probably the immediate source of this prescription in the *Constitutions*. While a student of theology at the University of Padua, he studied Erasmus's *Ecclesiastes* and wrote out excerpts from it for himself.[46] That treatise, the longest of Erasmus's works, was a diffuse compendium of his immense erudition as it pertained to preaching, the first major alternative to the medieval *Artes praedicandi* from humanist circles.[47] Although Polanco was the only important Jesuit who we know studied the *Ecclesiastes,* all the first ten companions had to a greater or lesser degree been influenced by aspects of the humanist tradition at Alcalá, Paris, or both places; Nadal and others who joined the Society later were in some cases even more deeply influenced by it.

Incontrovertible evidence substantiates, moreover, that at least Salmerón had assimilated humanist principles in a way that enabled him to deliver at Trent on the feast of Saint John the Evangelist in 1546 a Latin oration constructed according to them.[48] By 1556, Jesuits were being invited to preach in the presence of the pope during the *cappelle pontificie* in the Sistine Chapel and eventually were assigned Good Friday on an annual basis, just as the mendicant orders had their own assigned days to preach *coram papa*.[49] Given the humanistic style of preaching then favored at the papal court, the Jesuits surely strove to conform to it.[50] Most evidence indicates, however, that during this period the Jesuits were guided by no single theory or viewpoint in their preaching in the vernacular to general audiences, which of course is how most of it was done.[51] The Dominican Luis de Granada and the Franciscan Diego de Estella would in 1576 produce their great classics on the art of preaching.[52] It would take the Jesuits a long time to catch up.

Ignatius wanted Laínez to compose a commentary on the Sunday Gospels to help Jesuits with their preaching, but Laínez never got around to it.[53] Sometime in the 1550's Borja wrote his *Tratado breve del modo de predicar el santo Evangelio,* published posthumously by Ribadeneira in 1592.[54] The most often reprinted and translated of Borja's writings, it presents preaching as a religious act, effective only insofar as God operates through it. The treatise therefore contains reflections on the dignity and exalted character of the preaching office and on the virtues required in the preacher. Although it offers practical hints about preparation and delivery, it does not address technical issues of rhetoric. As part of preparing a sermon, however, it recommends use of "the holy fathers Augustine, Jerome, Gregory, and Chrysostom" and an interlinear gloss of the Bible.

A more ambitious work of 1563 by Juan Ramírez entitled *Monita pro iis, qui concionandi munus suscipiunt,* long attributed to Laínez, had some circulation in manuscript in the Society.[55] Ramírez was a feisty ascetic, a former disciple of Juan de Avila. Almost immediately upon his entrance into the Society in 1555, he became well known for his preaching, which was controversial because of his outspoken criticism of public figures. His *Monita* is best interpreted as mirroring in some limited way practice and ideals current in the Society at the time. It consists of injunctions and suggestions and, though different from the *Artes,* is a far cry from the *Ecclesiastes* and works influenced by it.

Even though Ramírez insisted on the necessity of scholastic theology for effective preaching and recommended some medieval sources to help the preacher, he did not mention or advocate the "thematic" style developed by the *Artes.* In its stead he endorsed in an understated way the homiletical form of the patristic age. He took great pains to indicate how the preacher differs from the secular orator, even as he presupposed some correlation of preaching with the most general principles of classical rhetoric. He himself wrote in a straightforward Latin style purged of medieval traces.

Other evidence indicates that most vernacular sermons by the Jesuits were what Ramírez's treatise suggests—a genial or uneasy mix of patristic, medieval, and Renaissance elements, with now one and now another predominating. Polanco's notes on his own preaching in Padua, Bologna, and Pistoia in 1545–47 show that he sometimes studied a homily of Saint Bernard and then used it as a model for what he wanted to say. At other times he took the Gospel passage from the mass of the day, explained it, applied it to his listeners in a way that made it revolve around a single subject such as loving Christ, bearing tribulation, receiving the Holy Spirit, or achieving contrition of heart.[56] Andrés de Oviedo, in three sermons near Gandía on Good Friday,

1550, borrowed at least some features of the scholastic "thematic" structure, and in so doing he probably represents the rule rather than the exception for this generation of Jesuits.[57]

Beginning with Ignatius himself, however, on one issue there was no ambiguity. The younger members of the Society were to study the Greek and Latin orators and the classical treatises on rhetoric. The Jesuits needed to know these works for many reasons, but paramount among them was their utility for training preachers. More specifically, the early Jesuits seized upon the classical tradition of rhetoric for its power to teach the preacher how to touch and arouse the emotions. When Nadal commented on the provision of the *Constitutions* about not preaching in the scholastic style, he indicated that the problem with that style was precisely that it was "speculative" and dry.[58]

Nadal, like others of his age, looked forward to a time when a "properly Christian" art of oratory might be composed, but he believed such an art would still have to draw on the parts of the classical treatises that deal with "moving the affections."[59] The ancient dispute about whether the classics were compatible with Christianity was a dead issue with the Jesuits, as it was by this time with most of their contemporaries. The provision in the *Constitutions* about not preaching "in the scholastic manner" may not have perfectly reflected the actual practice of the first generation, but it presaged the future.[60]

The Jesuits agreed with Cicero, Quintilian, and other writers on rhetoric that, if a person did not have innate talent for the orator's art, no amount of training could supply it; hence, not all Jesuits were expected to become preachers.[61] They were also convinced that proper training enhanced talent and that this training included what could be learned from the classics.

Training also meant listening to good sermons and analyzing them, practicing before one's confreres, and asking for criticism and help.[62] In Jesuit houses young Jesuits regularly delivered sermons during the midday and evening meals and received advice and correction on them. Those same Jesuits several times a week had to practice the "tones" *(toni)*, short set pieces of which Ignatius was the reputed author, designed as exercises in the plain, middle, and grand or vehement styles of oratory.[63] In 1551, however, the Jesuits at the new college in Vienna wrote back to Rome that they ran into difficulty in the application of the tones to their sermons because the people were accustomed to a more sedate approach.[64] We can assume that in Vienna and elsewhere adjustments were made because, according to Nadal, Ignatius himself maintained that the tones learned in Rome may not be suitable everywhere.[65]

Underlying the rhetoric, of course, had to be solid learning. As early as 1548, Canisius wrote to Leonard Kessel in Cologne that the principal reason for the years of study enjoined upon members of the Society was to make them effective preachers.[66] Nadal insisted that Jesuits chosen for this office be especially learned—*doctissimos*.[67] He reported that Ignatius taught and prescribed that no academic discipline that could help preachers was to be neglected by them.[68]

The learning required for preaching surely included theology, but in fact Jesuit scholastics who had yet to study theology did a great deal of preaching. Other Jesuits also preached from a surprisingly short fund of theology and sometimes seem to have been capable of not much more than repeating sermons by other Jesuits like Laínez and Salmerón that they had obtained in manuscript.[69] We have no evidence that this glaring discrepancy between theory and practice ever received comment. It reveals something about how the Jesuits looked upon theology and also about what they understood "the Word of God" to be that they preached.

The Jesuits of course believed that the "Word of God" was both Testaments of the Scriptures, and they prescribed direct study of the Bible as an essential part of the theology for members of the order. That goes almost without saying. Important for them as well, however, was the Word of God spoken within. Ignatius's experience at Manresa of being directly taught by God was not something they believed was reserved exclusively to him.

For the Jesuits, truly effective ministry rested first and foremost, as the *Constitutions* insisted, not on natural talent and acquired learning and skills, but on the union *(familiaritas)* of the minister with God in prayer and on similar realities that made him an instrument of divine grace in God's hands.[70] The first Jesuits accepted this traditional teaching without question but sometimes gave it surprising interpretations and applications.

In a letter to one of his subjects in 1554, Ignatius congratulated him on beginning his study of Scripture, but also assured him that in his preaching the Holy Spirit would compensate for the years of theological study that he lacked.[71] When the young Estrada preached while studying philosophy at the University of Louvain, he was supplied by Favre with some rudiments of theology for his sermons, but he also preached from inspirations derived from his daily prayer and meditations.[72] Once, in Sicily, Nadal encountered a lay brother who did not know anything—"que no sabia cosa." Nadal taught him how to meditate and told him to ask God for help. When on a later occasion the man was sent by Nadal to preach, he said "marvelous things."[73]

In Messina in 1548 a thirteen-year-old boy who had "a special gift of God" for preaching was recommended to the Jesuits by Leonor Osorio.[74] The Jesuits befriended him and with Ignatius's approval began to give him some instruction. Two years later, however, he disappointed them by showing that he was more interested in money than in promoting piety. Polanco observed that experience was teaching the Jesuits that not much confidence could be placed in even the most gifted of preachers until they had reached maturity, at which time their virtues could be more closely examined.[75]

In the Jesuits' orphanage for about two hundred children in Brazil, however, they boasted in 1552 that the way the boys assimilated the training they gave them in preaching in both Portuguese and their native tongue demonstrated that the education there was equal to what was given in Portugal.[76] In Goa they also encouraged preaching by boys in their charge; in 1552, for example, the Jesuits had an orphan boy preach on Christ's sufferings on the steps outside a church.[77] In instances like these, of course, there was no question of extraordinary charismatic gifts, but there was also no question of any learning beyond basic catechism.

The charismatic aspect of the Jesuits' appreciation of preaching needs to be underscored because it is so often overlooked and because it reflects the charismatic origins of the Society itself. In the Jesuits' understanding of what they were about, that aspect was an essential component. It was a straightforward expression of the central role that conversion of heart and its results were meant to play in their own lives and in the lives of those to whom they ministered.

Did they, then, share any common theology of preaching or of the ministry of the Word of God? Surely not, if the question implies a systematic and fully articulated program. The question itself would have been almost unintelligible to them, for, despite all the tracts and treatises that the Middle Ages produced on theology of the sacraments, the Jesuits would have encountered no similar treatments of preaching in the sources they habitually read. They did, however, share a practical conviction that nature and grace somehow worked together—in this case, natural and acquired gifts in conjunction with supernally derived powers to touch the heart. The conviction pervades the *Constitutions* and would also otherwise have been conveyed to them, if they did not have it already. The primacy went without question to the gifts from above, communicated within.

Nadal explained in a few passages what those gifts meant for preaching. In his journal, for instance, he noted, "Power in the Spirit means to speak from the heart and to speak with the forceful grace of the sacred word"[78] and "The power of the Gospel cannot be explained by the words we utter, but it can be felt or relished or understood in heart and spirit."[79] While discussing preaching in one of his exhortations late in his life, he said: "May Christ speak in you, may his word be efficacious in and by means of you, for, infinite as it is, it contains all the divine majesty, sweetness, power, and consolation."[80]

In that same exhortation he provided another understanding of the "Word of God" of which the Jesuits were ministers. This time it was not the word of Scripture or the internal word communicated in the heart, but Christ himself, the *logos,* or Word of God, as described in the opening verses of the Gospel of John (1:1–18):

> It is a great grace and excellent office in the church of God to be ministers of the Word of God. We know in the Spirit, my brothers, that Christ is also the infinite Word of God. We are ministers of that Word—for he sends us [to preach]; he teaches us; he is the Word inside us; he grants that we hear the Word of his teaching and know that it proceeds from him; he gives us our effectiveness, and he supplies love and divine power to our utterance.[81]

Sentiments like these are occasionally found in other Jesuit documents, including Ramírez's *Monita.*[82] In a sermon in Rome in 1561, Estrada elaborated on the preacher's office as exemplified by John the Baptist and on the compelling power of the Word of God. The effect of preaching the Word of God, he said, was to give hope to the fainthearted and console them.[83] Polanco and surely others, moreover, admired those Jesuits who preached seemingly "inflamed with the fire of the Holy Spirit."[84]

Did this fire of the Spirit imply the prophetic gift of confronting the mighty with their misdeeds? Ramírez affirmed in the *Monita* of 1563 that it did and that this was one of the differences between preachers and secular orators.[85] He had the previous year complained in a letter to Laínez, then general, that the Jesuits in Spain subscribed to lax moral opinions and had in their preaching become "pale with the spirit of prudence," like "mute dogs, unable to bark" (Is. 56:10). He lectured Laínez on how Jesuits should be ready to die for the truth by denouncing evil in high places, even in Rome.[86]

When Laínez replied, he described his own conduct in Rome, having easily detected the implied criticism of himself in relationship to the papal court. He said that in private conversations and in his public preaching, heard by cardinals, he had spoken out "against the abuses of that court" and that he had done the same elsewhere. He could not resist noting for Ramírez that he had not as yet been put to death for it.[87]

Preaching that denounced abuses in the church was, therefore, considered an obligation by some Jesuits of this generation, and they sometimes engaged in it. But the change in religious atmosphere, especially in Rome, from the middle of the sixteenth century onward put a damper on public criticism and rendered it less common and ever less tolerable.[88] The tenth of the "Rules for Thinking with the Church" anticipated the new atmosphere by advocating that such criticism be offered behind closed doors.[89]

During this period from 1540 to 1565, the Jesuits produced no truly outstanding preachers according to the standards of their day. But many of them consistently attracted large crowds, and some few were more than ordinarily successful—Ramírez, for instance, in Spain, and Estrada in Spain, Portugal, and elsewhere. Laínez, Salmerón, and Benedetto Palmio were the most esteemed in Italy.[90] What was important about members of this first generation, however, and for the most part characteristic of them was the combination of good academic training with an enthusiasm that carried them to places where others with comparable backgrounds did not bother to go.

Sacred Lectures

Sometime before 1485 the humanist Aurelio Brandolini, while commenting on the liturgies in the Sistine Chapel *coram papa,* deplored that some preachers there did not know the difference between a lecture *(lectio)* and a sermon or sacred oration *(oratio).*[91] The first Jesuits knew this distinction well, as the latter version of the *Formula* indicated by listing lecturing as a distinct ministry, right after preaching. Although "lecturing" was an extremely important component of the Jesuits' pastoral activity, it has been little noticed and never studied.[92]

The Council of Trent in its Fifth Session, 1546, legislated the establishment of benefices in cathedrals and parish churches for lectureships on Scripture.[93] The lectures were to be open to the laity. Little is known about the origins of this decree and its implementation (or lack of implementation), but, like most Tridentine legislation, the decree did not create something new but promoted a practice already known in certain localities. Since "lecturing" was not explicit in the *Formula* until 1550, we may think the addition was due to Tridentine influence, but Jesuits were delivering such lectures well before the enactment of the decree.[94] The addition must be taken as simply a codification of earlier Jesuit practice, independent of the Council, engaged in by the Jesuits from the very beginning.

Just how widely practiced such lectures were by others before then is not clear, partly because scholars, sometimes misled by the sources themselves, have consistently failed to make the distinction between lectures and sermons. Evidence suggests, however, that lectures were fairly common in some cities of Italy in the churches of the mendicants. Savonarola, for instance, delivered in Florence series of lectures on the Apocalypse, the First Epistle of John, and other books of the Bible. Some of these lectures were published in both Latin and the vernacular by 1536, four decades after his death.[95] Moreover, Jesuit sources occasionally mention that in the same city where they were lecturing a mendicant was doing the same.[96] In 1540, for instance, Favre stated in a letter to Codure and Xavier that in Bressanone a certain Fray Raphael had been preaching for eighteen months and also lectured every day on Scripture.[97] In 1541, before he entered the Society, Nadal gave a series of lectures on Romans and another on the Canon of the mass in the cathedral of Majorca.

Lectures were not unknown in northern Europe. Erasmus described John Colet's custom during the first two decades of the century of delivering series of lectures *(conciones)* for layfolk in Saint Paul's cathedral in London on continuing subjects such as the Gospel of Matthew, the Creed, and the Lord's Prayer. Erasmus implies that this practice was an innovation in England.[98] In 1519 Luther, while still an Augustinian friar, began for the people of Wittenberg two series of "sermons" *(gemina concio)* on Genesis and the Gospel of Matthew.[99]

The Jesuits did not, therefore, invent the lectures. What they contributed was, in the first place, a more widespread diffusion of them. Everywhere they preached, they also lectured, and at least in some localities they began to be imitated, as by the Dominicans in Messina in 1549.[100]

According to the Jesuits, their lectures differed from the others' in that they were directed to devout living. When Polanco compared the lectures delivered by Jesuits with those given by others, he judged the former better because they were infused with greater devotion and with more frequent exhortation to "all that is good."[101] The lectures were not, therefore, a mere transfer of material out of a university classroom, which is what Polanco implies they were for others; rather, they were an adaptation of this material to the questions and needs of ordinary folk. Generally delivered to the laity in a church, they must be clearly distinguished from lectures on books of the Bible intended for a university audience, of which Luther's are the best known from the period. Nadal allowed that the term in the *Formula* included such academic lectures, but neither he nor others commented much on them, probably because they made up such a well-defined genre.[102]

Despite the exhortatory element the Jesuits cultivated, they still saw that a lecture differed principally from a sermon in that a lecture had instruction as its primary aim. The sermon was of course also supposed to instruct, but its objective was to touch the emotions in order to accomplish a goal directly related to religious practice or sentiment. The more instructional character of the lecture was indicated by the fact that members of the audience sometimes came equipped with writing materials in order to take down what they heard.[103] The few series of lectures by Jesuits still extant from this period are not from their authors but from notes of those in the audience.[104]

In Jesuit theory and practice there were other differences between a lecture and a sermon. Lectures were delivered as part of a series and, when they were on Scripture, independent of the liturgical lectionary. The difference most readily manifested itself, however, in that the lecturer sat on a bench or chair in the body of the church on the same level with his audience, unless the crowd was so large as to require the pulpit; the preacher always spoke from the pulpit, if one was available.[105] The preacher always wore a surplice and, when it was the local custom, also a stole; the lecturer wore no liturgical vestment.[106] The lecturer used a simpler, more direct style, but a style "pleasant and agreeable."[107] As with their sermons, however, the Jesuits sometimes paused in the middle to allow their listeners a short intermission.[108]

Because of these differences, the Jesuits realized that some of their members might be capable of delivering lectures effectively but not have the talent needed for preaching, and vice versa.[109] In general, however, Jesuits performed both ministries, but were warned not to confuse one with the other.[110] Polanco, even while secretary to Ignatius, often preached in the Jesuit church in the morning and lectured in the afternoon. The Jesuits obviously considered these lectures the indispensable complement to their preaching.

They in fact generally delivered lectures in conjunction with a preaching assignment in a church. Polanco's pattern was typical. In the morning, for instance, Jesuits would preach on the Gospel of the day either before, during, or after mass and, in the afternoon, deliver one of the lectures in their series. Although they usually delivered the lectures in a church to an audience of lay women and men, often with some admixture of clergy, they on occasion delivered them to an exclusively clerical audience, or some other designated group. But this was by far the exception rather than the rule.[111] On even rarer occasions they might deliver the series in a setting other than a church, as when in 1554 Bobadilla lectured on the Epistle to the Galatians in the episcopal residence at Ancona to the bishop, his chapter, and a large audience of lay notables.[112]

Whereas direct evidence about the specific content of the lectures is sparse, evidence about the frequency with which they were delivered and about the topics considered is abundant. A series might contain twenty or more lectures, typically delivered on Sunday, Tuesday, and Friday, usually in the afternoon but sometimes in the morning. The lectures might, however, be delivered only on Sundays and feast days; in Rome on those days they followed vespers once the chanting of that liturgical Hour was introduced into the Jesuit church.[113] Elsewhere they accommodated to other patterns according to local preferences. Whenever Jesuits were attached to a church for more than a week or so, however, they lectured almost as much as they preached.

In general the lectures were supposed to deal with a book of the Bible or a specific pericope like the "Sermon on the Mount," but they sometimes were on "Christian Doctrine," that is, topics from the catechism, and often on "cases of conscience"—both so important as to constitute almost distinctive genres. The lectures occasionally dealt with general topics such as prayer, bearing tribulation, the Eucharist, or the life of Christ.[114] When Jesuits spoke about "lecturing," however, they usually meant lecturing on the Bible.

In 1556 Jesuits lectured on the Canticle of Solomon in both Syracuse and Florence, and the series was so popular in the latter city that it had to be transferred to the cathedral.[115] In that same year Borja lectured in Valladolid on the book of Lamentations.[116] In Naples in 1552 Bobadilla gave forty lectures on Jonah.[117] Jesuits sometimes lectured on other books from the Old Testament, but they more generally lectured on the New.

Probably because they preached more often from passages from the four Gospels according to the liturgical texts of the mass, they tended to choose other parts of the New Testament for their lectures and showed a special preference for the Pauline Epistles. At Regensburg in 1542, for instance, Jay lectured on Galatians;[118] at Messina in 1549, André des Freux lectured on one of the Epistles to the Corinthians;[119] that same year Salmerón lectured at Belluno on Ephesians;[120] in Naples in 1551 Laínez lectured four or five times a week on Galatians.[121] Sometimes all we know is that they lectured "on Paul."[122]

Within the Pauline corpus, they preferred the Epistle to the Romans.

Bobadilla lectured on it, for instance, at Vienna in 1542 and again in the Kingdom of Naples in 1550 and 1552;[123] Laínez did the same in Naples in 1549,[124] as did Nikolaas Floris (Nicolaus Gaudanus) at Ingolstadt the next year;[125] in 1551 André des Freux lectured on Romans in Venice, and Paolo d'Achille in Palermo;[126] another Jesuit lectured on it in Ferrara in 1554.[127] Nadal lectured on Romans in the cathedral in Messina in 1548 to a large audience that included the viceroy, and he repeated the series there during the summer of 1550.[128] In his other writings, moreover, he showed a special interest in Romans.

For Luther, the Epistle to the Romans was the most important book of the Bible, "the Gospel in its purest expression," the primary source for his teaching on justification by faith alone. The choice of cities in Germany and some of those in Italy in which the Jesuits lectured on that Epistle suggests that they used the occasion to refute Luther's interpretation. This suspicion is explicitly confirmed for Floris's lectures "on Paul" in Vienna in 1554. He "openly, briefly, and learnedly gave an exegesis of the difficult passages, overturning the errors of the heretics and splendidly confirming Catholic truth."[129] Floris was certainly not a lonely exception to the rule.

None of the Jesuits' many lectures on Romans from this period has survived, but Salmerón composed a huge commentary on the Epistle between 1575 and 1580 that surely reflects his lectures.[130] The commentary justifies the inference that lectures on Romans provided an irresistible occasion for entering into the religious controversies of the age, but it precludes the inference that this was the only, or even primary, reason Jesuits chose to lecture on it. Romans had long been recognized as special within the Pauline corpus and been the subject of much commentary in the decades just prior to the Reformation.

Salmerón in several places underscored the importance and preeminent "dignity" of Romans, but at the beginning of the commentary he summarized the reasons it deserved special esteem:

It contains the basic truths of Christian doctrine and the principles of our faith. It distinguishes the Gospel from the Law and philosophy. It makes manifest the benefits from Christ, by whose offering God was placated so as to bestow on us gratuitous remission of sins, liberation from death, true justification in God's sight, the gift of the Holy Spirit, sure hope of future immortality, patience and perseverance, and other fruits of good works, by which we attain eternal life. This Epistle describes the three human situations: life in the Gospel with our nature restored by Christ, life in Judaism under the Law, and life in the state of fallen nature and the old Adam where neither Law nor Gospel was known. In this Epistle, therefore, human pride that thinks we are deserving of some credit is utterly crushed, while Christ's grace is extolled in a way that shows that all glory is to be attributed to God.[131]

Nadal's imperative to himself in his journal is curt: "Study Paul!"—"Paulus legendus."[132] In the context of the entry it is clear Nadal was not thinking about Luther but about something important for his own spiritual life, which he several times in the journal described through expressions borrowed from Romans. On one occasion, true, he specifically differentiated Catholics from Lutherans in that for the former "our will" concurred in promotion to grace and glory.[133] But he seems more captivated by the passages that indicate the indwelling of the Holy Spirit in the hearts of the faithful (5:5; 8:11) and found in them the substance of the Pauline message.[134]

While commenting briefly on the third and fourth chapters of the Epistle, he described the origin of justification in a way that, typically for him, amounts to an anti-Pelagian statement: "We understand [from these chapters] nothing else than that the principle of justification is not the works of the Law or our works (if we extend Paul's meaning to our works and do not understand him to refer only to the works of the Old Law), as if they were from us; but we understand that the principle of justification and its sufficiency is from God through Christ, which is what we profess by faith, the principle and root of all justification."[135]

In another passage he said that the faith Jesus preached when he cured the sick was not the kind by which we believe in the Trinity, for instance, but a simple attachment to God.[136] Only chance passages like these provide glimpses into how he must have lectured on the crucial issues of the Epistle. Salmerón's commentary indicates the same basic interpretation, which was also a faithful and learned reflection of the teaching of the Council of Trent.

The form of the sacred lecture seems to have been a verse-by-verse exegesis, an *explication de texte*. To generalize from the surviving lectures of Salmerón and Laínez is to infer that the commentary would not have been conceived along humanist lines as a historico-critical examination of the text according to a consistent methodology. The lectures would be, rather, a loose concatenation of philological information, patristic commentary, medieval spiritual teachings, scholastic divisions of materials, digressions, and sage reflections into which were injected specific and practical applications to different groups of people that might be in the audience. Apostrophes were sometimes addressed to them—judges, doctors, mothers and fathers, benefice-hungry priests. The tone was unprepossessing and generally mild, the style conversational, even homely—"as when you women go to buy meat and the butcher throws in a bone for good measure," said Laínez.[137]

Of these lectures the only series on Scripture extant is Salmerón's on Psalm 118 (119), delivered in Rome in the winter of 1561–62.[138] While different in their nontechnical language from scholastic commentaries on Scripture, they still betray Salmerón's scholastic education and mind-set in a number of places. They are thus more typical of him than the classical heights to which he rose in the oration at Trent. Some of the same scholastic underpinnings are present in the two extant series by Laínez.

Laínez began his series of twenty-seven lectures "On Tribulation" in Rome in February 1558, shortly after he was elected general. He said he chose the topic not to add misery to misery—the Romans had suffered much that year—but to console those who were afflicted and to suggest some remedies.[139] This series immediately followed thirty lectures on prayer that he had begun the previous fall.

At some unknown date Laínez composed a brief work on "how to interpret Scripture well."[140] Besides Nadal's comments on sacred lectures in his exhortations on the *Formula,* this is the only extended statement from the period on how the lectures were to be done—more specifically, how the exegesis was to be done when the lectures dealt with Scripture. The lecturer was to expose the literal sense of the text and not much depart from it—the "mystical sense" was more appropriate for sermons. Laínez prescribed no particular doctrine to be expounded, but insisted that whatever was taught be solid, simple, and incontrovertible, based on the clear testimony of the Bible itself or on the traditions of the church that were certain.

Even if "sacred lectures" were known and practiced before the Jesuits took them up, they were given new zest and diffusion through the immense time and energy the Jesuits devoted to them. They constituted an essential part of the Jesuits' pastoral self-definition. Because they have been so little studied, it is difficult to assess them, but it is perhaps not too far from the mark to describe them as among the first attempts at "adult education" undertaken systematically and on a large scale.

Conversation and Publication

After the ministries of preaching and lecturing, the second version of the *Formula* added "and any other ministry whatsoever of the Word of God"— "et aliud quodcumque verbi Dei ministerium." From the experience of their first decade, the Jesuits saw that ministry of the Word extended beyond preaching and lecturing, and by this phrase they seemed to want to avoid premature foreclosure in defining its limits. No official document, however, stated clearly what these further ministries might be.

When Nadal was commissioned to promulgate the *Constitutions* and on other occasions had to speak about the Institute, he could not avoid commenting on the expression. By examining the activities of his colleagues even before the founding of the order, he was able to single out their practice of devout conversation among themselves and with others as something "any other" might denote. Although the practice is commended a number of times in the *Constitutions,* it had never attained the technical status of a ministry.[141] With Nadal it did, and it thereby more formally entered the canon of the *consueta ministeria.*[142] Moreover, it entered as a ministry of the *word,* which indicates once again that the Jesuits did not conceive such ministry as tied immediately to the text of the Bible.

In the two dialogues Nadal wrote in the 1560's, he implicitly provided lengthy and highly idealized models for such conversations taking place among people from different Christian persuasions.[143] Nadal was not, however, the only person to see such conversations as integral to Jesuit ministry. In 1583, late in his life, Peter Canisius wrote an important letter to Claudio Aquaviva, then general, in which he commended devout conversation and eulogized Pierre Favre as a model in its practice.[144] More important, Polanco's *Chronicon* relates thousands of examples of this ministry, accepted there as a normal and significant part of every Jesuit's daily round.

Nadal underscored its importance by interpreting it as the very origin of the Society. By such conversations Ignatius gathered his companions at Paris, and only afterward did he guide them through the *Spiritual Exercises.* In the general design of Jesuit pastoral practice, Nadal therefore saw them as often the first step. According to him they were a form of ministry of God's Word because they required "practically every skill of the preacher." But they differed from preaching and were in some ways more effective because through them one endeavored to enter gently and with love into the thoughts of a specific individual.

For this process Nadal took Ignatius as model and mentor. According to Nadal, Ignatius often spoke about such conversations and how to engage in them. He first required that one approach individuals with love and a desire for their well-being, while carefully observing each person's temperament and character. One began the conversation with subjects of interest to the other, so that with a merchant one spoke of trade, with a nobleman of government, and only gradually did one bring the discussion around to matters of the spirit. Ignatius often quoted the Spanish proverb that advised "going in by their door in order to come out by ours." If the Jesuit discovered that the individual consistently deflected the conversation from religious topics, he should then address them bluntly, turning from pleasant subjects to hell and divine judgment. The individual would either accept tue turn and profit from it or walk away and not waste the Jesuit's time further.[145]

This was a pastoral tactic, not the art of conversation, and the tactic implied control and calculation. It also exemplified the cardinal rule of Jesuit ministry: that it be accommodated to the circumstances of the persons concerned. The Jesuits in fact seemed to be more straightforward in their devout conversations than Ignatius's advice suggests. Those conversations fell into two categories. The first consisted of those that arose rather spontaneously among themselves and with others in which no specific agenda was operative besides mutual encouragement in "the things of God."

Erasmus's dialogue entitled "The Godly Feast" (Convivium religiosum) is the best-known model of such conversations to come down to us from the Renaissance, but the Jesuits were probably more directly influenced by models they found in the New Testament, one being that of the disciples whose "hearts burned warmly within them" as they conversed with Jesus along the way to Emmaus (Lk. 24:13–35).

They sometimes arranged situations where such conversation might take place. Shortly after they arrived in Messina to begin their first school, they organized a group from persons who frequented their church. One of these persons read aloud from a religious book supplied by the sacristan, and afterward they conversed among themselves on spiritual topics. Without explicitly naming him, Nadal gave credit to Filippo Neri, his contemporary and the founder of the Roman Oratory, for creating the model for such groups.[146] In 1549 a similar group met on Sunday afternoons at Valencia,[147] and, since Nadal recommended the practice in his exhortations on the Formula, others probably met elsewhere.

More characteristic of the Jesuits, however, was a second type of "conversation," best exemplified by their practice of "going fishing," usually two by two. Nadal used the expression in his exhortations, and Polanco in his circular letters to the Society. All the Jesuits understood what this allusion to Jesus' disciples being changed into "fishers of men" meant in the Jesuit context.[148] It was the practice of going out into the marketplace, prisons, ships in dock, and other places, not to preach to a group but to approach individuals.

In theory the purpose of fishing was simply to initiate a devout conversation and to exhort one's partner "to a spiritual and Christian life."[149] But in fact the purpose was usually quite specific—to get the other person to a sermon or to confession. At least one Jesuit besides the sacristan stayed behind in the church to continue the conversation as people arrived.[150] This was devout conversation, commando style.

A preferred time for fishing was the afternoons on Sundays and feast days when the Jesuits, whether priests, scholastics, or lay brothers, might have time at their disposal, and when a larger number of people would presumably be found in the streets and other public places. Although the Jesuits would fish for almost anybody, they seem to have cast their nets more often for persons from the lower social ranks—laborers, sailors, and "rustic folk" who might have come into the city for their day off.[151]

They kept track of their successes. In his circular letter to the whole Society on 20 July 1559, Polanco gave his eye-witness account of how within a five-day period the Jesuit scholastics from the Collegio Romano brought into the church for confession about four hundred people.[152] Such spectacular results were exceptional, but the Jesuits were sufficiently encouraged by the potential of this ministry to enlist others to follow their example.

Nadal promoted the idea, while cautioning that men and women should not go fishing together unless they were married and in general should restrict the practice to the circle of their relatives, friends, and servants.[153] In Modena in 1553, however, with Jesuit encouragement some "matrons" went fishing for both men and women to try to bring them to sermons, confession, and Communion.[154] In Padua in 1556 three or four women under Jesuit inspiration sought out prostitutes to exhort them to confession and to give them food if they needed it.[155]

The Jesuits sometimes turned the fishing expeditions into attacks on vice, especially gambling at card games. The moral problem was not the game but the loss by workers in a few hours on Sunday of their wages for the whole week. The Jesuits might swoop down upon these men while they were playing in order to persuade them to give up the vice.[156] Polanco reported one case of Jesuit scholastics specifically warning the card sharks and then "by the sword of God's Word" disrupting the game. They got some of the card players to confession and then to catechism. Others, supposedly, gave up the habit. The rest, we are told, simply fled every time they saw the scholastics heading down the street.[157]

In any case, whenever Nadal explained to his fellow Jesuits the meaning of the "any other" in the *Formula,* he spoke principally about "devout conversation" in its many forms—including how it was practiced in the sacrament of Penance and in "helping the dying." In his second Dialogue, 1562–63, he added a few other forms to the "any other." Among the principal ministries of God's Word, he believed, was the good example of the Jesuits because example generally spoke more powerfully than words, he knew not why. The idea that a good life was the best sermon was a Christian commonplace, but it had received new vigor in its adoption by humanists such as Erasmus. The Jesuits took it up from them and from the many other sources in which it was found. It was one of their favorite themes.[158]

Nadal also stated in this Dialogue that the Jesuit schools were a form of ministry of the Word. He thus created a place for them in the *Formula,* but he did not elaborate on the idea beyond the generality that the reason for their founding was to promote *pietas.* Without a word of elaboration he mentioned as well the writing of books, either to refute heretics or simply to "help souls."[159]

Given the immense amount of publication by Jesuits over the centuries and the amount eventually published even by members of this first generation, the slowness with which they grasped the usefulness of printing for their goals comes as a surprise, even though we have become accustomed to the idea that Protestants exploited the printing press with more imagination and vigor than their Catholic opponents.[160] In the first years of the Society, indeed, at least some Jesuits considered publication incompatible with their vocation. The printing of Salmerón's oration delivered at Trent in 1546 displeased him precisely for that reason, as he explained in a letter to Paolo d'Achille, a fellow Jesuit: "We are called to a way of life characterized chiefly by simplicity, modesty, and unrestricted charity to our neighbor. True, the publication of books is not in itself incompatible with these qualities; it nonetheless can be an obstacle to more excellent works of charity and at times a distraction from them."[161] Some years later even the *Constitutions* made only slight mention of "writing books useful for the common good."[162]

It was inevitable, however, that Jesuits turn to the printing press, and Ignatius himself gave an impetus to it that the *Constitutions* do not reflect. He came to support especially two categories of publication—writings to refute the heretics and writings to aid Jesuits in their ministry. In a letter to Canisius, 13 August 1554, he encouraged Jesuits in Germany to counter Protestant pamphlets with their own, and he did the same in a letter to Nadal the next year.[163] He encouraged Polanco to compile the manual for Jesuit confessors, Canisius to write his catechism, and Laínez to write a compendium of theology adapted to pastoral needs.

The categories began to broaden even in Ignatius's lifetime and surely with his approval. Just after Ignatius's death, for instance, Gaspar de Loarte published a short manual of Christian piety for lowly folk, *Esercitio della vita christiana,* and then continued to produce similar works.[164] By 1573 Nadal was explicitly commending the writing of books "that can guide souls to goodness and devotion."[165] At about that time he took his own advice by composing for publication *Adnotationes et meditationes in Evangelia.*

It was the schools, however, that sparked the biggest change in Jesuit attitudes and practice about publication. Textbooks were needed, at prices students could afford. With that end in view, Ignatius in the last year of his life went to immense trouble to secure a good press for the Collegio Romano, which was installed and in working order within a few months after his death.[166] Jesuit teachers in the meantime discovered that the texts available did not always suit them and began to compose their own. Among the first books published by this first press operated by the Society of Jesus was André des Freux's edition (1558) of a pagan classic, Martial's *Epigrams.*

By 1564 the press at the Collegio Romano had acquired Arabic characters, and by 1577, Hebrew. The Jesuits installed presses in other colleges, not without worry that they might seem to be running a business for profit.[167] These presses were of modest dimensions, but they performed important services for the Jesuits and their clients. In 1563, for instance, Nadal arranged for the press at the school in Vienna to print fifteen hundred copies of the *Spiritual Exercises.*[168] In 1556, the same year the press was put into operation in the Collegio Romano, the Jesuits introduced printing into India by installing a press in their college in Goa. Thus the first book printed in India was Xavier's *Doutrina Christam.*[169]

The Jesuits of this generation wrote and published influential books, including the catechisms by Canisius.[170] Nonetheless, the number published during their lifetimes and especially in the first two decades of the Society's existence was relatively small. The Jesuits were indefatigable writers, as the quantity and variety of documents cited in this book testify, but most of what they wrote was correspondence or documents internal to the Society, not intended for publication. Publication of theological works increased considerably in the 1570's. In their pastoral activities, however, the Jesuits preferred the spoken word to the written, direct human contact to a page of print.

Teaching Christianity

As we have seen, Ignatius had hardly arrived at Alcalá in 1526 when he began to teach "Christian Doctrine." He continued to do so in other places during his "pilgrim years." Pedro de Ribadeneira many years later recalled how as a boy in Rome he was among the young and old, men and women, learned and unlearned to whom Ignatius taught catechism and how he in the process corrected Ignatius's Italian.[171]

It is difficult to shake the prejudice that before Luther's publication in 1529 of both *Kleiner Katechismus* and *Grosser Katechismus* instruction in the rudiments of the Christian faith had completely died out and that upon his publications all subsequent catechesis was somehow dependent. It is now clear, however, that beginning in the fifteenth century a new concern about instructing the faithful in "the art of Christian living and dying" had begun to emerge in some parts of Europe.[172]

In Spain the concern began to gain momentum at the end of the century, due in part, of course, to the efforts of the great reformer, Cardinal Francisco Jiménez de Cisneros. Other initiatives followed, reaching a climax between about 1525 and 1550.[173] The established system of catechesis that Franciscans were employing in Mexico by 1525 indicates similar phenomena in their native Spain.[174] Juan de Avila, a reformer influenced by Erasmus, had perhaps as early as 1527 published his catechism, written in verse and meant to be set to tunes—*Doctrina cristiana que se canta*. Just as important, he articulated principles of catechetical pedagogy that stressed the necessity of accommodation of the teacher and lesson to the audience and insisted on the establishment of an affectionate and trusting relationship between teacher and pupil.[175] Other catechisms came into circulation, including in the 1540's those of Constantino Ponce de la Fuente, who was even more of an Erasmian than Avila.[176] By that same decade confraternities for teaching Christian Doctrine were being established.[177]

In Italy in the early 1400's Bishop Nicolò Albergati of Bologna organized a confraternity of teenaged boys and adults to teach catechism. One of the earliest and widely reprinted incunabula was *Libreto dela dotrina christiana per i putti piccoli e giovanetti*. Only in 1536, however, did Castellino da Castello organize in Milan "Schools of Christian Doctrine" that had lasting and widespread influence.[178] These "schools," which quickly spread to other Italian cities, were really just catechism classes taught on Sundays and feast days, mostly by lay men and women.

This context explains the early interest in catechesis of Ignatius and his companions and the fact that the first version of the *Formula* lists "the instruction of young and uneducated persons in Christianity" as a specific ministry of the Society. All Jesuit documents from the period clearly understood the expression to mean catechism, not the schools the Jesuits would eventually establish, an interpretation that only the later history of the Society sometimes erroneously imposed.

The sixteenth century marked, however, the great change in catechesis that has long been attributed to it and that cannot be considered simply a continuation of an earlier movement unmodified except in intensity. While we must avoid the fallacy that Luther's catechisms appeared without precedent, we must recognize that they symbolized and powerfully stimulated a radical change in the history of this traditional Christian institution. The Jesuits appeared just as this change was taking place, and they were initially an independent aspect of it. By about 1555, moreover, their catechesis began to be affected by concerns and assumptions stemming from the Reformation and from other modifications of religious sensibilities.

The sixteenth-century change in catechesis was essentially twofold. First, what was earlier the preoccupation of relatively few individuals and of elite circles exploded into widespread agitation and action that eventually touched every stratum of society. The teaching of catechism became a more highly organized enterprise than ever before. It moved from hearth to public space. The printing press and the new faith in education that characterized the age ignited the change and gave it much of its character. The enthusiasm for catechesis was part of the "war against ignorance and superstition" that both Protestants and Catholics waged so relentlessly.

The importance the nascent Society of Jesus attributed to catechetical instruction was thus typical of the era but perhaps even more emphatic. An articulation of it peculiar to the Society, for instance, was that, as the *Constitutions* came to determine, the fully professed members were required as part of their vow of obedience to give "special care for the instruction of children."[179] If this was explicit only for the professed, all the members observed it. When Ignatius died, only forty-eight Jesuits out of the thousand were solemnly professed, yet the Jesuits cultivated this ministry with the greatest intensity everywhere they went.

The First General Congregation approved, however, of sometimes obliging the professed by virtue of their vow to teach catechism, and it supported the position by recalling that Ignatius so obliged them to do it once for a continuous forty-day period.[180] The Second Congregation, 1565, extended the obligation of such a period to the spiritual coadjutors, thereby implicitly recognizing its paradigmatic role for all Jesuits and unwittingly suggesting the confusion already operative in the Society about the distinction between the two "grades," that is, modes of membership.[181]

The second feature in the sixteenth-century shift consisted in changes in the character of the catechesis from its medieval and even early Christian antecedents. These changes, though generally effective in both Protestant and Catholic catechesis as the century wore on, occurred in different forms, with different emphases and appreciations, and according to different time-tables among Protestants and Catholics—including, of course, the many sub-groups, like the Jesuits, within those extensive categories.

What were some of these changes? There was a movement away from the fundamentally oral character of catechesis, in which the lesson was conveyed by lectures or sermons and learned in verses often set to tunes, to study from printed texts. The question-answer format practically drove out other forms. Catechism was taught less to adults and, in many places, almost exclusively to children. Protestant pastors and in some places Catholic priests began to be seen as the preferred and proper teachers of catechism. Substructures governed by a particular theological viewpoint began to be introduced into texts, even though traditional materials like the Creed and the Decalogue were retained. This led to overt or covert attempts to turn the text into an instrument of religious polemics or a summary of confessional orthodoxy. What resulted was a tendency to make catechesis more an exercise of mind and memory than a continuation of its more traditional function as an initiation into Christian life and religious practice. The Jesuits came to reflect, promote, ignore, and sometimes resist these changes, and their practice of catechesis varied in different territories, even though the effective network of communication within the Society helped them maintain a certain common outlook. Especially in the first fifteen years they were more in touch with earlier traditions of catechesis, which they infused with energy and enthusiasm.

Aside from what Ignatius and other early Jesuits learned about catechesis in Spain, Paris, and northern Italy, they in 1554 accepted into the Society two talented disciples of Juan de Avila—Diego Guzmán and Gaspar de Loarte—who were forces even at that date for a continuation of the earlier traditions. From 1554 until his death in 1585 Guzmán labored as the most important and influential Jesuit catechist in Italy.[182] For the rest of the century, moreover, the Jesuit schools in Spain used Avila's catechism, not those composed by Peter Canisius or other members of the Society.[183]

In India by 1552 the Jesuits were using, among others, a catechism by Constantino in which Xavier, unlike the Spanish Inquisition, did not perceive any heterodoxy and wanted to take it with him into China.[184] But Xavier, drawing on the Iberian tradition as he knew it, had himself composed catechisms. He wove into his teaching elements that were taken directly from the *Spiritual Exercises*. He often taught without a text and used verse, song, dialogue, and "lesson" as occasion seemed to suggest.[185]

Especially in the earlier years the Jesuits made frequent use of the "lesson," essentially a form of sacred lecture, in which the teacher simply stated and explained the topic to pupils, who then might be asked to repeat in set formula the essence of what was taught. In 1546 Xavier wrote for catechetical purposes a "Declaration" on the Apostles' Creed. It is the only such document that has survived from the early Jesuits, as close as we can get to how they developed a "lesson" on this subject.[186] It proceeds article by article, basically by elaborating on the pertinent biblical stories and making frequent but brief applications to the life of the Christian.

The "lesson" seems, in fact, to have been the way most public catechesis was done in the late Middle Ages. Luther used it in Wittenberg in 1516 when he "expounded" the Decalogue and the Lord's Prayer.[187] He observed many years afterward that "to preach on the catechism was then a new and uncommon thing," but his experience was limited to Germany.[188]

Nonetheless, Polanco related that in Burgos in 1556 the teaching of "Christian Doctrine" was practically unknown. One of the Jesuits professed, therefore, to give a series of lectures on the Epistle of James, but in fact he substituted Christian Doctrine.[189] The audience, we presume, was predominantly adult. In that same year in Valladolid, Jesuits were lecturing on the Lamentations of Jeremiah, but the provincial determined that they should switch the subject to catechetical doctrine.

Ignatius's lesson on Christian Doctrine confirms that lecture was the format he used, and its content is typical of early Jesuit catechesis.[190] It begins with a few words about how to make one's confession to a priest, and then continues with a brief explanation of the Decalogue, of five so-called precepts of the church concerning matters such as the lenten fast, of the seven capital sins, of the five senses of the body, of the corporal and spiritual works of mercy. Like the late-medieval catechesis it reflects, it pretends to no literary unity and bespeaks no theological viewpoint. Although undated, it is probably from about 1540, but almost certainly reflects Ignatius's teaching from much earlier days. It contains nothing that suggests any awareness of Protestantism or efforts to counteract it. Perhaps more important, it is obviously geared to Christian life and sacramental practice, with notable attention given to fundamental issues of morality. It does not contain the Creed, but the omission is probably an accident of textual transmission, for we know Ignatius taught "the articles of faith" at Alcalà, 1526–27.[191]

The Jesuits, even after they began to use printed catechisms extensively, concentrated on the same elements as had Ignatius—not out of imitation but out of the force of tradition. Along with the Apostles' Creed, they also taught the "Our Father," the "Hail Mary," the Decalogue, remedies for sin, the works of mercy, the Beatitudes, and they concluded with a short exhortation.[192] They did this for boys and girls, for men and women. On occasion they substituted or included instruction on how to pray, as did Xavier in India in 1548 and Nadal in Messina in 1550.[193]

Whenever Nadal spoke of this ministry, he in fact insisted that, like the Jesuit vocation itself, catechesis not be "speculative, but practical," so that as the mind was instructed the will be moved to action and the soul become ardent in devotion.[194] This was a Jesuit adaptation of the earlier tradition, which would continue as a distinguishing mark of their understanding of genuine catechesis. Thus, once adults were sufficiently catechized, they were ready to move on to a somewhat more advanced book on the spiritual life, such as Loarte's *Esercitio*.[195]

When Jesuits lectured on Christianity, they sometimes varied the format. In Florence in 1553, for instance, two scholastics taught it by way of a dialogue between themselves.[196] When in 1555 Nikolaas Floris taught catechism to adults and children in the Jesuits' church in Venice, he installed two little pulpits from which two boys expounded the lesson for a while. He then took up where they left off. Nadal, who wrote to Ignatius about the incident, noted that the people liked it.[197]

During the Renaissance, Italians were accustomed, especially in their confraternities, to having boys preach to them. That surely explains why Floris did not shock local sensibilities. Moreover, as the Milanese "Schools of Christian Doctrine" show, the laity in Italy played a central role in the reactivation of this ancient ministry from the very beginning. Nonetheless, the extent to which the early Jesuits engaged the laity, especially young people, in helping them in their catechesis is striking. They seem altogether innocent of any concern that it should be reserved to priests, pastors, or members of religious orders.

Employing the laity generally meant alternatives to the lecture. One such alternative was teaching and learning the lesson set to verse, and another was teaching from a written text. The Jesuits made use of texts already in circulation and, when necessary, translated them into other languages, as when they put Avila's catechism into Italian verse. They also composed their own, as was the case with Laínez in Parma in 1540, Doménech in Sicily in 1547, Adriaan Adriaenssens in Louvain in 1550, Giovanni Araldo in Naples in 1552, and Polanco himself in Perugia in 1557.[198] Other

Jesuits wrote and published catechisms, about which we know nothing more than that.[199]

Inclined as the Jesuits were to report their successes to Rome, they outdid themselves in reporting their catechetical triumphs from countries where they were not competing with Luther or Calvin. Of all the *consueta ministeria,* they seemed most often and most genuinely to have enjoyed this one. This was particularly true once they discovered the exponentially multiplying effects they achieved by teaching their disciples how to teach, especially when the catechetical texts were set to tunes—a practice they learned in Spain and exported elsewhere. They surely must have taught those disciples that by imparting Christian Doctrine to others they were performing the important spiritual work of mercy of instructing the ignorant, for Avila's catechism made that point explicitly.[200]

In his *Chronicon* for 1555, Polanco narrated what was happening in distant Goa. Catechism was taught in many places by "Ours," but more frequently it was taught by their pupils, "who showed themselves also to be teachers." A "new and delightful spectacle" awaited Jesuits recently arrived from Portugal when they saw the variety of these pupil-teachers—some white, some black, some yellow, some clothed, some "naked, although a loin cloth covered their more private parts."[201] In 1550 the Jesuits imported to Brazil from Lisbon seven orphan boys who volunteered to be employed as catechists.[202] The Jesuits were more than satisfied with the success of the experiment. The next year nine orphans went to India for the same purpose.[203]

The Jesuits were doing similar things back home. Ignatius recommended to Canisius in 1554 that students at the Jesuit school in Vienna be sent out on Sundays and feast days to teach catechism.[204] In Plasencia in 1555, a Jesuit priest taught catechism to adults on Sundays and feast days, and a scholastic taught it to boys and girls daily. These children taught it in turn to others who, for one reason or another, could not come to the regular lessons.[205] By 1556 in Genoa children were helping lay adults in this ministry on a regular basis.[206]

It was with the help of tunes that the children came into their own. Polanco reported what happened in Gandía in 1554. One of the Jesuit scholastics, accompanied by two boys, walked through the streets ringing a little bell. The boys meanwhile sang parts of the catechism "in a sweet melody." As the children gathered behind their three leaders, they were led to a church, where classes were taught and the tunes learned. The tunes and lyrics became so popular that "day and night in the whole town nothing was sung by both adults and children but 'Christian Doctrine' "—by craftsmen and day laborers in the town, by farmers in their fields, by mothers, who had learned it from their children, in the homes. The lessons were taught in the church daily in the winter and once a week in the summer, sometimes to as many as four hundred children. Those who did particularly well received prizes, but the enthusiasm was so great that often seventy or eighty prizes had to be awarded.[207]

In Messina in 1555 the viceroy decreed that all ten parishes in the city offer catechism lessons for children between the ages of six and twelve. He committed the task to the Jesuit provincial, who designated two Jesuits for each parish. At the appointed hour on Sundays and feast days, the church bells were rung. About thirty or forty children usually gathered at each church, where "with such great enjoyment" the older children taught the tunes and lyrics to the younger that "night and day they sang nothing else in the streets and marketplaces of the town."[208]

In Valencia that same year parents were so impressed that they gathered to sing the catechism with their children in responsorial fashion—one group singing answers to the other.[209] In remote villages in northern Spain, no songs were sung "on those hills" except the "Our Father" and other prayers taught in the classes of Christian Doctrine. In Murcia, Syracuse, and other cities, children paraded through the streets singing their lessons.[210]

The Jesuits introduced singing into Germany only later and sparingly, but in their church in Vienna in 1569 it was the weekly practice after vespers on Sunday, with parents present. It might begin with a boy singing the "Our Father" from a raised platform, which the rest of the children then repeated. He would be followed by a girl singing the Apostles' Creed, and so forth until the lesson was completed. The service lasted about half an hour.[211]

A query was addressed to the First General Congregation, 1558: "Is it appropriate to teach Christian Doctrine in song, for experience teaches that children are more easily attracted to it that way and that greater success results?" The Congregation referred the question, which obviously begged an affirmative answer, to the newly elected Laínez. He responded that it was indeed appropriate wherever it seemed to work.[212]

The Jesuits' reports of their successes in catechesis raise, of course, a number of questions. The rhapsodic rhetoric in which they sometimes encased the reports leaves modern readers skeptical. Nonetheless, once allowance is made for exaggeration, the reports have the ring of truth in the basic information they convey and in their psychological insight into the fun children have in teaching one another and especially in teaching their parents and other adults.

Assessing pedagogical effectiveness is never easy. The only attempt to do so for catechetical instruction during this period has been for Lutheran parts of Germany. It led to negative conclusions, hotly contested, and to the surmise that an examination of catechesis in Catholic Bavaria would show the same results.[213] To speculate further would be inappropriate until more information is available. Moreover, despite similarities between all Protestant and Catholic catechesis, these two massive efforts at indoctrination did not altogether fall into the same mold, were not based on identical assumptions about human nature, evinced different attitudes toward established ways, sometimes interacted with their constituencies according to diverse patterns, and varied in different cultures.

When Jesuits worked in those parts of Europe where the catechisms of the Protestant reformers were in use, however, their own catechisms showed the effect and, as the catechisms devised by Peter Canisius to respond to Luther's gained wider currency in the Society, especially in its schools, the changes were to some extent felt in other places. That is why 1554 is a crucial date, the year in which Canisius delivered to King Ferdinand, the emperor's brother, a first version of his catechism entitled *Summa doctrinae christianae,* a project requested by Ferdinand and commended to Canisius by Ignatius.[214]

It was not this "large catechism" or its later revisions that enjoyed great success, or even Canisius's *Catechismus minimus* (1556–57), intended for very young children, but the *Catechismus parvus* or *minor,* an intermediate text published in 1558 and destined to run through innumerable editions and translations. This "Small Catechism" eventually drove most Catholic competitors in Germany off the market, and although not published until almost three decades after the first edition of Luther's *Kleiner Katechismus,* it became the preeminent Catholic response to it.[215]

King Ferdinand helped greatly in the dissemination of Canisius's catechisms through his edict, published as a preface to the first edition of the *Summa,* ordering all catechists in his domain to use it and no other. Nonetheless, Canisius's catechisms had certain features that distinguished them from their late-medieval antecedents and helped make them popular.

They adopted the question-answer format, which by this time had become widespread. Although they had a strong moral emphasis, they were not geared directly toward confession. They contained the traditional elements, but cast them into a framework of the two virtues of wisdom and justice, or righteousness *(justitia, Gerechtigkeit),* which appears to be at least an unconscious attempt to break with the preoccupation with sin in some earlier catechisms. Under wisdom Canisius treated faith (the Apostles'

Creed), hope (the "Our Father"), love (the Decalogue), and the seven sacraments. The sacraments were generally not given separate treatment in late-medieval catechisms but that situation had already changed in German Catholic texts. Canisius adopted and radically adapted the faith-hope-love scheme from the *Enchiridion* of Augustine. He divided justice into two parts: "avoid evil" (the capital sins, sins against the Holy Spirit, and so forth); and "do good" (the spiritual and corporal works of mercy, the cardinal virtues, the Beatitudes, and similar materials).

Canisius's catechisms were not overtly polemical, and in a different context they might pass as detached from contemporary disputes. They thus adhered to Ignatius's consistent advice to present Catholic teaching in a positive way and to avoid contention whenever possible. Nonetheless, the definition and treatment of faith and especially of righteousness were obviously a reply to Luther on these same issues. Moreover, Canisius's catechisms made explicit mention of the papacy in their descriptions of the church, a significant departure from most of their earlier counterparts.[216] In other words, although Canisius's catechisms looked to the practice of a devout Christian life, they were also statements of confessional bias.[217]

All these factors help account for the long-standing success of Canisius's catechisms among Catholics in Germany and, despite their implicit apologetics, made them suitable for export. But other Jesuits continued to compose catechetical texts. Shortly after the first edition of Canisius's catechisms, Diego de Ledesma published in Italy a catechism for the "very ignorant" and another for the "less ignorant." Ledesma, a man of many talents, had studied at the universities of Alcalá, Paris, and Louvain and was another great architect of the educational program for the Jesuit schools.[218] His catechisms seem to have been influenced by Canisius's in their general structure. They ran through many editions and translations well into the seventeenth century when, for instance, they were used with the indigenous peoples in New France.[219]

The merits of Canisius's and Ledesma's efforts become evident when they are contrasted with the *Catéchisme et sommaire de la doctrine chrétienne* published in 1563 by the French Jesuit Emond Auger.[220] Written expressly against "the errors of our times," it was a response to Calvin's *Formulaire d'instruire les enfants en la chrétienté* (1541), which it attempted to counter on a point-for-point basis. In so responding, it adopted the format and assumptions about the nature of catechesis of the enemy it was attacking. These were the reasons for the immediate success in France of the large and small versions and then for their rapid decline in popularity. By 1576 the latter had been displaced by translations of Canisius's "Small Catechism" even in Jesuit schools in France because it was too polemical and too involved with abstract notions, which is to say, not sufficiently oriented to "piety."[221] Nonetheless, Auger's larger version was early translated into Spanish, Italian, and Dutch, and it influenced later French catechisms.

Canisius's catechetical works, beginning with the *Summa*, began to be translated into Italian in 1558. Antonio Possevino was their great promoter in Piedmont and Savoy. Although Polanco had misgivings about using in Italy catechisms constructed for heretical territories, in 1565 he reported in his circular letter to the whole Society that the Jesuits had three thousand copies of, presumably, the "Small Catechism" printed in Rome on the press of the Collegio Romano along with two thousand of another *Dottrina cristiana*, probably Ledesma's, for distribution to the Jesuit catechetical centers in the city.[222] In a letter to Cristóbal Rodriguez two years later he noted that in Italy the Jesuits were using four different catechisms—two by Canisius and the two by Ledesma.[223]

After 1548 the Jesuits taught catechism to students in their schools, usually for an hour or so a week, and often to students from other schools as well. They sometimes tried to persuade instructors in other schools to teach catechism to their pupils.[224] This incorporation into a larger curriculum is a sign of the further formalization of the process that was part of the general development of the era. Moreover, location of catechism in a classroom helped promote a subtle—and for the Jesuits generally unintended—shift from "learning one's religion" (in order to practice it) to "learning truths about one's religion" (in order to have them in one's arsenal of information).

When the Jesuits taught catechism outside the schools, the use of printed texts often entailed teaching reading and writing as well, especially when they worked with the indigenous populations of India and Brazil. In this they were in concert with their contemporaries in Europe, where the cultural impact of the new catechesis was just as significant as the religious.

This brief survey of the early Jesuits' promotion of *Christianitas*, or "Christian Doctrine," perforce leaves many questions unanswered, but a few things are clear. This ministry was for the Jesuits in both theory and practice of the utmost importance from the very first hour. In this regard they generally acted on their own initiative, and their assistance to the viceroy of Sicily in 1555 was more the exception than the rule. Although in some parts of Europe their catechesis became an instrument for the defense of confessional orthodoxy, that was not its original purpose, nor did that defense even in those places substantially deflect the Jesuits from the earlier ideal of catechesis as instruction in Christian living and practice. *Christianitas* remained the fundamental goal and orientation.

The catechetical tradition of Juan de Avila remained strong in the order. Therefore, even though the Jesuits much appreciated Canisius's labors, they adopted no master text, just as they adopted no uniform format or process—they "accommodated to times, persons, places." Especially by 1565, however, their practice clearly showed characteristics of the new pedagogy and of the new assumptions about catechesis introduced in the sixteenth century.

Missions to the Countryside

One of the most distinctive pastoral strategies devised in Catholicism in the early modern period was the so-called mission to small villages and hamlets, which in the seventeenth century was extended to include cities and whole dioceses.[225] Eventually these missions incorporated a carefully, even elaborately designed program of preaching, catechesis, confession, and establishment or reform of confraternities, and they might engage several "missioners" in the same location for a month or longer. Although they had some vague precedents in the preaching of the friars in the cities in the late Middle Ages, they were in fact a new institution. They were religious "revivals," as their unwitting Protestant imitators would call them centuries later.

The Jesuits were among the first, if not the first, to develop this institution and were extremely influential in its evolution.[226] The rudiments appear almost with the founding of the Society, but neither Nadal nor any other contemporary singled out the mission as a special form of pastoral activity, for it was in too inchoate a stage.

It contained in itself practically all the *consueta ministeria*. What eventually made it a distinctive institution, however, was its marshaling them into an organized strategy with clearly defined objectives. At least the basic contours had emerged by 1556, when, for example, Jesuits from Seville concentrated on nine nearby villages. They stayed in the villages for a day, several days, or a week, living in local hospitals or any other suitable lodging they could find. In the morning they preached. In the evening, with the children gathered around them, they marched through the town singing catechism until they came to the church, where they lectured on it. At convenient times they heard confessions of both men and women. They founded or reactivated confraternities. Before they left the town, they chose a man who could read, gave him the catechism book, and then instructed him on how to teach it. Some of the people were so impressed, however, that they followed the Jesuits to the next town and even further—so it was reported—to repeat the experience.[227]

Jesuits began doing the same thing at about the same time in Italy, where Silvestro Landini had even earlier set an example of itinerant preaching in the countryside.[228] Rome and Loreto were the two centers out of which the excursions radiated during these experimental years. Jesuit scholastics from the Collegio Romano were among those who participated.

In 1564, four Jesuits engaged in a quite different kind of mission for six months in villages of Bavaria. The duke himself had requested the preachers from Canisius, for the express purpose of combating the Lutherans and, of course, confirming wavering Catholics. He gave the Jesuits wide authority to deal with convents, schools, and other institutions. The Jesuits were, as usual, thoroughly shocked by the ignorance of basic beliefs and the hatred directed at the Catholic Church. Their preaching was conditioned by this desperate and often polemical situation, and they had to defend the authority of the church, the nature of the sacraments, the sacrificial character of the mass, and other contested points of doctrine. But a social and political agenda promoted by the duke also manifested itself, for the Jesuits unfailingly preached on the duty to obey lawful secular authority.[229]

The Exercises in Practice

For their ministry the Jesuits possessed no more distinctive instrument than the *Exercises*.[230] The first generation, under the influence of Ignatius, knew they had in that book a unique instrument to "help souls." Polanco saw the *Exercises* as a "compendium" *(epilogus)* of all the means the Jesuits had for helping souls in spiritual growth.[231] From Ignatius's example and from the text itself, moreover, the Jesuits also knew that the *Exercises* were an extraordinarily pliable instrument that could be accommodated to a great variety of circumstances and individuals—"Multiplex est modus tradendi Exercitia," said a contemporary source.[232]

A landmark was passed in 1548 with the first printing of the text, issued in Rome by the press of Antonio Blado and paid for by the duke of Gandía, Francisco de Borja. Until then only a few copies of the Spanish text circulated in manuscript within the Society. They contained errors in transcription, which seems especially to have motivated Ignatius to have the text printed. André des Freux, an accomplished classicist, made the Latin translation of the edition, which some people began to take for the original language. (The Spanish text was not published until 1615.) The book carried an official approbation from Paul III, a protection experience had shown and would continue to show was needed.

With copies of the text now more or less readily available to them, the Jesuits made direct use of the *Exercises* more extensively in their ministries than before, but the basic patterns of accommodation or application did not substantially change. They ranged from the relatively simple or "light" *(leves)* exercises described in the eighteenth "Introductory Observation"[233] to the full-scale "retreat" of thirty days or more done in seclusion and in close conversation with a spiritual guide. Between these two extremes were numerous variations that either built upon the simplest possibility or scaled down the most elaborate.[234]

The eighteenth "Observation" tells how the *Exercises* can be adapted to persons who want help getting "some instruction and [reaching] a certain level of peace of soul." It recommends teaching things like examination of conscience and some methods of prayer found in the First Week and instructing the persons in the basic elements of the catechism. Weekly confession and Communion are also to be commended. This was the format Ignatius more generally followed himself at first—from Manresa until his arrival in Paris. Although on one level the *Exercises* seems to be only an intensified catechesis, the daily conversations Ignatius held with individuals doing it indicate that a deepening of religious sensibilities, a new level of commitment and appropriation, was the true goal.[235] The eighteenth "Observation" is thus of crucial importance for understanding not only this method of "giving the *Exercises*" but also for understanding Jesuit catechetical practice and the "other ministries of the Word of God" discussed in this chapter.

When, after 1540, other Jesuits began making use of the *Exercises* in their ministry, they too usually followed some form of this simple procedure. In Parma in 1540, for instance, Favre and Laínez reported on the large numbers who made the *Exercises*, and then reported that these disciples in turn led others in them—pastors thus helping their parishioners, teachers their students, and women their friends and acquaintances.[236] This easy enlisting of persons to guide others meant that a simplification even beyond Ignatius's early practice had taken place.

The simplification also meant that the *Exercises* early began to be given to more than one person at the same time, as when some orphan boys in Messina made the *Exercises* under Jerónimo Doménech in 1547.[237] The same would be true in Bologna in 1549, when Broët often gave them to young women, "sometimes to twelve or thirteen at a time,"[238] and in Chieti that same year when Landini gave them to eight priests or the next year to fourteen young women.[239] These examples are typical. In such cases the opportunity for private conversation with the Jesuit would perforce be much reduced, and the instructional element would presumably loom larger, probably conveyed in lectures.

In 1546, Polanco directed Bishop Pier Francesco Galigari da Gagliano of Pistoia in a course of the *Exercises* according to the nineteenth "Observation," which allowed continuing in one's ordinary occupations with the proviso of setting aside a few hours a day for this special purpose.[240] This is in fact probably how Ignatius usually gave the *Exercises* in the early years, especially when they were limited to the First Week.[241]

The better arrangement, surely, was for the individual to leave familiar surroundings and occupations for fuller concentration on the *Exercises*— and to continue this way for one or several weeks. The more arrangements like these could be secured, the more clearly the *Exercises* emerged as a self-standing program of ministry, distinct from lecturing and catechesis. But such arrangements were difficult to find, a major problem the Jesuits faced everywhere they worked.

One solution was for people to lodge and take food at a nearby convent or monastery. The men then came to see the Jesuit in his room or someplace else in the house, whereas the women, even if more than one were making the retreat at the same time, saw him in the church in a "confessional," which at this time was generally a simple armchair without any grill or enclosure.[242]

After a few earlier experiments, in 1553 the Jesuits built their first building at the college at Alcalá specifically for housing men doing the *Exercises,* and similar houses were later built elsewhere.[243] At Alcalá there was sometimes a waiting list of up to twenty.[244] Moreover, once the Jesuits began to acquire the more spacious houses needed for the faculties of their schools, they sometimes set aside rooms for this purpose, a practice approved by Polanco.[245] In Valencia by 1555, for instance, the Jesuits had three or four such rooms.[246] For reasons of propriety, no similar arrangements were even considered for women.

Nadal directed that the men lodged in Jesuit houses were to pay for what they ate and drank, but for nothing more. In the larger houses they were expected to eat the same meals as the community, but in smaller ones they could usually order what and how much they wanted, to be more in accord with the "Rules" in the *Exercises* about taking food. They ate in their rooms, not in the Jesuit refectory. One of the lay brothers was assigned to them to see to their material needs—to clean the room, make the bed, supply writing materials, and do whatever else might be needed.[247]

Reports arrived in Rome from Messina, Florence, Tournai, Prague, and other cities about the difficulties of finding persons to make the *Exercises,* and Ignatius had to prod Jesuits to be more diligent in inviting people to do so, a situation unusual for the *consueta ministeria.*[248] The novelty of the idea and the difficulty of finding appropriate locations were among the problems Jesuits faced in trying to comply. Moreover, the *Exercises* themselves indicated that their full course was not for everybody, and the *Constitutions* specified that to mean they were for a "few."[249]

Successes were reported, and the Jesuits cast their nets broadly. Queen Catherine of Portugal, sister of the emperor, made them in 1554, as did other members of the royal court.[250] Upon his arrival in Brazil in 1557 as governor general, Mem de Sá spent a week in the *Exercises* under the guidance of Nóbrega.[251] Whole convents of nuns began to request them, as did men from other religious orders.[252] When Nadal commented on the section of the *Constitutions* restricting the full course to a "few," he interpreted the word as broadly as possible: "We say 'few' in relationship to the total population, but we nonetheless hope in the Lord that those few will be many." He then indicated how different parts of the *Exercises* helped different people with different needs.[253] Polanco insisted the *Exercises* were intended for every class of society and in fact had helped every class—in ways that preaching, exhortation, and fear of damnation did not.[254]

By 1564 Nadal had begun to advocate that all—or at least the better—students in Jesuit schools not leave them until they had made the *Exercises* in some form.[255] This idea did not exactly square with the observation in a different context by Polanco in 1554 that experience had taught that the *Exercises* should always be undertaken by people "freely, and not quasi-coerced."[256] Relatively soon after the founding by the Jesuits of the Collegio Germanico in Rome in 1552, the students were expected to spend eight or ten days after entering the school in instruction in "things of the spirit"—which almost certainly meant a form of the *Exercises.* In any case, when the Collegio moved to new and more spacious quarters in 1563 some rooms were designated for outsiders who wanted to make retreats, so that it became the first "retreat house" in Rome.[257]

People had different reasons for making the *Exercises* even in their more extended form, so that the election did not always play the role in practice that the book indicates. Even the *Constitutions* allowed "an increase in devotion" as what might best be sought.[258] People engaged in the *Exercises,* therefore, to learn how to pray, to receive more intense spiritual counsel, to move further in their spiritual lives, to reform their lives within their station, and, of course, to make an "election" about a new station.[259] Some few possibly came out of curiosity. Because of this diversity of goals, as well as for other reasons, commentaries insisted that the person guiding the *Exercises* get to know the individual as best he could so that he might accommodate the *Exercises* to that person's particular needs and desires.

That person's function was threefold. He acted sometimes as a teacher—about some point of doctrine or about practical matters, such as how to pray. He engaged in a devout conversation by listening attentively and then giving spiritual counsel, paying special attention to movements of "consolation and desolation." He briefly and objectively proposed points for prayer and meditation, as the text itself prescribes.[260] Polanco only echoed the text and others when he said in that regard that "the points proposed for meditation should not be much elaborated upon because, as the second 'Preliminary Observation' indicates, individuals will more deeply relish what they discover for themselves and because thus greater room is left for enlightenment and [other] movements from above."[261]

The person who led others in the *Exercises* soon came to be known as the "director," and that remained the traditional term through the centuries. This designation does not occur in the text. Ignatius usually referred to the person as the one "who gives the *Exercises*" or, better, "delivers them over to another"—"el que da los exercicios," "tradens exercitia." This mode of expression, though generic and awkward, better captures the actual functions as they are delineated in the text and lacks the suggestion of predetermination that "director" conveys. Ignatius saw the relationship as basically conversational, like a "colloquy."[262] Once begun, the *Exercises* were to be fundamentally in the hands, or heart and mind, of the one undertaking them. That was their basic presupposition.

The delicacy of the "helper's" role was understood from the beginning. Besides the cautions Ignatius gave in the text of the *Exercises,* he frequently warned in conversation about how much spiritual guides harmed others by insisting that they follow in their ways and by believing that what was good for themselves was good for everybody.[263]

At least in the early years, therefore, the Jesuits who were deemed suitable for the role learned it in an apprenticeship system from other Jesuits, with Ignatius being the first master-teacher. When they gave the *Exercises* in

Rome during his lifetime, they conferred with him in the evening about how they had handled issues that arose and submitted themselves to his supervision. The same practice was followed elsewhere with others recognized for their skill and experience. In order to be more sensitive to the situation, Jesuits sometimes made the *Exercises* again themselves while directing others in them. In Vienna in 1560, Juan Alfonso de Vitoria, who had himself been supervised by Ignatius in Rome, gave to his fellow Jesuits a series of conferences on the director's role, after each of which they turned in a written composition to show they understood what they had heard and how they would apply it to particular cases. Similar series were later held elsewhere, but did not become widespread.[264]

The Jesuits acknowledged that retreats that included an "election" required more gifted and experienced directors, but even Ignatius early recognized that some elaboration of the counsel provided in the *Exercises* would be helpful for such persons in every situation. In 1552 Polanco composed a memorandum for him in which he indicated that one of his tasks as general was to compose a "directory" for the *Exercises*. When Ignatius died in 1556 he left behind some notes on the subject, but nothing more. The General Congregation of 1558 called for such a document, but no official text appeared until the *Directorium* of 1599, which was never revised or retracted.

Sometime between 1539 and 1541 Jean Codure had composed a commentary on the *Exercises* for the retreatant, not the director.[265] After 1556 other · Jesuits, including Polanco, produced commentaries or "directories" along the lines Polanco indicated to Ignatius either to fill the lacuna until the official directory appeared or as contributions toward it. Two traditions of interpretation early appeared, represented respectively by the directories of Polanco and Diego Miró. The former insisted on the need to accommodate to the individual and the situation and on the power of "reasons of the heart." The latter stood for a literal application of the details of the text and took as its norm a theoretical ideal of spiritual proficiency. Polanco and Miró found it impossible to work with each other in composing a common document, and Miró's text is in some particulars a covert counter-statement to Polanco's, which he had at his disposal when composing his own.[266] The *Directory* of 1599 was a compromise.

Many of the patterns of practice that began during Ignatius's lifetime continued and were expanded in succeeding years. Others began to change or deteriorate shortly after his death, of which two deserve special mention. First, the only category of persons in which the numbers of those making the *Exercises* diminished is that of women, due without doubt to ever-stricter regulations about how to deal with women in general. Second, despite the concern about careful selection of directors, their quality generally declined, and numerous complaints were heard about too literal, too mechanical interpretations of the text. The best-qualified people were now busy governing the growing provinces, teaching in the schools, or managing the ever-larger communities attached to them.[267]

WHEN JESUITS described themselves as primarily ministers of the Word of God, what did they mean? They meant of course that they were preachers, and then they meant that they were "lecturers." But by extension they came to include in the category practically every form of religious discourse or conversation. For Nadal it even included that part of the sacrament of Penance that could be considered "a kind of private sermon."

What was the "Word of God"? It was the text of Scripture, but it was, perhaps in some slightly mitigated sense, everything that was derived from Scripture or considered its equivalent, like the articles of the Creed or the works of mercy. On one level of content, therefore, it was the equivalent of *Christianitas.* On another level, it came more from inner light received through prayer, contemplation, and special visitations of the Spirit. The Jesuits assumed and taught that this light, if legitimate, would not contradict the teaching of Scripture or the church. But the teaching of the *Exercises* on this point nonetheless got them into trouble with some of their vigilant Catholic contemporaries.

The Word of God was for them not merely instruction for the mind. Although the mind may need instruction, the heart needed still more to be warmed, healed, and eventually turned to the needs of one's neighbor. Even "sacred lectures" had to take this reality into account, and catechism was not properly taught unless it had an effect on "Christian living and dying."

Most of these assumptions and most of the ways the Jesuits plied the ministries described in this chapter remained constant during these first twenty-five years, but important changes of various kinds were already under way—not always because the Jesuits deliberately decided to make them but because the situations in which they found themselves led them into such changes, sometimes unaware.

~ 4

Sacraments, Worship, Prayer

AFTER THE LIST of ministries discussed in the last chapter, the *Formula* of 1550 continued with "the spiritual consolation of Christ's faithful through hearing confessions and administering other sacraments." This was a change from the earlier version, which stated in more restrictive fashion "the spiritual consolation of Christ's faithful in hearing confessions." This latter phrase, in turn, had been added to the original "Five Chapters" in 1540, probably upon the suggestion of their papal revisor, Cardinal Girolamo Ghinucci. The "Chapters" had limited themselves to "ministry of the Word, *Spiritual Exercises*, works of charity, and expressly the education of children and unlettered persons in Christianity."[1]

The failure of the "Chapters" to mention the sacraments is important, for it suggests an emphasis on the ministries actually listed. Nonetheless, confession and Communion were in fact implicit in practically all of them, and confession was already a crucial centering point of the ministry of Ignatius and his companions. Among the other six sacraments, the Eucharist most immediately correlated with confession, that is, with the sacrament of Penance. The Jesuits believed that the Eucharist was the only sacrament besides Penance that they would under normal circumstances administer.

When Nadal commented on this part of the *Formula*, latter version, he restricted himself to these two sacraments and, because of the practical issues involved, devoted by far the most attention to Penance. Since Jesuits were forbidden by their Institute to accept prelacies of any form, Nadal maintained that the term "other sacraments" in the *Formula* meant only those that could be administered by "simple priests." He thus eliminated Confirmation and Orders, which only bishops could confer. He then eliminated Baptism, Matrimony, and even Extreme Unction (rites for the dying) on the grounds that, according to canon law, these were the realm of pastors of parishes. Jesuits were not "pastors" in that proper and canonical sense of the term. They could, therefore, officiate at these sacraments only in cases of necessity or when they were working in parts of the world where parishes had not been established. That left only Penance and the Eucharist, and even these could not be administered by Jesuits when they were received by the faithful in fulfillment of the annual obligation imposed by *Omnis utriusque sexus,* the decree of the Fourth Lateran Council, 1215, that stipulated reception from the pastors of parishes or their delegates during the Easter season.[2] This was the common understanding the Jesuits had of their relationship to the seven sacraments, and they in fact operated according to it.[3]

The Jesuits were priests in the Tridentine era, yet they did not quite conform to what the Council of Trent laid down as the normative duties of priests. The reason for the discrepancy is that the Council legislated for pastors of parishes and their curates. This meant that the Council was concerned to a large extent with the rights and duties of pastors in administering the sacraments of Baptism, Matrimony, Extreme Unction, and of Penance and the Eucharist when they were construed as fulfilling the Lateran decree. The Council was interested in the external discipline for both clergy and laity connected with all these sacred rites. Because Jesuits were not pastors, they did not fall under that legislation. They were careful not to trespass on what they understood belonged by right to pastors.

At the urging of Cardinal Ghinucci, a change was made in the "Chapters" on another liturgical issue. The "Chapters" stated that members of the Society who were priests were "obliged to recite the canonical Hours according to the rite of the church, not however in choir, lest they be impeded in the works of charity to which we have totally dedicated ourselves. Therefore, they will not use the organ or singing at mass and other sacred ceremonies." Whereas it was praiseworthy for others to use them, "we have found them to be a serious impediment because, according to the design of our vocation, we must be frequently occupied during large parts of the day and sometimes even the night in consoling the sick in body and in soul, as well as in other necessary undertakings."[4]

Ghinucci feared that such a statement would give comfort to the Lutherans in their criticism of Catholic worship. For these lines, which amount to almost a paragraph, was substituted simply that the priests of the order "were each singly obliged to [recite] the canonical Hours privately according to the rite of the church." The *Formula* of 1550 later specified "and not in common or in choir."

The first Jesuits were adamant about not being obliged to recite the Hours "in common or in choir," and they resisted as best they could later efforts to impose it on them. In the sixteenth century most Catholics could not conceive of a religious order without choral chanting of the Hours and, indeed, tended to see it as what most clearly distinguished members of religious orders from the rest of the population. The practical reason the ten companions offered in the "Chapters" was realistic and, with sometimes different emphases, would be frequently reiterated by them as the years wore on. Their forswearing of choir also served a deeper function. It stood as a concrete symbol of the very essence of their vocation: to be fully at the service of those in need in "the Lord's vineyard."

If the first Jesuits were ultimately successful in warding off the obligation of choir for themselves, they were notably less so in keeping music out of their churches for mass and vespers. Pressures inside and outside the Society proved too great to resist. Gradually, they themselves saw the pastoral function that more elaborate services might perform even in Europe, but they especially became aware of the power of music with the indigenous peoples of Brazil and elsewhere.[5] From being opposed to music in the worship in their churches, they soon came to tolerate and then promote it, but with restrictions and sometimes misgivings.

Confession and Casuistry

Frequent reception of the sacrament of Penance had been advocated by some theologians in the late Middle Ages. In the early fifteenth century, Jean Gerson recommended it for most people, even as often as every month or every week on feast days.[6] The idea had not caught on. Although in their early decades the Jesuits suffered much grief for their advocacy of more frequent reception of the Eucharist, they experienced resistance even for advocating more frequent confession. In certain localities their advocacy did not evoke animosity, but it elicited comment as a departure from custom.[7] Despite opposition and raised eyebrows, they persisted. Why did they attach so much importance to the frequent reception of this sacrament?

The Jesuits inherited and fully accepted the conclusions of medieval theologians about the necessity of confession to a priest for the forgiveness of serious sins, and they were utterly untouched by any of the questions Protestants adduced concerning the origins of the sacrament and the form it had taken over the course of the centuries. If those questions did anything, they led them to insist on the medieval and, in due time, the Tridentine teaching on the sacrament.[8] Anybody who deliberately committed a serious sin and, if a confessor was available, had not confessed it was damned. This persuasion was as fundamental for the Jesuits as it was unexceptional in Catholic teaching.[9]

Their advocacy of frequent confession and especially of what they called "general confession," however, cannot be reduced to promotion of a ritual periodically undertaken in order to be saved from the eternal consequences of one's repeated misdeeds. They never forgot the necessity of confession for the forgiveness of serious sins and generally assumed that for many persons such forgiveness might be required often in their lives. In conformity with late-medieval catechisms and texts for confessors, they provided for their penitents and for themselves lists of sins to assure that consciences were instructed in what was right and wrong and in what was required for the confession to be "integral," that is, that all serious offenses be clearly presented to the priest. Partly in view of confession, therefore, they advocated daily examination of conscience.

Their peculiar emphasis lay, however, in seeing confession as a means of beginning a new way of life, which may in some instances mean turning from serious sin more definitively than ever before. The best way to understand their approach is to examine the role they gave to "general confession." The term itself is confusing, for by the sixteenth century it designated several different but related things. It sometimes meant a text, namely, a detailed examination of conscience, a *modus confitendi.*[10] It sometimes meant a practice, of which at least three kinds were known. The first was the liturgical confession of sins at the beginning of mass.[11] The second was the confession of sins by an individual to a priest in the sacrament of Penance, which assumed that in previous confessions serious sins had been deliberately concealed, itself a sin. In such a case confession of the concealment was required and then confession of every other serious sin back to the time the deception began.

The third kind, recommended in the *Exercises,* was a review with a confessor of one's whole life, not undertaken because sins were concealed in some previous confession, but to attain a better knowledge of oneself and more firmly turn to God and away from what was wrong and harmful. Although one may infer from the *Exercises* that this was a once-in-a-lifetime experience, the Jesuits began to encourage it as something one might do periodically as an aid to spiritual growth. The *Constitutions* prescribed, for example, that Jesuit scholastics were to make such a confession every six months "because of the many benefits it entails."[12] In these instances, one reviewed not one's entire life, but what had happened in the past semester.

Priest hearing a man's confession in Germany before the introduction of enclosed confessionals in the late sixteenth century. Woodcut by unknown artist.

This third kind of general confession, it must be noted, bypassed under normal circumstances the tangle of medieval legislation pertaining to certain aspects of the sacrament, for it could be assumed that these juridical complications, if they existed, had been handled in earlier confessions. The crucial point is that this general confession was undertaken not in fulfillment of an obligation but out of a desire for spiritual progress. It was a devout practice, not a duty.

Where and how the practice originated is not known, and its history even in the post-Tridentine era remains sketchy.[13] If Ignatius had not heard about it before he went to Montserrat, which is probable, he learned about it there. At that date it seems to have been little known and practiced. Given the influence of the *Devotio Moderna* on Abbot Cisneros, it is reasonable to infer that its origins lay in that movement. Once Ignatius learned about it, he became its principal propagator, and through him it entered into the Catholic mainstream. Although no detailed studies as yet exist about its spread and practice even after that date, in devout circles it became common.

Besides enjoining the general confession on their own members, the Jesuits consistently recommended it to others from all walks of life as the keystone and expression of their conversion. Favre proposed it "more than anything else" as the foundation for a new and happier life.[14] In 1549 Francis Xavier recommended it to penitents along with meditations over several days from the First Week. He typically insisted that the confessor try not to incite fear in the penitents but move them by considerations of "the abundant mercy of God." To lessen the penitents' shame and confusion, he suggested that the confessor disclose "in general terms" something from his own sinful past.[15] Gaspar de Loarte's *Esercitio della vita christiana* was intended for simple folk, even for the illiterate, to whom it might be read by another. The very first chapter dealt with general confession, advocating it as a way "to begin to make a new book" of one's life.[16] The general confession provided the foundation for all that followed.

Loarte urged setting aside one or two days from one's usual occupation to review the past, a practice recommended by confessional handbooks even for the annual confession of obligation. He suggested using a learned but brief *confessionario* as a help in this review—if you cannot read, have somebody read it to you. Seek the most learned and virtuous confessor you can find, search for the best doctor for your soul. For this office he does not mention the pastor of the parish. In other words, he is not here interested in a ritual routine or an ecclesiastical obligation, but in the personalized guidance and counsel that the right confessor could presumably offer.

He specified what one might hope for in this and other confessions if one chose the confessor well: instruction when in doubt, strength when weak, encouragement when wavering, consolation when arid, calm when tempted, guidance when in danger, and, in general, direction in the right way. This is what the people of Israel found in Joshua as they were being led into the promised land.

Late-medieval works on confession gave due attention to the consolatory and therapeutic aspects of the sacrament, partly in compensation for the anxiety and reluctance so often associated with it—both Luther and Ignatius suffered much from obsessive doubts about the integrity of what they confessed and the adequacy of their sorrow.[17] Loarte and other Jesuits also stressed the therapeutic aspects of confession, but more characteristic of them was their specification of guidance, counsel, and encouragement as the means of accomplishing the healing.

Nadal was thus led in some of his exhortations to Jesuit communities to propose confession as a form of "ministry of the Word." He located that ministry not in the questions the confessor might ask about sins confessed but in the words of warning, advice, and comfort given to the penitent. The words were "sort of private sermons"—"privatas (ut ita dicam) conciones." On these occasions the confessor must help evoke not some mere velleity to do away with sin, as Nadal believed so often happened, but a fervent and confirmed desire to begin a new life and "put on a new soul."[18] Elsewhere, speaking of ministry of the Word, he described confession as an occasion "to soften the heart of the sinner and move it by the Word of God."[19]

The intrinsic relationship between preaching and confession that Nadal suggested in his exhortations other sources made explicit. Polanco reported that in India Xavier reaped in confession the fruit of his preaching.[20] When Nadal tried to explain in a letter to Ignatius in 1549 why people came to the Jesuits' church in Messina, he said it was "for counsel, confession, and to hear the Word of God."[21] For him the conversation with the penitent was but another form of the "loving and familiar" exchange that occurred in every devout conversation, and "just as the preacher sows [the seed of the Word of God] to the multitude, so do confessors and all others who engage people [in such conversation] reap it."[22] It was to a large extent due to these "conversations [in confession] that Ours hold" that spiritual counsel or spiritual direction, as it is sometimes called, began to enter into a new and classic phase in Catholicism in the latter half of the sixteenth century.[23] The Jesuits were not the first or only ones to use confession as an occasion for spiritual counsel. That they were skillful at it and sensitive to the uniqueness of each person's experience, however, is supported by the consistent encouragement many of them proffered Teresa of Avila beginning about 1555—Diego de Cetina, Francisco de Borja, Juan de Prádanos, Baltasar Alvarez, Dionisio Vázquez. The passages in Teresa's *Autobiography* concerning them are among the few sources that describe Jesuit confessional practice from the viewpoint of the penitent, and they are consistent in their praise.[24]

There was, however, another side to confessional practice. The sacrament had developed in the Middle Ages in tandem with the revival of canon law. Confession had come to be conceived as a tribunal in which the confessor was the judge and the penitent the accused—in this case, the self-accused. The model of the tribunal pervades much of what the Council of Trent decreed about the sacrament of Penance in its Fourteenth Session, 1551, and the ninth canon of that Session explicitly affirmed it.[25]

This interpretation of the sacrament of course affected the Jesuits, who did not have to wait for Trent to learn about it. Using three traditional categories, Nadal described the confessor's function as "sometimes encouraging with kind words like a father, sometimes expostulating and reprehending like a judge, sometimes applying remedies for sickness like a doctor."[26] Insistence upon the consolatory aspects of the sacrament within the juridical framework developed in the Middle Ages characterized the Jesuits' approach to confession and marked it with its many ambivalences.

The role that emerged most explicitly with the Jesuits was that of consoler or comforter. The explicit correlation between confession and consolation in the *Formula* unavoidably called the Jesuits' attention to this role. If they did not take the hint, Nadal was ready to prompt them. In one of his exhortations his message was unmistakable when he came to the words "especially the spiritual consolation of Christ's faithful." They refer, he maintained, to all the *consueta ministeria,* not just confession. This meant that Jesuits were not to rest content in their ministries with what was required for salvation but were always to strive for the spiritual improvement and consolation of those to whom they ministered. Consolation is indeed the best sign that a person is moving along the right path. When the *Formula* says "especially," it means that spiritual progress and its correlate, consolation, hold first place and must be the Jesuit's primary intention and goal.[27]

Somewhat less emphatically, similar ideas recur in other sources. In his *Breve directorium* for Jesuit confessors, Polanco stated that the task of the confessor was to console those who were trying to change their ways, and he stressed consolation more strikingly, as we shall see, in his work on assisting the dying.[28] In confession, said Loarte in his *Esercitio,* one receives counsel and consolation.[29] Not surprisingly, Jesuits liked to report that penitents left confession consoled and comforted, even joyful.[30] They also reported that they were sometimes so much in demand as confessors that they had to omit celebrating mass in order to accommodate those who came to them, a forceful commentary on the importance they attached to this ministry.[31]

They were aware, however, of the difficulty of the confessor's role, an awareness perhaps intensified by the abuses in the sacrament that at the time were being subjected to so much criticism and ridicule. This meant that, at least in theory, even in the Society this ministry was to be undertaken only by those qualified for it. In commenting on the *Constitutions,* Nadal warned that it was better to let confessions go unheard than to employ for them unsuitable persons.[32] In his *Directorium* Polanco provided a standard list of the qualities required for a good confessor—such as knowledge, humility, prudence. This last quality meant that the Jesuit confessor would know how to accommodate to individual cases, but that, when in doubt, he would "always incline in the more humane direction"—"semper in humaniorem partem declinando."[33]

Repeatedly, the Jesuits were advised to be "mild," to be "sweet, approachable, and sensitive," to be "meek, mild, gentle," to show "compassion and kindness."[34] In his *Memoriale* Favre reflected on a general confession he had just heard. Showing mercy to another in this sacrament brought tears to his eyes, for it helped him discover anew the mercy God granted Favre himself. He concluded by observing that if a person wanted God to show kindness and not act out of the rigor justice required, that person must be kind and indulgent to all, "not stringent and overly just."[35]

In Cologne in 1544 he composed a short work for confessors that circulated only in manuscript. The fact that it concluded by quoting from the famous thirteenth chapter of the First Epistle to the Corinthians—"Love is patient and kind"—indicates its tenor. Its basic theme was that confessors were "vicars of the mild Christ." They should never be harsh, but always sweet. They must ward off in themselves all pharisaic self-righteousness. Although penitents should be encouraged to confess in any manner they wished, they should be guided by the confessor in locating their most characteristic sin that gives rise to the others. The confessor should then indicate possible remedies and take care to instruct them in how to pray.[36]

When the first Jesuits wrote about the sacrament of Penance, they tended to consider it a way of "helping" individual Christians and spoke little about its social ramifications and impact. In an impassioned section in an exhortation, Nadal departed from this pattern. Sin, he said, is what defaces the church. "In the frequent administration and reception of this sacrament is to be found the reform of Christianity"—*reformatio Christianismi*. Through confession the church would have restored to it its beauty, splendor, perfection, and divine light and would be made stable in them.[37]

The passage from Nadal raises the issue of the ultimate impact on religion of the more systematic and widespread propagation of information about the necessity of the sacrament and the requirements for its proper reception, especially in the wake of the Council of Trent. It is clear that in the late Middle Ages and well beyond many Catholics deeply resented the obligation of annual confession to their pastor and in one way or another evaded it.[38] The issue is far too complicated to be addressed here, but the Jesuits were of course in the forefront of those who stressed the importance of the sacrament and gave instruction about its proper reception.

Once Polanco's *Directorium* was published in 1554, it assumed almost official status within the Society. Divided into two unequal parts, it ran to about 150 small pages. The shorter first part presented in a simple and straightforward fashion what was required of both confessor and penitent for an integral and spiritually helpful confession. The confessor was instructed in what questions to ask to attain both ends. Although this part was moderate in its counsel to the confessor about interrogation pertaining to integrity, it still evinced the problems inherent in a system based on such lists and moral measurements.

The much longer second part was a series of quasi-appendices. Many of them were more detailed inventories of sins according, for instance, to the Ten Commandments or the responsibilities of people from different walks of life—temporal lords, judges, lawyers, students, married persons, merchants, children, and so forth. By far the longest such list concerned bishops and priests. There was no section dealing with peasants or day laborers. There was little on sexual sins.

The other sections in this part, obviously intended as a reference handbook, dealt with social and juridical problems arising from certain kinds of sins—in cases of fraud and theft, when and how was restitution to be made; under what circumstances might heretics and other publicly excommunicated persons be reconciled to the church; how was one to deal with penitents in a locality under ecclesiastical interdict; and similar situations. The conception of confession as a tribunal and the confessor as a judge was nowhere clearer.

An immensely tangled mass of legislation concerning sins of this kind had emerged in the Middle Ages. The public and sometimes complex nature of such sins led to the practice of "reserving" them to the local bishop or, in some instances, even to the Holy See. In other words, an ordinary priest could not impart absolution except in cases of dire urgency, as with a dying person. If "social control" entered directly into the practice of confession during this era, it was most obviously with this legislation. Moreover, the impracticality of much of the legislation meant that the exceptions to it often far exceeded the rule.

These exceptions, these "privileges," had been granted by popes with open hand to the mendicant orders, especially from the last quarter of the fifteenth century onward. Each of the orders had its *Mare magnum* (Great Sea) of pastoral privileges, which sometimes exceeded the authority of bishops to deal with such cases and in other ways trespassed on what bishops considered their rights and obligations. The bishops' resentment erupted at the Fifth Lateran Council, 1512–17, and again at Trent. The orders turned to the papacy for protection, while they competed fiercely with one another in trying to augment their privileges.

In 1545 Paul III bestowed extensive privileges of this sort on the Society of Jesus, and he and his immediate successor confirmed and amplified them. In 1552, for instance, Julius III specifically granted priests of the Society permission to absolve anybody from the sin of heresy, thus allowing them to bypass the inquisitorial tribunals, and he forbade even bishops to interfere with this authority.[39] Such grants gave the Jesuits wide scope in their preaching and especially in their administration of the sacrament of Penance. They inevitably provided bishops and the older orders with grounds for resentment, just as they strengthened the bond of gratitude the Jesuits felt toward the papacy.

The privileges also gave rise within the order to speculation about just how and when they might prudently be employed, which joined the other body of speculation about how the confessor should deport himself in the most pastorally effective manner with specific cases of conscience and different types of penitents. The "spiritual consolation of Christ's faithful through the hearing of confessions" could be a complicated business indeed.

This brings us to casuistry, that is, to the study of "cases of conscience" (casus conscientiae). The need the Jesuits felt to study such cases grew out of the complex nature of the confessor's task. If the confessor was a judge, then he had to assess the morality of the penitent's actions and assign a suitable penance; if a doctor of the soul, he needed solid information for the instruction of the penitent's conscience. As had long been assumed in law and in ethics, circumstances differ from instance to instance, and they influence questions of culpability and morality. A crime committed in a moment of passion is not the same as one long calculated. Killing another human being is forbidden, but is it forbidden if done to save one's own life from an aggressor? The study of cases was meant, therefore, to facilitate the application of general norms like the Decalogue to different sets of circumstances according to consistent principles. Is what I am doing good or bad in *these* circumstances, and may I, or must I, continue to do it?

Confession was the sacrament in which the priest's role could most easily devolve into an exercise in manipulation and control. Casuistry, it is often charged, expressed and promoted the devolution. The charge is not implausible, but the basic impulse behind casuistry was the desire to clarify complicated moral issues, to sort out claims of seemingly conflicting moral obligations, and to bring moral absolutes down from the high heavens of abstraction to the more lowly human reality of "times, places, and circumstances." This was a noble and humane impulse, but it was itself caught in the "times, places, and circumstances" of its own history. The art of casuistry was developed and plied, that is to say, in the framework of a scholasticism that sought to tie up every loose end and resolve every possible doubt. Casuistry, meant to free the conscience, indulged in a chattering pursuit of resolution that, unawares, could just as easily bind it.

Casuistry was, in any case, the system of ethical reasoning the Jesuits inherited, accepted, and then advanced. A half century later it was the system they transformed by their widespread adoption of the principles of Probabilism, an extraordinarily important shift in approach to conscience and moral questions known to us better through Pascal's scorn than through serious study.

Even if the Jesuits' study of "cases of conscience" sometimes led them into pat answers and a prescriptive approach to the concrete issues arising in confessions they heard, such results were precisely what that study was supposed to prevent. In other words, at the center of casuistry was the rhetorical principle of accommodation to times, places, persons, and other circumstances. It is now clear that casuistry, despite its more immediate origin in medieval scholasticism, ultimately derived from the classical discipline of rhetoric. As a recent study has observed: "Rhetoric and casuistry were mutual allies. It is not surprising to find the Jesuits, who were dedicated to teaching classical rhetoric in their colleges, become the leading exponents of casuistry."[40]

More immediately, the Jesuits' commitment to the sacrament of Penance and their understanding of the "practical" nature of their vocation meant that the study of cases of conscience would inevitably appeal to them. They needed it for themselves as confessors, but they early began to lecture on cases, sometimes in their schools, sometimes in their churches or in the cathedral, for a broader audience, both lay and clerical.[41] By 1555 Jesuits lectured on them to mixed audiences of clergy and laity in distant Goa.[42] Such lectures were also being delivered by members of other orders, but we do not know to what extent.[43] A subset of the Jesuits' "sacred lectures," they were in much of their content an expanded and more sophisticated version of late-medieval catechetical lectures, which helps explain their appeal to the laity. The section of the *Exercises* dealing with the "General Examination of Conscience" gives some idea how they may have sounded.[44]

The lectures were especially appropriate for the clergy, who until this time had never had such opportunities available to them. Cases were not part of the curriculum of medieval universities, and, if priests wanted to study them, they did so on their own. In 1546 the episcopal vicar of Faenza arranged for Broët to lecture on them daily for his ignorant priests.[45] In such an instance, the lectures were geared especially to confessional practice.[46]

As the number of their own members grew, the Jesuits began to deliver lectures on cases in the Jesuit community. By 1556 at the Collegio Romano the rector prescribed daily lectures on the subject, and Diego de Ledesma was appointed professor of cases of conscience, a significant step in the curricular regularization of the discipline.[47] In 1557 Nadal prescribed them at the Collegio even on days when other lectures were not held.[48] In 1563, after years of experience with them for Jesuit scholastics, the Jesuits instituted a course open to all the students. It drew about two hundred, some of them Jesuits.[49] A year later the course had to be transferred to the church because it drew an audience of "no less than eight hundred," including pastors and curates from nearby parishes.[50] A powerful tradition was in the making.

Such lectures helped advance moral theology to a self-standing discipline within the theological curriculum.[51] Moreover, when delivered as a course in the Jesuits' universities, they were a concrete implementation of the Jesuits' desire to reshape the traditional curriculum by making it less "speculative," more responsive to pastoral concerns. As their schools multiplied, they were able to make this reshaping effective on a Pan-European basis.

In the years I am considering, the Jesuits lectured from available texts. The procedure was commentary, *explication de texte,* that moved along paragraph by paragraph or category by category. Among the texts, they preferred the *Summula peccatorum* by Cajetan (Tommaso De Vio, d. 1534), the famous Dominican commentator on Aquinas.[52] They also used other works by contemporary authors—especially the *Summa quae Aurea Armilla inscribitur* by Bartolomeo Fumo and the *Manual de confessores et penitentes* by Martín de Azpilcueta, known as "Navarro."[53] These were among the most important and influential texts of the day.

When Polanco studied theology at the University of Padua, he made use of the *Summa confessionalis* of Saint Antoninus of Florence and the *Summa de virtutibus et vitiis* of another Dominican, Guillaume Peyraut, as well as the work of Cajetan.[54] The Jesuits began, therefore, by building on the late-medieval and contemporary tradition as they found it.

The predilection for Cajetan, as well as for other Dominican authors, fitted with the Jesuits' early predilection for Aquinas. Ignatius specifically recommended to Jesuits the study of the second part of Aquinas's *Summa theologiae,* the part dealing with virtues and vices, and as early as 1548 he recommended Cajetan's *Summula* to Nadal for the lectures on cases that had been requested by the commune of Messina.[55] Some Jesuits took exception to Cajetan—Juan Ramírez thought him too lax, as did Laínez on some specific issues.[56]

Cajetan's *Summula* was arranged alphabetically according to topics, most of which were sins. As with the other topics, sins were first defined, then reasons were given why the action was sinful, and finally circumstances were briefly presented that rendered the action more or less sinful, or not sinful at all. The book manifested the penchant of scholastic theology for ever more precise refinement of concept and the preoccupation with sin of authors of texts like these.[57] By lecturing on such texts and granting their assumptions, the Jesuits became involved in a juggling act between the focus of the tradition on sin and law and their desire to emphasize the consoling aspects of the sacrament.

In the early years the Jesuits did nothing more than study the available texts on cases of conscience and, when the occasion arose, lecture on them. By about 1560 changes in procedure began to be introduced, such as a general discussion in which each participant presented his own resolution of the case.[58] A circular letter to the Society in 1563 reported that at the Collegio Romano a question period followed the lectures, and thus "one by one different cases were introduced."[59] Nadal suggested that every Jesuit confessor spend at least an hour every day in the private study of cases.[60] As has been correctly observed, the *casus conscientiae* played a much larger role in the Society of Jesus, almost from the beginning, than the *Constitutions* and other official documents indicate.[61]

The fullest indication of what these lectures by Jesuits were like at this time is to be found in the *Instructio Sacerdotum* by Francisco de Toledo.[62] Although not published until 1599, it was put together for the most part from students' notes taken at the Collegio Romano during the 1560's. Longer than Cajetan's *Summula* and organized on different principles, it is obviously in immediate continuity with that tradition of dealing with moral issues.

Aside from a privileged source such as Teresa's *Autobiography*, little information is available on how the Jesuits applied what they learned in the confessions they heard. The only evidence is indirect—from the frequency with which they were sought out by persons who had easy access to other confessors, from the style and content of the various "examinations of conscience" they composed for those who might come to them. Even with due allowance made for the bias in the sources, the Jesuits were from the beginning sought as confessors by all manner of people.

Throughout this first quarter century women came to them in great numbers to have their confessions heard—in some localities more frequently than the men. In the first dozen years or so, the Jesuits only noted the fact and on occasion resisted efforts to put any restrictions on hearing women's confessions. In 1551, for instance, one of their friends from the Venetian aristocracy tried to persuade the Jesuit rector to order his subjects to desist from hearing so many women's confessions because of the danger to their reputation in the Venetian senate. The rector refused to comply because the practice was "so essential and proper to our Institute." He then referred the matter to Ignatius, who confirmed the decision.[63] The Jesuits began to be concerned, however, with what the "sectarians," presumed Lutheran sympathizers, were saying about them in this regard.[64]

In 1553 another prominent Venetian friend urged the Jesuits gradually to stop hearing women's confessions because of possible calumny. Ignatius again replied that no curtailment should be considered; if some genuine scandal arose, appropriate measures could be taken at that point.[65] Polanco reported that in 1555, again in Venice, the Jesuits would have heard many more confessions from women had not the Inquisitors and the papal legate forbidden the practice to any priest under thirty-six years old.[66]

Nonetheless, they became more cautious. In 1552 Xavier wrote an instruction on "avoiding scandal" in hearing women's confessions that laid down restrictions which began to be insisted upon about the same time by his colleagues in Europe.[67] In 1553 Ignatius wrote to the Jesuits at Naples and some other places that when they heard the confessions of women and young men they should make sure that the penitents were kneeling at the side of their chair, not in front of it, and that confessors should hold their hand to their forehead so as not to see their penitents' faces.[68] In 1555 he warned the Jesuits in Genoa not to go without a companion to women's homes to hear their confessions when they were sick.[69] Nadal began to discourage altogether hearing women's confessions in their homes, proposing that they be referred to their pastors. Even if the case was urgent or special, Jesuits were according to him always to go with a companion.[70]

At least as late as 1561, Jesuits in Rome were still hearing women's confessions in their homes, and they seemed to be doing it frequently for persons of both sexes.[71] There is no evidence, moreover, that they at this time began to hear fewer confessions of women in their churches. In 1560 Laínez reprimanded Bartolomé de Bustamante, the provincial of Andalusia, for introducing the "new custom" of putting a grill or curtain between the confessor and women penitents.[72] Nonetheless, a new and sometimes stringent caution was coming into play. Desire to protect the good name of the Society from gossip was surely among the reasons for this change, but a more intense preoccupation with propriety had begun to mark the Society as well as Catholic culture in general.

Antonio de Araoz, soon to be the first provincial of Spain, had in 1545 written to Rome that nothing would be more helpful to the Society than to have a Jesuit reside in the royal court.[73] He was surely not the last to utter such a sentiment, but the irregularity of arrangements like this was not lost on his colleagues. Indeed, the Second General Congregation, 1565, forbade Jesuits to commit themselves to hearing the confessions of kings and other magnates, lay or clerical, if this entailed living in court or regularly accompanying princely entourages.[74] Early in his days in Lisbon, Simão Rodrigues had become confessor to John III and taken up residence in the court, whence he also functioned as provincial for the Jesuits in Portugal. This anomalous situation created difficulties, and word spread that Rodrigues was a man who could not live without the "palaces and pomp of the world."[75]

When Rodrigues was replaced as provincial of Portugal in 1553, the king asked Diego Miró and Luís Gonçalves da Câmara to act as his confessors. Neither of them wanted to accept the office because they thought it inconsistent with the humble nature of the Jesuit vocation, but Ignatius ordered them to accept.[76] Ignatius here gave warrant to a policy that would later bring the Society much grief, but the incident revealed a difference of opinion in the Society about the propriety of being "confessors to kings" that would surface again and again.

Surely among the reasons that impelled persons from widely different situations to frequent Jesuit confessors was the Jesuits' adamant refusal to charge for their services. As late as 1556 this practice shocked the Genoese, who thought they were not truly absolved from their sins unless they offered some money to the confessor.[77] Although in general the Jesuits tried to avoid even the appearance of accepting direct remuneration for any of their ministries, they were adamant about it for confession. Nadal insisted that a Jesuit accept no gifts of any kind from anybody whose confessions he had heard, even gifts that were later sent to him when no direct relationship to the sacrament was intended.[78]

What the Jesuits practiced themselves, they tried to inculcate in other priests. In the spring of 1544 Laínez guided in the *Exercises* about a dozen priests from the diocese of Bressanone. He was pleased when they afterward petitioned the episcopal vicar for permission thenceforward to hear confessions gratis.[79] The Jesuits' attitude regarding payment must be numbered as one of their major contributions to the "reformation" of confession.

We catch another glimpse of their practice through the examinations of conscience they offered to the faithful. Whereas they expected the confessor himself to be armed with detailed information about the various categories and sub-categories of sins and the juridical complications that might attend some of them, they were much less exigent of the penitents. Even the examination of conscience that Ignatius proposed for the general confession during the *Exercises* is notably undetailed.[80]

As we have seen, Ignatius's lesson on Christian Doctrine treats the traditional categories of the Decalogue, the five "commandments of the Church," the seven capital sins, the five senses, and the spiritual and corporal works of mercy. Although the very number of items on the list might suggest the omnipresent possibility of sin, the treatment of each heading is brief, nontechnical, and straightforward. "Thou shalt not commit adultery" forbids fornication in desire and deed. Ignatius says nothing more, even when he is instructing on the capital sin of lust.[81]

Loarte in his *Esercitio* recommended the use of an *interrogatorio* in preparation for one's periodic confessions, but he himself offered only the suggestion that one review one's thoughts, words, and actions or that one examine oneself with regard to the Decalogue.[82] He treated sins of the flesh with the utmost discretion and in the most general terms.[83] The review of the Decalogue and the examination of conscience in the catechisms of Canisius and Ledesma were also relatively brief, and they were similarly reticent concerning sexual sins.

Although in general the Jesuits strove to avoid extremes in their moral teaching, Laínez and Canisius took more rigorous positions on usury than some of their Catholic contemporaries.[84] In 1554 in the great commercial city of Genoa, Laínez composed *Disputatio de usura,* one of the most comprehensive treatments of the issue in the sixteenth century. In 1560 in Augsburg, the city of the Fuggers, Canisius launched a campaign against the so-called Triple Contract, according to which an investor could obtain 5 percent interest without risk. Although Canisius's opposition to the contract was not absolute, his stance then and later lost the Jesuits penitents and brought them other troubles as well. This happened just as Calvin's exegesis of the troublesome verses from Deuteronomy (23:19–20) that prohibited lending on interest, the locus classicus on which theological discussion of the issue centered, provided the solution to the problem that continued to elude Catholics.[85] In any case, even Laínez while general cautioned Canisius about his pastoral practice in this regard, and neither of their theoretical positions finally carried the day in the Society.

The daily examination of conscience that the Jesuits recommended so frequently in their works on piety did not necessarily look to confession. The examination was already a commonplace in the Christian tradition of asceticism. The contribution the Jesuits made was through their propagation of the so-called particular examination of conscience recommended in the *Exercises*.[86] Along with a general review of the day went concern for a "particular sin or defect," which, because especially frequent or characteristic, grounded the others. The bookkeeping Ignatius recommended for this sin or defect is another manifestation of the moral foundation he and his disciples considered essential for the spiritual edifice.

But such human calculation about moral performance was not meant to imply that God was an exacting bookkeeper. According to Nadal: "Father Ignatius says that God deals with us differently than do worldly human beings. They look to find whatever is bad or imperfect in our actions, they take note of it and then hold it against us. God, however, looks to see what good we have done, and closes an eye to our imperfections."[87]

In some localities where the Jesuits as members of an international organization found themselves, confession of sins presented peculiar problems when the confessor did not know the language of the penitent. By 1552 the Jesuits in Brazil had employed a practical solution. They trained boys to act as interpreters. The penitents told their sins to the boy, who in turn related them to the priest and then related what the Jesuit said back to the penitents.[88]

That year Pedro Fernandes Sardinha had been appointed bishop for Brazil. Although outwardly friendly to the Jesuits, he seemed to them in fact to be hostile. He particularly objected to this method of hearing confession because it was not customary in the church, "even if three hundred Navarro's and six hundred Cajetan's approve."[89] Nóbrega, the Jesuit provincial, defended the practice on the grounds that the boys were well instructed, that experience taught it worked well, and that learned theologians allowed it.[90] Two years later the Jesuits were still continuing the practice, still arguing that "experience taught that it was extremely useful."[91] Jesuit officials in Rome voiced no objection, insisting only that the secrecy of what was confessed be carefully guarded. Pressure on the Jesuits disappeared when Fernandes Sardinha was recalled to Portugal in 1556. After being shipwrecked on his way out of Brazil, he was killed and eaten by the natives of Caetité.

Even the bishop allowed that an interpreter may be used when necessity demanded it, but he insisted that it be an "upright and prudent man." He would have been shocked had he known that the Jesuits occasionally used Brazilian women for this task, about one of whom a Jesuit wrote in 1552, "I think she is a better confessor than I am."[92]

Holy Communion and the Eucharist

Within the context of the Eucharistic piety and theology of the late Middle Ages, most characteristic of the Jesuits was their promotion of more frequent reception of the sacrament.[93] Ignatius possibly learned about the spiritual advantages of the practice at Montserrat, but, in any case, by the time he was at Manresa he was receiving the Eucharist every Sunday.[94] At Manresa, moreover, he discovered *The Imitation of Christ,* and he and the early Jesuits recommended it to all who came to them. The entire fourth book of the *Imitation* is on the Eucharist, the fifth chapter of which recommends its frequent reception.

The idea of frequent Communion, therefore, was not new.[95] An effective advocacy originated in the Low Countries in the late fourteenth century, as the *Imitation* suggests. Although frequent reception was not characteristic of the spirituality of the *Devotio Moderna* as a whole, the *Imitation,* by far the most widely circulated document of the movement, gave the idea its greatest impulse.

By the beginning of the fifteenth century, others were also promoting it, including Jean Gerson. Since most of the early Jesuits believed him to be the author of the *Imitation,* their beloved "Gersonçito," they found double confirmation when they quoted his authentic works to that effect.[96] By "frequent" Gerson and others meant about once a month.

As with frequent confession, the idea had not taken hold widely. Most preachers never mentioned it. When the Jesuits came on the scene, few lay persons in most parts of Europe received Communion more than once or twice a year, and in many convents the nuns received only slightly more often. The great holiness of the sacrament, the great unworthiness of the recipients, and the great danger of frequency begetting contempt or indifference were the standard reasons given for restraint.

In the 1530's, however, Antonio Maria Zaccaria prescribed in the Constitutions for his Barnabites in Milan that they receive Communion at least every Sunday and every feast day. Gaetano da Chieti, co-founder with Carafa of the Theatines, supported similarly frequent reception, and shortly thereafter the eccentric Bonsignore Cacciaguerra took up the cause in Palermo, Naples, and Rome.[97] The Jesuits, therefore, became part of a movement already under way, but by sheer force of their numbers and international character they became its most effective spokesmen. Like most other advocates, they in these first decades recommended reception about once a week but, with the notable exception of Bobadilla, not daily. By the 1570's some of them, including Salmerón, promoted it even for some of the laity on a daily basis.[98]

Their exhortations to frequent Communion aroused suspicions against them and provided their enemies with a convenient excuse for denunciation. At Valencia in 1548, for instance, a Jesuit preaching on the matter caused such controversy in the pulpits of the city that the bishop convoked a consultation of theologians to settle it. After hearing the theologians, the bishop sided firmly with the Jesuits, but a year later "many ecclesiastics and educated persons" continued to voice their objections.[99]

In Bologna in 1550 members of other orders criticized the Jesuits for their stance, and two years later in Perugia no less important a person than a minister general of the Franciscans warned the episcopal vicar that because of Jesuit preaching and practice lay persons were receiving Communion too frequently. In Saragossa in 1554 critics were blunt: frequent Communion paves the road to hell.[100]

Despite much opposition, the Jesuits persisted. Why? Ignatius was early convinced that he and his companions were reinstituting in somewhat modified fashion a practice of the "primitive church," when the faithful communicated every day.[101] One of his immediate sources for this idea was the *Summa theologiae* of Aquinas.[102] Bobadilla, in his "Libellus" on the subject in 1551, referred to the same source.[103] The practice of the early church was a self-validating argument.

The first Jesuits nonetheless echoed traditional teaching about the spiritual benefits conferred by reception of the Eucharist. They generally added little to the fourth book of the *Imitation,* except perhaps more emphasis on spiritual consolation. Loarte's *Esercitio* was typical—the Eucharist is as necessary for the soul as food for the body; it brings health and strength, forgives sins, diminishes temptation; it confers sweetness and provides comfort and consolation.[104]

In his personal journal, Nadal drew more deeply on the sacramental and liturgical tradition: "When the blessed Eucharist is devoutly received, the mysteries not only of the passion and death of Christ are imprinted on us but also of his whole life and resurrection. Thus we can say that we live but, more, Christ lives in us [Gal. 2:20]. And even more is to be hoped for, so that we might say that we have the same mind and sentiments as Christ Jesus [Phil. 2:5]."[105] In his exhortations to the Jesuits on their ministries, however, he had little to say about the Eucharist and its benefits, perhaps because he assumed explanation was unnecessary.

Nonetheless, in recommending more frequent reception the Jesuits had to defend themselves against many opponents. Ignatius finally encouraged the publication of a book on the subject. In June of 1554 Salmerón hastily collected pertinent passages from the Fathers, but had to leave them behind when he left Rome for Spain a short while later. Andrés de Oviedo had to abandon his notes on the subject when he began to prepare for his departure for Ethiopia. Cristóforo de Madrid took up the project and published *De frequenti usu sanctissimi Eucharistiae sacramenti libellus* in a limited edition in Naples in 1555. After revisions, he published the definitive edition two years later with the press at the Collegio Romano. It was the first book ever published for the professed and exclusive purpose of defending and promoting more frequent reception of the Eucharist.

Written in classical Latin style but in unmistakably scholastic form, it was a polemical and apologetic work. In the *proemium* Madrid deplored Protestant attacks on the Eucharist, but he clearly aimed the work at Catholic opponents of frequent Communion. His special target was the idea that one must make oneself worthy before approaching the Eucharist. He countered that virtue and great devotion were not prerequisites, for these were precisely what the Eucharist imparted. In answer to the objection that the church did not urge frequent Communion, he invoked the practice of the early church—*nascentis ecclesiae.*[106] In good scholastic fashion he accordingly marshaled testimony from the Bible and the Greek and Latin Fathers, but, typical of the early Jesuits, he also argued from "experience." He of course opposed reception out of routine, "as we see today in many priests, who so irreverently and carelessly celebrate the Eucharist out of obligation or hope of financial gain."[107] He did not wish to condemn those who abstained out of reverence, but he argued for the increase of consolation and spiritual joy of those who frequently received.

In that regard he called upon "Christian liberty" in a way that, for all its differences, contained phrases reminiscent of Luther:

> Those who abstain because of some silly fear of irreverence are far removed from Christian freedom, which is altogether full of confidence in Christ and his promises. People like this become too scrupulous—they become sluggish for action, cold in love, tepid in prayer. Those who receive frequently, however, are filled with evangelical trust and confidence, rejoice in their Christian liberty, are rendered strong and sharp for action [and] ardent and fervent in prayer.[108]

Madrid's book ran through a number of printings and had fairly wide circulation outside the Society, especially in the joint editions with Polanco's directory on confession. Bobadilla's earlier work on Communion, the first by a Jesuit on the subject, circulated only in a few manuscripts and was not published until 1933.[109] Written in 1551, it was a response to a specific question by a certain Virgilio Zinguino: Can a pastor refuse to give Communion to the laity who want to receive it daily? Bobadilla responded with a resounding "no."

Although both Ignatius and Polanco saw the work and seemed to approve of it, they did not commission Bobadilla to revise and expand it into the defense later delivered into the hands of Salmerón, Oviedo, and, finally, Madrid. Bobadilla was already a somewhat controversial figure both inside and outside the Society, but his forceful position in favor of daily Communion was perhaps what tilted the scales against him in this instance. Ignatius and the other early Jesuits saw daily Communion as an exception to the rule, and the *Constitutions* repeatedly specified Communion received weekly, or slightly more often, as the norm even for non-ordained members of the Society.[110]

Bobadilla's work was basically a broadside against "worthiness" doctrines. His teaching was straightforward: Persons who have not repented of serious sin and confessed it cannot receive; otherwise they may. No priest, no bishop, no pope can take away the freedom to communicate—*libertatem communicandi*.[111] He especially attacked the idea that a certain period of time had to elapse after intercourse and other sexual acts, even involuntary "nocturnal pollutions," before one may approach the Eucharist:

> Theologians give another reason for abstaining from the Holy Eucharist— nocturnal pollution, about which they philosophize with a thousand distinctions. My opinion, however, is that neither nocturnal nor diurnal pollutions, neither those while asleep nor those while awake, neither those in legitimate matrimony nor those in lust outside it, neither mortally sinful nor venially sinful ones are in themselves obstacles, so long as the person has repented any sin and confessed it. Forgiveness does not happen over a period of time but in an instant.[112]

For validation of his advocacy of daily Communion, he cited Aquinas, but he more explicitly referred the reader to Gerson's "Magnificat" and the *Imitation of Christ*.[113] If you are cold, come to the fire. If you are sick, come to the medicine. In breaking with the worthiness doctrines, Bobadilla presented an image of God or Christ as friend and lover—constantly faithful, unremittingly merciful.

The first Jesuits did not settle within Catholicism the controversy over frequent Communion. The decree of the Council of Trent in its Thirteenth Session on the Eucharist, 1551, dealt directly with questions controverted with the Protestants, and it reiterated the decree *Omnis utriusque* of the Fourth Lateran Council obliging Catholics to receive annual Communion. Although in a passing mention the decree exhorted the faithful to "frequent Communion," it did not specify what "frequent" meant.[114] According to Gregory Martin, weekly and even daily Communion was practiced in many churches in Rome by the time of his sojourn there, 1576–78, but we have little solid information about how widespread the custom generally became.[115]

The controversy dragged on with diminished intensity in the sixteenth century, flared again between the Jesuits and the Jansenists in the seventeenth, and was finally resolved only in 1912 with a decree of Pope Pius X urging frequent, even daily reception of the sacrament. The Jesuits' advocacy of frequent Communion, in any case, did not originate as either an antidote to Protestantism or a response to the Council of Trent, which in fact showed no real interest in the issue. Moreover, when the Jesuits spoke in favor of frequent Communion, they meant precisely that—they were not talking about attendance at mass, a separate but related issue. They regularly administered the sacrament before or after mass, or at some other time in the morning, as was the widespread custom.[116] They reserved the sacrament, therefore, in their churches so that they would have hosts for people who wished to receive Communion. They did not have much to say about adoration of the reserved sacrament or other prayer in its presence. Not until 1562 did Francisco de Borja provide that the chapel of the Collegio Romano be enlarged and the sacrament reserved there so that the Jesuit scholastics could use it for prayer.[117]

Although in general the Jesuits showed relatively little interest in other forms of Eucharistic piety that had developed in the late Middle Ages, they surely did not oppose them.[118] They had a special fondness for the feast of Corpus Christi. Nadal urged solemn liturgy, with procession, in Jesuit churches for the feast. Even as he pointed out that elaborate ceremonies were "beyond the scope of our Institute," he allowed an exception in this case "because of the times," that is, because of Protestant criticism of what the feast implied.[119]

Jesuits probably did not need Nadal's encouragement to stage the great celebrations of Corpus Christi that became almost characteristic of them. The feast was too popular to be ignored, and it provided wonderful opportunities to engage all members of the congregation in the liturgy, especially the children.[120] The procession in Vienna in 1565 was typical. It stopped at four altars erected along the way, at which children followed the "Roman custom" of reciting verses and dialogues in honor of the Eucharist. In 1567 the children presented the "Sacrifice of Isaac" and in 1569, the "Offering of Melchizedek."[121] In a village near Bahia in Brazil in 1559, the procession wended its way through streets decorated with flowers and foliage while the children sang hymns in Tupi and Portuguese. The processions in Brazil on this and other feast days were often much more elaborate than those else-where—with poetry, dialogues, banners, torches, drums, flutes, trumpets, and dance.[122]

Besides advocating frequent Communion, the Jesuits also advocated fre-quent attendance at mass—a distinct, though obviously closely related, issue.[123] The *Constitutions* prescribed daily, or almost daily assistance at mass for non-ordained members of the Society and for students at Jesuit universities.[124] They recommended at least weekly celebration of mass for Jesuit priests, with the understanding that on other days they would attend mass.[125] Nonetheless, as early as 1554 Nadal informed Jesuits in Spain that daily celebration by the priests of the Society had already become a "firm custom."[126]

Holy Orders

Because the Society strictly forbade its members from accepting bishoprics, Jesuits obviously could not administer the sacrament of Orders. That prohi-bition helps account for the little mention of the sacrament in the sources. Most Jesuits were, however, either already ordained priests or destined for ordination. What is surprising about this fundamental reality is how seldom it is singled out for comment.[127] Ordination to the priesthood, for instance, is in effect not mentioned in the *Constitutions*. Certainly, the early Jesuits spoke so little about priesthood because they took it for granted. They inherited the medieval idea that the sacrament of Orders conferred the power to confect the Eucharist and provided the basis for the jurisdiction that allowed priests to hear confessions. Given the centrality of these two sacraments in the ministry of the early Jesuits, they obviously needed to be ordained to carry out that ministry as they understood it.

As should be clear by now, however, much of the ministry in the Society was in fact done by persons who were not ordained. More fundamentally, the warrant for all the ministries derived in their opinion not from ordination but from acceptance of the call to be a member of the Society of Jesus. The Jesuits discussed that call frequently and at length, but rarely, if at all, did they speak of a "call to priesthood."

They could find some substantiation for these attitudes in the *Summa* of Aquinas and the writings of other members of the mendicant orders. Moreover, they found them at least indirectly confirmed by the various papal documents that allowed all members of the order to preach and engage in all the *consueta ministeria,* except hearing confessions and distributing Communion.

When Nadal in his exhortations reviewed with his fellow Jesuits the outline of Ignatius's life, he therefore had practically nothing to say about his ordination, reflecting Ignatius's *Autobiography* in this relative silence. On one occasion Nadal began an exhortation with a telling apology for his narrative about what happened in Venice in 1537: "I must mention, by the way, that yesterday I forgot to tell you that Father Ignatius was ordained a priest."[128]

In a more considered passage, he described how in 1539 the ten companions had to give an account of their Institute when they asked for Paul III's approval. They said they followed a way of life in which "monasticism" was joined to priesthood.[129] "Monasticism" here had the broad meaning of life in a religious order.

For the first decade or so the situation was somewhat fluid. Polanco related how in 1550 in Tivoli a Spanish scholastic exercised a fruitful ministry of preaching and teaching catechism. People were so moved that they wanted him to hear their confessions, "even though he as yet had no sacred orders." As a response "to the pious desires of so many persons," he was ordained and began to hear "many confessions."[130]

In that same year in Meldola, an Italian scholastic preached, gave exhortations and the *Exercises,* and organized lay women to counsel younger women who planned to join a convent. He did so well that Ignatius asked him if he wanted to be ordained a priest. When he replied that he was "indifferent," that is, ready for either alternative, Ignatius decided for him in favor of ordination.[131] Some young Jesuits thought ordination brought with it the danger of honor and special privilege and, hence, said they did not want to be ordained unless their superiors expressly ordered them.[132]

Throughout these years, the pragmatic necessity of providing a sufficient number of confessors was often adduced as a reason for ordination.[133] As the course of studies for the scholastics became more regularized, so did provisions for their ordination. Polanco in his *Chronicon* began after a certain point occasionally to mention the first mass celebrated by a newly ordained Jesuit, but here and in other Jesuit sources priesthood as such never surfaced as a theme.

It cannot be said that the Jesuits, like the Somaschi, another religious order founded at about the same time, were a lay institution that became "clericalized." All the original ten companions were already priests in 1540, and, when Polanco some years later inquired of Ignatius whether all the professed should be priests, he was told emphatically that they should.[134] The Jesuits never tried to pass themselves off as anything else, nor did they entertain the possibility that most Jesuits would not eventually be ordained. They were by definition an order of "clerks regular." Nonetheless, the psychological reality that primarily grounded their lives and their ministry was membership in the Society, not being in orders.

Music and Worship

Cardinal Ghinucci's objections eliminated from the "Five Chapters" the explicit prohibition of musical instruments and the reasons for not chanting or reciting the Hours in choir, but those ideas continued to have force in the Society. Gradually, nonetheless, Ignatius and his successors had to make concessions. The pressure for change came from several sources.

The Jesuits had hardly arrived in Brazil when they discovered the natives' talent and enthusiasm for music. In a letter to Rome in 1549, Nóbrega told of the Brazilians' delight in hearing the Jesuits sing and play instruments. The next year he accepted the seven volunteers from the newly founded royal orphanage in Lisbon to help as catechists. The boys cut their hair in native style (much to the disgust of the bishop Fernandes Sardinha, who said it made them look like monkeys), used native tunes and instruments (to the great disgust of the bishop), and in general joined the Jesuits in launching a musical and liturgical tradition.[135]

At São Vicente by 1553 the Jesuits had founded "the first school of music in the Western Hemisphere," where besides reading and writing they taught children how to sing and play the flute.[136] By 1555 the provincial reported that at Bahia three different choirs were in operation for vespers on Sundays and feast days—one accompanied with organ, another with clavichord, the third with flutes. No questions were raised by the Jesuit leadership in Europe.

For the Jesuit churches in Europe, Ignatius tried to be stringent: on the one hand, as the *Constitutions* observed, there were already many other churches where the services were sung;[137] on the other, for the Jesuits to sing mass and the Hours well and on a regular basis would take them away from the *consueta ministeria*. Ignatius gradually permitted the singing of vespers on certain days for a good reason—in some places the people practically demanded it. The *Constitutions* fairly well summarized his attitude and practice:

> If it is judged expedient in some houses or colleges, at the time of the afternoon when a sermon or lecture is about to be given, vespers alone could be recited immediately beforehand or afterwards to please the people. This could also be done ordinarily on Sundays and feast days . . . in a devout, smooth, and plain tone. It is done for the purpose of attracting the people to more frequent confession and attendance at sermons and lectures and to the extent that it is judged useful for this end, and in no other manner.[138]

As late as 1556, however, he was angry that Jesuits were singing high masses in the church in Vienna, and he forbade it in the future.[139] After his death the First General Congregation was asked about sung masses, as was the Second in 1565.[140] Although in their responses both Congregations restricted to the general the granting of permission to do so on a regular basis, exceptions to the prohibition were obviously increasing.

By 1565, the end of the period I am considering, sung vespers on Sundays and feast days had become the norm rather than the exception in the Jesuit churches to which a sufficiently large community was attached. This phenomenon was in fact not quite so dramatic a deviation from the original prohibition as it at first seems. The prohibition looked to the members of the Society, especially the priests. Once the schools were founded, however, the students did the singing. This included the Jesuit scholastics, for whom, however, the amount of time spent practicing singing was restricted. In the schools, sung vespers became part of the regular spiritual program for the students who were not Jesuits, as it had been for the devout laity for centuries, and they were open to the public who frequented the college church.

The report the Jesuit provincial in India made in 1556 about what had happened in Goa is typical of what happened elsewhere: "Sung liturgies were introduced into our college because there was no hope of doing otherwise, so great is the people's attachment to them. However, except for one of our priests who presides on Sundays and feast days, all the singers are boys from the college."[141]

Nonetheless, in India the Jesuits had almost from their first moments there used music in religious services more frequently and elaborately than had their brethren in Europe. Special but not out of character was the mass opening the academic year at the college in Goa in 1558. The viceroy and other high officials of church and state were present. The celebrant was assisted by a deacon and a subdeacon. Not only was the mass sung, but shawms, kettledrums, trumpets, flutes, and violins provided the instrumental music. A procession through the streets followed the mass, during which the same instruments were used as well as "the usual music by the boys of the college."[142]

As reports concerning this issue imply, a fair number of the Jesuits could read music and play instruments with enough skill to teach others at least the rudiments, sometimes much more. In the colleges, however, when music came to be needed not only for mass and vespers, but also for academic celebrations and other occasions, the Jesuits called upon more sophisticated teachers. They undertook the management of the Seminario Romano for the archdiocese of Rome when it was founded in 1564 by Pope Pius IV. Two years later they hired for it as *maestro di capella* Giovanni Pierluigi Palestrina, who held the position for five years.[143] They had come a long way from what the companions had envisioned in 1540! Although the ambivalences that marked the first decades would never be fully resolved, Jesuit schools and churches began to sponsor impressive musical programs, for which they achieved renown.[144]

For the Jesuits themselves the issue of reciting or chanting the Hours in choir would not go away, not because they wavered in their resolve but because of outside pressure, especially from Pope Paul IV (1555–59). Their relations with the pope were at best uneasy, beginning in 1536 with that mysterious encounter of Ignatius in Venice with the then cardinal Giampietro Carafa. As a gesture toward placating him as pope and forestalling his tampering with the Institute, Ignatius decided in 1555 to allow vespers to be chanted by the Jesuits in Rome on Sundays and feast days, and he renewed the decision for Holy Week in 1556.[145]

Obviously intended as a temporary measure, it failed to ward off the pope. In 1558, just as the Jesuits felt that their difficulties with him from before and during their First General Congregation had abated, he informed them that henceforth the Society would be bound to recite or chant the Hours in common. Their objections availed them nothing.

When the pope died the next year, Laínez consulted "learned theologians" and won from them the opinion that the obligation ceased with the death of the pope. The Jesuits returned to their wayward practice—or, better, non-practice.[146] They later had to face and overcome similar problems with Pius

V (1566–72). The very length of Nadal's commentary on the paragraph of the *Constitutions* that prohibited choral or communal Hours suggests, however, that even Jesuits needed repeated instruction on why they in this regard differed so markedly from many other priests and members of all other religious orders.[147]

Underlying this whole complex matter, of course, was a particular vision of ministry, priesthood, and religious life. Whatever the first Jesuits understood by them, they did not define them as consisting primarily in cult as expressed in the celebration of the mass and the Hours. They inherited well-known medieval ideas about the mass that stressed its immolatory and impetratory aspects, especially as these might be useful or necessary to the individual believer—and the individual priest.[148] To say that for them the mass was basically one among many forms of prayer in which the individual might engage—the supreme and most powerful among those forms being "the Sacrifice of the Cross"—would be to oversimplify, but not by much.[149] They took a while to see how celebrations of mass and the Hours enhanced by music might be an instrument of their ministry.

On the prescriptive level, the first generation consistently assigned such celebrations an ancillary role. Nadal could not have been clearer. Where the custom has been established of singing mass and vespers on Sundays and feast days, Jesuits should participate only on condition that a sufficient number of priests "are not lacking for hearing confessions, preaching sermons, delivering lectures, and for all the other ministries that are proper to the Society. The ministries are never to be omitted for the sake of sung liturgies."[150]

Prayer

In their sermons, sacred lectures, confessional counsel, and catechesis, the Jesuits consistently recommended prayer to those with whom they dealt. This of course included liturgical prayer of the mass and Hours, and the *Exercises* simply assumed that persons making them assisted regularly or daily at both these functions.[151] Nonetheless, when the Jesuits spoke of prayer and encouraged it, they generally meant something else. They meant the recitation of set formulas such as the "Our Father" and other prayers found in the catechisms. They often commended recitation of the Book of Hours of Our Lady, a well-established and extremely popular form of devotion among the literate throughout Europe.[152]

By prayer they also meant meditation, contemplation, or some other form of interiorized prayer done by the individual. They often somewhat infelicitously termed these forms "mental prayer." They tried to teach them even to simple folk, as the many chapters dedicated to them in Loarte's *Esercitio* testify. Laínez's series of sacred lectures on prayer in Rome, 1558, commended formulaic prayers, daily recitation of the Hours of Our Lady, and recitation of other prayers found in books. But he particularly recommended mental prayer for his mixed audience of lay women and men.[153]

The Jesuits were not the first to do this. They borrowed or adapted the techniques and methods for such prayer from earlier traditions. However, their peculiar insistence upon it, their belief that it could be fruitfully practiced by persons of every station, and their access to the handy codification and explanation of methods in the *Exercises* all indicate that because of them a significant reshaping of the practices of the devout life was under way for many Catholics.

Erasmus's *Modus orandi Deum* (1524) provided examples of prayers that individuals might compose for themselves and especially tried to foster an attitude to assure that the heart as well as the lips prayed.[154] The *Modus* was widely diffused and still read in Rome in 1558, as a passing comment by Laínez makes clear.[155] It failed, however, to recommend or explain mental prayer, an omission typical of Erasmus.

But for the Jesuits the teaching and promoting of mental prayer was one of their special campaigns. They had learned how to do it in the *Exercises* and, presumably, had experienced its benefits. They then were expected to make those benefits available to others.

In explaining why the *Exercises* generally effected such great changes in persons who made them, Nadal said that the methods of prayer in the *Exercises* enabled individuals to penetrate in their hearts and spirit the inner mysteries of Christ's life, passion, death, and resurrection. Thence arose the historical significance of the *Exercises*: "Briefly, we see that today prayer has collapsed, devotion has disappeared, contemplation been forgotten, and spiritual sensibilities sent into exile . . . God wanted through the *Exercises* to rush assistance to this distressing situation in the church. But you object: this is too much!—as if we preach that we are the ones who through our *Exercises* are going to save prayer from utter collapse."[156] Nadal denied, of course, such an arrogant claim. He hoped, in fact, that God might inspire others to discover an even better method of teaching prayer to everybody— a discovery, we easily infer, that he thought highly unlikely to occur.

In passages like this we get about as close as we can to how the first Jesuits thought they brought succor to the "collapsed" religion of their times. Like the *Devotio Moderna* and similar movements, they wanted to promote a more intensified interiority, and they found in mental prayer the most direct and efficacious means of doing so on a long-term basis. They were not professedly anti-liturgical, as has sometimes been charged, but they certainly put an emphasis on other forms of prayer as constitutive of an authentic Christian life.

This emphasis perforce reflected the priorities they had established for themselves as Jesuits. Nadal revealed and somewhat overstated the priorities when he described for his fellow Jesuits the difference between public and private prayer:

> Public prayer consists principally in the mass, which has supreme efficacy as sacrament and sacrifice. It also consists in other prayers commonly held in churches, like litanies and similar things. Private prayer is the prayer that each one does in his room, and it . . . should always take order and priority over public prayer because of its power, and it especially befits us because we do not celebrate public prayer in common—we do not have choir. This means that for the Jesuit his room becomes his choir.[157]

In practice, however, Jesuits tried to find ways to correlate "private prayer" with the public prayer that was the mass. This first generation produced three lengthy works that illustrated in detail the correlation they fostered. It is significant that each of them took the texts from the Gospels read at mass during the annual liturgical cycle as the materials for these meditations. Borja, Nadal, and Canisius were the authors.

Between 1563 and 1566 Borja wrote *Meditaciones para todas los dominicas y ferias del año,* which was not published until 1675.[158] It seems to be the first collection of meditations ever written that was organized according to the texts of the liturgical cycle. As we have seen, about ten years later Nadal composed *Adnotationes et meditationes in Evangelia quae in sacrosancto missae sacrificio toto anno leguntur.*[159] The magnificent series of 153 copperplate illustrations that accompanied the text in the first edition (Antwerp, 1594) is the earliest such series of the whole of the New Testament of any size or importance ever produced; the text identified persons, places, and things in the illustrations and then used them as materials for the meditations. Although the last of these works to be written was Peter Canisius's *Notae in evangelicas lectiones,* it was the first published—in two volumes, 1591–93.[160]

~ 5

Works of Mercy

IN 1552 POLANCO noted that the women and men who regularly confessed to the Jesuits in Messina soon began to visit the sick in the hospitals, beg alms for the poor, and perform other works of charity or mercy.[1] This was not an isolated instance but the pattern the Jesuits expected themselves and others to follow as a consequence of a deeper spiritual life. Commitment to works of mercy completed the cycle that began with ministries of the Word. Preaching and the *Exercises* led to conversion, which was expressed in confession and nourished by prayer and reception of the Eucharist. The conversion, in turn, flowered into dedication to alleviating the physical and spiritual needs of other human beings. The "Contemplation for Love," as the last meditation of the *Exercises,* sent the individual back into the world with the observation that "love ought to manifest itself in deeds rather than words."[2]

The pattern was in itself unexceptional in the Christian tradition. As put into operation by the Jesuits, however, it manifested three special features. First, it was more powerful because it was so simply and clearly delineated in their foundational documents—the *Exercises* and the *Formula.* They knew, almost step by step, what they wanted to accomplish and the end toward which the process tended. Second, for some of the steps they adapted or created instruments such as the general confession to seal and formalize them for themselves and others.

Third, the works of mercy assumed a special character because of the particular context into which they were inserted and from which they drew much of their design. They were mentioned in the eighteenth "Observation" of the *Exercises,* but did not explicitly recur in the text.[3] They were prominent, however, in the "Five Chapters" and the *Formulae,* written later and intended specifically for Jesuits and their ministry.

Probably just as basic even for the Jesuits, the spiritual and corporal works of mercy were an essential aspect of *Christianitas,* explicit in the late-medieval catechesis of Spain and Italy. The *Doctrina cristiana* of Juan de Avila, so favored by the Jesuits, had put to verse the lists as well as the source of many works they contained. That source was, as we have seen, the pertinent section of the twenty-fifth chapter of Matthew's Gospel—when you clothe, feed, console, and do other kind deeds for the wretched and outcast, said Jesus, you are clothing, feeding, and consoling me.[4] The motivation was powerful.

Ignatius initiated some measures for poor relief in his native Azpeitia during his last visit there in 1535, but he and the companions took up these activities with intensity upon their arrival in Venice just a little later. Their status as students before this date put limits on the time and energy they could spend on such activities. The importance they eventually assigned to them in their new compagnia manifested itself in the section of the "Chapters" that adduced hospital service as a principal reason they could not be bound by choir.[5]

As the companions in Venice turned their attention to the corporal works of mercy, they would have discovered complex and variegated networks of assistance to the poor and sick in that densely populated city.[6] They would have become aware especially in Venice of the new problems created by the appearance of syphilis several decades earlier and the impact which that "incurable disease" continued to have on social consciousness and reality. In Venice and the other parts of central Italy in which they wandered between 1537 and 1540, they would have encountered the many and lively confraternities—or *compagnie* or *scuole*—that were among the most salient features of social and religious life in Italian cities, often the main or only vehicle supplying organized relief for communal needs.

Their recent experience of these social realities surely contributed to the formulation of the "Chapters" and the *Formula.* These institutions were the immediate context providing the basic instruments and mentality that gave shape to the works of mercy that the Jesuits themselves began to undertake and to encourage in others.[7] Jesuit attitudes and activities manifested three features in this regard.

In the first place, the Jesuits understood their imitation of the ministry of Jesus and his disciples to include or reproduce, in some way, the bodily healing that was a part of that ministry—"heal the sick" (Lk. 10:9). Favre spoke for them all when he said he wanted to bring help to others "not only for their spirit but also (if one may presume in the Lord) for their bodies."[8] The Jesuits' visits to hospitals and similar activities were more than "good works" meritorious unto salvation; they were intrinsic to their pastoral self-understanding.

The Jesuits in fact consistently worked to improve the physical circumstances of the needy they encountered, and they took for granted, without much explanation, that this was an integral part of their ministry. They expended great time and energy in the works of mercy. Nadal has justly been described, for instance, as "the premier organizer of social relief in Sicily" during his years there, 1548–53.[9] They just as consistently engaged others in these enterprises to labor alongside them or, eventually, to be left in charge.

Second, although in this aspect of their activities the Jesuits were inspired by the New Testament, they were also trained in medieval philosophy and canon law about their obligation to contribute to "the common good," as indicated by the prominent employment of that term in the *Formula*. This was not a biblical term or notion; rather, it reflected a social philosophy present in their thinking.

The social aspect of Jesuit ministry often took the form of direct physical or financial assistance to individuals suffering from occasional disasters like famine, flood, or plague; for example, during the bitter Roman winter of 1538–39, the companions begged food and clothing and procured lodging for hundreds of people for months at a time.[10] Nonetheless, its more striking form was grounded in institutions—hospitals, prisons, orphanages, refuges for women in trouble, and especially confraternities. This is the third particularly salient feature of their commitment to the works of mercy.

The Jesuits sometimes performed their social assistance within existing institutions, at other times they founded new ones. In both cases a confraternity managed by the laity almost invariably entered the picture sooner or later as the most natural and viable instrument to assure the continuance of the ministry or institution. The confraternity was thus generally "the institution behind the institution," and it provided a line of continuity among the Jesuits' diversified involvements as well as with the reality of the local situation.

One of the many stories related in this regard by Polanco will serve as introduction to the issue because it illustrates the different roles the Jesuits typically played, their relationships to local rulers and other laity, and the often spontaneous character of these projects. In Palermo in 1550 the Jesuits begged alms from the viceroy and others, by which they secured the liberation from prison of twenty debtors. When they discovered other prisoners ill almost to the point of death from a contagious fever, they used their influence to get some of them transferred to a hospital. The possibility that these criminals might take flight, however, meant that many of the sick remained in the prison.

A Belgian scholastic named Julian brought these sick prisoners "the sacraments and the Word of God," as well as further alms he had begged from members of the viceroy's household. He then began to build for them little huts or shelters *(habitatiuncula)* in or near the prison to provide them with better sanitary conditions. He soon contracted the fever himself and died. The viceroy was so impressed with what Julian had done that he ordered more such shelters to be built at his own expense and supplied with beds and medicine. He then summoned some public notaries and exhorted them to continue this work, suggesting that they seek the advice of Fathers Laínez and Doménech as to how best to do it, which they did. Soon thereafter the men met to frame the constitutions of their new confraternity, which began with over fifty members, and to elect the officers. The duties of the members were to visit the sick prisoners and care for them, beg and themselves contribute money in order to free debtors, and try to persuade creditors to remit debts. They reformed their own lives through more frequent confession. In all this, they contributed "not a little to the common good."[11]

The story manifests the pluriform character of Jesuit engagement with the works of mercy, designated in the *Formula* as "works of charity"—*opera caritatis.* This chapter describes the more important aspects of that engagement. There were other activities important in certain localities but not widespread or standard in the Society. The Jesuits supported and promoted, for instance, the *Montes pietatis,* the low-interest loan banks of Franciscan inspiration that originated in Italy at the end of the fifteenth century to relieve the poor, as well as the *Ufficio di Carità* in Sicily.[12] They begged money to ransom back prisoners taken by the Turks.[13] They served as chaplain-nurses on military and naval expeditions.[14] In 1551 in Brazil they preached so effectively against slave-taking raids by the Portuguese that, at least for the moment, the practice stopped, and they got some of the Brazilians released by their captors.[15]

Peacemaking

The *Formula* of 1540 mentioned "works of charity" without specification, unless we construe the phrase to indicate teaching catechism and hearing confessions. The version of 1550 expanded the list of ministries and some-what shifted their order. While it retained the generic *opera caritatis,* it spec-ified among them "reconciling the estranged" and "assisting and serving those found in prisons and hospitals." Whereas the latter category had ear-lier appeared in the "Chapters," as we have seen, reconciliation appears explicitly for the first time in 1550—and in first place. The experience of ten years of ministry surely prompted specific mention. "Pardoning offenses and injuries" was one of the seven spiritual works of mercy.

Although religious peacemaking figured in the ministry of the mendicants in the late Middle Ages and played a role in some confraternities, we do not know much about it either in detail or as a general phenomenon.[16] It is therefore impossible to make a comparative assessment of Jesuit peace-making beyond noting that the Jesuits had precursors in it and that, at least in certain localities, they were not defying people's expectations when they played this role but fulfilling them. When Nadal commented on this part of the *Formula* in his exhortations, he began of course with *dissidentium recon-ciliatio.* He recalled that this was the seventh Beatitude as listed in Matthew's Gospel—"Blessed are the peacemakers, for they shall be called sons of God" (5:9). He generalized: "When this Beatitude is taken in its full comprehen-sion, all the ministries previously mentioned are in its service."[17] Unfortu-nately, at least a full page of his text amplifying upon this judgment is missing. Nonetheless, the fact that he on one occasion pronounced that the Jesuits were fundamentally engaged in a "ministry of reconciliation" is important for understanding the other ministries and their strongly social character.

The correspondence and other reports from the early Jesuits do not rise to this level of generalization, but narrate tale after tale of how members of the Society effected reconciliations among warring factions, especially in remote villages in the two great peninsulas. Other sources from the period confirm how fierce the vendettas were in these places.[18] The Jesuits might sometimes exaggerate their own role and their success, but they do not exag-gerate the problem, incredible though some of these situations might seem. As early as 1540 Jay reported that through preaching and hearing confessions in Bagnorea, fifty miles north of Rome, he was able to convince the villagers to renounce the bloody feuds that had raged there for years.[19]

Polanco in his *Chronicon* described a number of dramatic instances, but he provided an especially detailed account of what happened in 1549 in Cor-reggio, hardly a remote village.[20] Landini began to preach there during the summer. The town was divided into two factions. This had led to forty-five murders or assassinations in recent years, three of the victims being priests. The men came to church fully armed. After Landini had preached there for a while, sometimes twice a day, he succeeded in getting the two leaders of the opposing factions to confession. They agreed to make peace and do whatever Landini indicated to effect it.

One evening a herald was sent through Correggio to summon people to church the next day. Once the crowd assembled, it eventually quieted down for mass and the sermon, and so many wanted to go to confession that more priests had to be called. After the sermon, in which "the Word of God softened the hearts of the leaders of the factions," Landini from the pulpit addressed by name one of the leaders, who asked, "Father, what do you want me to do?" Landini told him to single out his enemies, ask their forgiveness, and wish them peace. The man, after throwing his weapons to the floor, did so. Landini then came down from the pulpit and told him to follow his example; he began to embrace the man's enemies and give them the kiss of peace. Soon everybody in the church joined in. "The whole church—young and old, women and men, tears in their eyes—resounded with peace, and those hearts that only a few days earlier had like lions thirsted for nothing but revenge and murder now were reconciled like lambs in meek and reciprocal love." They decided to commemorate the day henceforth with an annual feast.

In Faenza in 1545 Broët gathered a hundred men in the cathedral for a similar liturgy of reconciliation, during which they forgave each other "the homicides, injuries, and other evils that flowed from hatreds of this kind."[21] In 1548 one of the Jesuits who was sent to a village in Portugal preached so as to reconcile twenty men with one another in the presence of all the inhabitants. The men did so with so many tears and charitable embraces that what the "power" (energia) of the divine word had effected internally was made externally manifest.[22]

In 1551 Landini preached in villages near Modena. The area was so torn by factions that in one place nearly fifty, in another sixty, and in yet another one hundred people had been killed. Murder, robbery, and the desire for revenge were the order of the day. In each of the villages Landini had some success, and before he left them he established a "Confraternity of the Body of Christ" (Corporis Christi Societas) made up of both men and women who agreed to weekly or at least monthly reception of Communion. They elected their own officers, among whom the most important were two whose task was to work for the "reconciliation of enemies."[23]

With variation in detail, the Jesuits reported scenes like these repeatedly.[24]

Jesuit peacemaking sometimes extended, however, beyond the elimination of brutal vendettas. At Valencia in 1549 Antonio de Araoz effected a reconciliation between estranged spouses—the duke and duchess of Calabria.[25] At Monreale, outside Palermo, Laínez at the behest of Cardinal Alessandro Farnese settled a long-standing dispute between the monks and the local clergy by a careful examination of archival documents.[26] Perhaps most remarkable, the Jesuits at Ingolstadt were able in 1550 to reconcile some of the professors at the university, whose mutual hatreds had even found their way into print.[27]

Hospitals and Prisons

By the middle of the sixteenth century in central Italy, hospitals, including those for the "sick poor," were often sophisticated institutions, seemingly well in advance of what prevailed in other parts of Europe.[28] The service by the original companions in the hospitals of Venice set an example for future members of the order. Wherever the Jesuits went, they eventually found their way to the hospitals, as the *Chronicon* testifies. They sometimes washed and fed the patients and otherwise tried to make them physically comfortable. They preached to them and, if they were priests, heard the patients' confessions. This became almost routine for members of a Jesuit community of any size.

In a few instances this commitment attained heroic dimensions. During the plague in Perugia in 1553, the Jesuits remained almost alone to nurse and minister to the sick in the hospitals and in their homes.[29] Because over the years the number of Jesuits who died under such circumstances began to rise, a more cautious policy was initiated while Laínez was general.[30] Even with the policy in place, Jesuits still sometimes put themselves in jeopardy to aid the sick. During the plague in Rome in 1566 and again in 1568, they went out in large numbers to care for the stricken, with each Jesuit assigned a street as his particular charge.[31] In Lisbon in 1569 seventeen Jesuits died while attending victims of the plague.[32]

As part of their concern for the sick, they sometimes undertook tasks we might not expect of them. For instance, in 1555 Father Bartolomé Torres, who was a doctor of medicine, established a pharmacy and small infirmary for the sick in Rome near the Torre Rosso.[33] In a Roman hospital a few years later, the Jesuits, besides sweeping the whole hospital twice a day, making beds, and serving food, tried to persuade the employees to be less spiteful toward one another and to deal with the sick "in a more helpful and humane way."[34] In Palermo in 1551 Nadal worked successfully to have endowment funds intended for a hospital for the poor returned to that purpose by the nobles who had diverted them to their own benefit.[35]

When the Jesuits arrived at Mozambique in 1548, they first lodged in a hospital where most of the 120 patients had contagious diseases. They begged medicines for them, and then one of the Jesuits undertook the threefold "function of cook, preacher, and pharmacologist."[36] In Goa by 1546 they were running a hospital for native Indians.[37] By 1576 enough Jesuits were doctors to prompt Pope Gregory XIII to issue a general exemption for them—provided that other doctors were not available—from the canons that forbade clerics and religious to practice medicine.[38]

As the number of schools increased, this time-consuming, fatiguing, and often dangerous ministry suffered some eclipse. Other factors contributed to greater caution and restraint. The *Constitutions* provided that one of the tests the novices had to undergo was a month of hospital service.[39] In the early years novices sometimes ate and slept in the hospital for the whole time, but the practice gave rise to many problems. In 1547 Cornelius Wischaven and a lay brother named Pascasio were sent as novices to Santa Maria della Consolazione in Rome, where they received a miserable welcome even from the patients. They had practically no time for sleep. Worst of all, the *ospedaliere* tried to seduce Pascasio and kept urging him to come live with him. Wischaven and Pascasio survived their ordeal, but not everybody did. A few died, more got sick, some simply left, and others yielded to seductions.[40] Gradually, therefore, the experiments for the novices were tempered, and, we infer, similar changes were made for other members of the order. Nadal later explicitly laid down the norm, for instance, that Jesuits should not nurse women, but only preach to them and hear their confessions.[41]

In 1542–43 Ignatius tried to initiate a major change in medical and pastoral practice. It failed, at least in Rome, but his attempt strikingly illustrates an aspect of the Jesuits' relationship to the sick that balances the stories of their humanitarian services. The Fourth Lateran Council in 1215 issued a decree, canon twenty-two, entitled *Cum infirmitas,* which forbade doctors to treat the sick until a priest had heard their confessions. Pope Gregory IX had later in the thirteenth century inserted the canon in his *Decretali,* thus giving it further promulgation, but by the sixteenth century it seems not to have been observed. Ignatius set about having it revived.[42] He argued that, since the decree was issued by a general and legitimate council, under the authorship and presence of the Holy Spirit, it could not possibly provide or determine anything against charity.[43]

When the doctors in Rome got wind of what was under way, they began to gather legal and theological opinion in opposition to the decree, basing their case on the argument that an exhortation to call a confessor was sufficient and that the doctor need not suspend his visits until the patient had done so. Ignatius in turn gathered opinions of bishops and theologians favorable to an interpretation of the decree that required the doctor to suspend his services after three days if the patient had not confessed. It is not surprising to find among these the Dominican zealot Ambrogio Politi (Catarino), but also favorable were Girolamo Seripando and the theologians of the General Chapter of the Augustinians over which he presided in Rome in the spring of 1543.

Sometime that year Paul III ordered observance of the decree in Rome, but it seems never to have been effectively enforced. Rodolfo Pio ordered its observance in his diocese of Faenza, as did the new bishop of Modena, Giovanni Morone. Juan de Vega, the great friend of the Jesuits, ordered as viceroy its implementation in Sicily, and Jerónimo Doménech reported from there in 1547 that the promulgation was "very beneficial."[44]

We do not know how thoroughly implemented the provisions were in these dioceses and territories, but they did not everywhere remain a dead letter. In any case, Paul III never ordered promulgation outside Rome itself, even though Ignatius hoped from him a "more universal" extension of the decree.[45] In chapter seventeen of his work on ministry to the dying, first published in 1575, Polanco made passing mention of the "salutary decree," nothing more.[46] In his *Directorium* for confessors, he did not speak of it even in the examination of conscience for doctors.[47] Nadal only alluded to it.[48] For whatever reason, the decree did not become a rallying cry even in the Society.

The Jesuits provided for prisoners in jail many of the same services they did for the sick in hospitals, and they assigned this work the same importance. In some ways ministry to prisoners was less exacting because the prisoners did not normally require sustained and round-the-clock attention. This made it more compatible with the schedules of Jesuits teaching in the schools.

Who were these prisoners? In the sixteenth century the incarcerated throughout Europe fell into two major categories—debtors and persons awaiting sentence or execution. Internment in jail for a specified period as an ongoing punishment for crime was for the most part unknown. In Rome after about 1550 over half of those detained were debtors from the poorer classes, even though the upper classes were also heavily in debt. Most of the other prisoners were awaiting trial or sentencing, and their guilt therefore often had yet to be established. In Venice, Rome, and elsewhere, delays, sheer inefficiency, and the corruption of officials received attention from governments and from religious activists like the Jesuits, but "prison reform" was just as difficult to effect in the sixteenth century as it is in the twentieth.[49]

This situation explains the character of Jesuit involvement with prisoners and the welcome from them they often received. For the most part they were not dealing with hardened criminals. They preached to the incarcerated, taught them catechism, heard their confessions, brought them food, begged alms for them. Nadal maintained that they should be more diligent in begging alms for prisoners than for the sick, because the hospitals were in general better provided for.[50] On at least one occasion, in Plasencia in 1556, they went to the prisoners' homes at Christmas and cleaned them for them.[51] They tried to get prisoners to give up gambling and cursing.[52] In Rome in 1565 they had some lives of the saints sturdily bound and then attached them to the walls of the jails with chains so that the prisoners could read them.[53]

Much of the Jesuits' effort in Italy and Spain was directed toward freeing debtors by begging alms to pay off their creditors or by dealing directly with the creditors themselves.[54] They sometimes successfully intervened to have the sentences of convicted criminals mitigated, and on a few occasions they got the death penalty suspended and the prisoner freed, as with a woman condemned to capital punishment for adultery in Valladolid in 1551.[55]

They had no plan for reform of the system. The institutional component of their activities was the traditional confraternity. The members performed more or less the same corporal and spiritual services as the Jesuits, except those reserved to priests. The only such confraternity that has been studied in detail is the Confraternità dei carcerati, founded in Rome in 1575 by the French Jesuit Jean Tellier.[56] Although it was established slightly later than the period I am considering, its statutes and activities reflect rather faithfully earlier counterparts. It was governed entirely by its lay members. Women were admitted, but not with the same status as men. Its considerable success sparked imitation in other Italian cities, including Naples, Turin, Florence, Milan, Bologna, and Rimini.

Ministry to the Dying

In hospitals and prisons the Jesuits frequently encountered the dying and those condemned to die, who were generally bereft of a regular pastor.

Although they would not administer the last rites of the church if the pastor was available, they obviously were free to do so in other cases. Moreover, ministry to persons in danger of death extended far beyond administering the sacraments to them. As we have seen, Nadal categorized it as a form of devout conversation.

Jesuits early began to look upon such ministry as especially appropriate for them because in no other circumstances was need more obvious and urgent. Polanco noted that some ministries were to help persons live well, others to die well. The latter were to be preferred.[57]

Most confraternities showed special concern for their moribund members and even for the equitable administration of their wills.[58] The fifteenth through the seventeenth centuries produced an immense amount of literature on "the art of dying well."[59] The fact that Erasmus undertook in 1534 to publish a work on "preparation for death" (De praeparatione ad mortem), translated into every major European language and reprinted in Latin or the vernacular some sixty times within the next twenty-five years, confirms the importance of the topic for his own age. The only work that today is read outside a narrow circle of specialists, however, is his colloquy "The Funeral" ("Funus"). In it Erasmus contrasts the fearful and superstitious death of George, who noisily departs this life surrounded by priests and laden with indulgences, with the serene death of Cornelius, who simply commends himself and his family to God.

Most of the literature about dying well—like the pertinent sections of Loarte's Esercitio and Borja's reflections entitled Algunos remedios para que los siervos de Dios no teman la muerte—was intended for persons who wanted to prepare for their own deaths.[60] Some, however, was for the ministers who attended people in their last days or hours, like sections from Nadal's exhortations on Jesuit ministries[61] and especially Polanco's Methodus ad eos adiuvandos, qui moriuntur. These four documents provide the most concrete information about Jesuit attitudes and practice.[62] Some inferences can be drawn, however, from the serene attitude Nadal adopted concerning his own death.[63] Favre's attitude was similar.[64]

Of thirty-two chapters, Loarte devoted one to "what a Christian ought to do in sickness and danger of death" and another to "remedies for temptations at time of death."[65] Like the rest of the book, these chapters assumed a relationship with God that was "familiar" and confident, close to what Erasmus depicted for Cornelius. Loarte repeated the accepted wisdom that at the moment of death the demons intensified their attack, and he briefly explained the standard remedies for temptations against faith and hope. He said that one must especially remember, however, that God, the angels, and the saints—over whom the devils cannot prevail—are on one's side. He finally advised the person, as death approached, to call in some devout friends who could console with their good words and read from some holy book, especially from the accounts of Jesus' suffering and death in the New Testament.

Borja's little leaflet, published posthumously, was written in 1568 while he was general, just a few years before he himself died. While acknowledging death as an evil, it presented considerations and practices to forestall or diminish fear of it in those who have tried to live as good Christians. Among the considerations was, of course, the remembrance of Christ, who "by dying destroyed our death, by rising restored our life." Filled with quotations from the Fathers, the piece reads almost like a patristic homily.

Nadal's advice to the minister was sober—indeed, cool and businesslike. It was also brief, as he referred his listeners for further advice to persons experienced in assisting the dying. Although he dismissed the idea that everybody at death's door is tempted in faith and sees the devil, he stated that these things did occur. The minister must help the sick person deal with such disturbances of spirit, make sure an honest will is prepared, and, if necessary, warn of approaching death. The person should of course be fortified by confession, Communion, and the last anointing.

The twenty chapters of Polanco's *Methodus* provide a fuller picture. As a handbook for those called upon to assist the dying, it represents a genre that extends back at least to Jean Gerson's *La médicine de l'âme* of the early fifteenth century. Polanco's book, first published in 1575, ran through a number of editions and became especially influential when, after 1591, it often joined his *Directorium* for confessors and Madrid's book on frequent Communion in one volume. It consistently suggested a preparation for death like Cornelius's, but, unlike Erasmus's *De praeparatione*, descended to practical details and suggestions to help the minister help the dying person.

Nowhere more emphatically than in the *Methodus* do those two consistently inculcated ideals of Jesuit pastoral theory receive expression—the minister's need to accommodate to the situation and his role as bearer and facilitator of consolation. Polanco enunciated these principles in the first chapter and frequently returned to them. He summarized them in two adverbs—the minister should always and down to the most minute detail act "prudently and lovingly" (*prudenter et amanter*).

The Latin style of the *Methodus* was correct according to classical usage but filled with scriptural allusions and imagery, as were the many prayers

Polanco had composed and suggested might be used or adapted to different situations found in the sickroom. In other words, these were not prayers according to set formulas. He proposed Christ as one's "brother," one's "truly faithful friend." What ultimately consoled a person at the hour of death, moreover, was "the love of our eternal Father." As the individual awaited death, the minister or one of those standing by might read an account of Jesus' suffering and death from one of the Gospels, the First or Second Epistle to the Corinthians, the Epistle to the Philippians, the Second Epistle to Timothy, or the last chapter from the Book of Revelation.

Indulgences were mentioned once in the book—the devils, as well as Mary and the saints, just slightly more often. Among the duties of anybody attending the dying was to make sure that the person had made a will that provided for his family. This was standard advice. Once obligations to one's family and creditors were satisfied, the person might wish to leave something for "the poor or some pious institute." If the individual wanted suggestions, the Jesuit should be careful not to mention the Society directly or indirectly; he could, however, indicate help for souls in purgatory, alms for the poor, for ransom of captives, for orphans of both sexes, for debtors held in prison, for hospitals.

Chapter eighteen, one of the longest in the book, dealt with how to help criminals condemned to death. It reflected and promoted the increased concern in the sixteenth century with such individuals.[66] We know, nonetheless, that confraternities had been engaged in this work of mercy for at least two centuries. One of the oldest and most important had been founded in Florence by a group of devout young men, *fanciulli*, in 1343. Its Roman counterpart was founded by expatriate Florentines in 1488. Named San Giovanni Decollato, its most famous member was Michelangelo, registered as a brother from 1514 until 1564. When Michelangelo died that year, the confraternity was in charge of his funeral rites in Rome. Like many other confraternities, those dedicated to comforting the condemned commissioned important works of art for their chapels, oratories, and meeting rooms.[67]

Polanco at least indirectly drew upon the experience of such confraternities. The difficult and delicate nature of their task led the confraternities to require training and indoctrination for lay members to whom this comforting was entrusted, and they committed their instructions to writing.[68] Especially after Polanco's book was translated into the vernacular (for example, Italian, in part, 1576; German, 1584; French, 1599), it influenced this literature, and thus had an impact beyond the clergy.

Historians have not been loath to point out the limitations and ambivalences of such activities by the confraternities, especially in the post-Tridentine period.[69] The confraternities represent, nonetheless, a notable effort to mitigate a harsh system of justice, and the eighteenth chapter of Polanco's book is a remarkably compassionate document in which the minister is, in keeping with the tradition, more consistently described simply as "the consoler" than in any other chapter. Never should he desert the condemned person, even up to the last moment. Once the criminal was executed, the minister continued his office of consoler by visiting the criminal's family to try to assuage their sorrow and lessen their shame.

Polanco paid so much attention to ministry to criminals condemned to death because by the early 1550's the Jesuits were very involved in it, sometimes in localities where other priests refused to minister because of superstition or fear of infamy, as in certain parts of Sicily.[70] In Seville in 1565 the Jesuits introduced the practice of allowing prisoners about to be executed to receive the Eucharist.[71] Although the Jesuits usually acted on their own initiative, in 1555 the cardinal inquisitor in Lisbon asked the Jesuit provincial to send somebody to hear the confessions of eight men condemned to death. The Jesuits did so and then stayed with them in prison three days and nights until their executions.[72] In Rome in 1561, two Jesuits attended the duke of Paliano and other disgraced and despised relatives of the recently deceased Pope Paul IV as they awaited execution for crimes committed during that pontificate.[73] Polanco also reported how Jesuits dissuaded "persons of both sexes" from suicide. In at least one case the Jesuit achieved success by persuading the man to make a general confession and thus put his past behind him.[74]

In their ministry to the dying, the Jesuits encouraged their disciples to do as they were doing when the occasion arose. Polanco in his circular letter to the whole Society in late 1565 told with obvious approval about a woman—"una donna devota"—who frequented the Jesuit church in Rome. "Finding herself at the bedside of a dying person, where there was no pastor, other priest, or anybody else to undertake the office of charity to help the person die well, she undertook to do it herself. To the great admiration of the bystanders, she comforted and helped the dying person and commended his soul to God."[75]

Ministry to Prostitutes

Prostitution, as well as Christian attitudes toward it and institutions to deal with it, has a long history.[76] By the beginning of the sixteenth century, especially in Italy, these histories entered a new phase.[77] In Venice and Rome the "courtesan" had emerged with a new social status and acceptability.[78] Alongside these relatively few were great numbers of other women who plied their trade in miserable conditions and out of sheer desperation.[79]

Almost everywhere, including Venice and Rome, prostitution elicited more official and unofficial concern than before. This was in part simply a result of urban growth—prostitutes were more numerous and more in evidence, and they seemed therefore more of a threat to public decency. But with the appearance of syphilis in the late fifteenth century, they became a threat to public health. The disease triggered an alarm that called attention to prostitutes in a new way and sparked additional efforts from local governments and other entities to deal with them.[80] In any case, they were unavoidably visible and often patently wretched.

By 1543 Ignatius had founded in Rome Casa Santa Marta, and Jesuits elsewhere followed suit by engaging in various ways in ministry to the women. The Jesuits, like other religious enthusiasts before them, believed that one of the best ways to persuade them to give up their sinful lives was through preaching. In many or most cities of Europe, municipal authorities had long supported this notion. In the sixteenth century they imposed on bordellos and the persons who managed them an increasing number of restrictions and regulations, some of which pertained to religious practice. In Seville, for instance, brothels were closed on Sundays and prostitutes required to assist at mass.[81] In other cities officials forced prostitutes on certain days to hear sermons directed especially at them.[82]

From our contemporary perspective, however, perhaps the most curious aspect of this whole phenomenon is the piety and regular religious practice of a fair number of prostitutes and courtesans. True, many of them went to church to find customers, a fact well known to both ecclesiastical and municipal authorities. Others were accused of being "pagan of heart although Christian of speech."[83] Nonetheless, it seems incontestable that some of these women, especially those driven to their situation by poverty or in it out of the inertia of family system, were sincerely religious.[84] This factor—plus ill health and the threat of disease, advancing age, economic insecurity, physical and financial abuse from their pimps—made them more susceptible to changing their ways than we might at first imagine, especially if a concrete alternative to their way of life was offered.

In Florence officials gathered the prostitutes of the city in the cathedral every year on Thursday of the fifth week of lent. During mass on this day the passage from Luke's Gospel was read about the sinful woman who washed Jesus' feet with her tears in the house of Simon the Pharisee (7:36–50). When Laínez preached on this occasion in 1548, he attracted a large number of prostitutes and ordinary citizens. Polanco related that as a result of Laínez's preaching seven or eight repented and were received "into the homes of honest matrons, who would help them find an honest way of life."[85] We infer, therefore, that part of Laínez's sermon proposed to the matrons what their responsibilities or opportunities were in this regard.

This is not the only instance of such assistance from "honest matrons." Pedro de Ribadeneira recalled how as a young man he saw Ignatius himself accompanying courtesans *(nobiles meretrices)* through the streets to the homes of some of the most prominent women of Rome.[86] He singled out by name Leonor Osorio, consort of Juan de Vega, then the ambassador of Charles V. She continued to take a special interest in these women when he became viceroy of Sicily, just as she had been especially supportive of the Casa Santa Marta in Rome.

Laínez preached in Palermo on the same Thursday in lent the very next year, 1549. The viceroy ordered the prostitutes to attend, and "many were converted to the Lord." Leonor took sixteen into her household. She intended to procure dowries so that some might get married, and she helped seven others, after they had a strange and emotional encounter with the nuns, to enter a monastery of *Conversae,* that is, of reformed prostitutes. She kept a few with her as part of her staff.[87]

Polanco's account of how the seven came to enter the monastery bears repeating. Leonor lodged nine of the prostitutes in the monastery with the promise they would remain there only until they could get married, but immediately upon arrival they said they wanted to become nuns. A few days later, on Monday of Holy Week, these prospective novices behaved so badly in choir that the nuns ordered them out of the chapel. One of the "more hardened" hid in a part of the monastery where, by accident, she was able unseen to watch the nuns take the discipline after choir. She was so touched by the Lord at what she saw that she was "filled with compunction and consolation" and declared that she wanted then and there to have her hair shorn and to take the veil. Six others shortly followed suit, and the nuns obliged their requests. The viceroy sent Laínez and Doménech a few days later to see that all was in order. Only two of the original nine decided in favor of matrimony.

These stories reveal three solutions to the reformed prostitute's dilemma—matrimony, service as a domestic in some large household, or entrance into a monastery of *Conversae.* Who would want to marry these women? Once they had a dowry, such a marriage might be attractive even to their former pimps, so that the task for reformers was to assure that the marriage was itself "honest." Although sordid motives were a constant danger, marriage to prostitutes surely did not everywhere carry the same stigma that in other times and places has been attached to it. In 1199 Pope Innocent III had declared that marriage to them was in fact a work of great piety and that persuasion persisted into the sixteenth century—marry a prostitute and save your soul![88]

No doubt respectable husbands could often be found for these women. Manuel da Nóbrega promised good marriages for prostitutes who emigrated to Brazil.[89] Although the Jesuits may have inflated the figures, they reported even from Goa their success in finding husbands for concubines.[90] An unusual case illustrates the point. In Rome in 1565 a Jew was thrown into jail on charges brought by a prostitute. One of the Jesuits discovered that the man wanted to become a Christian, so he went to the prostitute and told her that, as she had been the cause of the imprisonment, she should under these happy circumstances be the cause of his release. She dropped the charges and, further, volunteered to pay for all the expenses he had incurred in prison so that she might have a bigger part in his conversion. Then the neophyte, instructed by the Jesuit, went to her and said that, just as he had come to Christianity through her, she should leave her life of sin "for love of him." She did so, and soon married him "to live like a good, honest Christian."[91]

The monasteries of the *Conversae* had some medieval antecedents—there was one in Bologna, for instance, in the thirteenth century.[92] But they became more numerous toward the end of the fifteenth century and the beginning of the sixteenth. One was founded in Paris in 1492, and several opened in other French cities, in Lombardy, Piedmont, other northern provinces of Italy, and elsewhere.[93] In 1520 one opened in Rome. Generally under the patronage of Mary Magdalene, the repentant sinner, the monasteries imposed a life of severe penance and strict cloister—obviously not an attractive alternative for every woman who wanted to change her ways or escape from her situation.

Nonetheless, women sometimes chose this alternative—freely or out of desperation. In Ferrara in 1548 some prostitutes began, seemingly as a self-initiated group, to go to Jay for confession. As a result they resolved not only to give up prostitution but to enter a monastery of *Conversae*.[94] The Jesuits reported, however, that they themselves generally tried to locate these women according to their choice either in a convent or in matrimony;

sometimes all that is reported, whether about Gandía, Valencia, Goa, Palermo, Seville, or Rome is that they helped these women "take up a better state of life."[95] Entrance into a monastery of the *Conversae* did not, of course, guarantee perseverance or even moral probity, as the Jesuit Benedetto Palmio discovered to his dismay when a scandal broke out in 1561 at the Convertite alla Giudecca in Venice.[96]

Jesuits in Italy did a lot of preaching in the monasteries of *Conversae* and were sometimes involved in their reform. In Palermo in 1547, Doménech discovered that the monastery there was torn with strife. He managed to get rid of the abbess, roundly hated by all the nuns, and to install a "widowed matron" for the time being. Meanwhile, he begged alms for the nuns' temporal sustenance.[97]

In 1555 in Modena, where the Jesuits had no church, they began to hear confessions in the chapel of the monastery of the *Conversae,* but discovered that some of their other penitents refused to return to them because they did not want to be associated with such a location.[98] Some who frequented the Jesuit church in Ferrara undertook in 1556 exhorting prostitutes to a better way of life, which led to their being shunned by many of their peers.[99]

That same year in Venice the rector from time to time led groups of ten or twelve persons through the First Week of the *Exercises,* which on one occasion included a prostitute who made a general confession and gave up her former life.[100] In Goa and elsewhere in India Jesuits incurred the displeasure of the Portuguese for preaching against the selling of natives into slavery and concubinage.[101] In 1556 in some towns in the neighborhood of Seville, however, the Jesuits seemed gratified that the civil authorities imposed penalties on prostitutes who feigned repentance, and earlier at Evora in Portugal they were instrumental in securing other penalties for prostitutes.[102]

Two facts about how Jesuits dealt with prostitution are easily discernible: the sheer quantity of their involvement with these women and the variety of attitudes and relationships that this involvement entailed. The Jesuits often acted on their own initiative, but in general concert with the policies and expectations of other reformers and civil authorities. On a few occasions, as in India, they opposed official or quasi-official policy; on others, they acted almost as its agents or instigators.

They founded one institution, however, that was an innovation—the Casa Santa Marta in Rome and its imitators in other cities, including Florence, Pisa, Padua, Bologna, Modena, Milan, Palermo, Agrigento, Trapani, Valladolid, and Messina.[103] In late 1542 or early 1543, Ignatius conceived the idea of establishing a house that would admit women on a temporary basis and provide them with the situation and resources to make a choice about their future. He had two kinds of women in mind—unmarried prostitutes and women estranged from their husbands who had entered a life of prostitution. For the former, dowries were to be collected whereby they could freely choose either to get married or to enter a monastery of *Conversae* (or possibly some other monastery).[104] For the latter an opportunity was offered to work toward a reconciliation or, that failing, to live henceforth like nuns even though still bound by the marriage vows.[105] He won approval for the idea from Pope Paul III, who on 16 February 1543 established the Compagnia della grazia as the confraternity that would oversee and fund the institution, which was opened that year in a building facing the present Piazza Collegio Romano.

The most concise, reliable, and informative document about the origins and first years of the Casa Santa Marta is a memorandum, 1551, by Polanco. The house was founded, he reported, for single women who wanted to give up a life of sin and for married women who were discovered in sin outside their homes. He said that by 1546 the difficulty of placing in other monasteries women who wanted to become nuns led to constituting part of the Casa as a monastery for them. All who lived in the house were under a "mother abbess and her vicars," and they followed appropriate discipline for their life in common. A confraternity "of all sorts of persons" governed the house and was responsible for providing alms and counsel. Polanco reported that in the years it has been operating it has helped about three hundred women. At present there were about twenty nuns and four others in the house, but the number has reached as high as forty or more. The Society was the originator of the house and functioned in four ways: (1) for its founding: it expedited the papal bulls, collected alms, gave money from its own meager resources; (2) it sought the first women and selected the first directress *(gubernatrice);* (3) it organized the confraternity, into whose hands the work was entirely committed; (4) it helped in drawing up the rule of life and supplied preachers and confessors for the women's spiritual profit.[106]

Although Ignatius is generally credited with being the first person to conceive such an institution, it seems a woman by the name of Laura Baliarda had tried to establish a similar one in Modena in 1535.[107] In 1542 Giammatteo Giberti, the reforming bishop of Verona, made special provision for repentant prostitutes who did not want to become nuns.[108] Ignatius may or may not have known about these precedents, if precedents they were. In any case, Santa Marta emerges with much clearer contours because we have more ample documentation about it; it is more important because under Jesuit inspiration similar houses were opened in other cities. Santa Marta was, even with possible antecedents, a strikingly original institution of social assistance.[109] It sought to reinsert into society those who desired it.

The Santa Marta in Rome could house approximately sixty women. Its discipline was like that of a convent. Women who entered had to promise, under pain of losing the possessions they brought with them, not to leave until they were settled in one of the several alternatives to the satisfaction of the confraternity. When they applied for entrance, they were interviewed about their family, health, marital situation, and other factors required for a "case history" according to a rather sophisticated questionnaire.

The very name of the institution suggested how it was meant to differ from the *Conversae*. In the latter the women were under the patronage, as well as the stigma, of Magdalene, and were destined to a life of penance for their sins. The Casa was under the patronage of Martha, to whom no such stigma or destiny was attached. Ignatius chose Martha surely because, like many of his contemporaries, he believed that her sister Mary was Mary Magdalene.

The Casa Santa Marta was unable, however, to sustain its original character. Within four years of its founding, a dozen women housed there petitioned Paul III to allow them to remain on a permanent basis as, in effect, *convertite*. The house was divided into two sections, but within less than a decade the other women were moved to a so-called Casa Pia. By 1573 Santa Marta had become a full-fledged monastery reserved for virgins.[110]

The Casa Pia continued, however, the original tradition for at least several decades and even added to the two options for the women the further possibility of entering service as a domestic. The description of the Casa by Gregory Martin, 1576–78, is at present our unique source for the subsequent history of the enterprise:

> They make franke and free choise whether they wil live a simple life in service with noble wemen and honest matrones of the citie, or marry, or become Religious. A free choise I say of these three conditions, al very honest and sufficient, that no necessity of any one state might hinder their Conversion, but that they might esteme their owne free choise to their contentation, rather a reward of their present goodnes, then penance for their former naughtinesse. And see here the charity of the Romanes rejoycing upon one sinner repenting more then upon others nintiene. If it please them to serve in single life, how many noble matrones are desirous to have them and to feede Christ in his litle ones, such especially as before also neglected no occasion to helpe their Conversion. If they wil marry, neither dowries are wanting (of which I wil speake apart hereafter) nor

men of honest state and calling, who to make them or to keepe them honest and chast wemen, thincke it no stayne (although Italians and Romanes) to take them to wife; and if it be, yet they preferre the meritorious act therof. But if they choose with Marie Magdalen the best part, to sit at Christes feete in quiet contemplation, and by penance to wash his feete with their teares of true repentance and satisfaction of their former life, and love much bycause much is forgeven them: breefely if leaving worldly matters to Marthaes, they wil doe continuall penance with Marie by entering into Religion voluntarely (for to compel them by any meanes directly or indirectly is no lesse then a matter of Excommunication) then are they placed in the Nonnery of S. Marie Magdalen, and there continew for ever in the service of God day and night, as is before sayd generally of Religious wemen.[111]

The Casa del Soccorso, founded in Venice in 1577 along the lines of Santa Marta, survived in its original purpose until early in the seventeenth century, when it began to be assumed that the inmates would always move on to a monastery of the *Conversae*.[112] We have only scattered bits of information about the houses in other cities. For instance, Nadal related how in Messina "women of honest life" went through the city to try to bring prostitutes to repentance and, presumably, to enter the casa, which he founded there sometime before 1553.[113] The house founded in Palermo in 1554 settled about forty women in matrimony within the first five months of its existence.[114]

In Italy, Spain, and Portugal during this period, then, for all the restrictions placed on prostitutes, they were recognized as having certain rights as Christians that by and large were respected for even the most miserable among them, and they had an access to the church at least to the end of the period I am considering—a privilege that has surely not been accorded them in other times. To help them out of their predicament, religiously motivated persons devised concrete means that, for all their limitations, recognized the social, economic, and even psychological ramifications of a decision to try to begin a new way of life. The Jesuits both reflected and promoted a concern for these women that in the long history of prostitution seems, for complex reasons of demography and social attitudes, to have achieved a certain peak especially in Italy in the mid-sixteenth century.

Orphans and Daughters of Prostitutes

During the Middle Ages foundlings were the almost exclusive focus of efforts to provide for children who had no home or parents, a phenomenon about which we are reasonably well informed.[115] In the early decades of the sixteenth century, especially in Italy, attention began to be directed also to "street kids"—boys and girls either orphaned at an early age or abandoned by their parents to shift for themselves. Plague, famine, war, economic depression, and population growth in the urban areas—all contributed to a situation in which there seemed to be more such children than before. The problem and efforts to alleviate it have been little studied.[116]

Seemingly the first person to address the problem in an influential way was the Venetian patrician Gerolamo Miani (or Emiliani) through his Compagnia dei servi dei poveri. In 1525, when he was about forty years old, he underwent a religious conversion that led him to the poor and sick. After the famine of 1527–29 he began to give special attention to orphaned child beggars, and in 1531 he opened near San Rocco a shelter for them and then more adequate quarters in the Ospedale degli Incurabili. He is thus given credit for being the founder of separate institutions for such children, who up to that time had at best been lodged in often squalid appendages to hospitals. Miani soon thereafter left Venice to continue his work elsewhere. The program in these institutions was, besides to provide food and housing, to teach reading, writing, and a trade. Miani eventually settled in Somasca, outside Milan, where he died in 1537, but his compagnia (the "Somascans") lived after him.[117] From about this time records of similar institutions begin to appear.

While Ignatius and the others were in the Veneto in the late 1530's, five worked in the Ospedale degli Incurabili and thus experienced Miani's work firsthand. It is not surprising, then, that just a few years after the companions' arrival in Rome, Ignatius was among those instrumental in the establishment in 1541 of a Compagnia degli orfani to care for boys and girls in two separate institutions. The orphanage for boys at S. Maria in Aquiro near the Pantheon has been in continuous operation since its establishment.[118]

This first venture presaged others, about most of which we know practically nothing, although the founding of such institutions and their correlative confraternities is often mentioned in the sources. The Jesuits seem to have been especially active in Sicily. Jerónimo Doménech early on saw to the founding of an orphanage for boys and girls in Palermo, and in 1550 Laínez instigated a confraternity to fund and care for it.[119] In 1552 a similar confraternity was founded at Messina, and that same year Nadal arranged for the funding of orphanages in Catania and Caltagirone.[120] In 1549 Pedro Doménech founded under the patronage of Queen Catherine an orphanage for thirty boys in Lisbon. He was then a diocesan priest, but he worked in closest collaboration with the Jesuits, as we have seen. Under the inspiration of this orphanage, the Jesuits had by 1552 established similar institutions in the Portuguese dependencies of India and Brazil.[121]

At Gandía, Messina, and elsewhere they begged dowries for girls who wanted to be married, although it is not always clear whether the girls were affiliated with an institution or not.[122] The aspect of the Jesuits' activity about which we are best informed are the institutions for the young daughters of prostitutes.

By 1546 the Casa Santa Marta was financially and administratively stable enough for Ignatius effectively to turn his attention to these girls, who seemed almost predestined to continue in the profession of their mothers— a profession in which Rome abounded. He understood, therefore, that families transmit from generation to generation patterns of behavior difficult to modify or break. This led to the founding that year of the Conservatorio [Compagnia] delle Vergini Miserabili at the church of Santa Catarina de' Funari, sustained and managed, of course, by a confraternity of men and women founded for that purpose. The idea was to take in girls no younger than ten and no older than twelve, educate them in some modest way, and then provide dowries whereby, once again, they could either marry or enter a convent.[123] The institution seemed to thrive almost from the beginning, and by 1585 it was large enough to hold about 150 girls. We do not know how the girls were recruited for the Conservatorio, but we infer that until the pontificate of Pius V (1566–72) their mothers' permission was required. Pius determined that girls could be taken into the Conservatorio against parental wishes—by what process we know not.

Similar institutions were founded in other Italian cities either directly or indirectly under Jesuit influence. In Florence, for instance, between 1557 and 1558 a laywoman named Marietta Gondi established the Fanciulle della Pietà, and Francesco Rosati and his wife the Poverine di Borgo S. Niccolò. In 1564 a similar institution was founded in Naples and within a short time supposedly housed over four hundred girls.[124]

In 1560 Benedetto Palmio was primarily responsible for the founding in Venice of the Conservatorio [Casa] delle Zitelle Periclitanti. It opened that year with about 30 girls under the direction of some noble laywomen, principally Maria Bernardo and Isabella Contarini. It thrived, eventually developing an elaborate and full-scale program of assistance to the girls from the moment they entered until their marriage or entrance into a convent—and, to some extent, even thereafter. The girls normally stayed in the Conservatorio for five or six years. By 1567 there were 90 girls, and fifteen years later some 180.[125]

Brian Pullan's assessment of the Conservatorio is apposite and applies to additional institutions of social assistance with which the Jesuits and others were associated: "Palmio and his disciples were not attempting mere hand-to-mouth charity, by the temporary relief of physical needs: instead, they aimed at a take-over bid, at establishing an institution which would, in the interests of the soul, assume all the functions of a zealous and exacting parent."[126]

Jews and New Christians

The Jews, a minority group long beset by civil injustices, entered a particularly oppressive phase of their history in the Mediterranean world with the issuance of the decrees expelling them from Spain in 1492 and Portugal in 1496. The decrees dramatically focused attention on them and had repercussions in Italy, where, along with other factors, they gave impetus to an increased display and practical implementation of prejudice, including the establishment of the ghetto in places that had never known it. In 1516, for instance, Venice forced the Jews to live in a certain quarter of the city, and similar measures were beginning to be expedited elsewhere.[127]

The Jews had traditionally enjoyed more freedom and been subjected to less harassment in the Papal State than perhaps anywhere else in Europe, but the pontificate of Paul III marked the beginning of a new zeal to proselytize them. Proselytism advanced to persecution when, in 1555, Paul IV created the Roman ghetto and began to enforce some of the most stringent restrictions on the Jews' freedom in all of Italy and to countenance judicial atrocities against them in the Papal State.[128]

Even if they had wanted to, the first Jesuits could not avoid the issue.[129] In Spain the fierce hostility against the Jews extended to the "New Christians"—Jewish converts to Christianity and even their descendants for several generations.[130] The result by the middle of the sixteenth century was that all the major and most influential religious orders in Spain refused to admit novices of Jewish origin. The pressure on the new and fragile Society of Jesus to follow suit was almost overwhelming, so that some deliberate decision had to be made.

Ignatius refused to yield. If local conditions in Spain or Portugal made it inadvisable for "New Christians" to be received on the spot, he wanted them sent to Italy or some other neutral location for their training and ministry. He and his two immediate successors as general maintained the same policy for "Moriscos," Christians of Muslim ancestry in Spain.[131] Despite increasing pressure from within the Society, his policy prevailed in principle until 1593, when the Fifth General Congregation, in the wake of a severe internal crisis, absolutely excluded from entrance persons of Jewish or Muslim descent. Pedro de Ribadeneira and Antonio Possevino, now veterans of the early days, complained bitterly about the decision as a betrayal of Ignatius and the spirit of the Society. (Possevino was himself almost certainly of Jewish ancestry.)[132] The prohibition was mitigated in 1608 and again in 1923, but not fully rescinded until 1946. That Laínez was easily elected to succeed Ignatius as general indicates that, at least in the leadership of the Society, Ignatius's attitude prevailed during the period I am considering, and the lack of *limpieza de sangre* was not an obstacle to the highest position.

In Italy the Jesuits were in fact proud of Jewish recruits. Polanco related with satisfaction how a young Jewish man had begun catechism with Lutherans in Venice, but then had come under the influence of the Jesuits and been admitted to the Society in 1552 under the new and significant name *Baptista Romanus*. He was a marvel, for he could recite practically all of the Old Testament from memory in Hebrew, had traveled widely in Palestine and Germany, and knew Spanish, German, and Turkish.[133] This was, in fact, Giovanni Battista Eliano, grandson of the great Elijah Levita. He went on to teach Hebrew and Arabic at the Collegio Romano and then spent many years as a missionary in the Middle East among Copts and Maronites.[134] After 1563 he composed and published in Rome an extremely interesting document, a catechism for the illiterate consisting almost entirely of illustrations.[135]

Nadal, who often had to bear the brunt of Jesuit policy in Spain, faithfully implemented it and defended it to both clergy and laity. Among those he had to face on the issue was Silíceo, the formidable archbishop of Toledo, but he also repeatedly encountered opposition elsewhere. He noted in his diary, 1561, for example: "Count Rui Gómez took me seriously to task for our allowing 'neophytes' to be received into the Society. I answered him gravely with arguments to confirm our liberty in this regard."[136] After the king, Gómez was perhaps the most influential political figure in Spain.

While the polemic with Siliceo was at its height, 1552–54, the Society in Spain continued to accept New Christians, among whom two were outstanding. The first was Gaspar de Loarte, author of the *Esercitio*, whom Ignatius soon named rector of the college at Genoa. The second was Alfonso de Pisa, a well-known medical doctor and mathematician, whom Ignatius installed as professor of physics at the Collegio Romano in 1555.

In 1558 the Jesuits accepted Francisco de Toledo, a brilliant young professor at the University of Salamanca, who after a few months' novitiate at Simancas began to teach logic at the Collegio Romano in 1559 to become one of the most famous Jesuits in Italy for his preaching and learning. A number of Spanish and Portuguese New Christians became members in the Province of India, beginning with Henrique Henriques, who started working there under Xavier in 1547. Some of these missionaries joined in Europe, but some entered in India itself, where inside and outside the Society the same problems manifested themselves as in Portugal and Spain.[137] But we shall never know just how many New Christians the Jesuits took into the Society because they kept no consistent records.

A letter from the rector of the Jesuit college at Córdoba to Borja in 1572 reveals the reputation the Jesuits had earned. The school had nearly six hundred students, many of them from the best families of the city. All the boys who believed they had a vocation to a religious order entered the Dominican convent of San Pablo, which they said was a convent of *caballeros*. According to them, nobody entered the Jesuit order except "Jews."[138]

Before Nadal entered the Society he had become involved in a bizarre incident at Avignon. The Jews there wanted to make him their chief rabbi because he knew Hebrew so well, but he exploded with indignation at the invitation, calling them "diabolical spirits and heretics in the Law of Moses."[139] After several years in the Society he overcame at least some of his prejudices, but to the end he remained a product of his times.[140] Among the leading Jesuits of the first generation, Araoz was deeply prejudiced in favor of *limpieza de sangre* and opposed Ignatius's policy.

Ignatius on several occasions expressed the wish to be of Jewish blood so as to be of the same race as Christ.[141] He left at least the Spaniards among his listeners astounded, if not shocked. He was keen of course on active proselytism among the Jews, and, sharing other prejudices of his contemporaries, he supported some of the severe measures taken against them by Paul IV.[142]

From his earliest days in Rome he was responsible for some Jewish conversions, and he encouraged others to work for the same end. He was also largely responsible for the bull *Cupientes iudaeos* of Paul III in 1542 that allowed Jewish converts to retain their property, even that obtained by usury if it was impossible to return. This bull obviously removed a major obstacle to conversion and indirectly gave impetus to proselytizing by increasing the likelihood of its success.

When prospective Christians in Rome underwent instruction in their new faith from the Jesuits, they were at first housed with them in the community. By 1543, however, Ignatius had convinced Paul III to establish an independent institution where, in separate sections for men and women, they could be housed, fed, and instructed until their Baptism. Like the Casa Santa Marta, this was conceived as a half-way house designed to facilitate the converts' entrance into Christian society. Ignatius was much assisted in this enterprise by Margaret of Austria ("Madama"), bastard daughter of Charles V and wife of the pope's grandson, Ottavio Farnese, and by Giroloma Orsini, one of the pope's daughters-in-law, mother of the young cardinal Alessandro Farnese.[143]

When the Casa dei Catecumeni first opened, the Jesuits contributed to it their extra furniture and assigned to it the alms they had been collecting for that purpose. Ignatius retained some direct influence over the management of the Casa for several years. From the beginning, however, it was officially under a confraternity of priests, which within a year a papal constitution changed into a confraternity of lay persons.[144] The confraternity gradually assumed full responsibility for funding and management.

The Jewish community deeply resented the Casa. In 1554 Pope Julius III required each synagogue in Rome to contribute ten ducats per annum to its upkeep, and, when later the number of synagogues was reduced to one, Paul IV imposed a different kind of financial exaction on the Jewish community. The Casa continued through subsequent centuries as a source of tension between the papacy and the Jews of Rome.[145] Nonetheless, the idea was exportable, and similar institutions opened in Venice, Bologna, Ferrara, and Padua.[146]

In Italy the Jesuits gladly accepted opportunities to preach to the Jews when, like the prostitutes, they were herded together against their will. Polanco in one of his circular letters to the whole Society in 1561 told of an occasion when the cardinal vicar of Rome ordered all the Jews of the city to be present in Saint Peter's for a sermon by Laínez. From a pulpit set up in the nave, Laínez preached to them in the presence of fourteen or fifteen cardinals for two hours. As a result, Polanco reported, some of the Jews were disposed to accept Christianity, and others at least conceded that his sermon was the best they had heard in fifty years.[147]

One of the Jesuits in Rome at the end of this period seems to have made the conversion of the Jews his specialty, and Polanco several times narrated how he worked, sometimes with questionable tactics, first on one and then another to secure their conversion.[148] The Jesuits occasionally succeeded in having the death penalty lifted for Jewish criminals when they said they wanted to become Christians.[149] In early 1554 Bobadilla presided in Ancona at the burning of the Talmud, a measure recently ordered by the Roman Inquisition under Cardinal Carafa and sanctioned by Pope Julius III.[150]

The original ten companions and their first recruits in Italy were for the most part Iberian expatriates. They thus carried a special awareness of Jewish-Christian tension with them into Italy, where it also happened to be reaching new heights. The first generation of Jesuits were by no means innocent of the prejudices of their day, although in individual instances and in the official policy of the Society they rose above some of them.

They worked to make it easier for Jews who wished to do so to become Christians. Their interest in proselytizing promoted a shift in Rome in official policy in that regard and lent at least indirect support to the harsh measures against the Jewish community in Rome and the Papal State by Paul IV and subsequent popes. These Roman measures had repercussions in the rest of Italy, often as confirmation and intensification of anti-Jewish policies governments had already set in place. Important though the Jesuits' ministry to the Jews was in Italy, it was mostly confined there. In northern Europe the Jesuits were few and occupied with other problems. In the Iberian peninsula there were no Jews to convert.

Confraternities and the Marian Congregations

For several centuries confraternities had been deeply involved in social and religious life in all parts of Europe.[151] In Lyons, for instance, in 1496 there were at least thirty such associations "organized for reasons that were at least in part religious," and a similarly dense pattern prevailed in the cities of France and the Empire.[152] They were especially numerous in Spain, where as elsewhere they evinced, along with certain traits common to them all, an almost infinite variety in their patterns of piety, in the "works" they undertook for their own members and for others, in their relationships to civil and ecclesiastical institutions, and in the social and economic composition of their membership.[153]

Sometimes in practice the main purpose of these voluntary associations was mutual aid to their own members, or not much more than neighborliness and conviviality, but always within some religious framework. In most of them the religious element was dominant. The so-called Third Orders affiliated with the Dominicans and Franciscans were an integral part of this picture, and they were originally models for many of the confraternities.[154]

When Ignatius and his companions first arrived in Italy, they would have found religious confraternities to be such numerous and established realities that, viewed from one angle, they at times seemed almost to define the Italian church; viewed from another, they looked like civic or municipal institutions, religiously motivated—making distinctions practically meaningless in the sixteenth century.[155] From whichever angle, however, they were not branch offices of either the parish or the local town hall but self-governing and self-determining entities working in some self-defined way toward "the common good." The attention historians have paid to the confraternity known as the Oratory of Divine Love founded in Genoa in 1497 has badly obscured how it fits, granted its special traits and importance, into an older and almost indescribably widespread pattern.[156] In that city alone between 1480 and 1580, there were at least 134 such organizations.[157]

By the early sixteenth century, new confraternities, at least in major cities like Venice and Rome, were effecting shifts in the character of the institution that included in some instances a movement away from mutual aid toward more emphasis on assistance to nonmembers.[158] Further shifts were occurring during the century, but the Jesuits' role in the phenomenon has received little analysis and has, to say the least, "been underrecorded."[159] In any case, the confraternities continued to play an enormous role in religious and social life, as indicated by the fact that between 1540 and 1600 some sixty were founded in Rome alone.[160]

The Jesuits early established relationships with existing confraternities. In 1540 Ignatius by letter promoted in his native Azpeitia the Confraternity of the Blessed Sacrament, founded in Rome just two years earlier by the Dominican Tommaso Stella.[161] In 1541 he and five other Jesuits joined that same confraternity at the church of Santa Maria della Strada, where the Gesù stands today.[162] At about the same time, Ignatius joined the Confraternity of the Holy Spirit attached to the hospital of that name and paid enough money to guarantee membership for the next twenty years.[163] He probably joined these institutions because of spiritual benefits like the special indulgences to which members had access, for he does not seem to have played an active part in either of them.

The annals of the early Society are filled, however, with instances of Jesuits' more vital engagement with confraternities, of which only the most meager sample can be provided here. For instance, sometime around 1545 Polanco preached in Pistoia to a confraternity whose members gathered regularly for an hour in the evening before supper for exhortations and prayer; they wanted to elect him rector, but Ignatius refused permission.[164] At Gandía by 1550 the Jesuits provided a chapel for a confraternity of flagellants, and they sometimes preached to them.[165] In Palermo at the same time they preached to a women's confraternity dedicated to giving financial assistance to "incurables," that is, to victims of syphilis.[166] It was a confraternity in Foligno that in 1555 urged the Jesuits to open a school there.[167] A confraternity in Terni that provided relief for the poor heard about the Society and, in 1554, promising to provide a house and other necessities, asked Ignatius to send five or six Jesuits to do the *consueta ministeria,* a request later seconded by the bishop and civic officials.[168]

Ignatius's refusal to grant Polanco permission to assume the rectorship in Pistoia was consistent with his general policy. In 1551 a lay confraternity was formed at Salamanca to care for orphaned girls until they could be suitably married, and they wanted a Jesuit to assume direction of it; he was willing, but Ignatius "did not want him or any of Ours" to accept such offices.[169] The next year the episcopal vicar of Perugia wanted Jesuits to take charge of a confraternity, but they successfully resisted the request.[170] In Venice in 1556 members of a confraternity asked that some Jesuits at least be present when their officers were elected, but Ignatius denied the request and further stipulated that Jesuits were not to be present at any of their ceremonies or meetings.[171]

This policy, behind which lay the fear that the mobility of the Society would be compromised by the members' accepting offices in confraternities, found expression in the *Constitutions,* which at least implicitly discouraged Jesuits even from joining them, a change from Ignatius's stance in 1541.[172] The policy also indicated that the Jesuits believed the laity fully capable of managing on their own. To say the least, the Jesuits manifested no desire to take charge. Although closer clerical control over confraternities eventuated in the next two centuries, it took a long while to happen, even after the stipulations of Trent in 1562 and the provisions of Clement VIII in 1604 that gave official impetus to that development.[173]

The Jesuits not only collaborated with existing confraternities in a variety of ways, including helping "reform" them,[174] but they were also directly responsible for the founding of many new ones. They held to the same hands-off policy regarding the government of these latter confraternities, but in almost all cases influenced their statutory practices of piety in favor of frequent confession and Communion and in other ways that reflected the patterns prescribed for members of the Society itself. When time and circumstances permitted, in other words, they tried to shape these confraternities or *compagnie* into the image and likeness of their own Compagnia di Gesù.

In 1539–40 Pierre Favre founded a confraternity in Parma, surely among the very first for which the Jesuits were responsible. Members, both priests and laymen, bound themselves to daily meditation and examination of conscience, to weekly confession and Communion, and to works of charity, especially care of the poor, instruction of the ignorant in Christian Doctrine, and assistance to criminals condemned to death. Not without reason, therefore, the confraternity took the name Compagnia di Gesù. Within a short time some members joined the bigger Compagnia di Gesù—for example, Jerónimo Doménech, Paolo d'Achille, and Benedetto Palmio.[175]

In 1549 a group of students, influenced by Silvestro Landini, formed a confraternity and "gave it the name of our Society," namely, Compagnia di Gesù.[176] When Polanco designated the statutes or foundational documents of confraternities like these—their *vivendi formula*, or rule of life—he used the same term that designated the charter of the Society of Jesus, the [*vivendi*] *Formula*.[177] The confraternities that owed their origins to the Jesuits thus manifested a "family resemblance" no matter where in the world they were founded—whether the one begun in Goa in 1552, whose members by their "devout conversations" would attempt to dissuade persons from living in concubinage and to reconcile enemies, or the one founded in Messina that same year by men who frequently confessed at the Jesuit church, who at night visited the homes of the poor to help the living and bury the dead, or the one founded in Valencia in 1554, in which the men guaranteed that in turn two of them would work through each night at a hospital for the poor, or the one founded in Seville in 1555 to care for convalescents in their homes once they were released from hospitals.[178]

The *confrarias* founded by the Jesuits in Japan within a few years after their arrival eventually had male and female branches and devoted themselves to both the corporal and spiritual works of mercy. When the persecutions began in the seventeenth century, they proved to be the underground institution in which Christian faith and practices were maintained and transmitted to the next generation. The leader of the confraternity acted as a lay pastor.[179]

Membership in confraternities inspired by the Jesuits of the first generation followed different patterns. Sometimes men and women were separated, as in Messina in 1549, where both confraternities were dedicated to helping the poor and the imprisoned.[180] The confraternity of the Blessed Virgin of Charity founded in a Portuguese village in 1551 had both men and women—and of the first fifty members thirty were prostitutes who had converted that lent. Not surprisingly, therefore, some of the members were designated to "speak out against public sins."[181] At Evora in 1554 members bound themselves to confession four times a year as a "promiscuous" (*promiscue*) gathering that cut across social classes—nobles, their servants, townspeople, and people from the surrounding villas.[182]

Do these associations, nonetheless, evince at least in embryo characteristics that scholars attribute to "Counter-Reformation confraternities"? Do they, for instance, downplay or eliminate the convivial and fraternal aspects in favor of privatized pious practices and insist on moral discipline in the members, who then work toward an almost puritanical change in social patterns? Do they thus impose the piety of a religious elite on more popular patterns? Do they, wittingly or unwittingly, play into the plans of lay and ecclesiastical magnates to control social, religious, and political unrest by these and other means? Do they help begin the process whereby determination will pass out of the hands of the ordinary membership into the hands of those who "know better"?[183]

Until the evidence for the period I am considering is studied in a systematic and comprehensive way, the answer to these complex questions must be qualified. The establishment of the "Marian Congregations" in 1563 surely signaled a new phase for the Jesuits. Even at the outset, however, the Jesuits wanted the confraternities to support and promote a more deeply interiorized ethical and religious life. While earlier confraternities also sometimes had this purpose, Jesuit reliance on the *Exercises* gave it clear form, and their insistence on more frequent confession and Communion was special, but not unique to them, and it pointed to the future. Of crucial importance in the Jesuit phenomenon, however, was the fact that these confraternities were not attached to parishes. Membership was therefore more the result of a deliberate decision, and the religious practices proposed by the confraternity were presumably chosen more freely.

In any case, the Jesuits sometimes took it upon themselves to put an end to gambling at cards, mock-bishop ceremonies, and public singing and dancing near shrines during lent; they certainly conveyed these attitudes to their disciples.[184] At Valencia in 1556 the Jesuits and the archbishop, Tomás de Villanueva, worked together to "change the face" of the city from vice to piety, especially through the elimination of gambling and card playing. But, along with the elimination of vice came the works of mercy. The men of the city visited the hospitals, begged food and clothing for the poor, and some fifty of them formed a confraternity to collect dowries for honest marriages to save young girls from prostitution.[185]

In Naples in 1554, Giovanni Francesco Araldo founded both a male and female confraternity, which followed the usual Jesuit pattern in exercises of piety and works of mercy, including the women's receiving reformed prostitutes into their homes until they could be suitably placed elsewhere. However, nobody was admitted to either confraternity until after having made a general confession, and both confraternities, while electing their own officers, had official authorization from the bishop. The women, moreover, agreed not to wear rouge or to associate with others who did! Even the name that the male branch first bore indicated a change from medieval piety—The Congregation of [Eucharistic] Communicants.[186] It was in that regard not unique among confraternities of Jesuit inspiration.[187]

That same year in both Barcelona and Alcalá the Jesuits persuaded some men to found confraternities whose special aim was to counteract the vice of cursing and blaspheming, supposedly widespread in those cities. Members imposed penalties on themselves, for instance, if they slipped into it. In Alcalá the institution was called The Name of God Confraternity, a forerunner of the "Holy Name Societies" so characteristic of modern Catholicism.[188]

The members of the Confraternity of the Blessed Virgin of Charity who agreed to speak out against public sin in that Portuguese village determined that if they were unsuccessful they would appeal to the bishop and the king for help.[189] The confraternity associated with the Casa dei catecumeni in Rome had papal approval from the beginning. The Casa Santa Marta, to which the Compagnia della grazia was attached, was erected by a papal bull. But these are more the exceptions than the rule. In different places, therefore, the confraternities assumed different emphases and had different relationships to ecclesiastical and secular officials in ways that do not substantially deviate from what prevailed earlier.

Once the Jesuits began to found schools, they almost inevitably began to utilize and adapt the confraternity for their students. Student confraternities were not a new idea; they had existed, for instance, in Rome and Florence since the fifteenth century. As early as 1557 the Jesuits initiated one in their college in Genoa, and in 1562 in Perugia. The decisive institution, however, got under way at the Collegio Romano the following year under the leadership of a young Belgian Jesuit, Jan Leunis.[190]

The circular letter of 14 July 1564 from Rome to the whole Society described the new *societas*.[191] It was under the patronage of the Virgin Mary, and made up especially of younger boys *(pueri)* from the college, who agreed to daily mass, weekly confession, monthly Communion, as well as to a half-hour meditation each day and to some other pious exercises. They would also "serve the poor." This sounds familiar enough. The letter added, however, that "one of the Fathers directs" the confraternity, even though from among "the older and wiser" boys a prefect was elected. Since most of the members were no older than their early teens, the role of the Jesuit is not surprising, but it marked a change from previous practice. Although the letter mentioned service to the poor, both it and other contemporary documents suggest that the devotional life of the students was at the center of this "Marian Congregation," or Sodality of Our Lady, as it came to be called. Once again, the age of the members almost dictated this emphasis. What, then, did the student-prefect do? His principal task was to select twelve officials from among the boys to watch over the conduct of the other members and assure their application to their studies.

The choice of the patron reflected the strong Marian element in Leunis's personal piety, but it was also probably considered appropriate for the age of the members.[192] Up to this time, as we have seen, very few of the other confraternities with which the Jesuits had been associated were dedicated to the Virgin.

By 1563 the Collegio Romano was the international meeting place for Jesuit priests and scholastics from all of Europe, and the Collegio's particular adaptation of the confraternity to young students began to be diffused to other Jesuit schools and eventually became an integral part of the education offered in them. This led both to the idea that the others were or ought to be something like branch offices of the "primary" Marian Congregation in Rome and to the bull of Pope Gregory XIII in 1584 establishing that primacy.[193] Already "aggregated" to the Roman Congregation were some fifty others in places like Naples, Genoa, Barcelona, Madrid, Mexico, Prague, Cologne, Lisbon, and Lucerne.

What this development meant in the long run was that the Jesuits now had a confraternity, a "sodality," that was as recognizably theirs as were the "Third Orders" for the mendicants. It had its first home in the Jesuit schools, but the model soon extended to adults. As has recently been shown, the Marian Congregations were strikingly important in forming patterns of lay piety in many areas of Europe in subsequent centuries, and they must be clearly distinguished from other confraternities, especially those attached to local parishes.[194]

The papal bull of 1584 was taken up for the most part with the many and various indulgences to which members had access by virtue of the present document, but it also granted the general of the Society supervision over all the aggregated Congregations. Three years later Claudio Aquaviva, then general, clarified in the "Common Rules" which he established for the Congregations that the elected prefect was subordinate to the Jesuit director in all matters—"in tutte le cose."[195] This stipulation probably only codified actual practice by this time, but it and the role ascribed to the general in the bull indicate a great change from how the Jesuits dealt with confraternities in their earliest years.

The papal bull and the other official documents that followed upon it helped crystallize what confraternities would henceforth mean to members of the Society, and, in place of the congeries that had earlier prevailed, they promoted a normative model. The bull and the "Common Rules" helped give members of the Marian Congregations a sense of bonding that transcended the local scene. In this important development, as in so many others, the schools had played a determining role.

~ 6

The Schools

ON 10 AUGUST 1560, Polanco wrote in Laínez's name a letter to all superiors that revealed an immensely significant development in the way the ministries of the Society had come to be conceived by that date. He said that "generally speaking, there are [in the Society] two ways of helping our neighbors: one in the colleges through the education of youth in letters, learning, and Christian life, and the second in every place to help every kind of person through sermons, confessions, and the other means that accord with our customary way of proceeding." The letter thus explicitly recognized that the schools were by that date understood not simply as one ministry among many, but as a super-category equivalent to that into which all the other *consueta ministeria* fell.

For that super-category Polanco made his crucial point: "every Jesuit must bear his part of the burden of the schools"—"portar parte del peso delle schuole."[1] He duly qualified this generalization, but the whole orientation of the letter manifested the practical priority that the schools had assumed among the ministries. Since approximately 1551 the Jesuits had begun to open schools at the rate of about four or five per year and were on the way to opening many more. In roughly the first decade of their history, the Jesuits in effect had no schools. This is the major difference that distinguished that decade from all that followed.

We know a great deal about the origins of Jesuit commitment to formal schooling and the context in which it took place.[2] Not all questions have been answered, but the essential framework is clear. What is still surprising, however, is how easily the first Jesuits glided into a decision of this magnitude and how little account they seem to have taken of its manifold impact upon them. The sources never fully satisfy on this issue.

Once the Jesuits undertook this ministry, they did not falter. This was true of Ignatius himself, whose previous history as a "pilgrim" and chief architect of the *Formula* indicated a quite different orientation. Nonetheless, as Polanco observed in 1551 upon the prospect of opening a school in Bologna, "The idea pleased Ignatius, who was always very much inclined toward the idea of educating youth in letters and matters of the spirit."[3] In pursuit of this program, Ignatius relegated to a lesser status the "professed houses," one of his favorite ideas and main safeguards for the kind of poverty that was to mark the Society. As Polanco wrote to Borja in 1555, just a year before Ignatius's death, "Our father's intention is that, especially in these initial stages, the colleges must multiply rather than the houses."[4]

In other words, Ignatius was willing to make immense adjustments to accommodate this new ministry and to deal with the many problems and frustrations it entailed. He did not see the schools as incompatible with his original vision or with the Compagnia in which it resulted. Both the vision and the Compagnia had from the beginning, in fact, a plasticity that encouraged moving beyond a rigid interpretation of the *Formula*. Moreover, he and the original companions, graduates of the University of Paris, had always seen learning as related to the piety they embodied and wished to inculcate in others. They saw it as even more intrinsically related to their particular "way of proceeding" in ministry and, hence, essential for those who would later join the Society to engage in its ministries. These are the essential elements that allowed them to move gradually along a path that led in 1548 to the great turning point, the opening of the school in Messina.

Toward Messina and Beyond

Shortly after Laínez and Favre arrived in Rome with Ignatius in 1537, they lectured on theology at the University of Rome at the request of Paul III. In 1542–43 Favre lectured on the Psalms at the University of Mainz, and in 1543–44 Jay filled the chair of theology at Ingolstadt left vacant by the death of Johannes Eck.[5] In 1545 Ignatius agreed that Rodrigues become tutor to the son of John III of Portugal.[6]

The bull *Licet debitum* of 1547 granted permission for the general to depute members of the Society to teach theology and all other disciplines "anywhere," a permission difficult to obtain at the time.[7] In 1549 Ignatius responded to negotiations originating with Duke Wilhelm IV of Bavaria and assigned three Jesuits to teach theology at the University of Ingolstadt—Jay, Salmerón, and Canisius. He arranged through Cardinals Marcello Cervini and Giammaria del Monte for them to stand for a doctoral examination at the University of Bologna, which they passed in early October. Shortly after the Jesuits arrived in Ingolstadt, Canisius was elected dean of the theological faculty, then rector, and in 1551–52, vice-chancellor. But by February of that last year they had all received new assignments and moved elsewhere.[8]

It was not occasional assignments like these, however, that primarily grounded Jesuit engagement with formal education, but the *Formula*'s provision that the Jesuits establish colleges near universities where future members of the order might be trained. The idea possibly originated with Laínez, with discussion centering on how to fund the institutions in a way that accorded with the poverty the Jesuits professed.[9] Even before September 1540, the companions resolved the problem by allowing these "colleges"—unlike the other houses of the Society, which were to live off alms—to be endowed and thus have a fixed income.

Although classes were taught at the colleges of the University of Paris, with which the companions were familiar, the colleges for future Jesuits that they foresaw in 1539–41 would be simple domiciles, without any instruction—"no estudios ni lectiones en la Compañia."[10] The Jesuit college, which would have no formal relationship to the university, would provide lodging for the scholastics, who would take all their classes at the university or at its other colleges. The first scholastics were sent, in accordance with the predilection of the companions, to the University of Paris, where the house faltered for lack of funding and ran into further difficulties in 1542 when the outbreak of war meant that all subjects of the emperor had to leave Paris. Those Jesuits went to Louvain.

By 1544 there were seven such colleges—at the universities of Paris, Louvain, Cologne, Padua, Alcalá, Valencia, and Coimbra. Except for the last, they were all small and financially unstable. Under the generous auspices of King John III of Portugal, however, the college at Coimbra opened in 1542 with twelve scholastics. By 1546 it had almost a hundred and within a year was fully endowed—the only one of the seven that measured up to the original plan. The basic obstacle to funding was persuading benefactors to contribute to an institution reserved exclusively for Jesuits, a group of men untested and practically unknown.

Jay wrote to Salmerón from Germany in early 1545 about precisely this difficulty. Surely nothing, he believed, could be expected from the German bishops, whose own clergy badly needed such resources. Jay, convinced of the necessity of a reformed system for the training of the diocesan clergy in Germany, was an early, insistent, and lonely spokesman for the idea with

German bishops, as he showed during the first period of the Council of Trent.[11] His shock at the condition of the German clergy even led him to propose in the letter to Salmerón that the Society found or staff some colleges in Germany for their future training. He prefaced his idea with the important disclaimer that he was of this opinion even though he knew that "our vocation is not ordered to undertaking professorships or 'ordinary' lectureships in the universities."[12] No immediate action was taken on his proposal.

The idea that members of the Society might do some formal teaching on a restricted basis and in extraordinary circumstances, however, continued to surface. Since 1543 a few Jesuits had been teaching reading, writing, grammar, and catechism at a kind of "seminary" in Goa for about six hundred male students between ten and twenty years of age, and they were soon on their way to taking full responsibility for the institution, which they did in 1548. In 1545, moreover, Ignatius consulted Laínez about the possibility of having Jesuits give some instruction in the colleges to other Jesuits, somewhat like the pattern in the colleges at Paris.

The issue arose out of the situation at Padua, where Polanco and some other Jesuits were enrolled. Although Polanco found the teachers and the lectures good, he believed that they had to be supplemented if one wished to make fast progress, as he had learned to do while studying philosophy at Paris.[13] Ignatius decided that under such circumstances lectures, repetitions, drills, and similar exercises could be conducted by Jesuits for other Jesuits. This was an important departure from an earlier decision, but also a key moment in the Jesuits' growing awareness that the *modus parisiensis* had something distinctive to offer to Italian schools.

Meanwhile the duke of Gandía, Francisco de Borja, who had overseen the founding of the Jesuit college at the University of Valencia, had by late 1544 petitioned Paul III to assign certain ecclesiastical revenues to a Jesuit college in Gandía itself. But the college at Gandía was special in two ways: first, there was no university at Gandía, which meant that the Jesuits would give all the instruction; second, the duke wanted other students to be educated there along with the Jesuits—in fact, his principal aim was the education of the sons of his Morisco subjects.[14] Ignatius, always partial to the duke's suggestions, agreed, and in 1546 Jesuits began to teach "publicly," that is, to students who were not Jesuits. Soon thereafter Paul III granted this exceedingly modest institution the status of *Studium generale,* which meant it was a university.[15]

Jerónimo Doménech was meanwhile laboring in Sicily, where he found "such an immense ignorance in the clergy that you would not believe it unless you saw it." Aware of what had happened in Gandía, he told Ignatius that Leonor Osorio was eager for the Jesuits to found a college.[16] After some maneuvering, her husband, the viceroy, saw to it that not he but the officials of the city of Messina formally ask Ignatius on 19 December 1547 to send five Jesuit scholastics to study there and five teachers for classes in theology, cases of conscience, "arts," rhetoric, and grammar—"all disciplines," as Nadal said, "except law and medicine."[17] The officials promised they would supply food, clothing, and lodging for the Jesuits according to their need, so that the instruction could be given free of charge.

By March 1548, Ignatius had not only complied with the petition but had chosen the ten Jesuits—four priests and six scholastics. He selected some of the best talent available to him in Rome, but also seemed concerned to make the group as international as possible—the priests, for instance, were Nadal, Canisius, André des Freux, and Cornelius Wischaven. He allowed them to elect their superior, Nadal. Never before had a group of this size been gathered and "sent" for any ministry. Never before had so much talent been concentrated on a single undertaking. Ignatius obviously pinned high hopes on the venture. The solemnity of the enterprise was underscored by an audience with Paul III, who encouraged the Jesuits to combat the errors of the Lutherans.

For Ignatius the arrangement solved the problem of how to fund the education of younger members of the Society, but what further motivated him at this point is not clear. For the founders in Messina, the training of their sons in "good letters" was of course the paramount consideration. Almost from the moment the school opened its doors their priority prevailed. Both parties had heavy stakes in seeing the venture succeed. The energies of the young Jesuits, however, got directed to teaching other students rather than to their own education.

These factors, plus the palpable success of the undertaking from the very beginning, distinguished the college of Messina from its predecessors in Goa and Gandía.[18] Nadal's enthusiasm was contagious, and, although relatively few of his letters from this period survive, they must have helped convince Ignatius and others to move with bold, even precipitous speed along a path where previously they had taken only a few tentative steps.[19]

Within months after the Collegio di San Nicolò opened in Messina in 1548, the thirty members of the senate of Palermo petitioned Ignatius to establish a similar college in their city. In this petition they were warmly supported, as we have come to expect, by the viceroy, who wrote to both

Ignatius and Paul III about it, and especially by his wife, who had a large inheritance assigned to it as an endowment. On 1 June 1549, Ignatius responded positively to the senators, designated Laínez and Doménech to attend to the immediate details, and soon selected eleven Jesuits from five different nations to begin the school. On 25 November Pedro de Ribadeneira, a twenty-two-year-old scholastic, inaugurated the academic year in an assembly of municipal and regional dignitaries with a typical humanistic oration in praise of study. The Jesuits had chosen for the school a building they found admirably suited to their purposes, leading Father Paolo d'Achille to affirm that better classrooms were not to be found even in Paris.[20]

Word reached distant Cologne about what was happening at Gandía, Messina, and Palermo, and on 4 October 1549 Leonard Kessel, the rector of the college, wrote to Ignatius registering his surprise but also his enthusiasm. "If it has come to the point that the brethren have begun to teach publicly," he had the highest hopes for it as a way of "gaining all youth to Christ."[21] A college for students who were not Jesuits was in fact not opened in Cologne until 1557,[22] but at the very time Kessel wrote, Ignatius was already at work establishing colleges in Naples, Venice, and possibly elsewhere.[23] By the next year the offer of financial support by the duke of Gandía helped make possible on 22 February 1551 the opening under modest circumstances of the Collegio Romano. Over its door hung the inscription "School of Grammar, Humanities, and Christian Doctrine, Free"—"Schola di Grammatica, d'Humanità e Dottrina Christiana, gratis."

Enthusiasm for the colleges had within a few short years seized the Jesuit leadership in Rome. On 1 December 1551, Polanco on commission from Ignatius wrote a brief letter to Simão Rodrigues, then provincial of Portugal, encouraging him to open schools like those operating in Italy.[24] On that same date he wrote two other letters, even more important. The first, addressed to Antonio de Araoz, the provincial of Spain, similarly encouraged the opening of schools.[25] Polanco also reviewed some examples to show how they might be funded—by the city, as happened in Messina and Palermo; by some prince, as in Ferrara and Florence by their respective dukes, or as in Vienna by King Ferdinand; by some private individual, as in Venice and Padua by the prior of the Trinity, Andrea Lippomano; by a group of individuals, as in Naples, Bologna, and elsewhere.[26]

Aside from the different sources of funding, the very number of colleges opened or about to open between 1548 and 1551, of which this is not a complete listing, is an astounding revelation. Polanco's letter to Araoz is especially important, however, for other reasons. It succinctly described, for instance, how the curriculum was to be built up from the base of classes in grammar and what discipline and religious practice were expected of the students. It concluded with a list of fifteen goals the Society hoped to achieve through the schools.

The second letter, addressed to all members of the Society, outlined the religious program for both Jesuit students and others.[27] The Jesuits were not to be sent to the colleges to study unless they were firm in their vocation; they should assist at mass every day, set aside time for prayer and examination of conscience daily, receive the sacraments of confession and Communion every week, and attend sermons and catechism class every Sunday and feast day. They should also help in preaching and other ministries in the college. The program for the other students was simpler, but it moved along the same lines. Polanco began it with the statement: "First of all, we accept for classes and literary studies everybody, poor and rich, free of charge and for charity's sake, without accepting any remuneration."

Both documents obliquely but clearly reveal a new understanding of the broader pastoral potential of the colleges. Until about 1550 the theory prevailed that the *consueta ministeria* of the *Formula* would not be exercised in and from the colleges but would be reserved to the other houses. The experience of Messina defeated this theory when it was seen how successful a base for such ministries the colleges in their new form could be.

This meant, among other things, that even when the scholastics were sent to the colleges to continue their own studies they were expected to teach and help with the other ministries. In most of the colleges, because of their small size, this last expectation almost immediately overwhelmed the first, so that Jesuit scholastics in fact studied only in colleges with a large faculty and student body. They studied, therefore, alongside their lay peers. In this way, as well as others, their training was radically different from what eventuated for the diocesan clergy in most of the seminaries inspired by the legislation of the Council of Trent.[28]

The colleges became the principal centers for all Jesuit ministry, which helps explain why Ignatius's interest in the "professed houses" waned, despite the role he assigned them in the *Constitutions*. As time went on, he was reluctant to accept a college unless a church was attached.[29] In other words, although Polanco's letter of 10 August 1560 divided the ministries of the Society into the two categories of the schools and the *consueta ministeria*, these categories were not in practice so distinct as the letter suggested.

By the time Ignatius died, the Society operated thirty-five or more colleges, depending on one's definition of "college." Nineteen of these were in Italy, with negotiations for others under way in distant places.[30] By 1565 the Jesuits had thirty colleges in Italy alone and had just opened two in Poland, at Braniewo and Pułtusk. During the early years the number of students in the schools varied considerably. In 1556 enrollment ranged from a mere 60 in Venice to 800 in Billom and 900 in Coimbra. That same year there were 120 in Bologna, 160 in Naples, 170 in Perugia, 280 in Palermo, and 300 in Córdoba. In Vienna there were over 320, some of whose parents were "alienated from the Catholic faith," as was also true in Modena.[31] Enrollment tended to be larger in schools outside Italy, except for the Collegio Romano.

Protestant students were expected to follow the religious program, but concessions were made. In Prague, for instance, the Jesuits admitted Lutheran and Hussite boys along with Catholic without distinction (promiscue) and even accepted them as boarders. The Lutherans were exempted from reciting the Litany of the Saints. Hussite parents successfully insisted that Jesuits not speak to their sons about faith and exempt them from receiving Communion, but they agreed to the hearing of mass and in some instances even to confession. The Jesuits confiscated and burned any heretical books the boys had and then gave them others as compensation.[32]

They immediately saw, therefore, that the schools could in certain localities be instruments for winning young converts from Protestantism and for likewise influencing their parents. In those same localities, the schools could and would be powerful instruments for confirming wavering Catholics and, more important, for building the future through an articulate laity and clergy. When in 1554 Canisius inquired of Ignatius how the Society might best help Germany, he replied, "colleges."[33]

Nonetheless, despite the commission from Paul III for Messina, the Jesuits did not in the first instance undertake the colleges with an apologetic, much less a polemical, purpose. The original impulse came from the need to provide a certain amount of training for their own members, along with the need to devise a formula that would assure adequate funding for such a venture.

But even as Messina was being founded, other motives were already strong and becoming stronger. As Polanco's letter to Araoz demonstrates, the Jesuits soon became convinced that lay peers would derive from a program of study and devout practices the same benefits they hoped for their own members, a persuasion perfectly in accord with their "way of proceeding" from the beginning. Within a few years after 1548, most of the institutions in which this persuasion found incarnation were operated by

Jesuits exclusively for the education of lay persons. They saw this work as a ministry and clearly designated it as such.[34] Moreover, at least some of them realized that, although there were vague antecedents, they were undertaking something that had never before been done by any religious order.[35]

The *Constitutions* described the schools as a "work of charity."[36] By using that term, they suggested that it was a form of the traditional spiritual and corporal works of mercy—among the former of which was "instructing the ignorant." The extent to which the Jesuits consciously made such a connection is not clear, but the designation "work of charity" indicated the motivation they believed impelled them. It was an alternative formulation of their favorite description of their ministries, "the help of souls."

The Faith in Education

Ignatius related in his *Autobiography* that after his return from Palestine in 1524 he felt inclined to study for some time in order to "help souls" better. The belief in a relationship between learning and effective ministry that underlay this decision was traditional. Nonetheless, Ignatius was born into an age in which arguments for that relationship and, indeed, for an intrinsic relationship between education and an upright life had been propounded with new insistence and from a new viewpoint ever since Petrarch, "the Father of humanism," first made them popular in the mid-fourteenth century. That a relationship existed between "good literature" and virtue was a propelling assumption of the humanist movement.

Although by no means unrelated to educational traditions of the Middle Ages, that assumption challenged many medieval notions about texts, curriculum, and related matters, especially as those notions had since the twelfth century found expression in the universities. In their criticism of university (or "scholastic") education, the humanists were especially vociferous about its failure to relate learning to a life of virtue and public service.

The institutional embodiment of the humanists' educational concerns was the primary/secondary schools inspired by their ideals that began in Italy in the fifteenth century and then gradually spread to other parts of Europe. These institutions originated one of the great revolutions in education in the Western World, a revolution whose enduring influence was evident in the curriculum of Greek and Roman authors at the center of "the best" secondary education until well into the twentieth century.

We are well informed about the size and shape of these schools in sixteenth-century France, whence the Jesuits derived many elements of their pedagogy, and in Italy, where they founded their first schools and became dedicated to the venture.[37] In all cities of Italy were to be found schools of two types—the "Vernacular School," which imparted practical skills in reading, writing, and calculation needed for business or a trade, and the "Latin School," which operated more or less according to the principles propounded by the humanists.

The Latin Schools, no matter how many there might be in a town or city, often consisted in a single schoolmaster, with perhaps an assistant—hired by the municipality, by a confraternity, or by a group of parents. In many instances the schoolmaster simply "freelanced." He might be a layman or a priest, and he often gave instruction in his home. However elaborate or modest these schools might be in any given locality, they were established institutions in Italy by the time the Jesuits opened their collegio in Messina. Despite their Latin curriculum, some of them may have been relatively innocent of the high claims humanists were making for this style of education.

Did the Jesuits make the same claims? At the urging of Ignatius, Pedro de Ribadeneira wrote to Philip II of Spain on 14 February 1556 to explain why the Society was so deeply committed to its colleges. One sentence jumps from the page: "All the well-being of Christianity and of the whole world depends on the proper education of youth."[38] It was a humanistic commonplace. Ribadeneira's claim is noteworthy, therefore, not for originality but for indicating that the faith in the formative powers of good literature promulgated by the humanist movement found powerful echo in the Society. That faith motivated Jesuits, and they used it to motivate others.

However, the origins of the colleges for members of the Society and even for others cannot be precisely identified with that faith. The origins were more pragmatic and traditional for both these groups. They were thus basically in accord with the values of the social classes from which the first Jesuits mostly came—classes for whom literary and professional training was indispensable for maintaining their status. Furthermore, the academic program initiated at Messina included theology and cases of conscience, which were not disciplines in a strictly humanist curriculum. The former discipline was in fact taught only in universities, which therefore demanded a more elaborate institution than the Latin School and by definition implied one friendly toward scholastic—that is, university-style—theology.

Nonetheless, at Messina and in the schools that followed, the typically humanistic disciplines such as grammar and rhetoric and the cultivation of Latin, Greek, and, in many places, Hebrew became the most popular part of the curriculum—or its only part. The teaching of these disciplines and languages was by the mid-sixteenth century inseparable from some belief in the formative power of the educational program of which they were the most distinctive expression. The Jesuit program was a species within the genus, and it increasingly subscribed to the educational faith enunciated so forcefully by Ribadeneira.

The propaganda that in the Renaissance extolled the power of education to form or reform the *mores* of individuals and entire societies doubtless exceeded the reality and did not always correlate with the plodding and pedestrian methods of instruction in the classrooms.[39] Nonetheless, inflated though the claims sometimes were, they were not utterly unfounded, and they possessed a certain self-fulfilling dynamism. In any case, the Jesuits by and large came to subscribe to them. The claims provided an expansive aim for their educational undertakings as well as a lens through which to view what they actually accomplished.

The Jesuits were not of a disposition, however, to be swept along in the enthusiasm without more palpable and pragmatic reasons, especially for the study by Jesuits themselves of the *cosas de humanidad*. Shortly after Polanco was first appointed secretary in 1547, he wrote a letter to Laínez precisely on this subject in order to dispel Laínez's misgivings.[40] The reasons he adduced favoring such study were used by humanists, but they were not ones that made the broadest claims. The study of *humanidad*, said Polanco, helps in the understanding of Scripture, is a traditional propaedeutic to philosophy, provides a pedagogically sound entrance into other subjects, enables a person to express his thoughts better, fosters the skills in communication that Jesuit ministries require, and develops the facility in different languages that the international character of the Society demands.

Some of these arguments would be valid for lay students of *humanidad* while others would not, but the Jesuits, like the humanists, saw the civic and social applications for their students of the "humane" disciplines. When they opened their school in Tivoli in 1550, they did so for the "utility of the city"—"ad civitatis utilitatem."[41] When they urged the bishop of Murcia in 1555 to establish a college, they said it would be of great benefit to the "republic" by producing good priests, good civic officials, and good citizens of every status.[42] This was of course standard humanist talk, but its employment by the Jesuits indicates the breadth that marked their desire to "help souls." As with their other *opera caritatis*, their ministry of education had civic and societal dimensions that carried the Jesuits beyond the evangelical models that principally inspired them.

When Polanco indicated in 1552 for Valencia that colleges were powerful instruments "for the reform of cities," he adduced an article of faith.[43] The faith derived not from a confessional stance but from a broad consensus among the learned elite of Europe about the power of education. On the one hand, the faith assumed standards formulated by that elite, but on the other, the standards could not be imposed without the assent of the parents because of the voluntary character of enrollment in the schools. If the Jesuits were ultimately interested in using their schools to exercise "social control," as has been passionately argued by some critics, they were in that regard far from unique among their contemporaries.[44]

The Jesuits' ideals were socially conservative. It never occurred to them that they should make concerted efforts to break down traditional roles and class structures. As we have already seen, they depended for the endowment of their schools on the wealthy and powerful. They opened their schools, however, to all who were qualified and who would abide by their rules. They were to be "for everybody, poor and rich," Ignatius enjoined upon the Jesuits in Perugia in 1552—"per tutti quanti, poveri et ricchi."[45] Polanco told the Jesuits at Ingolstadt in 1556 to accept "every kind of person"—"ogni sorte di persone"—in order to "animate and console them."[46]

With a notable exception or two, the Jesuit schools during the period I am considering did not favor the sons of the rich over other students. While they generally had a mix of social classes, some catered especially to the poor, even the rural poor. Nadal in 1561 described the college at Monreale, outside Palermo, as "small, uncomfortable, without a church and without endowment . . . From neighboring hamlets come some four hundred students, mostly of the humble poor [pauperculi]."[47] Although not social revolutionaries, the Jesuits in theory and practice supported improvement of status through education.

Their decision to adopt the humanist rather than the vernacular curriculum, however, directed their schools toward the classes of society for whom that curriculum had particular appeal.[48] Moreover, in 1551 Ignatius decided for the Collegio Romano that boys had to attain the basic skills in reading and writing before they were admitted because he believed the Society did not have the manpower to expend on such instruction; later that year he made the rule general.[49] The *Constitutions*, which were being composed at about the same time, stated more mildly that Jesuits did not "ordinarily" teach those skills.[50] Many exceptions therefore continued to be made, but wherever the provision was enforced it tended to exclude from Jesuit schools boys from the lower social classes, who had little opportunity otherwise to learn the skills prerequisite to admission. The Jesuits' determination to minister to all members of society regardless of rank had to do battle, therefore, with the dynamism intrinsic to the humanist program as such and with the repercussions of not teaching the so-called ABC's.[51]

The Jesuits adopted the humanistic program for a number of reasons, but especially because, like their contemporaries, they believed that humanistic studies formed upright character, *pietas*. Although different in many ways from the *Christianitas* that the Jesuits wanted to instill by their teaching of catechism, *pietas* correlated with it in that the truths learned were expected to have an impact on the pupil's behavior and outlook. In this regard their schools correlated with that earlier inspiration.

When in 1552 Nadal asserted the primacy of *pietas* in the educational system the Jesuits were undertaking, he spoke for them all—"Omnia vero selecte ita ordinanda, ut in studiis primum locum pietas obtineat."[52] He merely echoed one of the most prevalent sentiments of his day.[53] Moreover, the Jesuits took for granted that learning and literacy were goods in and of themselves, and they felt at home in promoting them.

The motivation behind the Jesuits' decision to undertake formal schooling as one of their ministries cannot, therefore, be reduced to a simplistic formula, as Polanco's list of the fifteen benefits conferred by the schools indicates.[54] The list is relevant as much for what it did not mention as for what it did. Polanco divided it into three parts—benefits for the Society, for the students, and for the locality:

For the Society

1. Jesuits learn best by teaching others.
2. They profit from the discipline, perseverance, and diligence that teaching requires.
3. They improve their preaching and other skills needed in ministry.
4. Although Jesuits should not try to persuade anybody to enter the Society, especially not young boys, their good example and other factors will, nonetheless, help gain "laborers in the vineyard."

For the students

5. They will make progress in learning.
6. The poor, who could not possibly pay for teachers, much less for private tutors, will be able to do the same.
7. Students will be helped in spiritual matters by learning Christian Doctrine and hearing sermons and exhortations.

8. They will make progress in purity of conscience and every virtue through monthly confession and the instilling of good habits.

9. They will draw much merit and profit from their studies by learning to direct them to the service of God.

For the locality

10. Parents will be relieved of the financial burden of educating their sons.

11. They will be able to satisfy their consciences of their obligation to educate their children.

12. The people of the area will be helped by the Jesuits' preaching and administration of the sacraments.

13. Parents will be influenced by the positive example of their children to live as good Christians.

14. Jesuits will encourage and help in the establishment of hospitals, houses of *convertidas,* and similar institutions.

15. Those who are now only students will grow up to be pastors, civic officials, administrators of justice, and will fill other important posts to everybody's profit and advantage.

The practical viewpoint that underlay this list seems poles apart from Ribadeneira's grandiloquent claims to Philip II, and it better captured what originally steered the Jesuits toward this form of ministry and later sustained them in it. The list betrays no preoccupation with orthodoxy, and it does not mention "reform." It expects of the colleges only benefits they might realistically be hoped to deliver. It is straightforward in its recognition of the advantages they will procure for the Society itself.

The Jesuits were moved in this direction by other considerations. The advantages of labors sustained with the same group of people over a long period of time, instead of the pastoral blitz, came to be noted and commended in the *Constitutions,* and they balanced the emphasis on mobility.[55] Like so many educators, Jesuits also came to believe that the values they espoused could be communicated more easily and effectively to the young not yet corrupted by other influences.[56]

From the beginning, the Jesuits produced for their schools a huge amount of documentation. Almost all this material dealt with curriculum, textbooks, pedagogical principles and techniques, and the role of religious practices such as mass and confession. Influential as an early codification of such materials was the letter to Polanco from Annibal du Coudret, 14 July 1551, which described in detail the program at Messina.[57] Documentation like this occasionally expressed in aphoristic fashion the ideal and goal toward which such great energy and effort were being expended—for example, the hope of instilling a "learned piety" *(docta pietas)* or producing "good citizens," but going little further. In other words, despite the Jesuits' great faith in education, they did not elaborate a philosophy of education in the ordinary sense of that term, probably because the humanists had already done it for them.[58]

Among the exceptions to that generalization, however, was the *Ratio studendi,* written at the Collegio Romano in 1564 by the Spanish professor of philosophy Benito Pereira.[59] Pereira began with the important statement that the goal of study was knowledge of the truth, which is the perfection of the human mind. He recalled that Aristotle said that, although it was fine to be a friend of Socrates and Plato, it was more important to be a friend of the truth. This meant that one sometimes had not only to disagree with others but, if truth demanded it, to change and retract one's own opinions.

He continued with other reflections that went beyond techniques on what made for effective teaching and effective learning and described how both body and mind were to be disposed for study. He provided rules for literary criticism. He took for granted that the goal of schools was to cultivate the intellectual talents of the individual and to bring them to the highest point of perfection. There were three such talents—intelligence, memory, and judgment. All were necessary, but what was most valued in a mature person was good judgment; education should concentrate its efforts in the cultivation of that faculty. Pereira here captured something central to the Jesuits' educational endeavors. Under the influence of Quintilian and other theorists, the Jesuits looked more to formation of mind and character, to *Bildung,* than to the acquisition of ever more information or the advancement of the disciplines.[60]

Pereira's *Ratio* is a synthesis of classical, medieval, and Renaissance ideas on education. Not therefore original, it is important in the Jesuit context because it rose above details of curriculum and pedagogical technique without claiming education to be the panacea for all the ills of church and society. Pereira ended with a section on "topics" or "commonplaces" for speaking and writing, which climaxed with typically humanist considerations about "human dignity." That theme accorded with the benign relationship between nature and grace that the Jesuits espoused and, hence, fitted in a generic way with the positive view of human nature that, at least in theory, undergirded Jesuit enthusiasm for education in the humanistic mode.[61] The last words of the treatise were typical of such an appreciation:

"Because of the excellence and almost divine quality of their virtues and deeds, many men were in bygone days honored with not only the highest human but even divine honors, and by the ancients were numbered among the gods."

Transcending the Modus Parisiensis

The *Constitutions* indicated two basic kinds of educational institutions that the Society might operate.[62] The first was the college, in which "humane letters, languages, and Christian Doctrine," as well as possibly "cases of conscience," formed the curriculum.[63] The second was the university, where the higher disciplines would also be taught—logic, metaphysics, ethics, the sciences, mathematics, and theology.[64] Excluded from universities operated by the Society were, under normal circumstances, the faculties of law and medicine.[65] In this Fourth Part of the *Constitutions,* directives were given on the order of teaching the disciplines, the techniques for teaching them, the texts to be used, the degrees to be conferred, the moral and spiritual values to be inculcated, and the duties to be fulfilled by the officials in charge of the institution.

One of the earliest sources for these provisions was a long document composed about 1552 by Nadal, fresh from his experience in Messina, but with his eyes on the greater potential of the Collegio Romano. *De studii generalis dispositione et ordine* was among the first of his many important writings dealing with the general topic.[66] The detail and sophistication of *De dispositione* could have come only from somebody like Nadal, who had broad experience of educational institutions across Europe—the universities of Alcalá, Paris, Avignon, Majorca, and the Jesuit experiment at Messina.

The *Constitutions* and other prescriptive documents including the *De dispositione* can be deceiving, however, when they suggest that many or most of the schools that the Jesuits operated contained all the disciplines they describe. Few of the schools during this period taught anything more than the "lower disciplines," which meant three years of "grammar," another of *humanitas* (poetry, history), and another of "rhetoric," that is, classical oratory. The best of them, like Messina, were *trilingue* in that besides Latin and Greek they also taught Hebrew. (In Italy the Jesuit curriculum differed most notably from earlier Italian practice in that it elevated Greek to a secure place in the syllabus.)[67]

The students entered at about ten years of age for an approximately six-year program. These "colleges" thus resembled most immediately the American high school, but to the degree they prepared students for the professional schools the university incorporated, they also corresponded to American undergraduate colleges.

In these early days the outstanding example of a school that did more than teach the "lower disciplines" was the Collegio Romano, which within a few years of its inception taught the full curriculum described in the *Constitutions* and was, in effect, a "university."[68] This meant, however, that it also taught the "lower disciplines." The two stages beyond "humane letters" taught at the Collegio Romano, the future Gregorian University, were "arts," or "philosophy"—logic, metaphysics, ethics, mathematics, and physics, according to the texts of Aristotle for the most part—and, finally, theology, considered the apex of the curriculum.[69]

As has often been pointed out, the model for this pyramid culminating in theology was the University of Paris that the architects of the Jesuit system knew so well.[70] The pyramidal structure was only one element, however, in the complex reality of the *modus parisiensis* that the Jesuits introduced into their schools in Italy and thence exported, as modified by their Italian experience, to their schools elsewhere in the world. Their early persuasion of how much it differed from the *mos italicus* and their belief in its superiority gave them a sense of cultural mission in propagating it. In many parts of Europe the difference was a major factor in making their schools distinctive and attractive.

In 1553, just two years after the opening of the Collegio Romano, Polanco wrote to all Jesuit superiors about the hopes the Society entertained for the new institution.[71] Among them was that "it be academically distinguished for having professors who are not only erudite but also diligent pedagogues, who will introduce into the college the style of academic exercises used at the University of Paris. This will be a marvelous help to Italy, in whose schools two things are notably lacking—a well-ordered program of lectures and exercises to assure the assimilation of the materials. Diligent students, we therefore hope, will achieve more with us in a short time than elsewhere in a long time; and perhaps other schools will improve, inspired by our example."

In describing the Italian system Polanco drew on his experience at the University of Padua, but he and other Jesuits applied the same criticism also to primary and secondary education in Italy: it was not sufficiently structured according to the age and competence of the students, and it did not make sufficient use of drill and other ways of actively engaging the students to assure assimilation of information and skills.

The *modus parisiensis* was, as the Jesuits saw it, the polar opposite of much of what they found in Italian schools and schoolmasters. It was based on an exacting program of lectures, complemented by a full array of drills, repetitions, and disputations—*exercitia,* or *exercitationes*—in which the student demonstrated mastery of the materials. Students at all levels were divided into classes according to a set plan of progression from mastery of one skill or author to mastery of the next. Examinations determined who was ready to move to the next class. A "class" represented a unit of work to be mastered, not a period of time. Hence, brighter boys could move through the curriculum more quickly than others. If the classes were large, students were divided into groups of ten under a more accomplished peer (the *decurio*), who drilled them and reported to the teacher on their progress or lack of it.[72]

These principles and techniques, though applied to "humane letters," developed at Paris as part of the scholastic tradition, with its great penchant for order, system, and "disputation."[73] The *modus parisiensis* encompassed many things, but what it most broadly gave to the Jesuit system was an organized plan for the progress of the student through increasingly complex materials and a codification of pedagogical techniques designed to elicit active response from the learner.

Despite the "Parisian" designation, these principles and practices had undergone significant development in the Low Countries in the fifteenth century with the Brethren of the Common Life, who themselves had been influenced by developments in France and Italy. From the Brethren, they were exported back to France—to some of the *collèges* at the University of Paris, including the Collège de Montaigu, where Ignatius first studied, as well as to other schools in the kingdom.[74] They were exported elsewhere, as to the humanistic school founded by Johannes Sturm in Strasbourg in 1535.[75] They were introduced into Coimbra by King John III of Portugal.[76] They had found their way to the University of Alcalá, where Ignatius, Laínez, Salmerón, Bobadilla, Nadal, Ledesma, and other early Jesuits had studied. In other words, the so-called *modus parisiensis* or elements of it were already on their way to becoming an international phenomenon by the time the Jesuits introduced them into Italy, and they had themselves encountered them even before they studied in Paris.

The similarity between the Jesuit schools in Italy and Sturm's in Protestant Strasbourg led to allegations that the Jesuits borrowed their ideas from him. There is no evidence indicating that this is what happened. Even before the Jesuits thought of opening their own schools, Polanco as a student at

Padua had pointed out the advantages of the *modus parisiensis*. The similarity between Sturm and the Jesuits was due to a common origin, as scholars now recognize. The similarity points, moreover, to the assumption generally shared by leaders in sixteenth-century Europe of the necessity of the "war against ignorance" for the good of religion and society. The necessity was so patent for these generations that it needed no justifying arguments.

Polanco noted instances where in Italy the new methods introduced by the Jesuits positively influenced other teachers. In Palermo in 1552 one of the older schoolmasters came to the Jesuits' classes to learn firsthand the "right way to teach," by which boys made so much progress in so little time. It did not escape Polanco, however, that others preferred to remain ignorant, an oblique indication of the resentment the schoolmasters often felt toward the Jesuits, who were taking away their students.[77] After the Collegio Romano had been in operation for a few years, Polanco said that people began to regard the teaching at its rival institution, the University of Rome, as "cold and, in comparison, useless," but even there teachers began to be more diligent because of the Jesuits' example—and competition.[78]

When the college opened in Vienna in 1551, the Jesuits offered a mishmash of courses, which "displeased Ignatius" when he heard of it. He made it clear that students were to lay a foundation in "humane letters," then give their attention to "philosophy," and only then move on to theology.[79] Two years later the *modus parisiensis* was seen in Vienna as distinctive of the instruction given by the Jesuits.[80] In Córdoba in 1554 people gave the Jesuits credit for introducing the "new" practice of frequent written and oral exercises.[81]

There were other features in the colleges, however, that find no exact counterpart in the *modus parisiensis*. One of these was the introduction into the curriculum of classes in Christian Doctrine once a week. Although in theory theology was the discipline toward which the others pointed, it was not taught in the colleges, that is, in the secondary schools, and its place was taken in a certain sense by this much more elementary exercise. Sturm also introduced catechism into the curriculum, requiring more of it than did the Jesuits.[82]

Another difference was the widespread practice of offering classes in "cases of conscience" even in these lower schools, although who the students were and how these classes functioned is not always clear. In 1553 the colleges at Evora and Lisbon offered only the lower program in "humane letters," but "cases of conscience" were also taught.[83]

Although the program of classes and academic exercises in Jesuit schools was demanding and the academic year long, there were regular and frequent holidays, and the Jesuits showed themselves in other ways sensitive to the students' need for relaxation, recreation, and sports.[84] In boarding institutions, the "prefect of health" was to provide "good meals, well seasoned, from food of good quality."[85]

Some cities and communes in Europe had devised means to provide education without "direct cost" to children of their citizens, but even in these places the Jesuit schools generally accepted more students and were much cheaper for the municipality, since the Jesuits required no salaries, needing only enough money to cover food and clothing expenses. In this aspect of their venture, they were true innovators. They inaugurated in Italy and many other places the first systematic and widespread effort to provide free education for large numbers of students in a given town or city.[86] Moreover, the Jesuits granted free of charge all advanced degrees, which could cost "a small fortune at regular universities."[87] They refused to charge tuition out of the religious motives that from the beginning led them to refuse payment for any of their ministries. This stance made Jesuit schools financially attractive to parents and local governments and was a powerful factor contributing to their spread.

The Jesuits installed in their schools the spiritual program whose basic elements Polanco described in his letter of 1 December 1551, summarized above. The program's precedents were the practices in the colleges at the universities of Alcalá and Paris, where they varied from college to college but included frequent or daily attendance at mass, fasts and other penances, daily participation in at least part of the liturgical Hours, daily examination of conscience, and confession and Communion at determined intervals.[88]

The Jesuits employed many of the same elements, but, as we have seen, with a sense of some intrinsic cohesion among them. Moreover, they extended the program to students who continued to live at home or somewhere else outside the institution—which was the vast majority, since few of the schools at this time had provisions for boarders. This factor, plus the general tenor of Jesuit spirituality, meant that the program eliminated or mitigated some of the practices of Alcalá and Paris. The program had no counterpart in the pre-university schools run by municipalities and, for the most part, by other educators. At least in theory the program was voluntary, and the *Constitutions* forbade expelling students simply for not complying with it.[89]

Polanco described the program at the college at Palermo the year after it was established.[90] All students went to confession every month, some every two weeks. They assisted at mass daily and heard a sermon on Sundays and feast days. In the afternoons of class days, a number of them went privately and spontaneously to the Jesuits to talk about their spiritual lives. But what was especially important, reported Polanco, was the weekly talk given by Laínez "about matters concerning them related to their progress in virtue and learning."

Vespers on Sundays and feast days became standard, daily examination of conscience inculcated, and eventually in some places, students encouraged or obliged to do part of the *Spiritual Exercises.* Taken for granted all along was encouraging students, as far as their age allowed, to practice the works of mercy that the Jesuits favored.[91] Further extension and intensification of the program resulted from the introduction of the Marian Congregations into the schools after 1563. Like the *modus parisiensis,* those Congregations became a distinctive mark of the Jesuit schools.

Gioseffo Cortesono was rector of the Collegio Germanico in Rome from 1564 until 1569. Sometime late in his term of office, he composed at the order of Borja the *Constitutiones Collegii Germanici,* another document that rose above stipulation of particulars.[92] Somewhat misnamed, it was less a juridical instrument than a reflection on broad educational issues, "based on experience." The several sections dealing with the spiritual program spoke of course of the devout practices expected of the students, but also manifested a concern for the interiorization of religious and moral values through those practices and through the guidance that the students, young Italian laymen for the most part, were to receive from the Jesuits.

In the "entrance interview" for the students, for instance, the Jesuit should explain what piety *(il spirito)* consists in—liberation from the tyranny of sin, peace of conscience, friendship with God, "walking in the light," and "tasting the sweetness, joy, and contentment of things of the spirit."[93] This was another paraphrase of what the Jesuits meant by consolation.

The Jesuits should encourage students to go to the sermons in the Jesuit church, but not do so in a way or to a degree that would annoy them. The students should then be encouraged to take special note of the parts of sermons that "moved their affections" and afterward to discuss them with one another. Of even more help would be the exhortations delivered in the college that were intended specifically for them—either for all of them assembled together or for special groupings among them.[94] From the Collegio Germanico at about the same time came a recommendation from Michele Laurentano to employ the older students to talk to the younger ones about the spiritual life as well as to give them examples of how to make progress.

He described what seems to have been the practice, for he observed: "This method of helping the laity by means of the laity results in good success when it is done well, and they generally accomplish more than [do the] religious."[95]

Concern for the spiritual well-being of students was supposed to be manifested in the classroom. The *Constitutions* put the matter simply: "The masters should make it their special aim, both in their lectures when occasion is offered and outside of them too, to inspire the students to the love and service of God our Lord and to a love of the virtues by which they will please God."[96]

Favre related how, when he was a boy, his teacher made "Christians" out of the classical authors he was studying.[97] Official Jesuit educational documents never go quite that far, but Nadal repeatedly urged teachers to find *pietas* in all the authors and subjects studied and to draw out the "spiritual" meaning imbedded in the texts.[98] Polanco reported that these "little digressions," which he considered a form of devout conversation, produced great effect even with boys "much addicted to the vices of youth."[99]

The "humane letters" to which a spiritual interpretation was applied were the classics, and, although the Jesuits did not in principle exclude works by the Fathers of the Church, such as Augustine, Jerome, and Gregory the Great, they in fact never formed part of the curriculum.[100] Calvinist schools were at this time turning more decidedly in favor of the Bible and Christian texts.[101] The Jesuits fully appropriated, moreover, the humanists' persuasion that culture and moral responsibility were inseparably connected.[102]

Jesuit educational documents spoke of the spiritual well-being of students without regard for the religious controversies of the age, but in their correspondence the Jesuits sometimes betrayed that they saw sound spirituality as a bulwark against the "errors of the times," subscribing to the traditional view that immorality was the hotbed and prerequisite for heresy. This view surfaced of course more often concerning northern Europe, but was not unknown elsewhere. Luís Gonçalves da Câmara, a leader in the more rigorous party in the Portuguese province, wrote to Nadal from Lisbon, for instance, on 29 May 1561: "I desire that our schools concern themselves especially with the virtues necessary for this kingdom and in particular [work] against the vices . . . for they seem to open the door and provide the disposition that allows heresy to enter."[103]

Classes and the program of religious practices formed the backbone of the Jesuit schools, but also important from the beginning were the plays and academic celebrations in which students displayed their talents and skills to a wider public. At Paris and elsewhere the early Jesuits had learned that such events were part of the *exercitium* required of students by good pedagogy and, hence, an integral part of their education.[104] The Jesuits brought memories of such "spectacles" with them into Italy, where some of these events, like orations in the universities to open the academic year, had long been practiced. The Jesuits were conscious, however, whence they derived their model, for they opened the academic year at Ferrara in 1552 with Latin poems and orations recited by the students in a program "celebrated in the Parisian style."[105] From their experience they saw the enthusiasm thus engendered especially in younger students, and they set about exploiting it as an aid for appropriating skills learned in the classroom.[106] These events were also effective advertisements for the school and won public support for it.

In Florence that same year for the same occasion, three Jesuits delivered panegyrics on the virtues, on the Latin language, and on the relationship between them—a significant but traditional theme.[107] The academic year opened at the Collegio Romano in 1553, just two years after it was founded, with disputations on philosophy, theology, and rhetoric, which were attended by a number of "cardinals, bishops, and other men of great authority."[108] Two years later public celebrations lasted for eight days—three days devoted to theology and the rest to "arts" (logic, ethics, physics, mathematics, metaphysics) and to "humane letters."[109]

The awarding of doctoral degrees at the Collegio Romano quickly emulated ceremonies in other universities, as we see from Polanco's descriptions for 6 February and 2 May 1556, and for one celebrated *valde solemniter* on 1 September 1557, at which Nadal presided.[110] But "recitals" were interspersed throughout the academic calendar both in Rome and in the humbler *collegia*. At Bologna in 1555, for example, a student, age eleven, delivered a Latin oration on "The Boy Jesus" at the opening of the year, another did the same at Christmas on "The Birth of Christ," and others at Pentecost on "Christ's Ascension," on "The Descent of the Holy Spirit," and similar topics.[111]

Students were sometimes sent to other locations to demonstrate their accomplishments. In 1556 the bishop of Genoa expressed to the Jesuits a desire to hear an oration on "Good Government." On Pentecost Sunday in the cathedral after a long liturgy a twelve-year-old student delivered an oration on the subject written by a Jesuit teacher. He was such a success, Polanco reported, that Andrea Doria, the great admiral and political master of Genoa, summoned the boy to repeat it for him privately.[112] A few weeks later the bishop invited two more boys to deliver orations after vespers on the feast of Corpus Christi.[113]

Within the schools orations like these were combined with other exercises, even with catechism, as Polanco reported—again for Genoa that same year:

> People came eagerly to an event where the students recited Christian Doctrine and interspersed the recitation with the delivery of Latin orations they had written, which aroused great admiration in the audience because it was something not done in other schools. The chance to deliver their orations engenders enthusiasm in the boys and is also an incitement to the parents to send them to school. The rector afterward praised the "orators," who had performed so well, and explained the necessity of actual practice of the rules of the art of oratory they had studied.[114]

Orations and poetry were employed in all the schools for celebratory occasions, and in the larger ones philosophical and theological disputations according to the standard scholastic style were also used. In some schools more elaborate forms like "dialogues," where verses set to music were sung between the "acts," began to appear.[115] At Bologna in 1556 during the Christmas season, the students appeared in a *sacra representatio,* a kind of pageant portraying the birth of Christ and the arrival of the Magi, and at Easter in another, accompanied by verses, portraying Christ's deposition from the cross.[116] Italians were quite familiar with the genre, for their confraternities had been producing such pageants for many generations.[117] From these *rappresentazioni* it was but a short step to full-fledged drama.

There are numerous studies of Jesuit theater, including a detailed, multivolume work on it in German-speaking lands from 1554 until almost the end of the seventeenth century, as well as a two-volume repertoire into the eighteenth.[118] In general these studies do not pay sufficient attention to music and dance (including ballet), usually an integral part of the performance that with the passing of time became ever more cultivated and important.[119] They show, in any case, that the significance of theater in all its aspects for Jesuit colleges can hardly be overestimated. Again, the Jesuits did not invent the "school drama," but they cultivated it to an especially high degree over a long period of time in a vast network of schools almost around the globe. They were involved in it within a few years after they opened the school in Messina.

One of the first plays of which there is clear record was *Jephthah Sacrificing His Daughter,* written by the Jesuit scholastic José de Acosta and produced at Medina del Campo in 1555. The play was well received—all the more so, Polanco tells us, because Acosta was born and raised in Medina.[120]

The next year Acosta wrote and produced two more, one of which was *Joseph Sold into Egypt*.[121] From a family of New Christians, Acosta was fifteen years old when *Jephthah* was produced and had already been a member of the Society for three years. He went on to a brilliant career in Spain and Peru as administrator and writer. His best-known and most celebrated work was *Historia natural y moral de las Indias* (1590).[122]

In 1556 a "comedy" entitled *On Good Morals* was produced at the school in Syracuse. Word about it spread and some leading citizens from a nearby town asked the rector to let the students present it there. The rector denied the request on the grounds that plays were produced in the schools "to encourage love of literature in the students, not as spectacles for the public."[123] This opinion did not prevail. By the 1560's elements of such productions were given in the vernacular to accommodate the wider audience,[124] and occasionally entire plays were produced in the vernacular.[125] In Munich in 1561, two years after the college was founded, the play was first performed for the general public and then for the duke and his court. Two years later in Innsbruck the first performance was in the Rathaus, the second in the imperial court before the emperor and empress.[126]

When Robert Claysson wrote back to Rome in 1558 about the plays, eclogues, academies, and similar events in the college at Billom, the first Jesuit school in France, he interpreted their purposes broadly and positively by affirming that their spiritual impact was the equivalent of a good sermon.[127] Most Jesuits shared his enthusiasm, but not all. That same year a Jesuit in Bologna complained that the boys spent their time on nothing else but getting ready for the play and that it was improper for members of religious orders to sponsor such events; in fact, children ridiculed the Jesuits in the streets with the cry "Here come the comedy priests!"—"Ecco li preti delle comedie!"[128]

Other Jesuits, including the ever-vigilant Juan Ramírez, complained that the plays were too costly to produce and caused scandal.[129] In the Collegio Germanico in 1570 a brawl broke out between the students and the actors from the Collegio Romano. Weapons were brandished. The incident led the general, Borja, to remove the rector from office and to expel one of the students, "the author of the sedition."[130]

From about 1560, Jesuit authorities imposed on the plays a number of regulations, which were inconsistently enforced and sometimes reversed; on rare occasions they discouraged plays altogether, but in general enthusiasm for them was high. Two or even three plays per year were regularly produced in some schools during the sixteenth century.[131]

The Jesuits wrote their own plays and produced those written by others—ancients and contemporaries. In Vienna, for instance, an adaptation of Terence's *Adelphi* was produced in 1556 and 1566, and an adaptation of Plautus's *Aulularis* in 1565.[132] Under Nadal's aegis, in 1557 the students at the Collegio Romano produced Terence's *Heautontimorumenos*. Twenty-five plays written between 1556 and 1572 by the Spanish Jesuit Pedro Acevedo still survive.[133] At Messina, Stefano Tucci wrote and produced in 1562 *Nabuchodonosor* (Nebuchadnezzar) when he was a scholastic only twenty-one years old; he followed in successive years with *Goliath* and *Judith*.[134] At Como about the same time students acted in *The Rebels* by the Dutch neo-Latin playwright Georgius Macropedius (1486–1558).[135] In 1555 *Acolastus* by the Dutch humanist Gnaphaeus was produced at the colleges in Córdoba and Lisbon.[136] *Euripus: Tragedia Christiana* by the Franciscan Levin Brecht was especially popular in German schools.[137] Seemingly peculiar to Cologne were overtly polemical pieces, with Luther, Calvin, and the Devil among the principal characters.[138]

These are but samples of a phenomenon that within a year or two of the inception of a given school became a staple of its educational program. The aesthetic limitations of "school drama" are well known, but to put them into perspective we need to recall that Lope de Vega, Calderón, Andreas Gryphius, Jacob Bidermann, Corneille, and Molière received their first training in theater in Jesuit schools.

Jesuit Education

Despite problems, sometimes severe, the Jesuit schools enjoyed success in most localities even during these early years, and they soon assumed the preeminent place among the ministries of the Society that Polanco attributed to them in 1560. Some reasons for their success should by now be clear. The Jesuits at times founded schools where there were none before. More often they simply offered something that seemed better than its alternatives. As was often true of them in other endeavors, the Jesuits created relatively few of the components of their educational program, but they put those parts together in a way and on a scale that had never been done before.[139] It was the combination, not any single feature, that distinguished the education offered in the Jesuit schools from what was offered elsewhere.

The Jesuits produced an immense amount of documentation concerning their educational enterprise as they moved toward the definitive edition of *Ratio studiorum* in 1599. The very quantity of their writings makes it difficult to find the forest amidst the trees. The Jesuits themselves often could not find it. The documents tend, moreover, to jumble together features that today would be neatly sorted out into charters, job descriptions, "mission statements," "profiles of the ideal graduate," class schedules, curricula, pedagogical techniques, and syllabuses.

Nonetheless, at least ten characteristics can be identified as contributing to the Jesuits' initial success and to a new, international educational style. First, the schools charged no tuition. Second, at least in principle they welcomed students from every social class. Third, especially the schools of "humane letters" conformed to the emerging consensus of the age in curriculum, the importance of character formation, and similar matters. The disciplinary regulations by and large conformed to the same consensus. Fourth, the Jesuits postulated compatibility between an education in "humane letters" on the one hand and in Aristotelian philosophy/science and Thomistic theology on the other, a compatibility vaguely adumbrated in the "Rules for Thinking with the Church" in the *Exercises*.[140]

Fifth, from the *modus parisiensis* they implemented division into classes (each with its own teacher), ordered progression from class to class according to clear curricular goals, and similar provisions. Sixth, again from the "Parisian Mode" they borrowed the insistence on active appropriation of both ideas and skills—*exercitium!*—that consisted not only in written compositions and oral repetitions in the classroom, but also in plays, disputations, and other "spectacles" open to the public.

Seventh, they sponsored a clear, coherent, and basically simple religious program, adaptable to students of different ages and backgrounds—a program that in principle sought to move the student beyond pious practices to an inner appropriation of ethical and religious values. Eighth, through their Marian Congregations they gave further articulation to their religious program by adopting and adapting one of the most popular institutions of the day, the confraternity.

Ninth, they were on the way to creating an international network of schools, the largest by far under a single aegis the world had ever seen, in which information was effectively shared about what worked and what did not. Their normative documents with their sometimes obsessively detailed stipulations pushed them toward conformity, especially once the *Ratio* was published in 1599, but the Jesuits could never forget the necessity of accommodation to times, places, and circumstances.

Finally, most difficult to calculate, the "teaching under the teaching" was different coming from this special group of men. The Jesuits were on the whole better educated and motivated than most pre-university schoolmasters almost anywhere in Europe. Further, they tried to influence their students more by their example than by their words. They repeatedly inculcated in one another the importance of loving their students, of knowing them as individuals, of enjoying a respectful *familiaritas* with them.[141] Whenever these ideals were achieved, they were crucially important in contributing to a school's success. Failure to achieve them would perhaps be even more telling.

The blend of these features resulted in an educational program that in some parts of Europe appeared as a notable improvement on practices already in operation, in other parts as a stunning innovation. It resulted in a program that in its totality transcended the designation *modus parisiensis*. An inversion of terminology began to take place, as the Jesuits now occasionally used *modus italicus* to indicate the style of *their* schools in Italy, which they in turn wanted to introduce into Paris.[142] "Our way of proceeding" had developed its educational component.

Failures, Frustrations, and Crisis

"The Society is being ruined by taking on so many schools." That was the frank judgment of Cortesono at the end of the period I am considering. He gave his reasons: the schools were such a burden that the Jesuit scholastics were sent to teach in them at the price of curtailing their own studies; in order to ensure a supply of teachers, the Jesuits accepted unsuitable candidates into the Society; for the same reason they tolerated within their midst even rogues *(discoli);* this was leading to a loss of the Society's true spirit; the financial problems of the schools would lead to the adoption of choir (with benefices), and so forth. He further judged that although the Society undertook the teaching of letters to form youth in Christian piety, experience showed little evidence of the success of such formation, except with boarders. His remedy in this apologia for the Collegio Germanico was to curtail drastically the number of schools, so that each province have no more than two or three, and whenever possible to turn them into boarding schools—like the Germanico, of which he was the rector.[143]

Plausible as Cortesono's charges may have been, they did not exhaust the list of questions and problems. In almost every conceivable way the Society was unprepared to open in rapid-fire fashion as many schools as it had in the first years after Messina, which by 1553 had led to a crisis in personnel that became almost endemic. There were too few Jesuits for the number of schools, as well as for other commitments. Many among those few performed badly in the classroom, either because they did not know the subject or because they were incompetent pedagogues. Practically none were ready by training and temperament to assume the administrative duties these institutions required.

These were the almost desperate sentiments of Miguel de Torres, provincial of Portugal, conveyed to Ignatius in 1553 and then repeated to Laínez eleven years later.[144] As provincial of Andalusia, he in 1555 estimated that among those who were in charge of schools in that area no more than two had the talent requisite for the job.[145] Similar sentiments were expressed by others elsewhere in the Society and justified by the facts.[146] Although Jesuit headquarters in Rome heard about how well things sometimes were going, complaints also poured in.

A common complaint from students and their parents was that the Jesuits changed teachers too often, and almost as often replaced them with less competent ones.[147] Foreigners sometimes had only a rudimentary grasp of the local language and spoke Latin with accents to which the natives were unaccustomed—a sensitive issue in Italy.[148] The manpower situation was exacerbated by the necessity of supplying teachers for distant places. In 1561, for instance, Nadal searched the Iberian peninsula for six qualified Jesuits to be sent to India—a rector for Goa, three teachers of Latin, a teacher of philosophy *(las artes),* and a teacher of theology.[149] Moreover, Jesuits in the schools sometimes had to be reminded that their primary responsibility was to their students, not to adults who came to them for confession or counsel.[150]

The difficulties in opening new schools were so overwhelming that some Jesuits simply abandoned their vocation to the Society, and Polanco warned as early as 1553 that "experience teaches" that only the "most proven and constant" should be sent into these situations, a warning with scant possibility of being heeded.[151] Some of those sent occasioned disturbance of the peace *(perturbationes)* in their communities, and sending them elsewhere did not solve the problem.[152]

Older Jesuits began to complain that the scholastics sent to the colleges, especially from the highly touted Collegio Romano, knew their Terence better than their Aquinas. The scholastics had become accustomed to niceties in food and clothing, showed favoritism in dealing with students, had little interest in teaching, were "arid in things of the spirit," and dreamed of the "honor of a chair." In a word, "The colleges are being ruined by the disorder they cause, and every year one must begin again to repair the damage done by the end of the previous year."[153] In his letter of 10 August

1560, Polanco required that all Jesuits do their part in "bearing the burden of the schools," but not all Jesuits were equal to the task.

What about the students? From many schools came enthusiastic reports about the progress the students made in studies and virtue and about the hope they inspired for the future.[154] Although the Jesuits were proud of their triumphs, they were also pragmatic observers and frank communicators to each other of what succeeded or failed. When they reported success, as they often did, they must be taken more or less at their word. The same assumption applies for failures. Some schools reported intractable problems with discipline. A scholastic at Ferrara in 1556 could handle classes of no more than nine or ten students, but another sometimes had only two or three. That year enrollment in the school seriously declined, and occasionally no students showed up for some of the classes. Polanco conceded that part of the reason was the poor quality of instruction, but added that the youth of Ferrara was less disciplined *(liberior)* than the Jesuits had hoped.[155]

In Florence the "insolence" of some students caused ongoing problems for the Jesuits.[156] As early as 1548 Nadal laid down the rule in Messina that students could not enter the school buildings bearing arms. This was a somewhat standard regulation for educational institutions of the day, but the Jesuits kept repeating it for their schools.[157] The boys at Gubbio were tough—"unmanageable and like beasts, who have been known to kill each other."[158] Especially when there were boarders, as in the Germanico, the Jesuits had suspicions, seemingly not ungrounded, about the sexual *mores* of the students, and they feared that, unless something was done, "our schools will end up like the others in Italy." Some Jesuits thought, rather, that too much surveillance in this regard was making matters worse.[159]

Although the Jesuits did not particularly favor schools that accepted boarders, they had undertaken some, especially in northern Europe. They did so to protect the boys from a Protestant environment. Within a few years of opening, the college at Vienna had 6 boarders.[160] By 1562 the college at Tournai, for instance, had 125 boarders, 120 day students; the college at Cologne, 51 boarders and 444 others.

A composite list of problems consistently arising in such institutions, which has an almost timeless quality to it, went somewhat as follows: Jesuits talked with students about things concerning the school that students had no right to know; the students complained about the quantity and quality of the food; prefects were so overburdened as to lose all privacy, and by their frequent contact with the students, lost their respect; the boys invented cruel nicknames for their teachers and prefects and united against them; students had a lingo of their own in which they communicated to frustrate those in charge of them.

How to discipline unruly students was no less a problem for the Jesuits than it has been for educators through the ages. The Jesuits were repeatedly admonished to do so gently, sparingly, by word rather than deed, to prefer rewarding good behavior to punishing bad. Like their contemporaries, however, they believed that physical punishment was sometimes required, at least for the younger boys. When in Messina in 1557 they experimented with abolishing corporal punishment, the boys' parents objected, and the Jesuits had to reinstitute it.[161]

But who was to administer the blows? According to Ignatius, the Jesuits themselves were never, under any circumstances, to do so. It would be difficult to find a single issue on which he was more adamant, unbudging, intransigent than this one, and behind which he more repeatedly threw the full weight of his authority. In the reputedly militaristic discipline of the Society of Jesus, commands issued "under holy obedience," that is, in virtue of the vow, were extraordinarily rare. But, once Ignatius realized by 1553 that he was not being heeded in the matter of physical discipline, he imposed on all Jesuit teachers in Italy precisely such an injunction, from which he would not tolerate the slightest deviation.[162] Could Jesuits at least strike students on the palms of their hands? The answer was negative.[163] Why was he so insistent on this issue? He believed that physical punishment diminished respect for the one administering it and ruptured the bond of affection between Jesuits and those they were trying to "help." His stance caused the Jesuits untold minor agonies in trying to be faithful to it.

The solution Ignatius suggested was to hire a "corrector," but some schools were too poor to do so or could not find somebody at the price they were willing to pay.[164] At Venice in 1556 some "pious matrons" said they would supply funds until the position could be endowed.[165] Some schools resorted to having the older boys punish the younger—with bad results. Parents objected, and little improvement was noted in the offenders.[166] At Gubbio the outcome was utterly disastrous; the younger boys, "armed," ganged together and beat up on their oppressors.[167] The problem dragged on in the Society without satisfactory resolution, although in 1558 the First General Congregation mitigated Ignatius's prohibition by allowing the general to dispense from it "when necessary."[168]

Some of the problems I have been describing are endemic to secondary schools, even if not in the aggravated degree to which they sometimes afflicted the Jesuit colleges during this period. But the schools had opened at such a hectic pace and raised so many new issues that by 1553 a systemic crisis ensued. In that year Polanco composed a document dealing with the problem of their rapid multiplication, and Ignatius set down norms for the number and competence of Jesuits required to establish a school, for its endowment, and for other necessities before the Society would accept an invitation to open a school.[169]

The First General Congregation, 1558, ratified the provisions concerning the number of Jesuits needed for a school and reiterated the same interesting distribution of tasks: two or three priests for confession and ministry of Word, four or five teachers, a few others as substitutes in case of sickness and other emergencies, and two temporal coadjutors to take care of material needs. This added up to about a dozen or more, less than half of them full-time teachers.[170] In those few teachers considerable versatility was required; Nadal himself taught Greek, Hebrew, and mathematics in the first years at Messina.

Meanwhile, schools began to close—at Argenta, Gubbio, Frascati, Foligno, Montepulciano, Modena, and elsewhere, sometimes amid great bitterness. Some schools made a poor showing against already established institutions, as in Florence, and many incurred overwhelming debts.[171] In some localities the resentment of local schoolmasters raged against them, causing the Jesuits to lose students and the financial support they so desperately needed.[172] At Segovia in 1570 the citizens withdrew their financial support from the school of "humane letters," and it had to close.[173]

Whereas some towns sought out the Jesuits because their schools would fill a vacuum, others resented them and considered their schools superfluous. Modena, for instance, seemed to have plenty of schoolmasters, and its citizens never warmed up to the Jesuits, partly because of their hard line against persons suspected of Lutheranism.[174] The bishop held out little hope for the college because the teachers were not Italians.[175] In France the Jesuits in general had difficulty gaining acceptance.[176]

In any case, if a great strategy was operative behind decisions when and where to establish schools, it is far from apparent, except for a preference for schools in larger and more important cities.[177] Ignatius did not wait for an invitation from Duke Cosimo I to establish a school in Florence, for example, but in 1551 had Laínez try to persuade the duke that it was a good idea.[178] It is true, moreover, that in 1555 Ignatius began to show himself less inclined to open more colleges in Italy, hoping to divert some of the available manpower to places like Hungary, Transylvania, Bohemia, Poland, France, and of course Germany, with an obvious eye to the struggle in those places against heresy.[179] It is also true that Antonio Possevino a few years later formulated a strategy for Piedmont and Savoy.[180]

Otherwise opportunities were seized or created without benefit of a master plan and, it seems, often without adequate consideration of what the market would bear and what Jesuit talent could sustain. In 1565, in any case, the Second General Congregation decreed a drastic slowdown in opening new schools, no matter how important they may seem, until the Society had a more adequate supply of teachers and other persons to staff them.[181]

Perhaps the major remedy the Society applied to bring order out of the many problems raised by the schools and to coordinate efforts in this far-flung enterprise was, besides an avalanche of written documents, the employment of "commissaries," those representatives of the general with practically plenipotentiary powers. As we have seen, the first and most out-standing of these was Nadal, appointed by Ignatius himself for Spain and Portugal, 1553–54, and then reappointed by him and his two immediate successors. Although in that first visitation Nadal was to promulgate and explain the *Constitutions* and to resolve doubts about "our way of proceeding," the first task listed for him was to give order and method to the schools. This task continued to engage Nadal's energies in subsequent visitations—to the Empire and Italy in 1555, to Spain and Portugal in 1561, to France, Belgium, and the Empire in 1562–63, and to the same regions in 1566–68. Problems persisted, but through commissaries and other means a measure of stability was achieved, and some schools that earlier foundered began to flourish.[182]

Training the Clergy

The Jesuit educational venture originated with concern for the training of younger members of the Society, whose education the first companions hoped would be at least the equivalent of their own. Those companions must themselves be numbered among the clergy that benefited from the best their age had to offer. From their observations, however, and from many other sources as well, we know that the training of the diocesan clergy followed an extraordinarily haphazard pattern across Europe.[183] Although a small percentage were well educated and devout, the seemingly vast majority were so ill-trained as to constitute a major scandal, and some were ignorant almost beyond description. It was almost inevitable that the Jesuits would be drawn into attempts to alleviate the situation.

They did so before the famous decree on seminaries of the Council of

Trent, 1563, and would continue to do so afterward. Although after 1563 the Jesuits were surely influenced by the Council, their most typical institution did not fall into the pattern of the "Tridentine Seminary," that is, a free-standing and programmatically integral institution reserved exclusively for the future diocesan clergy under the direct jurisdiction of the local bishop. The Jesuits' preferred instrument for the training of their own members and young diocesan clerics was a school they themselves managed, perhaps with residences attached, that was open to both of those groups and also to lay students.

The best way to get a sense of their thinking in this regard is to look at three Roman institutions—the Collegio Romano, the Collegio Germanico, and the Seminario Romano. Almost immediately upon its founding, the Collegio Romano assumed a special position because Ignatius urged Jesuit superiors around Europe to send scholastics there for training, and he entertained the hope that it would be the preeminent educational institution of the Society.[184] By 1555 it had Jesuit students from Italy, Spain, Portugal, France, Flanders, Germany, Bohemia, Dalmatia, Greece, and elsewhere, housed in the Collegio apart from the *casa professa*.[185] Moved from location to location until finally settled in 1560 in the present Piazza del Collegio Romano, it was school building and residence for both Jesuit teachers and Jesuit students.[186]

From the beginning its financial status was precarious, often desperate. The endowment from Borja fell far short of expectations and need. Polanco wrote to all Jesuit superiors in 1553 telling them that the Collegio would be an "ornament for the Holy See," but until the much later pontificate of Pope Gregory XIII (1572–85) financial support for it from the popes was sporadic and paltry.[187] Begging money for the Collegio was invariably one of Nadal's assignments on his Iberian trips. When in the fall of 1555 Ignatius sent some hundred Jesuits out of Rome to other colleges in Italy, Spain, and Portugal, he did so at least partly because he was constrained by the dire financial situation. He could not afford to feed them at the Collegio.[188]

Among the colleges, however, the Collegio Romano was the apple of Ignatius's eye. He tried to provide for it the best teachers, drawn from Jesuit provinces throughout Europe. His successors continued the policy, which ensured the preeminence Ignatius had desired. Francisco de Toledo, for instance, arrived in 1559 to teach logic, but moved on to teach physics, metaphysics, cases of conscience, and scholastic theology; he eventually became one of the most important Catholic theologians of his day. As early as 1561, he published *Introductio in dialecticam Aristotelis*.[189] That same year, Juan de

Mariana began at age twenty-four to teach Scripture and then scholastic theology. He remained at the Collegio until 1565, and many years later published his great masterpiece, *Historia general de España,* and the work for which he is best known, *De rege et regis institutione,* with its famous thesis on the permissibility of regicide. Cristoph Clavius, the distinguished German mathematician and astronomer, began teaching there in 1564. Moreover, regulations, procedures, and textbooks adopted at the Collegio were held up as the norm and ideal for schools elsewhere.[190] Although other students were admitted to the Collegio Romano in great numbers, in Jesuit eyes it had a special character because of its role in educating Jesuits. Almost from the beginning, it was conceived as a center from which Jesuits would be sent on various pastoral missions and from which "new colonies" would be formed for the founding of other schools.[191]

The year after the Collegio Romano opened its doors, so did its closely related institution the Collegio Germanico.[192] The idea for the school originated with Cardinal Giovanni Morone, who proposed it to Ignatius. Assisted by Cardinal Marcello Cervini, Morone soon won approval for it from Pope Julius III. Its purpose was to provide training in Rome as future diocesan priests for young men from Germany and other areas of northern Europe "infected with heresy," such as Bohemia, Poland, and Hungary.[193] In a letter in 1554 in which Ignatius tried to win financial support for the Germanico from Emperor Charles V, he argued unsuccessfully that more was to be expected for the restoration of Catholicism in the Empire from the school than from arms or even from the Council of Trent.[194] Later that year in a letter to a Spanish Jesuit, Nadal expressed his enthusiasm for young men of "northern" nations being trained there "to preach and guide souls" by their example and learning, for there was a great lack of such pastors in those regions.[195]

The Germanico opened with twenty-four students, who took their classes at the Collegio Romano. In other words, the Germanico was basically a residence. The Jesuits were in charge, and some resided there, overseeing the discipline, the religious program, and the academic repetitions, disputations, and similar exercises. The rules for the students were similar to those for the Jesuit scholastics. "Protectors" of the Germanico who sent students to it were expected to provide the financing for poor youths who wanted to be priests.[196]

Even an institution of this simple design faltered. Except among the Jesuits, it failed to spark enthusiasm. Neither the German bishops, the Italian cardinals, nor Popes Julius III and Paul IV provided any consistent financial aid, and by 1556 the whole financial burden fell on the Society. There were also disciplinary problems.[197]

The number of German students had meanwhile fallen below even the originally modest number. The Germanico admitted only one new student in 1555, none in 1556 and 1557. In an effort to save the institution at least in principle, Laínez in 1558 allowed admission of other students as paying boarders. Most were Italians. They were not expected to be candidates for holy orders. Within a few years and after several changes of location, the expedient resulted in a great influx of these new students. They were all under fifteen years old. The costs of boarding meant that they had to come from wealthy backgrounds; indeed, some of them were from the most distinguished families of their locality—the Dorias of Genoa, the Bentivoglios and Buoncompagnis of Bologna, the Fuggers of Augsburg. Names like these confirm the good reputation the Jesuits had already achieved as educators. By 1565 the Germanico had students from many countries of Europe, including Poland, England, and Scotland, and even two from Turkey.[198]

Wealthy though the students were, they of course paid no tuition to the Collegio Romano, but they had to pay for their meals and the other expenses of a boarding school.[199] They had to pay for any servants in their own employ.[200] Between 1563 and 1573 the number of students resident in the college was about two hundred, with the ratio of about one German seminarian to ten of the others.[201] This means that the Germanico had devolved during this period into an institution reserved largely to the wealthy elite.

The disciplinary problems arising from this mix of nationalities and from the sometimes recalcitrant students get due attention in the abundant documentation that has survived.[202] The Germans, according to Nadal, were "disobedient and trouble-makers."[203] The Italian *putti* were often bad when they first arrived, but the Jesuits saw them change for the better with time.[204] However, they often resented the Jesuit scholastics who were sent there to help with the discipline of the house and other matters.[205]

Despite problems and the reservations about the enterprise entertained by some Jesuits, Polanco painted an optimistic picture in his circular letter to the Society in 1565, emphasizing how fond the students had grown of their collegio.[206] About 1567, Cortesono, who was the rector and ought to have been better informed, went so far as to suggest the abandonment of the institution as it was originally conceived, because "Germany is not so much in need as before."[207] By 1570 Laurentano, soon to be rector himself, vigorously supported the direction the Germanico had taken: "Just as the ecclesiastical seminaries are ordered for the reform of the clergy, so does this college serve for the reform of the lay nobility . . . The Society does not have a better means to help the nobility and great lords and magistrates of our times."[208] Two years later, on the eve of the transfer of the non-German boarders to the Seminario, he argued the same position.[209]

The original purpose of the Germanico was thus largely thwarted during this period, and some Jesuits did not see great urgency in its recovery. Other counsels prevailed. When Pope Gregory XIII gave moral support to the original purpose and backed it up with substantial financing, the non-German boarders were moved out in 1573. Bishops of the Empire had meanwhile begun to send students in greater numbers. From this time forward the Germanico became an important instrument in the restoration of Catholicism in many parts of Germany through the pastors and especially the theologians and future bishops it trained. Jesuit universities elsewhere often followed the same pattern of having colleges for diocesan clergy attached to them. The Germanico also served as a model for the establishment of papal seminaries in Germany in the 1570's and 1580's.[210]

The Germanico and its parent institution, the Collegio Romano, were the first institutions of international scope established in Rome for the training of future Catholic clergy. After 1573, the Germanico became the model for other national colleges of clerical students attached to the Collegio Romano that would become characteristic of the city.[211] These two colleges were the first and decisive steps in a process that eventually turned Rome into the center for training clergy that it has remained to this day.

In 1564 Pope Pius IV founded the Seminario Romano for the archdiocese of Rome in conformity with the Tridentine decree of the previous year.[212] Although he was at the time annoyed with the Jesuits, he confided its direction to them, an action that set off widespread resentment in the Roman clergy against the Society, not least because the pope taxed them to support the new institution. In that context Bishop Ascanio Cesarini proclaimed that he could not bear having Roman youth taught by Germans and Spaniards— that is, heretics and Jews! Nonetheless, in February 1565, after the death of Laínez the previous month, the Seminario opened its doors to some eighty students.[213]

The Seminary was basically a residence like the Germanico. The students took classes at the Collegio Romano, up to but not including courses in theology. The Jesuits found the students extremely difficult to handle and complained that, unlike at the Germanico and other schools fully under the aegis of the Society, they had no control over admissions and dismissals. In

1568 the Roman province of the Jesuits decided to ask Pope Pius V to relieve the Society of the Seminario and give it to others, but to no avail.[214]

Sometime around 1570 the Jesuit rector and his assistant wrote reports that made the seminarians sound like outlaws. Although they came from the lowest rungs of Roman society, they were nonetheless filled with an over-weening pride. They were liars, cheats, ingrates, utterly untrustworthy, cor-ruptors of the few good among them, devoid of any pastoral or religious motivation, intent only upon gaining fat benefices with no pastoral duties attached. They called the seminary a "prison" and the Jesuits "spies and hypocrites," their "jailers and executioners." In the rector's opinion, the Germanico was in comparison "a paradise."[215]

Through many vicissitudes the Jesuits continued in their role at the Seminario until the Society was suppressed in the late eighteenth century. At least in the sixteenth century they were disinclined toward undertaking other institutions of this type. In 1565 the Second General Congregation, which was convoked to elect a successor to Laínez, took up the issue for-mally and decreed that the Society not assume responsibility for "episcopal seminaries about which the Council of Trent decreed," even if the bishops were willing to commit their full governance to the Society. The Congrega-tion allowed the general to make exceptions, but only under certain strin-gent conditions.[216] Why this reluctance?

The furor and ill will aroused by their acceptance of the Seminario Romano surely made an impact on the Jesuits gathered for the Congrega-tion, and an even more complicated imbroglio in Milan surrounding the new seminary sponsored by Carlo Borromeo had to increase their misgiv-ings.[217] But there were deeper reasons. Even when assurances to the contrary were given them, the Jesuits worried about losing in such institutions their independence to act as they saw fit. They may have feared implication in matters proper to diocesan officials. In any case, in 1568 Borja, now general, stated that the "statutes prescribed for seminaries by the Council of Trent" made them incompatible with the Jesuit Institute.[218]

Even more fundamentally, the Jesuits believed that their own colleges were already "true and excellent seminaries," as Polanco wrote to Nadal from Trent on 6 July 1563, an idea allowed by the Tridentine decree.[219] As early as 1553, Ignatius agreed as part of the statutes to accept as students at the college of Compostela four candidates for ordination from that arch-bishopric and eight from other bishoprics of Galicia.[220] More generally, the Jesuits prided themselves on the number of the students in their colleges who decided to become priests or enter religious orders. When in 1550 Ignatius described to Ercole d'Este, duke of Ferrara, the college he wanted to establish there as "a seminary, from which will come regularly new laborers in the vineyard of the Lord," he surely meant to include such students in that description.[221]

The colleges were in fact far superior in both their academic and religious programs to the diocesan seminaries that eventuated from the legislation of Trent. Concerned though the Jesuits were with the proper training of the diocesan clergy, they much preferred to promote it through their own institutions.[222]

The model Jesuits envisaged for the education of the diocesan clergy even after Trent, therefore, was an adapted form of the late-medieval practice of special residences for the clergy, which might also contain lay students, located in the vicinity of an educational institution like a university and attached to it. At the Jesuit university at Pont-à-Mousson in the early seventeenth century, for instance, there were three "seminaries" for students from three different dioceses, as well as several convents for students from other religious orders.[223]

There was another way, however, in which Jesuits contributed to the training of the diocesan clergy in several parts of the world. Building on the early pattern of the temporary teaching assignments of Laínez and Favre at the University of Rome and of Jay, Salmerón, and Canisius at Ingolstadt, Jesuits began to accept more long-term assignments to teach especially philosophy and theology in universities not under the aegis of the Society. Only priests or candidates for ordination studied theology at universities, and many students of philosophy were drawn from that same group.

At Ingolstadt beginning in 1556, for instance, the number of Jesuits teaching theology, small though it was, equaled or surpassed the number of others. From 1560 until 1575 three Jesuits taught theology at the University of Cologne. In Trier as early as 1561 Jesuits had in effect taken over the faculties of philosophy and theology and were soon on the way to doing the same at Mainz. The pattern continued into the seventeenth century. The number of Jesuits thus engaged was relatively modest, but their influence through their students, who often became teachers themselves, was significant.[224]

As we have seen, the Jesuits inserted into the formal university program courses on cases of conscience—courses that had a direct bearing on pastoral practice. Their insistence on the study of rhetoric, on the "Tones," and on similar exercises to help develop preaching skills broke, on the one hand, a pattern of university training that ignored such skills and, on the other, a pattern of apprenticeship training that lacked the means to communicate them effectively. In codifying these developments among Catholics, the Jesuits were pioneers.

The Impact of the Schools

The Jesuits opened a new era for formal education in Roman Catholicism. The Society was the first religious order to undertake systematically, as a primary and self-standing ministry, the operation of full-fledged schools for any students, lay or clerical, who chose to come to them. It marked a decided break with earlier patterns of relationship between the church and educational institutions.[225]

Over the course of the next two centuries, the Society established its remarkable network of more than eight hundred educational institutions, primarily in Latin Europe and Latin America, but also in other parts of the world, a truly unique phenomenon in the history of education that ended with the suppression of the order in 1773. When the Jesuits were restored by Pope Pius VII in 1814, they resumed the task. Moreover, since the latter part of the sixteenth century their example encouraged many other religious orders of men and women to do the same, down to the present century.

Jesuit schools greatly influenced religion and culture in many areas of the world, but the very immensity of the Jesuit educational enterprise and the complexity of the questions it raises practically preclude a comprehensive assessment. We must be content with studies limited to specific territories, chronologies, and issues—and thence draw larger, highly qualified conclusions.[226]

A somewhat more tractable problem, and more pertinent to this book, is the impact the schools had on the Society of Jesus itself. The Jesuit *Constitutions* stipulated that "the first characteristic of our Institute" was for the members to be free to travel to various parts of the world.[227] The foundational model for this characteristic was the itinerant preachers of the Gospel described in the New Testament. Although the evangelical model was dominant in the early years, it was of course not the only one, for stable residences were foreseen from the beginning. Nonetheless, that model now had to be further tempered by the reality of being resident schoolmasters. The tension between the continuing insistence on the necessity of mobility and the long-term commitment required by the schools would remain throughout Jesuit history.

Even in the early years the schools were comparatively large and complex institutions that required the best talent for their management and faculty.

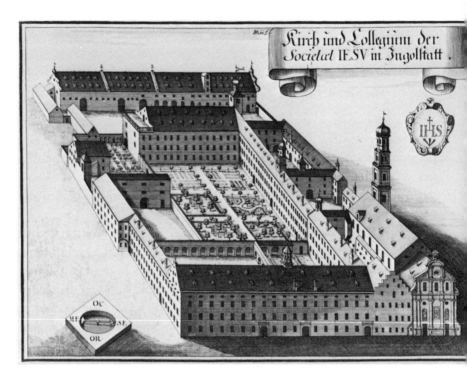

The Jesuit school and church at Ingolstadt, from an engraving of 1701.

Their governance and the officials needed for it became a special focus of attention and legislation. The Jesuit communities attached to them grew to considerable size, and this development hastened and conditioned the usual sociological repercussions of transition from an informal situation to something larger and more regularized. The fact that most members of the Society would be housed in the endowed institutions that were the schools changed an important aspect of the vow of poverty described in the *Constitutions*. Moreover, the Jesuits became property owners on a large scale, for their schools with their classrooms, observatories, theaters, and courtyards were often huge establishments, to which were attached a Jesuit residence and church.

While in many ways the schools enhanced the other ministries, which so often used them as a base, they also absorbed manpower and talent to an extraordinary degree. This meant that an increasing amount of Jesuit energy would be spent on adolescent boys. Those boys were often, but by no means exclusively, drawn from the middle and upper classes of society, and the Jesuit schools to some extent drew the other ministries along with them in that direction. From these classes of society, moreover, the Jesuits would tend to attract their own new members. The Jesuits never lost their concern for the poor and "outcast," and some would expend great energies on them. But with the passage of years it was indirect asssistance through the Marian Congregations and other confraternities they inspired that became increasingly important.

Until the Collegio Romano opened in 1551, the Jesuits intended that their own members would be taught by university teachers who were not Jesuits. After that date they began to take for granted, though the *Constitutions* suggest otherwise, that Jesuits would be trained by other Jesuits in schools run by Jesuits. This change helped forge a clearer sense of identity for the members of the Society, but it also meant a more closed intellectual atmosphere.

Perhaps the most important change the schools wrought within the Society, however, was the new kind and degree of its members' engagement with culture beyond the traditionally clerical subjects of philosophy and theology. The earliest Jesuits from the beginning wanted their recruits to have a first-rate education, but with the schools came the obligation to train their members to teach what they had learned, and therefore to appropriate it in a more profound way. Moreover, much of what they taught related only indirectly to the Christian religion as such.

The *Constitutions* of the Dominicans from the thirteenth century stipulated that student-members of the order were not to read books by pagans or learn any "secular sciences" except by dispensation: "let these student-members and all others read only books of theology."[228] The Dominican *Constitutions* allowed exceptions, which subsequent General Chapters authorized, but the stipulation continued to be observed and to have effect into the sixteenth century and beyond.[229] The history of the first six or seven years of the Jesuits did not preclude a similar route for them, especially given the conservative turn taken in Catholic circles at about that time. However, by force of their vocation as teachers of the humanities and of "natural philosophy," that is, the physical sciences, the Jesuits had to move in precisely the opposite direction.

Ignatius foresaw Jesuits writing books on ministry and in refutation of "the heretics," which they did, but many of the first books that Jesuits produced were textbooks on grammar, rhetoric, and the Latin and Greek classics—subjects that almost every Jesuit taught at some point in his career. *De arte rhetorica* by Cipriano Soares, first published in 1562, ran through more than two hundred editions into the nineteenth century.[230]

Jesuits taught mathematics, astronomy, physics, and other sciences, wrote on these subjects, ran observatories and laboratories, and attained renown in these fields.²³¹ The schools also brought theater with them, and with theater came dance and music, so that the early misgivings about music were challenged from another direction and gradually overcome. In some places they brought training in fencing and horsemanship. The large buildings that Jesuit schools required led members of the Society into a new relationship with architects and architecture. The schools, though run under Jesuit auspices, were institutions of civic import that gave the Jesuits an access to civic life that their churches alone could never provide.

Thus began an engagement with secular culture, modest enough at first, that became a hallmark of the order and an integral part of its self-definition, not present at the beginning. That engagement was not occasional or incidental, but systemic. It became interwoven with the very fabric of the Jesuits' understanding of their ministry, of their "way of proceeding." Their religious mission remained basic to them, but, especially as a result of the schools, they also began to see themselves as having a cultural mission.

A basic premise of the humanist tradition in the Renaissance was that religious and moral inspiration could be found even in pagan authors. The Jesuits subscribed to that premise, which generically correlated with the tendency in Thomistic theology to find as much harmony as possible between "nature and grace," also a theme of the Jesuit *Constitutions*. Although the Jesuits were not uncritical in their engagement with secular culture, they tended in general to be welcoming of it.

When the Jesuits first embarked on their educational venture about a decade after their founding, they could not have foreseen its impact on them. They treated the schools as if they were one more—although an especially important—ministry added to an already long list. They did not grasp that this ministry had an intrinsic dynamism that would change the organization undertaking it.

～ 7

Religious and Theological Culture

ALTHOUGH THE decision to undertake schools inserted the Jesuits into the culture of their day in unanticipated and quite special ways, they would never have moved in that direction had their background not already inclined them to it. With the schools they began to be recognized as excellent pedagogues even in subjects unrelated to religion. In most of their schools, in fact, theology was not a subject in the curriculum. Because it was not at the base but at the peak of the academic pyramid of the *modus parisiensis,* it was taught only in Jesuit universities, of which there were but a handful.

Nonetheless, the Jesuits saw themselves and were seen by others as "theologians." In an important instruction to the Jesuits at Alcalá in 1561 on the program of studies in the Society, Nadal referred to Ignatius as "our father, the theologian."[1] A professor of theology at Paris reportedly said that he had never heard anybody speak so well on theological questions. This was Martial Mazurier, whom Ignatius guided in the *Exercises* while he was at Paris as a student.[2]

Peter Canisius described Favre in almost identical terms.[3] Paul III's appointment of Favre and Laínez to teach theology at the University of Rome immediately upon their arrival in the city and the subsequent appointments of Laínez, Salmerón, and Jay as theologians to the Council of Trent are but two instances of a general persuasion that members of this new *compagnia* were well suited to deal with pressing religious and theological issues. Understanding the Jesuits, therefore, obviously entails understanding how they envisaged the theological enterprise and their role in it.

The Jesuits often described the theology they espoused as "mystical" and contrasted it with the "purely speculative" theology of some of their Catholic contemporaries, such as Domingo de Soto.[4] By mystical they meant not the transports and ecstasies usually connoted by the term, but, according to Nadal, an inner understanding and relish of the truth translated into the way one lived.[5] Nadal here articulated in a different context the most basic orientation of the *Spiritual Exercises*.[6]

Despite the Jesuits' sometimes harsh words against speculative theology, that is, much of the scholastic theology of their day, they did not reject what they saw as its accomplishments. This would have meant rejecting the formal training they had themselves received and that they came to prescribe for others. It would have run counter to the appreciation for scholastic theology in the "Rules for Thinking with the Church."[7] The Jesuits wanted, however, to provide that theology with a new casing and to direct it more effectively to ministry. Nadal expressed their ideal succinctly: "to join speculation with devotion and with spiritual understanding . . . This is our desire. This is the underlying premise of the plan of studies in the Society."[8]

The Jesuits were more adept at indicating with whom they differed in this regard than in clearly articulating just how they realized their ideal. As Nadal saw it, they had to distinguish themselves from four groups. With two they differed principally in content: they had to avoid the errors of the Lutherans, especially concerning justification and church authority, and then they had to be careful not to be taken as *alumbrados,* which meant they had to watch how they spoke about prayer and the devout life.[9]

With two other groups they differed in method. They had first to avoid the mistakes of those who practiced theology as if it were a purely speculative or purely academic discipline, thus deviating from the earlier and more genuine tradition of the church. By this they meant those scholastics "who totally immerse themselves in speculation, so that they leave no room for devotion, for the Spirit, and for spiritual understanding." Then they had to shun the arrogance and hyperbole of the "grammarians," that is, the humanists who believed that their skill in "humane letters" gave them warrant to pronounce on theological and doctrinal issues.[10]

As far as the Lutherans and *alumbrados* were concerned, the Jesuits simply had to make clear how much they differed from them. But for scholasticism and Renaissance humanism their task was much more complex, for the Jesuits espoused much of the form and content of both.

Scholasticism

The formal and advanced education of the first companions took place for the most part in the arts faculty of the University of Paris. This meant that much of their time and effort in Paris was directed to "philosophy," a late-medieval program of logic, dialectics, physics, astronomy, metaphysics, ethics, psychology, and other subjects based for the most part either directly or indirectly on the works of Aristotle.[11]

The Jesuits later prescribed a similar program for each of their own schools that had a Faculty of Arts, where they insisted that Aristotle always be studied directly from his texts, not from compendia.[12] Teachers in the Society were to indicate where Aristotle deviated from Christian teaching, so as to observe the decree in that regard of the Fifth Lateran Council, 1513.[13] Since "natural philosophy" was such a strong component in this program, Jesuit proficiency in mathematics and science developed out of this philosophical segment of studies integral to the *modus parisiensis*.

By the time the first companions left Paris, they all had degrees in philosophy. Favre and Xavier were awarded their licentiates in 1530, for instance, and Ignatius in 1533. In 1535 Ignatius earned his Master of Arts degree. Laínez had a degree from Alcalá even before he arrived in Paris. They were, therefore, entitled to be addressed as "master" and often referred to each other by that title—"Master Francis," "Master Ignatius," or, once they were priests, "Father Master Ignatius."

None of them took a degree in theology at Paris. The doctorate required twelve to fourteen years, and even the baccalaureate took five. This was more time than they wanted to spend. In the years after they received their degrees in philosophy, however, they attended lectures in theology at the four colleges that offered them—at the Dominican and Franciscan convents, at the Sorbonne, and at the College of Navarre. Because Ignatius did not receive his licentiate in philosophy until 1533 and left Paris early in 1535, he spent less time on theology than the others.

From Rome in 1538 Favre wrote a letter to Diogo de Gouveia, the old principal of the Collège de Sainte-Barbe, which concluded with greetings in the name of all the companions to seven professors of theology at the university.[14] Only from indirect evidence like this can the character of theology they studied at Paris be reconstructed. The letter allows the assumption, for instance, that the companions followed courses in all four colleges where theology was taught.

The theologians singled out by Favre were important, but they were not the best-known figures in the university. The Franciscan Pierre de Cornibus, much esteemed by Bobadilla, was a sworn enemy of Erasmus, an active opponent of the Lutherans, and in 1530 a supporter of Catherine of Aragon in the famous case brought by Henry VIII.[15] From about 1520 until 1543

Jacques Berthelemy was the *conscriptor* of the Sorbonne, which meant he was in effect its head.[16] François Le Picart was best known for his preaching, so effective that it was said to have saved Paris from Lutheranism.[17]

Robert Wauchope, a diocesan priest from Scotland, had been guided in the *Exercises* by Favre. More important for his later ecclesiastical diplomacy than for any activity at the university, he was present at the Diets of Worms in 1540 and Regensburg in 1541, and he headed the commission that authored the decree on justification at the Council of Trent. He kept in close contact with the Jesuits during these years, and while he was at Worms with Favre he guided some clerics in the *Exercises*.[18]

The seven professors of theology were not the only persons at the university with whom the companions were associated.[19] With a few the relationship was unfriendly, as with Doctor Pedro Ortiz, who later took them under his wing in Rome.[20] But Ignatius himself directed in the *Exercises* both Mazurier and Alvaro Moscoso, later bishop of Pamplona.[21]

Mazurier had a stormy career at Paris and suffered severe strictures from his colleagues for his heterodoxy. A disciple of Jacques Lefèvre d'Etaples and associated with Bishop Guillaume Briçonnet in his suspect reform of the diocese of Meaux, Mazurier had some of his teachings condemned as heretical by the Faculty of Theology in 1523. In 1525 he had to yield his pulpit under threat of being declared a relapsed heretic; in 1530 he was accused of teaching that God did not approve the veneration of the saints and their images, that all Christians were priests, and that there was no need to make satisfaction for sin. In 1550 the Faculty censured his book on confession and placed it on its list of forbidden books. His colleague René Benoist deemed it more Protestant than Catholic.[22]

Ignatius led Mazurier in the *Exercises* just at the time the animus of the Faculty against him was at its height. Ignatius must have known him rather well, probably better than he knew any other member of the Faculty. In any case, although Mazurier—of all people!—praised Ignatius for his grasp of theology, many decades later Ribadeneira told how Laínez spoke freely about Ignatius's "little learning and eloquence" *(pocas partes)*. Ribadeneira's account suggests that what Laínez said was simply taken for granted by those closest to Ignatius.[23]

When Laínez's assessment is placed in the context of the mystical and pastoral nature of theology that the first Jesuits espoused, it does not necessarily contradict the positive assessments. The context of Nadal's epithet "the theologian" was decidedly pastoral: "Here, then, you see the necessity for the course of studies in the Society: to be able to preach and become skilled in those ministries that the Church deems ordered for the help of our neighbor . . . Here is our father, the theologian. His desires were always to seek how he might better employ himself in the service of God."[24] "Theologian" here had a special meaning and did not imply technical proficiency.

For a man who came to the university late in life, Ignatius competently grasped what he was taught and well assimilated basic principles of the disciplines, but he lacked intellectual curiosity. Although a theological vision underlay the *Constitutions* and his correspondence, Ignatius rarely addressed theological issues in a direct and technically explicit way. When he did so, responsibility for the wording usually fell to Polanco. Ignatius's genius and passion lay elsewhere. To his contemporaries he was a theologian in that he possessed extraordinary gifts for reflecting upon his religious experience, communicated what he had learned in a pastorally effective way, and taught others to do the same.[25]

Other companions at Paris assimilated more profoundly the technicalities of the academic theology they studied. Laínez and Salmerón were outstanding. From their preaching and writing they continued to learn throughout their lives, and, although not particularly original, they merit recognition as being among the truly learned theologians of the midsixteenth century.

The very diversity of the Parisian colleges in which the companions heard lectures points, however, to the eclectic nature within the scholastic tradition of the theology they all imbibed. Through his textbooks and popular lectures, the most influential theologian at Paris for years was John Mair (or Major, d. 1550), known as "the Prince of the Nominalists." He left Paris for good in 1531, where he had most recently been associated with the Collège de Sainte-Barbe—which is where Favre, Xavier, and Ignatius were enrolled.[26]

Favre's *Memoriale* contains clearly Occamist traits, which in fact supported the Jesuits' emphasis on the primacy of religious experience.[27] When Laínez first lectured in Rome at the university, he chose the Nominalist Gabriel Biel's commentary on the Canon of the Mass as his text.[28] In his strenuous objection at Trent in 1546 to the doctrine of "double justification" proposed by Girolamo Seripando and others, he seems closer to a Nominalist understanding of the relationship of grace to God's *potentia absoluta* and *potentia ordinata* than to the position of Thomas Aquinas.[29] In time, nonetheless, the Jesuits definitively settled on Thomas Aquinas as their preferred author "for scholastic doctrine," a decision Ignatius enshrined in the *Constitutions.*[30] Even so, they meant to allow themselves leeway, as Salmerón explained three decades later, and never intended to be more a friend to Thomas than to truth.[31]

Several extrinsic factors had to incline them toward Aquinas. At the beginning of the sixteenth century, the Dominicans in Paris had displaced Thomas's early commentary on the Sentences of Peter Lombard with the *Summa theologiae,* the work of his maturity, as the subject of their lectures. This was an important innovation that helped determine the character of the Thomistic revival in Catholicism later in the century. Its relative novelty probably attracted the attention of the companions during their stay in Paris and drew them to the lectures at the Dominican convent of Saint Jacques. At least some of them heard lectures there by Matthieu Ory, Thomas Laurent, and Jean Benoist, and Ignatius seems to have been particularly favorable toward the Dominicans.[32]

Nadal, who, unlike the original companions, actually received a licentiate in theology from Paris, went on to earn a doctorate in theology at the University of Avignon in 1538, seven years before he entered the Society. He was deeply influenced by Bonaventure but also knew and read Thomas.[33] Canisius developed an admiration for Thomas while doing his baccalaureate in the Faculty of Arts at Cologne.[34]

Polanco studied the *Summa* and Cajetan's commentary on it while pursuing his theological studies at Padua, 1542–46.[35] Although he of course studied other authors, he gave special time and attention to these texts and seems not to have been exposed to any Nominalists. Given Polanco's important role in the composition of the *Constitutions,* especially the parts dealing with education, he was surely instrumental in assigning Thomas his place in that document, but only in seconding what seems to have been Ignatius's predilection. In such an important matter, however, a consensus had to have been developing. As early as 1549 at the University of Valencia, for instance, the Jesuits reported studying "nothing but Scripture and Saint Thomas."[36]

Surely inclining the Jesuits in this direction once the Society was established in Rome was the liturgical and theological preeminence Thomas had long enjoyed there.[37] His feast was celebrated annually in the Dominican church of Santa Maria sopra Minerva with unparalleled solemnity and with the participation of the papal court. Cardinal Oliviero Carafa had brought Cajetan to Rome earlier in the century precisely so that his commentaries on Aquinas might be composed there. The Dominicans, who as Masters of the Sacred Palace held the chief theological position in the *Studium* of the papal curia, of course favored their confrere.

By far the single most palpable and approved theological influence in

Rome throughout the sixteenth century, therefore, even long before the impetus given him by Pius V between 1566 and 1572, was the Angelic Doctor. The Jesuits could hardly have been unaware of this fact or unmoved by it. Their own adoption of Thomas furthered a movement already well under way. When Francisco de Toledo began teaching at the Collegio Romano in 1559, he brought with him from the University of Salamanca the tradition of the brilliant revival of Aquinas initiated there earlier in the century by Francisco de Vitoria, Domingo de Soto, and others.[38]

Important though these extrinsic factors were, the Jesuits would never have selected Thomas unless they found in him elements compatible with their religious vision. His unquestioned orthodoxy would be chief among these. The clear organization and comprehensiveness of the *Summa* made it relatively easy to follow and teach. Thomas's understanding of the relationship of Aristotle (or "philosophy") to Christian doctrine was consonant with the teaching of the Fifth Lateran Council. His Christian adaptation of Aristotle's teaching that virtue took a middle path between two extremes provided intellectual grounding for Ignatius's teaching on moderation in ascetical practices. In any case, the Jesuits and Ignatius himself especially liked and recommended the *Pars secunda,* where this idea was a leitmotif.[39] There may have been other features they found attractive, but the surviving documentation does not provide any apodictic evidence explaining why they rejected the eclectic program the companions followed at Paris and settled on Aquinas.

Nonetheless, the basic assumption of the compatibility between "nature and grace," between "reason and revelation" that underlay the Thomistic synthesis coincided with the Jesuits' conviction that in their pastoral activities they should not only rely upon God's grace but also use all the "human means" at their disposal, as the *Constitutions* prescribed.[40] Thomistic reasoning would also help rationalize this conviction, which was intimated early in their history by seemingly trivial decisions such as Ignatius's abandoning at Manresa his purposely disheveled appearance.

Intimately related to the Thomistic assumption that "grace perfects nature" was an understanding of the relationship between grace and "free will" that allowed for human activity under the influence of grace. In this view, the will was wounded and enfeebled by Original Sin, but not vitiated or destroyed. Grace, always the primary factor, allowed the will to "cooperate" with it, so that in some mysterious way human responsibility played its part in the process of salvation. This theology is much more easily reconciled with the language of the *Exercises* and the *Constitutions* than a more

Augustinian viewpoint. The danger was that one could slip into semi-Pelagianism, the "save yourself" heresy of which the Jesuits were often later accused. In any case, the Jesuits' understanding of Thomas's teaching on this point positioned them for their later stance against Jansenism, presaged as early as 1570 by the young Roberto Bellarmino's attack at Louvain against Michel de Bay (Baius).

Thomas's teaching on human nature and free will was only a specification of his positive appreciation of all created reality and human institutions even after the Fall of Adam. God was thus ubiquitously present and operative and had pronounced all things good, sin alone excepted. God could thus be "found in all things," as the *Constitutions* stated,[41] succinctly summarizing the essence of the "Contemplation to Obtain Divine Love" that closes the *Exercises.*

Taken in the large these teachings on nature, grace, will, and creation were not unique to Thomas among scholastic theologians. Moreover, a cooperative understanding of the relationship between grace and free will was formally adopted by the Council of Trent in its famous decree of 13 January 1547, which rested on a broad consensus in the Council that transcended "the schools." Nonetheless, Thomas expounded these teachings with particular forcefulness and clarity and used them as the basic underpinnings of his system.

When Nadal spoke to his many Jesuit audiences or wrote for them over the course of his long career, he unfailingly proffered this interpretation of these complex issues, which was in many ways at the center of his message. Although he may not always have derived it directly from Thomas, he explained it in ways that made it compatible with the teaching of the *Summa theologiae.* Nadal's understanding of the basic goodness of human nature as created by God and of its potential as redeemed by Christ led him frequently to console himself and others with thoughts about human dignity, a theme fundamental to this theology.[42] He was possibly influenced by the new prominence that the Renaissance revival of classical rhetoric occasioned for the theme, but he always rooted it in theological ground. He applied his insistence on the primacy of grace in the work of salvation to the ministry that the Jesuits and others performed in the church: "Spiritual ministry is efficacious not through human effort but through the power of God. It is not the minister who does it, but in and through him Christ performs it."[43] This expressed in different words a fundamental theme of the *Constitutions:* in the ministry the Jesuit was but an instrument in the hands of God.[44]

Despite the convergence between basic assumptions in Aquinas and major emphases in the theological teaching of the early Jesuits, on one crucial point they surely differed with how some contemporaries interpreted Aquinas's affirmation in the opening question of the *Summa* that theology was principally a "speculative" discipline.[45] The theological speculation of the "schools" was supposedly directed ultimately to pastoral effectiveness, especially in preaching, but the intrinsic dynamics of the enterprise made little allowance for it. Moreover, the highly intellectualized character of its notions, now removed from the pulpit of the patristic age and the chapel of the medieval monasteries and transferred to the lecture hall, meant that the message was addressed to the head, not the heart. Erasmus was basically correct in seeing scholastic theology as a break with the earlier patristic and monastic tradition, effecting in his opinion a baneful distinction between theology on the one hand and spirituality and ministry on the other.[46]

When the first Jesuits inveighed against reducing theology to "speculation alone," they sometimes directed their criticism specifically against teachers at Paris. They of course made exceptions for theologians such as Le Picart and Wauchope, whom they admired especially for their pastoral concern. But Nadal excoriated others for not "going out into the cities and towns to announce the Kingdom of Heaven according to the example of Christ and the Apostles" and for being "only speculative theologians and treating all disciplines in only a speculative fashion."[47] In such criticisms he echoed sentiments Xavier had expressed in the letter from India that led Nadal to join the Society.[48]

When Nadal described in general terms "our way of proceeding," he reduced it to the triad of acting "in the Spirit, from the heart, practically"—"spiritu, corde, practice."[49] This was one of his most telling summaries of the ideal of the Jesuit life. To act "in the Spirit" meant to refer all to God and divine grace. To act "from the heart" meant to bring the feelings to bear on whatever was being done, and never to act "only speculatively"—"Ut speculative tantum ne agamus." To act "practically" meant that a Jesuit's affectivity was not like that of a "contemplative," but was directed to helping others. In a word, to act "practically" meant to act pastorally. "Mystical theology" expressed a central aspect of the Jesuits' way of proceeding.

Although scholastic theologians always professed that the human mind could never fathom divine mystery, they often seemed to their critics to construct their systems as if it could. Among the Jesuits, Nadal was acutely conscious of how little the intellect could achieve in this realm. Dependent upon the treatise *On Mystical Theology* of Pseudo-Dionysius, he felt most comfortable with a "negative theology," with a "learned ignorance," with the idea that we understand most about God when we understand that we know nothing.[50] For him, "mystical theology" was a matter of the heart, not the brain: "Seek God in the inmost movements of your heart, where he is found in serene quiet and sweet intimacy along with an unfathomable sense of his infinite energy. If you seek him in your intellect, you will become entangled in difficulties, and you will not find him. Mystical theology is in the heart— 'In corde est mystica theologia.' "[51]

Neither Nadal nor any other of the first Jesuits left a clear explanation of how they proposed to effect the blend of mystical with speculative theology. Although Erasmus never said it in so many words, his solution was to jettison the scholastic enterprise and replace it with the more rhetorical theology of the Fathers. This solution was far too radical for the first Jesuits.

Moreover, their criticism of purely speculative theology probably first derived from the scholastic tradition itself. Not all scholastics were purely speculative, even before the humanists' attack on their system. Nadal and the others likely got some of their ideas and at least confirmation of the very term "mystical theology" from Gerson. Gerson, writing in the early fifteenth century, could have been speaking for the Jesuits a century and a half later when he said: "If Cicero describes the orator as 'a good man skilled in speaking,' we describe the theologian as 'a good man with learning in sacred letters'—not with the learning of the intellect alone but even more of the affections, so that what he understands through theology he through constant reflection transfers into the feelings of his heart and into Christian practice."[52]

The Jesuits did not attempt to formulate a theory that would conjoin speculation with affectivity, for they were more interested in content and conclusions than in reconciling methods or analyzing systems. Even when in 1552 Nadal prescribed the study of Thomas for Jesuits, he complained of Thomas's "prolixity." He hoped that somebody would compile a compendium of scholastic theology containing everything the scholastics taught concerning basic doctrine and reconciling their disagreements so as to break down the "factions of Thomists, Scotists, and Nominalists" into which they were divided.[53]

The next year Ignatius, at the entreaty of King Ferdinand and with the encouragement of Nadal, commissioned Laínez to put together such a compendium. Laínez dutifully began the project and sent to the Jesuits in Rome for their review the parts he managed to write, which they judged good but, again, too prolix. His many occupations prevented him from ever completing the book.[54] Had it been finished and found satisfactory, it might have qualified the special place Thomas enjoyed in the *Constitutions*.

The first Jesuits committed themselves and those who later joined them to the scholastic theological tradition. They were urged in this direction by many factors, not least of which would have been Ignatius's affirmation in the "Rules for Thinking with the Church" of its utility for "our times" in defining issues and stating them clearly, in refuting errors and exposing fallacies.[55] In an intervention at Trent in 1563 while he was general of the Society, Laínez "praised the scholastics, for scholastic learning greatly illumines the intellect."[56] Although Jesuit teachers at the Collegio Romano sometimes had to be warned not to poke fun at Aquinas and scholastic theology, the tradition had been firmly set in the Society.[57]

Renaissance Humanism

The revival of classical literature that occurred during the Renaissance, though based on a few simple assumptions, manifested at different times and in different circumstances a remarkable variety of expressions.[58] Neither Renaissance humanism itself nor its relationship to the Jesuits' theological culture can be facilely summarized.

From its origins in the fourteenth century and thereafter, the humanist movement advocated a displacement of the "barbarous" Latin style of the Middle Ages with a style more in accord with classical or patristic usage. This was the most obvious postulate of the movement. Although such a shift in style might seem to be superficial, like all major mutations in language it signaled and effected a change in sensibilities and mentality, a change in ways of appreciating and conceptualizing reality. The more eminent humanists had some understanding of what was at stake, while many other practitioners of the new style seem to have believed they were merely adorning old truths with more attractive dress.

Rhetoric, the central discipline cultivated by the movement, was in its primary form the art of oratory. Thus by definition the movement was concerned with an art of persuasion that entailed engagement of the imagination and emotions as much as the intellect. Rhetoric was thus a direct and sometimes explicit challenge to the centrality of dialectics in the scholastic system. When Erasmus stigmatized scholastic theology as "frigid," which he often did, he hit the system at one of its most vulnerable points.

In keeping with the classical tradition, the humanists saw the "good style" that rhetoric helped one cultivate as intrinsically supportive of "good morals." Good style persuaded—persuaded, indeed, to some positive action. Although of course concerned with the truth, worthwhile literature led from an intellectual assent to a translation of truth into one's whole style of thinking, feeling, and behaving. That was the theory, and that was precisely, in the opinion of some, what scholastic theology tragically failed to do.

Many persons influenced by the humanist movement were, however, little concerned with scholastic theology, and many of those who were concerned did not see the two enterprises as essentially antagonistic. The leading Jesuits of the first and subsequent generations fell into this latter category.[59] In various ways and in varying degrees, they had imbibed elements of the humanist phenomenon, which, however, was not yet so deeply rooted in the cultures from which they came as it was in Italy, where the movement had begun two centuries before their arrival there.

Most of the Jesuits of the first generation could speak and write in a humanistic style of Latin, and at some point they became convinced of an intrinsic relationship between *Christianitas* and the curriculum of classical authors that the humanists advocated for formal instruction in secondary schools. The very fact that the Jesuits so easily accepted these aspects of the humanists' agenda indicates how effective the humanists' propaganda had been on a Pan-European scale. No doubt, as we have seen, the humanist movement influenced the Jesuits most profoundly and pervasively through the secondary schools based on humanistic principles that the Jesuits undertook after 1548.

Unlike Jesuits in succeeding generations, however, some in this first did not have a full and thorough grounding in the tradition of "good letters." Certainly, the more potent influences upon Ignatius—but also upon Laínez, Salmerón, Borja, Canisius, and others—were medieval and late-medieval. Moreover, at the time the Society was founded the religious and theological dimensions of Renaissance humanism were precisely the ones under rabid attack, with Erasmus the chief symbol of all that was wrong. He laid the egg, as his Catholic opponents put it, that Luther hatched.[60] These are reasons for the hesitancies in the first Jesuits' response to humanism amid their enthusiasm for most aspects of it.

Nadal could be speaking for almost all of them when he said in his response to Pedroche's attack on the *Exercises* that he once took delight in being able to speak in the "scholastic style" and was still perfectly capable of doing so.[61] He in fact used a classicizing Latin that self-consciously avoided the pedantry criticized by Erasmus in *Ciceronianus*.[62] He argued, moreover, that whereas in the "primitive church" an artless style was required to make clear that the power of the Gospel was not due to human persuasion, now it was appropriate to extol with every human art what was established on divine foundation.[63] Polanco was, as usual, more practical and less sweeping when he defended classical eloquence by criticizing scholastic theologians for their inability to express their ideas persuasively.[64]

In 1565 Pedro João Perpinyá, a distinguished Portuguese teacher of rhetoric at the Roman College, argued in a memorandum intended for the Jesuit leadership in Rome that, if unadorned truth excited love for it, how much more were the feelings inflamed when the language that expressed it was more commensurate with the sublimity of the subject.[65] This was a typical humanistic argument for the classical ideal of eloquence. There is no need to belabor how appealing the argument would be to the Jesuits, who from the beginning were convinced that engagement of the emotions was critical for successful ministry; nor is there a need to belabor how nicely the argument coincided with the inner appropriation of truth advocated by the Jesuits' "mystical theology."

Although the Jesuits never worked out a theoretical solution to the problem of making scholastic speculation pastorally meaningful, their practical solution was to translate its teachings into a humanistic rhetoric, which meant its transformation. They probably thought they were doing nothing more than putting old truths into new dress, but any new way of talking means a new way of thinking, a new *forma mentis*. It means different sensibilities and sensitivities.[66] In comparison with the constitutions of older religious orders, for instance, the language of the Jesuit *Constitutions* frequently manifests the new reality, beginning with the opening paragraph of the Preamble. Nadal's two humanistic *Dialogues* manifest it more consistently. The same was almost surely true for much of the Jesuits' preaching.

One aspect of the rhetorical *forma mentis* was its imperative for accommodation, an aspect that coincided with the Jesuits' way of proceeding on a profound and pervasive level. In the classical treatises, rhetoric was geared to produce the successful orator. Essential to this success was the orator's ability to be in touch with the feelings and needs of his audience and to adapt himself and his speech accordingly. Beginning with the *Exercises* themselves, the Jesuits were constantly advised in all their ministries to adapt what they said and did to times, circumstances, and persons. The "rhetorical" dimension of Jesuit ministry in this sense transcended the preaching and lecturing in which they were engaged and even the rhetorical foundations of the casuistry they practiced—it was a basic principle in all their ministries, even if they did not explicitly identify it as rhetorical. The *Constitutions* identified it as a hallmark of "our way of proceeding":

In general, they ought to be instructed in the way of proceeding proper to a member of the Society, who has to associate with so great a diversity of persons throughout such varied regions. Hence they should foresee the inconveniences that may arise and the opportunities that can be grasped for the greater service of God by using some means at one time and others at another. Although all this can be taught only by the unction of the Holy Spirit and by the prudence that God our Lord communicates to those who trust in His Divine Majesty, nevertheless the way can at least be opened by some suggestions that aid and dispose one for the effect that must be produced by divine grace.[67]

The Jesuits did not explicitly make the connection between rhetoric and this aspect of their way of proceeding. When they professedly argued in favor of the study of the classics, they had at their disposal more standard reasons, such as those Polanco proposed to Laínez in his letter of 21 May 1547 about the study of *humanidad*.[68] Nonetheless, the study of rhetoric reflected and promoted the accommodation central to the Jesuits' pastoral style.

Still, not everybody in the Society was convinced that such study was appropriate, and in 1555, for instance, Ignatius needed to remind a certain "good Father" of the traditional patristic argument that the classics were the "spoils of Egypt." Ignatius took for granted, of course, that some of the classical authors needed to be purged of *dishonestà*.[69] In an earlier letter to Andrea Lippomano of Venice, great benefactor of the Society, he argued more positively for the ethical content of authors such as Virgil and Terence—they had much that is "useful for doctrine, and much not unuseful, indeed helpful, for a devout life."[70] With such a stance Ignatius in effect accepted the humanists' tenet that good literature was essentially didactic. Nadal characterized the goal of the program of studies followed by young Jesuits as "a conjoining of good letters with theology."[71]

The ethical content of the classics and their necessity for the cultivation of a pleasing and persuasive style of discourse for ministry were therefore the principal basis on which the Jesuits justified the classics for themselves. But they also argued that study of the classics was helpful for understanding Scripture, and when they taught Hebrew in their schools it was with that purpose in mind. They were still in accord with standard humanistic arguments for the revival of good letters, but here they betrayed more caution than Erasmus and some Protestant reformers.

By the sixteenth century, Erasmus, following the path blazed earlier by Lorenzo Valla, had developed a sophisticated historical and philological approach to the text that culminated in 1516 in his critical Greek edition of the New Testament along with his new Latin translation.[72] He continued to revise the Greek text and to provide his *Paraphrases* in Latin. This work substantially challenged the Vulgate edition, and it also raised questions that had doctrinal implications for certain passages. At this point the Jesuits became hesitant. Enthusiastic about the rhetorical and literary dimensions of the *studia humanitatis,* they were more conservative about just when and how historical and philological criticism was to be applied to sacred teachings, texts, and traditions.

Nadal voiced their misgivings. Probably while he was at Paris he learned how the humanists were stigmatized as mere "grammarians" when they intruded into the realm of doctrine.[73] Thus had spoken the Faculty of Theology in its condemnation of Erasmus, and by the middle of the sixteenth century others, especially some Italian churchmen, had taken up the cry with a vengeance. Nadal urged the study of scholastic theology because otherwise one "hesitated in perplexity" over grave issues of doctrine. He was pointing an accusing finger at the humanists.[74]

His attitude was conservative but not entirely negative on the emendations of the biblical text that the humanists advanced. In 1554 he distanced himself from the "insolence and temerity of the grammarians" but said he approved the light their studies shed on the Bible. Study of languages was, he maintained, absolutely necessary in the Catholic Church. Writing after the decree of Trent in its Fourth Session, 8 April 1546, that the Vulgate was to be the "received" edition in the church, he of course agreed that it was "necessary to hold the *editio vulgata* as most holy," but argued that the study of Hebrew and Greek were needed to make its meaning clear.[75] Years later in another passage he added that those languages should be used to defend the Vulgate against its calumniators.[76]

Ignatius went so far as to say that languages were studied to defend the Vulgate on every single point—"deffender en todo."[77] Laínez and Salmerón, who had been present for the debates at Trent and understood how qualified the Council had been in its approbation of the Vulgate, rushed to change Ignatius's obvious intent by interpreting him to mean "everything that with reason and honesty can be defended."[78] Ignatius accepted their qualification for incorporation into the pertinent section of the *Constitutions,* but the First General Congregation deleted it.[79]

How the first Jesuits would have reacted in a different religious climate is a matter of speculation, but they in fact were cautious about other Latin translations or antagonistic toward them.[80] When Canisius discovered at

Ingolstadt in 1556 that Erasmus's translation of the Epistles and Gospels read during mass was in circulation, he had "Jerome's version," that is, the Vulgate, printed to displace it.[81]

Nonetheless, the Jesuits were much more open-minded than many of their Catholic contemporaries. From 1523 until his death in 1559, Robert Estienne published a number of editions of the Bible that purported to be revisions of the Vulgate along lines that at least on the surface seemed to be what the Jesuits desired.[82] While basing his text on ancient codices of the Vulgate, he also employed Erasmus and other contemporary translations. He ran into so much opposition from the Faculty of Theology, however, that he fled to Calvin's Geneva, where in 1551 he published a small portable edition that included Erasmus's Latin translation of the New Testament.

Between 1550 and 1556 Ignatius showed positive interest in Estienne's annotations and in the portable edition of the New Testament.[83] Jesuit leaders in Rome were fully aware of the strictures in Paris and had to know of the Genevan origins of the book. They were, therefore, circumspect, but as late as 1556 Ignatius gave Gaspar de Loarte permission to use it.[84] He also gave permission to use Melanchthon's annotations.[85]

The Jesuits did not comment much on vernacular translations of the Bible. The invention of the printing press and especially the encouragement by humanists like Erasmus of the reading of the Bible as a central exercise of piety had given added impetus in the early sixteenth century to this traditional practice. The first Jesuits explicitly commended such reading, as did Loarte in his *Esercitio*, but they did not elaborate upon it.[86] Their "sacred lectures" on books of the Bible seem to presuppose that members of the audience had texts at hand and were going to read them, but this is mere surmise. Students in at least some Jesuit schools were expected to have copies of the Epistles and Gospels used at mass.[87]

The *Exercises* were for the most part based on the Gospels and specifically recommended that they be read, which some people surely would have to do in vernacular translations. Nonetheless, in keeping with the tradition of the *Devotio Moderna,* the *Exercises* did not so much confront the individual with a text as with an image or scene. Although persons might read parts of the Gospels while making the *Exercises,* they could just as well read a "life of Christ."[88]

The Jesuits had to be affected by the misgivings and outright fear associated with vernacular versions of the Bible and the reading of them by the laity that even antedated the outbreak of the Reformation, but their sources record little about the issue. The misgivings and fear culminated in the

Roman Index of 1559, which forbade all vernacular translations. Although the prohibition was later mitigated, it drew an important line of demarcation for the future between Catholic and Protestant piety.[89]

Jesuits from this generation wrote a number of biblical commentaries, all of which were published later in the century, some of them posthumously. From 1569 to 1579, Salmerón labored on his commentary on the New Testament, first published in sixteen volumes in Madrid in 1597–1602, one of the largest such undertakings in the sixteenth century.[90] It shows an excellent command of the biblical languages and of ancient and contemporary commentaries, including those of Valla, Erasmus, Cajetan, and Luther. Although based on traditional assumptions about church and sacraments, its erudition is outstanding even for such a learned age and its judgments balanced for such a contentious one.[91]

To Salmerón's commentary must be added those of Juan de Maldonato, who taught at the Collège de Clermont in Paris until the Faculty of Theology censured him in 1574, of Francisco de Ribera, confessor to Teresa of Avila and one of her first biographers, and those of three professors at the Collegio Romano—Francisco de Toledo, Benito Pereira, and Manuel de Sá. They all approached the text through knowledge of the original languages and utilized the philological techniques developed by the humanists.[92]

Erasmus advocated a return not only to the biblical text but also to the theological style of the Fathers of the Church. His critical editions of their works from 1516 until his death in 1535 are one of the great monuments of Western scholarship, and they mirrored and powerfully promoted a renewed interest in the Fathers in the sixteenth century. The Jesuits echoed the enthusiasm, but only faintly in these early years.

Canisius made frequent and competent use of patristic sources in his writings, and he in some ways felt more affinity with them than with the scholastics. He even published a few editions of their works. His edition of the *Contra Julianum* of Cyril of Alexandria, 1546, basically a revision of the Latin translation by the Lutheran Johannes Oecolampadius that appeared in print two decades earlier, was among the first works published by a Jesuit. Like the *Contra Julianum,* his other editions reflect a grasp of critical technique and principles, but they do not make significant advances over what was already known.[93]

Since Ignatius, Favre, and Nadal kept spiritual journals, we might expect them and other Jesuits to manifest interest in Augustine's *Confessions,* but, except possibly for Canisius and Ribadeneira, this does not seem to be the case.[94] A Directory composed by Diego Miró for the *Exercises,* however, rec-

ommended the book for persons making the *Exercises*.[95] Ignatius occasionally exhorted his fellow Jesuits to read "some of the doctors like
Chrysostom, Bernard, and Jerome" for their utility in preaching.[96] While
Laínez, Salmerón, and Bobadilla were students at Paris, they on their own
initiative studied some patristic texts but in order to mine them for proof-
texts to be used in disputation and controversy—in other words, with a
basically scholastic mind-set.[97]

In the "Rules for Thinking with the Church," Ignatius delineated a basic
difference between the theology of the Fathers and the "scholastic doctors,
such as Saint Thomas, Saint Bonaventure, and the Master of the Sentences
[Peter Lombard]."[98] The former were distinguished from the latter by their
ability to "rouse the affections so that we are moved to love and serve God
our Lord in all things." That description was a fair statement of what Ignatius thought was most important in theology, and it would have pleased
Erasmus.

What was, then, the attitude of Ignatius and other members of the Society
toward Erasmus? This is a question that transcends the biblical and patristic
issues. It is a complicated one about which a great deal has been written,
much of it until recently badly misleading.[99] Two purported facts about
Ignatius have generally been used to ground the argument. First, he was
turned against Erasmus during his studies in Spain, either at Barcelona or at
Alcalá, by a reading of the *Enchiridion (The Handbook of the Christian Soldier)*, according to Ribadeneira because it chilled his inner devotion.
Second, he much later as general forbade all Jesuits to read anything
Erasmus wrote.

The accuracy of the first fact has been questioned.[100] Among the reasons
for not accepting it at face value is the style and content of the *Enchiridion*
itself, which especially in the Castilian translation contained so much that
was compatible with Ignatian *pietas* and little or nothing that ran counter
to it.

Moreover, when Nadal in 1557 reviewed the life of Ignatius in his *Apologia*
for the Society against the condemnation of the Parisian Faculty of Theology, whose anti-Erasmian sentiments were well known, he made no mention of the incident. He related, as well, that when Ignatius was interrogated
by the Dominicans at Salamanca in 1527 about "the many errors of Erasmus
and others that fill the world," he refused to answer unless compelled by
some competent authority.[101] This would have been an excellent occasion for
Nadal to distance Ignatius from Erasmus—or Nadal could simply have
omitted the story.

There is no problem, however, in imagining that other popular works of Erasmus, including the *Praise of Folly* and some of the *Colloquies,* would have been distasteful to Ignatius for their caustic and sarcastic criticism of the abuses, venality, and superstition in the church. Such criticisms of the church he loved so much, although they appeared in mitigated form in the preaching and other public utterances of some of his Jesuit brethren, could indeed have cooled Ignatius's ardor. But, with the possible exception of the *Enchiridion,* there is also no evidence that he had firsthand knowledge of these works or of anything else Erasmus wrote.

The second "fact" is false. Ignatius never issued to the Society a universally binding prohibition of Erasmus's works. Nonetheless, by 1552 he began to register reservations and restrictions. This development must be attributed to two causes. First, he and his companions had been exposed to the vilification of Erasmus almost endemic to the Faculty of Theology at the University of Paris during their days as students, which might even have influenced some of the wording of the "Rules for Thinking with the Church." Moreover, when they came to Rome they found the same sentiments orchestrated into a mighty and vicious vendetta by certain churchmen, especially those connected with the Roman Inquisition. By 1554–55 that tribunal was clearly tending toward a condemnation of the *opera omnia,* which in fact was fully promulgated by Paul IV in the Index of Prohibited Books of 1559.[102]

The second and more immediate reason for the development lay in the Jesuit schools, which were then just getting under way. In a number of letters after 1552 Ignatius discouraged and even forbade the use of Erasmus's works such as *De octo partium, De conscribendis epistolis, De copia,* and the *Colloquies* not for Jesuits to read but for them to use as textbooks. He absolutely prohibited their use at the Collegio Romano, but showed himself more flexible in other circumstances.[103] As late as 1554, for instance, he praised the method of classroom correction of compositions "recommended by Erasmus."[104]

At least in Italy Erasmus was used in many "grammar schools" similar to those founded by the Jesuits, and these schools were therefore stigmatized by Erasmus's enemies as hotbeds of heresy.[105] For any number of reasons the Jesuits wanted to avoid running the risk of such labeling for their own new and fragile institutions. Although on occasion Ignatius expressed a more general desire that Jesuits abstain from reading Erasmus, he for the most part raised the issue only for textbooks.[106] In his correspondence he never elaborated on the reasons for his restrictions and prohibitions. A letter to

Giambattista Viola in 1555 stated simply: "Since the author is not in favor, it is not appropriate for students to get to like his books."[107] On several occasions he linked Erasmus with Terence and Juan Luis Vives as authors to be avoided.[108]

Ignatius also discouraged Jesuits from reading Savonarola. He wrote in 1549 that Savonarola, "a man of great and exceptional gifts," had been misled by the devil into uttering prophesies, none of which had been fulfilled as he predicted.[109] In a letter in 1553 Polanco put him and Erasmus in the same category, stating simply, "Father Ignatius does not want the works of Savonarola and Erasmus read."[110] Later that year Polanco explained the prohibition of Savonarola, which in this instance would apply in part to Erasmus:

> The reason for prohibiting the books of Savonarola is not because some of his books, like *Il triompho della croce* and others, are not good, but because the author is an object of controversy—some people saying that he is a saint, others that he was justly executed, which is the more common opinion. Since there are so many books by good authors that are not controversial, the Society does not want us to have those that are. It does not, however, condemn or otherwise stigmatize them.[111]

That passage is as close as we can come with some certainty to what lay behind Ignatius's restrictions. As such, it is perfectly in character and reveals his reluctance to pronounce on specific theological issues. It also reveals his deep caution in matters theological and his classicist mentality in matters intellectual. Nonetheless, entirely missing in him and his closest associates in the governing of the Society is any suggestion of the scurrilous epithets hurled at Erasmus by his Catholic enemies—"infamous heretic," "son of the devil," "captain of apostasy," "evil spirit," "rabid dog."[112]

Beginning with Messina in 1548, the Jesuits made ample use of Erasmus in their classrooms, as Ignatius knew well.[113] They were at the same time using his *De copia* even in Goa.[114] Despite Ignatius's later misgivings, the Jesuits continued to use Erasmian texts in some of their schools all through the period I am considering and well beyond. In 1557 while he was vicar general of the Society after the death of Ignatius, Laínez wrote to Jesuits at Ingolstadt and Padua to quiet their scruples. He stated that Erasmus was not to be considered a heretic and made it quite clear that Ignatius's prohibition of his writings in the schools was not absolute.[115]

Once the dust began to settle after the Index of 1559, Nadal, who had originally built Erasmus into the curriculum at Messina, continued in his official capacity as *commissarius* to authorize the use of Erasmian texts, but with certain restrictions.[116] In Cologne in 1562 the Jesuit school produced a dialogue, *De civiltate morum,* almost certainly an adaptation of Erasmus's work by the same name.[117] Typically, however, Nadal insisted at Dillingen in 1566 that the students use the Vulgate version of the New Testament, not Erasmus's.[118] Moreover, Jesuits were themselves beginning to write textbooks that could replace Erasmus in the classroom.[119]

Outside the Erasmian works that could be used as textbooks, it is not clear how much familiarity the Jesuits had with the rest of that immense *corpus,* although we must assume that after a certain point Ignatius's attitude and the general climate of opinion in Catholicism tended to reduce it to a minimum. As we have seen, Laínez had read the *Modus orandi Deum,* and Polanco the *Ecclesiastes.* At Padua Polanco had also studied Erasmus's *Paraphrases on Matthew.*[120] What we know of the Jesuits' libraries suggests that many of them possessed his editions of the Fathers, even though in 1567 Nadal prohibited them at Louvain.[121] Canisius's edition of a selection of Jerome's letters in 1561 had in fact been intended as a corrective to Erasmus's. In his preface he said that Erasmus should have restricted himself to humane letters, where he was justly admired, and "either have left sacred studies entirely alone or else have shown himself less supercilious in his judgments on the writings of the Fathers. As soon as he begins to play the theologian he becomes unduly self-confident and arrogant."[122] Canisius never retracted that judgment, but years later showed an appreciative, though critical, grasp of Erasmus's writings on Mary. One of the leading Jesuits of the first generation, he is among those who were most familiar with Erasmus's religious writings.[123]

None of the early Jesuits, however, understood what Erasmus fully intended in those many works. Had they done so, they would have found much in him that was congenial to their own *pietas* and much that was helpful in dealing more effectively with the "mystical theology" they espoused. But their own training and the hatred for Erasmus that filled the atmosphere around them prevented them from appreciating his religious and theological message.

Salmerón assiduously studied Erasmus's *Paraphrases* and other works related to Scripture, and he seems as well to have read some of his other works, such as the *Praise of Folly* and the *Ecclesiastes.* But in the sixteen volumes of his commentary on the New Testament, he could not bring himself to say a good word about Erasmus and took every possible occasion to criticize his exegesis.[124] At least by the 1570's when he was writing the commentary, Salmerón was solidly established in the egg-that-Luther-hatched school of interpretation.[125] He even more deeply resented Erasmus's supposed failure to take a stand in the subsequent religious controversies and his thereby committing the terrible "crime of neutrality"—*crimen neutralitatis.*[126]

Toward the end of the century the still active Antonio Possevino launched a virulent attack on Erasmus.[127] Given the ambivalences of the Jesuits toward him in their early decades and the ever more vicious vituperation of him by other Catholics, it is easy to understand why in the course of time a belligerence toward Erasmus was attributed to the Jesuits and why Jesuits began to claim it for themselves and act upon it.

Catholic Piety

Scholasticism and humanism were powerful influences on the Jesuits, but the literature of medieval and late-medieval piety was at least as important. Upon Ignatius and others, the influence of *The Imitation of Christ* and similar works antedated scholasticism and humanism and was more profound. Jesuits of this first generation read and sometimes commended to their clients devotional writings such as *Dieta Salutis* and *Stimulum divini amoris* (wrongly attributed to Bonaventure), the letters and dialogues of Catherine of Siena, the writings of Ludolph and Dionysius the Carthusians, occasionally works of Henry Herp, Johann Tauler, and others from the Rheno-Flemish mystical tradition and from the *Devotio Moderna.*[128]

They read and commended the *Meditationes vitae Christi,* attributed to Bonaventure but written about 1300 by his Franciscan confrere Giovanni de Caulibus.[129] Although they did not realize it, this book was the remote source for the method of "contemplation" on the life of Christ in the *Exercises,* transmitted to Ignatius through the *Vita Christi* of Ludolph the Carthusian and possibly through other works in the tradition of the *Devotio.*[130]

Without doubt, however, the work they most frequently acclaimed was *The Imitation of Christ.* The privileged place that the *Imitation* enjoyed in the *Exercises* as the only work besides the New Testament and the life of Christ recommended for reading during their course very much inclined them to the book.[131] When Nadal entered the Society in 1545, Ignatius advised him to read a chapter every day.[132] Years later in Córdoba its price doubled in the bookstores because of Jesuit endorsement.[133] In 1558 almost every student at the Jesuit college in Cologne owned a copy.[134]

Jesuit predilection for the *Imitation* is in some ways curious. Ignatius discovered it at Manresa during a crucial period in his life, which helps explain his attachment to it. Its widespread distribution after it first appeared about 1415 and the fact that its orthodoxy had never been in question surely commended it to the Jesuits. Its untechnical language, its axiomatic structure, and the simplicity of its sentiments made it easily accessible to them and to the broad categories of persons to whom they ministered. Yet in important particulars the piety it enjoined was little congruous with the Jesuits'.

The *Imitation* was a work redolent of monastic values, and it extolled the solitary sweetness of the monk's cell.[135] It never mentioned ministry or bringing succour to others as a constitutive element of Christian calling. When the author affirmed that "those who travel much seldom achieve holiness,"[136] he was practically contradicted by the Jesuit *Constitutions*: "Our vocation is to travel through the world and to live in any part of it whatsoever where there is hope of the greater service of God and the good of souls."[137]

The *Imitation* had, moreover, a decided bias not only against scholastic philosophy and theology but to some extent against learning as such.[138] It presented a piety several steps removed from the text of the New Testament and from the concrete deeds and ministry of Jesus and his disciples offered for meditation in the *Exercises*. It spoke of "nature and grace" with heavily Augustinian overtones—they "move in contrary directions." Human nature was corrupted *(vitiata)* by the sin of Adam; it is most wicked *(pessimam naturam meam)*.[139] Although these statements received some qualification, they could not be reconciled with the more positive Thomistic (and also Tridentine) understanding of the relationship between nature and grace that the Jesuits appropriated not only as a theological position but as a premise for their pastoral engagement.[140]

Despite these discrepancies, the Jesuits commended the *Imitation* enthusiastically and without reservation. This means that, as was true for other works that were not objects of controversy among Catholics, they read it less with an analytical and critical eye than with the hope of utilizing what supported their spirituality. In the *Imitation* they found in fact a great deal that was supportive and that confirmed certain directions they had taken; the book contained at least in embryonic form some of the first Jesuits' great themes. It encouraged frequent confession and Communion, though without defining what "frequent" meant.[141] It encouraged daily examination of conscience.[142] The whole of Book Three was entitled "The Book of Consolation" and emphasized the significance of the presence and absence of inner devotion—rudiments of ideas elaborately and systematically articulated in the "Rules for the Discernment of Spirits" in the *Exercises*.[143] Like many other works of piety, including Erasmus's *Enchiridion,* it anticipated the meditations on "Christ the King" and the "Two Standards" by speaking of "our Commander" and "our King," for whom we must "be prepared to die bravely in battle and not stain our glory by deserting the cross."[144]

Of greatest importance to the Jesuits must have been the *Imitation's* most general message: the call to inwardness, to reflection and self-awareness, to personal appropriation of religious truth in holiness of life. The *Imitation* purported to speak to the heart and from the heart. It and works like it that the Jesuits cultivated were not, therefore, extrinsic to their theological enterprise, but helped undergird it.

The *Imitation* explicitly and implicitly called for a simplification in the practices of the devout life. Such demands were a popular theme of the age, found also in the humanists. By the sixteenth century many religious reformers advocated the elimination or drastic reduction of popular practices of piety that had proliferated at the end of the Middle Ages to the obfuscation or destruction, in their view, of the essentials of Christianity. For some reformers these practices and reliance upon them were the equivalent of superstition—scapulars, fasting, relics, pilgrimages, rosaries, indulgences, some (or all) aspects of devotion to the saints.

What role did the Jesuits play in this "war against superstition"? According to the sixth of the "Rules for Thinking with the Church": "We should show our esteem for the relics of the saints by venerating them and praying to the saints. We should praise visits to the Station Churches, pilgrimages, indulgences, jubilees, crusade indults, and the lighting of candles in churches."[145] In their ministry and in their own lives, the Jesuits acted upon this rule and others like it that advocated fasting, sacred images, "long prayers in church," and similar practices. They did so, however, in their own "way."

The *Exercises* provided the basic framework for Jesuit piety. They focused on Jesus and the trinitarian God. Aside from some biblical saints that appear in the Gospel narratives, no others are mentioned in the body of the text. At a few junctures Mary plays an important, but quite subordinate, role.[146] Reading the lives of the saints, or some other pious book, is twice briefly recommended.[147]

The *Exercises* assume rather than prescribe that during their course the individual will assist daily at mass and participate in at least some of the liturgical Hours, especially vespers. They assume that some bodily penance is appropriate during most of the *Exercises* and for the life one will lead afterward, but the counsel is mild.[148] The basic rule for penance and, by extension, for other pious practices is that they be used to the extent that they promote an inward appropriation of godliness.

As Loarte's *Esercitio della vita cristiana* demonstrates, the Jesuits believed some degree of appropriation was possible for all, regardless of education or social class. They made no distinction between piety for an intellectual and social elite and piety for the masses, even though they recognized that on other grounds different people had different capacities.[149]

By and large Jesuits who dealt with more ignorant segments of the population showed themselves tolerant of local religious practices and even made use of them in their ministries. They drew the line at what they believed was gross superstition. In his lectures on prayer in Rome in 1557, Laínez gave examples of unacceptable practices, such as insisting that the outcome of prayer was secure if certain formulas were used, or that it depended on the person's being in a certain place or reciting the formulas at a certain time, or on gathering certain herbs on that day before sunrise, or on tying the herbs with a certain kind of string.[150]

In 1556 in a small town in Sicily, Jesuits tried to break the hold of a curious burial custom. Relatives of the deceased induced or paid women to stand alongside the corpse, sometimes with hands extended, sometimes singing "silly songs," sometimes pulling their hair and scratching their faces. During the two or three years of mourning, they did not go to mass or receive the sacraments, or enter the church from which the body had been buried.[151]

Even as sixteenth-century reformers waged campaigns against superstitious and obsessive religious practices, they enjoined a sometimes stern moral discipline. Erasmus consistently decried the weak moral fiber of his times, and in this regard he surely had a profound influence on the religious culture of several generations. As we have seen, the Jesuits occasionally took a strong stand against gambling, blasphemy, and other public excesses. In Spain in 1562 Nadal encouraged the Jesuits to work for the elimination of bullfights.[152] The Jesuits generally followed Ignatius's advice about moderation of bodily penance, however, and at Bologna in 1553 Francesco Palmio persuaded some persons to turn over to him their hairshirts and scourges, which according to him they had been using to excess.[153]

Canisius and other Jesuits in German-speaking lands believed in witches and supported their prosecution, but Jesuits from the Mediterranean world showed practically no concern with them.[154] They believed in diabolical possession, however, and they performed exorcisms to free individuals from it.[155] They did not seem to consider that possession might be a matter for the

Inquisition. Cornelius Wischaven, much given to exorcisms even before his entrance as a priest into the Society, performed so many in Rome in 1557–58 that Polanco had to assure the cardinal protector of the Society that he could be trusted.[156]

Jesuits recognized the difference between ordinary psychological stress and more serious psychic malady. Near Venice in 1553, for instance, a Jesuit was asked to visit a man suspected of being possessed. He diagnosed the man, a twenty-two-year-old student, as depressed from too rigorous a program at the university and "helped him" simply by his conversation.[157]

Along with probably most other Jesuits, Polanco assumed that certain persons, like a young Spanish Jesuit named Miguel de Ochoa, received "gifts of healing from the Lord." When sick with a fever in Rome in 1548, Polanco with Ignatius's approval asked Miguel for help.[158] As was Miguel's custom in such instances, he wrote out, in the presence of the Eucharist, the Lord's Prayer and the Hail Mary three times and then applied the paper to Polanco's neck. The fever immediately subsided. Polanco persuaded him to exercise his gift henceforth simply with a blessing and imposition of hands, without making use of the written prayers. Miguel followed Polanco's counsel and continued to use his special gifts with great success in Tivoli and later in Spain.[159]

One day a man in India asked a Jesuit to cure his wife who "was possessed and half-dead." Since the Jesuit was too busy to go to her, Polanco related, he sent a copy of John's Gospel, prescribing that the husband suspend it around his wife's neck. When this was done, she was "liberated and healed."[160] As these examples make clear, for the Jesuits the line between superstition and a supernal gift for healing was sometimes thin.

If there is little about the veneration of the saints in the *Exercises,* there is also relatively little about it in the other documentation that has survived from these early decades. But the Jesuits of course practiced it and inculcated it in others. Recitation of the "Litany of the Saints" was a common practice in their schools. In the early 1560's Canisius imposed, for the needs of the church, the daily recitation of the litany on the Jesuit communities in Germany, and it was eventually adopted elsewhere in the Society as practically the only occasion when Jesuits gathered together regularly for prayer.[161] In 1563 Nadal prescribed in Venice that there be sacred images in all the classrooms and that the boys be taught to pause for a little prayer in front of them as they entered.[162] A practice similar to this came to be more or less the norm for all the schools.

Veneration of the saints stood, the Jesuits believed, on its own merits, but they began to interpret it as a statement against the Protestants. In 1549, for instance, they effected the transference of the heads of two of the eleven thousand virgin martyrs of Saint Ursula from Cologne to their church in Messina.[163] Nadal reported to Ignatius about his sermon on the veneration and invocation of the saints during the solemn ceremony of welcome. He was consoled at the devotion of the people toward the two relics, "to the confusion of the heretics."[164] As this story makes manifest, the Jesuits took the authenticity of relics more or less for granted. Late in life Nadal defended the authenticity of "Veronica's Veil," the cloth preserved in Saint Peter's basilica in Rome on which the facial image of Christ had supposedly been imprinted as he made his way on foot to Calvary. "Let no one tell me," Nadal said, "that this story is apocryphal. To a person unmoved toward accepting this devotion by the tradition, usage, and veneration of the Roman Church, I would respond: let him be on guard lest some bitter root lurk in his soul that will bring harm to him and others."[165] Nadal similarly believed in the authenticity of a relic from the column on which Christ was scourged, found in the church of Santa Prassede in Naples.[166] He seems never to have been shaken in his conviction that Pseudo-Dionysius was a disciple of Paul.[167] Not until the seventeenth century did the Jesuits sponsor through the Bollandists in Antwerp—a learned society still functioning today—a systematic and critical examination of the lives, miracles, and relics of the saints.

When even Nadal described the atrocity of Christ's suffering, as he did with imagination and in some detail in his *Meditationes,* he never utilized any of the late-medieval "revelations" concerning it purportedly made to Saint Bridget of Sweden and others. Just as the Jesuits were reserved about predictions concerning the "end times," they were reserved about many other special phenomena connected with holy persons. On one occasion when Nadal recounted the wonderful physical recovery that Ignatius experienced at the point of death at Loyola on the vigil of the feast of Saints Peter and Paul, he attributed it to intervention from on high, but with the disclaimer that he was little inclined to see miracles everywhere—"Et ancor ch'io non sia amico de far miracoli delle cose."[168]

The piety the Jesuits learned in the *Exercises* prevented them from confusing veneration of the saints with what was more fundamental to Christianity. Nadal voiced their general sentiment when he said, "Take care lest devotion to the saints and their invocation weaken devotion to God and invocation of him, which ought always to be on the increase. The latter differs totally from the former and altogether excels it."[169]

Among the saints the Jesuits not surprisingly mentioned the Virgin Mary most frequently—although not so frequently as one might expect. They were pleased when their students had rosary beads and prayed with them.[170] Sometime before 1557 Borja wrote a set of "points" to guide meditation on the fifteen "mysteries" of the rosary.[171] Although it was not published until 1964, its focus as much on Christological as on Marian realities and its emphasis on the virtues were probably typical of how the Jesuits instructed people in this devout practice.

Jesuits assiduously commended the Hours of Our Lady to others and prayed them themselves.[172] When after 1563 the specifically Jesuit form of confraternity, the Marian Congregation, or "Sodality of Our Lady," began to spread, it obviously highlighted the role of Mary for those who were enrolled. Ledesma's catechisms provided more space, within their extremely modest scope, for Mary and Marian prayers than was common in earlier catechisms.

Not until 1577 did Canisius publish the first book by a Jesuit on Mary, *De Maria Virgine incomparabili*, also known as *Opus Marianum*. It was the second part of a projected larger work refuting the Magdeburg Centuriators that Borja as general had, in the name of Pius V, commissioned him to write. Nadal ended his book *Adnotationes et meditationes* with a long section entitled "On the Praises of the Virgin Mother of God."[173] Like Borja's earlier and shorter work, Loarte's meditations on the rosary, published in Italian in 1573 in both Venice and Rome, dealt more explicitly with the life of Christ than with Mary.[174]

Seemingly all the early Jesuits took for granted the authenticity of the Holy House at Loreto, the habitation of Mary at the time of the Annunciation, transferred miraculously to Italy by angels in 1295, and they were much devoted to it. Part of their ardor stemmed, however, from the opportunities for ministry that the large number of pilgrims provided. Besides Mary, however, no other saint appeared with any frequency in Jesuit records as an object of devotion. At the castle of Loyola during his convalescence, Ignatius felt the desire to emulate the achievements of Francis and Dominic. As Jesuits gradually began to see that Ignatius was inspired by the example of these two saints in founding the Society, they showed special respect for them, but never particularly commended their invocation.

Ignatius's healing on the vigil of Peter and Paul and his emphatic respect for the papacy helped establish a special devotion to these two Apostles, who according to tradition ended their days in Rome. No doubt the itinerant and evangelizing Paul provided a model for what Nadal envisioned as the ideal of the Jesuits' "fourth vow." In his journal he said pointedly: "Peter signifies firmness and direction in our Society, and Paul signifies for us its ministries."[175]

Pilgrimage had been a Christian practice from the earliest centuries, but as a journey to the shrines of the saints it was among those practices especially criticized in the sixteenth century for its excesses. When in his *Autobiography* Ignatius referred to himself simply as "the pilgrim" and dreamed of Jerusalem as his goal, he suggested the biblical sense of the term (Heb. 11:13–16) and the late-medieval *viator,* not a seeker of devotion at the shrine of a local saint. The same was true for the pilgrimage later prescribed for novices of the Society, which was also intended as a kind of introduction to the itinerant preaching "in poverty" to which they were called.[176] In fact, in early Jesuit writings "pilgrimage," "travel," "mission," and "journey for ministry" were often almost synonyms.[177] "Pilgrim" thus had deep roots in the Jesuit tradition, and that fact perhaps helped incline them to foster pilgrimages in the more conventional sense. Their experience of Rome and Loreto as pilgrims' goals did the same. Until Loarte published his book on the subject in 1575, however, they did not single it out for special attention.[178]

Loarte's book was a direct result of his sojourn in Loreto in 1572, where he saw how useful it might be. Although it contains polemic against "the Lutherans" and a fervent defense of the authenticity of the Holy House, it begins by setting the idea of pilgrimage in its biblical context and then asks, "Are we not all pilgrims upon this earth?" A pilgrimage is essentially an act of hope and love, which both need to be fostered on the holy journey by prayer and meditation. Confession and Holy Communion are essential parts of it.

Intimately connected with such pilgrimages were indulgences, as Loarte's full title implied. The Jesuits believed in and defended this hotly contended practice. In 1555 Canisius as episcopal administrator of Vienna used the papal Jubilee upon the accession of Mary Tudor to the English throne as an occasion to insist on their great spiritual value.[179] Except in such polemical situations, however, the Jesuits' attention to them was peripheral. The *Exercises* seem once again to have set the direction, where they play no role in the body of the text.

What was characteristic of the Jesuits in general applied also to their traditional practices of piety. They ruled out what they deemed grossly superstitious. Otherwise, if the practices were sanctioned by custom or ecclesiastical authority, they made pragmatic use of them as occasion suggested. They subordinated them, however, to their own vision of the essentials of Christian devotion. If the practices were under attack by Protestants, the Jesuits defended them and gave them more prominence than they did in other situations. They made them into symbols of loyalty. This tendency became more obvious beginning about 1555 and continued to intensify. Not always well schooled in the critico-historical methods developed by the humanists or unwilling to apply them, they sometimes resorted to defenses of practices and institutions that in fact lacked the historical or theological warrant they attributed to them.

Lutheranism and the Empire

In October 1540, just a few weeks after the approval of the Society by Paul III, the now friendly Pedro Ortiz invited Pierre Favre to accompany him as part of Charles V's diplomatic entourage to the religious colloquies being held at Worms and Regensburg. Favre was thus the first Jesuit to enter Germany, where he spent a lot of time until his death in 1546, but he went there neither on his own initiative nor as part of some Jesuit plan, but upon the invitation from Ortiz. Hampered by his inability to read and speak German and by his general inexperience with the situation, he contributed nothing to the colloquies or to any other high-level efforts to determine political or ecclesiastical policy.

For the future of the Society in the Empire, however, his sojourns in Germany and the Low Countries had a lasting impact. He made the existence of the Society known to some important Catholics and guided a few of them, including the controversialist Johann Cochlaeus, through the *Spiritual Exercises*. He conveyed to his brethren in Italy and the Iberian peninsula vivid images of the appalling condition of the Catholic Church—not so much of the aggressiveness of the Lutherans as of the lassitude and confusion among Catholics and the shocking ignorance and other problems besetting the clergy. In 1542 he wrote to Ignatius that the situation was so bad that he was amazed there were not even more Lutherans.[180] At Louvain, aided by the young Francisco Estrada, who was then studying as a Jesuit at the university, he gained some novices for the Society, eight of whom he sent to Coimbra and one to Cologne for further studies.

Most important, he guided a young Dutch student of theology named Peter Canisius through the full course of the *Exercises* and admitted him to the Society in 1543. In no other part of Europe where the Society established itself did it owe its success and identity so manifestly to a single individual as it did to Canisius in the German Empire. In no other part of Europe did the

Society, especially in the person of Canisius, so early come to play such a pivotal role in determining the character of modern Catholicism.[181] During the first ten or twelve years of the Society's existence, however, this role was barely adumbrated. In 1542 Cardinal Giovanni Morone as papal nuncio took Bobadilla and Jay with him to Germany as the first step in implementing a program of itinerant preaching occasioned by the fears aroused by the failure of the religious colloquies. The two Jesuits remained in the Empire for several years. Jay won from King Ferdinand, Charles V's brother, admiration and support for the Society that would persist, through thick and thin, until his death as emperor in 1564. In 1546 Ferdinand used all his influence with Paul III to have Jay named bishop of Trieste, only to be frustrated by Ignatius's adamant resistance to the idea that any member of the Society assume a position in the hierarchy. Jay was already present at the Council of Trent and would not return until late 1549 to the other side of the Alps, where he died at the Jesuits' new college in Vienna just two years later.[182]

In 1547 Bobadilla tried to marshal forces against the Augsburg *Interim*, the concessions Charles V had made to the Lutherans upon the unilateral decision of Paul III to transfer the Council from Trent to Bologna. Neither pope nor emperor, he argued, could issue decrees against what is right. He so angered Charles that he was ordered to leave the Empire. Bobadilla's return to Rome placed Ignatius in an embarrassing quandary, for the general did not want to alienate the imperial party in Rome by seeming to support Bobadilla, yet he knew of Paul III's opposition to the *Interim*. Ignatius received Bobadilla with a cool propriety that prevented either party from claiming Ignatius as his own— and prevented Bobadilla from passing himself off as a martyr to the Catholic cause.[183] Bobadilla's resentment against Ignatius "the tyrant" possibly began to smolder at this time, only to burst into full flame after Ignatius's death at the time of the First General Congregation.

Canisius was ordained a priest in 1546 at Cologne, where the Jesuits had a small community. He engaged in the *consueta ministeria* there and took an active part in the controversy that surrounded Hermann von Wied, the Lutheranizing archbishop. Ignatius summoned him to Rome the next year and almost immediately dispatched him to Messina as one of the ten founders of the school, an experience that had a profound effect on him. Canisius's departure from Germany practically coincided with the departures of Jay, Bobadilla, and Cornelius Wischaven. Favre had died in 1546.

By 1548, therefore, Jesuit presence in Germany was sparse indeed, and outside Cologne, practically non-existent. Foundations had in fact been laid for the future of the Society in the Empire during this first decade, but they were shaky, haphazard, and perceptible only with hindsight. Although Ignatius and his advisers were alerted by Favre, Jay, and Bobadilla to the desperation of the Catholic situation, they assigned it no priority. They responded to requests for help but took little initiative themselves. The fact that almost none of the Jesuits at this time spoke or even read German and, as time would tell, that few seemed capable of learning the language helps account for this seeming disinterest.

The Jesuits were not, however, otherwise insensitive to the progress of the Reformation. Laínez and Favre had hardly arrived in Rome in 1538 when they discovered an Augustinian friar named Agostino Mainardi preaching Lutheran ideas, and the Jesuits a few years later launched a persistent and temporarily successful campaign to win back to orthodoxy the duchess of Ferrara, Renée of France, who was the cousin of King Francis I and the wife of Duke Ercole d'Este II, one of the Jesuits' great benefactors.[184] They tried to counter Protestantism elsewhere in the Italian peninsula.

In 1542 Salmerón and Broët spent a brief and fruitless few months in Ireland as papal legates in the wake of Henry VIII's schism. Ignatius was eager to have some Jesuits accompany Philip II when in 1554 he went to England espoused to Mary Tudor, but none were invited by that prince, who like his father showed little enthusiasm for the Society. Nadal and Borja were chagrined at this slight *(discrédito)* and believed that Araoz's negligence in pursuing the matter was at least partly to blame.[185] The Jesuits did not enter England until 1580, and even then there were just three of them—Robert Persons, Ralph Emerson, and Edmund Campion. The next year Campion was apprehended and executed for "treason."

The Jesuits began to work in Poland only in 1564, but within ten years they were already operating five schools there.[186] France was a special situation, as we shall see. The Jesuits' major field of endeavor in holding back or reversing the tide of Protestantism during these early years, therefore, was the Empire, including the parts of the Low Countries under Habsburg dominion. This is not surprising, but neither was it preordained, since it hinged so much on the contingency of having the right man, Canisius, in the right place at the right time.

The decade beginning in 1550 was determinative. That year "the defense of the faith" appeared prominently in the new version of the *Formula*. Ignatius had a few months earlier acceded to the request of Duke Wilhelm IV of Bavaria and dispatched Jay, Salmerón, and Canisius to the University of Ingolstadt. For all practical purposes Canisius, who did not die until 1597, never again left Germany.

With the support of King Ferdinand, Jay had by 1551–52 established at Vienna the first Jesuit college in the Empire.[187] When Jay died, Canisius assumed leadership and soon had under him at Vienna twenty-five Jesuits sent by Ignatius, most of whom were incapable of communicating with the Viennese except in Latin. Undaunted, Canisius, with Ignatius's permission, settled with Duke Albrecht V of Bavaria in 1555 the terms for the eventual establishment of a Jesuit college at Ingolstadt, and on 5 July 1556 eighteen Jesuits entered the city for that purpose.[188] In 1553 Canisius had narrowly escaped becoming archbishop of Vienna and was forced to compromise by acting as administrator of the diocese until a bishop could be named. In 1556 Ignatius, who had meanwhile opened the Germanico in Rome, established the German province of the Society and named Canisius its first provincial. The previous year Canisius had published the first of his catechisms.

Upon the request of Pope Julius III, Ignatius in 1555 dispatched Laínez and Nadal as papal theologians to the Diet of Augsburg in the entourage of Cardinal Morone. He simultaneously named Nadal *commissarius*, with practically plenipotentiary powers, for the Jesuits in the Empire. It was the first time Nadal had set foot in this territory and, like his Jesuit predecessors, was utterly dismayed at what he found. His sense of disaster could only have been intensified that year by the terms of the Peace of Augsburg, which spelled the defeat of the Catholic cause as it had been pursued up to that point and meant the end of the career of its leader, Emperor Charles V.

Nadal returned to the Empire for two more long visitations—1562–63, 1566–67. But from the time of this first trip in 1555, he labored as best he could to make Germany a special priority among his brethren in southern Europe.[189] "Woe unto us," he wrote, "if we do not help Germany."[190] Another turning point in the history of the Society had decidedly been reached.

By 1555 there were about 50 Jesuits in the Empire—15 at Cologne and practically all the rest in Vienna. Within twenty years there were about eight times that number, many of whom were natives, but many others were sent there by the general. Two tart letters from Jesuit headquarters in Rome in 1562 reveal both how importunate Canisius was in demanding reinforcements and how in practice Germany had become a special concern of the Jesuit leadership. On 16 May Francisco de Borja, acting as vicar for Laínez, who was then at Trent, wrote to Canisius: "To speak plainly to your Reverence, I think you ought to be more content with the men sent to you in Germany, partly because they are suitable and partly because no province of the Society is being treated more liberally than yours." Two weeks later he wrote to him in the same vein: "You ought not to be so persistent in asking us for a new man every hour of the day. We are not rich in experienced teachers and are therefore obliged to send you such as we have. I can tell your Reverence for a fact that we do more for your one province than, perhaps, for all the other provinces put together."[191]

By dint of such tactics with the general and by reason of the Germans that he and others recruited for the Society, Canisius was directly or indirectly responsible during his long lifetime for the founding of eighteen Jesuit schools. This included the college in Prague in 1556. That college began with twelve Jesuits, but that same year eighteen more arrived—five priests and thirteen scholastics.

Under Canisius, the Jesuits in the Empire engaged in the *consueta ministeria* as they did elsewhere, but of course with more apologetical and polemical intent. They entered into controversy with Protestants and tried in other ways to win them back, but their major energies were directed to Catholics. In this they took the long view in seeing the schools as the key factor in preparing future generations who would be as devout as they were well instructed in their tradition. The difficulties with financing and personnel that these establishments entailed were perhaps as great as they anywhere encountered. While they had the support of some ecclesiastical and lay leaders such as Ferdinand, they had a much cooler reception from others, including Ferdinand's son Maximilian.

Despite his own reluctance and the persuasion of the Jesuits in Rome that his talents would be better engaged elsewhere, Canisius appeared briefly at Trent in 1562, where he worked for a mitigation of the Index of Prohibited Books issued by Pope Paul IV in 1559. To a degree unusual for Jesuits in other parts of the world, he labored more directly for the implementation of the Tridentine decrees, beginning in 1565 with his appointment by the pope as his special envoy to carry them to the German bishops. Although this appointment indicated the esteem and trust that Canisius by then enjoyed, it also conveniently coincided with the fact that he was on his way back to Germany after being in Rome to cast his vote for the successor to Laínez as general.

This brief sketch of how the Society first established and bore itself in Germany raises the more general question of how the early Jesuits understood the Reformation. In the first place, they accepted as given the basic thesis that it was heterodox. Second, they resorted to the standard practice of their day for explaining major calamities by attributing them to the sins of Christians. That explanation was in use long before their time; for instance, it was employed to explain the success of Turkish incursions into

Europe earlier in the century.[192] When applied by the Jesuits to the Reformation, it missed and obscured deeper issues but had some verisimilitude because of the undoubted impact on religious consciousness of the scandal caused especially by ignorant and immoral clergy. Nadal in particular recurred often to this explanation.[193] Among the first and principal causes of the calamity that afflicted Germany, he said, were the depraved morals and vices of ecclesiastics.[194]

The conclusion was obvious. If the bad lives of Christians were the cause of the Reformation, good lives must be the cure—and not only the good lives of clerics. A passage from Laínez's thirtieth lecture on prayer to his Roman audience of laywomen and men in 1557 stated the thesis with clarity. Having finished the first part of the lecture, he digressed just before the intermission to inform his audience that seven or eight German soldiers, seemingly Lutherans, were stranded in Rome after the truce between Paul IV and Philip II. After a brief condemnation of even a "just war" because of the great damages it inflicts especially on women and children, he appealed for alms for the German soldiers, who were from a nation "scandalized by our sins." He continued:

I am not a Lutheran, but I believe that we have given occasion for this trouble by our pomp, sensuality, avarice, simony, and by usurping for ourselves the goods of the church. And now what? We can now restore what we have ruined and scandalized, but how do we do it? In my opinion we cannot do it with beautiful words alone or with conferences and similar things without accompanying them with deeds, because it was with the deeds of a bad life that we did evil. All right, now we want to do better? Contraries are cured by contraries. We must therefore lead good lives. We can provide good example and begin by giving alms to these soldiers, so that they can leave Rome consoled, praising God for the edification they have received.[195]

"Contraries are cured by contraries." Earlier in that same series Laínez had quoted that medical axiom to somewhat the same effect, except that his depiction of the Lutherans was even less flattering than of the Catholics. "If they are proud, impatient, without charity, and impure, let us be humble, patient, pure, and obedient. Thus we will better cure this evil" than by commissioning agents to collect money to oppose it. The Christian faith was planted in Germany with humility, patience, and suffering, and by these means will it be restored.[196]

Laínez here gave utterance to the deepest persuasion among his brethren that the primary means of healing the religious division was to instill in Catholics the desire for a more devout life. That was the fundamental principle animating their efforts against the spread of heresy in Germany and elsewhere, and they believed that in their way of proceeding in their ministries they had a particularly appropriate means to accomplish their goal.

But the goal of course assumed a polemical and confessional character, which is how the Reformation began to have its most palpable impact on the religious and theological culture of the Jesuits. In the passage quoted above, Laínez immediately moved into an imaginary dialogue with a Lutheran in which he descended to greater detail: You will not pray the rosary, and I will pray it more often and with greater devotion; you damn indulgences, and I will esteem them more highly than ever; you ridicule prayers and masses for the dead, and I will double their number; you condemn confession, and I will confess my sins all the more frequently. If we behave thus, Laínez assured, God will certainly help us.[197]

Many years later Nadal, while discussing the meaning of "the defense of the faith" in the second version of the *Formula*, repeated the same kind of argument with special application to the Jesuits: The heretics rely on vain eloquence and human learning, but Jesuits cultivate simplicity in both; they prefer their heresiarch to the doctors of the church, but Jesuits adhere to the teaching of the doctors and the councils; they teach new doctrines and contaminate the old, but Jesuits do not permit such novelty; they hate the pope and the Apostolic See, but Jesuits have a special vow to obey the pope; they have abolished confession, but Jesuits promote its frequent reception.[198]

The passage reveals, among other things, a fateful shift in interpretation by Jesuits of the earliest years of the Society. Practices that grounded the Society on their own merits without reference to Protestantism were by 1576 adduced specifically as antidotes to it. Nadal had earlier begun to promote among Jesuits the idea that the Society was founded precisely to counter the Reformation.[199] In 1554 even Ignatius had come close to saying the same thing in a letter to Canisius.[200] Not without a grain of truth, the idea was fundamentally a retrospective distortion. It did not emerge with any clarity or insistence until after the death of Ignatius.

Once Ignatius was dead, however, the temptation to compare him with Luther was too great to resist. Nadal did so, for instance, in the exhortation at Alcalá in 1576, but he had suggested the theme as early as 1557 in an exhortation to the Jesuits at the Collegio Romano.[201] In his second *Dialogue* some five years later, he portrayed Ignatius as the new David pitted against Luther, the Goliath.[202] He reminded the Jesuits at Cologne in 1567, with some confusion of dates, that the year Luther was called by the devil Ignatius heard the call from God.[203]

With more chronological precision, Polanco later noted that the year Luther appeared before Charles V at Worms, 1521, was the year of Ignatius's conversion.[204] As Pedro de Ribadeneira prepared notes for his biography of Ignatius, the first ever published (1572) and the most influential, he paralleled the two men: Luther and his followers were destroying the faith, but Ignatius and his were raised up by God to confirm and defend it.[205] A convenient and favorite theme of historians for the next four hundred years, this paralleling was first created and promoted by the Jesuits themselves.

In 1541 Favre's list of those for whom he explicitly prayed included "the pope, the emperor, the king of France, the king of England, Luther, the sultan, Bucer, and Philipp Melanchthon."[206] By the grace of God he had great love for heretics and for the whole world, especially for Germany— "esta pobre nación."[207] Laínez told the Romans in 1557 that, although some persons maintained the contrary opinion, it was praiseworthy to pray for heretics, schismatics, and excommunicates, and he especially exhorted them to do so for the first group, misled because of their own sins but also "scandalized by our rottenness and simony."[208]

Like Laínez, many Jesuits considered the rank and file of Lutherans misguided and worthy of compassion, but by about 1560 they fell into explicit vilifications of Luther that did occur while Ignatius was alive. Ignatius was unusual among both his Protestant and Catholic peers in his abstinence from name-calling, and his example seems to have kept a damper on it among the Jesuits. But by 1577 Canisius was calling Luther a "hog in heat"— "subantem porcum."[209] Laínez said he was perverse.[210] Nadal was perhaps the worst and most consistent offender, for whom Luther was "disturbed and diabolical," "an evil and bestial man," "a wicked, proud, enraged, drunken, and devilish monk."[211] He did not invent the bad-monk interpretation of Luther. It had been in circulation among Catholic polemicists for decades before he adopted it. Besides being a simple example of the vituperative rhetoric common to all religious parties of the day, it was based upon the ancient persuasion that heterodox thinking was the result of immorality and willful blindness to the truth.

Nadal's opinion of Protestants was not improved by his several encounters with them in his travels, and especially not by his being held captive by them with threats to his life, as he was for some three hours outside Toulouse in 1562.[212] Like some other Jesuits, moreover, he thought that the Germans ate and drank too much, were domineering when they had authority and servile when they did not, and were generally cold and difficult to deal with.[213] To Nadal's credit, he forbade at Louvain the reading, in both the Jesuits' refectory and that of their pupils, Cochlaeus's *Commentarium de actis et scriptis Martini Lutheri.*[214] First published in 1549, it was a book that, barely managing to rise above the worst legends about Luther, dwelt on his alleged sins and immoral conduct rather than dealing with his teaching or program of reform.

How well did the first Jesuits understand that teaching and program? Whatever they read of Luther—and for the first several decades only a few were able to read his works written in German—they read with hostile mind and polemical intent. It seems Ignatius never read anything by Luther or other Protestants. Except for Jesuits working in northern Europe and a few others, he was typical.

Although among the many "privileges" the Society enjoyed from the Holy See was permission under certain conditions to read the writings of the heretics, even Jesuits like Canisius worried that other papal decrees, like the Index of 1559, had in fact rescinded that permission. His worry showed, however, that he did read them, and he in fact cites Luther, Calvin, Bucer, Bullinger, Chemnitz, and of course the Centuriators verbatim.[215] By his own account Bobadilla read works of "the heretics Luther, Philipp Melanchthon, Pellicanus, Oecolampadius, and others" when he was in Germany during the mid-1540's.[216]

Favre recommended to his brethren in Rome the "Augsburg Confession" with Melanchthon's commentary but, suffering from the same scruple about reading heretical material, never said explicitly that he read it himself.[217] Especially after about 1553 Ignatius's correspondence returned with some frequency to the issue, at times assuring Jesuits that no permission was needed to read books that were merely "suspect," at other times urging caution, but generally confirming that their permission to read heretical books had not been revoked by the Holy See.[218] Ignatius allowed for use in the schools classical texts commented on by Protestant authors if the books did not contain the "poison" of their religious doctrine and if their authorship could be concealed.[219]

While a student at Padua, Polanco read Catholic controversialists such as Albert Pigge and Ambrogio Catarino, but at least at that time he does not seem to have read any Protestants.[220] When he described Jay in Vienna in 1551 as "carefully studying the opinions of the heretics," he implied that Jay did so directly from Protestant sources.[221] From what we know about certain assignments that Laínez and Salmerón received at Trent in 1547 and 1551, they surely at those times studied Lutheran works written in Latin.[222] In 1562 Nadal made a special trip to Antwerp to buy books, including some "by heretics, which will be useful to our Fathers at Trent."[223] Laínez and Polanco met Theodore Beza and Peter Martyr Vermigli face-to-face at the Colloquy of Poissy in 1561 and heard their arguments.[224] By the time Salmerón wrote his commentary on the New Testament, he had acquired a knowledge of Protestant commentators, including Calvin and Beza, that was dazzling in its breadth and precision.[225]

But it was from Nadal that most Jesuits received their first lessons in the Society about what Luther and subsequent Protestants taught. Nadal had read Martin Chemnitz's *Theologiae Iesuitarum praecipua capita* (1562), for he professedly wrote his second *Dialogue* in defense of the Society as a response to it, and he probably read some other Protestants. His description of Protestant teaching, scattered in short passages in a number of his works, manifested only an approximate and superficial grasp of it. Sometimes indiscriminately, sometimes with specific reference to Calvin, he accused Protestants of denying the Real Presence of Christ in the Eucharist.[226] According to him, the Lutherans denied the doctrine of the Communion of Saints and the efficacy of the saints' prayer for wayfarers here below.[227] He asked in rhetorical fashion questions that had been commonplace at least since Erasmus's *De libero arbitrio* of 1524: "Why do the German princes believe these heretical preachers? Are these preachers more learned, more virtuous? . . . If the Holy Spirit speaks in them, why not in others?"[228]

As might be expected, however, Nadal recurred most often to the issue of justification. He believed that the Lutherans denied any cooperation between grace and human will in the process of justification, which led him to brand them as Manichees, an accusation often hurled at them by Catholics.[229] Without qualification he described them as "excluding our good works" and "destroying free will." He warned Jesuits that when they spoke of trust and confidence in God's mercy they should be careful not to give the impression that "faith alone" justified.[230]

The Lutherans taught, according to Nadal, that justification was only imputed, not intrinsic, and that all Protestants—Lutherans, Calvinists, Anabaptists—taught that sins remain in the just.[231] It was this aspect of their doctrine that most offended him, for it seemed to deny that by the full remission of sin and the infusion of grace a "new creation" (Gal. 6:15) came into being by which we were made "sons of God, brothers of Christ, co-heirs with him, and partakers of the divine nature" (Rom. 8:16–17; 2 Pet. 1:4).[232] From the very first moment leading to the "new creation," Nadal, like Trent, asserted that grace was operative and that it enabled the human cooperation that was also essential to the process. The result in the moment of justification was that the individual could boast with Paul, "I live, now not I, but Christ lives in me" (Gal. 2:20).[233] Thus was established the deepest foundation of human dignity, a dignity that Lutheran teaching denied.[234] He referred the basic idea to Ignatius: "Father Ignatius often used the expression 'in our Lord' because he wanted to indicate the spiritual origins of our actions. That is, we do not in our actions do what we do from our own strength but in Christ, in his grace, and out of his power, as if to say: I labor, but it is not I; Christ labors in me, and I in Christ."[235]

Nadal was on much firmer ground in this Catholic interpretation of justification and sanctification that pervades almost everything he wrote than in his brief, occasional, and prejudiced excursions into Lutheran theology. Salmerón wrote in his commentary on Galatians a similar but more extended and systematic explanation of the Tridentine teaching on justification.[236] In positively emphasizing Catholic teaching, they followed Ignatius's most consistent advice on how to deal with doctrinal controversies—whenever possible, avoid public polemics and confrontations and be content with an exposition and confirmation of Catholic doctrine.[237] Ignatius was astute enough to recognize that polemics gave free advertising to bad ideas, but the advice also resonates with his belief that the heart, not the head, was where the problem lay.

But even Ignatius wanted Jesuits to refute Protestant doctrines when the situation called for it.[238] After a private encounter with two Lutherans in Vienna in 1551, André des Freux concluded that in his sermons and sacred lectures he needed to refute explicitly the "opinions and novelties of the sectarians."[239] Nadal believed that such refutations had been the tradition of the church in every age and therefore should be the practice of his own.[240] From Vienna in 1555 he urged Ignatius to send Laínez to Germany precisely so that he might write books against the Lutherans.[241] The establishment at about this time of a chair of "controversialist" theology at the Collegio Romano indicated beyond a shadow of a doubt that the Jesuits were readying to go on the offensive.[242]

Although Jesuits seemed to agree that punitive measures against heretics would not effect their conversion, they advocated civil disabilities and coercive measures for the protection of others against the contagion or when nothing else seemed to work and the situation was especially dangerous. On 13 August 1554, Ignatius responded to a letter from Canisius asking what he should recommend to King Ferdinand concerning the religious situation in the Empire.[243] The moment was delicate. Charles V, acknowledging his military defeat by the Protestant princes, was preparing his abdication in favor of Ferdinand. The solution to the religious controversies codified the next year at Augsburg seemed inevitable—"cuius regio eius religio."

Ignatius divided his answer into two parts. In the first he described how the sickness of heresy could be driven out, in the second how the patient could be nursed back to health. The recommendations in the second part included ensuring good appointments to bishoprics, importing good preachers and pastors, seeing to the publication of good catechisms, and especially developing four kinds of seminaries to assure good clergy in the future.

The recommendations in the first part were severe and, in that respect, typical of the times. Canisius should try to persuade King Ferdinand, among other things, to remove all heretics from his Council, to deprive all Protestant professors of their positions in the University of Vienna, to search out all heretical books in bookstores and have them burned. All preachers and "heresiarchs" convicted of spreading heresy should be subjected to heavy penalties like deprivation of office and other rights and privileges. In these cases exile, imprisonment, and even execution might be called for.

Both sides in the religious controversies were long hardened in their positions. Europe had already experienced the first of its many religious wars, and execution for heresy, blasphemy, and "treason" was by 1554 no longer a novelty. Although religion was often only a convenient mask for other motives, the spilling of blood in its name had begun decades earlier and would continue for a century longer.

~ 8

The Jesuits and the Church at Large

WITH THE BULL *Regimini militantis ecclesiae* of 27 September 1540, the Society of Jesus acquired official status within the Catholic Church at a crucial juncture in the church's history. Whereas the Jesuits' opposition to Protestantism increasingly contributed to their self-understanding, their interaction with Catholic institutions and personalities gave them even sharper definition.

The Catholic Church of the sixteenth century was a complex and lumbering association of interlocking but independent or semi-independent institutions in which papacy, episcopacy, episcopal synods, monarchies and dukedoms, city councils, confraternities, cathedral chapters, religious orders, theological faculties of universities, and other social bodies boasted rights and advanced claims that often brought them into conflict with one another.

By 1540 many of these institutions had begun to rally around the cry for "reform of the church" and shared some assumptions as to how that reform might be realized. These common assumptions led, after many delays, to the inauguration of the Council of Trent by Pope Paul III in December 1545. Even at this point and well beyond it, however, opinions were sharply divided about what reform of the church really meant. The issue exacerbated old jealousies and provoked new ones. Moreover, fear of Turks, *alumbrados, conversos,* "Erasmians," and especially Protestants generated in some circles an atmosphere of suspicion and corporate paranoia that ill served a judicious approach to the reform that was on everybody's agenda.

Into this situation the Society of Jesus was born. Many Catholics welcomed the Society's efforts to "help souls" and approved of its "way of proceeding," but others did not. Still others vacillated. What was to be feared or hoped for from this new and untested organization? Where on the many spectrums of claims, loyalties, enmities, and understandings of religion and social weal did the Jesuits fit?

Ignatius repeatedly advised Jesuits to deport themselves as neutral on issues where Catholics were divided. As he said to Jay, Salmerón, and Canisius on their way to Germany in 1549, "Where there are different factions and sects, members of the Society will not oppose either party but show love for both."[1] The sixteenth-century situation, however, often did not allow this advice to be realized, especially not when the Jesuits themselves became the object of controversy.

The juridical status of the Society within the Catholic Church was the Jesuits' defense against their enemies, but in some cases it was the very reason they needed a defense. When the companions obtained papal approval of their compagnia in 1540, they were following a pattern well established since the thirteenth century when Saint Dominic and Saint Francis did the same for their orders. What did this approval entail?

The papal bull, that is, the *Formula,* was the charter of the order. As a charter it served the same purpose as today the approval by some governmental agency does for the incorporation of any benevolent or educational institution. The approval acknowledges that the general purposes for which the institution stands are legitimate and fundamentally consonant with the ethos of the commonwealth, and, as long as the institution observes the laws of the land, the charter guarantees the institution the right to function independently in pursuit of those purposes, within the limits stated in the charter. The bull was a license to operate.

Although it was issued by a pope, the charter did not constitute the Society as a sort of bureau within the papal curia or make the superior general of the order the vice-president of a special division under the pontiff as chief executive officer. This is a modern, often implicit and unexamined misconception that some statements of the first Jesuits themselves seem to support when taken out of context. Those Jesuits had in fact the more traditional understanding of their charter and at times had to defend themselves even against popes who wanted to change elements in it.

Papal approval did, nonetheless, establish a special relationship between the Society and the papacy. Among other things, the papacy was the source of the Jesuits' permission to preach and administer the sacraments. As we have seen, the popes almost immediately enhanced that permission with a number of "privileges." Some of the episcopacy's attacks against the Jesuits were occasioned by these very pastoral privileges that the Jesuits and members of the other orders enjoyed.

The bull *Regimini* meant that the Jesuits were in fact "exempt" from the jurisdiction of bishops, that within certain limits they could function independently of episcopal hierarchy even in their ministries. The origins and anomalies of this arrangement in the Catholic Church antedated the Jesuits by several centuries.[2] Alongside the juridical fact of exemption, moreover, was an ambivalence: the Jesuits defended the legitimacy of episcopacy, hierarchy, and even benefices, yet they fought desperately to evade nominations of themselves to any prelacy or to any position that entailed benefices. Although similar attitudes can be found in many religious enthusiasts in the history of Christianity, few corporations took such an adamant and official stand against their members' accepting prelacies as did the Society of Jesus.[3]

Their own origins and their abstention from such positions meant that their concerns, even regarding "reform," did not perfectly coincide with those of the bishops assembled at Trent or with those of prelates in the Roman curia, even of their friends there like Cardinals Contarini, Cervini, and Morone. For bishops and other prelates, "reform of the church" meant first and foremost the reform of the disciplinary and juridical structures of papacy, episcopacy, pastorate, and parochial practice. It was to these that they principally directed their attention and hope, whether they were "intransigents" or "spirituals," for they were by choice professional churchmen. Their starting point was the institution. From this reform they surely hoped to accomplish the moral and spiritual betterment of the faithful, but their primary focus was on the church as an organization of bishops and pastors of parishes.

This was not the Jesuits' primary focus. Their starting point was not the institution but the individual or voluntary groupings of individuals, beginning with themselves. They had forsworn participation in precisely the institutions with which the others were primarily concerned. Polanco reported that when Paul III saw the "Five Chapters" in 1539 he was moved by a prophetic spirit to say that the Society would do "much for the reform of the church," but reform as an aim of the Jesuits is nowhere found in the official documents of the Society defining its purpose.[4] When equivalent terms occur in the writings of some Jesuits, they generally do not bear the same meaning as they did at Trent.

In 1545 Pierre Favre hoped and prayed that Christ would use present and future members of the Society as instruments to "cleanse his house," the church.[5] Other Jesuits spoke in similar terms, but they generally referred to some local situation. What Favre meant is clear from a short instruction he wrote in 1541. In it he indicated that true reform meant the reform of the individual through a general confession, daily examination of conscience, weekly reception of the Eucharist, study of the catechism and inner appropriation of its lessons, and other practices and attitudes the Jesuits consistently promoted.[6]

As early as 1546 Ignatius complained that some people accused the Jesuits of "wanting to reform the whole world."[7] According to a later comment by Ribadeneira, Ignatius acknowledged some truth in the accusation about such "zealots" ("zelosos") who got mixed up in politics ("meterse en cosas de governo"), and he said they should, like good religious, better occupy themselves with preaching and confessions.[8]

But then as now a line of demarcation between religion and politics, including ecclesiastical politics, was easier to propose as an ideal than to implement in practice. By actively seeking the friendship of princes and prelates, moreover, the Jesuits were almost perforce drawn into policy and partisanship. The fact that some Jesuits acted as theologians at the Council of Trent meant that, sooner or later, they would take positions with which other members of the Council would bitterly disagree. Often enough, however, the Jesuits ran into trouble with their fellow Catholics not because of a particular position they defended or attacked but because their very Institute was considered suspect or subversive.

Bishops and Theologians

Besides local skirmishes with other Catholics over issues like frequent Communion and the opening or closing of schools, the Jesuits were involved in conflicts of wider import. Few were more shocking to the members of the Society or deemed by them potentially more dangerous than the active opposition they encountered in Paris in 1554—from Bishop Eustace du Bellay, from the French Parlement, and especially from the Faculty of Theology of the university. The rebuff from the Faculty, still considered the most prestigious voice in the theological world, was a major setback. It was emotionally painful because of the pride the first companions and other Jesuits took in their earlier association with the university. The Society did not in fact gain legal entrance into France until 1562, and its ministries there were much hampered until that time.[9] This meant that it officially entered the kingdom at a particularly difficult moment, the very eve of the long wars of religion in France in which the houses of Valois, Guise, and Bourbon fought out their rivalries.

Ignatius had sent a colony of young Jesuits to study at the University of

Paris in the spring of 1540, well before the formal approval of the Society that September. They were under the superiorship of Diego de Eguía, soon succeeded by Jerónimo Doménech. Doménech eventually settled the Jesuits at the Collège des Lombards. Among the Jesuits who studied at Paris in these early years were some destined to play important roles in the history of the order—Jean Pelletier, Olivier Manare, Robert Claysson, Paolo d'Achille, Francisco Estrada, Andrés de Oviedo, Diego Miró, Pedro de Ribadeneira, and Everard Mercurian, who succeeded Borja as the fourth general of the Society.

For the first decade of their presence in the capital, the Jesuits suffered a number of vicissitudes in that disturbed political and religious atmosphere but were able to pursue their studies and carry on a modest ministry.[10] They had a few powerful friends. Guillaume du Prat, bishop of Clermont, had met and come to esteem Jay, Salmerón, and Laínez during the first period of Trent. In 1550 he persuaded the Jesuits in Paris to abandon their quarters at the Collège des Lombards and take up residence in his palace on the rue de la Harpe, which he in fact planned to give to them. This was the origin of what became the famed Collège de Clermont, later Collège Louis le Grand.

To take possession of real property like the palace, the Jesuits needed official admission as a body into the kingdom, the *droit de naturalisation*. It was over this issue that the storm broke against them. Backing the Jesuits' request for the *droit* at the court of King Henry II was the young cardinal Charles de Guise, to whom Ignatius had recommended the Society when he came to Rome for the conclave of February 1550. The cardinal offered to be the protector of the Society in France. The friendship of de Guise was itself enough to arouse antagonism toward the Society from du Bellay. Their families were old political rivals.

The Jesuits had, meanwhile, presented the several papal bulls approving the Society and granting it extensive privileges—a bad miscalculation if the Jesuits thought such documents would favorably incline toward them the Parlement, a body that vaunted "the liberties of the French church." Gallican sentiment in the French capital would be a prevailing undercurrent in the opposition the Jesuits experienced there.

When Bishop du Bellay took a public stand against the Society, the Parlement and the Faculty followed suit. On 1 December 1554, the theologians published their condemnation, which to a large extent repeated the objections raised by du Bellay—the name of the Society was arrogant; the Jesuits interpreted the three vows of poverty, chastity, and obedience in an inadmissable way; they had cast off all the usages of religious life; their privileges infringed on the pastoral rights of bishops, pastors of parishes, universities and other religious orders; and similar objections. The document concluded: "This Society appears to be a danger to the Faith, a disturber of the peace of the church, destructive of monastic life, and destined to cause havoc rather than edification."[11] To its well-known condemnations of Luther and Erasmus, the Faculty now added the Society of Jesus.

In a letter from Rome about a month later, in late January 1555, Ignatius reduced the arguments against the Society to two—its name and the number of its privileges from the Holy See.[12] But political, professional, and religious rivalries had won the condemnation its support and brought into the open many Dominicans, Franciscans, Carmelites, and others who upon its promulgation cried that Jesuits should be beaten out of France with sticks and clubs.[13] Placards against them appeared on churches and other buildings all over Paris, and Jesuits were denounced from the pulpit.

In May 1555, the episcopal tribunal of Paris summoned Paschase Broët, the Jesuit provincial of France, to inform him that members of the Society were forbidden under pain of excommunication to do ministry in Paris. Whereas word of the condemnation and this measure circulating throughout Europe deeply distressed the Jesuits, it heartened their other enemies to speak out against them, even as far away as at the court of Charles V at Yuste.[14] According to Polanco, by the fall of 1556 "everybody" in Spain was talking about the condemnation.[15]

How to respond? Ignatius feared that a direct response would only engender further rancor and be contrary to the Society's mission as peacemaker.[16] He interpreted the attack as more "against the Apostlic See than against us," for the Jesuits saw the Faculty paying only lip service to the papal bulls. But by the time Broët was threatened with excommunication, Paul IV had become pope. From him, as Polanco later put it, "it did not seem opportune to request a remedy," although both Ignatius and Broët made at least some gestures in that direction.[17] The Jesuits feared further offending the bishop of Paris through such an intervention. They also feared that the pope harbored objections to the Society similar to those listed in the condemnation.

Ignatius decided that the best redress was to seek testimonials from around Europe about the good work the Jesuits were doing, and he ordered superiors to do so where they thought it would yield the desired results.[18] A number of such letters were eventually obtained—for example, from King Ferdinand and King John, from the dukes of Tuscany, Ferrara, and Bavaria, from the universities of Valladolid, Gandía, Coimbra, Louvain, Vienna, and from the bishops of Messina, Genoa, and Bologna.

Before these testimonials could be effectively marshaled, however, Ignatius died, and the long crisis occasioned by the First General Congregation lasted even beyond its conclusion on 10 September 1558. Meanwhile in France the continuing opposition of the bishop, the death of King Henry II in 1559 and of his successor in 1560, the turmoil after the Conspiracy of Amboise, and other factors consistently frustrated efforts to resolve the issue in the Society's favor. Not until 1561, at the time of the Colloquy of Poissy, in which Laínez played a leading role, did the Assembly of the Clergy in its concern over Protestant advances finally lend its support to the Jesuits. This development led du Bellay to soften his opposition. In 1562 the Parlement granted the Society legal existence in France, even though it imposed some severe limitations. The Faculty of Theology never formally retracted its condemnation, but it had even earlier ceased pressing it.

On the official level the Jesuits achieved their objective. At Paris, nonetheless, they continued to experience opposition and distrust from the university, the bishop, pastors of parishes, members of the mendicant orders, and others, which in the spring of 1564 erupted into attacks on the Collège, opened the previous year, and the smashing of its windows.[19] But by 1565 the violence and more aggressive opposition had died down.[20]

Even during this period, the Jesuits functioned relatively undisturbed in the diocese of Clermont under the auspices of du Prat. In 1553 he invited Jesuits to undertake there the *consueta ministeria* and shortly thereafter wrote to Ignatius requesting the establishment of a university in Billom. After appropriate negotiations, the school opened on 26 July 1556 with five hundred students, which almost immediately grew to some eight hundred under fourteen professors. By 1563 the students numbered about sixteen hundred. Upon the unexpected death of du Prat in 1560, the Jesuits successfully defended in court the college's right to the endowment he left it, another factor that eased the acceptance of official recognition of the Society into the kingdom.

The college at Billom was the Jesuits' first major establishment in France. The college they opened at Pamiers in 1559 had to be closed two years later. In 1561 the cardinal de Tournon turned over to them his already established school in Tournon, and the cardinal d'Armagnac effected the same arrangement for the collège in Rodez the following year. Under threat of Huguenot violence, the Jesuits abandoned Tournon the year after it opened but were soon able to return. The college had fifteen Jesuits, four of whom were priests. In 1563 they established a college at Mauriac in Auvergne, for which du Prat had also provided in his will, and they sent there, besides the rector, three professors of "letters," a preacher, a catechist, and a lay brother for the domestic chores. A year later Armagnac brought the Jesuits to Toulouse, and in 1565 they took over the collège in Lyons—in both cities in the aftermath of much bloodshed. At about the same time they opened schools in Verdun, Avignon, and Chambéry.

During these same years in the south of France, in Piedmont, and in the diocese of Geneva, Emond Auger, Louis du Coudret, and especially the young Antonio Possevino, a novice, tried to marshal Catholic institutions against Protestants and found considerable support for their efforts from Emmanuel-Philibert, duke of Savoy, and other Catholic leaders.[21] By the mid-1560's, therefore, the Society had overcome the initial resistance to it from Parisian officialdom and had begun to pursue its ministries in a number of francophone territories.

The decree of the Sorbonne provoked from the Jesuits three attempts to refute it. The first two, undertaken with Ignatius's blessing, were résumés by Polanco and Martín de Olabe of conversations held in Rome in the autumn of 1555, when four Parisian theologians accompanied the cardinal of Lorraine, Charles de Guise, there on a political visit.[22] After the conversations the theologians protested that they were now better informed and agreed the decree had been hasty; the conversations and the Jesuit documents weakened opposition to the Society in the university.

Polanco and Olabe argued that the name of the Society was not unprecedented, for there was in Italy an order of "Gesuati," and other orders had names of the Blessed Trinity and the Holy Spirit. They then tried to show that the pastoral privileges of the Society were like those of the mendicants and were not, therefore, a threat to bishops and pastors. The Society "a danger to the Faith"? How could such an accusation be reconciled with its papal approval and with the favor extended to it by many bishops and Catholic princes?

The arguments and tone of both documents were conciliatory. The same cannot be said of Nadal's *Apologia* against the censure, written in 1557 amid the stress surrounding the summoning of the First General Congregation.[23] This long document—incomplete, unrevised, and never circulated—is divided into two parts: a preface in which he directly addressed the issue, followed by a retelling of the origins of the Society up to 1545. Nadal was obviously convinced that the best apology for the Society was its story, especially the life and accomplishments of Ignatius. In this context he seized the occasion implicitly to defend Ignatius and the *Constitutions* against the attacks just launched by Bobadilla that jeopardized the Congregation and engaged Pope Paul IV against it.[24]

Nadal argued against the Faculty that the censure was useless because in the intervening years the Society had thrived throughout the world. But his basic argument against the censure was the familiar one that it was really an attack on the authority of the papacy that had approved the Society. From that premise he launched a reckless frontal offensive that attributed all France's territorial losses in Italy to its support of the conciliarism of the Pragmatic Sanction of Bourges and of the Council of Basel—all promoted by the theologians of Paris. Nadal mentioned Gerson by name among the conciliarists of Paris—perhaps the only place in early Jesuit documents in which Gerson was not invoked with reverence.[25]

The indignation with which the document resounds betrays how deeply the censure was felt by this alumnus of the university even as he tried to discount its effectiveness. On a larger plane, the document shows how the Jesuits' defense of their existence and of their pastoral legitimacy came to be identified with defense of certain papal prerogatives, about whose extent and authenticity not all Catholics agreed.

This same issue of papal authority had earlier arisen in Spain, when the Jesuits ran into a complicated web of opposition originating with the distinguished Dominican theologian Melchor Cano and Silíceo, archbishop of Toledo and primate of Spain.[26] The recent discovery of a manuscript by Cano in the British Library entitled *Censura y parecer que dio contra el Instituto de los PP. Jesuitas* has provided new information about the origins of Cano's rabid opposition to the Society and has also confirmed that his fear of anything resembling the teaching of the *alumbrados* was a crucial part of it.[27] He found echoes of that teaching in the *Exercises*. Cano was a master of the scholastic theology he taught at Salamanca and loved its clarity and objectivity, just as he feared the subjectivity of those who placed confidence in internal inspiration.[28] He also believed that the Jesuits' refusal to chant the Hours in choir, their seeming disregard for the tradition of cloister, and their neglect of bodily penance made them as dangerous in Spain as Luther was in Germany.

Personal reasons exacerbated Cano's antipathy. In his *Censura y parecer* he describes having met Ignatius several times in Rome, probably in 1542. He found Ignatius vain, given to speaking about the revelations he had received from God, and lacking in good judgment. Cano stated the principle that for the Society to be the work of God its founders had to be holy men, for God builds on rock. Ignatius fell short of Cano's standards. Moreover, in 1552 at Trent Laínez and Salmerón had paid him a visit to try to dispel his hostility, but the two-hour conversation ended in anger. Laínez lost his temper and responded to one of Cano's criticisms with "That's shit!"—"istas merdas."[29] His almost immediate repentance did not remove the sting of the insult. Cano afterward loved to repeat the story about the "horrid lewdness" ("atrox crimen") in which Laínez indulged.

In any case, beginning as early as 1548, Cano's attacks on the Jesuits from the pulpit and elsewhere were furious. He obviously believed that Ignatius and many of his followers were deluded by the devil, and he satirized them by joking that the *Exercises* promised sanctity on the short order of thirty days. For Cano, papal approval of the order extended only to recognition that it had a good purpose—preaching—but no further. He denounced the Jesuits for undue familiarity with women and for laxity with penitents in confession. They had to be stopped.

The situation deteriorated so rapidly that in 1549 Ignatius obtained from the master general of the Dominicans in Rome a circular letter forbidding such attacks on the Society and a brief from Paul III naming the bishops of Cuenca and Salamanca as judges against detractors of the Society. Meanwhile, influential people such as Juan de Avila and Juan de la Peña came to the public defense of the Jesuits. Cano held his peace for the time being, and the papal brief was not used against him.

Cano eventually renewed his attacks, in veiled but unmistakable ways, and by 1555 other Dominicans in Spain were following suit.[30] The Dominicans at the University of Salamanca published the decree of the Paris Faculty against the Society.[31] A Dominican preacher in Seville in 1556 accused the Jesuits of ruining psalmody in the church, of fostering the teaching of the *alumbrados,* of preaching the certainty of grace, of being precursors of the Antichrist.[32] Cardinal Morone, friend of the Jesuits and official cardinal protector of the Dominicans, interceded with the master general to get more effective implementation of the earlier decree against such attacks.[33] The master general was sympathetic but found it difficult to turn the tide. However, Luis de Granada, one of the most respected Dominicans in Spain, publicly and privately defended the Jesuits.

Cano influenced some powerful persons outside the Dominican order against the Jesuits. Notable among these were the duke of Alba, who came as viceroy to Naples in 1556, and especially the duchess, his consort. They were convinced the *Exercises* were heretical, the Jesuits in Spain too familiar with women, and they spread word in Naples about the condemnation by the Faculty of Theology.[34]

Cano's most serious threat was probably never realized. He composed *Censura y parecer* sometime between 1552 and 1556, while Ignatius was still alive. In 1558 at just about the time the troubled First General Congregation of the Jesuits was coming to a close, he considered sending it to Pope Paul IV, who had himself given ample evidence of antipathies toward the Society, some of which were identical with Cano's. There is no evidence that the pope ever received the document, but, if he did, it would have been consonant with his worst suspicions about Ignatius and the institution he had founded.

Silíceo became archbishop of Toledo around the time Cano first began attacking the Jesuits. He had earlier been friendly toward them, but grew increasingly suspicious and began to restrict their preaching and administration of the sacraments in the archdiocese. In 1551 he forbade their ministry altogether. Although there were a number of reasons for this change of attitude, two were especially important. Like so many other bishops, Silíceo resented the pastoral privileges of the Jesuits. When Francisco de Villanueva, rector of the Jesuit college at Alcalá, the only Jesuit house in the diocese, tried to explain to Silíceo the papal privileges, Silíceo, contemptuous of papal nepotism and other abuses, replied that in Toledo there was no need for a pope.[35]

When Villanueva attempted a second conversation on the subject, Silíceo revealed that the Society's practice of admitting New Christians into its ranks was perhaps the major source of his antagonism.[36] According to Polanco, the archbishop spoke as if practically all Jesuits were such *conversos*.[37] Silíceo indicated to Villanueva that if the Jesuits were to impose on themselves the same restrictions of *limpieza de sangre* that he imposed on his diocese, they would have no greater friend than he.

This time Ignatius approached Pope Julius III and requested letters both to Silíceo ordering him to desist from actions against the Society and to the papal nuncio telling him to see that the mandate was obeyed. With little choice left him, Silíceo in substance complied. Meanwhile, however, Cano had delivered to Silíceo his copy of the *Exercises* with notations on the parts he considered heretical and scandalous. This led Silíceo in 1553 to establish a commission to examine the *Exercises* headed by the Dominican Tomás de Pedroche, which, as we have already seen, found parts of them unorthodox.

Silíceo did not press Pedroche's verdict. Villanueva and Araoz made their rounds in Toledo and Alcalá showing the approval of the *Exercises* by Paul III in 1547, and their action had effect. By 1554 the furor had considerably abated. When it was then suggested to Nadal that, to be on the safe side, he submit the *Exercises* to the Spanish Inquisition for approval, he replied that papal approbation was sufficient.[38] Nonetheless, he himself undertook an *Apologia* for the *Exercises,* in which he became preoccupied with refuting every accusation of heterodoxy.[39] Despite the problems with Cano, Nadal in his commentary on the *Constitutions* later explicitly recommended Cano's important and influential work *De locis theologicis* for Jesuits studying theology.[40] Cano died in 1560.

In 1564 Nadal, possibly in collaboration with Polanco, undertook another defense of the Society in response to the uproar in Rome caused by the attack by Bishop Ascanio Cesarini.[41] Word of the attack spread abroad, especially to Germany. Cesarini resented being displaced by a Jesuit in an office dealing with the restoration of churches in Rome, had the usual problems with the pastoral privileges of the Society and its new style of life, but especially despised the huge foreign presence in Rome and Italy that the Jesuits, that "diabolical sect," represented. Woe to the church! Woe to our Latin civilization! Woe to our Italian fatherland! He found support among many of the clergy and other "true Romans" especially at this moment when the Jesuits had just agreed to staff the Seminario Romano.

Cesarini circulated a number of unsigned pamphlets and verses in which the standard objections against the Jesuits were raised, as well as accusations of sexual perversions, disregard for church law, financial speculation, and insatiable greed for gold. There were also specific accusations of pastoral malpractice, especially in hearing confessions and recruiting novices to the order. The Jesuits in Rome did nothing to counter the charges, but the seriousness of the situation became clear when, from Germany, Cardinal Otto Truchsess von Waldburg wrote to Pope Pius IV asking him to take action against the damage being done even so far away. Pius submitted the matter to a commission of cardinals, who after an investigation exculpated the Jesuits but suggested they write a clarification about the charges—the origin of the *Apologia* by Nadal. The pope deprived Cesarini of his offices and threatened to imprison him if he stirred up any more trouble. He also wrote briefs to the emperor, the duke of Bavaria, and a number of German bishops announcing the verdict and vindicating the Society.

The body of Nadal's document is structured according to extremely brief statements of the accusations followed by a response of about a paragraph. Concerning confession, Nadal said that the Jesuits followed standard practices and were diligently instructed to be discreet when dealing with sexual matters. Nadal maintained that Jesuits did not put undue pressure on people to join the order and would not accept novices until convinced they had a "divine call" to the order. He refuted the charge that Jesuits favored novices from rich families and discouraged the poor from joining by asserting that the vast majority came from "poor" families.

The problems that erupted with the Society in Paris, Salamanca, Toledo, and Rome were especially threatening because they transcended the local scene, but they were also indicative of problems the Jesuits often faced elsewhere with their coreligionists. The repeated pressure on them to defend their orthodoxy reinforced an already deeply felt concern for orthodoxy. The necessity they felt to recur to the papal approbations they had received reinforced a bond with the papacy that had been forged in their very earliest years.

The Papacy and the Popes

Of all Catholic institutions, the Jesuits identified themselves most closely with the papacy and have been most closely identified with it by others over the course of the centuries. In his second *Dialogue* Nadal had his Lutheran interlocutor object to the Jesuits as *papistissimi*—"as papal as papal can be."[42] Nadal did not answer the objection directly, but used it as an entrance into broader ecclesiological issues. At about the same time that Nadal was working on the *Dialogue*, Polanco in effect answered the allegation by saying that Jesuits were "papalists [*papistas*] only in what they have to be and nothing more, and even then only with an eye to the glory of God and the general good."[43] In 1549 Ignatius himself had prescribed for the three Jesuits going to the University of Ingolstadt: "Let them defend the Apostolic See and its authority and draw people to authentic obedience to it in such a way that they not make themselves, like papists [*tamquam papiste*], unworthy of credence by exaggerated defenses."[44] Important though qualifications like these are, they confirm the substance of what they qualify.

Nonetheless, the relationship of the Society to the papacy was more complex than at first appears. The most obvious, the most elemental level of the relationship was the ongoing need of the Jesuits to invoke the authority of the papacy for their own protection, as we have many times seen. This was a relationship of dependency for sheer survival, as well as for the freedom they wanted to perform their ministries according to their own "way of proceeding." Because popes like Paul III and Julius III had in fact provided such protection, a strong relationship based on gratitude was also established and extolled.

Another level was the apologetic task the Jesuits took upon themselves of defending the Catholic faith. Although Protestants differed among themselves on many issues, all of them rejected the papacy more or less outright, and many Catholics considered that rejection the essence of their teaching. It was inevitable, therefore, that the "defense of the faith" of the second *Formula* often devolve into defense of the papacy and lend the papacy a prominence in Jesuit thinking that under different circumstances it would not have enjoyed.

These levels represent only the most superficial aspect of the Jesuits' relationship to the papacy and do not take into account the ecclesiological and pastoral framework that structured it. Despite what most writings about the Jesuits suggest, however, reconstruction of the ecclesiology that was the lived reality of the order is not a simple task. The Jesuits shared certain assumptions about the church and, perhaps even more important, about *Christianitas*, but they had no official or fully articulated ecclesiology. Attempts to discover their ecclesiology and pastoral vision have too often rested on a few proof-texts, usually taken from the "Rules for Thinking with the Church," or have probed no further than the recognition that certain Jesuits, such as Laínez, Nadal, Canisius, and Ignatius himself, attributed broader jurisdictional authority to the papacy in certain particulars than did many of their Catholic contemporaries. If the issue is to be addressed satisfactorily, a broader methodology is required.

The best way to begin is with the terms, usually metaphors, with which the Jesuits referred to the church. In the *Exercises* Ignatius twice described the church as "hierarchical."[45] No doubt important, the description is rare in the corpus of his writings. In the same sentences in the *Exercises,* moreover, he also calls the church "the true spouse of Christ" and "our holy mother." He in fact used a number of other traditional metaphors. Not unlike many of his contemporaries, Protestant and Catholic, he showed some preference for the Pauline "body of Christ," in which Christ is the head and every member solicitous for the care of every other.[46] In his catechesis, the church was simply "a congregation of the Christian faithful, illumined and governed by God our Lord."[47] This was one of the most traditional descriptions of the church, found equivalently in both Augustine and Aquinas, but employed to advantage by conciliarists in the fifteenth and sixteenth centuries.[48]

Gaspar Loarte used the expression several times in his *Esercitio* and also spoke of the church as "the house of God," in which all members communicate to the others the gifts they have received and help one another spiritually and corporally as parts of one body.[49] Nadal of course employed the same image of the body of Christ[50] but presented a unique description when he said: "Holy Scripture, the virtues, right reason, and edification—in a word, the church."[51]

The early Jesuits thus often described the church without reference to juridical structure and gave as much emphasis to the reciprocity of relationship among all members as they did to management from the top down. In other words, the horizontal dimension of the church was as strongly represented in what they wrote—as well as in how they operated—as was the vertical. What these scattered descriptions and metaphors point to, therefore, is the ecclesiological assumption found on practically every page of what they wrote. They projected from their own self-understanding: the church was "to help souls." Like themselves, the church accomplished this task in a variety of ways and through a variety of persons, relationships, and institutions.

A fundamental metaphor for the church that came close to capturing this pastoral reality was "the vineyard of the Lord." The term occurs insistently in Jesuit documents, including Ignatius's correspondence and Polanco's *Chronicon*, but most significantly in the title of Part Seven of the *Constitutions*, which deals with how members of the Society were to be deployed throughout the world, as well as with the criteria for their deployment. As the title of what is in many ways the heart of the document, it underscores the centrality of the metaphor in the thinking of Ignatius and Polanco.

That Part of the *Constitutions* begins with a discussion of the famous "Fourth Vow," by which the professed members of the Society oblige themselves to "special obedience to the sovereign pontiff regarding missions."[52] As we have seen, this vow raised questions in the papal curia when it was first proposed in the "Five Chapters" in 1539 and, despite the simplicity of what it intended, has raised questions and been variously interpreted ever since. Whatever the vow's meaning, Ignatius indicated its importance early on, in 1545–46, by referring to it as "our beginning and the principal foundation of the Society."[53] That description did not, however, find its way into the *Constitutions* or any other official document.

Confusion about the meaning of the vow even among Jesuits has stemmed from inattention to the obvious. First of all, it was not a vow "to the pope," as is sometimes said elliptically, but, like all religious vows, a vow to God.[54] Second, the vow was not even about the pope, but about "missions"—*circa missiones*. "Missions" here clearly meant itinerant ministry, or ministry "throughout the world" for the "greater help of souls."[55] The vow was "our beginning" because the companions had pronounced its equivalent in Paris in 1534 as the fall-back alternative to the trip to Jerusalem. It was the "principal foundation" of the Society because it concerned what was utterly central to the Jesuit calling—ministry.

The vow of stability was what made the man a monk, in other words, the promise to live his entire life in the monastery, where he would seek his own sanctification. The Jesuits' Fourth Vow was in essence a vow of mobility, that is, a commitment to travel anywhere in the world for the "help of souls." The *Constitutions* in fact assume that these "missions" would generally last not longer than three months.[56] The Fourth Vow was thus one of the best indications of how the new order wanted to break with the monastic tradition.

The vow assumed, moreover, that the pope had the broad vision required for the most effective deployment in the "vineyard of the Lord," which by definition extended throughout the world. The implicit model, again, was Jesus sending his disciples—the "vicar of Christ" (the vicar of Jesus) sending the Jesuits. The *Constitutions* were explicit on the historical origin and intent of the vow:

> The intention of the fourth vow pertaining to the pope was not to designate a particular place but to have the members distributed throughout the various parts of the world. For those who first united to form the Society were from different provinces and realms and did not know into which regions they were to go, whether among the faithful or unbelievers; and therefore, to avoid erring in the path of the Lord, they made that promise or vow in order that His Holiness might distribute them for the greater glory of God. They did this in conformity with their intention to travel throughout the world and, when they could not find the desired spiritual fruit in one region, to pass on to another and another, ever intent on seeking the greater glory of God our Lord and the greater help of souls.[57]

This Part of the *Constitutions* immediately moves on, however, to attribute the same vision and role to the general of the order, who somehow by reason of the vow can deploy members in the same way as the pope.[58] Once the vow was interpreted in the *Constitutions* to apply to the general as well as to the pope, its ultimate character was more clearly revealed and an important development in Jesuit reality signaled. As early as 1542, Ignatius, seemingly to forestall any misunderstanding, petitioned from the pope "express" authorization to send Jesuits anywhere in the world among Catholics, and in 1549, just when the *Constitutions* were in the crucial stage of construction, he did the same for "among infidels."[59]

It is in fact ironical that the initiative for the Jesuits' most spectacular "missions" during these early years—to India, Brazil, Ethiopia—came not from the reigning pope but from King John of Portugal. Ignatius in his correspondence with the king sometimes seemed to concede him authority over the Society equal to that of the papacy. In 1549, for instance, he told him that it was his prerogative to make decisions where Jesuits should be sent and that it was "our duty to submit ourselves to Your Majesty and carry out everything you desire with all our will."[60]

During the deliberations in 1539 that led to the decision to found a new order, those taking part saw serious problems with a vow of obedience, which seemed to be superfluous because they had decided to place themselves at the disposal of the pope. But they answered that problem realistically by saying that the pope could not be expected to be responsible for the many details and contingencies inevitable in such assignments. It in fact almost immediately became clear that few Jesuits would either directly or indirectly have the location of their ministry determined by the reigning pope. Jesuits were given their assignments by the general or by their provincials, even though for particularly large or important ventures the blessing of the pope might be sought, as for the group setting off to found the school in Messina in 1547.

It is remarkable, even astounding, how seldom Ignatius in his correspondence directly referred to what he had at an early date called the "principal foundation" of the Society. For the Jesuits and for their relationship to the papacy, the vow was of the utmost importance, but from the beginning it was, with a few exceptions, a symbol rather than a practical instrument for deployment of manpower.

Nadal provided the clearest and most eloquent explanation of what the vow symbolized.[61] As we have seen, for him as for his confreres, "missions" and "journeying for ministry," and sometimes even "pilgrimage," were synonymous.[62] In his exhortations to Jesuit communities he described such missions and journeyings as the "principal and most characteristic 'dwelling'" for the Jesuit, as their "most glorious and longed-for 'house.'" He loved this paradox that he saw entailed in the vow.[63]

His commentary on the opening words of Part Seven of the *Constitutions* was typical:

"When they are dispersed to any part of Christ's vineyard." This dispersion of the professed and coadjutors will indeed take place in the founding of professed houses, and also of colleges and houses of probation [novitiates], in important cities as well as in large and populated towns. But we must always look to and strive for that great goal of the Society, which is not only that Ours live in our houses and from them come to the aid of the city or town or even nearby countryside, but that the professed and coadjutors be engaged in journeys that are undertaken by commission either from the supreme pontiff or from our superiors. They do this so that help might be brought to souls wherever they are found—in whatever way and in whatever situation they need spiritual help, whether we are sent to idolaters, to Muslims, to heretics, or to Christians who are perishing or in danger because of a lack of ministers or their neglect.[64]

A rhetorically more powerful statement about missions and journeyings appears at the end of his second *Dialogue:*

That is altogether the most ample place and reaches as far as the globe itself. For wherever they can be sent in ministry to bring help to souls, that is the most glorious and longed-for "house" for these theologians. For they know the goal set before them: to procure the salvation and perfection of all men and women. They understand that they are to that end bound by that Fourth Vow to the supreme pontiff: that they might go on these universal missions for the good of souls by his command, which by divine decree extends throughout the whole church. They realize that they cannot build or acquire enough houses to be able from nearby to run out to the combat. Since this is the case, they consider that they are in their most peaceful and pleasant house when they are constantly on the move, when they travel throughout the earth, when they have no place to call their own, when they are always in need, always in want—only let them strive in some small way to imitate Christ Jesus, who had nowhere on which to lay his head and who spent all his years of preaching in journey.[65]

The vow implied for the Jesuits, therefore, the basic vision of the church, "the Lord's vineyard," in which they were called to imitate the apostles and disciples of Jesus in the exercise of their *consueta ministeria.* It specified the pope as, in effect, "the bishop of the universal church," assigning him a primarily pastoral and caring position.[66]

But Protestants denied the papacy any function whatsoever. In the first edition of his Large Catechism, Canisius described the church in one place by using the traditional formula "the congregation of all the Christian faithful," but in another he added the unwonted qualification that it was under the governance and pastoral care of Peter and his successors. In his subsequent catechisms the two descriptions were consistently combined.[67]

Canisius's was not the first of the German Catholic catechisms of the sixteenth century to add the papal qualification to the traditional descriptions of the church.[68] While this emphasis in Canisius was connected to his broader ecclesiological vision, it was also obviously apologetical.[69] The circulation and authority that his works enjoyed made them one of the first instruments for a major shift in popular mentality and for a new indoctrination among ordinary Catholics about the institutional aspects of the "congregation of the faithful" to which they belonged. Given the belligerencies of the sixteenth century, it was inevitable that when Catholics in many parts of the world thought about the church they would think about the papacy, but Canisius's catechisms reflected and promoted the new mentality that became characteristic of "Roman Catholicism." In this regard Canisius's work was typical of the Jesuits.

But there was another aspect to the issue. The papacy was an object of controversy among Catholics themselves. Although all who called themselves Catholics acknowledged that the papacy had an essential role in the church, theologians and canonists were often bitterly divided about the precise nature and extent of that role. Despite Ignatius's warnings about not taking sides in disputes among Catholics, the Jesuits were unable to avoid taking sides in this one. They were too well instructed in theology and canon law to advocate any form of papal absolutism, but in certain specifics they argued for more authority for the papacy than other Catholics allowed.

Nadal, surely echoing the sentiment of his confreres, as well as many reputable theologians outside the Society, repeatedly affirmed that the pope could not err when he approved a religious order.[70] In his *Apologia* for the *Exercises* against Pedroche, he went so far as to insinuate that Paul III's approbation of them was "infallible."[71] In 1556 Ignatius, smarting under the censure of the Society by the Theological Faculty of Paris, wrote that to call into question the right of the Holy See to grant pastoral privileges to religious orders was "against the faith."[72]

The Jesuits used the authority and even inerrancy of the Holy See as a club with which to beat their enemies. They also brandished it as a defense when the Holy See itself threatened to change important provisions of the *Formula.* In 1572, for instance, Nadal argued in the face of such possibilities that it would be against the authority of the Holy See for the Holy See to impose choir and make other changes.[73] This kind of argument had for centuries been traditional with religious orders and in fact had helped generate the idea of papal infallibility.[74]

Jesuit proclivity for stretching the extent of papal prerogatives found its most public expression in Laínez's intervention at the Council of Trent on 20 October 1562, when he argued that bishops' jurisdiction did not derive from their office but was granted them by the papacy.[75] Laínez's position was perfectly in line with Ignatius's views, clearly stated in his letter to the king of Ethiopia, 23 February 1555.[76] Nadal held the same opinion.[77]

The Council rejected Laínez's thesis. Some who heard him speak questioned his motives, for by exalting the prerogatives of the papacy he appeared to be indirectly protecting the privileges of the Society. Those who knew him best rejected these suspicions as inconsistent with his character.

He was about to take another unpopular position on a related issue. By the summer of 1563 the Council had reached almost the breaking point over the relationship of episcopal to papal authority that had resurfaced with the explosive issue of the reform of the papal curia. Was that reform to be undertaken by Pope Pius IV himself, as he promised, or should the Council take it into its own hands? On 16 June 1563, Laínez spoke in favor of the former course in a way and at a moment that threw the Council into an uproar and that even Morone, the chief papal legate, judged imprudent and inopportune.[78] The large number of both Spanish and French prelates at the Council were outraged, as some of them were by another intervention by Laínez on 2 October.[79]

Laínez's intervention on 16 June reflected the cautiously deferential attitude toward the papacy typical of the first Jesuits. Nonetheless, the Jesuits' position on this occasion was less predetermined than at first appears.[80] When Laínez made his controversial intervention, he was general of the Society and had been accompanied to Trent by his secretary, Polanco. Sometime before he made his speech, Polanco, presumably at Laínez's behest, drew up a memorandum on the reform of the curia that looked to having the pope threatened with deposition if he failed to undertake the reform.[81] The basic thesis of the document was that the principal cause for the disorders in the church was the disorder in the head, that is, in the papacy. Polanco listed the lands that because of papal malfeasance had already fallen into heresy and those that probably would (Poland, Flanders, France); he also indicated his fear even for Spain and Italy.

Polanco based his case on a standard interpretation of the canonical axiom "The pope is to be judged by no one, unless he should deviate from the faith." "Deviation from the faith" had for centuries been interpreted by respected canonists to mean not only heresy but also grave scandal.[82] Polanco began with an indictment of papal practice by listing the scandals—today nobody seeks the papacy except with the intention of enriching his relatives; this has resulted in unworthy members in the college of cardinals and, in turn, unworthy candidates for the papacy; reservation of benefices has resulted in the absence of bishops from their dioceses; avarice and simony rule in payments for dispensations, regressions, bulls, and briefs; and similar abuses. These were standard grievances against the papacy, proclaimed by preachers and reformers since the fourteenth century but more urgently and stridently since the advent of the Reformation.

Polanco's remedy was to have the leading Catholic princes of Europe—the emperor, the doge of Venice, the kings of France, Portugal, Spain, and Poland, as well as some prelates from different nations—obtain a guarantee from Pius IV that reform "in head and members" be undertaken. The pope, a man easily frightened, will probably comply—"tiene poco animo." If he should refuse, they should point out to him that the scandals are so great that even theologians who most favor the authority of the Holy See agree that a council can be held "even without his acquiescence" and that it could proceed to depose him on the grounds of incompetence. If Pius surrenders at this point, then a select committee drawn from every nation should construct a plan for reform and submit it to the council, so that it would thus have both conciliar and papal support.

Polanco was not alone in such views. Probably about the same time, Salmerón, present with Laínez and Polanco at Trent, wrote an even stronger statement.[83] He repeated the standard arguments about the duty of a council to depose a heretical pope but then explicitly refuted the idea that heresy was the only crime meriting deposition. Among the other crimes, for instance, were a long-standing practice of simony or toleration of it, a tyrannical regime, and failure to engage in due consultation on grave matters affecting the entire church.

Laínez's intervention betrayed no suggestion that such ideas were entertained by Jesuits at Trent. Although it should not automatically be assumed that he at any point fully agreed with either Polanco or Salmerón, his theological training at Paris and the circumstances of the statements by his two colleagues suggest that on a theoretical level his position would have been similar. The first Jesuits, despite their "special vow" and their general policy of supporting papal authority, remained within the theological and canonical mainstream even regarding the papacy.

How to explain Laínez's intervention? He seems to have moved gradually to his more curialist position for several reasons. He acted on the misinformation that Pius IV had already begun to take action, and he was possibly otherwise not persuaded that Pius was displaying the obstinacy that would warrant such drastic measures. More fundamentally, he became convinced that many bishops were using the issue of reform to advance the doctrine of a constitutional superiority of council over pope, that is, conciliarism in the strict sense of the term. In other words, these bishops were not looking to the emergency situation that both Polanco and Salmerón envisaged but were maintaining as a constitutional principle that even in normal circumstances a pope was in all matters subject to a council. The Jesuits were adamantly opposed to this position, which they considered patently heterodox.

Moreover, Laínez grew increasingly pessimistic on a practical level about the ability of the Council to manage such a complex undertaking. Not reform but further chaos would ensue. The results would be disastrous. Nadal and Canisius, though not present at Trent at the time, shared this opinion—in fact, they were utterly convinced of it.[84] They were probably right. Nadal predicted further schism; Canisius, who feared similarly dire results, recommended that the problem be handled by direct negotiations between the emperor and the pope.

Laínez's intervention most certainly did not mean that he was unconcerned about reform of the papal curia. In 1556 he had already addressed the issue in a "Tractatus de simonia" that he drew up at the request of Pope Paul IV.[85] Paul, though he had no intention of reconvening the Council of Trent, seriously intended to reform the papal Datary, and he wanted Laínez to remain in Rome to advise him on it. Since it was clear that the pope was to do the reforming, Laínez dealt with what needed to be done and why. He did not restrict himself to the Datary but ranged widely, in basically scholastic style, over the general scandal of the buying and selling of ecclesiastical offices and favors.

The "Tractatus" was a strong and straightforward document, at times deliberately reminiscent of Saint Bernard's *De consideratione,* which dealt with similar issues four centuries earlier. Laínez made his arguments contemporary, however, by asserting that the sins, mistakes, and scandals of the papacy had been responsible for the defection from the Catholic Church of northern Europe; he warned, as Polanco did later, that southern Europe would follow suit unless drastic measures were taken. He conceded that a minister could legitimately be sustained by the freewill offerings of the faithful but insisted that money could never be exacted as a price for spiritual goods and services. In this unholy traffic, unfortunately, the popes had provided the worst example of all, and unless "the head" was reformed there was no hope for the reform of "the members." The pope had to remember that, although he was the shepherd of the Lord's sheep, he was at the same time one of the sheep.[86] The popes and the members of the papal curia had become the scribes and pharisees "devouring the substance of widows" denounced by Jesus in the Gospels (Matt: 23:14).[87]

The basic point of the document was hardly new by the mid-sixteenth century. These ideas had already been proposed in a generic way to Pope Paul III in 1537 in the *Consilium de emendanda ecclesia*.[88] However, the length of Laínez's document, its strong tone, and the details to which it descends make it noteworthy, even though it was submitted to a pope who presumably listened with willing ears. It was not thereby submitted without risk to the Society for, even if it did not offend the pope, it surely would upset some members of the curia.

In brief, while the leading Jesuits of this period tended to favor a strong papal authority in the church, their ecclesiological vision had a breadth that tried to put that issue in a pastoral framework, and their position on great issues of ecclesiastical polity remained grounded in the canonical thinking broadly respected in their day. They of course had to deal not only with the papacy as a theological issue and ongoing institution but also with the individual popes themselves. They were eager to please. They did not always succeed.

During this quarter century there were five popes, including Marcellus II, who in 1555 died within a month of his election. After approving the Society in 1540, Paul III consistently supported it until his death in 1549. His successor, Julius III, did the same until he died in 1555. That year the Jesuits rejoiced at the election of Marcellus II, Marcello Cervini, not only because they knew of his friendship over the years but because they also had high expectations for what he would do for the church as a whole. Ignatius wrote enthusiastically on 13 April 1555 to a fellow Jesuit: "God has given us an excellent pope."[89] Polanco rejoiced that Marcellus had been elected not by human machinations but by inspiration of the Holy Spirit. Marcellus was a man of grave piety and morals who refused favors to his relatives and forbade his only brother to come to Rome.[90]

After a bitter election a month later, Marcellus was succeeded by Paul IV, Giampietro Carafa. Carafa, proud scion of one of the leading families of Naples, co-founder of the Theatine order with Gaetano da Chieti and active for most of his eighty years in reform circles in Italy, had had an ambivalent relationship with the Society and its founder since those early days in

Venice. Precisely what transpired at that time is not clear, although Carafa probably resented what seems to have been unsolicited advice from Ignatius about the Theatines and about Carafa's own style of life.[91]

When years later, in 1545, the Theatines suggested that the two orders amalgamate, Ignatius turned down the offer, which made the relationship with Carafa even more delicate.[92] Ignatius also successfully resisted at the papal court Carafa's efforts to force a novice named Ottavio Cesari to leave the Society because of his parents' objections.[93] What was well known in Rome and elsewhere, however, was Carafa's hatred and suspicion of all things Spanish, born of his resentment of Spanish occupation of his native Naples for over half a century. Meanwhile, as Carafa advanced in age, his religious zeal grew ever fiercer and more intransigent.

No doubt the Jesuits in Rome, including Ignatius, were apprehensive about the possibility of Carafa's election, partly for the reasons already mentioned and partly because they were suspicious that he would try to make changes in the Institute, like obliging the Jesuits to communal chanting of the Hours.[94] Luís Gonçalves da Câmara reported as an eyewitness that when Ignatius first heard about Carafa's election "he shook in every bone in his body."[95]

Over the course of the summer Ignatius dispatched a number of letters to Jesuits reassuring them that all was well, but the letters sometimes had a perfunctory ring.[96] He was straightforward with Araoz on 29 May 1555: "We believe that he will show good will toward the Society . . . but we will be better able to judge with the passage of a little time."[97] On that very point the Jesuits in Rome became perturbed: whereas Marcellus had received Ignatius in audience almost immediately upon his election, several months passed with Ignatius having no access to Paul. Even when he was finally received in July, he was not able to get satisfaction on any business, especially on the desperate financial straits of the Collegio Romano and the Germanico.[98] Perhaps the best indication of the apprehension of the Jesuits in Rome was Ignatius's intention to use the testimonial letters not only to change the decision of the Faculty of Theology of Paris but also to influence the pope "if he should attempt anything against the Society."[99]

Not until early December did Carafa overtly betray hostility toward the Jesuits. Probably motivated by his chronic fear of Spanish conspiracies against him, he sent the papal police, led by the governor of Rome, to search the *casa professa* for weapons. Fortunately, the governor was friendly toward the Jesuits, and upon his arrival he left the police at the door and asked to see Ignatius, to whom he explained his assignment. Ignatius summoned

Polanco and had him lead the governor and some other officials who accompanied him through every corner of the house. They found no weapons, and that was the end of the extraordinary incident.[100]

During the last year of Ignatius's life, therefore, an unpredictable, sometimes ominous, relationship existed with the reigning pope. Paul IV showed confidence in individual Jesuits, such as Laínez and Bobadilla, and occasionally was quite cordial toward Ignatius. But the intemperate arbitrariness that marked all the pope's dealings also marked his relationship with the Society. Only after Ignatius's death and the First General Congregation was convoked to elect his successor did the Jesuits' relationship to Paul IV devolve into full crisis. This led Nadal to pray that the Lord soon bestow on the pope his eternal reward.[101]

Two years elapsed between the death of Ignatius and the successful completion of the Congregation.[102] This lapse of time was due in part to the slowness of travel and to disagreement among the Jesuits as to how to proceed in this first-time situation, but it was primarily due to the threats and interventions of the pope, which left the Jesuits confused and disoriented. When they decided to hold the Congregation in Spain in order not to be "under his eyes," the pope forbade them to leave Rome because he feared they would support Philip II, with whom he was about to go to war.[103] Philip in turn forbade his Jesuit subjects, including Francisco de Borja, to go to Rome.

Bobadilla meanwhile got the pope's ear and convinced him that the inner circle of Laínez, Polanco, and Nadal were organizing the Congregation in a way that denied the role of original companions like himself. He vented his long-standing grievances against Ignatius and his style of leadership. He called him a "tyrant." The pope echoed Bobadilla and threw the epithet back at Laínez. He then demanded to see the *Constitutions*, which were as yet unratified by a Congregation of the Society, and informed the Jesuits that he could change anything his predecessors had ratified.[104] Now that the Jesuits had lost Ignatius, their "idol," they had to learn to place their trust not in him or any other human being but in God alone.[105]

On 10 August 1557, Nadal gathered the Jesuits of the Collegio Romano to alert them to the seriousness of the situation, which he described as "tending to the destruction of the whole Society."[106] The "conspiracy of Bobadilla," as Nadal termed the crisis, was at its height. Within a few days, however, things took a decided turn for the better when Brouët and Rodrigues, early companions who had at first abetted Bobadilla, saw the error of their ways and threw in their lot with Laínez, Polanco, and Nadal. Through the whole crisis Laínez had been acting as vicar general of the order and continued to have access to the pope. Once Bobadilla stood practically alone in his accusations and demands, Laínez was able to persuade Paul IV to allow the Congregation to convene.

Only after peace was concluded between Spain and the Holy See did the Congregation open—on 19 June 1558.[107] On 2 July, the date set for the election of the new general, Cardinal Pedro Pacheco appeared and informed the Jesuits that the pope had deputed him to oversee the election and count the votes. Laínez was elected with thirteen votes out of twenty, and Nadal was next with four. There is no reason to doubt that the Jesuits voted according to their consciences, but they also knew that Laínez was as acceptable to the pope as practically any Spaniard could be.

Still persuaded that Ignatius had governed the Society as a tyrant, Paul IV demanded that Laínez's term be not for life as the *Constitutions* stipulated, but for only three years, so as to prevent a recurrence of the supposed abuses under Ignatius. The Congregation demurred and sent through Laínez and Salmerón a letter to the pope telling him it was their unanimous desire that the *Constitutions* not be changed in this regard. Paul received them coldly and, once informed of the substance of the letter, accused them of insubordination, saying that he expected every kind of disorder from the Society. He refused to change his decision.

As the Jesuits feared from the beginning, the pope also imposed upon them the obligation of chanting the liturgical Hours every day in choir. Laínez saw to it that the Jesuits in the *casa professa* in Rome complied fully, but elsewhere, especially in the colleges, recitation of all the Hours in common was practically impossible and could not be observed. Before this anomaly had time to attract papal wrath, Paul IV died, on 18 August 1559. Laínez immediately consulted canonists in Rome about the binding power of Paul IV's orders regarding the Hours, which contradicted the *Formula,* and, as seen, happily accepted and implemented the opinion that under that circumstance it bound only for the lifetime of the pope imposing it. Laínez moved with much more hesitancy about the general's term of office, not satisfied until Pius IV formally abrogated his predecessor's orders in 1561.[108]

Thus ended the tangled and often turbulent relationship of the Jesuits with Giampietro Carafa, Paul IV. With his successor, Pius IV, they found more consistent favor, but they did not fail to incur his occasional displeasure, as on the occasion of Carlo Borromeo's conversion and when Laínez argued passionately against allowing priests in Germany to marry and allowing German Catholics to receive Communion in the form of both bread and wine. Pius IV died in December 1564, just two months before Laínez. Although Jesuit relations with the new pope, Pius V, were good, they once again had to defend their Institute against him on several points.

Ignatius saw even Paul III as a threat to the Institute when there was danger that Jay and Canisius might be made bishops. He did all in his power to prevent such appointments and was successful.[109] What the first Jesuits feared was that any change in their Institute, in their substantial "way of proceeding," was a threat to the integrity of the whole—thus their resistance even to the papacy on what might seem to be secondary matters like the Hours, the general's term of office, and the appointment of Jesuits to the episcopacy.

When Nadal commented, therefore, on the section of the *Constitutions* dealing with the vow that the professed members of the Society pronounce not to accept any prelacy, his words had a broader application:

> Only the Supreme Pontiff can compel the Society in this regard. In such instances every manner and means of resisting and impeding such an intention of the Pontiff are to be expended and exercised, every stone (as they say) to be turned lest such a dignity be imposed. We are not to cease working toward this end or give up our efforts until we have exhausted every possibility. This will not be verified until the Apostolic See expressly obliges us under pain of mortal sin and will obviously brook no further resistance.[110]

Nadal here clearly showed that Jesuit promptitude in obeying the pope "regarding missions" was not understood to extend to every area where papal authority might possibly reach.

Inquisitions and the Banning of Books

By the late Middle Ages the apparatus of tribunals that investigated heresy and that in its papal form had functioned with regularity in certain parts of Europe, especially in the thirteenth and early fourteenth centuries, had for the most part fallen into desuetude. That situation began to change when in 1478 the Spanish Crown won special concessions from the Holy See that placed the correlative institution there under the sovereigns, giving it a new vigor. When the threat of Protestant infiltration into Italy led Paul III to place Italian tribunals directly under the Roman Inquisition (or Holy Office) that he established in 1542, they too began to play a much more vigorous role in ecclesiastical life than ever before, and a new age opened with virtually new institutions. In some other parts of Europe, such as France and the Low Countries, similar changes occurred, but patterns of operation and offices bearing responsibility differed widely from place to place.[111]

In Spain by the time Ignatius was a young man, the Inquisition was a firmly established institution that, as we have seen, pursued New Christians and *alumbrados* and was increasingly turning its attention to Erasmians and Lutherans.[112] Ignatius and sometimes those associated with him had had to defend themselves against institutions like this, even after arriving in Rome in 1537–38.[113] Other Jesuits, including somebody from such high social rank as Francisco de Borja, the former duke of Gandía, would later experience a similar fate.

Under these circumstances it might be expected that the first Jesuits would show more reserve in relation to these tribunals than they did. True, they had a privilege that allowed them to absolve in confession persons who admitted their guilt, and they preferred this kind of private reconciliation to a judicial procedure. Collaboration with various inquisitions was far from a major aspect of their activities even in Spain and Portugal. But where inquisitions were in place they accepted them as part of their general acceptance of Catholic institutions as they found them, and they felt a responsibility to bring persons suspected of heterodoxy to the attention of the inquisitorial tribunals. Although by and large they seem to have acted upon this responsibility only when there was substantial grounding for their suspicions, some were notable in their zeal.[114]

From several remarks by Polanco the inference could easily be drawn that Ignatius had not only importuned from Paul III the establishment of the Roman Inquisition but was principally responsible for it.[115] Actually, the decision was made quite independently of Ignatius and was the direct result of the breakdown of the final attempt at reconciliation with the Lutherans at the Colloquy of Regensburg in 1541 and related events.[116] The failure of Regensburg practically coincided with panic in central Italy about the infiltration of Protestantism into the peninsula, especially in the wake of the notorious apostasies of Bernardino Ochino and Peter Martyr Vermigli.

By his own account, nonetheless, Ignatius had interceded "strongly and many times" at the papal court for something like the institution Paul III created. Among those he approached concerning it was, in fact, Cardinal Giampietro Carafa, who hardly needed a spur in that direction and who became the most active member of the Congregation of the Inquisition that

Paul III instituted by the bull *Licet ab initio*. Ignatius expressed satisfaction with the bull.[117]

For many years King John III of Portugal, the great friend of the Jesuits, tried to obtain from the Holy See privileges for the Portuguese Inquisition similar to those conceded to Ferdinand and Isabella in 1478—that is, he wanted to put the institution directly under the crown. Ignatius, in a series of letters in 1542 and 1543, expressed approval of the king's idea and promised him his aid "in such a just and holy enterprise."[118]

Ignatius's efforts probably contributed to Pope Paul III's granting the king his request on 16 July 1547 with the brief *Meditatio cordis nostri*. In 1555 the king asked Ignatius to allow the Jesuits in Portugal to assume, under royal patronage, direction of the Inquisition in Lisbon. He found support for his proposal in the enthusiasm of Diego Miró, then provincial superior of the Jesuits in Portugal. Ignatius had reservations—he feared that engaging in the apprehension of the suspect and the eventual condemnation of the guilty was contrary to "our way of proceeding" and that the Jesuits involved would in effect be released from their vow of obedience. He asked six Jesuits in Rome to consider the matter and submit to him their recommendations—Polanco, Bobadilla, Salmerón, Madrid, Martín de Olabe, and Laínez. All except Laínez favored the proposal, and Ignatius himself became persuaded that such activity was compatible with the Society's ways. In the end the matter came to naught because of complications at the royal court that led the king to change this aspect of his plans.[119]

Individual Jesuits joined in the direct pursuit of heretics. In 1552 in Modena, for instance, Landini worked energetically to have citizens inform on suspected persons.[120] A decade earlier Salmerón had preached there against presumed heresy in a way that brought him into conflict with the bishop, Giovanni Morone. In Valladolid in 1558 Juan de Prádanos, one of the Jesuit confessors of Teresa of Avila, seems to have informed the inquisitors about Lutheranizing circles in the city, whose discovery was one of the factors leading to the extreme measures against heresy taken by the Inquisition and the king in 1559 and 1560. The Jesuits were themselves soon caught in the wake of those measures.[121]

There was, however, another aspect to their activities. They generally tried to work for the easiest possible reconciliation. In 1545, for instance, Ignatius tried to establish contact with Bernardino Ochino, the apostate minister general of the newly founded Capuchin branch of the Franciscan order, to effect for him a reconciliation with Paul III that would bypass the Inquisition.[122] At the behest of the Holy Office, Cristóforo Rodríguez went to Calabria in late

1565 to investigate cases of heresy, where he was in fact able to work out reconciliations with the church that avoided criminal proceedings.[123]

Nadal provided one of the few extended statements that reveal a general attitude on the issue:

> Our neighbor is first of all to be urged through devout and gentle conversations to approach the sacrament of Penance. If this is unsuccessful, we should use other means like prayers and masses for him, and then we should try to get somebody else, like his father or brother, to be solicitous for him. If he is not sufficiently warned in this way, we should not therefore inform the bishop but turn the matter over to our superior, and let him judge what is to be done and how the person is further to be helped.[124]

Nadal of course did not oppose in principle turning suspects over to the inquisitors.[125] In an exhortation to the Jesuits at Alcalá in 1561, he went so far as to say that anybody who set his own judgment above that of the Inquisition came close to heresy himself.[126] He was perhaps trying to dispel criticism because at that precise moment Francisco de Borja was so deeply and notoriously in trouble with the Inquisition. Years earlier, in 1553, Nadal, along with Araoz and Borja, had found himself at odds with the Spanish Inquisition over the tribunal's pursuit of the two disciples of Juan de Avila who wanted to join the Society—Guzmán and Loarte.[127]

Related to the inquisitorial tribunals, though sometimes effected independently of them, were measures taken against publishers and sellers of presumably heterodox books. In 1550 Nadal refused to collaborate with an episcopal inquisitor because he understood that the bishop intended to put the accused on trial. They worked out a compromise, however, according to which the Jesuits would examine suspect books in bookstores and indicate those to be burned. The bishop, in turn, gave the Jesuits permission to absolve in confession anybody who possessed such books, so that the whole undertaking could be concluded "without injury to anybody's good name"—"sine cuiusdam infamia."[128]

The most damaging measures were not such local initiatives but the Indexes listing titles and publishers that began to be compiled and broadly promulgated in mid-century. The Indexes published by the theological faculties of the universities of Paris and Louvain and others published in some Italian cities like Milan and Venice were well known in Rome when Paul IV early in his pontificate set about through the Roman Inquisition to draw up a papal list.[129]

At one stage of the process in Rome, the pope summoned Laínez to collaborate on the project, at which time he was delegated the task of investigating the writings of the long-dead Savonarola. Paul IV harbored a particular dislike for the Florentine reformer, fanned by the determination of Dominicans like Catarino to see Savonarola posthumously condemned as a heretic. Laínez disliked the role assigned him and did no more than point out passages that might be investigated. In the Society itself he as general never took any measures to curtail the reading of Savonarola or to have Jesuit houses rid their libraries of his works.[130]

When Paul IV finally published the first papal "Index of Prohibited Books" in 1559, he was largely unsuccessful in his attempt against Savonarola but managed, nonetheless, to create one of the most fanatical documents of even that fanatical pontificate. The Jesuits had supported the idea, but when it was realized it shocked them by its indiscriminate inclusiveness. Nadal had even before publication intervened with the Roman Inquisition for moderation.[131] After publication Canisius wrote to Laínez from Germany that it was "intolerable" and a "scandal."[132] Jesuits feared that Madrid's book on frequent Communion and Loarte's *Esercitio* might experience a similar fate.

Even as the Index stood, it posed immense problems for them. Among its many sweeping condemnations, as we have seen, were the works of Erasmus—*opera omnia.* The Jesuit college at Loreto had some fifty volumes of Erasmus in its library, and other colleges had similar collections. But what caused them the most consternation was their need for Erasmian texts in their classrooms. When the rector at Perugia registered his alarm, he epitomized the quandary of many Jesuit schools: "We have no books [for certain classes] except those of Erasmus!"[133] The Jesuits feared at the same time that the permission they had obtained for themselves from Paul's predecessors to read heretical books was rescinded by this new papal decree.

The pope's death shortly after the publication of the Index somewhat eased the situation for all concerned. Even earlier Laínez obtained permission from the Roman Inquisition for the Jesuits to use and read certain books and got explicit license for *De octo partibus* of Erasmus. In 1561 he approached Pius IV to add his voice to those protesting the extremes of the document.[134] When the Council of Trent reconvened the next year, it preempted the issue from the pope, but in its haste to finish its business in late 1563 it referred it back to him. The Index of Pius IV, 1564, was notably milder than his predecessor's, even regarding Erasmus, but on particular items the Jesuits, like others, continued to have questions and scruples.

Because the Jesuits had problems with the Index of Paul IV of course does not mean they were tolerant of books they considered dangerous or genuinely heretical. They policed themselves. When Nadal visited Jesuit houses, he often gave instruction on the matter. If heretical books were useful in teaching or preaching, they could be retained—but under lock and key. Otherwise, they were to be burned. Books about which there was uncertainty were to be set aside for further consideration.[135]

Outside their own houses they seem relatively rarely to have taken the initiative in pursuing others with the intent of burning their books, but there were exceptions. In 1553 Ignatius gave Bobadilla permission to do whatever ministry he wanted, and Bobadilla won for himself an appointment as *commisarius* of the Holy Office for the March of Ancona, where he was to seek out heretical and Jewish books for destruction.[136] It was common, however, for Jesuits to exhort their listeners to hand over their suspect books for burning, as did Laínez at Bressanone in 1544.[137]

The Jesuits abstained entirely from the furious campaign of proscription waged in the early 1540's in Italy against *Beneficio di Cristo,* the work of devotion stemming from the circle of the so-called *spirituali,* or "Italian evangelicals."[138] Among the leaders against the *Beneficio* was Cardinal Giampietro Carafa. The campaign began the long crisis in the highest level of religious authority in Rome between the *spirituali* and the *zelanti* that more or less culminated in the trial for heresy of the Jesuits' old patron Cardinal Giovanni Morone.[139]

This dedicated and brilliant churchman was part of the *spirituali* circle, which had centered on Cardinal Gasparo Contarini until his death in 1542.[140] Contarini more than any other person, of course, had won from Paul III approval for the nascent Society of Jesus and had made the full course of the *Exercises,* probably under the direction of Ignatius himself. The Jesuits had other friends in this circle. Moreover, the primacy the Jesuits attributed to religious experience and interior illumination had at least generic counterparts in the teaching espoused by the *spirituali.* In the vocabulary of both groups, "consolation" figured large.[141]

A heavy cloud of suspicion and distrust hung over Contarini after the failure of his efforts at reconciliation with the Lutherans at Regensburg in 1541. Many in Rome considered him guilty of heresy himself because of purported concessions to the Lutherans, especially on the doctrine of justification. The same cloud hung over those associated with him, however loosely—a cloud darkened by the defection to Protestantism in 1542 of Vermigli and Ochino. Even in this atmosphere, Ignatius's gratitude and devotion to Contarini's memory never seem to have wavered.[142]

In the aftermath of Contarini's death and the other fateful events of 1542, Cardinal Reginald Pole gradually assumed leadership of this ever more beleaguered group. Although both Pole and Morone continued to enjoy the confidence of Paul III and Julius III, Morone was accused of being soft on heresy while he was bishop of Modena at the time of the defections and had to answer Paul III's queries.[143]

Carafa, convinced that the *spirituali* were crypto-Lutherans, could not contain his zeal for their undoing. When elected pope in 1555, he almost immediately instigated the juridical process against Morone, cardinal though he was. The pope was never able to win his conviction, but in 1557 he arrested and imprisoned him in Castel Sant'Angelo for the rest of his pontificate. Embarrassing to the Jesuits was the fact that Salmerón was summoned by the tribunal in both 1555 and 1557 to give testimony because of his confrontation with Morone over the justification issue when in 1543 as a young man he had preached in Modena.[144]

Salmerón was not eager to testify, but presented his recollection of the incident as a difference with Morone over the role of good works in justification, which had led to Morone's forbidding him to preach. The attorney for Morone's defense, Marcantonio Borghese, disputed Salmerón's version of the events of 1543 and maintained that Morone forbade him to preach because he mentioned individuals by name from the pulpit.

In 1558 Salmerón was called upon to play a more congenial role in the affair. By this time Paul IV and Philip II had ended their war and more or less settled their differences. While Salmerón was at the court of Philip in Brussels, therefore, Laínez wrote to him and Ribadeneira exhorting them to use their influence on behalf of Cardinal Reginald Pole, who, though safe in Mary Tudor's England as papal legate appointed by Julius III and now archbishop of Canterbury, was sought for heresy by Paul IV. But Laínez especially urged them to try to help Morone.[145] The "cautious but intense" activity of the two Jesuits probably influenced Philip's decision not to further the pope's designs.[146] Pole was saved from them by his death later that year.

When Paul IV died the following year, the college of cardinals immediately released Morone from prison, and Paul's successor appointed him three years later one of his legates to the reconvened Council of Trent, where he proved more important than any other individual in bringing the Council to a successful conclusion. When Morone regained his freedom, he expressed to Laínez his resentment over Salmerón's testimony used against him.[147] The magnanimous Morone soon resumed his friendly attitude, however, and it prevailed through his occasional disagreements with the Jesuits at Trent.

Even before the death of Paul IV and Morone's rehabilitation, the Jesuits found themselves involved in another spectacular prosecution for heresy, a *cause célèbre* indeed. This time the accused was the primate of all Spain, Bartolomé Carranza, a Dominican and successor to Silíceo as archbishop of Toledo.[148] The attack centered on his *Catechismo* but was motivated less by zeal for orthodoxy than by professional and personal animosities. Leading the attack was Fernando de Valdés, inquisitor general and archbishop of Seville, who resented the conferral on a Dominican of the most prestigious see in Spain. He was principally aided and abetted by Carranza's Dominican confrere, Melchor Cano, who nursed long-standing personal and theological resentments against him.[149] Some of Cano's theological objections were generically similar to his objections to the Jesuits. Ardently leading the defense was Martín de Azpilcueta ("Navarro"), the canonist and casuist so admired by the Jesuits.

Registering their support or condemnation of Carranza were some of the most prestigious persons and institutions of the age. Few cases reveal so clearly the overheated religious atmosphere of Spain and Rome in the middle of the sixteenth century or illustrate so dramatically the confusing and overlapping networks of jurisdictions, loyalties, and ecclesio-political policies and antagonisms within Catholicism. Few cases reveal such patent injustice.

Arrested and imprisoned in Spain in 1559, Carranza was, after a papal intervention, brought to Rome in 1567, where he was again imprisoned, this time in Castel Sant'Angelo. On 4 April 1576, nearly seventeen years after Carranza's arrest, Pope Gregory XIII handed down an ambiguous verdict. Carranza, finally released, died a few days later in the Dominican convent of Santa Maria sopra Minerva, in the center of Rome.

The Spanish Inquisition had begun its process against him in 1558, in which the key element was a condemnation of Carranza's *Catechismo* by Cano. Although the Spanish Inquisition was for all practical purposes independent of its Roman counterpart and almost a rival institution, Valdés won approbation for his measures from Paul IV. Once the pope learned that the *Catechismo* had been written by Carranza in England and had the sympathy of Cardinal Pole, he had no further need of witnesses. Paul's successors were more ambivalent on the issue, for any number of reasons, but the process had got under way with papal blessing.

In 1559 the Spanish Inquisition issued its own Index of Prohibited

Books, which of course included the *Catechismo.* It also included works of two staunch friends of the Jesuits—*Audi, filia,* by Juan de Avila, and *Guía de pecadores* and *Libro de la oración y meditación,* both by Luis de Granada. Immensely more disconcerting to members of the Society, however, was the inclusion of a book entitled *Obras del cristiano,* purportedly written by the most prestigious and best-known Jesuit in Spain, Francisco de Borja.[150] This book and two other compilations attributed to Borja were pirate editions.

Valdés was suspicious of Borja also because Carranza had invoked his name as part of his defense. The inquisitor and his minions showed no interest in sorting out in these compilations the works actually written by Borja from those that were not. Meanwhile King Philip, just returned to Spain, had become annoyed with Borja on several counts, not the least being a rumor in the royal court that, in the king's absence during his marriage to Mary Tudor, Borja had lived in concubinage with Philip's sister and regent, Princess Juana. (Juana was of course a Jesuit, unbeknownst to Philip.) He had other grievances against the Jesuits, including their efforts to persuade Spaniards to support with benefactions a foreign institution, the financially faltering Collegio Romano.

The intractible attitude of the Inquisition and the hostility of the royal court led Borja, fearing arrest, to accept an invitation from Cardinal Henrique to visit Portugal. In the tense months before his departure, Borja felt, quite correctly, that the well-connected Antonio de Araoz was doing less than his utmost to help him. Word about the unpleasantness between these two Jesuits—"quasi schisma," according to Nadal—reached as far as the court.[151]

Borja's plight sent a shock through his confreres about the situation of the Society in Spain, and, with good reason, they also began to expect another assault on the *Exercises.* Jesuit correspondence about the Borja affair, abundant, had to be carried on in code.[152] In this indirect but significant way, the Jesuits early got linked to the process against Carranza.

Jesuit involvement had, however, slightly antedated the publication of the Index. When Carranza got wind of the forces being marshaled against him, he tried to enlist advocates for his cause. He had known and admired Laínez and Salmerón at Trent and, ironically, had been approached in Brussels by Salmerón and Ribadeneira to intercede at court for the hapless Morone. As archbishop of Toledo, he had reversed the policies of his predecessor against the Society. He was also fully aware of the Jesuits' bad relationship with Cano. In late 1558, therefore, he turned to the new general of the Society to help him in Rome, supported in this endeavor by leading Spanish Jesuits including Borja and especially Bartolomé de Bustamante, who considered Carranza a veritable replication of "the good shepherds of the primitive church."[153]

Laínez was a step ahead of Carranza and had already requested and received from Salmerón a theological judgment on the *Catechismo* that was altogether positive. At first Laínez was inclined to send Salmerón's verdict to Spain, but, after reading part of the *Catechismo* himself, he judged it inappropriate "for these times."[154] On three occasions between 5 February and 5 March 1559, he instructed Salmerón that the Jesuits were not to throw their influence, such as it was, behind Carranza, and he told Salmerón that if he had read the book judiciously he would have arrived at the same judgment as he himself had.[155] This was well before the publication of the Spanish Index in October of that year.

Even if we give Laínez the benefit of the doubt and concede that he was genuinely convinced the *Catechismo* was heterodox or at least misleading, as he continued to insist over the course of the years,[156] we must also reckon with the certainty that he was much concerned that intervention on behalf of Carranza would result in reprisals against the Society by the Spanish Inquisition and by the still fiercely reigning Paul IV. Those fears surely influenced the way he judged the *Catechismo*. Most disconcerting in the whole affair is the letter he wrote through Polanco on 5 March, in which he proposed to Salmerón various strategies for extricating himself from his embarrassment with Carranza, which included pleading that he was ill and inattentive when he first read the book.[157] We do not know what action Salmerón took, if any, but this was certainly not Laínez's finest hour. Laínez and Salmerón almost got involved in the Carranza affair again a few years later when it surfaced at the reconvened Council of Trent, but they were spared rendering an opinion.[158] The Jesuits played a minor but active role in the practical rehabilitation of Granada, finalized in 1566, but during Laínez's generalate they maintained a hands-off policy toward Carranza.[159]

With the support of Pius IV, Laínez was able in 1561 to summon Borja from Portugal to Rome, thus beginning his rehabilitation by simply distancing him from his enemies in Spain. After Borja's death as general of the Society, the *Obras* appeared again on the Spanish Index of 1583, but with a curious disclaimer applied also to other authors on the list like Avila and Granada—like John Fisher and Thomas More!

During Borja's generalate, 1565–72, Jesuits in Rome gave signs of support to Carranza. On 4 January 1568, for instance, Carranza was invited to a festive dinner at the Collegio Romano, and his jailers let him attend. (Part of the celebration consisted in fifteen "little sermons" in fifteen different languages—Hebrew, Arabic, Greek, Latin, English, Scotch, Irish, Flemish, French, German, Bohemian, Polish, Italian, Spanish, and Portuguese.)[160]

In 1570 the Roman Inquisition asked Francisco de Toledo, already highly esteemed for his theological accomplishments, to render an opinion on the accusations against Carranza. Through a painstakingly careful examination, he arrived at conclusions diametrically opposed to Cano's, and his final judgment vindicated the orthodoxy of the archbishop. This did nothing, however, to secure Carranza's release from prison. Carranza's Spanish enemies tried to discredit Toledo's opinion, including pointing out that it had come from a "Jew."[161]

The case against Carranza was a symbol of the great religious crisis seeking solution in Iberia and Italy in the 1560's and 1570's. Cano discovered the heresies of Luther and the *alumbrados* on every page of Carranza's catechism. Toledo, even in the face of Cano's strictures, pronounced the book sound. Cano typified those Catholics who on the same grounds attacked Erasmus, Contarini, Morone, and Carranza, who put their utmost trust in moral discipline and in a highly objectified truth, and who defined orthodoxy as a narrow gate through which few truths passed. Toledo saw things differently. The contrast between the judgments of these two theologians did not really reflect a conflict between orthodoxy and heterodoxy but something more profound. It reflected, as has well been said, a conflict "between two different ways of understanding Catholicism itself."[162]

In any case, the Jesuits related in varying degrees and in a variety of ways to institutions responsible for the extirpation of heresy and the banning of books. They were at different times and places accusers, accused, and agents for the defense in complex situations in which concern for their own survival sometimes influenced their conduct and judgment.

Inquisitions and related topics are not mentioned in the *Constitutions*. If Nadal's comment quoted above represented the best Jesuit thinking in this regard, it indicated a "way of proceeding" that tried within the assumptions of the age to steer a moderate course. It expressed an attitude and ideal that seems to have been widely, but by no means universally, appropriated and practiced by the Jesuits. Although they were therefore sometimes more reserved and evenhanded in such matters than many of their peers, both Catholic and Protestant, no Jesuit, surely, wanted to be found lacking in his zeal for "the defense of the faith."

Reform and the Council of Trent

In an age in which political, intellectual, and religious leaders consistently and vociferously demanded "reform of the church," the Jesuits spoke of it seldom.[163] From time to time the phrase appeared in documents emanating from Jesuit headquarters in Rome, where it generally meant first and foremost reform of the papal curia. Ignatius, Polanco, Laínez, and the others who used the term of course understood its broader meaning, but, like so many of their contemporaries, they believed that "reform of the head" was the indispensable precondition for "reform of the members," which would follow almost perforce after the former had been accomplished.

Why did the Jesuits speak of this burning issue so rarely? Not because of unconcern. Two reasons especially account for their reticence. First, they disliked expressing or even implying criticism of the church and churchmen except in situations where it could reasonably be expected to have a positive effect, as the "Rules for Thinking with the Church" inculcated.[164] Indiscriminate criticism of abuses caused more harm than good, they believed. They had complaints about the status quo and some definite opinions about how it might be bettered, conventional though most of them were. They knew that occasionally public denunciation was called for, and they sometimes acted accordingly. But generally they were reserved about broadcasting their criticisms concerning what was wrong with the church.

The second reason was deeper, more fundamental. Although the Society of Jesus is often described as having been founded to reform the church, the early Jesuits did not in fact see "reform of the church" as their direct concern. When the Jesuits spoke of church in this context, they meant, despite their generally broader ecclesiological vision, the institutional structure comprising the offices of pope, bishops, and, to a certain extent, pastors of parishes. They professedly eschewed participation in that structure. The "way of proceeding" of those offices, even when there was no question of scandal or abuse, was different from their "way of proceeding." For one thing, the offices entailed benefices.

Jesuit documents, consequently, never indicate "reform of the church" as a task of the Society. "Reform of the church" is here obviously to be taken in a technical sense. If "reform" were understood more broadly, it would encapsulate the objectives of the *Formula* and state the ultimate goal of all the *consueta ministeria*. But in that sense it would mean personal conversion or spiritual improvement as presented in the *Exercises,* not the direct emendation of ecclesiastical procedures and structures, which is what Jesuits and their contemporaries understood by the expression "reform of the church."

Some of those contemporaries could not see the reform happening except as fulfillment of apocalyptic predictions. The Jesuits were fundamentally untouched by such speculation and by the idea that what was needed was the long-awaited "angelic pope" who would set things right. A few Spanish Jesuits, including Borja, had early on shown themselves susceptible to prophecies about the "angelic pope," mediated to them through the Franciscan visionary Juan Texeda.[165] There were those who speculated that Borja himself might be that holy pontiff. In 1549 Ignatius addressed the matter in a long document to Borja and pronounced such visions "very suspect."[166] That in principle settled the matter.[167]

Leading figures of the sixteenth century, including Luther, believed that the end was nigh. Even when they did not go that far, they passionately decried their times as fundamentally, even desperately, distressed, as probably or surely the worst the world had ever seen—a sentiment that seems almost an essential ingredient in the constitution of a "reformer."[168] In the vast documentation he left behind, however, Ignatius did not echo the sentiment. If he found his times utterly corrupt, he allowed no anguished cry bemoaning them to escape his lips. The same was true for the other leading Jesuits of these early decades.

They were of course shocked and scandalized by certain things—by the venality of the papal curia, for instance, and by the degraded condition of the Catholic clergy in Germany, by the ignorance of religion they found in remote areas of Italy and the Iberian peninsula. But, unlike many of their contemporaries, they rarely uttered generalized exclamations of dismay about their times or about the condition of the Catholic community. This peculiarity was consonant with other aspects of their corporate personality, including their pragmatic and straightforward approach to their ministries and their fundamental optimism about human nature.

But on occasion they spoke of "reform of the church" and showed their concern for it. The expression occurred with unaccustomed frequency in Ignatius's correspondence at the time of the election of Pope Marcellus II in the spring of 1555.[169] As Cardinal Marcello Cervini, the new pope had been friendly to the Jesuits at Trent when he was papal legate, as well as in other circumstances. Ignatius and his collaborators knew him well, therefore, and their expectations were high that abuses in the papal curia would be effectively addressed.

The issue seems to have come up in informal conversation in the *casa professa* after the election. Ignatius reportedly said that if the pope reformed himself, the papal "household," or curia, and the cardinals in Rome, everything else would fall into place.[170] The idea was hardly original, but it indicated a significant strain of thinking in the Society not confined to Ignatius.

When Marcellus was succeeded by Paul IV, the Jesuits tried to look on the bright side, which was the zeal for the reform of the church for which Carafa had been known for decades. The new pope initiated a flurry of activity in this regard, in which he employed Laínez and some other Jesuits, as we have seen. A year later Polanco was realistic: "They are beginning to deal with the reform [of the curia], and it seems in earnest, even if the procrastinations of the past prove that we should not easily believe these things until we see them accomplished."[171]

In Rome itself the Jesuits on occasion publicly denounced the evils that needed remedy. Laínez affirmed that he did so, and evidence corroborates him. The best evidence to survive is from 1558. Polanco reported that on 13 March Laínez, still vicar general, preached "against heretics and Roman abuses."[172] In both of his series of sacred lectures before a lay audience that fall and winter, Laínez denounced "sinful Rome."

Much of what he said applied generally to a population notorious in many circles for a rich variety of vices.[173] Some of it applied directly to ecclesiastics—their piling up of benefice upon benefice, their panting after "dignities and honors, and their enriching themselves with bishoprics and cardinalates." After they acquire their bishopric, cardinalate, or papacy, Laínez warned, hell awaits them.[174] He could be more specific: "[Prelates become rich on benefices] at the expense, as they say, of the crucified Lord. Do you think God wants this? No! One man gets himself made bishop. Another gets himself made pope—some do it with the help of France, some with the help of Spain. And what do they do? They elect the pope—sometimes like now they elect a good man, but for the most part they elect the worst possible candidate. Ah, God does not will but merely permits it."[175]

Standard though these criticisms were, they targeted the most notorious abuses and in their substance corresponded to ideas found in more studied documentation extant from Laínez and other Jesuits. By 1563 at the latest, Laínez and Nadal—and with some qualification, also Polanco and Canisius—were convinced that the "reform" would be best undertaken by the pope himself, but they were not deluded that this would be an easy task or that success was assured.

It was principally to the Council of Trent, of course, that concerned persons looked for the reform of the church, which in that context included but was much broader than reform of the papal curia. Like the Jesuits, the official decrees of the Council avoided using the term itself, probably because of the radical meaning with which Protestants and others had invested it. From the beginning, in any case, the Council understood itself as having a twofold task—the "affirmation of doctrine" against the new heresies and the "reform of morals" against long-standing disciplinary abuses. Its decrees were divided accordingly into two categories—those dealing with doctrine and those entitled *de reformatione.* The reform of morals was to be accomplished through a strong assertion of the duties, rights, and jurisdiction of bishops and pastors, with enforcement guaranteed by newly stringent canonical penalties. Although the Council was ultimately prevented from addressing the reform of the papacy, the "reform of morals" was soft rhetoric for the traditional expression "reform of the church."

As it turned out, two Jesuits had official commissions as theologians for the first period of the Council, 1545–47—Laínez and Salmerón, designated by Ignatius upon a request by Paul III. At the behest of Otto Truchsess von Walburg, bishop of Augsburg, Jay acted as his procurator. In 1547, just as the Council was approaching its bitterly contended translation to Bologna, Peter Canisius appeared briefly at the behest of Truchsess. The other three Jesuits made important contributions to the Council on both doctrinal and reform issues, including especially, through Jay, a raising of awareness about the necessity of better training for the clergy. They were not, however, the pivotal figures.[176]

Ignatius was manifestly pleased at the respect shown his new compagnia by these requests by the pope and an important bishop for the services of his confreres. In early 1546 he sent to Laínez, Salmerón, and Jay an instruction as to how they should deport themselves at Trent.[177] The document, divided into three parts, is as important for what it does not say as for what it does. The first part counseled that they be modest in presenting their opinions, listen with respect to the viewpoint of others, always review and consider both sides of any disputed point, and show deference for judgment better than their own.

The second part instructed them to carry on at Trent the *consueta ministeria*—preaching, catechism, the *Exercises,* visiting the sick and poor, "even bringing them a little gift if possible." Ignatius designated these ministries the principal reason, at least as far as he was concerned, that the Jesuits were at Trent, and, hence, this must be considered the most important part of the letter. The three Jesuits faithfully followed Ignatius's directive, and they were even successful in guiding a few bishops through some form of the *Exercises.*

The third part concerned the Jesuits' lifestyle and regimen, which included meeting each evening to discuss their experiences of the day, to decide on the agenda for the next, and to take measures to correct anything that might be wrong in their conduct. Missing in Ignatius's letter, of course, was any word concerning the great issues facing the Council. He obviously had confidence that, whatever those issues were, the Jesuits would have something helpful to say when occasion required. He looked upon the Jesuits, however, more as mediators than as proponents of specific agenda. If Laínez, Salmerón, and Jay had a program, they surely did not receive it from Jesuit headquarters. For Ignatius these appointments to Trent were also an opportunity, as is easily inferred, to secure good will for the Society from the prelates gathered there.

Polanco's account of the Jesuits' contribution to the first period manifested the same detachment from specific issues under debate in the Council. In that regard he noted merely that Ignatius wanted the Jesuits to avoid favoring any positions like those held by "heretics and sectarians," but nothing more. He added the significant detail that in 1546 Ignatius considered recalling Laínez and assigning him to Florence because he thought the Council was moving at a snail's pace.[178]

On 3 July Ignatius had in fact written to all three Jesuits at Trent, asking whether it might not be for God's greater glory for them to withdraw from the Council and go about the *consueta ministeria* elsewhere. Salmerón replied that, although they were ready to do what Ignatius thought best, they were of the unanimous opinion that they should stay at Trent.[179] Ignatius acquiesced. Before the Council adjourned in 1547, however, he assigned and sent Jay to Ferrara at the request of Duke Ercole d'Este, seemingly without second thought that the Council ought to have priority.[180]

When the Council was finally reconvened in 1551, Laínez and Salmerón resumed their earlier assignments. After the arrival of the Lutherans began to make itself felt in early 1552, the Council stalled to a virtual standstill. In a reversal of roles, a disheartened Salmerón asked Ignatius if it would not be better for him to leave Trent.[181] There was no time to take action on the request because within a month the threat to Trent by the army of the Protestant Schmalkaldic League forced the Council to suspend its labors.

In a letter of 29 November 1551, Ignatius for the first and only time had proposed to the Jesuits an item for the agenda of the Council. Because in some parts of the Catholic world the authority of a Council was held in higher regard than that of the Holy See, would it not be advisable to seek approbation or at least confirmation of the Society from the Council?

Within a month the two Jesuits replied in the negative—no other religious order had ever received such approbation, the Council had too much other business, the *Constitutions* needed further work and were not yet translated into Latin.[182] Ignatius again acquiesced, but the incident reveals a curiously domestic perspective on the great Council.

Salmerón and Laínez returned to Trent for its third period, 1562–63, among the very few figures consistently present over the long eighteen years of the Council's history. By this time Laínez, accompanied by his secretary, was present by virtue of being general of the Society. During this period, however, the Jesuits began to pursue the approbation of the Society by the Council that they had earlier judged inappropriate. They were partly motivated by the still precarious situation of the Society in France, where their papal approbations seemed to do them more harm than good. They were also perturbed by the direction the Council was taking on certain issues. Laínez's right to membership in the Council as general of the Society had been challenged because of the seemingly indeterminate nature of the Jesuits' Institute. More important, the Council, set on a course of strengthening the authority of the episcopacy, threatened to diminish or abolish the pastoral privileges the religious orders had received from the papacy. Confirmation by the Council would base the Jesuits' rights to existence and engagement in ministry on a broader approbation. Moreover, the *Constitutions* had been completed and ratified by the First General Congregation—that objection to consideration of the Society by the Council was no longer valid.

The Jesuits never obtained the full-fledged approval they had come to desire. They were satisfied, however, with explicit mention of the Society in the part of the decree on religious orders that dealt with "profession," full commitment through solemn vows. The decree required that members of religious orders make their profession immediately after the novitiate, whereas in the Society the profession did not take place until many years later—after ordination, in fact, if the Jesuit was a priest. The pertinent part of the decree reads: "By these enactments the holy council does not wish to introduce any innovation or to prevent the religious institute of clerics of the Society of Jesus from serving the Lord according to their constitution, which has been approved by the holy apostolic see."[183] The Council did not directly approve the Society, but it recognized its papal approbation. In the decree on seminaries, moreover, the Jesuits were successful in avoiding taxation of their schools for the financing of the seminaries—implicit recognition even without express mention of their name.[184]

A few important Jesuits were thus deeply engaged with the Council of Trent, and at a certain point the relationship of the Society to the Council became itself a concern to them. Laínez as general was obviously far more involved in the Council than had been Ignatius, who never attended, never considered that he might attend, and otherwise remained surprisingly disengaged from beginning to end. In the immense amount of Jesuit documentation that has come down to us from this period, the Council is little discussed in proportion to its general importance. The reasons for this relative inattention should by now be clear. The Jesuits, never doubting that they were orthodox Catholics, knew that the doctrinal decrees were drawn up with the Protestants in view. Although they of course wanted to teach and preach in accord with them, they did not see them as directed at the Society. The decrees *de reformatione* pertained hardly at all to their situation in the church.

Besides Laínez and Salmerón, other Jesuits paid close attention to what was happening at Trent. Ignatius reported in 1546 that he had heard that Paul III intended to have the decree on justification examined by Jesuits in Rome, but nothing seems to have happened.[185] Nadal, who never held any official position at the Council, certainly studied that decree and assimilated it profoundly into his thinking and teaching. He also knew the other doctrinal texts of the Council. After the Council had finally adjourned in December 1563, some Spanish Jesuits heard disquieting reports from bishops returning to Spain about Laínez's intervention on reform of the papacy, and Polanco felt constrained to write to them justifying what had ensued.[186] We must not picture the Jesuits of this period, however, as determining the substance or manner of their ministry by reference to the decrees of the Council of Trent.

The Jesuits found their center in *Christianitas,* not "reform of the church." They were not bishops. They were not pastors of parishes. During this early period, in fact, Ignatius expended considerable energy avoiding episcopal and prelatial appointments for the Society—for Jay as bishop of Trieste, despite the importunate insistence of King Ferdinand; for Canisius as bishop of Vienna; for Borja and Laínez as cardinals.[187]

On only one occasion did Ignatius depart from this principle, cooperating in 1554 with King John III of Portugal in promoting to the episcopate João Nunes Barreto, Andrés de Oviedo, and Melchor Carneiro for an ill-fated mission to Ethiopia.[188] King Galawdewos (also known as Claudius), hard-pressed by the Muslims, sought military help from Portugal. The Portuguese, badly misinterpreting the king, believed he was willing to allow a union of the Ethiopian and Roman churches as part of the deal. Ignatius was enthusiastic at the prospects of the expedition and showed his enthusiasm by giving permission for the episcopal ordination of the three Jesuits and by designating twelve other Jesuits to accompany them into Ethiopia. He believed that in these instances there was no danger of the episcopacy's being sought because of any honor or benefice attached—indeed, the future promised only extreme hardship.

Once Claudius became fully aware of the Portuguese missionary project, he repudiated it outright. That left most of the Jesuits stranded in Goa, their gateway to Ethiopia. Of the three bishops, only Oviedo ever set foot in Ethiopia, where he died in destitution in 1577. The mission, for which Ignatius entertained the highest hopes, was a total failure.

The Ethiopian misadventure only highlights the Jesuits' resistance to episcopal appointments in places where the Catholic hierarchy was already established. Nonetheless, Jesuits were often engaged by bishops to help them with "reform," the term understood by the Jesuits in these cases as something different from "the reform of the church," although obviously related to it. This "reform" meant that the Jesuits instructed and exhorted diocesan clergy, examined candidates for ordination, and helped in other ways with the discipline and morale of diocesan institutions.[189] They often acted as episcopal visitors to convents of nuns.[190]

When Jesuits were welcomed into a diocese by a bishop, such collaboration almost inevitably followed and was so characteristic of the Jesuits that it almost deserves listing among the *consueta ministeria*. Although the Jesuits on relatively rare occasions found themselves seriously at odds with the local bishop, they more often tried to join with him in "reform"—but reform that accorded with "our way of proceeding."

~ 9

Prescriptions for the Future

THROUGH CORRESPONDENCE, visitations, exhortations, and similar means, leading Jesuits such as Ignatius, Laínez, and their closest collaborators sought to instill an *esprit de corps* in their fellow Jesuits and to communicate to them a proper understanding of the Society and its way of proceeding. Not every Jesuit agreed on every issue, but the campaign of indoctrination for the most part succeeded remarkably well.

More was required. The movement from *Gemeinschaft* to *Gesellschaft* that formally began on 27 September 1540 moved forward ineluctably; but with rapid growth ever-clearer determination of institutional mechanisms was essential for survival. That determination accelerated rapidly about 1553 under the pressure of several factors, not least of which was the great crisis with the provincial of Portugal, Simâo Rodrigues, companion of Paris. The results of the accelerated and intensified flow of prescriptive documents received an implicit confirmation in the outcome of a potentially more disastrous crisis set off just a few years later by Nicolás Bobadilla, another of the first companions.

Even given the sometimes idyllic nature of Jesuit reports on their activities and achievements, the first dozen years of the Society were relatively unmarked by concerted opposition from the outside or by major crises from within. In their ministries, in their new schools, in the respect they had won from high and low, in the degree of communication achieved with one another, the Jesuits seemed to be doing splendidly.

In 1553, however, Pedroche launched his attack on the *Exercises,* which gave center to the earlier criticisms of the Society by Cano and the opposition of Archbishop Silíceo. The next year brought the condemnation at Paris by the Faculty of Theology, and the next the advent to the papacy of the at best ambivalent Paul IV. By this time certain problems on the inside began to be keenly felt—the strain the schools put on personnel and resources being only the most obvious.

At that precise moment the first major crisis internal to the Society came to a head in Portugal.[1] Although the crisis resulted from a particular convergence of circumstances and personalities, it sounded a warning that the organization had reached a point where more formalized means of cohesion had to be employed if it was to survive. When Nadal set out for the Iberian peninsula in 1553, dealing with the aftermath of the Portuguese crisis was just as important a part of his agenda as the promulgation of the *Constitutions,* from which task it was not altogether distinct. The crisis was one of authority and self-understanding.

Simão Rodrigues had been acting as superior of the Jesuits in Portugal from the time he arrived in Lisbon in 1540, even though Ignatius did not formally designate that territory a province until 1546. The prosperity of the province in numbers and reputation was due in part to royal favor but also to Rodrigues's charm and ability. From the beginning Ignatius received fewer letters from him than he liked, and he began to get reports from others about inconsistency and arbitrariness in governing and especially about Rodrigues's tolerance or promotion of penitential practices among Jesuits that caused wonderment among friends and enemies. The practices included severe fasting and self-flagellation in the streets, not a common practice in Portugal at the time, but letters also reported instances of truly bizarre behavior—such as taking a corpse to one's room to meditate on death.[2] Reports also cited instances of young Jesuits openly contesting the wishes and orders of their superiors. Meanwhile Simão himself continued to reside in the royal court as confessor and confidant of John III. He was without doubt one of the most important religious personages in the realm.

When Ignatius attempted to call Rodrigues to Rome in 1545 to discuss the situation in the Portuguese province, the king intervened and supported Simão's reluctance to make the journey. Ignatius let the matter ride, but in May 1547 he addressed a long letter to the Jesuits studying at Coimbra counseling them to moderate their penances and the time spent in prayer and to direct their fervor to study and ministry.[3] The letter was a veiled criticism of Rodrigues's permissiveness in these matters. The next year he wrote to them again, urging obedience.[4]

In 1548, Rodrigues began to talk about going to India or Brazil as a missionary and taking some dozen Jesuits with him. Because these plans had the approval of "neither the pope, nor the king, nor Father Master Ignatius," they aroused misgivings in Jesuit headquarters in Rome.[5] Simão did not act on his plans.

When Ignatius called the original companions and a few other Jesuits to Rome two years later to comment on the preliminary draft of the *Constitutions,* he wanted to use the occasion to discuss the Portuguese situation with Rodrigues. This time Simão came and stayed for a month in early 1551, but virtually nothing is known about what happened except that he was critical of parts of the *Constitutions.*

At the end of the year, Ignatius decided that Rodrigues had to be replaced as provincial and that this also meant persuading him to leave Portugal, at least for the time being. Before making these moves, however, he consulted some members of the province, as well as the king and queen, who by this time had become less protective of Rodrigues. To ease the blow to Rodrigues's pride, Ignatius appointed him provincial of the new province of Aragon.

Even with this palliative, not every disinterested person thought that Ignatius had found the best solution. Borja, well informed about the Portuguese situation, wrote to Ignatius on 19 September 1552 clearly intimating that if he had been better informed he would have acted differently.[6] Araoz, out of whose territory Aragon had been carved, was sympathetic to Rodrigues's cause and gave him moral support after he was removed from office.

In any case, Ignatius appointed Diego Miró provincial of Portugal, an unfortunate choice for the delicate situation in which resentments were building against Ignatius for the supposed injury done Rodrigues, who continued to tarry in Portugal. While the province seethed with rumors and intrigue, Miró vacillated between severity and disinterest. Ignatius had in the meantime named Miguel de Torres visitor, with plenipotentiary powers. In July 1552, Torres in the name of Ignatius ordered Rodrigues to leave Portugal and to assume the government of the province of Aragon. When the king and queen wrote to Rodrigues exhorting him to obey, Simão had little choice.

The unstable leadership of Miró, who continued to govern the province, and the departure of Rodrigues under such peremptory marching orders only exacerbated the divisions within the province. Finally, in December, Torres began a thorough visitation of the province, determined to force the issue of the authority of the general: accept it or leave the Society. He interviewed every Jesuit. The visitation took two months. It resulted in the departure or dismissal from the Society of an extraordinarily large number of members—even today estimates range from thirty-three to well over a hundred.[7] Nadal put the number at "about sixty" from the college at Coimbra alone.[8] A lower estimate is almost certainly closer to the truth, but even that number would be stunning, representing nearly 20 or 25 percent of the province or more.

The "tragedy," as Polanco called it, did not end there. In February, just as the visitation by Torres ended, Rodrigues pleaded ill health and returned to Portugal, where his presence was sure to open old wounds. When Miró forbade him to set foot in any house of the Society and the king let it be known that he was not welcome in the palace in Lisbon, Rodrigues took refuge with his friend the duke of Aveiro. On 20 May 1553, Ignatius wrote Rodrigues two letters—the first more conciliatory, but the second ordering him "under holy obedience" to come to Rome.[9]

Probably even before that letter arrived, Miró on his own, after consulting some members of the province, issued a similar order, threatening excommunication if Rodrigues failed to obey. Bereft of support, Rodrigues complied and departed from Lisbon on 28 June. Ignatius, unaware that Rodrigues had finally obeyed, dispatched to Miró on 24 July and again on 3 August authorization to dismiss this early companion from the Society unless he now did what he was told.[10]

When Rodrigues finally arrived in Rome a tardy five months after his departure from Lisbon, he complained that he had been maligned by other Portuguese Jesuits, especially Luís Gonçalves da Câmara. Ignatius thereupon confided adjudication of the matter to four Jesuits who Rodrigues agreed would be impartial judges.[11] One of them was Polanco.

For over two months the judges heard testimony and gathered evidence. In the end they unanimously recognized the great services Simâo had rendered in Portugal and the exaggerations of some of his critics, especially da Câmara. They concluded, however, that he bore principal responsibility for the chaotic situation in Portugal and had been guilty of disobedience to the general and other faults. The penances they proposed included two years of semi-seclusion and, most painful, perpetual exile from Portugal.

At first Rodrigues accepted the verdict in good part, and of the penances, Ignatius imposed only the prohibition of his returning to Portugal. Within a short time, however, Rodrigues began to resent what had occurred and, among other things, threatened Ignatius that he would take his case to the pope. Ignatius thereupon forbade him to leave the house. This led to a stand-off in the *casa professa,* and only Salmerón and Bobadilla, called to the *casa* by Ignatius, were able to restore some calm to the scene. Their intervention induced another acknowledgment of responsibility from Rodrigues.

When in July 1554 plans for the pilgrimage to Jerusalem for which Rodrigues had won Ignatius's approval fell through, he betook himself with ill grace to Bassano in self-imposed exile. Nadal visited him there twice and believed he had helped somewhat toward a reconciliation. Nadal had to listen, however, to Rodrigues's lengthy complaints about the injuries done him and to his assertions that he was as much a founder of the Society as Ignatius.[12] With that interpretation of the Society's origins, Nadal of course had no sympathy whatsoever.

In the wake of Rodrigues's removal as provincial, Nadal began the promulgation of the *Constitutions* in Portugal in July 1553. It was in this context that Ignatius dispatched to the members of the Portuguese province his letter on obedience, dated 26 March of that year, perhaps the best-known letter in all his correspondence.[13] No doubt the events in Portugal prompted a more decided emphasis on obedience in the Society and occasioned closer definition of it as a religious ideal. The letter itself soon appeared in print and became required reading at table in Jesuit houses on a regular basis. There can also be little question that Nadal's insistent inculcation with his fellow Jesuits that Ignatius founded the Society was intensified by the Portuguese crisis and the crisis of the First General Congregation a few years later, 1556–58.

The former crisis was in fact related to the latter, to that series of interventions by Pope Paul IV that followed the death of Ignatius.[14] Although the pope was the principal protagonist, he was instigated to intervene by Bobadilla, who was initially supported by two other of the first companions—Rodrigues and Broët. That left only Salmerón among the five original companions still alive to stand with Laínez.

Personal resentments played a part with Bobadilla and Rodrigues. Ignatius had never confided to Bobadilla a major role in the internal government of the Society, for which Bobadilla showed a consistent disdain, and he in effect excluded him in 1555 as a candidate for vicar-general. As early as 1543 Bobadilla wrote to Ignatius that he was too busy to read his letters and was surely too busy to conform his correspondence to the format Ignatius prescribed. Ignatius bristled at the insinuation that he was a fussbudget and sent him a tart riposte.[15] In 1548 Ignatius offended Bobadilla's pride by the way he received him after the Germans had sent him back to Rome because of his opposition to the *Interim,* as we have seen.

Two years earlier, Salmerón reported to Ignatius from Trent disquieting rumors he had heard about the way Bobadilla deported himself in Germany, and he indicated he had also heard that Bobadilla was trying to inveigle an invitation from German bishops to attend the Council. Salmerón obviously dreaded the prospect of being joined by Bobadilla, and he almost certainly was speaking for Laínez and Jay as well.[16] When Ignatius then tried indirectly to suggest to Bobadilla that his efforts might improve if he took a more critical look at them, Bobadilla shot back a reply detailing the dangers he was encountering "while others sat comfortably in their garden or kitchen in Rome."[17]

At the peak of the "sedition" in 1557, Nadal let fly against Bobadilla a scathing indictment betraying that his grievances against Bobadilla had long been festering. The list of offenses was extensive, but most damning among them were the following: "He was always alienated from Father Ignatius; he is ignorant of our Institute and disdainful of his colleagues in the Society; . . . the German princes took him for a clown, even while he insisted he was enjoying their highest respect; he verbally abused others, calling them children or asses—not remarkable, since he called Father Ignatius an evil sophist, a Basque corrupted by flattery."[18]

Bobadilla had to be at least somewhat aware of the reservations, misgivings, and antipathies of some of his brethren concerning him even before the events of 1556–57. He was particularly incensed that in preparation for the Congregation Laínez, Polanco, and Nadal huddled together as a decision-making team that excluded him. Rodrigues was of course still smarting under the verdict on his governance of Portugal and hoped to have it reversed.[19]

But the "sedition" of 1557 suggests more than an occasion to settle personal grievances. The prerogatives of the "founding fathers" went unrecognized in the *Constitutions,* constructed for a phase of development in an organization that had moved well beyond informal bonding in a common cause. More important, the sedition indicated resistance to the ever more objectified procedures that the prospect of a General Congregation brought unmistakably to the fore, especially with Polanco and Nadal present.

First Broët and Rodrigues and then eventually Bobadilla came to accept at least implicitly the wisdom or inevitability of what was happening, but the incident again calls attention to the style and degree of regulation that was being put into operation and to the high measure of authority Ignatius assumed was his once he was elected general. In the heat of the crisis, Bobadilla accused Ignatius of being a "tyrant," as we have seen, and he said the *Constitutions* were a "prolix labyrinth" that neither superiors nor subjects would ever be able to understand.[20] He also let slip the telling observation that "Laínez was a good man, but he allowed himself to be managed by two of his sons, who led him into a host of errors."[21] The "sons" were Polanco and Nadal. The former was, after Ignatius himself, the principal architect of the *Constitutions,* and the latter their official promulgator and interpreter, commissioned by Ignatius.

Bobadilla's sedition had no concrete consequences. By mid-October, once Paul IV had lost interest in pursuing the matter as he became ever more aware that he had lost his war with Philip II and Bobadilla himself began to realize he had no chance of success, he tacitly sought reconciliation with his brethren, which was granted him by Laínez without further ado. Nadal and Polanco, however, were not able to forgive and forget so easily.

Bobadilla never apologized or retracted a word he said, and he continued afterward to speak frankly and straightforwardly on issues that concerned him. Until he died in 1590, reverenced as the last survivor among the original companions of Paris, Bobadilla and his brethren in the Society chose to act as if the sedition had never happened.

From 1540 until at least 1557, however, Bobadilla clung to the idea that the Society could continue more or less in the informal ways of its origins and that it was those ways that Ignatius had been subverting.[22] Polanco and Nadal were Ignatius's henchmen, who showed their true colors after Ignatius's death by how they managed arrangements for the First General Congregation.[23] Although Bobadilla's desire for a less structured organization was unrealistic and his criticisms of Ignatius, Polanco, and Nadal distorted, the crisis he provoked was in part caused by a proliferation of regulatory documents, by an increasing emphasis on the virtue and vow of obedience, by a growing insistence on conformity in details of lifestyle, by a new sense of discipline and "observance." These all became part of "our way of proceeding." Inevitable and even necessary though some of these developments were, they marked a significant change.

Constitutions, *Rules, and Traditions*

The *Formula* prescribed that a more detailed instrument for the governance of the order be constructed, and by 1549 Polanco had collected the rules and constitutions of other orders to aid Ignatius in the task, already well under way.[24] Compared with such documents, the Jesuit *Constitutions* would be considerably longer. Accounting in part for the length was the attention given to issues like the education of members of the Society and the institutions responsible for it, treated much more briefly, if at all, in correlative documents of other orders.

Also accounting for the length were the many qualifications that hedged almost every principle. While protracting and complicating the text, the qualifications lent the document a flexibility that stood it in good stead, a flexibility in accord with the essentially missionary character of the order that was clear from the beginning.[25] The *Constitutions* explicitly prescribed "moderation"—*moderatio, mediocridad*—as the principle according to which they were to be interpreted, with neither "extreme rigor" nor "extreme laxity."[26]

The combination of sheer length, the many escape clauses, the large number of detailed but qualified stipulations, and some confusing and not altogether consistent repetitions probably made the *Constitutions* seem a "labyrinth" to Bobadilla. They in fact required explanation, as was recognized from the beginning. Not only did Ignatius send Nadal to the Iberian peninsula in 1553 to elucidate them, but in 1555 he sent Ribadeneira to Cologne, Louvain, and Tournai to do the same.[27] Nadal did not want the *Constitutions* taken to the Indies in 1554 because nobody prepared to explain them was making the trip.[28] The following year, however, Antonio de Quadros, practically trained for the task by Nadal, set off for the East with the *Constitutions* in hand.[29] In 1559 Laínez delivered a series of sixteen exhortations on them to about two hundred Jesuits in Rome,[30] and other Jesuits did the same in similar circumstances.[31] By 1561 Nadal had composed a full draft of *Scholia in Constitutiones*, a detailed commentary that the Second General Congregation, 1565, recognized as enjoying special but not prescriptive authority.[32]

Despite their complexity on certain levels, the *Constitutions* had a formal organization in their ten Parts that made their design patent. Each of the Parts was subdivided into chapters. Goals were clearly stated, even while the many means to attain them were packed into relatively few words. The religious inspiration that was to animate members of the Society and that was the basis for all that was prescribed was apparent even in the sober vocabulary. The "Preamble" stated the fundamental assumption that "the interior law of charity and love that the Holy Spirit writes and engraves upon hearts" was more important for the welfare of the Society than this written document.[33] Other theological assumptions—for instance, that grace perfects nature—also imbued the *Constitutions* with a cohesion more than formal. Unlike the constitutions of the older religious orders, therefore, the Jesuit *Constitutions* were far from being simply a collection of ordinances.[34] They were, more profoundly, an attempt to express a spiritual wisdom.[35]

In fact, the originality of the *Constitutions* was nowhere more striking than in the developmental design according to which they followed the Jesuit from entrance into the Society through to his commissioning for ministry explained in Part Seven, which concerns "the distribution of members in the vineyard of the Lord." Like the *Exercises,* the *Constitutions* were based on a presupposition that psychological or spiritual growth will take place, and they provided for it by prescribing certain things as appropriate for beginners and suggesting others as appropriate for more seasoned members.

A few provisions, such as where the fully professed were to reside, proved impracticable almost from the beginning, as the exceptions became the rule.[36] The distinction between fully "professed members" (whether of four or three solemn vows) and the "spiritual coadjutors," while relatively clear in theory, soon begat confusion as to what it meant in practice. Some specific injunctions, including the requirement to study the *Sentences* of Peter Lombard,[37] were probably never observed, and others simply cluttered the text. But in general the *Constitutions* represented a faithful, though quite detailed, articulation into system of the bold strokes sketched in the *Formula.* In their content and structure, they differed from the constitutions of older orders in that they presented a clear orientation toward ministry as the purpose of the order and as the context in which the members would attain their own "salvation and perfection."

The Jesuit *Constitutions* broke new ground in the rationalized structure of their organization, in the psychological undergirding of their development from Part to Part, in their attention to motivation and general principles, in their insistence in particular and in general on flexible implementation of their prescriptions, in having an implicit but detectable theological foundation, and in conveying a sense of overall direction. They had beginning, middle, and end.

Because many of the specific provisions of the *Constitutions* have been discussed earlier, there is no need to review them again. But even more particulars were envisaged by Ignatius and others as necessary to give the Society shape and coherent routine. During Nadal's first visitation, he left behind extracts from the *Constitutions* but also "some rules based on them, so that it might be possible to accommodate the *Constitutions* to the use of those colleges."[38] This was the basis of the most fundamental set of "rules," the so-called Rules of the Summary, a collection of excerpts from the *Constitutions* meant to serve as a handy *vade mecum,* or "summary," of their ideals and goals.

Another basic collection, eventually known as the "Common Rules," was in the making even earlier. It originated about 1549 with directives Ignatius drew up for "the domestic discipline" of the *casa professa* in Rome.[39] As early as 1550 these had been adopted by some of the houses elsewhere and soon became an integral part of the packet that promulgators of the *Constitutions* explained and left behind to be observed.[40] Much more specific in their provisions than the "Rules of the Summary," they acted to some extent like traffic regulations for larger communities and also allowed Jesuits to adapt easily and feel at home as they moved from house to house, from country to country.

By 1555 Ignatius had drawn up a short collection entitled "Rules of Modesty" or, better, "Rules of Deportment" that because of his authorship were accorded great respect.[41] Besides these three collections of a general nature, many others that were basically job descriptions flowed from the pens of the early Jesuits, especially from Nadal's. At Padua in 1555, for instance, he left rules for the scholastics, for the master of novices, for the novices, for the rector, for the buyer, for the treasurer, and for several others. As he on this occasion rather understated to Ignatius, "I have not hesitated to provide more rules."[42]

Although leaflets containing the Rules of the Summary, the Common Rules, and a few others were printed in Rome in 1560 and in Vienna in 1561, the definitive corpus did not emerge until two decades later. However, the rules' character and the persons to whom they were directed were fairly well established by the time Ignatius died.[43] Although the rules were imposed from above, they were essentially a distillation of practice and experience. In the earliest years, some superiors and communities had found it necessary to manufacture rules of their own and had even petitioned that more precise directives be given them about how they were to conduct their affairs.[44] Nonetheless, once official promulgation of rules began, complaints reached Ignatius about their excessive number. Although the early Jesuits awarded Nadal high marks for his ability during his visitations to kindle their enthusiasm for their vocation, many criticized him to the general for prescribing routines of management and discipline with almost obsessive detail.[45] In 1554 a Jesuit at Córdoba reported that Nadal left behind more than three hundred regulations, of which some eighty pertained to the rector, who could not find the time even to read them.[46]

Two years earlier in Naples, Bobadilla and Nadal had already had a characteristic confrontation over the issue. Bobadilla openly volunteered his opinion that "some of the usual rules of the Society" need not be observed and that Jesuits should cultivate a spirit of "Christian liberty" regarding them. When Nadal visited the new college in Naples, he found both it and the Jesuit community in considerable disarray, to his way of thinking. He held the "too great liberty" permitted by Bobadilla responsible and soon received orders from Ignatius to "dispute" with Bobadilla over his opinions on this and related matters.[47]

Nadal himself liked to insist that the Jesuit walk "in the Spirit" and, indeed, that regarding external discipline Jesuits needed and had "more liberty" than members of other orders.[48] In Andalusia he found much discontent over the government of Bartolomé de Bustamante because it smacked of "monasticism" in its cultivation of seclusion and emphasis on observance of the rules.[49]

Bustamante entered the Society in 1552, already a priest. He underwent a surely rigorous but brief and informal novitiate under Borja's direction. Appointed master of novices at Simancas in 1554, he was made provincial of Andalusia in 1555, just three years after becoming a Jesuit. As early as 1556 the rector at Córdoba complained that Bustamante made a nuisance of himself because he would not let pass the slightest infraction of discipline; every "jot and tittle" had to be observed.[50]

On 30 January 1560, Laínez wrote Bustamante a letter severely criticizing his performance as provincial. In the first place, Bustamante was introducing new practices like insisting that the sacristan of the church speak to women only through a grill or veil and that confessors do the same; he was also forbidding Jesuits to take meals outside the house except with bishops or in monasteries. About the latter Laínez said, "This is something new in the Society and can mean we lose many opportunities for good in the divine service." Second, Bustamante seemed to have forgotten that, although the *Constitutions* were to be observed exactly, they granted to the superior authority to dispense from them in many particulars and left much to his discretion. Laínez then commented that "observance, generally to be commended, in some cases impedes the better service of God, which is what the *Constitutions* and all the rules ultimately look to."[51]

By this time criticism of Bustamante's rigidity had swelled to such a crescendo that shortly thereafter he simply abandoned his province and took refuge with Borja at Oporto, whither Borja himself had fled from his troubles with the Spanish Inquisition and Philip II. Bustamante tried without success to justify his actions to Laínez, but he still remained away from the province he was supposedly governing until the fall of 1561. In December Nadal finally relieved him of his office.[52]

At issue in the Society, therefore, was not so much the quantity and quality of the rules as the significance assigned them. In that regard Bobadilla represented one extreme, Bustamante the other. For the former the rules were little more than suggestions. For the latter a literal observance of them almost constituted the Jesuit vocation, an idea that in differing degrees animated the various "observantist" reforms of established religious orders from the late Middle Ages well into the sixteenth century. Despite the unhappy end of Bustamante's provincialate, ideas like his about obeying rules gained ground within the Society.

Polanco once described Ignatius as "not very exacting" about the observance of minor regulations.[53] While he was probably correct for the most part, Ignatius could occasionally be cross and exigent about details. Especially as he grew older, he demanded a close discipline in the *casa professa,* possibly because of the presence of the novices.[54] Even in a trivial matter he reprimanded somebody already as inclined to "observance" as Gonçalves da Câmera with "Observe the rule!"[55]

Nadal, for all the rules he produced, seems to have maintained a pragmatic appreciation of them and not to have invested their observance with an importance disproportionate to a rule's specific content. He faithfully echoed the *Constitutions* when he insisted that Jesuits who had finished their training not be bound by the same norms for exercises of piety—like the length and forms of their prayer—as the younger members. They were to have freedom to pursue whatever satisfied them spiritually.[56] Nadal believed, however, that those older Jesuits should observe the other rules, and he was a fervent creator and propagator of them. He was also a propagator of what he called "the traditions and customs" of the Society. These were practices that had not found their way into the *Constitutions* or rules but that were— and, according to Nadal, should be—"universally observed" in the Society.

For Nadal, a "tradition" was a practice that had originated with Ignatius—for instance, Jesuits prayed in the privacy of their rooms, not in the chapel or a chapter room; if a Jesuit fell sick on a journey, one of the others stayed behind to nurse him; Jesuit houses had a garden or vineyard for recreation; the Hour of matins was sung on the vigil of Christmas. A "custom" was a practice of uncertain authorship that had authority simply through widespread usage—for instance, the *Roman Martyrology* was read every day at supper; Friday abstinence from meat was not observed if a fast day occurred earlier in the week; despite the less exact indications in the *Constitutions,* priests celebrated mass every day.[57]

The seedbed for most of the traditions and customs was the Jesuit houses in Rome—the *casa professa* and the Collegio Romano.[58] As early as 1548 Ignatius urged that young Jesuits be sent to Rome "that they might better learn the Institute of the Society and its style of life," and, when the Collegio Romano was founded, he wanted it to be the "form and exemplar" for all the others.[59] "El modo de Roma" of which Nadal and the others spoke reflected to some extent the ancient ideal, classical and Christian, of Rome as exemplary center. But in this instance the center was Jesuit Rome, not the Rome of classical antiquity or of the papal curia.

Nadal's intention was to foster cohesion, not lock-step uniformity, but, like all the early Jesuits, he loved to descend to concrete particulars. He was clear in principle, however, that no universally binding format was either possible or desirable in the Society: "There are many things that must of necessity be different according to the differences in places and peoples."[60]

In 1556 the Jesuits at Louvain were apprehensive about Ribadeneira's visitation, fearing he would make them conform to the Roman way of doing things. Ribadenira reassured the superior, Adrianus Adriaenssens, that the *Constitutions* recognized that such uniformity was not possible or desirable. If his interpretation of any part of the *Constitutions* imposed a change that Adriaenssens deemed unsuitable, he would defer implementation until Adriaenssens had a chance to consult Ignatius himself.[61] This was typical of their procedure.

On some matters the *Constitutions* and other documents prescribed adaptation to the local situation. Like the Theatines but unlike members of other religious orders, Jesuits had no distinctive garb or habit. The *Constitutions* laid down only three conditions for clothing—that it be appropriate, that it conform to usages of the locality, and that it be in keeping with a vow of poverty.[62] Ignatius had learned from his early experience that what one wears "makes little difference."[63] Perhaps even closer to the mark and wittingly or unwittingly close to the sentiments of Erasmus was Polanco's opinion that those who understood the issue realized that Jesuits should be distinguished not by their "external habits but by the example of their lives."[64] Nadal explained that Jesuits had this "freedom of dress" so that they might labor more fruitfully and easily in the Lord's vineyard and that many people to whom they were to minister found a religious habit repugnant.[65]

Although Nadal allowed for exceptions, he and his contemporaries interpreted the first condition mandated in the *Constitutions* to mean that Jesuits should follow the practice of good priests of the locality.[66] This meant that for the most part Jesuits wore cassocks. In Rome these were black (gray inside the house—*viridis*) and unbuttoned in the front, held together by a sash-like cincture. This style was encouraged, later sometimes imposed, elsewhere, as by Borja for Germany.[67] But in Spain, except for Aragón, cassocks might be gray, black, violet, possibly even brown—and they were buttoned.[68] In 1554 the Jesuits in Brazil reported that they dressed like the Jesuits in Portugal.[69]

By 1605 when Ribadeneira commented on this feature of Jesuit life in his treatise *De ratione instituti Societatis Jesu,* a colony of Jesuits led by Matteo Ricci had been established in Beijing for two decades and were wearing Mandarin dress.[70] It is not clear how detailed Ribadeneira's information was on this point, but he knew that the Jesuits' wearing "clothing not much different from the Chinese custom" had been essential for their winning entrée and acceptance at the imperial court.[71] Their dress was in fact only the most obvious sign of an adaptation to local customs and mentality that was as radical as one could possibly imagine by Europeans of the time. For well over a century the Jesuits in the Chinese mission carried their pastoral principle of accommodation to times, places, and circumstances to its utmost expression.

According to Nadal, it was permissible for Jesuits to wear academic regalia when circumstances indicated it.[72] At least in the early years, novices continued to wear within the house the clothes they brought with them, "unless something else seems better to the superior."[73] The temporal coadjutors had considerable latitude in how they dressed, for the First General Congregation stipulated simply that their clothing should conform to styles of the locality and be such as to distinguish them from "our priests" and from "men in the world."[74]

For food and drink, Jesuits were to follow local custom, and when in doubt they should consult local doctors—a piece of advice often given.[75] Unlike the practice of other orders, obligatory fasts were not imposed beyond what the church prescribed for everybody. Ignatius was, in fact, notably cautious about fasting even in those cases. In 1550 he wrote to Nadal in Messina about fasting on the Fridays of advent: "Let the community observe it as we do in Rome, that is, let each one impose upon himself the limits he thinks best."[76] In 1555 he had a doctor examine every Jesuit in the *casa professa* who would normally be obliged to observe the regular lenten fast to make sure it would do no harm, and he himself restricted all those under nineteen to fasting only one day a week.[77]

Ignatius was particularly sensitive on this issue because the fasting and austerities he had undertaken after his conversion had undermined his health. He and his associates recurred to the idea that the body was a gift of God and should be cared for as such. In an exhortation to Jesuits in Rome in 1559, Laínez quoted Ignatius to the effect that other religious orders followed

The Jesuit astronomer and mathematician Johann Adam Schall von Bell
(1591–1666), who lived more than forty years in China and was an
important figure at the imperial court.

the example of the austerities of John the Baptist, whereas the Jesuits followed the milder example of Christ. Both ways could be helpful to one's
neighbor. Ignatius, he further observed, believed that until individuals surrendered to God, they took delight in penances and dealing roughly with
their bodies, but once that point was past, they treated their bodies better, as
gifts received from God.[78]

When the *Constitutions* commended to Jesuits care of their health, they then indicated more specifically what this meant regarding diet, living quarters, clothing, exercise, recreation, and amount of sleep.[79] Even before the Collegio Romano opened its doors, Ignatius's rules for the rector specified that he should retain a doctor for the students and faculty on an annual contract.[80] He ordered that every college where Jesuits themselves studied have a farm or house in the countryside where they might go for a day's recreation during the week.[81] In a word, for everything that refers to health or "standard of living," Nadal said that the norm in the Society was *mediocridad*—simplicity, a middle way between two extremes.[82] This norm, consistently inculcated, was consonant with Thomistic-Aristotelian teaching on the moral life.[83]

From the beginning the Jesuits, unlike members of some other orders, retained both their baptismal and family names. According to Nadal, Jesuits could change their family name if it had a strange ring to it.[84] Jesuits referred to each other by either their baptismal or family name, but prefixed it with a title if the person had an academic degree or was ordained. In February 1555, Ignatius voiced the opinion that even titles like "Father" should be eliminated in the Society, "for we are all brothers in our Lord," and in June he ordered that nobody be called "Father" except superiors. He may not have meant ideas like these in full earnest, but, if he did, they were too contrary to convention to have had a chance of being observed. Nadal in fact promoted formal styles of address within the Society.[85]

Older religious orders had jail cells within their monasteries as a way of dealing with seriously recalcitrant members, whom they might also whip or scourge if other means of correction failed. The *Constitutions* were silent on the issue for, unlike the correlative documents of almost all the earlier orders, even the Benedictine Rule, they contained no penal code.[86] Ignatius on one occasion said he would not hesitate to establish jail cells in the Society for the "pertinacious," but for the present they were not needed.[87]

After Ignatius's death the First General Congregation took up the matter and chose not to decide on it, leaving it to the discretion of the general.[88] The next year Laínez stated his opposition on principle: "In the Society there are no jails, and it is forbidden to punish anybody with blows."[89] There was under Borja and even later some vacillation on the issue, but Laínez's stance ultimately prevailed.[90]

Thus, in various ways Jesuit discipline evolved into a form that notably differentiated it from the discipline of older orders, even while it began to take on contours that generically resembled it. The *Constitutions* had nothing to say about the observance of silence in the house except as it pertained to novices, for instance, but it soon came to be understood that outside the time for recreation chatting with one another was discouraged.[91]

The pattern for the general order and discipline within the community seems to have been drawn partly from what the Jesuits had observed in the collegia of the various universities they attended and partly from what they knew about convents and monasteries. Jesuit houses were most clearly distinguished from the latter, of course, by the absence of regular chapter, of the conventual mass, and of choral recitation of the Hours.

The Vows and Grades of Membership

The vows of poverty, chastity, and obedience that the Jesuits pronounced were what identified them most closely with the conventual and monastic traditions. The Jesuit vows, as was true for those of other orders as well, had specific meaning according to specific determinations contained in the official documents of the order—in this case, the *Formula* and the *Constitutions.* They are one of the most technically complicated aspects of the Institute of the Society, intimately related to the equally complicated issue of "grades," or graduated membership.

Almost immediately after the approval of the Society in 1540, priests wanted to join who had the character and good will that made them suitable for some of the ministries of the Society but who lacked the academic training considered prerequisite to the more delicate and difficult ministries, especially preaching, and for the strange circumstances in which the Jesuits' special vow to do ministry anywhere in the world might place them. They could "help" the Society in some, but not all, of its ministries.[92] Laymen who lacked either the desire or the background to be ordained but who wanted to help "in temporalities" were also invited to join, as we have seen.

In 1546 with the bull *Exponi nobis,* Paul III gave permission for the Society to admit both "spiritual and temporal coadjutors."[93] This was the origin of the distinction in the order between these "coadjutors" and the "professed." At the very beginning the former seem to have been considered not much more than helpers, as the name indicated—a kind of corps of volunteers or an auxiliary branch—but their position immediately evolved into something much closer to full membership.

The second version of the *Formula* and even the *Constitutions,* while clear on certain principles, were composed during these early years of evolution. The most important change that was occurring was that ever more applicants entered the Society at a young age and, if they were going to be ordained, received their education in the Society and under its supervision. This development could have led to the elimination of the distinction between spiritual coadjutors and professed, but it did not. A somewhat mitigated course of studies was soon elaborated for those who were going to be spiritual coadjutors, but, because of an early error of interpretation by Nadal, a satisfactory solution continued to elude the Society all through its history.

Ignatius did not leave behind clear precedents. In 1548 he admitted Francisco de Borja to full profession, even though Borja had yet to study theology and would not be ordained a priest until 1551.[94] By the time Ignatius died, he had admitted to final vows only forty-eight out of a thousand Jesuits as fully professed and a mere five as spiritual coadjutors.[95] Nadal then misinterpreted the degree of theological competence Ignatius required in the professed and passed the error along by word and deed.[96] The training that all members received in the Society would have fulfilled what Ignatius wanted, but Nadal demanded something more. This was his only major mistake in interpreting Ignatius, but it had grave repercussions. Instead of the grade of spiritual coadjutor disappearing, as even Ignatius probably envisaged happening, it grew ever larger.

The distinction in grade manifested itself in several ways. As we have seen, some ministries were supposedly reserved to the professed. This restriction never worked. Whenever Nadal, Laínez, and other early Jesuits tried to explain the distinction in grades through a distinction in ministries, their very explanation betrayed that in practice it was not holding up.[97] Because this was a major basis for the differentiation in the first place, the whole structure rested on a shaky foundation.

The supposedly inferior training or intellectual gifts of the coadjutors made them unsuitable for participation in the government of the Society at the highest level. This was the other basis for the differentiation. The offices of general and provincial were, therefore, reserved to the professed, and, for the most part, only the professed could take part in provincial and general Congregations. The spiritual coadjutors could, however, be rectors of local communities and hold other offices. Sometimes they were made provincials, but with a quick change in grade.

Only after many years of ministry in the Society and after ordination did the general make the decision about grade for the individual concerned. In the mendicant orders the equivalent "profession" took place much earlier, sometime after the year of novitiate but always before ordination. The Society's departure from this tradition was based on the idea that long-term testing in ministry was prerequisite to such a final commitment, but it was taken by critics as another instance of Jesuit refusal to conform to the standard usages of the church.

Once the decision on grade was made for an individual, the distinction was manifested in the vows themselves. These were the so-called final vows, as distinct from the "first vows" all Jesuits pronounced after the two years of novitiate. At the time of "final vows," the coadjutors pronounced the three vows of poverty, chastity, and obedience—essentially the same as their still binding "first vows." The most important change in the practical realm that these vows effected was that they could not be so easily dispensed with at the request of the individual, and the Society could not so easily dismiss those it found unsatisfactory.

For the professed these final vows were more complicated. Besides the three vows of poverty, chastity, and obedience traditional in most religious orders, the professed pronounced the special vow "concerning missions." To these were added five further vows: (1) not to make any changes in the Society's legislation concerning poverty except to make it stricter; (2) never to seek any position of authority within the Society; (3) never to seek any prelacy outside the Society; (4) to report to superiors anybody guilty of either of these actions; (5) and, if obliged by a direct papal command to accept a prelacy, afterward to listen to (though not necessarily accept) the counsel of the general of the Society on any matter he determines.[98] The last was occasioned by Julius III's naming João Nunes Barreto patriarch of Ethiopia in 1554.[99]

If the practice and legislation of the Society was labyrinthine on any issue, it was on the distinction between the two grades of professed and spiritual coadjutor and the vows connected with them. Guarded though the sources are, they show that even in these early years the elitism within the brotherhood that this distinction codified caused confusion and took a psychological toll.[100]

In the day-by-day life of the Jesuit, however, much more important were the three vows of chastity, poverty, and obedience that all Jesuits shared and that they all were expected to observe from the moment of their entrance as novices until their dying breath. Even for aspects of these vows, some confusion persisted well into the 1550's, but definite solutions were on the way.[101]

In 1553 Ignatius wrote a provision into the *Constitutions* that stipulated that after a period as novices, which already was supposed to last about two years, these men were to pronounce simple vows of poverty, chastity, and obedience, as well as a promise "to enter the Society [fully]" after they completed their studies.[102] These "first vows" designated persons more solidly members of the Society than the novices, but it was understood that they were still in a period of probation as Jesuits and could be rather easily dismissed if found unsuitable—a situation that would continue for them until "final vows."

Of the three vows, the early Jesuits had the least to say about chastity. The vow formally precluded marriage, and to that extent it was clear-cut and needed no explanation. Besides the obligation of celibacy, however, the vow implied a life that was chaste in every way. About that aspect of the vow, the *Constitutions* stated simply that "it is evident how perfectly" it was to be striven for.[103] Ignatius, Nadal, and others offered standard counsel on how to deal with temptations to lust—they sometimes seem to have had masturbation in mind.[104] Moreover, Jesuits were to sleep one to a bed, even if this meant extra expense while they were traveling, and they were not to show fraternal affection for each other by embracing, except upon departure for a journey or returning from one.[105] Persons who consistently suffered "vehement carnal passions," especially if they sometimes gave in to them, could not continue in the Society.[106] Provincials from both India and Brazil warned that the special circumstances in those places meant that anybody known to have a weakness in this regard should not be sent from Europe.[107]

As with other religious orders, the vow of poverty was understood as essentially a response to the words of Jesus to the rich man: "If you would be perfect, go, sell what you have, and give it to the poor." In the *Exercises*, the movement of the Second Week looked especially to the imitation of Christ in poverty, either "poverty of spirit" or "actual poverty," and Ignatius had himself lived in voluntary "actual poverty" as a layman during his pilgrim years. The Franciscan influence upon him, direct or indirect, is nowhere more palpable than in this emphasis on the surrender of material goods.

Ignatius's personal experience fairly early persuaded him that too severe an understanding of "actual poverty" hindered his attempts "to help souls," and later he and his colleagues in the Society saw even more clearly the impracticability of such an understanding for the institution they were founding. The depiction of the disciples of Jesus in chapter four of the Acts of the Apostles holding all their goods in common provided a model of "evangelical poverty" more appropriate to such a situation. The stress thus fell less on being in want than in having nothing to call one's own. The Jesuits were hardly the first or the last Christians to fasten onto this idea as providing the basic design for the economic reality of their life together.

Most noteworthy about the early Jesuits, however, was the pastoral specification they gave to the vow of poverty. For them the crucial biblical passage was Jesus' injunction to the Twelve for their preaching mission (Matt. 10:8–10): (1) the Twelve were not to have money to call their own; (2) they were to live off alms; (3) they were to accept no direct recompense for their preaching.[108]

The Jesuits tried to incorporate all three of these ideals into their way of life, but they saw the last as especially distinctive of them and their way of proceeding—no direct recompense in the form of stipends or honoraria, much less in any kind of salary or benefice. The *Constitutions* explicitly cited the pertinent verse from Matthew: "You received without pay, give without pay."[109]

Besides the words in Jesus' commission, Nadal and others invoked the example of Paul, who preached "free of charge" (1 Cor. 9:1–18).[110] Tithes and benefices are legitimate, Nadal conceded, but Paul did not operate that way and neither do we, "so that our ministries might be performed with the greatest possible liberty, in the greatest possible purity, and find the greatest possible welcome."[111] At Alcalá in 1561, he put the matter simply and forcefully: "Now let us get to the point of what is particular about our poverty and proper to it. Proper to the poverty of the Society . . . is that nothing can be accepted for any of its ministries"—"cosa ninguna por alguno de sus ministerios."[112] He and others insisted on this point time and time again.[113] In this case, Jesuit practice conformed almost without exception to theory.

The Second General Congregation went so far as to forbid the installation of "poor boxes" and similar receptacles for any other causes in Jesuit churches, lest people have grounds for thinking that money was in any way expected from them in return for Jesuit ministrations.[114] In other situations, as we have seen, the Jesuits begged money for the poor and needy.

Even without explicitly saying so, the Jesuits clearly considered their stance a strong statement against contemporary abuses.[115] Few things did they consider so characteristic of their way of proceeding. Refusal to accept recompense lent a further "apostolic" dimension to their ministry while imbuing the ascetical tradition of poverty with a pastoral character.

The pastoral character of their poverty determined that the Jesuits' use of material goods in the lives and houses was to be modest and moderate because their pastoral engagement obliged them to have care for their health and to make use of material goods for the sake of their ministries. As Nadal said, "We are not supposed to seek the worst clothing or the worst food, because it is in accord with the [pastoral] purpose for which we exist that regarding clothing, food, and sleep we hold to the mean [*mediocridad*] that we are now actually observing"; otherwise, he added, Jesuits could not sustain the labors the Institute imposed.[116] The norm was, as he elsewhere stated, "that we be neither oppressed by destitution nor desirous of abundance."[117] In 1551 Ignatius allowed that Jesuits on their way to founding a new college need not beg their way but that the founders of the institution would provide them with some money so that they might travel "in modest comfort."[118]

Especially in some of the schools, however, the Jesuits found themselves in considerable want. In Florence they at first had to rent beds because they did not have enough money to buy them.[119] Situations like this were not regarded as ideal.[120] Laínez felt called upon in 1564, however, to write a letter to all provincials warning them that he had heard that some Jesuits were offending poverty by seeking the best in food and clothing, by acquiring too many books, and by other ways, and, when they were denied, they became resentful. He urged superiors to take measures to deal with abuses like these, but he also warned them to beware of the contrary fault, that is, withdrawing what was necessary or useful.[121]

Specific issues arose as to just what *mediocridad* entailed. In 1553 Ignatius wrote to the provincials of Spain and Portugal that they were not to have a mule reserved exclusively for their own use. Nadal modified the order by allowing them temporarily, and he also said that some colleges could have "their own mule."[122] His travels in the Iberian peninsula forced him into buying, selling, and trading mules, transactions about which he sometimes suffered scruples.[123]

Nadal's official visitations raised the question, moreover, as to who was to pay the expenses of his travels. When in 1554 Ignatius told Nadal that, like the Portuguese province, the Spanish should contribute to them, Nadal hesitated because he realized how hard-pressed some of the colleges were and "how tender their sensibilities in financial matters."[124]

In determining what their "use" of poverty meant in particulars like these, negotiations were inevitable. On more general issues, the answers were clear. For instance, no dowries were to be accepted for novices.[125] No matter how poor the house, Jesuits were not to accept money from their families.[126]

It was fundamental that upon "first vows" the Jesuit renounce all revenue due him from any goods or properties he might hold and divert it to some good purpose, and then, upon "final vows," that he completely divest himself of ownership and definitively dispose of the goods or properties. He was free to make the disposal as he judged fit, but was reminded of the evangelical injunction to "give to the poor."[127]

Begging from door to door for the needs of the "professed houses" was practiced at first, but it was soon discouraged.[128] The *Constitutions* clearly distinguished between the "professed houses" and the colleges.[129] As we have seen, the latter were to be endowed, and those who resided in them—as they were originally conceived, Jesuit scholastics—might live off the revenue of the endowment. The former were not simply for the professed in the strict sense but for all who were not in training and had pronounced their "final vows." They were to be without endowment, supported by alms. The *Constitutions* seem to assume that most of the Society would live in residences like these, an assumption based on the original idea that the Society would undertake "colleges" only for the benefit of its own members.

The reality fast outstripped the theoretical design. Once schools were opened for students who were not Jesuits, they multiplied at such a fast pace that their number soon overwhelmed the alternative—with Ignatius's own encouragement. As we have seen, Polanco wrote to that effect to a superior the year before Ignatius died.[130]

This "intention" of Ignatius's became the design for the future. Within a very short time most Jesuits lived in the "colleges" and were supported by the revenues from the endowment. "Professed houses" did not cease to be founded or exist, but they were soon the exception rather than the rule. Moreover, sometimes a foundation begun as a school continued to be designated a "college" even after it had ceased offering instruction.[131]

With the multiplication of the schools and with the quantity and quality of personnel they required, the further provision in the *Constitutions* that the professed not live in them became a dead letter.[132] This was an outstanding instance of how an idea central to an earlier understanding of poverty suffered a radical but silent transformation by the middle of the second decade. No one was more responsible for the change, however, than Ignatius.

Ignatius in the meantime gradually began to give a new emphasis to the vow of obedience. Although he treated it in the *Constitutions* less extensively than poverty, several letters written under his inspiration went into considerable detail. He wanted obedience of "execution, will, and understanding" to be a hallmark of the Jesuit. The context in which this emphasis arose is essential for understanding what he meant and for avoiding the distortions found in most discussions of it.

As early as 1542 Ignatius in a brief letter reproached Giambattista Viola for proposing to him a course of action in a way that left him little choice.[133] In July 1547, he wrote to the Jesuits at the inchoate college at Gandía with a threefold purpose. First, he informed them that he thought they should have a superior, and he gave his reasons. Second, he commended obedience to them as especially necessary in the Society, "which is made up of highly educated men, some of whom are sent on important missions by the pope and other prelates, others scattered in remote places, far from any superior, associating with great personages—and for many other reasons. Now, if their obedience is not of a very high quality, such men could hardly be governed at all." Third, he asked them to elect a superior from among their number. Every member of the community was to have a vote, and he would accept whomever they chose.[134]

While Ignatius dealt with obedience in passing in other letters, he had Polanco elaborate on it extensively to Andrés de Oviedo the next year in response to Oviedo's request to spend seven years in "retirement and solitude."[135] He told Oviedo to do what his provincial thought best. For his part, he feared that permission might establish a precedent inconsistent with the commitment of the Society to ministry, but he was also concerned about the importunity with which Oviedo advanced his petition.

This context allowed an idea to surface that would become a Jesuit theme: others might practice Christian self-denial in their great austerities or long periods of prayer, but Jesuits did so through the abnegation implied in obedience to their superiors. Given the nature of the crisis in Portugal just a few years later, it is not surprising that this theme predominated in the longer and famous "letter on obedience" in 1553 to that province, written in the wake of the crisis and occasioned by it. The letter followed the general contours of the earlier letter to Oviedo, composed by Polanco.[136] It was, therefore, in discussion and controversy over the asceticism proper to a Jesuit that obedience rose to prominence.

Both letters repeated standard principles about obedience in religious orders that circulated widely in the late Middle Ages. As was explicitly stated to Oviedo, the elaboration from these sources came not from Ignatius but from Polanco, who at precisely this time was examining the official documents of other orders as a help for the *Constitutions*. Both letters dealt with the motivation that should inspire obedience, if it was to be a truly religious virtue, and with the ways it could be ever better practiced—from simple execution of an order to appropriating for oneself the reasons that moved the person giving it. Neither letter even hinted that a Jesuit was a soldier.

Nonetheless, they and the correlative section of the *Constitutions* employed strong metaphors and similes—obedience should be blind, the person obeying should be like a staff in another person's hand, like a corpse.[137] These figures of speech were traditional in this context—the figure of the corpse, for instance, came from Bonaventure's life of Francis of Assisi.[138] No special force should be attached to them simply because they appear in Jesuit documents. There is no getting around the fact, however, that the general teaching contained in these letters and in the *Constitutions* reflected, sometimes in exaggerated form, the prevalent sixteenth-century worldview in which the universe was ordered from the top downward, in which the benefit of every doubt was enjoyed by persons in authority, and in which both religious and secular authority was invested with a sacral character. The Jesuit documents made clear, of course, that no one was to be obeyed who commanded something sinful, an obvious qualification often repeated.

It is incontestable that the early years of the second decade, culminating in the letter of 1553, marked an important development in the Jesuits' understanding of obedience and of the importance of its role in the Society. In response to Nadal's questionnaire administered to the Iberian Jesuits in 1561–62, none of those who entered before 1552 mentioned obedience in relationship to their Jesuit vocation, but for a number of those who entered later obedience figured obviously in the way they spoke about themselves.[139]

Nadal often expounded on the vow of obedience and its special importance in the Society in terms reminiscent of Ignatius's letter of 1553. After his major visitations began in that year, he indicated that in Jesuit communities the superior or somebody chosen by him should deliver an exhortation on obedience once a month, a practice begun in Rome under Ignatius.[140] Nadal's penchant for detail led him in 1562 to construct a long, dreary list of the many ways a Jesuit might offend against the kind of obedience expected in the Society.[141]

Because of the traditions about religious orders that the Jesuits inherited and the immediate circumstances in which the issue arose in the Society, the first Jesuits spoke about obedience as a surer way of finding God's will and as a higher form of the asceticism and self-denial intrinsic to the Christian life. This manner of speaking bypassed the most obvious reason for assigning obedience a particular importance in the Society—the specific nature of the Jesuits' pastoral engagement, which even required members by virtue of a special vow to be ready to be sent anywhere in the world.

Availability for ministry provided, therefore, an overriding reason for an emphasis on obedience, but the context in the Society in which the emphasis arose and the force of explanations for the vow inherited from a more monastic tradition sometimes hindered the Jesuits from expressing this reason with the clarity it deserved. But at other times they expressed it well, as when Nadal spoke about the special vow "concerning missions."

The Jesuits realized at the same time that ministry was a practical, "rhetorical," and cooperative enterprise whose success could not depend on some master plan imposed from above or on orders issued from on high by somebody commanding in isolated splendor. Moreover, Jesuits were often not within striking distance of their superiors, and means of communication were slow and imperfect. They had to make decisions on their own. The actual practice of obedience therefore correlated poorly with the authoritarian vocabulary the Jesuits used when they spoke of it in theoretical terms.

Although Ignatius in his later years sometimes invoked obedience over niggling details of deportment or house management, he practically never imposed a single course of action in matters of greater importance.[142] Those to whom he wrote were to use their own judgment about what he advised or even prescribed.[143] He sometimes sent Jesuits blank sheets of paper with only his signature, to be filled in as they thought best in a given situation.[144] While Laínez was general, he made generous allowance for situations where rules and regulations could not be observed.[145]

Nadal described the general style of obedience and governance in the Society as "sweet and moderate" or, more often, as combining "firmness and sweetness."[146] It was firm in the general goals to be achieved, but mild or sweet in dealing with the individuals concerned, in taking account of their physical and psychological situation by showing patience and moderation toward them and making ample use, when necessary, of epikeia and dispensations from general norms.[147] Expressions like "I command" or "I order" were never—or only in the most urgent cases—to be used by superiors.[148] Even should a Jesuit refuse to do something he was asked, the superior should not think less of him but try to inquire into the reasons for the refusal so that he might better understand and help him.[149] Nadal was setting norms and ideals, but he was also to a large extent reflecting actual practice, the actual way of proceeding.

To indicate their break with the capitular governance of the monastic and mendicant orders, Jesuits described theirs as "monarchical."[150] Their monarchy was moderated in several crucial ways. As we have seen, the General Congregation, not the general, was the highest authority in the Society. Moreover, written *Constitutions* stipulated the limitations according to which every superior had to govern, the performance of the general himself was subject to review, and provisions were in effect whereby he could be removed from office.[151]

Perhaps even more qualifying of this monarchical character was the obligation of all superiors to consult designated persons on certain matters. On serious questions the consultation might be broad indeed. Ignatius wrote: "The superior, according to his greater or lesser doubts about the matters over which he has authority, ought to have greater or lesser recourse to those who are his brothers or sons in the Lord—the more difficulty he experiences, the more he ought to consult and discuss with other persons or with all those who live together in the house, as the matter becomes more involved."[152]

We have seen a number of instances of how Ignatius himself conducted consultations among leading Jesuits in Rome, but he also consulted more broadly, as in 1555 when he got the consent of "all" in the *casa professa* before appointing Nadal vicar-general.[153] When Nadal was appointed "visitor" to the Collegio Germanico in 1570, he asked all the Jesuits—"tutti i nostri"—to write him their opinions about the institution at a particularly critical moment in its history.[154] This procedure was not frequent but neither was it uncharacteristic.

In a less clearly defined way, the insistence on frequent and frank communication through letters extended the consultative base to almost every member. Perhaps even more important were the interviews with their subjects at stated intervals that the *Constitutions* prescribed for every superior, the so-called manifestation of conscience.[155] These interviews were a crucial element in how obedience was meant to function in the Society and in how the Society was governed, as the *General Examen* indicated:

> Further still, in conformity with our profession and way of proceeding, we should always be ready to travel about in various regions of the world, on all occasions when the supreme pontiff or our immediate superior orders us. To proceed without error in such missions, or in sending some persons and not others, or some for one task and others for different ones, it is not only highly but even supremely important for the superior to have complete knowledge of the inclinations and motions [of soul] of those who are in his charge and to what defects or sins they have been or are more moved and inclined; that thus he may direct them better, without placing them beyond the measure of their capacity in dangers or labors greater than they could in our Lord endure with a spirit of love; and also that the superior, while keeping to himself what he learns in secret, may be better able to organize and arrange what is expedient for the whole body of the Society.[156]

In 1554 Ignatius issued an instruction to Jesuits describing the modesty but firmness with which they might impress their viewpoint upon their superiors, which could be done in these "manifestations" or on some other occasion.[157] The responsibilities and decision-making prerogatives of superiors were unambiguously delineated in official Jesuit documents, but they presupposed close, honest, and lively communication between superiors and subjects. The surviving Jesuit correspondence indicates that this was the kind of communication that took place.

The Houses of the Society

Even as the Jesuits acquired their own houses in different parts of the world, they often took lodging for shorter or longer periods in hospitals, convents, inns, and other places. If they did so for a good reason, they considered the practice much in accord with their way of proceeding. Jesuits were otherwise expected to live in a house of the Society and, if traveling, to seek lodging in one. The relatively large communities that the schools required meant building or adapting large edifices for that purpose. These developments meant that thought had to be given to arrangements of time and space inside them.

The "professed houses" were not reserved for the "professed" in the proper sense of that term, but for all those who had completed their training. These tended to be smaller than the houses attached to colleges, with perhaps as few as two or three members. Jesuits sometimes expressed prejudice against such small numbers because of the difficulty of maintaining the discipline and communal life deemed proper for a religious order.[158] By about 1555 at the latest, most Jesuits lived in the colleges, which meant they lived in communities of a dozen or many more members. Practically everything that was prescribed for the houses of the Society had that situation principally in mind.

After the death of Ignatius, the First General Congregation ratified what was already the norm when it legislated that the houses of the Society were to be "sturdy, practical, and conducive to good health" and at the same time be modest enough not to be confused with the palaces of the nobility.[159] The Congregation hesitated to pass similar legislation concerning Jesuit churches, saying that the matter needed further reflection.

The fact that for a short period in June 1554 the Jesuits engaged Michelangelo as the architect for the future church of the Gesù means that in practice they had at least implicitly determined on some principles.[160] The early plans for the church and the attached house show clearly that the huge dimensions of both were ordained from the beginning.[161] They would very much influence Jesuit architecture elsewhere. Construction of the church began in

1568 under the patronage and at the expense of Cardinal Alessandro Farnese and under the architectural direction of Vignola. Giacomo Della Porta designed the facade. It was probably the most important church building of the late sixteenth century.[162]

Gregory Martin left a description of its impression on him a decade later: "New Churches a building, first that of the Jesuites very large and fayre, by the Cardinal Farnese uncle to the prince of Parma: which being but halfe built had forthwith Masses, and preaching, and confessions, etc.; bycause they wil leese no time, whiles the rest is a building: and thou wouldest have thought this halfe part to have been a very goodly Church."[163]

Bustamante, unsuccessful in governing, was in architecture an autodidact of some talent, even influencing in a modest way the development of sixteenth-century Spanish style. Much affected by time spent as a young man in Italy, he had already used his skills in Spain before entering the Society in 1552. During his travels as Borja's secretary from 1553 to 1555 while Borja founded the colleges at Burgos, Medina del Campo, Plasencia, and Córdoba, he helped plan the buildings, and he later did the same for others. In 1565 at the Second Congregation he was the person principally responsible for establishing norms for major Jesuit buildings.[164]

The key figure for the architecture of the early Jesuit churches and houses, however, was Giovanni Tristano. A widower, he entered the Society in Rome in early 1556 as a temporal coadjutor. He came from a family of successful architects in Ferrara and almost immediately upon entrance began applying his skills to the many Jesuit projects in Italy. Soon adviser to the generals for buildings around the world *(nostro architetto),* he was not particularly inspired or original, but his influence was considerable in assuring that churches and houses were built "our way."[165]

The expression, applied to Jesuit buildings by the early 1560's, did not directly indicate a style of architecture but meant that they were to be "practical," that is, to look to effective pastoral practice. Whereas the houses were to be "sturdy, practical, and conducive to good health," the churches were to have good acoustics, dispense with side aisles and other complicated designs, be located in a part of the city easily accessible to the populace, and so forth.[166] The Gesù in Rome reflected these norms, where they were more obvious before the baroque decoration was added to the interior in the seventeenth century—"its original state: austere, even dour, with its great barrel vault crowning the cool classicism of Vignola's design."[167]

During this period in this indirect way Jesuits influenced the aesthetic quality of their buildings and the way they were decorated. Like so many religious figures active in Rome during the Cinquecento, they were remarkably detached from the artistic ferment and controversy of the city. For instance, in 1541 Michelangelo completed in the Sistine Chapel his *Last Judgment,* which excited great admiration but also much criticism because of the nudity of many of the figures. Jesuit sources say not a word about the painting or the controversy, or about any other artistic or architectural monument of the day. For all the Jesuits' cultivating of the imagination, their culture was most directly a culture of the book and the word.

Within the houses every Jesuit was to have his own room, large enough to fit comfortably his bed, desk, books, and whatever else he needed. Nadal insisted that, in contrast with the monastic and mendicant traditions, these rooms not be called "cells."[168] Not much further was prescribed for the interior of the house except that on the four walls of the refectory paintings of the finest quality—*optimae imagines*—were to be hung, one of which was to be of the Last Supper.[169]

The main meal, taken at midday, ordinarily consisted of three courses—an *antipastum* of soup or noodles, a second course of meat, fish, or eggs, served in covered dishes "family style," and finally fruit or, on more festive days, a sweet. The sick had a separate table with different food as needed. The rector provided that what was left over from dinner and supper be given to the poor. Wine was served at both meals.[170]

At the beginning of both meals a chapter was read in the vernacular from a book of the New Testament. At dinner this was followed by a reading from a book chosen by the superior. Among the titles Nadal recommended were Eusebius's *Ecclesiastical History;* the letters of Jerome, Augustine, Ambrose, and Gregory the Great; the *Dialogues* of Gregory; works of Bernard, Bonaventure, and Gerson; *The Imitation of Christ;* the *Summa Historialis* of Antoninus of Florence; the letters of Catherine of Siena and her "life," presumably the one by Raymond of Capua. Edifying letters from "the Indies" and the circular letters from Rome by Polanco were read when they arrived. Once a month some of the Jesuit rules were to be read, for which Ignatius's letter on obedience of 1553 could from time to time be substituted.[171] Instead of reading, Xavier occasionally had Jesuits in Goa tell each other the stories of their lives and vocations.[172]

In communities of more than fifty members, a Jesuit delivered a sermon every evening at supper, sometimes in Latin, sometimes in the vernacular. Where numbers were smaller, this was done less often, but at least once a week. On fast days, however, supper was taken in silence.[173]

The Jesuits hired cooks for themselves if they did not have a lay brother in the community to perform the task, but in some of the smaller communities everybody took his turn.[174] Although they also took turns waiting table and washing dishes, teachers and some others were exempt from such duties on class days.[175]

After both meals, an hour or so was set aside for recreation, and each house had a room designated for this purpose.[176] On feast days and special occasions reading at table was suspended at least for dinner.[177] On these days some hours could be spent singing, playing the flute, or in general passing the day pleasantly—"con molta allegrezza in Domino."[178]

When vespers was celebrated in their churches on Sundays and feast days, members of the community were expected to be present. They supposedly had no other prayer in common, but in fact the daily recitation together of the Litany of the Saints was fast becoming an exception to the rule. On Friday afternoons either a member of the community delivered to the others an exhortation on some aspect of the Jesuit vocation or, with seemingly decreasing frequency, the community as a whole engaged in a "collation"—a devout conversation—on a suitable topic.[179]

Jesuits who were priests were obliged by virtue of their ordination to pray the Hours every day, which they of course did privately. In 1542 Ignatius got permission from the Holy See for Jesuits to use for that purpose the so-called Holy Cross Breviary, or Breviary of Cardinal Quiñónes, first approved by Paul III in 1536.[180] Shorter than the Roman Breviary, it appealed to many devout priests because it was composed almost entirely of Scripture. Although condemned by the Theological Faculty of Paris and attacked at Trent in 1551 as smacking of Wyclif and Luther, it survived until Paul IV proscribed it in consistory on 8 August 1558. The decree was never properly promulgated, however, and as late as 1561, Laínez was still allowing Jesuits to use it.[181]

All members of the Society were expected to spend time each day in other prayer or meditation. For those in studies, the time was not to exceed an hour, normally broken up into two or three segments throughout the day. For the others, except novices, no time was prescribed. Superiors, kept informed, were to allow individuals to follow their own inspiration.[182] What concerned Ignatius, Nadal, and others was that Jesuits, especially in Spain, spent too much, not too little, time in prayer. The First General Congregation resisted pressure to make any further determination. In 1565 the Second allowed some discretion to Borja, newly elected general and inclined to prescribe more time.[183] The issue of the length and kind of prayer did not disappear, however, but erupted into a crisis a decade later.[184]

According to Nadal, at any rate, Jesuits were free to use the time in whatever way led to "peace and serenity and consolation." That might mean meditation, recitation of set formulas like the rosary, or some other way of spending time alone with God. Prayer did not consist in "dry speculation" but in a deepening of love and devotion.[185] Nadal assumed, in the tradition of the *Exercises,* that meditation or contemplation would most often begin with a text from the four Gospels.[186] Thence it might be raised to a more perfect form: "We set the perfection of our prayer in the contemplation of the Holy Trinity, in loving union, which through the ministries of our vocation is extended to our neighbor."[187]

Fundamental in Jesuit thinking about prayer for themselves was the "Contemplation for Divine Love" in the *Exercises* and the correlative exhortation in the *Constitutions* "to seek God in all things."[188] God's love expressed itself in everything that was, in everything that happened. The Jesuit's prayer should attune him to this reality and, according to the ideal, render every moment an act of contemplation of divine goodness.[189]

One of Nadal's most lasting and important innovations in Jesuit prayer was his strong suggestion in 1557 that the scholastics at the Collegio Romano repeat the *Exercises* in an abbreviated form during the summer vacations, a practice that by the 1570's most Jesuits were following.[190] In 1606 the Sixth General Congregation made this annual repetition of at least a week's duration mandatory for all members of the Society.

Besides professed houses and colleges, the only other type of house allowed by the *Constitutions* was that in which recruits were first trained, the novitiate. Some period of testing of a year or more for those who wanted to join had been envisaged from the beginning, but only gradually did the persuasion evolve, especially after about 1547, that recruits required an intensive program of indoctrination that could best be achieved in institutions established specifically for that purpose.[191] Polanco's study at that time of the documents of older religious orders seems to have confirmed for Ignatius an idea already taking shape. The term "novice" then began to appear in Jesuit writings.

As was so often true, Nadal gave the idea its first practical expression. In 1549 he wrote to Ignatius from the newly founded school in Messina to suggest that part of the house be set aside for ten young men desirous of entering the Society and that Cornelius Wischaven be put in charge of them. With Ignatius's approval, the plan was executed the following year. This was the first Jesuit novitiate, 1550, and it was deemed successful.

From that time forward, novices tended to be segregated from older

Jesuits. Complaints to superiors that younger Jesuits were undisciplined were accompanied by recommendations that their period of "probation" be extended, which quickly led to protracting the period of novitiate to two years.[192] When Ignatius died these arrangements had already been established in Goa, Vienna, and nine other locations in Spain, Portugal, and Italy. The Second General Congregation decreed that every province have such a "house of probation."[193]

The tendency to segregate the novices progressed to the point where in 1554, upon the request of Francisco de Borja, Ignatius agreed to the establishment of a novitiate at Simancas in a house entirely independent of any other Jesuit community.[194] Although such independent institutions eventually became the norm, in the *casa professa* in Rome the novices continued as part of the regular community until 1564 and even thereafter continued to live in the same building.

More important than this gradual process of segregation was the evolution of the program of training, already sketched in the *Constitutions*.[195] The cornerstone was the requirement that the novices follow the full course of the *Exercises* for about a month. During the two years, the novices would be instructed, supervised, and "tested" by a Jesuit soon referred to, in the traditional term, as "the master of novices."

Nowhere were the novices put through a more exacting routine than at Simancas under Bartolomé de Bustamante, not yet provincial, who typically insisted on "full observance" of various rules and regulations. He prescribed for his novices, moreover, an hour of meditation in the morning and another in the afternoon, an examination of conscience for a half hour at midday and another in the evening, two further hours for the recitation of the Hours of the Blessed Virgin, and a half hour for the rosary. In the morning he gave them an instruction on the Beatitudes and in the afternoon another on the rules and *Constitutions*. He allowed the novices six hours of sleep.[196]

The situation at Simancas was extreme, but altogether symptomatic of the kind of regimen toward which other novitiates were tending, including Goa. By the end of the First Congregation, in fact, a highly regulated discipline was well on its way to codification for all the novitiates of the Society.[197] Nadal, in general agreement with this development, nonetheless continued to insist that what was distinctive about Jesuit novitiates was not a rigorous discipline, much less long hours of prayer, but the preparation for ministry that the paragraphs in the *Constitutions* concerning them prescribed.[198] The records leave no doubt that the former were the object of much concern, but they are not so clear about the relative amount of attention given in actual practice to the direct pastoral engagement of the novice.

It was easier to draw up a program for novices than to accomplish, or even insist upon, every aspect of its implementation. As late as 1567 Nadal allowed that three or four months was long enough for the training of a novice in a novitiate, after which he could be sent to a college to teach or study.[199] Decades later it was still unusual in some novitiates for the novices to remain more than a year.[200] In the late 1560's Nadal discovered Jesuits in Germany who had never made any part of the *Spiritual Exercises,* and he demanded that they take time to complete at least the First Week and part of the Second.[201]

In any case, the *Constitutions* prescribed, besides the *Exercises,* a month or two of service in a hospital, another period teaching *Christianitas,* then, if the novice was already a priest, some extended experience in preaching and in hearing confessions. The novice also had to spend time "on pilgrimage," begging his way.[202] This experience was enjoined not to promote the medieval devotional practice by that name but to give the novice a taste of the discomfort entailed in itinerant ministry. It was based, as Laínez said, "on the example of Our Lord, who preached and taught while journeying on foot from place to place, . . . and also on the example of Saint Paul and the other Apostles, . . . and on Saint Dominic and Saint Francis."[203]

All these prescriptions for the novices obviously harked back to those early days before the official founding of the Society of Jesus, when the ten companions of Paris engaged in precisely these activities, now seen in retrospect as foreshadowing the essential elements of the way of life to which in 1540 they would commit themselves irrevocably. Formalized and artificially structured though these activities now were for the novices, they were meant to help them capture for themselves the experience of the original band.

Conclusion

HOW DID THE Society of Jesus come to be? For some nineteenth-century historians, it originated as part of a larger plot, diabolical and Spanish, to wage war on humane and liberal values or as something similarly sinister. For apologists on the other side, it was a providential happening at just the moment the Roman Catholic Church required rescuing from the paganism of the Renaissance and from the heresy and babel of Protestantism.

Less contentious historians have, in the meantime, simply recounted the story of Ignatius and his companions up to the fateful day in 1540 when, for better or worse, Paul III issued the papal bull of approval. With the *Formula* thus created and ratified, the original ten (now twenty or twenty-five) companions had become the Society of Jesus. This is a respectable answer to the question except that it does not go far enough.

By 1540 the companions had made a number of decisions, establishing for the new compagnia a basic character that would persist through the 450 years of its subsequent history. The most obvious and fundamental decision was the commitment to ministry, more exigent and clear-cut than the stated goals of any previous religious order. What the early companions did made them what they were, and they did ministry. A less obvious but also profound influence was the enthusiasm, dedication, and sense of identity and cohesion that the religious experience of the *Spiritual Exercises* inspired in them. Ignatius of Loyola stood among them, moreover, as mentor and instigator, as listener and learner.

But in 1540 the character of the Society of Jesus was in many important ways still plastic, still on the way to further determination in even its fundamental aspects. That further determination was forged through experience, forged in reaction to problems the Jesuits had to resolve and to opportunities they wanted to seize.

Le style est l'homme même. If style is but the surface expression of deepest personality, then the steps by which the Jesuits developed their style, or way of proceeding, tells how the Society of Jesus came to be what it was up to and beyond 1540. That is what this book has tried to do, but the journey described in these many pages has been tortuous. For a sense of its general movement, we now need to retrace the more important or symptomatic steps, to bring the story to closure.

The prehistory of Ignatius's conversion and his composition of the *Spiritual Exercises* was of course the pivot on which everything that later happened turned. The story of the Society as an identifiable social reality did not begin, however, until the gathering of the six companions in Paris and their vows on 15 August 1534. The story thereafter, until 1565, unfolded in four imperfectly distinct phases.

In the first phase, which concluded in 1540 with *Regimini militantis ecclesiae,* the companions made the *Exercises;* they banded together "to travel" to Jerusalem for ministry; in the Veneto they undertook together "in poverty" intensive ministries that adumbrated many of the later *consueta ministeria;* with the journey to Jerusalem impossible, they offered themselves to Paul III for ministry wherever in the world he saw fit; they finally decided to stay together on a permanent basis and therefore to elect a superior from their number. Up to that point they made their decisions communally, they had no house to call their own, they lived to a large extent in diaspora. Theirs was a charismatic band.

The second phase lasted from 1540 until about 1547 or 1548. It was distinguished by directly pastoral activities with all levels of society. Everywhere the members of the new *compagnia* went, they assiduously engaged in preaching and lecturing, in every form of "ministry of the Word of God" that they could devise. Especially in this way did they consider themselves imitators of Jesus, his disciples, and the evangelizing Paul.

They were chary of any assignment that might involve long-term commitment. They fulfilled their ideal of being missioned for ministry by travel from city to city, from hamlet to hamlet, but exemplified it most strikingly through Xavier and his companions in India. During this phase, Salmerón and presumably other Jesuits maintained that writing and publishing were inconsistent with the directly pastoral and largely itinerant scope of their Institute.

By undertaking for the most part ministries earlier developed by the mendicant friars, they gradually expanded upon them and created the repertoire of their own *consueta ministeria.* They delivered "sacred lectures" and practiced street preaching more diligently than had the friars. They considered teaching Christianity to children and adults, through lectures, tunes, and printed texts, among their more urgent and characteristic tasks. Their ministries were related to one another by an underlying design that in fact derived largely from the catechetical tradition. As performed by the Jesuits under the influence of the *Exercises* those ministries had, at least ideally, further character and cohesion, especially as they looked to "the spiritual consolation" of the persons involved.

Their ministries were characterized by discourse. The many "ministries of the Word" manifested this feature most obviously—preaching, delivering sacred lectures, "fishing." It was also manifested in their catechizing. Discourse was critical to the proper functioning of the *Exercises* in the ongoing conversation between the individuals and the persons guiding them and, more fundamentally, between them and God. But the Jesuits saw even the administration of the sacrament of Penance more as personalized discourse than ritual routine. They cultivated, not surprisingly, both rhetoric and casuistry. In their various forms of discourse, moreover, they sought to inculcate *Christianitas* and *pietas,* not merely intellectual comprehension.

They established their headquarters in Rome, where they first founded some of their most distinctive institutions of social assistance—the Casa Santa Marta, the orphanage at Santa Maria in Aquiro, and the Conservatorio delle Vergini Miserabili. These establishments exemplified the fundamental importance of the spiritual and corporal works of mercy in Jesuit ministry and self-understanding. Often in trying to further these works they created the patterns of their relationships to hundreds of new or established confraternities. Thus, directly and indirectly they worked to alleviate the situations of orphans, the sick poor, imprisoned debtors, condemned criminals, prostitutes and their daughters.

At this time they had no specifically Jesuit texts to guide them except for a few manuscript copies of the *Exercises.* They gained a relatively large number of recruits, especially in Portugal, but Ignatius also decided there would be no female branch. They encountered opposition for their stance on frequent confession and Communion, but none that transcended the local scene. They had early won a faithful friend in John III of Portugal, who proposed to them their great overseas ventures. Meanwhile, the Society began to receive recognition on a wider stage, especially with the appointment of Laínez, Salmerón, and Jay as theologians to the Council of Trent.

The third phase was the longest, lasting slightly over a decade, from 1547 or 1548 until the election of Laínez, 1558, or the death of Paul IV, 1559. The last five of these years, although greatly prosperous in many ways, became a crucible fired by internal and external crises. The significance of the decade can perhaps best be illustrated by taking a cue from Polanco and following the chronicler's method, year for year—listing some events as important in and of themselves and listing others as symptomatic of larger realities.

In March 1547, Polanco became secretary. Of the almost 7000 letters in Ignatius's extant correspondence, all but 175 were written after this date, in the last nine years of Ignatius's life. In May Ignatius wrote a long letter to the Jesuits at Coimbra, counseling them to moderate their penances and time spent in prayer. In December he received the request to open a school for lay students in Messina. By March 1548, he had agreed to establish the school and selected the ten Jesuits for the venture. Nadal was elected superior, and the school opened in the fall. This same year the *Exercises* were printed and distributed throughout the Society. Meanwhile in Spain Melchor Cano began his attack, assailing the Jesuits on precisely those things about which they were proudest—their pastoral practices and their trust in the direct experience of God. Ignatius wrote to Coimbra, again, and to Andrés de Oviedo stressing the importance of obedience for members of the Society. Ignatius and Polanco set to work in earnest on the *Constitutions*.

In 1549 the success at Messina begat the college at Palermo, and the schools moved quickly to highest pastoral priority. Canisius returned to Germany, whence he began to stress with the Jesuit leadership in Rome the urgency of the German situation and to importune reinforcements. Xavier entered Japan, and Nóbrega Brazil. By the next year Ignatius had, with Polanco's aid, brought the *Constitutions* to the point where they could be reviewed by others, and at Nadal's urging he opened the first novitiate in Messina. Pope Julius III issued the revised version of the *Formula,* which added "defense of the faith" as a primary goal of the Society and ratified a diversity of "grades" within it.

In 1551 Ignatius decided to remove Rodrigues as provincial of Portugal. The Collegio Romano opened—"School of Grammar, Humanities, and Christian Doctrine, Free." The Germanico opened the following year, as did the college in Vienna, the first to open north of the Alps. Ignatius began cautioning Jesuits against using Erasmus as a textbook in the schools. In Portugal the crisis over Rodrigues finally erupted, challenging the authority of the general.

The next year, 1553, the "tragedy" in Portugal was resolved, and in its wake

Ignatius wrote to that province the "letter on obedience." He invested Nadal with plenipotentiary powers and sent him to Portugal and Spain to explain and promulgate the *Constitutions* and to handle other business. "Rules" of various kinds had begun to appear, and documents concerning education and the schools multiplied. Ignatius began dictating his *Autobiography.* Tomás de Pedroche, commissioned by Archbishop Silíceo and encouraged by Cano's continued attacks, denounced parts of the *Exercises* as heretical. Ignatius reasserted his firm stand in favor of admitting New Christians. The strain on personnel caused by the schools begged for remedy, and Ignatius in effect ordered a slowdown in the acceptance of schools by prescribing norms for endowment, number of Jesuits required, and similar matters. At Alcalá the Jesuits built their first house exclusively for the use of men who wanted to spend time there in the *Exercises.*

In January 1554, Polanco sent copies of his newly published *Directorium* for confessors to all the Jesuit rectors in Italy, explaining that it was the result of collaboration among a number of Jesuits. Diego Guzmán arrived in Italy to propagate there for the next thirty years the catechetical tradition of Juan de Avila. The Jesuits briefly engaged Michelangelo as architect for their new church in Rome, and, despite Ignatius's reluctance, almost everywhere vespers were being sung in their churches on Sundays and feast days. Their schools began to produce plays, open to the public. In December, the Theological Faculty at Paris condemned the Society as "a danger to the faith, a disturber of the peace of the church."

Early the next year, Ignatius ordered the collection of testimonial letters to counter and help reverse the Paris condemnation. After the election of Giampietro Carafa in May as Paul IV, the Jesuits feared they might need the letters for protection against the pope. In the context of the Peace of Augsburg, Nadal made his first trip to the Empire, after which he assigned it high priority among the Society's tasks and promulgated the idea that the Jesuits had a God-given role in countering the Reformation. The first edition of Madrid's book on frequent Communion appeared, as did Canisius's Large Catechism. The following year Ignatius saw to the installation of a printing press in the Collegio Romano, and the Jesuits introduced the press into India. Loarte had ready for publication his *Esercitio* as a handbook of piety for humble and illiterate folk.

On 31 July 1556 Ignatius died, and the two-year crisis over the First General Congregation ensued, with much more at stake than Bobadilla's wounded sensibilities or the personal, nationalistic, and political antipathies of the pope. Bobadilla challenged, at least indirectly, the degree and style of authority that Ignatius had assumed as general and the increasing regularization of life in the Society, for which he held Nadal and Polanco much responsible. Even after Bobadilla's reconciliation with his brethren and the election of Laínez as general in 1558, the pope continued to challenge those aspects of their life that the Jesuits considered essential and had thought were guaranteed them in the *Formula*. Both these challenges ultimately failed.

Their failure meant in effect ratification on an even broader scale of directions—in ministry, self-understanding, internal discipline—that the Society had taken under Ignatius. Such was the obvious intent of the Congregation in its approval of the *Constitutions* almost as they stood and in its election of Laínez as general. Jesuit leaders in Rome and elsewhere were immensely relieved that they had finally been able to hold a Congregation at all and elect a general.

Thus, in 1558 or 1559, began the fourth phase, a confirmation and consolidation of the stipulations of the *Formula* and the *Constitutions* but also a routinizing of the interpretation they had been given in the past decade. Polanco remained in his post, and Nadal served the next two generals as interpreter to his brethren throughout Western Europe of every aspect of "our way of proceeding."

In this phase, some individuals who had given the Jesuits trouble died—Paul IV, Cano, Silíceo. Their friend Cardinal Morone was released from prison, but Archbishop Carranza was not. The juridical situation of the Society in France improved, and the Faculty of Theology no longer pressed its condemnation. The Jesuits won an oblique recognition from the Council of Trent, and they successfully got Borja out of his Spanish imbroglio and into Italy. Bishop Cesarini's machinations against Jesuit management of the Seminario Romano were thwarted.

Toledo and Clavius began teaching at the Collegio Romano, where in 1563 Jan Leunis founded the first Marian Congregation. In that same year the Collegio, which had for years offered a course in "controversialist theology," instituted one in "cases of conscience," open to all students. In 1564 the Jesuits entered Poland. Two years later they landed in present-day Florida, where they remained only until 1571.

Like any historical reality, the Society would continue to change after 1565, influenced by changes in culture and sensibilities in society at large and by changes within Catholicism itself. In important particulars it moved almost inexorably and ever more definitively into modalities characteristic of the Counter Reformation as such. The first Jesuits, moreover, were not later

Jesuits. As in every social body, subsequent generations magnified to distortion certain aspects of the earlier tradition, while they minimized others, let some atrophy, and even repudiated a few, like the policy on New Christians. By Laínez's death in 1565, however, the directions and major decisions taken in the third phase had become set; by and large they would be determinative for the future.

During the fourth phase, a few issues already resolved in theory continued to be troubling in practice. As the Jesuits tried to establish their legitimacy as the latest in a long tradition of religious orders, for instance, they had to deal with misunderstandings in their own ranks about what this aspect of their vocation meant, forcing Nadal to repeat again and again, "We are not monks." The distinction between "coadjutors" and "professed" became more, not less, problematic. The special vow to obey the pope "concerning missions" functioned ever less according to the original intention, especially as the general became better informed through his immense correspondence about pastoral needs around the globe. The attacks the Jesuits continued to suffer from fellow Catholics made them more circumspect; thus they became more concerned with stressing for themselves and others how they fit with the tradition, how they were anything but troublemakers.

There were other inconsistencies, polarities, "creative tensions," or paradoxes more or less present from the beginning that persisted as cause for confusion among friends and enemies, sometimes among Jesuits themselves. They wanted to be peacemakers, but their very commitments led them into controversy. As others rallied around "reform of the church," the Jesuits gave them unstinting support and undertook parts of that task consonant with their way of proceeding, but they defined themselves in other terms, as helpers of souls in the vineyard of the Lord. Born in the so-called Tridentine era, the Society abstained from the two institutions the Council utilized to propel its agenda—the episcopacy and pastorates. Ardent defenders of papal authority, the Jesuits did not believe that authority was absolute or could with impunity be exercised irresponsibly.

Doctrinally cautious, they nonetheless often had a closer spiritual affinity with the persecuted, like Morone and Carranza, than with the persecutors. Becoming ever more antipathetic toward Erasmus, they yet retained many religious and cultural ideals almost identical with his. Appreciative of the clarity and intellectual rigor of scholasticism and among the forces leading to a further revival of the system, they more profoundly wanted what they called a "mystical theology" that would "rouse the affections so that we are moved to love and serve God our Lord in all things," as Ignatius described the theology of the Fathers. Opposed to the Reformation on doctrinal grounds, they tended to see it more fundamentally as a pastoral problem, as a result of sin needing cure by virtue. "Jesuitical" in their belief in the necessity of accommodation to times, places, and circumstances, they accepted institutions as they found them.

In an organization built on a network of frank consultation and relying for its success on the enterprise of its members, an autocratic vocabulary gained greater currency. The Jesuits sought inner consolation for themselves and others but inherited and promoted a system of moral reasoning driven by codification of sin. Even as they subscribed to the stern morality of their day, they still followed Aristotle and Aquinas in defining virtue as a middle way between two extremes and were part of a revolution in piety by their insistence on moderation in austerities and on care for the body.

Teachers of prayer, they were told that the world was their house. Enthusiasts for formal education, they retained a reverence for the charismatically inspired preacher. They had the usual prejudices of their culture against women, but they for the most part ministered to them in the same way and degree as they did to men, and they invited them to join them as helpers in many of their ministries. Spurred to achievement by the magniloquent "greater glory of God," they often operated most in accord with their stated ideals when influenced by the more lowly "help of souls."

Perhaps the most telling paradox of all was their cultivating fidelity to the divine inspiration within while defending the laws, institutions, and usages of the church. In their own eyes they struck a balance between these two poles, in a kind of healthy dialectic. In the eyes of their critics, they betrayed one or the other. The two poles had counterparts even inside the order itself.

In 1558 the *Constitutions* were ratified, and in 1559–60 they were printed and circulated. Rules and regulations proliferated. These changes expressed and codified many aspects, large and small, of the Jesuits' way of proceeding. Jesuits such as Bustamante defined observance of procedures as almost the essence of that way. But with Ignatius, Polanco, Nadal, and others *nuestro modo de proceder* connoted something much larger, and specific procedures had validity only insofar as they expressed it. The "way," manifested variously, was the *style*—not a set of mannerisms and not superficial affectation. It was a manifestation of the character and of the deepest values and sensibilities of the organization. *Le style est l'homme même.*

Jesuits tried to identify the constitutive elements of their style by indicating traits of personality that defined it. Thus the traits singled out for "the ideal general" in Part Nine of the *Constitutions* captured part of "our

way"—large-minded, courageous, compassionate, of good judgment, energetic in undertaking and in seeing tasks to completion, and, above all,
"closely united with God our Lord and intimate with Him in prayer and all
activities."

They described the Jesuit (and, therefore, the way) as "flexible, not rigid,"
and as "approachable" *(familiaris)*. The cultivation of *mediocridad* as a norm
for institutional aspects of their life suggested a style of personal life
straightforward and unpretentious. Although the early Jesuits never said so
explicitly, the way manifested an optimism that was due to many factors—to
their teaching on consolation, to their theology of nature and grace, to their
rhetoric of edification and congratulation, to the success their ministries and
exploits generally enjoyed, to the abiding sense of gratitude to God encouraged by the "Contemplation for Divine Love."

It fell most often to Nadal to articulate for his brethren what the way
meant. He perhaps most succinctly and effectively captured the fundamental
aspects of the ideal with his triad "in the Spirit, from the heart, practically"—"spiritu, corde, practice."

"In the Spirit" meant that a direct and ongoing sense of God's presence,
practically the same thing as consolation, was the first premise of the way.
This was what Jesuits hoped for for themselves and tried to excite in others.
Although this may seem to be an obvious postulate for religious enthusiasts,
it was not shared by all Catholic theologians and reformers in the sixteenth
century. Some of them actually distrusted and repudiated it, at least as it was
understood by the Jesuits in their teaching on consolation, indifference, and
discernment of spirits. For many of the Jesuits' Catholic enemies, religion
consisted in right thinking on dogma, strict practice of morality and discipline, and stern legislation and sanctions to guarantee both the right
thinking and the strict practice. The Jesuits considered these things important, but they did not take them as either their starting or their ending
point, much less as their center.

"From the heart" signaled how Jesuits were to deal with others in their
preaching and every other way and also how they hoped individuals and
groups would respond to them and their message—from the bottom of the
heart. Persons completed the *Exercises,* as Polanco said, "with hearts
changed." The cultivation by the Jesuits of classical rhetoric, the discipline
that taught how to touch the human heart, was not simply conforming to
the received wisdom of the day but a pursuit that correlated with their
deepest pastoral impulses.

For Nadal "practical" was synonymous with "pastoral." For him the more effective and encompassing pastoral orientation was what particularly distinguished the Jesuit way from the way of the older orders, whether monastic or mendicant. The "help of souls"—no expression was more characteristic of Jesuit writing, thinking, and action. The ultimate model for the Jesuits' pastoral engagement was the disciples of Jesus—sent on journey for preaching and for healings in body and soul, not seeking or accepting direct recompense for their labors. The Jesuits saw this pattern replicated in Ignatius and his companions, and they "tested" the novices they admitted by having them replicate it on a smaller scale.

They saw their style as in this sense "apostolic." Like so many of their contemporaries, they were inspired by a sense of the immediacy of the New Testament and by the direct relevance of biblical realities and events for their lives and their age. They were not moved by apocalyptic thinking, nor did they believe in some myth of cyclical return. But the contemplations in the *Exercises* encouraged them to transport themselves in their imaginations back to the biblical events and then to interpret their lives as in some sense a reenactment of them—or, better, as their continuation. In the concrete this meant intense cultivation of preaching (and all other ministries of the Word of God) and of various forms of healing (in body and soul), the resolution not to accept direct recompense, and a life together in which all goods were held in common.

The Jesuits saw their style as constitutive of their identity and as distinctive of them as an organization. No doubt characteristics like the above that they cultivated in themselves helped distinguish them from others, to a greater or lesser degree. Some of these traits, however, were also cultivated by others in almost identical terms. They were, moreover, ideals. They were hopes and aims, which are never the same thing as the lived reality.

As the Jesuits tried to describe to themselves and to others just what made them what they were, they sometimes missed or failed to stress the obvious. They were too close to see it. With the hindsight of over four hundred years, we see more clearly than they did that the *Spiritual Exercises* and the schools were the two most important institutional factors that, when taken in their full implications, shaped the distinctive character of the Society of Jesus.

The first Jesuits recognized the importance of the *Exercises* and occasionally spoke of them as giving their life and ministries their fundamental orientation. Polanco called them the compendium of all the means the Jesuits had for helping souls. Behind Nadal's exhorting Jesuits to regular repetition of them in abbreviated form had to lie an intuition of their conclusive importance for motivation and for corporate cohesion. Often, however,

Jesuits spoke of them as simply one among the many *consueta ministeria,* without pinpointing how the *Exercises* articulated principles and designs that tended to permeate everything they undertook. Jesuit commentators have sometimes said that the *Constitutions* were a translation of the *Exercises* into institutional form. That is an exaggeration, but it contains more than a grain of truth.

Luther claimed that the doctrine of justification by faith alone was the quintessence of the Gospel, the core of the Christian message. It was certainly the central doctrine for him, the doctrine upon which his theology rested and according to which his practical and pastoral decisions were made. Did the Jesuits have a doctrine or teaching that they similarly singled out or exalted? If so, was it good works, papal primacy, seven sacraments, Real Presence?

The Jesuits never professed to have one. In fact, Luther's designation of a "doctrine"—an *idea*—as bearing the burden of the Christian message ran contrary to the traditional persuasion that the life of Christ was the best expression of what Christianity was all about. Luther shifted the focus from the synoptic Gospels to the Epistle to the Romans. This represented and promoted a subtle but extraordinarily significant change in religious sensibilities. Although the Jesuits would not be unaffected by the change, they were, through the *Exercises* and many other factors, firmly rooted in the earlier tradition. In any case, they were reluctant to pronounce one doctrine more important than another, even though the controversies of the day brought them to speak about some more frequently and to give them a new emphasis—a phenomenon that made the Jesuits agents in the practical imbalance in confessional professions of orthodoxy in post-Reformation Christianity.

There was, however, one "doctrine" that was fundamental for them, one that gave orientation to all their ministries and to the way they wanted to lead their own lives. It was the basic premise of the *Exercises,* even though it was buried unobtrusively in the fifteenth "Preliminary Observation": the Creator deals directly with the creature, and the creature deals directly with the Creator—heart to heart, one might say. Upon this teaching Jesuits based their more characteristic themes—indifference, discernment, and inner devotion, or consolation.

It was this teaching that in one form or another brought Ignatius into question with ecclesiastical authorities at Alcalá, Salamanca, Paris, Venice, and Rome. It was this teaching that sounded to many like the teaching of the *alumbrados,* Erasmians, and Lutherans. It was this teaching that set the

Jesuits off from some of their fellow Catholics who sought a better church—from people like Cano, Catarino, and Carafa. The rage of those who abhorred teaching like this as almost ipso facto heretical drove Catholicism in Italy and Spain into major crisis.

The Jesuits did not suffer as much in the wake of the crisis as did others, like the *spirituali* and Carranza. Ignatius and the Jesuits, at least, understood the teaching within the safe boundaries of Catholic tradition, and they were anything but founders of a Church of the Free Spirit. The fact that the teaching could be questioned or, indeed, attacked so vigorously is a window into sixteenth-century Catholicism. That it received general acceptance is yet another. Later in the century, however, Everard Mercurian, the fourth general, adopted even inside the Society of Jesus a cautious policy that tended to reduce the devout life to moralizing calculation and safe asceticism.

Besides the *Exercises,* what particularly distinguished the Jesuits was their schools. Within a few years of Messina they assigned them, in fact if not always in theory, a preeminent priority among their ministries. This meant some diminution in quantity and intensity of the other *consueta ministeria,* but not so much as we may at first imagine because the schools served as their bases. Not in that way, therefore, did the schools have their greatest impact on the Society.

Part of "our way," part of Jesuit style, was learning. Ignatius and his companions from the beginning advocated and exemplified a learned ministry. This did not, taken in the abstract, distinguish them from their contemporaries but conformed them to the consensus of their age. With the schools, however, came an intensification—as the Jesuits learned in order to teach. Along with intensification came a new modality—as the Jesuits became professionals in the teaching of the pagan classics, the natural sciences, and the performing arts, somehow or other in relationship to *pietas,* somehow or other in relationship to *Christianitas.* The Jesuits—as a group, systemically—became learned clergy their "way." The schools inserted them into secular culture and civic responsibility to a degree unknown to earlier orders. The *Formula* had committed them to work for the "common good," but the schools gave that commitment an institutional grounding that was quite special.

The most important impact the schools had upon the Society was, therefore, cultural. More easily tracked, however, was their sociological impact—on the size of communities, on the practical demotion suffered by professed houses, on the implicit redefinition of aspects of Jesuit poverty when the vast majority of Jesuits began to live in endowed institutions, on a closer bonding with the socioeconomic elite. Last but far from least, the schools recast the ideal of itinerant ministry, the ideal symbolized by the special vow "concerning missions"—the "beginning and principal foundation" of the Society, as Ignatius said of it in 1545.

Ignatius—how did he fit in the ongoing transformation of the Society of Jesus, especially after 1540 or 1547? Remarkable in the nascent Society was the talent and especially the intense and unwavering dedication of so many who joined it. Nonetheless, there would be no Society of Jesus, even after *Regimini militantis ecclesiae,* without Ignatius of Loyola. Rodrigues and Bobadilla were correct in a formal sense when they clamored that the founding was a corporate venture. But Ignatius was the leader.

He inspired confidence and won affection. When Xavier voted for him as general, he voted for "our old leader and true father, Don Ignacio, who, since he brought us together with no little effort, will also with similar effort know how to preserve, govern, and help us advance from good to better."[1] While Ignatius was general, his subjects respected him especially for listening to them with care until they were sure they had been understood.[2] Salmerón burst into tears when he heard of his death.[3] Nadal confessed in his journal that he never visited the room where he died without "spontaneous and sweet tears."[4]

Ignatius was, however, a complex man. He on occasion dealt in harsh and seemingly arbitrary ways with those in Rome who were closest to him. He did not always bear criticism gracefully. Once when Laínez insisted too strongly, he exploded with, "Here, you take the Society and govern it!"[5]

His natural reticence about himself and his stilted and conventional style of writing drew a curtain across much that we would like to know. Early on, moreover, his Jesuit contemporaries began to speak and write of him with a reverence that rendered edifying his every act, making it particularly difficult for later historians to find the man behind the hagiographical veil.

In this atmosphere Bobadilla's taunts can feel like a breath of fresh air. More important, they also raise again the difficult question of where, in the practical governance of the Society, Ignatius's part ended and Polanco's began. It is absolutely clear, however, that even toward the very end of Ignatius's life, when he was chronically sick, he made every major decision. He delegated a great deal, but he continued in charge to the end. His importance for the order looms of course much larger, as by now must be clear. No one more than he helped create its way of proceeding, and, in the eyes of his contemporaries, nobody better exemplified it.

But he did three things that were utterly crucial for the ethos of the

Society. First, he wrote the *Exercises* and made them the basic book of the institution. Second, he was the force behind a most remarkable instrument of governance, the *Constitutions*. Third, when the proper moment arrived for making a decision about the schools, he opened the throttle to full speed ahead.

Leadership is a gift difficult to analyze, but it consists to a large extent in vision, in the ability to see how at a given juncture change is more consistent with one's scope than staying the course. It consists as well in the courage and self-possession required to make the actual decision to change and to convince others of the validity and viability of the new direction. Such was Ignatius's vision and courage about the schools.

He had another ability that is equally important for a leader. He could recognize and utilize talents that complemented his own. The caliber of the provincials and rectors throughout the order, many of whom were hand-picked by him, were by and large proof of this gift. More striking, however, were the roles Ignatius conceded to Polanco and Nadal—without doubt the two Jesuits who, after himself, most effectively animated the young Society and gave it shape. It would be difficult to imagine two better choices or more open-handed delegations of responsibility.

How did the Society of Jesus come to be? The answer is dense and complicated, but at a certain point it devolves onto the human factor—the companions of Paris, the great recruits like Borja and Canisius, the many others, such as Ribadeneira, Loarte, Possevino, Doménech, Araoz, Bustamante, Toledo, Ledesma, Nóbrega, and Anchieta. In this regard, however, three outstrip the others by far—Polanco, Nadal, and Ignatius. According to Polanco, Ignatius possessed "in an uncommon degree certain natural gifts from God: great energy in undertaking extraordinarily difficult tasks, great constancy in pursuing them, and great prudence in seeing them to completion."[6] What he said of Ignatius could be applied as well to himself and Nadal, which makes it another important key to the character and development of the early Society of Jesus.

Abbreviations

Monumenta Historica Societatis Iesu (MHSI)

Chron. Juan Alfonso de Polanco, *Vita Ignatii Loiolae et rerum Societatis Jesu historica* [*Chronicon*], 6 vols. (Madrid, 1894–98)

Epist. Mixtae Epistolae mixtae ex variis Europae locis ab anno 1537 ad 1556 scriptae, 5 vols. (Madrid, 1898–1901)

FN Fontes narrativi de S. Ignatio de Loyola et de Societatis Jesu initiis, 4 vols. (Rome, 1943–65)

Litt. Quadr. Litterae Quadrimestres ex universis praeter Indiam et Brasiliam locis in quibus aliqui de Societate Jesu versabantur Romam missae, 7 vols. (Madrid and Rome, 1894–1932)

M Bobad. Nicolai Alphonsi de Bobadilla sacerdotis e Societate Jesu Gesta et scripta (Madrid, 1913)

M Borgia Sanctus Franciscus Borgia quartus Gandiae Dux et Societatis Jesu Praepositus Generalis tertius, 5 vols. (Madrid, 1894–1911)

M Bras. Monumenta Brasiliae, 5 vols. (Rome, 1956–68)

M Broët Epistolae PP. Paschasii Broëti, Claudii Jaji, Joannis Codurii et Simonis Roderici (Madrid, 1903)

M Fabri B. Petri Fabri primi sacerdotis e Societate Jesu Epistolae, memoriale et processus (Madrid, 1914)

MI Const. Monumenta Ignatiana. Sancti

Ignatii de Loyola Constitutiones Societatis Jesu, 3 vols. (Rome, 1934–38)

MI Epp. Monumenta Ignatiana. Sancti Ignatii de Loyola Societatis Jesu fundatoris epistolae et instructiones, 12 vols. (Madrid, 1903–11)

MI Ex. Monumenta Ignatiana. Exercitia spiritualia S. Ignatii de Loyola et eorum directoria, 2nd ed. rev., 2 vols. (Madrid, 1919; Rome, 1969)

MI Font. Doc. Monumenta Ignatiana. Fontes documentales de S. Ignatio de Loyola (Rome, 1977)

MI Reg. Monumenta Ignatiana. Regulae Societatis Jesu (1540–1556) (Rome, 1948)

MI Scripta Monumenta Ignatiana. Scripta de Sancto Ignatio de Loyola, 2 vols. (Madrid, 1904–18)

M Lain. Epistolae et acta Patris Jacobi Lainii, 8 vols. (Madrid, 1912–17)

M Nadal Epistolae P. Hieronymi Nadal Societatis Jesu ab anno 1546 ad 1577, 4 vols. (Madrid, 1898–1905), and *Commentarii de Instituto Societatis Jesu* (Rome, 1962)

M Paed. Monumenta paedagogica Societatis Jesu, 2nd ed. rev., 5 vols. (Rome, 1965–86)

M Rib. Patris Petri de Ribadeneira Societatis Jesu sacerdotis Confessiones, epis-

tolae aliaque scripta inedita, 2 vols. (Madrid, 1920–23)

M Salm. *Epistolae P. Alphonsi Salmeronis,* 2 vols. (Madrid, 1906–7)

M Xav. *Epistolae S. Francisci Xaverii aliaque eius scripta,* 2nd ed. rev., 2 vols. (Rome, 1944–45)

P Co. *Polanci Complementa. Epistolae et commentaria P. Joannis Alphonsi de Polanco,* 2 vols. (Madrid, 1916–17)

Other Sources

AHSI Archivum Historicum Societatis Iesu (journal)

ARSI *Archivum Romanum Societatis Iesu* (central archives)

Autobiography Ignatius's account of his early life, without title, critically edited in *MI Scripta,* 1:31–98

Const. The *Constitutions* of the Society of Jesus, critically edited in *MI Const.*

Nadal, *Orat. Obs.* Jerónimo Nadal, *Orationis observationes,* ed. Miguel Nicolau (Rome: Institutum Historicum Societatis Iesu, 1964)

Nadal, *Pláticas* Jerónimo Nadal, *Pláticas espirituales del P. Jerónimo Nadal, S.I., en Coimbra (1561),* ed. Miguel Nicolau (Granada: Facoltad Teologica de la Compañía de Jesús, 1945)

Nadal, *Scholia* Jerónimo Nadal, *Scholia in Constitutiones S.I.,* ed. Manuel Ruiz Jurado (Granada: Facultad de Teologia, 1976)

SpEx. The *Spiritual Exercises* of Ignatius of Loyola, critically edited in *MI Ex.,* 1:140–417

Notes

In the notes, the *Spiritual Exercises,* the so-called *Autobiography* of Ignatius of Loyola, and the *Constitutions* of the Society of Jesus are cited by the standard paragraph numbers. For those first two works, quotations in English are from *Ignatius of Loyola: The Spiritual Exercises and Selected Works,* ed. George E. Ganss (New York: Paulist Press, 1991), and for the last they are from *The Constitutions of the Society of Jesus,* trans. George E. Ganss (St. Louis: The Institute of Jesuit Sources, 1970). I have on rare occasions slightly modified these versions. All other translations are my own unless otherwise indicated.

Introduction

1. John Addington Symonds, *The Catholic Reaction,* 2 vols. (vols. 5–6 of *Renaissance in Italy*) (London: Smith, Elder, and Company, 1886), 1:65.

2. See, for example, John W. O'Malley, ed., *Catholicism in Early Modern History: A Guide to Research* (St. Louis: Center for Reformation Research, 1988), and Anne Jacobson Schutte, "Periodization of Sixteenth-Century Italian Religious History: The Post-Cantimori Paradigm Shift," *The Journal of Modern History,* 61 (1989), 269–284.

3. See, for example, Steven Ozment, ed., *Reformation Europe: A Guide to Research* (St. Louis: Center for Reformation Research, 1982).

4. See the review of literature by John Patrick Donnelly, "Religious Orders of Men, Especially the Society of Jesus," in O'Malley, *Catholicism,* pp. 147–162. The most important and comprehensive bibliographical instrument is László Polgár, *Bibliographie sur l'histoire de la Compagnie de Jésus, 1901–1980,* 3 vols. (Rome: Institutum Historicum Societatis Jesu, 1981–90). For current scholarship, see the listings in *AHSI.* For works written by Jesuits, the basic reference is still Carlos Sommervogel, *Bibliothèque de la Compagnie de Jésus,* 11 vols. (Brussels: O. Schepens; Paris: A. Picard, 1890–1932).

5. The most compendious of recent biographies is Ricardo García-Villoslada, *San Ignacio de Loyola: Nueva biografía* (Madrid: Biblioteca de Autores Cristianos, 1986). Concise and factually reliable is Cándido de Dalmases, *Ignatius of Loyola, Founder of the Jesuits: His Life and Work,* trans. Jerome Aixalá (St. Louis: The Institute of Jesuit Sources, 1985). A thoughtful study dealing with the period with which this book is concerned is André Ravier, *Ignatius of Loyola and the Founding of the Society of Jesus,* trans. Maura Daly, Joan Daly, and Carson Daly (San Francisco: Ignatius Press, 1987). For discussion of the scholarly problem, see Marjorie O'Rourke Boyle, "Angels Black and White: Loyola's

Spiritual Discernment in Historical Perspective," *Theological Studies,* 44 (1983), 241–257, and Philip Endean, "Who Do You Say Ignatius Is? Jesuit Fundamentalism and Beyond," *Studies in the Spirituality of Jesuits,* 19/5 (1987). See also William W. Meissner, "Psychoanalytic Hagiography: The Case of Ignatius of Loyola," *Theological Studies,* 52 (1991), 3–33, and *Ignatius of Loyola: The Psychology of a Saint* (New Haven: Yale University Press, 1992). A number of important studies concerning Ignatius and his generation of Jesuits are contained in Andreas Falkner and Paul Imhof, eds., *Ignatius von Loyola und die Gesellschaft Jesu, 1491–1556* (Würzburg: Echter Verlag, 1990), and Juan Plazaola, ed., *Ignacio de Loyola y su tiempo* (Bilbao: Ediciones Mensajero, 1992). Also useful, but ranging more widely, is Michael Sievernich and Günter Switek, eds., *Ignatianisch: Eigenart und Methode der Gesellschaft Jesu* (Freiburg: Herder, 1990). For the comprehensive bibliography, see Ignacio Iparraguirre, ed., *Orientaciones bibliográficas sobre San Ignacio de Loyola,* 2nd ed., rev. (Rome: Institutum Historicum Societatis Jesu, 1965), continued in two subsequent volumes edited by Manuel Ruiz Jurado, 1977 and 1990.

6. Mario Scaduto, *L'epoca di Giacomo Laínez (1556–1565),* 2 vols. (Rome: Edizioni la Civiltà Cattolica, 1964–74).

7. See Dominique Bertrand, *La politique de s. Ignace de Loyola: L'analyse sociale* (Paris: Editions du Cerf, 1985), p. 39.

8. The most concise and reliable commentary is Antonio M. de Aldama, *The Formula of the Institute: Notes for a Commentary,* trans. Ignacio Echániz (St. Louis: The Institute of Jesuit Sources, 1990).

9. See Manuel Ruiz Jurado, "Nadal y Polanco sobre la Fórmula del Instituto de la Compañía de Jesús," *AHSI,* 47 (1978), 225–239.

10. Ganss, *Constitutions,* pp. 66–67.

11. Ibid., p. 68.

12. See Antonio M. de Aldama, *The Constitutions of the Society of Jesus: An Introductory Commentary on the Constitutions,* trans. Aloysius J. Owen (St. Louis: The Institute of Jesuit Sources, 1989), pp. 2–11.

13. See Ganss's comments, *Constitutions,* pp. 35–59.

14. *M Nadal,* 5:304–305. See *Const.,* #152, 216.

15. *FN,* 1:354–507. The work has been translated into English a number of times, most recently by Joseph N. Tylenda under the title *A Pilgrim's Journey: The Autobiography of Ignatius of Loyola* (Wilmington, Del.: Michael Glazier, 1985), and by Parmananda R. Divarkar in *Ignatius of Loyola: The Spiritual Exercises and Selected Works,* ed. George E. Ganss (New York: Paulist Press, 1991), pp. 65–111. For the other translations and the origins of the document, see Tylenda, *Autobiography,* pp. ix–xiv.

16. See the comments of the editors, *FN,* 1:330–331.

17. See Miguel Nicolau, *Jerónimo Nadal, S.I. (1507–1580): Sus obras y doctrinas espirituales* (Madrid: Consejo Superior de Investigaciones Científicas, 1949), pp. 148–151, and John H. Wright, "The Grace of Our Founder and the Grace of Our Vocation," *Studies in the Spirituality of Jesuits,* 3/1 (1971).

18. The only major study is Bertrand, *La politique.* See also Joseph A. Munitiz, "Communicating Channels: Letters to Reveal and to Govern," *The Way,* supplement no. 70 (1991), 64–75. There are several English translations of selected letters, such as *Letters of St. Ignatius of Loyola,* trans. William J. Young (Chicago: Loyola University Press, 1959). The most copiously annotated is Hugo Rahner, ed., *Saint Ignatius Loyola: Letters to Women,* trans. Kathleen Pond and S. A. H. Weetman (Edinburgh and London: Nelson, 1960).

19. The best guide, though outdated and limited in scope, is Jean-François Gilmont, *Les écrits spirituels des premiers jésuites: Inventaire commenté* (Rome: Institutum Historicum Societatis Jesu, 1961), pp. 113–166. See also, of course, Sommervogel, *Bibliothèque de la Compagnie de Jesús.*

20. See James Brodrick, *Saint Peter Canisius* (Chicago: Loyola University Press, 1962). Unlike that of the other early Jesuits, his correspondence is not in the MHSI, but was independently undertaken by Otto Braunsberger, *Beati Petri Canisii Societatis Jesu Epistulae et Acta,* 8 vols. (Freiburg: Herder, 1896–1923). See also Gilmont, *Ecrits,* pp. 209–231.

21. See Cándido de Dalmases, *Saint Francis Borgia, Grandee of Spain, Jesuit, Saint,* trans. Cornelius Michael Buckley (St. Louis: The Institute of Jesuit Sources, 1991). See also Gilmont, *Ecrits,* pp. 169–192.

22. For basic biographical information, see Antonio M. de Aldama, *Imagen ignatiana del jesuita en los escritos de Polanco* (Rome: Centrum Ignatianum Spiritualitatis, 1975), pp. 7–30, and Constance Jones Mathers, "Early Spanish Qualms about Loyola and the Society of Jesus," *The Historian,* 53 (1991), 679–690. Of special importance is Angelo Martini, "Gli studi teologici di Giovanni de Polanco alle origini della legislazione scolastica della Compagnia di Gesù," *AHSI,* 21 (1952), 225–281. See also Clara Englander, *Ignatius von Loyola und Johannes von Polanco: Der Ordensstifter und sein Sekretär* (Regensburg: F. Pustet, 1956).

23. See Gilmont, *Ecrits,* pp. 196–208.

24. Juan Alfonso de Polanco, *Breve directorium ad confessarii et confitentis munus rite obeundum* (Rome: A. Blado, 1554).

25. Polanco, *Methodus ad eos adiuvandos qui moriuntur* (Macerata: Sebastiano Martellini, 1575).

26. See André Ravier, *La Compagnie de Jésus sous le gouvernement d'Ignace de Loyola (1541–1556): D'après les Chroniques de J.-A. de Polanco* (Paris: Desclée de Brouwer, 1990).

27. See Dennis Edmond Pate, "Jerónimo Nadal and the Early Development of the Society of Jesus, 1545–1573" (Ph.D. diss., University of California, Los Angeles, 1980); Manuel Ruiz Jurado, "Cronología de la vida del P. Jerónimo Nadal, S.I. (1507–1580)," *AHSI,* 48 (1979), 248–276; William V. Bangert, *Jerome Nadal, S.J. (1507–1580): Tracking the First Generation of Jesuits,* ed. Thomas M. McCoog (Chicago: Loyola University Press, 1992).

28. *MI Epp.,* 5:109.

29. *M Nadal,* 1:144.

30. See "Nadal, Jerôme," in *Dictionnaire de spiritualité.*

31. See Gilmont, *Ecrits,* pp. 232–249, which is especially outdated for Nadal.

32. See Nicolau, *Nadal.*

33. *M Nadal,* 5:524–774.

34. *Scholia in Constitutiones S.I.,* ed. Manuel Ruiz Jurado (Granada: Facultad de Teologia, 1976).

35. See John W. O'Malley, "To Travel to Any Part of the World: Jerónimo Nadal and the Jesuit Vocation," *Studies in the Spirituality of Jesuits,* 16/2 (1984).

36. The thesis is sharply formulated by Gottfried Maron, "Das Schicksal der katholischen Reform im 16. Jahrhundert: Zur Frage nach der Kontinuität in der Kirchengeschichte," *Zeitschrift für Kirchengeschichte,* 88 (1977), 218–229. See also Paolo Simoncelli, "Inquisizione romana e Riforma in Italia," *Rivista Storica Italiana,* 100 (1988), 1–125.

37. See John W. O'Malley, "Was Ignatius Loyola a Church Reformer? How To Look at Early Modern Catholicism," *The Catholic Historical Review,* 77 (1991), 177–193. See also Roberto Rusconi, "Gli ordini religiosi maschili dalla controriforma alle soppressioni set-

tecentesche: Cultura, predicazione, missioni," in *Clero e società nell'Italia moderna,* ed. Mario Rosa (Bari: Editori Laterza, 1992), pp. 207–274.

38. *SpEx.,* #316.

39. *FN,* 2:338.

40. See, for example, Jean Delumeau, *Sin and Fear: The Emergence of a Western Guilt Culture, 13th-18th Centuries,* trans. Eric Nicholson (New York: St. Martin's Press, 1990). For a discussion, see Robert Bireley, "Two Works by Jean Delumeau," *The Catholic Historical Review,* 77 (1991), 78–88. As Bireley points out, Delumeau also develops themes of peace and security, which are perhaps most prominent in his recent *L'aveu et la pardon: Les difficultés de la confession XIIIe–XVIIIe siècle* (Paris: Fayard, 1990). For a recent study that challenges part of the thesis, see Larissa Taylor, *Soldiers of Christ: Preaching in Late Medieval and Reformation France* (New York and Oxford: Oxford University Press, 1992).

41. See Agostino Borromeo, "The Inquisition and Inquisitorial Censorship," in O'Malley, *Catholicism,* pp. 253–272.

42. See Jean Delumeau, *Un chemin d'histoire: Chrétienté et christianisation* (Paris: Fayard, 1981).

1. Foundations before the Founding

1. The most detailed accounts of Ignatius and his companions up to 1540 are in the first volume of Georg Schurhammer, *Francis Xavier: His Life, His Times,* trans. M. Joseph Costelloe, 4 vols. (Rome: The Jesuit Historical Institute, 1973–82), and Ricardo García-Villoslada, *San Ignacio de Loyola: Nueva biografía* (Madrid: Biblioteca de Autores Cristianos, 1986).

2. *Chron.,* 1:10, 13. For the cultural context of these early years, see Rogelio García-Mateo, "Ignatius von Loyola in seiner sozio-kulturellen Umwelt: Spanien 1491–1527," in *Ignatianisch: Eigenart und Methode der Gesellschaft Jesu,* ed. Michael Sievernich and Günter Switek (Freiburg: Herder, 1990), pp. 19–41. For the religious context, see Mark Rotsaert, *Ignace de Loyola et les renouveaux spirituels en Castille au début du XVIe siècle* (Rome: Centrum Ignatianum Spiritualitatis, 1982).

3. See Anselmo M. Albareda, "Intorno alla scuola di orazione metodica stabilita a Monserrato dall' abate Garsías Jiménez de Cisneros (1493–1510)," *AHSI,* 25 (1956), 254–316.

4. *FN,* 2:344.

5. *Autobiography,* #29.

6. *Autobiography,* #27. See also *Chron.,* 1:25.

7. See Pedro de Leturia, "Génesis de los ejercicios de San Ignacio y su influjo en la fundación de la Compañía de Jesús (1521–1540)," *Estudios Ignacianos,* ed. Ignacio Iparraguirre, 2 vols. (Rome: Institutum Historicum Societatis Jesu, 1957), 2:3–55.

8. *Autobiography,* #50.

9. *Autobiography,* #57.

10. On the *alumbrados,* see Melquíades Andrés Martín, *Los recogidos: Nueva visión de la mística española (1500–1700)* (Madrid: Fundación Universitaria Española, 1975), and Massimo Marcocchi, "Spirituality in the Sixteenth and Seventeenth Centuries," in *Catholicism in Early Modern History: A Guide to Research,* ed. John W. O'Malley (St. Louis: Center for Reformation Research, 1988), especially pp. 164–166. For the later period, see Alvaro Huerga, *Historia de los Alumbrados (1570–1630),* 4 vols. (Madrid: Fundación Universitaria Española, Seminario Cisneros, 1978–88).

11. See Luis Fernández, "Iñigo de Loyola y los alumbrados," *Hispania Sacra,* 35 (1983), 585–680.

12. *Autobiography*, #85.

13. See I. Rodriguez-Grahit, "Ignace de Loyola et le Collège Montaigu: L'influence de Standonk sur Ignace," *Bibliothèque d'Humanisme et Renaissance*, 20 (1958), 388–401.

14. See Gabriel María Verd, "De Iñigo a Ignacio: El cambio de nombre en San Ignacio de Loyola," *AHSI*, 60 (1991), 113–160.

15. There is a popular biography by William V. Bangert, *To Other Towns: A Life of Blessed Peter Favre, First Companion of St. Ignatius* (Westminster, Md.: Newman Press, 1959). I have not been able to consult E. Niemann, *Pierre Favre, Priester der Gesellschaft Jesu, und die Anfänge der katholischen Reform in Deutschland* (Innsbruck, 1963). For further bibliography, see Brian O'Leary, "The Discernment of Spirits in the Memoriale of Blessed Peter Favre," *The Way*, supplement no. 35 (1979).

16. The most reliable edition to date, with an introduction, is not the Latin text in the MHSI but the French translation by Michel de Certeau, *Mémorial* (Paris: Desclée de Brouwer, 1960).

17. See Schurhammer, *Xavier*, 1:1–273.

18. See Mario Scaduto, *L'epoca di Giacomo Laínez, 1556–1565,* 2 vols. (Rome: Edizioni la Civiltà Cattolica, 1964–74).

19. See William V. Bangert, *Claude Jay and Alfonso Salmerón: Two Early Jesuits* (Chicago: Loyola University Press, 1985).

20. The edition I used is *Commentarii in Evangelicam Historiam, et in Acta apostolorum,* 12 vols., and, considered a continuation, *Commentarii in omnes Epistolas B. Pauli et canonicas,* 4 vols. (Cologne: A. Hierat and I Gymnicus, 1612–15). See John D. Willis, " 'Love Your Enemies': Sixteenth-Century Interpretations," (Ph.D. diss., University of Chicago, 1989).

21. See José Carlos Monteiro Pacheco, *Simão Rodrigues: Iniciador da Companhia de Jesus em Portugal* (Braga: Editorial A. O., 1987).

22. There is no biography or full-scale study. See, however, Arthur L. Fisher, "A Study in Early Jesuit Government: The Nature and Origins of the Dissent of Nicolás Bobadilla," *Viator*, 10 (1979), 397–431.

23. *MI Epp.*, 1:148–151.

24. On Jay, see Bangert, *Jay and Salmerón*. There are no full-scale studies of Broët and Codure. For chronologies for all ten members of the original band, with references to the sources, see the contributions by Giuseppe Mellinato and others, *AHSI*, 59 (1990), 179–344.

25. *M Broët*, p. 475.

26. *FN*, 1:204.

27. See Jesús Iturrioz, "Compañía de Jesús: Sentido histórico y ascético de este nombre," *Manresa*, 27 (1955), 43–53.

28. *M Broët*, pp. 495–496.

29. *M Bobad.*, p. 616.

30. *P Co.*, 2:720. See Thomas M. Lucas, "The Vineyard at the Crossroad: The Urban Vision of Ignatius of Loyola" (Ph.D. diss., Graduate Theological Union, Berkeley, 1991), especially pp. 67–79.

31. See Jean-Claude Guy, "Les 'Exercices Spirituels' de saint Ignace: L'achèvement du texte," *Nouvelle Revue Théologique*, 107 (1985), 255–260.

32. The bibliography is huge. For works in English, see Paul Begheyn and Kenneth Bogart, "A Bibliography on St. Ignatius's *Spiritual Exercises*," *Studies in the Spirituality of Jesuits*, 23/3 (1991).

33. *SpEx.*, #1.

34. See Juan Alfonso de Polanco, *MI Ex.*, 2:277, 279, 285, 286, 293. At one point Canisius makes them sound Stoic, ibid., 2:134.

35. See Louis Dupré, "Ignatian Humanism and Its Mystical Origins," *Communio*, 18 (1991), 164–182.

36. *SpEx.*, #135–189.

37. *SpEx.*, #18.

38. *SpEx.*, #19.

39. *M Nadal*, 4:849–852; 5:843–844.

40. See Ignacio Iparraguirre, *Historia de la práctica de los Ejercicios Espirituales de San Ignacio de Loyola*, 3 vols. under slightly different titles (Rome: Institutum Historicum Societatis Jesu, 1946–73), 1:136.

41. *SpEx.*, #23.

42. *SpEx.*, #18.

43. *MI Ex.*, 2:306–307; *SpEx.*, #170–174.

44. *SpEx.*, #91–99.

45. *SpEx.*, #136–148.

46. *SpEx.*, #4.

47. *SpEx.*, #230–237.

48. *SpEx.*, #337–351.

49. *SpEx.*, #313–336.

50. See Hugo Rahner, *Ignatius the Theologian*, trans. Michael Barry (New York: Herder and Herder, 1968), pp. 136–180. Recent literature on them is abundant. See, for example, Michael Schneider, *"Unterscheidung der Geister": Die ignatianischen Exerzitien in der Deutung von E. Przywara, K. Rahner, und G. Fessard* (Innsbruck and Vienna: Tyrolia-Verlag, 1983), and Jules J. Toner, *A Commentary on Saint Ignatius' Rules for the Discernment of Spirits: A Guide to the Principles and Practice* (St. Louis: The Institute of Jesuit Sources, 1982).

51. *SpEx.*, #234.

52. *SpEx.*, #55, 87, 195.

53. *SpEx.*, #175–188.

54. *MI Ex.*, 2:314–315.

55. *MI Ex.*, 2:279.

56. *SpEx.*, #327.

57. The text of the journal is in *MI Const.*, 1:86–158. See *Inigo: Discernment Log-Book—The Spiritual Diary of Saint Ignatius Loyola*, ed. and trans. Joseph A. Munitiz (London: Inigo Enterprises, 1987).

58. *SpEx.*, #100.

59. *SpEx.*, #15.

60. *SpEx.*, #14.

61. See Iparraguirre, *Historia*, 1:83–115.

62. See, for example, my introduction to vol. 66 (*Spiritualia*) of the *Collected Works of Erasmus* (Toronto, Buffalo, London: University of Toronto Press, 1988), pp. xviii–xix, xxxiii–xxxiv, xlviii–xlix.

63. *MI Ex.*, 2:314.

64. *SpEx.*, #145.

65. *MI Ex.*, 2:78–79, 81. See also ibid., 2:313.

66. *MI Ex.*, 2:95.

67. See Miguel Nicolau, *Jerónimo Nadal, S.I. (1507–1580): Sus obras y doctrinas espirituales* (Madrid: Consejo Superior de Investigaciones Científicas, 1949), pp. 350–355.

68. *M Nadal,* 5:289.

69. *M Nadal,* 5:297.

70. *M Nadal,* 5:295.

71. See Antonio M. de Aldama, *The Formula of the Institute: Notes for a Commentary,* trans. Ignacio Echániz (St. Louis: The Institute of Jesuit Sources, 1990), p. 38.

72. *SpEx.,* #230–237.

73. *Const.,* #288.

74. *M Nadal,* 5:364–365, 469–470. See John W. O'Malley, "To Travel to Any Part of the World: Jerónimo Nadal and the Jesuit Vocation," *Studies in the Spirituality of Jesuits,* 16/2 (1984).

75. *MI Ex.,* 2:60–64; *Chron.,* 1:25.

76. H. Outram Evennett, *The Spirit of the Counter-Reformation* (Cambridge: Cambridge University Press, 1968), p. 45.

77. See Emmerich Raitz von Frentz, "Ludolphe le Chartreux et les Exercises de S. Ignace de Loyola," *Revue d'Ascétique et de Mystique,* 25 (1949), 375–388; Andreas Falkner, "Was las Iñigo de Loyola auf seinem Krankenlager? Zum Prooemium der 'Vita Jesu Christi,'" *Geist und Leben,* 61 (1988), 258–284; Johannes Beutler, "Die Rolle der Heiligen Schrift im geistlichen Werden des Ignatius," in Sievernich, *Ignatianisch,* pp. 42–53; George E. Ganss, ed., *Ignatius of Loyola: Spiritual Exercises and Selected Works* (New York: Paulist Press, 1991), pp. 19–26.

78. On the *Meditationes,* see Daniel R. Lesnick, *Preaching in Medieval Florence: The Social World of Franciscan and Dominican Spirituality* (Athens: The University of Georgia Press, 1989), pp. 143–171. See also Ewert H. Cousins, "Franciscan Roots of Ignatian Meditation," in *Ignatian Spirituality in a Secular Age,* ed. George P. Schner (Waterloo, Ontario: Wilfrid Laurier University Press, 1984), pp. 51–64.

79. See Manuel Ruiz Jurado, "Hacia las fuentes del principio y fundamento de los Ejercicios," *Gregorianum,* 58 (1977), 727–756.

80. See de Leturia, "El 'Reino de Cristo' y los prólogos del 'Flos Sanctorum' de Loyola," *Estudios,* 2:57–72, especially 62–64.

81. See Terence W. O'Reilly, "The Exercises of Saint Ignatius Loyola and the 'Exercitatorio de la vida spiritual,'" *Studia Monastica,* 16 (1974), 301–323, and Manuel Ruiz Jurado, "¿Influyó en S. Ignacio el Ejercitatorio de Cisneros?" *Manresa,* 51 (1979), 65–75.

82. See the comments by the editors, *MI Ex.,* 1:34–60.

83. See Dupré, "Ignatian Humanism"; Terence W. O'Reilly, "The Spiritual Exercises and the Crisis of Medieval Piety," *The Way,* supplement no. 70 (1991), 101–113; and Mark Rotsaert, "L'originalité des Exercises Spirituels d'Ignace de Loyola sur l'arrière-fond des renouveaux spirituels en Castille au début du seizième siècle," in *Ignacio de Loyola y su tiempo,* ed. Juan Plazaola (Bilbao: Ediciones Mensajero, 1992), pp. 329–341.

84. See "Retraites spirituelles," in *Dictionnaire de spiritualité.*

85. See Iparraguirre, *Historia,* 1:32*–34*.

86. See "Direction spirituelle," in *Dictionnaire de spiritualité.*

87. *M Nadal,* 5:787.

88. *Chron.,* 3:552–554.

89. *M Nadal,* 5:484.

90. *SpEx.,* #238–260.

91. *MI Ex.,* 2:185.

92. *MI Ex.,* 2:170.

93. *MI Ex.,* 2:198.

94. *SpEx.*, #10.

95. *Chron.*, 3:543.

96. *M Nadal*, 5:93.

97. *SpEx.*, #352–370.

98. See Pascual Cebollada, "Loyola y Erasmo: Aportaciones al estudio de la relación entre ambos," *Manresa*, 62 (1990), 49–60, especially 56–59.

99. See Paul Dudon, *St. Ignatius of Loyola*, trans. William J. Young (Milwaukee: The Bruce Publishing Company, 1949), pp. 457–462.

100. *MI Ex.*, 2:327–328. See Philippe Lécrivain, "Ignace de Loyola, un réformateur? Une lecture historique des 'Règles pour avoir le vrai sens de l'Eglise,'" *Christus*, 37 (1990), 348–360.

101. See Marjorie O'Rourke Boyle, "Angels Black and White: Loyola's Spiritual Discernment in Historical Perspective," *Theological Studies*, 44 (1983), 241–257.

102. See Iparraguirre, *Historia*, 1:100–101. The controversy caused the Jesuits much anguish; see *MI Epp.*, 8:258, 343, 413; *Chron.*, 3:335–336, 523–524; 4:416, 473–474.

103. *MI Ex.*, 2:292, 281.

104. *MI Ex.*, 2:403, 458, 505, 742.

105. *MI Ex.*, 2:743.

106. *M Paed.*, 2:129–133.

2. Taking Shape for Ministry

1. *Const.*, #661. See John Carroll Futrell, *Making an Apostolic Community of Love: The Role of the Superior according to St. Ignatius Loyola* (St. Louis: The Institute of Jesuit Sources, 1970), pp. 76–79.

2. See Antonio M. de Aldama, *Unir a los repartidos: Comentario a la octava parte de las Constituciones de la Compañía de Jesús* (Rome: Centrum Ignatianum Spiritualitatis, 1976); Francisco Javier Egaña, *Orígines de la Congregación General en la Compañía de Jesús: Estudio histórico-jurídico de la octava parte de las Constituciones* (Rome: Institutum Historicum Societatis Jesu, 1972). See also J. Amadeo, "La Congregación General de la Compañía de Jesús: Permanece o cambia en sus lineamientos básicos? Notas al libro del P. Francisco Javier Egaña, S.J.," *Stromata*, 35 (1979), 275–295.

3. *Const.*, #677.

4. *Chron.*, 1:360.

5. *Chron.*, 2:5–6.

6. *Chron.*, 2:419.

7. *Chron.*, 3:5.

8. See Egaña, *Orígines*, pp. 163–164.

9. *MI Epp.*, 9:182; 8:584, 657.

10. *P. Co.*, 1:550.

11. *Chron.*, 1:419, 454.

12. *Chron.*, 6:781.

13. *Chron.*, 2:35.

14. *Chron.*, 1:169.

15. See Thomas Vance Cohen, "The Social Origins of the Jesuits, 1540–1600," 2 vols. (Ph.D. diss., Harvard University, 1973), 1:7, 186–212, and "Why the Jesuits Joined, 1540–1600," *Historical Papers* (The Canadian Historical Association, 1974), pp. 237–258.

16. *Chron.*, 4:410–415. See Ignacio Iparraguirre, *Historia de la práctica de los ejercicios espírituales de San Ignacio de Loyola*, 3 vols. under slightly different titles (Rome:

Institutum Historicum Societatis Jesu; Bilbao: El Mensajero del Corazón de Jesús, 1946–73), 1:144.

17. See Cohen, "Social Origins," 1:134–159.

18. *M Nadal*, 4:547–552.

19. *M Nadal*, 1:789–795.

20. See Cohen, "Social Origins"; "Why Jesuits Joined"; "Sociologie de la croyance: Jésuites au Portugal et en Espagne (1540–1562)," in *Les jésuites parmi les hommes aux XVIe et XVIIe siècles: Actes du Colloque de Clermont-Ferrand (avril 1985)*, ed. G. and G. Demerson, B. Dompnier, and A. Regond (Clermont-Ferrand: Association des Publications de la Faculté des Lettres et Sciences Humaines, 1987), pp. 21–34; and "Molteplicità dell'esperienza religiosa tra i primi 1259 Gesuiti, 1540–1560," *Annali Accademici Canadesi*, 1 (1985), 7–25.

21. See Cohen, "Why Jesuits Joined," pp. 243–247.

22. *Chron.*, 1:248.

23. *Chron.*, 1:410.

24. *Chron.*, 2:316.

25. *Chron.*, 1:256.

26. *Chron.*, 4:274–275.

27. *Chron.*, 6:223.

28. *Chron.*, 1:272, 285.

29. See Manuel Ruiz Jurado, "Noticias inéditas sobre la casa profesa de Roma en tiempos de san Ignacio," *AHSI*, 53 (1984), p. 291.

30. *Chron.*, 2:327–328, 351.

31. See Ruiz Jurado, "Noticias," p. 291.

32. *M Nadal*, 4:482.

33. See Cohen, "Why Jesuits Joined," p. 251.

34. See Cohen, "Social Origins," 2:566–619, and A. Lynn Martin, "Vocational Crises and the Crisis in Vocations among Jesuits in France during the Sixteenth Century," *The Catholic Historical Review*, 72 (1986), 201–221, especially 205–206.

35. See Martin, "Vocational Crises," pp. 205–206.

36. See Cohen, "Social Origins," 2:567–580, and Mario Scaduto, "Il 'Libretto consolatorio' di Bobadilla a Domènech [*sic*] sulle vocazioni mancate (1570)," *AHSI*, 43 (1974), 85–102.

37. *MI Scripta*, 1:505–506.

38. See Georg Schurhammer, *Francis Xavier: His Life and Times*, trans. M. Joseph Costelloe, 4 vols. (Rome: The Jesuit Historical Institute, 1973–82), 4:546.

39. *Chron.*, 6:200.

40. *MI Epp.*, 1:344–345. See William J. Bouwsma, *Concordia Mundi: The Career and Thought of Guillaume Postel (1510–1581)* (Cambridge, Mass.: Harvard University Press, 1957), pp. 10–13.

41. *MI Epp.*, 12:635; *MI Scripta*, 1:708–712; *M Broët*, p. 289.

42. *M Lain.*, 6:268–271. See *FN*, 3:753–765.

43. See Cohen, "Social Origins," 2:600–619.

44. *Chron.*, 3:60.

45. *Chron.*, 5:203–204.

46. *Chron.*, 6:54.

47. See Bernhard Duhr, *Geschichte der Jesuiten in den Ländern deutscher Zunge im XVI. Jahrhundert* (Freiburg: Herderische Verlangshandlung, 1907), p. 546.

48. For an unusual but illustrative case, see A. Lynn Martin, "Madness among the Early Jesuits: The Case of Hans Winckler," *AHSI*, 56 (1987), 293–297.

49. Cohen, "Social Origins," 2:606–612.

50. *Chron.*, 5:169.

51. *MI Epp.*, 11:275–277.

52. *Chron.*, 5:126.

53. *Chron.*, 3:178.

54. *Chron.*, 1:248; 5:562.

55. *FN*, 2:475–476; 3:611; *P Co.*, 2:772; see especially *MI Scripta*, 1:444–446.

56. *Chron.*, 3:20; 5:103. See also Cohen, "Social Origins," 2:580–582; Duhr, *Geschichte der Jesuiten*, p. 545.

57. See Martin, "Vocational Crises," pp. 213–216.

58. See Cohen, "Social Origins," 2:573.

59. *Const.*, #223–229.

60. See Scaduto, " 'Libretto consolatorio,' " p. 101.

61. See Cohen, "Social Origins," 1:214–274.

62. *Chron.*, 6:311–312.

63. *P Co.*, 1:517; *M Nadal*, 4:160. For a special case, see Hugues Didier, "Une vocation guidée par saint Ignace de Loyola: Juan de Mendoza, S.I.," *AHSI*, 46 (1977), 362–376.

64. *P Co.*, 1:285–286, 517.

65. *MI Epp.*, 6:569–570.

66. *Chron.*, 2:359.

67. See *O Colégio de "Jesus" dos meninos órfãos da Mouraria* (Lisbon: Arquivo Histórico de Portugal, 1959), pp. 22–23.

68. See Josef Wicki, "Der einheimische Klerus in Indien (16. Jahrhundert)," in *Der einheimische Klerus in Geschichte und Gegenwart: Festschrift P. Dr. Laurenz Kilger OSB*, ed. Johannes Beckmann (Schöneck-Beckenried: Administration der Neuen Zeitschrift für Missionswissenschaft, 1950), pp. 17–72, and "Franz Xavers Stellung zur Heranbildung des einheimischen Klerus im Orient," *Studia Missionalia*, 5 (1950), 93–115; Serafim Leite, *História da Companhia de Jesus no Brasil* (Lisbon: Livraria Portugália, 1938), 2:424–454. I am indebted to John Correia-Afonso of Bombay for allowing me to read his unpublished paper, "Ignatius and Indian Jesuit Vocations."

69. See C. R. Boxer, *The Christian Century in Japan, 1549–1650* (Berkeley and Los Angeles: The University of California Press, 1951), pp. 72–90.

70. See Cohen, "Social Origins," 1:58, 214, 241.

71. *Const.*, #117.

72. *P Co.*, 2:765; *M Nadal*, 4:366; 5:737; *M Lain.*, 4:76–77.

73. *M Nadal*, 5:452. See also *M Paed.*, 3:30.

74. *Chron.*, 6:387.

75. *M Nadal*, 4:633–635.

76. On Estrada, Araoz, and others, see Antonio Astrain, *Historia de la Compañía de Jesús en la Asistencia de España*, 7 vols. (Madrid: Administración de Razón y Fe, 1912–25), 2:482–500.

77. *Const.*, #673–676.

78. *Chron.*, 1:371; 2:33, 61.

79. *Chron.*, 1:263. See Mario Scaduto, "La corrispondenza dei primi Gesuiti e le poste italiane," *AHSI*, 19 (1950), 237–253.

80. *MI Epp.*, 8:481–483.

81. *MI Epp.*, 1:236–239.

82. *P Co.*, 2:593; *Chron.*, 1:422.

83. *M Nadal*, 1:187.

84. *Chron.*, 1:160, 257–258; 4:335; 6:541; *MI Epp.*, 6:171.

85. See Antonio M. de Aldama, *Imagen ignaciana del jesuita en los escritos de Polanco: Extractos* (Rome: Centrum Ignatianum Spiritualitatis, 1975).

86. See Dennis Edmond Pate, "Jerónimo Nadal and the Early Development of the Society of Jesus, 1545–1573," (Ph.D. diss., University of California, Los Angeles, 1980), and Manuel Ruiz Jurado, "Cronología de la vida del P. Jerónimo Nadal, S.I. (1507–1580)," *AHSI*, 48 (1979), 248–276.

87. *M Nadal*, 5:223.

88. *M Nadal*, 1:803–806; 2:73.

89. *M Nadal*, 1:798–818; *Chron.*, 4:395.

90. *FN*, 1:70–145.

91. *FN*, 1:151–297.

92. *M Nadal*, 5:287. See Miguel Nicolau, *Jerónimo Nadal, S.I. (1507–1580): Sus obras y doctrinas espirituales* (Madrid: Consejo Superior de Investigaciones Científicas, 1949), pp. 138–151, and John H. Wright, "The Grace of Our Founder and the Grace of Our Vocation," *Studies in the Spirituality of Jesuits*, 3/1 (1971).

93. *M Nadal*, 5:780. See also ibid., 5:623.

94. *Const.*, #812.

95. *M Nadal*, 5:41, 287, 490, 623; *Orat. Obs.*, #136.

96. *M Nadal*, 5:233–235, 552–564, 778–779.

97. *M Nadal*, 5:778.

98. *M Nadal*, 5:346, 414, 588, 817; *Chron.*, 3:536–537.

99. Nadal, *Orat. Obs.*, #609, 699, 1003, 1004.

100. *M Nadal*, 4:842–843.

101. *M Nadal*, 5:591–592.

102. Nadal, *Pláticas*, pp. 80–81.

103. Nadal, *Orat. Obs.*, #379. See also *M Nadal*, 5:125–127.

104. Nadal, *Orat. Obs.*, #459.

105. *M Nadal*, 5:37, 111, 335–336.

106. *M Nadal*, 4:165–181; See also Nadal, *Scholia*, p. 164.

107. *M Nadal*, 4:175; 5:54, 195–196, 364–365, 469–470, 673, 773–774; Nadal, *Scholia*, p. 175. See John W. O'Malley, "To Travel to Any Part of the World: Jerónimo Nadal and the Jesuit Vocation," *Studies in the Spirituality of Jesuits*, 16/2 (1984).

108. *M Nadal*, 5:126–127.

109. *M Nadal*, 5:413, 608.

110. *M Nadal*, 5:325.

111. *M Nadal*, 5:54, 364–365, 469–470, 773–774. See O'Malley, "To Travel," pp. 6–12.

112. *Chron.*, 2:187; 3:31; *MI Epp.*, 1:197.

113. *Const.*, #6. See Michel Dhortel-Claudot, *Le genre de vie extérieur de la Compagnie de Jésus* (Rome: Università Gregoriana Editrice, 1971).

114. *Chron.*, 1:322, 444; 2:362; 3:21.

115. *M Nadal*, 5:756.

116. *Chron.*, 1:444; 3:181; 5:523–524. See also *FN*, 1:299; 2:17, n4.

117. *Chron.*, 5:523–524; *P Co.*, 1:65–68.

118. *M Nadal*, 5:646–647; *FN*, 2:294–295.

119. *Chron.*, 1:444; 6:533.

120. See Emmerich Raitz von Frentz, "Ludolphe le Chartreux et les Exercises de S. Ignace de Loyola," *Revue d'Ascétique et de Mystique*, 25 (1949), p. 388.

121. See Pietro Tacchi Venturi, "La prova dell'indifferenza e del servizio negli Ospedali nel Tirocinio ignaziano," *AHSI*, 1 (1932), p. 18, n4.

122. *M Nadal*, 5:348.

123. *M Nadal*, 4:650.

124. Nadal, *Orat. Obs.*, #324; *M Nadal*, 5:322–323.

125. *Formula*, #3.

126. *MI Epp.*, 1:386–389.

127. See António Lopes, "Ignace de Loyola, François Xavier et Jean III du Portugal," in *Ignacio de Loyola y su tiempo*, ed. Juan Plazaola (Bilbao: Ediciones Mensajero, 1992), pp. 636–682.

128. *Const.*, #622d-e, 824.

129. *MI Epp.*, 1:442–444.

130. *MI Epp.*, 3:255, 261–262.

131. *Chron.*, 4:478.

132. *Chron.*, 2:653; 4:486.

133. *M Nadal*, 5:195–196; Nadal, *Scholia*, pp. 167–168, 175. See also O'Malley, "To Travel."

134. Nadal, *Orat. Obs.*, #316.

135. *M Nadal*, 5:126, 195–196.

136. *Const.*, #304.

137. Nadal, *Orat. Obs.*, #414.

138. *Const.*, #622–626, 650.

139. *Const.*, #324–325, 588.

140. Nadal, *Scholia*, pp. 167–168, 378, 440.

141. *Chron.*, 1:286.

142. *P Co.*, 2:786.

143. *Chron.*, 2:21.

144. See Iparraguirre, *Historia*, 1:137–138; *Chron.*, 2:683–684.

145. *Chron.*, 2:193–194.

146. See Gabriella Zarri, "La Compagnia di Gesù a Bologna: Dall'origine alla stabilizzazione (1546–1568)," in *Dall'isola alla città: I gesuiti a Bologna*, ed. Gian Paolo Brizzi and Anna Maria Matteucci (Bologna: Nuova Alfa Editoriale, 1988), pp. 119–123.

147. *P Co.*, 2:656.

148. Diego Laínez, "De fuco et ornatu mulierum," in *Disputationes Tridentinae*, ed. Hartmann Grisar, 2 vols. (Innsbruck: F. Rauch, 1886), 2:464–500. It was written at the suggestion of Ignatius, but never published until this edition. See Mario Scaduto, *L'epoca di Giacomo Lainez*, 2 vols. (Rome: Edizioni la Civiltà Cattolica, 1964–74), 2:485–487.

149. See *Saint Ignatius Loyola: Letters to Women*, ed. Hugo Rahner, trans. Kathleen Pond and S. A. H. Weetman (Edinburgh and London: Nelson, 1960). See also Pedro de Leturia, "Damas vascas en la formación y transformación de Iñigo de Loyola," *Estudios Ignacianos*, ed. Ignacio Iparraguirre, 2 vols. (Rome: Institutum Historicum Societatis Jesu, 1957), 1:69–85.

150. See Charmarie J. Blaisdell, "Calvin's and Loyola's Letters to Women: Politics and Spiritual Counsel in the Sixteenth Century," in *Calviniana: Ideas and Influence of Jean Calvin*, ed. Robert V. Schnucker (Kirksville, Mo.: The Sixteenth Century Journal Publishers, 1988), pp. 235–253.

151. *MI Font. Doc.*, pp. 696–711. See Rahner, *Ignatius: Letters*, pp. 276–295.

152. See Rahner, *Ignatius: Letters*, pp. 52–67.

153. "De oratione," ARSI, cod. Opp. NN 73, fol. 151v.

154. For the full details of his career, see Schurhammer, *Xavier*. See also Stephen Neill, *A History of Christianity in India: The Beginnings to* A.D. 1707 (Cambridge: Cambridge University Press, 1984), pp. 134–165.

155. See Boxer, *Christian Century;* Neil S. Fujita, *Japan's Encounter with Christianity: The Catholic Mission in Pre-Modern Japan* (New York: The Paulist Press, 1991); and especially Josephus Franciscus Schütte, *Introductio ad historiam Societatis Jesu in Japonia, 1549–1650* (Rome: Institutum Historicum Societatis Jesu, 1968).

156. Quoted in Boxer, *Christian Century*, p. 37.

157. See Fujita, *Japan's Encounter*, pp. 52–54.

158. For the sixteenth century, see the first two volumes of Leite, *História*. See also Robert Ricard, "Les Jésuites au Brésil pendant la seconde moitié du XVIe siècle (1549–1597): Méthodes missionnaires et conditions d'apostolat," *Revue d'Histoire des Missions*, 4 (1937), 321–366, 435–470, and "Aux origines de la mission du Brésil," *Etudes*, 239 (1939), 191–204.

159. *Chron.*, 1:200; 2:383, 393–394; 3:463; 5:618, 656. Their confreres in Europe made similar comparisons. See Adriano Prosperi, " 'Otras Indias': Missionari della Controriforma tra contadini e selvaggi," in *Scienze, Credenze occulte, Livelli di cultura: Convegno internazionale* (Florence: Olschki, 1982), pp. 205–234.

160. *Chron.*, 1:461–464.

161. *Chron.*, 4:649.

162. *Chron.*, 5:657.

163. *Chron.*, 1:474.

164. See Leite, *História*, 2:194–206. For Jesuit policy under Francisco de Borja (1565–72), influenced by Bartolomé de las Casas, see Ernest J. Burrus, "Pius V and Francis Borgia: Their Efforts on Behalf of the American Indians," *AHSI*, 41 (1972), 207–226, and Helen Rand Parish, *Las Casas as a Bishop: A New Interpretation Based on His Holograph Petition in the Hans P. Kraus Collection of Hispanic American Manuscripts* (Washington: Library of Congress, 1980), p. xxiii, n74. The title of Parish's book referred to in that note has been changed to *The Untold Story*, forthcoming from the University of California Press. I am indebted to Francis P. Sullivan for these references.

165. *Chron.*, 1:469–470; 2:159, 384, 393; 5:622, 624, 639.

166. *M. Paed.*, 1:523–524.

167. *M Nadal*, 5:323.

168. *Chron.*, 6:761–762.

169. *Chron.*, 2:418; 5:619; 6:831–833.

170. *Chron.*, 5:632–633.

171. *Chron.*, 4:634; 5:626, 633–634.

172. See Ricard, "Jésuites au Brésil," pp. 337–342.

173. See the tables for 1556 in Ladislao Lukács, "De origine collegiorum externorum deque controversiis circa eorum paupertatem obortis: Pars prior, 1539–1556," *AHSI*, 29 (1960), 242–243.

174. *M Nadal*, 5:820–865.

175. "Cum inter cunctas," in *Institutum Societatis Jesu*, 2 vols. (Prague: Typis Universitatis Carolo-Ferdinandeae, 1757), 1:11–12.

176. *Chron.*, 2:244–245, 445–446.

177. *Chron.*, 1:248; 6:513. See also Iparraguirre, *Historia*, 1:33.

178. *Chron.*, 2:330.

179. *M Nadal,* 1:593; 5:465; *Chron.,* 5:374.

180. *M Nadal,* 4:175.

181. *Const.,* #723–735.

182. *P Co.,* 2:729.

183. *P Co.,* 2:624, 748–753.

184. *Chron.,* 1:455; 3:99.

185. *Chron.,* 1:455.

186. *Chron.,* 5:523–524.

187. *M Fabri,* pp. 688–689.

188. Nadal, *Orat. Obs.,* #526. See also ibid., #14, 30.

189. *P Co.,* 2:729–730.

190. *P Co.,* 1:449–451.

191. Nadal, *Pláticas,* p. 191.

192. *M Fabri,* p. 569.

193. See Thomas N. Tentler, *Sin and Confession on the Eve of the Reformation* (Princeton: Princeton University Press, 1977), especially pp. 12–15, 347–349.

194. See Mark S. Burrows, *Jean Gerson and De Consolatione Theologiae (1418): The Consolation of a Biblical and Reforming Theology for a Disordered Age* (Tübingen: J. C. B. Mohr [Paul Siebeck], 1991).

195. See, for example, George W. McClure, *Sorrow and Consolation in Italian Humanism* (Princeton: Princeton University Press, 1991).

196. *Const.,* #30, 813–814.

197. Nadal, *Annotationes et meditationes in evangelia* (Antwerp: Martinus Nutius, 1595), p. 65.

198. Nadal, *Orat. Obs.,* #1005.

199. See Ricardo García Villoslada, *Storia del Collegio Romano, dal suo inizio (1551) alla soppressione della Compagnia del Gesù (1773)* (Rome: Pontificia Università Gregoriana, 1954), pp. 75–76.

200. *SpEx.,* #366–367.

201. See Aquinas, *Summa theologiae,* 1–2.109.6 ad 2am.

202. *SpEx.,* #18.

203. *SpEx.,* #238–260.

204. *MI Epp.,* 12:666–673.

205. On the paramount significance of *Christianitas,* see John Van Engen, "The Christian Middle Ages as an Historiographical Problem," *American Historical Review,* 91 (1986), 519–552.

206. See Tentler, *Sin and Confession,* p. 84.

207. See John Bossy, "Moral Arithmetic: Seven Sins into Ten Commandments," in *Conscience and Casuistry in Early Modern Europe,* ed. Edmund Leites (New York: Cambridge University Press, 1988), pp. 214–234.

208. See the German pre-Reformation catechism by Dietrich Kolde in Denis Janz, *Three Reformation Catechisms: Catholic, Anabaptist, Lutheran* (New York and Toronto: The Edwin Mellen Press, 1982), pp. 31–130.

209. See Alvaro Huerga, "Sobre la catequesis in España durante los siglos XV–XVI," *Analecta Sacra Tarraconensia,* 41 (1968), 299–345; José-Ramon Guerrero, *Catecismos españoles del sigle XVI: La obra catequética del Dr. Constantino Ponce de la Fuente* (Madrid: Instituto Superior de Pastoral, 1969); and Carlos Maria Nannei, *La "Doctrina Cristiana" de San Juan de Avila (Contribución al estudio de su doctrina catequética)* (Pamplona: Ediciones Universidad de Navarra, 1977).

210. See Maureen Flynn, *Sacred Charity: Confraternities and Social Welfare in Spain, 1400–1700* (Ithaca: Cornell University Press, 1989), especially pp. 44–74; Linda Martz, *Poverty and Welfare in Habsburg Spain* (Cambridge: Cambridge University Press, 1983), pp. 159–168; and Christopher F. Black, *Italian Confraternities in the Sixteenth Century* (Cambridge: Cambridge University Press, 1989), especially pp. 151–233.

211. See Roberto Rusconi, "Dal pulpito alla confessione: Modelli di comportamento religioso in Italia tra 1470 circa e 1520 circa," in *Strutture ecclesiastiche in Italia e Germania prima della Riforma*, ed. Paolo Prodi and Peter Johanek (Bologna: Il Mulino, 1984), pp. 259–315.

212. See Bossy, "Moral Arithmetic," and E. Delaruelle, E.-R. Labande, and Paul Ourliac, *L'Eglise au temps du Grand Schisme et de la crise conciliaire (1378–1449)*, 2 vols. (Paris: Bloud & Gay, 1964), 2:871–874.

3. Ministries of the Word of God

1. *M Nadal*, 5:343.

2. *Const.*, #645.

3. See, for example, John W. O'Malley, "Luther the Preacher," in *The Martin Luther Quincentennial*, ed. Gerhard Dünnhaupt (Detroit: Wayne State University Press, 1985), pp. 3–16; "Erasmus and the History of Sacred Rhetoric: The *Ecclesiastes* of 1535," *Erasmus of Rotterdam Society Yearbook*, 5 (1985), 1–29; and *Praise and Blame in Renaissance Rome: Rhetoric, Doctrine, and Reform in the Sacred Orators of the Papal Court, ca. 1450–1521*, Duke Monographs in Medieval and Renaissance Studies 3 (Durham: Duke University Press, 1979). See also John M. McManamon, "Innovation in Early Humanistic Rhetoric: The Oratory of Pier Paolo Vergerio (the Elder)," *Rinascimento*, NS 22 (1982), 3–32; Hervé Martin, *Le métier de prédicateur en France septentrionale à la fin du Moyen Age (1350–1520)* (Paris: Editions du Cerf, 1988), and Larissa Taylor, *Soldiers of Christ: Preaching in Late Medieval and Reformation France* (New York and Oxford: Oxford University Press, 1992). For broad lines of development as exemplified in Italy, see Roberto Rusconi, "Predicatori e predicazioni (secoli ix–xviii)," in *Storia d'Italia: Annali 4*, ed. Corrado Vivanti (Turin: Giulio Einaudi, 1981), pp. 951–1035, and Lina Bolzoni, "Oratoria e prediche," *Letteratura italiana*, ed. Alberto Asor Rosa, 9 vols. (Turin: Giulio Einaudi, 1984), 3/2:1041–1074.

4. *Const.*, #623f.

5. *P Co.*, 2:805; *Chron.*, 1:141, 196, 397; 2:98; 3:31; 5:559.

6. Alfonso Salmerón, Bibliotheca Apostolica Vaticana, cod. Urb. lat. 561, fol. 348v. See also *Chron.*, 1:209; 2:178.

7. *MI Epp.*, 7:39; 8:412.

8. *MI Epp.*, 7:39.

9. *MI Epp.*, 1:139.

10. *Chron.*, 6:554.

11. *Chron.*, 4:147.

12. *Chron.*, 2:20–21; 4:200; 5:183; 6:277. See also ibid., 6:81, and Pietro Tacchi Venturi, *Storia della Compagnia di Gesù in Italia*, 2 vols. in 4 (Rome: Edizioni la Civiltà Cattolica, 1938–51), 1/1:229–248.

13. *Chron.*, 1:324–325.

14. *Chron.*, 1:162, 222, 384; 2:113, 192–193; 3:24; *MI Epp.*, 6:268–269; 7:256; 9:535; 10:9; *M Nadal*, 1:81.

15. *Chron.*, 1:234.

16. *Chron.*, 2:521.

17. *Chron.*, 3:309.

18. *M Fabri*, pp. 340–341.

19. *Chron.*, 2:651.

20. *Chron.*, 1:394.

21. *Chron.*, 2:87–88.

22. See Saint Francis of Assisi, *Writings and Early Biographies: English Omnibus of the Sources for the Life of St. Francis*, ed. Marion A. Habig (Chicago: Franciscan Herald Press, 1977), p. 63.

23. See Norman P. Tanner, ed., *Decrees of the Ecumenical Councils*, 2 vols. (Washington: Georgetown University Press, 1990), 2:669.

24. *MI Epp.*, 7:612.

25. *SpEx.*, #18.

26. *Chron.*, 2:26.

27. *MI Epp.*, 9:404–405; 12:677.

28. *P Co.*, 2:749–750.

29. *MI Reg.*, pp. 276–280.

30. *Const.*, #404.

31. See, however, Mario Scaduto, *L'epoca di Giacomo Laínez*, 2 vols. (Rome: Edizioni la Civiltà Cattolica, 1964–74), 2:469–531.

32. *FN*, 2:420.

33. *MI Epp.*, 9:404–405; 12:677.

34. *MI Epp.*, 10:690–691.

35. See John W. O'Malley, "Luther the Preacher" and "Content and Rhetorical Forms in Sixteenth-Century Treatises on Preaching," in *Renaissance Eloquence: Studies in the Theory and Practice of Renaissance Rhetoric*, ed. James J. Murphy (Berkeley and Los Angeles: University of California Press, 1983), pp. 238–252; Bernd Moeller, "Was wurde in der Frühzeit der Reformation in den deutschen Städten gepredigt?" *Archive for Reformation History*, 75 (1984), 176–193.

36. *Chron.*, 1:396; 2:28.

37. *Chron.*, 2:504.

38. *MI Epp.*, 6:663.

39. *Chron.*, 1:192–193, 284, 291, 322; 4:147; 6:299.

40. *Chron.*, 2:113; 5:502.

41. *Chron.*, 2:73.

42. *Epist. Mixtae*, 5:78.

43. Gregory Martin, *Roma Sancta (1581)*, ed. George Bruner Parks (Rome: Edizioni di Storia e Letteratura, 1969), pp. 71–72.

44. Ibid.

45. *Const.*, #402.

46. See Angelo Martini, "Gli studi teologici di Giovanni de Polanco alle origini della legislazione scolastica della Compagnia di Gesù," *AHSI*, 21 (1952), 266.

47. See O'Malley, "Erasmus and Sacred Rhetoric."

48. Alfonso Salmerón, *Oratio . . . nuper in Concilio Tridentino habita, in qua ad exemplar divi Ioannis Evangelistae vera praelatorum forma describitur* (Rome: S. Nicolinus, 1547).

49. *P Co.*, 2:582, 615, 686–687.

50. See O'Malley, *Praise and Blame*, pp. 36–76.

51. See, for example, the sermons of Salmerón in ARSI, cod. Opp. NN 63 (198 fols.; see Scaduto, *Laínez*, 2:506n); see also ibid., cod. Instit. 110, fols. 73–82v; Bibliotheca Apos-

tolica Vaticana, cod. Urb. lat. 561, fols. 338–361v; the sermons of Francisco Estrada in the Biblioteca Casanatense, Rome, cod. 476, fols. 70–110.

52. See O'Malley, "Content and Rhetorical Forms."

53. *MI Epp.*, 11:283. For a work on preaching by Benedetto Palmio, never circulated, see Scaduto, *Laínez*, 2:514–517.

54. For the modern edition of this work, see San Francisco de Borja, *Tratados espirituales*, ed. Cándido de Dalmases (Barcelona: Juan Flores, 1964), pp. 438–459.

55. In Diego Laínez, *Disputationes Tridentinae*, ed. Hartmann Grisar, 2 vols. (Innsbruck: F. Rauch, 1886), 2:506–542.

56. See Martini, "Studi Polanco," pp. 262–264.

57. *Chron.*, 2:98.

58. Nadal, *Scholia*, p. 111.

59. Nadal, *Scholia*, pp. 386–387; *M Nadal*, 5:828. See also ibid., 4:645; 5:824–830; Nadal, *Orat. Obs.*, #7.

60. See, however, Marc Fumaroli, "Définition et description: Scholastique et rhétorique chez les jésuites des XVIe et XVIIe siècles," *Travaux de linguistique et de litterature*, 18 (1980), 37–48.

61. *M Nadal*, 5:827.

62. *P Co.*, 2:749–750.

63. *MI Epp.*, 12:686–688; *M Nadal*, 4:594, 5:826–827; Nadal, *Scholia*, pp. 74–75.

64. *Chron.*, 2:279.

65. *M Nadal*, 5:826–827.

66. *M Paed.*, 1:382.

67. *M Paed.*, 2:112.

68. *M Nadal*, 5:826.

69. See Scaduto, *Laínez*, 2:524–530.

70. *Const.*, #813.

71. *MI Epp.*, 7:440.

72. *M Fabri*, pp. 458–459.

73. Nadal, *Pláticas*, pp. 196–197.

74. *Chron.*, 1:288.

75. *Chron.*, 2:51–52.

76. *M Paed.*, 1:546.

77. *Chron.*, 2:735.

78. Nadal, *Orat. Obs.*, #568.

79. Nadal, *Orat. Obs.*, #610.

80. *M Nadal*, 5:826.

81. *M Nadal*, 5:832. For some related passages, see Nadal, *Orat. Obs.*, #568, 914; Nadal, *Scholia*, p. 111. See also *M Fabri*, p. 548.

82. Juan Ramírez, *Monita pro iis, qui concionandi munus suscipiunt* (1563), pp. 512–514.

83. Biblioteca Casanatense, Rome, cod. 476, fols. 84v–90v.

84. *Chron.*, 2:363.

85. Ramírez, *Monita*, pp. 507–508.

86. *M Lain.*, 6:313–325.

87. *M Lain.*, 6:509–513. See Scaduto, *Laínez*, 1:369.

88. Compare, for example, O'Malley, *Praise and Blame*, pp. 195–237, with Frederick John McGinness, "Rhetoric and Counter-Reformation Rome: Sacred Oratory and the

Construction of the Catholic World View, 1563–1621" (Ph.D. diss., University of California, Berkeley, 1982).

89. *SpEx.*, #362. See *MI Scripta*, 1:467–468.

90. See Scaduto, *Laínez*, 1:316–325; 2:469–521.

91. See O'Malley, *Praise and Blame*, pp. 41, 48n.

92. See, however, Scaduto, *Laínez*, 2:532–534.

93. Tanner, *Decrees of the Councils*, 2:667–670. See G. Pelliccia, *La preparazione ed ammissione dei chierici ai santi ordini nella Roma del secolo XVI* (Rome: Pia Società San Paolo, 1946), pp. 155–157.

94. *Chron.*, 1:150.

95. See Armando F. Verde, "Le lezioni o i sermoni sull' 'Apocalisse' di Girolamo Savonarola (1490): 'Nova dicere et novo modo,'" *Memorie Domenicane*, NS 19 (1988), 5–109, and Elettra Giaconi, "Il volgarizzamento toscano dei 'Sermoni sopra la Prima Lettera di S. Giovanni' di Frate Girolamo Savonarola," ibid., 111–189. See also Rusconi, "Predicatori," p. 990, and Adriano Prosperi, *Tra evangelismo e controriforma: G. M. Giberti (1495–1543)* (Rome: Edizioni di Storia e Letteratura, 1969), p. 242.

96. *Chron.*, 1:408; 4:201; 5:116.

97. *M Fabri*, p. 27.

98. See *Opus Epistolarum Des. Erasmi Roterodami*, ed. P. S. Allen, H. M. Allen, and H. W. Garrod, 12 vols. (Oxford: Clarendon Press, 1906–58), 4:516. See also Paul S. Seaver, *The Puritan Lectureships: The Politics of Religious Dissent, 1560–1662* (Stanford: Stanford University Press, 1970), especially pp. 72–87.

99. See *D. Martin Luthers Werke: Kritische Gesamtausgabe* (Weimar: H. Böhlau, 1893), 9:321–323.

100. *Chron.*, 1:372.

101. *P Co.*, 2:804.

102. *M Nadal*, 5:832.

103. *P Co.*, 1:290.

104. For example, Laínez, "De tribulatione," ARSI, cod. Opp. NN 73, fols. 23–91v; "De oratione," ibid., fols. 63–204v; Salmerón, "Lettioni" (on the Eucharist), Bibliotheca Apostolic Vaticana, cod. Vat. lat 4625, fols. 76–243v; "Lectiones super psalmum 118," Biblioteca Casanatense, Rome, cod. 476, fols. 1–67v. Some excerpts from Laínez's "De oratione" were published in his *Disputationes Tridentinae*, 2:543–560.

105. *Chron.*, 1:408.

106. See *Institutum Societatis Jesu*, 2 vols. (Prague: Typis Universitatis Carolo-Ferdinandeae, 1757), 1:478.

107. *M Nadal*, 5:831.

108. Laínez, "De oratione," fol. 163v.

109. *M Nadal*, 5:831.

110. *MI Epp.*, 5:696.

111. *Chron.*, 1:383, 489, 490.

112. *Chron.*, 4:141.

113. *P Co.*, 1:375.

114. *Chron.*, 2:175, 220; 3:59; *M Nadal*, 5:342. See also note 104 above.

115. *Chron.*, 6:149, 152, 299.

116. *Chron.*, 6:579, 663.

117. *Chron.*, 2:519.

118. *Chron.*, 1:100.

119. *Chron.*, 1:369.

120. *Chron.*, 1:412.

121. *Chron.*, 2:168.

122. *Chron.*, 2:573; *M Nadal*, 1:81.

123. *Chron.*, 1:100; 2:27–28, 519.

124. *Chron.*, 1:390.

125. *Chron.*, 2:80.

126. *Chron.*, 2:210, 242.

127. *Chron.*, 4:83.

128. *Chron.*, 1:282; 2:33.

129. *Chron.*, 2:573.

130. Volume 13 of *Commentarii in Evangelicam Historiam, et in Acta Apostolorum; Commentarii in omnes Epistolas B. Pauli et canonicas*, 16 vols. (Cologne: A. Hierat and I. Gymnicus, 1612–15).

131. Salmerón, *Commentarii*, 13:10.

132. Nadal, *Orat. Obs.*, #507.

133. Nadal, *Orat. Obs.*, #444.

134. Nadal, *Orat. Obs.*, #304, 449.

135. Nadal, *Orat. Obs.*, #713.

136. Nadal, *Orat. Obs.*, #716.

137. "De oratione," ARSI, cod. Opp. NN 73, fol. 156v.

138. "Lectiones super psalmum 118," Biblioteca Casanatense, Rome, cod. 476, fols. 1–67v.

139. "De tribulatione," ARSI, cod. Opp. NN 73, fol. 23.

140. Laínez, "Documenta ad bene interpretandas scripturas," in *Disputationes Tridentinae*, 2:501–505.

141. *Const.*, for example, #115, 349, 648.

142. His most extended treatment is in his exhortation, 1573–76, *M Nadal*, 5:832–837, translated into English by Thomas H. Clancy, *The Conversational Word of God* (St Louis: Institute of Jesuit Sources, 1978), pp. 51–56. See also Dario Restrepo Londoño, *Dialogo: Comunión en el Espíritu, La "conversación espiritual" según San Ignacio de Loyola (1521–1556)* (Bogotá: Centro Ignaciano de Reflexión y Ejercicios, 1975).

143. *M Nadal*, 5:524–774.

144. *Beati Petri Canisii, Societatis Jesu, Epistulae et Acta*, ed. Otto Braunsberger, 8 vols. (Freiburg: Herder, 1896–1923), 8:117–154; the pertinent sections are translated by Clancy, *Conversational Word*, pp. 57–67.

145. *M Nadal*, 5:833–835.

146. *M Nadal*, 1:81, 123; 5:836–837. See Louis Ponnelle and Louis Bordet, *St. Philip Neri and the Roman Society of His Times (1515–1595)*, trans. Ralph Francis Kerr (London: Sheed and Ward, 1979), pp. 171–173.

147. *Chron.*, 1:444.

148. *M Nadal*, 1:92, 121, 123, 496; 4:496; *P Co.*, 1:209–212, 263–264; *M Paed.*, 3:115.

149. *M Nadal*, 1:121.

150. *M Nadal*, 1:123.

151. *P Co.*, 1:209–211.

152. *P Co.*, 1:209–210.

153. *M Nadal*, 5:836.

154. *Chron.*, 3:149.

155. *Chron.*, 6:233.

156. *Chron.*, 5:95, 110–111.

157. *Chron.,* 6:167–168.

158. *Const.,* #637; *M Nadal,* 5:666; *MI Epp.,* 6:131–132; 7:284–285; *Chron.,* 1:236.

159. *M Nadal,* 5:665–666. See also ibid., 5:841, and Nadal, *Scholia,* pp. 188–189.

160. See Mark U. Edwards, Jr., "Catholic Controversial Literature, 1518–1555: Some Statistics," *Archive for Reformation History,* 79 (1988), 189–205.

161. *M Salm.,* 1:46–47.

162. *Const.,* #653. See Antonio M. de Aldama, *The Constitutions of the Society of Jesus: An Introductory Commentary on the Constitutions,* trans. Aloysius J. Owen (St. Louis: The Institute of Jesuit Sources, 1989), p. 262.

163. *MI Epp.,* 12:261–262; 9:116.

164. Gaspar de Loarte, *Esercitio della vita christiana* (Genoa, 1557). On Loarte, see Jean-François Gilmont, *Les écrits spirituels des premiers jésuites: Inventaire commenté* (Rome: Institutum Historicum Societatis Jesu, 1961), pp. 260–268.

165. *M Nadal,* 5:841.

166. See G. Castellani, "La tipografia del Collegio Romano," *AHSI,* 2 (1933), 11–16, and Ricardo García Villoslada, *Storia del Collegio Romano dal suo inizio (1551) alla soppressione della Compagnia di Gesù (1773)* (Rome: Pontificia Università Gregoriana, 1954), pp. 44–46.

167. See *Institutum,* 1:477.

168. See Dennis Edmond Pate, "Jerónimo Nadal and the Early Development of the Society of Jesus, 1545–1573" (Ph.D. diss., University of California, Los Angeles, 1980), p. 308.

169. See J. B. Primrose, "The First Press in India and Its Printers," *The Library,* 4th Series, 20 (1939), 241–265, and Jean Muller and Ernst Róth, *Aussereuropäische Druckereien im 16. Jahrhundert: Bibliographie der Drucke* (Baden-Baden: Verlag Librairie Heitz, 1969), pp. 39–44.

170. See, for example, the works listed in Gilmont, *Ecrits spirituels,* which does not include theological works or textbooks.

171. *FN,* 2:340–341.

172. See Martin, *Métier de prédicateur,* pp. 295–351; Guy Bedouelle, "Das Entstehen des Katechismus," *Internationale katholische Zeitschrift,* 12 (1983), 25–40; Alvaro Huerga, "Sobre la catequesis en España durante los siglos XV–XVI," *Analecta Sacra Tarraconensia,* 41 (1968), 299–345; Jean-Claude Dhotel, *Les origines du catéchisme moderne d'après les premiers manuels imprimés en France* (Paris: Aubier, 1967); Elisabeth Germain, *Langages de la Foi a travers l'histoire: Mentalités et catéchèse approche d'une étude des mentalités* (Paris: Fayard-Mame, 1972), and *Deux mille ans d'éducation de la Foi* (Paris: Desclée, 1983); Pierre Colin, Elisabeth Germain, Jean Joncheray, and Marc Venard, eds., *Aux origines du catéchisme en France* (Paris; Desclée, 1989); Robert I. Bradley, *The Roman Catechism in the Catechetical Tradition of the Church: The Structure of the Roman Catechism as Illustrative of "Classic Catechesis"* (Lanham, Md.: University Press of America, 1990); Paul F. Grendler, *Schooling in Renaissance Italy: Literacy and Learning, 1300–1600* (Baltimore: The Johns Hopkins University Press, 1989), pp. 333–362.

173. See Huerga, "Catequesis," and Jean Pierre Dedieu, " 'Christianisation' en Nouvelle Castille: Catéchisme, communion, messe et confirmation dans l'archevêche de Tolède, 1540–1650," *Mélanges de la Casa de Velazquez,* 15 (1979), 261–294.

174. See Robert Ricard, *The Spiritual Conquest of Mexico: An Essay on the Apostolate and the Evangelizing Methods of the Mendicant Orders in New Spain: 1523–1572,* trans. Lesley Byrd Simpson (Berkeley and Los Angeles: The University of California Press, 1966), pp. 96–108.

175. See Carlos Maria Nannei, La *"Doctrina cristiana" de San Juan de Avila: (Contribución al estudio de su doctrina catequética)* (Pamplona: Ediciones Universidad de Navarra, 1977), and Jodi Bilinkoff, *The Avila of Saint Teresa: Religious Reform in a Sixteenth-Century City* (Ithaca: Cornell University Press, 1989), pp. 80–87.

176. See José-Ramón Guerrero, *Catecismos españoles del siglo XVI: La obra catequética del Dr. Constantino Ponce de la Fuente* (Madrid: Instituto Superior de Pastoral, 1969).

177. See Maureen Flynn, *Sacred Charity: Confraternities and Social Welfare in Spain, 1400–1700* (Ithaca: Cornell University Press, 1989), p. 124.

178. See Grendler, *Schooling in Renaissance Italy,* pp. 333–362; Roberto Rusconi, "Dal pulpito alla confessione: Modelli di comportamento religioso in Italia tra 1470 circa e 1520 circa," in *Strutture ecclesiastiche in Italia e Germania prima della Riforma,* ed. Paolo Prodi and Peter Johanek (Bologna: Il Mulino, 1984), p. 297; Miriam Turrini, " 'Riformare il mondo a vera vita christiana': Le scuole di catechismo nell'Italia del Cinquecento," *Annali dell'Istituto storico italo-germanico in Trento,* 8 (1982), 407–489; Christopher F. Black, *Italian Confraternities in the Sixteenth Century* (Cambridge: Cambridge University Press, 1989), pp. 223–228.

179. *Const.,* #527, 532. See Antonio M. de Aldama, "Peculiarem curam circa puerorum eruditionem," *Cahiers de spiritualité ignatienne,* 13 (1989), 147–164.

180. *Institutum,* 1:481.

181. *Institutum,* 1:498.

182. See Scaduto, *Laínez,* 2:614–621.

183. See Nannei, *Juan de Avila,* pp. 96–99, 183–196.

184. *M Xav.,* 2:443. See Guerrero, *Catecismos,* pp. 338–339. On the turbulent relationship between the Jesuits and Constantino some years later in Seville, see Antonio Astrain, *Historia de la Compañía de Jesús en la Asistencia de España,* 7 vols. (Madrid: Administración de Razón y Fe, 1912–25), 2:94–98.

185. *M Xav.,* 1:93–116, 303–307, 348–370, 441–460. See Georg Schurhammer, *Francis Xavier: His Life, His Times,* trans. M. Joseph Costelloe, 4 vols. (Rome: The Jesuit Historical Institute, 1973–82), 1:218–224; 3:153–154, and John Hofinger, "Saint Francis Xavier, Catechist," *Lumen Vitae,* 8 (1953), 537–544.

186. *M Xav.,* 1:348–370.

187. See *Luther's Works,* ed. Helmut T. Lehmann (Philadelphia: Fortress Press, 1963), 48:113n.

188. Ibid. (1967), 54:282.

189. *Chron.,* 6:584.

190. *MI Epp.,* 12:666–673.

191. See Ignacio Iparraguirre, *Historia de la práctica de los ejercicios espírituales de San Ignacio de Loyola,* 3 vols. under slightly different titles (Rome: Institutum Historicum Societatis Jesu; Bilbao: El Mensajero del Corazón de Jesús, 1947–73), 1:3.

192. *Chron.,* 2:395, 560; 5:97; *M Fabri,* p. 122.

193. *M Xav.,* 1:441–460; *Chron.,* 2:33.

194. *M Nadal,* 5:850.

195. See Scaduto, *Laínez,* 2:620–621.

196. *Chron.,* 3:70–71.

197. *M Nadal,* 1:313.

198. Scaduto, *Laínez,* 2:619; *Chron.,* 2:86.

199. *Chron.,* for example, 6:84, 88, 98.

200. See Nannei, *Juan de Avila,* p. 234.

201. *Chron.,* 5:658.

202. See *O Colégio de "Jesus" dos meninos órfãos da Mouraria* (Lisbon: Arquivo Histórico de Portugal, 1959), pp. 16–24.

203. Ibid., pp. 24–27.

204. *MI Epp.*, 12:261.

205. *Chron.*, 5:469.

206. *Chron.*, 6:162.

207. *Chron.*, 4:350–351.

208. *Chron.*, 5:184–185.

209. *Chron.*, 5:362.

210. *Chron.*, 4:432–433; 6:301–302, 555, 697.

211. See Bernhard Duhr, *Geschichte der Jesuiten in den Ländern deutscher Zunge im XVI. Jahrhundert* (Freiburg: Herdersche Verlagshandlung, 1907), pp. 455–456. Singing the catechetical text is not mentioned, however, in Karl Schrems, "Der 'modus catechizandi' der katholischen Kirchenkatechese in Deutschland im 16. und 17. Jahrhundert," in *Beiträge zur bayerischen und deutschen Geschichte: Hans Dachs zum Gedenken* (Regensburg: Historischen Verein für Oberpfalz und Regensburg, 1966), pp. 219–241.

212. *Institutum*, 1:481.

213. See Gerald Strauss, *Luther's House of Learning: Indoctrination of the Young in the German Reformation* (Baltimore: The Johns Hopkins University Press, 1978), especially pp. 171–172, 288–291, and "The Reformation and Its Public in an Age of Orthodoxy," in *The German People and the Reformation*, ed. R. Po-Chia Hsia (Ithaca: Cornell University Press, 1988), pp. 194–214. See also, however, J. M. Reu, *Catechetics, or Theory and Practice of Religious Instruction* (Chicago: Wartburg Publishing House, 1918), especially pp. 83–136. On Protestant catechesis in general, see William P. Haugaard, "The Continental Reformation of the Sixteenth Century," in *A Faithful Church: Issues in the History of Catechesis*, ed. John H. Westerhoff III and O. C. Edwards, Jr. (Wilton, Conn.: Morehouse-Barlow Co., 1981), pp. 109–173.

214. *MI Epp.*, 12:259–262.

215. For a collection of pertinent texts, see Christoph Moufang, ed., *Katholische Katechismen des sechzehnten Jahrhunderts in deutscher Sprache* (1881; reprint ed., Hildesheim: Georg Olms, 1964).

216. Ibid.; Martin Ramsauer, "Die Kirche in den Katechismen," *Zeitschrift für katholische Theologie*, 73 (1951), 129–169, 313–346, especially pp. 134–140; Karlheinz Diez, *Christus und seine Kirche: Zum Kirchenverständnis des Petrus Canisius* (Paderborn: Verlag Bonifatius-Druckerei, 1987), pp. 250–255.

217. See Dhotel, *Origines*, pp. 66–82, and Franz Josef Kötter, "Zur Eucharistiekatechese des 16. Jahrhunderts: Dargestellt an den Katechismen des Petrus Canisius und dem Catechismus Romanus," in *Reformatio Ecclesiae: Beiträge zu kirchlichen Reformbemühungen von der Alten Kirche bis zur Neuzeit*, ed. Remigius Bäumer (Paderborn: F. Schöningh, 1980), pp. 713–727.

218. *M Paed.*, 2:686–762. See Allan P. Farrell, *The Jesuit Code of Liberal Education: Development and Scope of the Ratio Studiorum* (Milwaukee: The Bruce Publishing Company, 1938), pp. 153–187.

219. See Dhotel, *Origines*, pp. 99–101.

220. Ibid., pp. 44–64. Still useful, especially for the long excerpts from Auger, is Friedrich H. Brand, *Die Katechismen des Edmundus Augerius, S.J., in historischer, dogmatisch-moralischer und katechetischer Bearbeitung* (Freiburg: Herder, 1917).

221. See Guy Bedouelle, "L'influence des catéchismes de Canisius en France," in *Aux origines du catéchisme*, pp. 67–86.

222. *P Co.,* 1:561; 2:4. See Scaduto, *Laínez,* 2:619.

223. *P Co.,* 1:653.

224. *Chron.,* 1:242; 4:183–184.

225. See, for example, Rusconi, "Predicatori," pp. 1006–1007; Jean Delumeau, *Catholicism between Luther and Voltaire: A New View of the Counter-Reformation,* trans. Jeremy Moiser (London and Philadelphia: Burns & Oates, Westminster Press, 1977), pp. 189–194; E. Dos Santos, "Les missions des temps modernes au Portugal," in *Histoire vécue du peuple chrétien,* 2 vols., ed. Jean Delumeau (Toulouse: Editions Privat, 1979), 1:431–455.

226. See, for example, C. Faralli, "Le missioni dei Gesuiti in Italia (sec. XVI–XVII): Problemi di una ricerca in corso," *Bolletino della Società Valdesi,* no. 138 (1975), pp. 97–116; E. Novi Chavarria, "L'attività missionaria dei Gesuiti nel Mezzogiorno d'Italia tra XVI e XVII secolo," in *Per la storia sociale e religiosa del Mezzogiorno d'Italia,* ed. G. Galasso and C. Russo, 2 vols. (Naples: Guida Editore, 1982), 2:159–185; Raimondo Turtas, "Missioni popolari in Sardegna tra '500 e '600," *Rivista di Storia della Chiesa in Italia,* 44 (1990), 369–412; and especially Armando Guidetti, *Le missioni popolari: I grandi Gesuiti italiani* (Milan: Rusconi, 1988).

227. *Chron.,* 6:692.

228. See Guidetto, *Missioni popolari,* pp. 21–35.

229. See Duhr, *Geschichte der Jesuiten,* pp. 471–472.

230. Iparraguirre's *Historia* is the basic study, reliable and comprehensive.

231. *MI Ex.,* 2:274.

232. Probably to be attributed to Nadal; see *MI Ex.,* 2:176.

233. *SpEx.,* #18.

234. *MI Ex.,* 2:220–223.

235. See Iparraguirre, *Historia,* 1:3–5, and Cándido de Dalmases, "The Exercises according to the 18th Annotation: History and Method," in *The 18th Annotation: The Exercises and Catechesis,* 2nd ed. (Rome: Centrum Ignatianum Spiritualitatis, 1983), pp. 11–21.

236. See Iparraguirre, *Historia,* 1:25.

237. *Chron.,* 1:241–242.

238. *Chron.,* 1:489.

239. *Chron.,* 1:397; 2:24.

240. See Martini, "Studi Polanco," p. 266.

241. *FN,* 1:163–164, 440, 446; *Chron.,* 4:545–546; *MI Ex.,* 2:106.

242. See Iparraguirre, *Historia,* 1:147–148, and Wietse de Boer, " 'Ad audiendi non videndi commoditatem': Note sull'introduzione del confessionale soprattutto in Italia," *Quaderni Storici,* NS 77 (1991), 543–572.

243. See Iparraguirre, *Historia,* 1:144.

244. *Chron.,* 4:410.

245. *MI Ex.,* 2:281.

246. *Chron.,* 5:367.

247. See Iparraguirre, *Historia,* 2:247–253.

248. *Chron.,* 4:160, 198, 301; 6:171, 275, 378.

249. *Const.,* #649.

250. *Chron.,* 4:545–546. See Iparraguirre, *Historia,* 1:267–296.

251. See Robert Ricard, "Les Jésuites au Brésil pendant la seconde moitié du XVIe siècle (1549–1597)," *Revue d'Histoire des Missions,* 4 (1937), p. 461.

252. *Chron.,* 5:201.

253. Nadal, *Scholia,* p. 446.

254. *MI Ex.*, 2:106, 275.

255. See Iparraguirre, *Historia*, 2:221.

256. *Chron.*, 4:49–50.

257. See Iparraguirre, *Historia*, 2:6–8.

258. *Const.*, #277.

259. See Iparraguirre, *Historia*, 1:168.

260. Ibid., 1:174–180.

261. *SpEx.*, #2, 6–16; *MI Ex.*, 2:287. See Nadal, *Scholia*, p. 159.

262. *MI Epp.*, 1:388.

263. *MI Scripta*, 1:470.

264. See Iparraguirre, *Historia*, 2:378.

265. See Cándido de Dalmases, "Juan Codure autor probable de la explanación de los ejercicios atribuida a Polanco," *AHSI*, 37 (1968), 145–152.

266. See Iparraguirre, *Historia*, 1:129–130; 2:351–373, 415–461, and Antonio Alburquerque, "Los directorios de Ejercicios: Síntesis histórica y de contenidos. Utilidad y posibilidades de actualización del los Directorios hoy," *Manresa*, 62 (1990), 401–438.

267. See Iparraguirre, *Historia*, 2:213–227, 389–398.

4. Sacraments, Worship, Prayer

1. See Antonio M. de Aldama, *The Formula of the Institute: Notes for a Commentary*, trans. Ignacio Echániz (St. Louis: The Institute of Jesuit Sources, 1990), pp. 2–3, 42–43, and Pietro Tacchi Venturi, *Storia della Compagnia di Gesù in Italia*, 2 vols. in 4 (Rome: Edizioni la Civiltà Cattolica, 1938–51), 1/2:192n.

2. *M Nadal*, 5:850–852.

3. *P Co.*, 2:749.

4. See de Aldama, *Formula*, pp. 18–19, 91–92.

5. *P Co.*, 2:658.

6. See D. Catherine Brown, *Pastor and Laity in the Theology of Jean Gerson* (Cambridge: Cambridge University Press, 1987), pp. 57–58.

7. *Chron.*, 1:175; *FN*, 2:443.

8. The most extensive and considered treatment of the sacrament from a Jesuit of the first generation occurs in Alfonso Salmerón's *Commentarii in Evangelicam Historiam, et in Acta Apostolorum: Commentarii in omnes Epistolas B. Pauli et canonicas*, 16 vols. (Cologne: A. Hierat and I Gymnicus, 1612–15), 11:134–211.

9. For a judicious review of the state of the question, with special attention to the Jesuits, see Giancarlo Angelozzi, "Interpretazioni della penitenza sacramentale in età moderna," *Religioni e Società*, 2 (1986), 73–87. The most recent and comprehensive study of the many issues related to the sacrament as they manifested themselves in books published in Italy is Miriam Turrini, *La coscienza e le leggi: Morale e diritto nei testi per la confessione della prima Età moderna* (Bologna: Il Mulino, 1991). See also Thomas N. Tentler, *Sin and Confession on the Eve of the Reformation* (Princeton: Princeton University Press, 1977); Hervé Martin, "Confession et contrôle social à la fin du Moyen Age," in *Pratiques de la confession, des Pères du désert à Vatican II: quinze études d'histoire*, ed. Groupe de la Bussière (Paris: Editions du Cerf, 1983), pp. 117–136; John Bossy, "The Social History of Confession in the Age of the Reformation," *Transactions of the Royal Historical Society*, ser. 5, 25 (1975), 21–38; Roberto Rusconi, "Dal pulpito alla confessione: Modelli di comportamento religioso in Italia tra 1470 circa e 1520 circa," in *Strutture ecclesiastiche in Italia e in Germania prima della Riforma*, ed. Paolo Prodi and Peter Johanek (Bologna: Il

Mulino, 1984), pp. 259–315; Robin Briggs, "The Sins of the People: Auricular Confession and the Imposition of Social Norms," in *Communities of Belief: Cultural and Social Tensions in Early Modern France* (Oxford: Oxford University Press, 1989), pp. 277–338. The classic but badly biased history is Henry Charles Lea, *A History of Auricular Confession and Indulgences in the Latin Church*, 3 vols. (Philadelphia: Lea Brothers and Company, 1896).

10. See Pierre Michaud-Quantin, *Sommes de casuistique et manuels de confession au moyen âge (XIIe–XVIe siècles)* (Louvain, Lille, Montreal: Edit. Nauwelaerts, etc., 1962), pp. 71–72, 86–91; Leonard E. Boyle, "The Setting of the *Summa theologiae* of Saint Thomas," The Etienne Gilson Series, 5 (Toronto: Pontifical Institute of Mediaeval Studies, 1982); and especially Roberto Rusconi, " 'Confessio generalis': Opuscoli per la pratica penitenziale nei primi cinquanta anni dalla introduzione della stampa," in *I Frati Minori tra '400 e '500: Atti del XII convegno internazionale, Assisi, 18–19–20 ottobre 1984* (Assisi: Università di Perugia, Centro di Studi Francescani, 1986), pp. 189–227. More specifically related to Ignatius is J. Calveras, "Los 'confesionales' y los Ejercicios de San Ignacio," *AHSI*, 17 (1948), 51–101.

11. See Tentler, *Sin and Confession*, pp. 111–113, and Nicole Lemaître, "Pratique et signification de la confession communautaire dans les paroisses au XVIe siècle," in *Pratiques de la confession*, pp. 139–164.

12. *Const.*, #98.

13. See, for example, "Pénitence" in *Dictionnaire de spiritualité*, 12/1:985–986, and Lucien Ceyssens, "La pratique de la confession générale: La 'confession coupée' suivant le P. Christophe Lutbrewer," in *Jansénius et le Jansénisme dans les Pays-Bas: Mélanges Lucien Ceyssens*, ed. J. van Bavel and M. Schrama (Louvain: University Press, 1982), pp. 93–113. See also Pierre Gervais, "Ignace de Loyola et la confession générale," *Communio* [French edition], 8 (1983), 69–83.

14. *M Fabri*, pp. 119–120.

15. *M Xav.*, 2:89–90.

16. I used the Spanish translation, Gaspar de Loarte, *Exercicio dela vida christiana* (Cagliari: V. Sembenino, 1567 [1568]), fols. 5–7.

17. See, for example, Lawrence G. Duggan, "Fear and Confession on the Eve of the Reformation," *Archive for Reformation History*, 75 (1984), 153–175; Jean Delumeau, *L'aveu et le pardon: Les difficultés de la confession XIIIe–XVIIIe siècles* (Paris: Fayard, 1990).

18. *M Nadal*, 5:811–812, 838.

19. *M Nadal*, 5:787.

20. *Chron.*, 1:105.

21. *M Nadal*, 1:70. See Rusconi, "Dal pulpito alla confessione."

22. *M Nadal*, 5:786.

23. *MI Ex.*, 2:91. See also *Chron.*, 2:272, and *M Paed.*, 2:875–876. See "Direction spirituelle en occident," in *Dictionnaire de spiritualité*, 3:1106–1119.

24. See *The Collected Works of St. Teresa of Avila*, trans. Kiernan Kavanaugh and Otilio Rodriguez, 3 vols. (Washington: Institute of Carmelite Studies, 1976–85), 1:157–161, 187–188, 223–224. See also Jodi Bilinkoff, *The Avila of Saint Teresa: Religious Reform in a Sixteenth-Century City* (Ithaca: Cornell University Press, 1989), pp. 116–123.

25. See Turrini, *La coscienza*, pp. 190–212. On the Tridentine legislation, see Hans-Peter Arendt, *Busssakrament und Einzelbeichte: Die tridentinische Lehraussagung über das Sündenbekenntnis und ihre Verbindlichkeit für die Reform des Busssakramentes* (Freiburg: Herder, 1981), and especially Louis Vereecke, *De Guillaume d'Ockham à saint Alphonse de*

Liguori: Etudes d'histoire de la théologie morale moderne 1300–1787 (Rome: Collegium S. Alfonsi de Urbe, 1986), pp. 495–508.

26. *M Nadal,* 5:343.

27. *M Nadal,* 5:862.

28. Juan Alfonso de Polanco, *Breve directorium ad confessarii et confitentis munus recte obeundum* (Liège: H. Hovius, 1591), pp. 8, 9, 29.

29. *Exercicio,* fol. 92v.

30. *Chron.,* 2:484; 5:78, 82.

31. *Chron.,* 1:103; 5:80.

32. *Const.,* #407; Nadal, *Scholia,* p. 388.

33. Polanco, *Directorium,* pp. 11–16.

34. *M Nadal,* 5:812; *M Paed.,* 2:909; *M Fabri,* p. 251; Polanco, *Directorium,* p. 26.

35. *M Fabri,* pp. 655–656.

36. *M Fabri,* pp. 245–252: "Monita P. Fabri circa confessiones."

37. *M Nadal,* 5:860–861.

38. See Vereecke, *De Guillaume d'Ockham,* pp. 468–472; Bernard Dompnier, "Missions et confession au XVIIe siècle," in *Pratiques de la confession,* pp. 201–222; and Jean Delumeau, *Un chemin d'histoire: Chrétienté et christianisation* (Paris: Fayard, 1981), pp. 173–180.

39. *Institutum Societatis Jesu,* 2 vols. (Prague: Typis Universitatis Carolo-Ferdinandeae, 1757), 1:11–20, 26–28.

40. See Albert R. Jonsen and Stephen Toulmin, *The Abuses of Casuistry: A History of Moral Theology* (Berkeley and Los Angeles: The University of California Press, 1988), p. 88. Despite what the title seems to imply, the book argues for the validity of the basic premises of casuistry. See also Edmund Leites, ed., *Conscience and Casuistry in Early Modern Europe* (New York: Cambridge University Press, 1988).

41. See Johann Theiner, *Die Entwicklung der Moraltheologie zur eigenständige Disziplin* (Regensburg: F. Pustet, 1970), pp. 119–122, and Giancarlo Angelozzi, "L'insegnamento dei casi di coscienza nella pratica educativa della Compagnia di Gesù," in *La "Ratio Studiorum": Modelli culturali e pratiche educative dei Gesuiti in Italia tra Cinque e Seicento,* ed. Gian Carlo Brizzi (Rome: Bulzoni Editore, 1981), pp. 121–162.

42. *Chron.,* 5:654, 661.

43. *Chron.,* 5:466.

44. *SpEx.,* #32–42.

45. *Chron.,* 1:176.

46. See Theiner, *Entwicklung,* pp. 119–122.

47. On these developments, see Angelozzi, "Casi"; Theiner, *Entwicklung,* pp. 97–145; and Vereecke, *De Guillaume d'Ockham,* pp. 501–508.

48. Angelozzi, "Casi," pp. 144–145.

49. *P Co.,* 1:422.

50. See Ricardo García Villoslada, *Storia del Collegio Romano dal suo inizio (1551) alla soppressione della Compagnia di Gesù (1773)* (Rome: Pontificia Università Gregoriana, 1954), p. 71.

51. See Theiner, *Entwicklung;* Vereecke, *De Guillaume d'Ockham;* Bernard Häring and Louis Vereecke, "La Théologie morale de s. Thomas d'Aquin à s. Alphonse de Liguori," *Nouvelle Revue Théologique,* 77 (1955), 673–692; John Mahoney, *The Making of Moral Theology: A Study of the Roman Catholic Tradition* (Oxford: Clarendon Press, 1987); and John A. Gallagher, *Time Past, Time Future: An Historical Study of Catholic Moral Theology* (New York: Paulist Press, 1990).

52. *Chron.*, 4:445; Angelozzi, "Casi," pp. 140–145.

53. On these three works, see Theiner, *Entwicklung*, pp. 77–88, and Turrini, *La coscienza*, especially pp. 151–155, 262–265. See also Michaud-Quantin, *Sommes de casuistique*; Leonard E. Boyle, "The Summas for Confessors as a Genre, and Its Religious Intent," in *The Pursuit of Holiness in Late Medieval and Renaissance Religion*, ed. Charles Trinkaus and Heiko Oberman (Leiden: E. J. Brill, 1974), pp. 126–130, as well as the responses by William J. Bouwsma and Thomas N. Tentler, ibid., pp. 131–137.

54. See Angelo Martini, "Gli studi teologici di Giovanni de Polanco alle origini della legislazione scolastica della Compagnia di Gesù," *AHSI*, 21 (1952), 247–250. On Peyraut, see A. Dondaine, "Guillaume Peyraut: Vie et oeuvres," *Archivum Fratrum Praedicatorum*, 18 (1948), 162–236.

55. *MI Epp.*, 2:153; 12:186; see Theiner, *Entwicklung*, p. 117.

56. *M Laín.*, 6:319–322; Laínez, *Disputationes Tridentinae*, ed. Hartmann Grisar, 2 vols. (Innsbruck: F. Rauch, 1886), 2:487.

57. See Mahoney, *Moral Theology*, especially pp. 27–36.

58. See Theiner, *Entwicklung*, pp. 122–124.

59. *P Co.*, 1:373.

60. *M Nadal*, 4:520–521.

61. See Angelozzi, "Casi," p. 139.

62. The edition I used was Francisco de Toledo, *Instructio Sacerdotum locupletissima* (Lyons: Fr. Anissoniorum & Joan. Posvel, 1679).

63. *Chron.*, 2:211.

64. *Chron.*, 2:209.

65. *Chron.*, 3:122.

66. *Chron.*, 5:169.

67. *M Xav.*, 2:431–434.

68. *Chron.*, 3:189. See Wietse de Boer, " 'Ad audiendi non videndi commoditatem': Note sull'introduzione del confessionale soprattutto in Italia," *Quaderni Storici*, NS 77 (1991), 543–572.

69. *Chron.*, 5:115.

70. *M Nadal*, 5:854–856.

71. *P Co.*, 1:255–256.

72. *M Laín.*, 4:649. See de Boer, " 'Ad audiendi.' "

73. *Chron.*, 1:160.

74. *Institutum*, 1:496.

75. See Antonio Astrain, *Historia de la Compañia de Jesús en la Asistencia de España*, 7 vols. (Madrid: Administración de Razón y Fe, 1902–25), 1:619–621 [this is rev. ed. of first vol., 1912].

76. *MI Epp.*, 4:625–628.

77. *Chron.*, 6:165.

78. *M Nadal*, 5:855.

79. *Chron.*, 1:131.

80. *SpEx.*, #32–42.

81. *MI Epp.*, 12:670, 672.

82. *Exercicio*, fols. 73v–75v. For *confessionarios* then in use in Italy, see Anne Jacobson Schutte, "Consiglio spirituale e controllo sociale: Manuali per la Confessione stampati in volgare prima della Controriforma," in *Città italiane del '500 tra Riforma e Controriforma* (Lucca: Maria Pacini Fazzi, 1988), pp. 45–59.

83. In 1579 Loarte published his own book on hearing confessions, *Avisi di sacerdoti et confessori* (Parma: apud Sethum Viottum, 1579). See Turrini, *La coscienza,* pp. 200–201, 207–210.

84. See John T. Noonan, Jr., *The Scholastic Analysis of Usury* (Cambridge, Mass.: Harvard University Press, 1957), pp. 202–229; Klaus Hansen, "Petrus Canisius's Stand on Usury: An Example of Jesuit Tactics in the German Counter Reformation," *Archive for Reformation History,* 55 (1964), 192–203; and especially Clemens Bauer, "Rigoristische Tendenzen in der katholischen Wirtschaftsethik unter dem Einfluss der Gegenreformation," in *Adel und Kirche: Gerd Tellenbach zum 65. Geburtstag dargebracht von Freunden und Schülern,* ed. Josef Fleckenstein and Karl Schmid (Freiburg: Herder, 1968), pp. 552–579.

85. See Benjamin N. Nelson, *The Idea of Usury: From Tribal Brotherhood to Universal Otherhood* (Princeton: Princeton University Press, 1949), pp. 73–82.

86. *SpEx.,* #24–31.

87. *Orat. Obs.,* #6.

88. See Serafim Leite, *História da Companhia de Jesus no Brasil* (Lisbon: Livraria Portugália, 1938), 2:282–287.

89. See *M Bras.,* 1:357–366, his letter summarizing his many objections to Jesuit pastoral practice.

90. *Chron.,* 3:465–466.

91. *Chron.,* 5:630.

92. See Leite, *História,* 2:282, n5.

93. For the context, see Miri Rubin, *Corpus Christi: The Eucharist in Late Medieval Culture* (New York: Cambridge University Press, 1990).

94. *Autobiography,* #21.

95. See "Communion fréquente," in *Dictionnarie de spiritualité,* 3:1261–1273.

96. See Cristóforo de Madrid, *De frequenti usu Sanctissimi Eucharistiae Sacramenti libellus* (Rome: in aedibus Societatis Jesu, 1557; rpt. Vienna, 1909, ed. J. P. Bock), pp. 10, 18, 64, 73, 74; Paul Dudon, "Le 'Libellus' du P. Bobadilla sur la communion fréquente et quotidienne," *AHSI,* 2 (1933), 273.

97. See Tacchi Venturi, *Storia,* 1/1:249–290, and "Cacciaguerra, Bonsignore," in *Dizionario biografico degli italiani,* 15:786–788.

98. Salmerón, *Commentarii,* 9:355–356. See also ibid., pp. 343–361, for arguments in favor of frequent reception.

99. *Chron.,* 1:308, 445.

100. *Chron.,* 2:53; 4:154–155, 363–364.

101. *MI Epp.,* 1:164, 275–276.

102. Aquinas, *Summa,* 3.80.10, ad 5am.

103. Dudon, " 'Libellus' Bobadilla," p. 269.

104. *Exercicio,* fols. 75v–78v, 166v–177v.

105. Nadal, *Orat. Obs.,* #742.

106. Madrid, *De frequenti,* pp. 30–31.

107. Ibid., p. 35.

108. Ibid., p. 75.

109. Dudon, " 'Libellus' Bobadilla."

110. *Const.,* #80, 261, 342, 343, 584.

111. Dudon, " 'Libellus' Bobadilla," p. 274.

112. Ibid., pp. 267–268.

113. Ibid., p. 273.

114. See Norman P. Tanner, ed., *Decrees of the Ecumenical Councils*, 2 vols. (Washington: Georgetown University Press, 1990), 2:697.

115. See Gregory Martin, *Roma Sancta (1581)*, ed. George Bruner Parks (Rome: Edizioni di Storia e Letteratura, 1969), pp. 65–68.

116. *Chron.*, 2:589; 3:133; 5:532.

117. *P Co.*, 1:326.

118. *Chron.*, 2:56.

119. *M Nadal*, 4:494.

120. See Rubin, *Corpus Christi*, pp. 243–287.

121. See Bernhard Duhr, *Geschichte der Jesuiten in den Ländern deutscher Zunge im XVI. Jahrhundert* (Freiburg: Herdersche Verlagshandung, 1907), pp. 325–326.

122. See Robert Ricard, "Les Jésuites au Brésil pendant la seconde moitié du XVIe siècle (1549–1597)," *Revue d'Histoire des Missions*, 4 (1937), 321–366, 435–470, especially 347–353.

123. Nadal, *Orat. Obs.*, #278.

124. *Const.*, #342, 343, 481.

125. *Const.*, #80, 584.

126. *M Nadal*, 5:79, 805; Nadal, *Scholia*, p. 161. See Manuel Ruiz Jurado, "La santa misa diaria en la espiritualidad Ignaciana," *Gregorianum*, 72 (1991), 349–356.

127. The only major study is Luis de Diego, *La opción sacerdotal de Ignacio de Loyola y sus compañeros (1515–1540): Estudio histórico e interpretación teológico-espiritual* (Caracas: Centrum Ignatianum, 1975). See also André de Jaer, "Ignace de Loyola et le ministère des prêtres," *Nouvelle Revue Théologique*, 109 (1987), 540–553; and John W. O'Malley, "Priesthood, Ministry, and Religious Life: Some Historical and Historiographical Considerations," *Theological Studies*, 49 (1988), 223–257.

128. Nadal, *Pláticas*, p. 71.

129. Nadal, *Pláticas*, p. 69. See also *M Nadal*, 5:549.

130. *Chron.*, 2:17.

131. *Chron.*, 2:21.

132. *Chron.*, 2:127.

133. *Chron.*, 1:388; 2:629; 4:372.

134. *MI Const.*, 1:310, 329. See de Aldama, *Formula*, p. 91.

135. *Chron.*, 3:460; *M Bras.*, 1:357–366.

136. See Thomas D. Culley and Clement J. McNaspy, "Music and the Early Jesuits (1540–1565)," *AHSI*, 40 (1971), 213–245, especially p. 238.

137. *Const.*, #587.

138. *Const.*, #587.

139. *Chron.*, 6:353.

140. *Institutum*, 1:464, 491.

141. *Chron.*, 6:834.

142. See Josef Wicki, "Gesang, Tänze und Musik im Dienst der alten indischen Jesuitenmissionen (ca. 1542–1582)," in *Missionskirche im Orient: Ausgewählte Beiträge über Portugiesisch-Asien* (Immensee: Neue Zeitschrift für Missionswissenschaft, 1976), pp. 138–152, especially p. 144.

143. See Ricardo García Villoslada, "Algúnos documentos sobre la música en el antiguo seminario romano," *AHSI*, 31 (1962), 107–138, and T. Frank Kennedy, "The Musical Tradition at the Roman Seminary during the First Sixty Years (1564–1621)," in *Bellarmino e la Controriforma: Atti del simposio internazionale di studi* (Sora: Centro di Studi Sorani "V. Patriarca," 1990), pp. 631–660.

144. See Villoslada, "Algúnos documentos"; Culley and McNaspy, "Music"; Thomas D. Culley, *Jesuits and Music: I. A Study of the Musicians Connected with the German College in Rome during the 17th Century and Their Activities in Northern Europe* (Rome: Institutum Historicum Societatis Jesu, 1970); Culley, "Musical Activity in Some Sixteenth-Century Jesuit Colleges with Special Reference to the Venerable English College in Rome from 1579 to 1589," *Analecta Musicologica,* 19 (1980), 1–29; G. Dixon, "Musical Activity in the Church of the Gesú in Rome during the Early Baroque," ibid., 49 (1980), 323–337; T. Frank Kennedy, "Roman Seminary," and "Jesuits and Music: Reconsidering the Early Years," *Studi Musicali,* 17 (1988), 71–99.

145. *Chron.,* 5:33; 6:8.

146. See Scaduto, *Laínez,* 1:116–120.

147. *Const.,* #586; Nadal, *Scholia,* pp. 162–167.

148. See Joseph A. Jungmann, *The Mass of the Roman Rite: Its Origins and Development,* trans. Francis A. Brunner, 2 vols. (New York: Benziger Brothers, Inc., 1950, abridged and revised edition, 1961), and John Bossy, "The Mass as a Social Institution, 1200–1700," *Past and Present,* no. 100 (1983), 29–61.

149. *M Fabri,* p. 524; *M Nadal,* 4:511; Nadal, *Pláticas,* p. 200; Nadal, *Orat. Obs.,* #278.

150. *M Nadal,* 4:492.

151. *SpEx.,* #20.

152. *Const.,* #342. See Pedro de Leturia, "Libros de Horas, Anima Christi y Ejercicios Espirituales de San Ignacio," in *Estudios Ignacianos,* ed. Ignacio Iparraguirre, 2 vols. (Rome: Institutum Historicum Societatis Jesu, 1957), 2:99–148, and Roger S. Wieck, *Time Sanctified: The Book of Hours in Medieval Art and Life* (New York: George Braziller, 1988).

153. "De oratione," ARSI cod. Opp. NN 73, fol. 183–188.

154. See Hilmar M. Pabel, "Prayer in Erasmus's Pastoral Ministry through the Printing Press" (Ph.D. diss., Yale University, 1992).

155. "De oratione," ARSI, cod. Opp. NN 73, fol. 188.

156. *M Nadal,* 5:844–845.

157. Nadal, *Pláticas,* pp. 189–190.

158. Francisco de Borja, *Meditaciones para todas los dominicas y ferias del año,* modern edition, *El evangelio meditado,* ed. F. Cervós (Madrid: Administración de Razón y Fe, 1912).

159. Jerónimo Nadal, *Adnotationes et meditationes in Evangelia quae in sacrosancto missae sacrificio toto anno leguntur,* first edition, ed. D. Ximénez (Antwerp: Martin Nutius, 1594).

160. Peter Canisius, *Notae in evangelicas lectiones,* modern edition, ed. F. Streicher, 2 vols. (Munich: Off. Salesiana, 1939–55).

5. Works of Mercy

1. *Chron.,* 2:535.

2. *SpEx.,* #230.

3. *SpEx.,* #18.

4. See Carlos Maria Nannei, *La "Doctrina cristiana" de San Juan de Avila (Contribución al estudio de su doctrina catequética)* (Pamplona: Ediciones Universidad de Navarra, 1977), pp. 225–226.

5. See André de Jaer, "Ignace de Loyola et le ministère des prêtres," *Nouvelle Revue Théologique,* 109 (1987), 540–553.

6. See Brian S. Pullan, *Rich and Poor in Venice: The Social Institutions of a Catholic State to 1620* (Cambridge, Mass.: Harvard University Press, 1971).

7. The phenomenon has not been systematically studied. See, however, Pietro Tacchi Venturi, *Storia della Compagnia di Gesù in Italia*, 2 vols. in 4 (Rome: Edizioni la Civiltà Cattolica, 1938–51), 2/2:147–209; Mario Scaduto, *L'epoca di Giacomo Laínez, 1556–1565*, 2 vols. (Rome: Edizioni la Civiltà Cattolica, 1964–1974), 2:631–650; Pedro de Leturia, *Estudios Ignacianos*, ed. Ignacio Iparraguirre, 2 vols. (Rome: Institutum Historicum Societatis Jesu, 1957), 1:257–283; Abel Athouguia Alves, "The Christian Social Organism and Social Welfare: The Case of Vives, Calvin, and Loyola," *The Sixteenth Century Journal*, 20 (1989), 3–21.

8. *M Fabri*, p. 569. See Karlheinz Diez, *Christus und seine Kirche: Zum Kirchenverständnis des Petrus Canisius* (Paderborn: Verlag Bonifatius-Druckerei, 1987), pp. 86–91, 178, 367–368.

9. See Dennis Edmond Pate, "Jerónimo Nadal and the Early Development of the Society of Jesus, 1545–1573" (Ph.D. diss., University of California, Los Angeles, 1980), p. 105.

10. See Georg Schurhammer, *Francis Xavier: His Life and Times*, trans. M. Joseph Costelloe, 4 vols. (Rome: The Jesuit Historical Institute, 1973–82), 1:445–446.

11. *Chron.*, 2:37–38.

12. *Chron.*, 2:537; *M Nadal*, 1:132–133. See Scaduto, *Laínez*, 2:647–650.

13. *Chron.*, 1:448; 2:44, 137.

14. *P Co.*, 1:547–549; 2:699, 712–713.

15. *Chron.*, 2:380, 384.

16. See, however, Daniel R. Lesnick, "Civic Preaching in the Early Renaissance: Dominici's Florentine Sermons," in *Christianity and the Renaissance: Image and Religious Imagination in the Quattrocento*, ed. Timothy Verdon and John Henderson (Syracuse: Syracuse University Press, 1990), pp. 208–225, and Ronald F. E. Weissman, *Ritual Brotherhood in Renaissance Florence* (New York: Academic Press, 1982), pp. 44–45, 50–56, 89–90.

17. *M Nadal*, 5:862.

18. See Lauro Martines, ed., *Violence and Civil Disorder in Italian Cities, 1200–1500* (Berkeley and Los Angeles: The University of California Press, 1972).

19. *M Broët*, pp. 265–267.

20. *Chron.*, 1:399–401.

21. *Chron.*, 1:152.

22. *Chron.*, 1:322.

23. *Chron.*, 2:199.

24. *Chron.*, 2:246; 3:89; 5:471–472. See Nigel Griffen, "A Curious Document: Baltasar Loarte, S.I., and the Years 1554–1570," *AHSI*, 45 (1976), 56–94.

25. *Chron.*, 1:441.

26. *Chron.*, 1:382.

27. *Chron.*, 2:78.

28. See Pullan, *Rich and Poor*, pp. 197–215; Katharine Park, *Doctors and Medicine in Early Renaissance Florence* (Princeton: Princeton University Press, 1985); Park, "Healing the Poor: Hospitals and Medical Assistance in Renaissance Florence," in *Medicine and Charity before the Welfare State*, ed. Jonathan Barry and Colin Jones (London: Routledge, 1991), pp. 26–43; Park with John Henderson, " 'The First Hospital among Christians': The Ospedale di Santa Maria Nuova in Early Sixteenth-Century Florence," *Medical History*, 35 (1991), 164–188.

29. *Chron.*, 3:44.

30. *M Nadal*, 2:133, n8; *Beati Petri Canisii, Societatis Jesu, Epistulae et Acta*, ed. Otto Braunsberger, 8 vols. (Freiburg: Herder, 1896–1923), 3:547–548; 4:264. I am grateful to

A. Lynn Martin for a conversation concerning his forthcoming study on the Jesuits and the plague.

31. *P Co.*, 2:666, 691.

32. *P Co.*, 2:707. For an encomiastic presentation, see Philippus Alegambe, *Heroes, et victimae charitatis Societatis Jesu* (Rome: Ex typographia Varesii, 1658), especially pp. 1–40.

33. *Chron.*, 5:21–22.

34. *P Co.*, 1:295–296.

35. *Chron.*, 2:247.

36. *Chron.*, 1:340.

37. *Chron.*, 1:474–475. See Schurhammer, *Xavier*, 3:459–465.

38. *Institutum Societatis Jesu*, 2 vols. (Prague: Typis Universitatis Carolo-Ferdinandeae, 1757), 1:53–54.

39. *Const.*, #66.

40. See Pietro Tacchi Venturi, "La prova dell'indifferenza e del servizio negli Ospedali nel Tirocinio ignaziano," *AHSI*, 1 (1932), 7–23.

41. *M Nadal*, 5:863.

42. See Tacchi Venturi, *Storia*, 2/2:190–195.

43. *MI Epp.*, 1:265.

44. *Chron.*, 1:240.

45. *MI Epp.*, 1:286.

46. Juan Alfonso de Polanco, *Methodus ad eos adiuvandos, qui moriuntur* (Liège: H. Hovius, 1587), p. 133.

47. Polanco, *Breve directorium ad confessarii et confitentis munus recte obeundum* (Liège: H. Hovius, 1591), pp. 77–78.

48. *M Nadal*, 2:3.

49. See Pullan, *Rich and Poor*, pp. 394–397; Vincenzo Paglia, "*La pietà dei carcerati*": *Confraternite e società a Roma nei secoli XVI–XVIII* (Rome: Edizioni di Storia e Letteratura, 1980), pp. 3–73; Christopher Black, *Italian Confraternities in the Sixteenth Century* (Cambridge: Cambridge University Press, 1989), pp. 214–223.

50. *M Nadal*, 5:863–864.

51. *Chron.*, 6:608.

52. *P Co.*, 1:425.

53. *P Co.*, 1:559.

54. *Chron.*, 1:241, 283, 425–426; 6:565.

55. *Chron.*, 2:322; 3:58; 6:306–307.

56. Paglia, "*La pietà dei carcerati.*"

57. *P Co.*, 2:783.

58. See James R. Banker, *Death in the Community: Memorialization and Confraternities in an Italian Commune in the Late Middle Ages* (Athens: The University of Georgia Press, 1988), and Nicholas Terpstra, "Death and Dying in Renaissance Confraternities," in *Crossing the Boundaries: Christian Piety and the Arts in Italian Medieval and Renaissance Confraternities*, ed. Konrad Eisenbichler (Kalamazoo: Medieval Institute Publications, 1991), pp. 179–200.

59. See, for example, Mary C. O'Connor, *The Art of Dying Well: The Development of the Ars Moriendi* (New York: Columbia University Press, 1942); Rainer Rudolf, *Ars moriendi: Von der Kunst des heilsamen Lebens und Sterbens* (Cologne: Böhlau, 1957); Roger Chartier, "Les arts de mourir, 1450–1600," *Annales Economies Sociétés Civilisations*, 31 (1976), 51–75; Remo L. Guidi, *La morte nell'età umanistica* (Vicenza: L. I. E. F., 1983);

Erik Lips, "Sur la popularité de l'*Ars moriendi* aux Pays-Bas (1450–1530)," *Revue du Nord,* 70 (1988), 489–500. More broadly, see Jean Delumeau, *Sin and Fear: The Emergence of a Western Guilt Culture, 13th-18th Centuries,* trans. Eric Nicholson (New York: St. Martin's Press, 1990), pp. 55–66, 317–326, 348–356.

60. In *Tratados espirituales,* ed. Cándido de Dalmases (Barcelona: Juan Flors, 1964), pp. 461–469.

61. *M Nadal,* 5:838–841.

62. See also, however, Martin, *Jesuit Mind,* pp. 172–183.

63. Nadal, *Orat. Obs.,* #571, 691, 964. See also *M Nadal,* 1:47–50.

64. *M Fabri,* p. 612.

65. Gaspar de Loarte, *Exercicio dela vida christiana* (Cagliari: V. Sembenino, 1567), fols. 130–143v.

66. See Black, *Confraternities,* pp. 217–221.

67. See Samuel Y. Edgerton, Jr., *Pictures and Punishment: Art and Criminal Prosecution during the Florentine Renaissance* (Ithaca: Cornell University Press, 1985), especially pp. 165–221.

68. Ibid., pp. 165–210; Giancarlo Angelozzi, *Le confraternite laicali: Un'esperienza cristiana tra medioevo e età moderna* (Brescia: Editrice Queriniana, 1978), pp. 184–220; Adriano Prosperi, "Il sangue e l'anima: Ricerche sulle Compagnie di Giustitia in Italia," *Quaderni Storici,* 51 (1982), 959–999; Kathleen Falvey, "Early Italian Dramatic Traditions and Comforting Rituals: Some Initial Considerations," in Eisenbichler, *Crossing the Boundaries,* pp. 33–55; Jean S. Weisz, "*Caritas/Controriforma:* The Changing Role of a Confraternity's Ritual," ibid., pp. 221–236; Nicholas Terpstra, "Piety and Punishment: The Lay Conforteria and Civic Justice in Sixteenth-Century Bologna," *The Sixteenth Century Journal,* 22 (1991), 679–694.

69. See, for example, Prosperi, "Il sangue e l'anima"; Terpstra, "Piety and Punishment"; Vincenzo Paglia, *La morte confortata: Riti della paura e mentalità religiosa a Roma nell'età moderna* (Rome: Edizioni di Storia e Letteratura, 1982). See also Lionello Puppi, *Lo splendore dei supplizi: Liturgia delle esecuzioni capitali e iconografia del martirio nell'arte europea dal XII al XIX secolo* (Milan: Berenice, 1990).

70. *Chron.,* 6:308.

71. *P Co.,* 2:655.

72. *Chron.,* 5:559.

73. *M Nadal,* 1:408.

74. *Chron.,* 3:117; 5:360.

75. *P Co.,* 1:554.

76. See Charles Chauvin, *Les chrétiens et la prostitution* (Paris: Les Editions du Cerf, 1983), and Jean-Guy Nadeau, *La prostitution, une affaire de sens: Etudes de pratiques sociales et pastorales* (Montreal: Fides, 1987).

77. The literature is ample. See, for example, Elisabeth Pavan, "Police des moeurs, société et politique à Venise à la fin du Moyen Age," *Revue historique,* 264 (1980), 241–288; R. C. Trexler, "La prostitution florentine au XVe siècle," *Memoria,* 17 (1986), 983–1015; Sherrill Cohen, "Convertite e Malmaritate: Donne 'irregolari' e ordini religiosi nella Firenze rinascimentale," ibid., 5 (1982), 46–63.

78. See Cathy Santore, "Julia Lombardo, 'Somtuosa Meretrize': A Portrait by Property," *Renaissance Quarterly,* 41 (1988), 44–83.

79. See Paglia, "*La Pietà dei carcerati,*" pp. 69, 214.

80. See Pullan, *Rich and Poor,* pp. 374–394; Black, *Confraternities,* pp. 206–213; Sherrill Cohen, "Asylums for Women in Counter-Reformation Italy," in *Women in Reforma-*

tion and Counter-Reformation Europe: Public and Private Worlds, ed. Sherrin Marshall (Bloomington: Indiana University Press, 1989), pp. 166–188, and *The Evolution of Women's Asylums: Ex-Prostitutes and Unhappy Wives* (New York: Oxford University Press, 1992).

81. See Vern Bullough and Bonnie Bullough, *Women and Prostitution: A Social History* (Buffalo and New York: Prometheus Books, 1987), pp. 153–154. See also Mary Elizabeth Perry, " 'Lost Women' in Early Modern Seville: The Politics of Prostitution," *Feminist Studies*, 4 (1978), 195–214.

82. *Chron.*, 2:349–350. See Paul Larivaille, *La vie quotidienne des courtisanes en Italie au temps de la Renaissance (Rome et Venise, XVe et XVIe siècles)* (Paris: Hachette, 1975), pp. 163–165.

83. See Rita Casagrande di Villaviera, *Le cortigiane veneziane nel Cinquecento* (Milan: Longanesi, 1968), pp. 32–33.

84. See Larivaille, *Vie quotidienne*, pp. 158–165; Casagrande, *Le cortigiane*, pp. 32–33; Santore, "Julia Lombardo," pp. 56–57.

85. *Chron.*, 1:271.

86. *FN*, 2:346.

87. *Chron.*, 1:377–378. See also ibid., 1:289.

88. See Chauvin, *Les chrétiens*, pp. 79–80; A. Rabutaux, *De la prostitution en Europe depuis l'antiquité jusqu'a la fin du XVIe siècle* (Paris: A. Duquesne, 1869), p. 131.

89. *M Bras.*, 1:120, 166.

90. *Chron.*, 2:740–741.

91. *P Co.*, 1:563.

92. See Gabriella Zarri, "I monasteri femminili a Bologna tra il XIII e il XVII secolo," cited in Lucia Ferrante, " 'Malmaritate' tra assistenza e punizione (Bologna secc. XVI–XVII)," in *Forma e Soggetti dell'intervento assistenziale in una città di antico regime* (Bologna: Istituto per la storia di Bologna, 1986), p. 72.

93. See Chauvin, *Les chrétiens*, pp. 80–81.

94. *Chron.*, 1:278.

95. *Chron.*, 2:342, 349–350, 740–741; 3:204–205; *P Co.*, 2:655, 669.

96. See Scaduto, *Laínez*, 2:643–644; Pullan, *Rich and Poor*, pp. 385–394.

97. *Chron.*, 1:238–239, 381.

98. *Chron.*, 5:149.

99. *Chron.*, 6:192.

100. *Chron.*, 6:224–225.

101. *Chron.*, 2:147.

102. *Chron.*, 4:515; 6:694.

103. *Chron.*, 1:127–128; 3:204–205; 5:101. See Scaduto, *Laínez*, 2:641-643; Tacchi Venturi, *Storia*, 1/2:284–313; 2/2:160–182; and especially Charles Chauvin, "La maison Sainte-Marthe: Ignace et les prostituées de Rome," *Christus*, no. 149 (January 1991), 117–126; and "Ignace et les courtisanes: La Maison Sainte Marthe (1542–1548)," in *Ignacio de Loyola y su tiempo*, ed. Juan Plazaola (Bilbao: Ediciones Mensajero, 1992), pp. 551–562.

104. On dowries, see Black, *Confraternities*, pp. 178–184.

105. *FN*, 2:348–349; Laínez, "De oratione," ARSI cod. Opp. NN. 73, fol. 168v.

106. *P Co.*, 1:63–65.

107. See Scaduto, *Laínez*, 2:641.

108. See Adriano Prosperi, *Tra evangelismo e controriforma: G. M. Giberti (1495–1543)* (Rome: Edizioni di Storia e Letteratura, 1969), p. 265.

109. See Chauvin, "La maison Sainte-Marthe," p. 121.

110. Tacchi Venturi, *Storia*, 2/2:175–176.

111. Gregory Martin, *Roma Sancta (1581)*, ed. George Bruner Parks (Rome: Edizioni di Storia e Letteratura, 1969), pp. 144–145.

112. Pullan, *Rich and Poor*, pp. 391–394.

113. *M Nadal*, 1:275; *Chron.*, 3:204–205.

114. *Chron.*, 4:208.

115. See John Boswell, *The Kindness of Strangers: The Abandonment of Children in Western Europe from Late Antiquity to the Renaissance* (New York: Pantheon Books, 1988), and Philip Gavitt, *Charity and Children in Renaissance Florence: The Ospedale degli Innocenti, 1410–1536* (Ann Arbor: The University of Michigan Press, 1990).

116. See, however, Black, *Confraternities*, pp. 178–184, 200–206.

117. See "Gerolamo Miani," in *Dizionario degli Istituti di Perfezione;* "Jérôme Miani," in *Dictionnaire de spiritualité;* Pullan, *Rich and Poor*, pp. 259–263.

118. *FN*, 1:127. See Tacchi Venturi, *Storia*, 2/2:195–198.

119. *Chron.*, 1:240; 2:39; *Litt. Quadr.*, 1:51.

120. *Chron.*, 2:543, 556.

121. *M Bras.*, 1:25–26; *M Paed.*, 1:546–547. See *O Colégio de "Jesus" dos meninos órfãos da Mouraria* (Lisbon: Arquivo Histórico de Portugal, 1959), pp. 1–29.

122. *Chron.*, 2:100, 543.

123. See Tacchi Venturi, *Storia*, 2/2:185–189; Scaduto, *Laínez*, 2:645–647; Pullan, *Rich and Poor*, p. 385; Jean Delumeau, *Vie économique et sociale de Rome dans la seconde moitié du XVIe siècle*, 2 vols. (Paris: E. de Boccard, 1957), 1:429.

124. See Tacchi Venturi, *Storia*, 2/2:189; Scaduto, *Laínez*, 2:645.

125. See Pullan, *Rich and Poor*, pp. 385–391.

126. Ibid., p. 390.

127. Ibid., pp. 486–488.

128. See Kenneth R. Stow, *Catholic Thought and Papal Jewry Policy, 1555–1593* (New York: The Jewish Theological Seminary of America, 1977), and Nicolas Davidson, "The Inquisition and the Italian Jews," in *Inquisition and Society in Early Modern Europe*, ed. and trans. Stephen Haliczer (London and Sydney: Croom Helm, 1987), pp. 19–46.

129. See Francisco de Borja Medina, "Ignacio de Loiola y la 'limpieza de sangre,' " in *Ignacio y su tiempo*, pp. 579–615. See also José Luis Orella Unzue, "La provincia de Guipúzcoa y el tema de los judíos en tiempos del joven Iñigo de Loyola (1492–1528)," ibid., pp. 847–868; Eusebio Rey, "San Ignacio de Loyola y el problema de los cristianos nuevos," *Razón y Fe*, 153 (1956), 173–204; James W. Reites, "St. Ignatius of Loyola and the Jews," *Studies in the Spirituality of Jesuits*, 13/4 (1981); John Patrick Donnelly, "Antonio Possevino and Jesuits of Jewish Ancestry," *AHSI*, 55 (1986), 3–31; and the still useful summary by Salo Wittmayer Baron, *A Social and Religious History of the Jews*, rev. ed. (New York and London: Columbia University Press, 1969), 14:9–17.

130. See Stephen Haliczer, "The First Holocaust: The Inquisition and the Converted Jews of Spain and Portugal," in Haliczer, *Inquisition and Society*, pp. 7–18, and Catherine Brault-Noble and Marie-José Marc, "L'Unification religieuse et sociale: La répression des minorités," in *L'Inquisition espagnole, XVe–XIXe siècle [sic]*, ed. Bartolomé Bennassar (Paris: Hachette, 1979), pp. 143–195.

131. See Francisco de Borja de Medina, "La Compañía de Jesús y la minoría morisca (1545–1614)," *AHSI*, 57 (1988), 3–136.

132. See Ribadeneira's "De prognatis genere hebraeorum societatis aditu non excludendis," *M Rib.*, 2:374–388, and Donnelly, "Antonio Possevino."

133. *Chron.*, 2:216.

134. See José C. Sola, "El P. Juan Bautista Eliano: Un documento autobiográfico inédito," *AHSI*, 4 (1935), 291–321.

135. The edition I used was published under the name Giovanni Battista Romano, *Dottrina christiana nella quale si contengono li principali misteri della nostra fede rappresentati con figure per instruttione de gl'Idioti, & di quelli che non sanno leggere* (Rome: Vincentio Accolti, 1587).

136. *M Nadal*, 1:69.

137. See Josef Wicki, "Die 'Cristãos-novos' in der indischen Provinz der Gesellschaft Jesu von Ignatius bis Aquaviva," *AHSI*, 46 (1977), 342–361.

138. ARSI, cod. Epist. Hisp. XVIII, fol. 314, quoted in Rey, "Ignacio y cristianos nuevos," p. 191.

139. *M Nadal*, 1:29–31.

140. *Adnotationes et meditationes in Evangelia*, ed. D. Ximénez (Anvers: Martin Nutius, 1594), p. 378.

141. *FN*, 2:476–477; *M Rib.*, 2:375.

142. *MI Epp.*, 9:351, 362–363; *P Co.*, 1:181–182.

143. See Stow, *Catholic Thought*, pp. 51–54.

144. See Tacchi Venturi, *Storia*, 1/2:270–273; 2/2:149–160.

145. See A. Milano, "L'impari lotta della Communità di Roma contro la Casa dei catecumeni," *La Rassegna mensile di Israel*, 16 (1950), 355–368, 408–419.

146. See Tacchi Venturi, *Storia*, 2/2:159.

147. *P Co.*, 1:254.

148. *P Co.*, 1:61–62, 561–563, 624–627.

149. *Chron.*, 1:191–192, 235.

150. *MI Epp.*, 6:308; *Chron.*, 4:141–142. See Stow, *Catholic Thought*, pp. 54–58, and "The Burning of the Talmud in 1553, in the Light of Sixteenth-Century Catholic Attitudes toward the Talmud," *Bibliothèque d'Humanisme et Renaissance*, 34 (1972), 435–459.

151. The bibliography on medieval confraternities is extensive. Still basic is Gilles-Gerard Meersseman, *Ordo Fraternitatis: Confraternite e pietà dei laici nel medioevo*, 3 vols. (Rome: Herder, 1977). See also more recent studies like Banker, *Death in the Community*; Eisenbichler, *Crossing the Boundaries*; Lester K. Little, *Liberty, Charity, Fraternity: Lay Religious Confraternities at Bergamo in the Age of the Communes* (Northampton: Smith College, 1988); *Le fraternite medievali di Assisi: Linee storiche e testi statuari*, ed. Ugolino Nicolini, Enrico Menestò, and Francesco Santucci (Assisi and Perugia: Accademia Properziana del Subasio e Centro di Ricerca e di Studio sul Movimento dei Disciplinati, 1989). More general in their considerations and chronological scope are, for instance, Angelozzi, *Confraternite laicali*; Isidor Moreno, *Cofradías y hermandades andaluzas: Estructura, simbolismo e identidad* (Seville: Editoriales Andaluzas, 1985); see especially Roberto Rusconi, "Confraternite, compagnie e devozioni," in *Storia d'Italia: Annali 9*, ed. Giorgio Chittolini and Giovanni Miccoli (Turin: Giulio Einaudi, 1986), pp. 469–506, with ample bibliography for Italy.

152. See Philip T. Hoffman, *Church and Community in the Diocese of Lyon, 1500–1789* (New Haven: Yale University Press, 1984), p. 25; Jean Delumeau, *Rassurer et protéger: Le sentiment de sécurité dans l'Occident d'autrefois* (Paris: Fayard, 1989), pp. 248–254; R. Po-chia Hsia, *Society and Religion in Münster, 1535–1618* (New Haven: Yale University Press, 1984), pp. 98–102.

153. See Maureen Flynn, *Sacred Charity: Confraternities and Social Welfare in Spain, 1400–1700* (Ithaca: Cornell University Press, 1989).

154. See Meersseman, *Ordo Fraternitatis*, especially 1:355–409; 2:578–920.

155. See Pullan, *Rich and Poor*, pp. 33–193, and "The *Scuole Grandi* of Venice: Some Further Thoughts," in *Christianity and the Renaissance*, pp. 272–301; Weissman, *Ritual Brotherhood*, and "Sacred Eloquence: Humanist Preaching and Lay Piety in Renaissance Florence," in Verdun, *Christianity and the Renaissance*, pp. 250–271; John Henderson, "Penitence and the Laity in Fifteenth-Century Florence," ibid., pp. 229–249; Black, *Confraternities*; Paglia, *"La pietà dei carcerati"*; *Le confraternite romane: Esperienza religiosa, società, committenza artistica*, ed. Luigi Fiorani (Rome: Edizioni di Storia e Letteratura, 1984); Danilo Zardin, "Le confraternite in Italia settentrionale fra XV e XVIII secolo," *Società e Storia*, 10 (1987), 81–137; Alison Bideleux, "Devozione popolare e confraternite a Lucca nel Cinquecento," in *Città italiane del '500 tra Riforma e Controriforma* (Lucca: Maria Pacini Fazzi, 1988), pp. 165–180.

156. See Rusconi, "Confraternite," pp. 481–482.

157. See Zardin, "Le confraternite," p. 84.

158. See Pullan, *Rich and Poor*, p. 280, and especially Terpstra, "Death and Dying," pp. 187–190.

159. Black, *Confraternities*, p. 70. See, however, Scaduto, *Laínez*, 2:624–629; Paglia, *"La pietà dei carcerati"*; Luigi Fiorani, "L'esperienza religiosa nelle confraternite romane tra Cinque e Seicento," in Fiorani, *Le confraternite romane*, especially pp. 160–166.

160. See Paglia, *"La pietà dei carcerati,"* pp. 86–87.

161. *MI Epp.*, 1:162–163; *MI Font. Doc.*, pp. 655–657.

162. *MI Font. Doc.*, pp. 647–650.

163. *MI Font. Doc.*, pp. 642–647.

164. *Chron.*, 1:173.

165. *Chron.*, 2:97.

166. *Chron.*, 1:381; 2:50–51.

167. *Chron.*, 5:65.

168. *Chron.*, 4:145.

169. *Chron.*, 2:324.

170. *Chron.*, 2:440–441.

171. *Chron.*, 6:225. See also *MI Const.*, 1:181.

172. *Const.*, #651.

173. See Paglia, *"La pietà dei carcerati,"* p. 79, and Norman P. Tanner, ed., *Decrees of the Ecumenical Councils*, 2 vols. (Washington: Georgetown University Press, 1990), 2:740.

174. *Chron.*, 1:279. See Scaduto, *Laínez*, 2:627–628.

175. *M Fabri*, pp. 39–43. See Scaduto, *Laínez*, 2:625.

176. *Chron.*, 1:395.

177. *Chron.*, 1:69–71, 150.

178. *Chron.*, 2:539, 742–743; 4:334; 5:489.

179. See Neil S. Fujita, *Japan's Encounter with Christianity: The Catholic Mission in Pre-Modern Japan* (New York: Paulist Press, 1991), pp. 168–171.

180. *M Nadal*, 1:68–69.

181. *Chron.*, 2:368–369.

182. *Chron.*, 4:518.

183. See, for example, Weissman, *Ritual Brotherhood*, pp. 195–235; Black, *Confraternities*; Flynn, *Sacred Charity*, pp. 115–145; Rusconi, "Confraternite"; Robert R. Harding, "The Mobilization of Confraternities against the Reformation in France," *The Sixteenth Century Journal*, 11 (1980), 85–107; Andrew W. Barnes, "Religious Anxiety and Devotional Change in Sixteenth-Century French Penitential Confraternities," ibid., 19 (1988),

389–405; Nicholas Terpstra, "Women in the Brotherhood: Gender, Class, and Politics in Renaissance Bolognese Confraternities," *Renaissance and Reformation*, 26 (1990), 193–212.

184. *Chron.*, 3:306; 5:80, 422.

185. *Chron.*, 6:502–504.

186. *Chron.*, 4:174–175, 181–182.

187. See Scaduto, *Laínez*, 2:624.

188. *Chron.*, 4:358–359, 423. See Jean Delumeau, *La peur en Occident* (Paris: Fayard, 1978), pp. 400–403, and *Un chemin d'histoire: Chrétienté et christianisation* (Paris: Fayard, 1981), pp. 152, 172–173; but see also Jean-Pierre Dedieu, "Le modèle religieux: Les disciplines du langage et de l'action," in Bennassar, *L'Inquisition espagnole*, pp. 241–267.

189. *Chron.*, 2:369.

190. See Scaduto, *Laínez*, 2:464–467; Emile Villaret, *Les Congrégations mariales, I: Des origines à la suppression de la Compagnie de Jésus (1540–1773)* (Paris: Beauchesne, 1947); Josef Wicki, *Le père Jean Leunis, S.J. (1532–1584): Fondateur des Congrégations Mariales* (Rome: Institutum Historicum Societatis Jesu, 1951). For a collection of official documents, see Elder Mullan, *The Sodality of Our Lady: Studied in the Documents* (New York: P. J. Kennedy, 1912).

191. *P Co.*, 1:470–471.

192. See Wicki, *Leunis*, p. 42.

193. *Institutum*, 1:88–91. The bull is also in Mullan, *Sodality*, pp. 5*–11*.

194. See Louis Châtellier, *The Europe of the Devout: The Catholic Reformation and the Formation of a New Society*, trans. Jean Birrell (Cambridge: Cambridge University Press, 1989).

195. See Mullan, *Sodality*, pp. 36*–37*.

6. The Schools

1. *M Paed.*, 3:305–306.

2. For the general background, see R. R. Bolger, *The Classical Heritage and Its Beneficiaries: From the Carolingian Age to the End of the Renaissance* (New York: Harper and Row, 1964); Paul F. Grendler, *Schooling in Renaissance Italy: Literacy and Learning, 1300–1600* (Baltimore and London: The Johns Hopkins University Press, 1989), especially pp. 363–381; Gerald Strauss, *Luther's House of Learning: Indoctrination of the Young in the German Reformation* (Baltimore and London: The Johns Hopkins University Press, 1978); Anthony Grafton and Lisa Jardine, *From Humanism to the Humanities: Education and the Liberal Arts in Fifteenth- and Sixteenth-Century Europe* (Cambridge, Mass.: Harvard University Press, 1986); George Huppert, *Public Schools in Renaissance France* (Urbana and Chicago: University of Illinois Press, 1984); Marie-Madeleine Compère, *Du collège au lycée (1500–1850): Généalogie de l'enseignement secondaire français* (Paris: Editions Gallimard, 1985), and the bibliographical review edited by Grendler, "Education in the Renaissance and Reformation," *Renaissance Quarterly*, 43 (1990), 774–824. On the Jesuits, see especially Allan P. Farrell, *The Jesuit Code of Liberal Education: Development and Scope of the Ratio Studiorum* (Milwaukee: Bruce Publishing Company, 1938); George E. Ganss, *Saint Ignatius' Idea of a Jesuit University* (Milwaukee: Marquette University Press, 1954); Ladislaus Lukács, "De origine collegiorum externorum deque controversiis circa eorum paupertatem obortis," *AHSI*, 29 (1960), 189–245; 30 (1961), 1–89; John W. Donohue, *Jesuit Education: An Essay on the Foundation of Its Idea* (New York: Fordham University Press, 1963); Mabel Lundberg, *Jesuitische Anthropologie und Erziehungslehre in der Frühzeit des Ordens (ca. 1540–ca. 1650)* (Uppsala: Almquist & Wiksells, 1966); Gabriel Codina Mir, *Aux*

sources de la pédagogie des jésuites: Le "Modus parisiensis" (Rome: Institutum Historicum Societatis Jesu, 1968); François de Dainville, L'éducation des jésuites (XVIe–XVIIIe siècles), ed. Marie-Madeleine Compère (Paris: Les éditions de minuit, 1978); Karl Hengst, Jesuiten an Universitäten und Jesuitenuniversitäten: Zur Geschichte der Universitäten in der Oberdeutschen und Rheinischen Provinz der Gesellschaft Jesu im Zeitalter der konfessionellen Auseinandersetzung (Paderborn: Ferdinand Schöningh, 1981); Gian Paolo Brizzi, ed., La "Ratio studiorum": Modelli culturali e pratiche educative dei Gesuiti in Italia tra Cinque e Seicento (Rome: Bulzoni Editore, 1981); Aldo Scaglione, The Liberal Arts and the Jesuit College System (Amsterdam and Philadelphia: John Benjamins Publishing Company, 1986).

3. Chron., 2:195.

4. MI Epp., 9:83.

5. See Hengst, Jesuiten, pp. 80–86.

6. Chron., 1:156–157.

7. Institutum Societatis Jesu, 2 vols. (Prague: Typis Universitatis Carolo-Ferdinandeae, 1757), 1:18.

8. Chron., 1:410. See Hengst, Jesuiten, pp. 86–90.

9. FN, 1:610. See Antonio M. de Aldama, The Constitutions of the Society of Jesus: An Introductory Commentary on the Constitutions, trans. Aloysius J. Owen (St. Louis: The Institute of Jesuit Sources, 1989), p. 147, n29.

10. See Lukács, "De origine," (1960), 197–199.

11. See James A. O'Donohoe, Tridentine Seminary Legislation: Its Sources and Formation (Louvain: Publications Universitaires de Louvain, 1957), pp. 35–37, 64–73.

12. M Broët, pp. 286–291.

13. See Angelo Martini, "Gli studi teologici di Giovanni de Polanco alle origini della legislazione scolastica della Compagnia di Gesù," AHSI, 21 (1952), p. 272.

14. See Francisco de Borja de Medina, "La Compañía de Jesús y la minoría morisca (1545–1614)," AHSI, 57 (1988), 3–136, especially 32–38.

15. M Paed., 1:373–375.

16. Litt. Quadr., 1:51.

17. M Nadal, 2:3. See also FN, 3:746–753.

18. See Dennis Edmond Pate, "Jerónimo Nadal and the Early Development of the Society of Jesus, 1545–1573" (Ph.D. diss., University of California, Los Angeles, 1980), pp. 53–136, and Mario Scaduto, "Le origini dell'Università di Messina: A proposito del quarto centenario," AHSI, 17 (1948), 102–159.

19. M Nadal, 1:53–63.

20. Chron., 1:385.

21. Litt. Quadr., 1:172.

22. See Hengst, Jesuiten, pp. 99–109.

23. Chron., 1:390, 404–405.

24. MI Epp., 4:11–12.

25. MI Epp., 4:5–9.

26. See Miguel Batllori, Cultura e Finanze: Studi sulla storia dei Gesuiti da S. Ignazio al Vaticano II (Rome: Edizioni di Storia e Letteratura, 1983), especially pp. 121–138.

27. MI Epp., 4:9–11.

28. See, for instance, Thomas Deutscher, "Seminaries and the Education of Novarese Priests, 1593–1627," The Journal of Ecclesiastical History, 32 (1981), 303–319, and "The Growth of the Secular Clergy and the Development of Educational Institutions in the Diocese of Novara (1563–1772)," ibid., 40 (1989), 381–397.

29. *M Paed.*, 1:606; Nadal, *Scholia*, p. 384.

30. *Chron.*, 5:550. Lukács gives the number as forty-six, "De origine," (1960), p. 241. Scaglione gives thirty-three for 1556, *Liberal Arts*, p. 61.

31. See Lukács, "De origine," (1960), 242–243; *Chron.*, 2:460; 6:340–341.

32. *P Co.*, 2:657; *Chron.*, 6:373–374, 379–380.

33. See Lukács, "De origine," (1960), 234–235.

34. *M Nadal*, 5:462, 832.

35. *M Paed.*, 2:872.

36. *Const.*, #440, 451.

37. See Huppert, *Public Schools*; Grendler, *Schooling in Italy*; Codina Mir, *Aux sources*; Scaglione, *Liberal Arts*.

38. *M Paed.*, 1:475.

39. See Grafton and Jardine, *From Humanism*, pp. 1–28.

40. *MI Epp.*, 1:519–526. See Mario Fois, "La giustificazione cristiana degli studi umanistici da parte di Ignazio di Loyola e le sue conseguenze nei gesuiti posteriori," in *Ignacio de Loyola y su tiempo*, ed. Juan Plazaola (Bilbao: Ediciones Mensajero, 1992), pp. 405–440.

41. *Chron.*, 2:19.

42. *Chron.*, 5:535.

43. *Chron.*, 2:651.

44. See Gian-Mario Anselmi, "Per un' archeologia della *Ratio:* Dalla 'pedogagia' al 'governo,' " in Brizzi, "*Ratio studiorum*," pp. 11–42.

45. *MI Epp.*, 12:310.

46. *M Paed.*, 1:485.

47. *M Nadal*, 2:71.

48. On these two types of schools in Renaissance Italy, see Grendler, *Schooling in Italy*, pp. 111–329.

49. *M Paed.*, 1:89–90, 284–285, 526; *MI Epp.*, 3:722–724.

50. *Const.*, #451.

51. See Scaglione, *Liberal Arts*; Grendler, *Schooling in Italy*, pp. 381–399; Gian Paolo Brizzi, *La formazione della classe dirigente nel Sei-Settecento: I seminaria nobilium nell'Italia centro-settentrionale* (Bologna: Il Mulino, 1976); Gian Paolo Brizzi, Alessandro D'Alessandro, and Alessandra del Fonte, *Università, Principe, Gesuiti: La politica farnesiana dell'istruzione a Parma e Piacenza (1545–1622)* (Rome: Bulzoni Editore, 1980).

52. *M Paed.*, 1:136; *M Nadal*, 5:462, 832.

53. Scaglione, *Liberal Arts*, p. 43.

54. *MI Epp.*, 4:7–9.

55. *Const.*, #623g.

56. Nadal, *Pláticas*, p. 132.

57. *M Paed.*, 1:93–106.

58. See Donohue, *Jesuit Education*, pp. 125–136, and Strauss, *Luther's House of Learning*, pp. 48–70.

59. *M Paed.*, 2:670–685.

60. See, for example, Scaglione, *Liberal Arts*, p. 57.

61. See Lundberg, *Jesuitische Anthropologie*.

62. See de Aldama, *Constitutions*, pp. 139–187.

63. *Const.*, #394, 392–439.

64. *Const.*, #446–451, 440–509.

65. *Const.*, #452.

66. *M Paed.*, 1:133–163.

67. See Grendler, *Schooling in Italy*, p. 379.

68. See Ricardo García Villoslada, *Storia del Collegio Romano dal suo inizio (1551) alla soppressione della Compagnia di Gesù (1773)* (Rome: Pontificia Università Gregoriana, 1954).

69. *Const.*, #446.

70. See Codina Mir, *Aux sources*, pp. 282–288.

71. *M Paed.*, 1:425–426.

72. See Farrell, *Jesuit Code*, pp. 119–121, and Scaglione, *Liberal Arts*, pp. 13–14.

73. See Codina Mir, *Aux sources*, pp. 109–131.

74. See Huppert, *Public Schools*, pp. 47–60, and James K. Farge, "The University of Paris in the Time of Ignatius of Loyola," in *Ignacio y su tiempo*, pp. 221–243, especially pp. 230–231. See also Scaglione, *Liberal Arts*, for correctives to Codina Mir, *Aux sources*.

75. See Anton Schindling, *Humanistische Hochschule und freie Reichsstadt: Gymnasium und Akademie in Strassburg, 1538–1621* (Wiesbaden: Franz Steiner Verlag, 1977).

76. *M Paed.*, 1:599–602.

77. *Chron.*, 2:544.

78. *M Paed.*, 1:458.

79. *Chron.*, 2:270.

80. *Chron.*, 3:241.

81. *Chron.*, 4:445.

82. See Codina Mir, *Aux sources*, pp. 220–221.

83. *M Nadal*, 2:8.

84. See Scaglione, *Liberal Arts*, pp. 92–93, and Jacqueline Lacotte, "La notion de jeu dans la pédagogie des jésuites," *Revue des Sciences Humaines*, no. 158 (June 1975), 251–268.

85. *M Paed.*, 2:910.

86. See Grendler, *Schooling in Italy*, p. 365.

87. See Scaglione, *Liberal Arts*, pp. 68–69.

88. See Codina Mir, *Aux sources*, pp. 141–147.

89. *Const.*, #482.

90. *Chron.*, 2:37.

91. *Chron.*, 2:223–224.

92. *M Paed.*, 2:864–934.

93. *M Paed.*, 2:877.

94. *M Paed.*, 2:911.

95. *M Paed.*, 2:949.

96. *Const.*, #486.

97. *M Fabri*, p. 491.

98. *M Paed.*, 1:158; 2:29, 95; *M Nadal*, 4:490; Nadal, *Scholia*, p. 383.

99. *Chron.*, 2:242–243.

100. See Codina Mir, *Aux sources*, p. 306.

101. See Scaglione, *Liberal Arts*, pp. 48–49.

102. See, for example, Charles Trinkaus, "Themes for a Renaissance Anthropology," in *The Scope of Renaissance Humanism* (Ann Arbor: The University of Michigan Press, 1983), pp. 364–403.

103. *M Nadal*, 1:473.

104. See Codina Mir, *Aux sources*, pp. 128–130.

105. *Chron.*, 2:501.

106. *Chron.*, 6:164.

107. *Chron.*, 2:514.

108. *Chron.*, 3:8. See Villoslada, *Collegio Romano*, p. 29.

109. *M Nadal*, 1:271.

110. *P Co.*, 2:582, 584, 605.

111. *Chron.*, 5:120–121.

112. *Chron.*, 6:163–164.

113. *Chron.*, 6:164.

114. *Chron.*, 6:163.

115. *P Co.*, 1:267–268; 2:582.

116. *Chron.*, 6:179.

117. See, for example, Nerida Newbigin, "The Word Made Flesh: The *Rappresentazioni* of Mysteries and Miracles in Fifteenth-Century Florence," in *Christianity and the Renaissance: Image and Religious Imagination in the Quattrocento*, ed. Timothy Verdon and John Henderson (Syracuse: Syracuse University Press, 1990), pp. 361–375; Cyrilla Barr, "Music and Spectacle in Confraternity Drama of Fifteenth-Century Florence," ibid., pp. 376–404; Paola Ventrone, "Thoughts on Florentine Fifteenth-Century Religious Spectacle," ibid., pp. 405–412; Konrad Eisenbichler, ed., *Crossing the Boundaries: Christian Piety and the Arts in Italian Medieval and Renaissance Confraternities* (Kalamazoo: Medieval Institute Publications, 1991), pp. 11–107, 237–262.

118. Jean-Marie Valentin, *Le théâtre des jésuites dans les pays de langue allemande (1554–1680)*, 3 vols. (Bern: Peter Lang, 1978), and *Le théâtre des jésuites dans les pays de langue allemande: Répertoire chronologique des pièces représentées et des documents conservés (1555–1773)*, 2 vols. (Stuttgart: A. Hiersemann, 1983–84). See also "Gegenreformation und Literatur: Das Jesuitendrama im Dienste der religiösen und moralischen Erziehung," *Historisches Jahrbuch*, 100 (1980), 240–256; Ruprecht Wimmer, *Jesuitentheater, Didactik und Fest: Das Exemplum des ägyptischen Joseph auf den deutschen Bühnen der Gesellschaft Jesu* (Frankfurt am Main: Vittorio Klostermann, 1982); Géza Staud, "Les décors du théâtre des jésuites à Sopron (Hongrie)," *AHSI*, 46 (1977), 277–298; Jan Okon, "Sul teatro dei Gesuiti nell'antica Polonia: Dopo i primi volumi di una pubblicazione fondamentale," ibid., 51 (1982), 319–328; L. E. Roux, "Cent ans d'expérience théâtrale dans les collèges de la Compagnie de Jésus en Espagne," in *Dramaturge et société: Rapports entre l'oeuvre théâtrale, son interprétation et son public au XVIe et XVIIe siècles*, ed. Jean Jacquot, 2 vols. (Paris: Centre national de la recherche scientifique, 1968), 2:479–523; Florencio Segura, "El teatro en los colegios de los jesuitas," *Miscellanea Comillas*, 43 (1985), 299–327; for France, see de Dainville, *L'education des jésuites*, pp. 473–517. A comprehensive study in English, reliable but outdated, is William H. McCabe, *An Introduction to the Jesuit Theater: A Posthumous Work*, ed. Louis J. Oldani (St. Louis: The Institute of Jesuit Sources, 1983). See as well Michael C. Halbig, *The Jesuit Theater of Jacob Masen: Three Plays in Translation with an Introduction* (Bern: Peter Lang, 1987); Joseph Simons, *Jesuit Theater Englished: Five Tragedies of Joseph Simons*, ed. Louis J. Oldani and Philip C. Fisher (St. Louis: The Institute of Jesuit Sources, 1989), and especially Nigel Griffin, *Jesuit School Drama: A Checklist of Critical Literature* (London: Grant & Cutler, 1976), and the supplement under the same title, 1986. For comparisons, see Edith Weber, "Le théâtre humaniste protestant à participation musicale et le théâtre jésuite: Influences, convergences, divergences," in *Les jésuites parmi les hommes aux XVIe et XVIIe siècles: Actes du Colloque de Clermont-Ferrand (avril 1985)*, ed. G. and G. Demerson, B. Dompnier, and A. Regond (Clermont-Ferrand: Association des Publications de la Faculté des Lettres et Sciences Humaines, 1987), pp. 445–460, and Marguerite Soulié, "Le théâtre et la Bible au XVIe

siècle," in *Le temps des Réformes et la Bible*, ed. Guy Bedouelle and Bernard Roussel (Bible de tous les temps, 5) (Paris: Beauchesne, 1989), pp. 635–658.

119. See, however, Raymond Lebègue, "Les ballets des jésuites," *Revue des cours et conférences*, 37 (1935–36), 127–139, 209–222, 321–330, and Judith Rock, "Terpsichore at Louis Le Grand: Baroque Dance on a Jesuit Stage in Paris" (Ph.D. diss., Graduate Theological Union, Berkeley, 1988).

120. *Chron.*, 5:421–422.

121. *Chron.*, 6:567.

122. See *Obras de P. José de Acosta de la Compañía de Jesús: Estudio preliminar y edición*, ed. Francisco Mateos (Madrid: Ediciones Atlas, 1954).

123. *Chron.*, 6:303.

124. See Segura, "El teatro," pp. 326–327; Bernhard Duhr, *Geschichte der Jesuiten in den Ländern deutscher Zunge im XVI. Jahrhundert* (Freiburg: Herdersche Verlagshandlung, 1907), p. 337.

125. See Villoslada, *Collegio Romano*, p. 77. For examples from a later period, see Staud, "Les décors à Sopron," pp. 279–282.

126. See Duhr, *Geschichte der Jesuiten*, pp. 339, 342.

127. *M Paed.*, 3:269–271.

128. *M Paed.*, 3:267–268.

129. *M Paed.*, 3:390–392, 439–440.

130. *P Co.*, 2:710. See Villoslada, *Collegio Romano*, pp. 76–77.

131. See Valentin, *Le théâtre: Répertoire*, 1:1–48.

132. Ibid., 1:1–7.

133. See Melveena McKendrick, *Theatre in Spain, 1490–1700* (Cambridge: Cambridge University Press, 1989), p. 52.

134. See Scaduto, *Laínez*, 2:358.

135. Ibid., 2:432.

136. See Segura, "El teatro," p. 324.

137. See Duhr, *Geschichte der Jesuiten*, pp. 331–332, 337, 339, 340.

138. Ibid., pp. 337–338.

139. See Donohue, *Jesuit Education*, pp. 39–40.

140. *SpEx.*, #363. See Marc Fumaroli, "Définition et description: Scholastique et rhétorique chez les jésuites des XVIe et XVIIe siècles," *Travaux de linguistique et de litterature*, 18 (1980), 37–48.

141. *Chron.*, 4:507; 5:563; *M Paed.*, 2:883, 946.

142. *Chron.*, 3:294.

143. *M Paed.*, 2:870–871.

144. *Chron.*, 3:391; *M Paed.*, 3:362–365.

145. *Chron.*, 5:528.

146. *Chron.*, 3:158. See, for example, A. Lynn Martin, *The Jesuit Mind: The Mentality of an Elite in Early Modern France* (Ithaca: Cornell University Press, 1988), pp. 53–57.

147. *Chron.*, 4:58, 100–101; *M Paed.*, 3:342, 374–375.

148. *Chron.*, 2:524; 4:100.

149. *M Nadal*, 1:367.

150. *Chron.*, 3:60.

151. *Chron.*, 3:47.

152. *Chron.*, 3:161.

153. *M Paed.*, 3:341–342, 373–375, 377–382, 443–444.

154. *M Paed.*, 3:261–262.

155. *Chron.*, 6:196, 199–200.

156. *Chron.*, 5:101.

157. *M Paed.*, 1:21, 200, 637; 3:32.

158. *Chron.*, 3:28.

159. *M Paed.*, 2:977, 993.

160. See Duhr, *Geschichte der Jesuiten*, pp. 295–296.

161. See Pietro Tacchi Venturi, *Storia della Compagnia di Gesù in Italia*, 2 vols. in 4 (Rome: Edizioni la Civiltà Cattolica, 1938–51), 2/2:356.

162. *Chron.*, 3:23–24; *M Paed.*, 1:423–424; *Const.*, #397, 488, 489.

163. *Chron.*, 4:204.

164. *Chron.*, 6:178–179, 226; *M Paed.*, 1:464, 591.

165. *Chron.*, 6:226.

166. *Chron.*, 4:62; 5:140; *M Paed.*, 1:591.

167. *Chron.*, 3:28; *M Paed.*, 1:553.

168. *Institutum*, 1:464.

169. *M Paed.*, 1:446–449; Lukács, "De origine," (1960), 238–241. See also Miguel Batllori, "Su la fondazione del collegio di Sassari: 1562. Nel IV centenario della Università turritana," *AHSI*, 31 (1962), 360–377; Jan Korewa, "Les débuts de la Compagnie de Jésus en Pologne, 1549–1564," ibid., 34 (1965), 3–35; John Patrick Donnelly, "The Jesuits at Padua: Growth, Suppression, Attempts at Restoration, 1552–1606," ibid., 51 (1982), 45–79.

170. *Institutum*, 1:469–470.

171. *P Co.*, 2:680, 704; *M Nadal*, 2:7. See Scaduto, *Laínez*, 2:440–449, 462.

172. *Chron.*, 2:459, 480–481; 4:148–150; 5:161.

173. *P Co.*, 2:715.

174. *Chron.*, 4:99–103; 5:151.

175. *Chron.*, 5:146–149. See Susanna Peyronel Rambaldi, *Speranze e crisi nel Cinquecento modenese: Tensioni religiose e vita cittadina ai tempi di Giovanni Morone* (Milan: Franco Angeli, 1979).

176. *P Co.*, 2:637–638; Scaglione, *Liberal Arts*, pp. 55–56, 111–133.

177. *Const.*, #622e. See, for example, Marc Venard, "Y-a-t-il un stratégie scholaire des jésuites en France au XVIe siècle?" in *L'université de Pont-á-Mousson et les problèmes de son temps* (Nancy: Université de Nancy, 1974), pp. 67–85.

178. See Tacchi Venturi, *Storia*, 2/2:420–433.

179. *Chron.*, 5:11.

180. See Mario Scaduto, "Le missioni di A. Possevino in Piemonte: Propaganda Calvinistica e restaurazione cattolica, 1560–1563," *AHSI*, 28 (1959), 51–191.

181. *Institutum*, 1:489.

182. See Farrell, *Jesuit Code*, pp. 187–216.

183. See, for example, Deutscher, "Seminaries," and "Growth of Clergy"; Maurilio Guasco, "La formazione del clero: I seminarii," in *Storia d'Italia: Annali 9*, ed. Giorgio Chittolini and Giovanni Miccoli (Turin: Giulio Einaudi, 1986), especially pp. 634–658, and Guerrino Pellicia, *La preparazione ed ammissione dei chierici ai santi ordini nella Roma del secolo XVI* (Rome: Pia Società San Paolo, 1946).

184. *MI Epp.*, 4:684–690.

185. *Chron.*, 5:24–25.

186. See Villoslada, *Collegio Romano*, pp. 49–55.

187. *MI Epp.*, 4:685.

188. *MI Epp.*, 9:638–640; 10:60–61, 167. See Pate, "Nadal," pp. 178–180.

189. See Justo Fernández Alonso, "El Cardenal Francisco de Toledo, S.J., y su fundación en Santa María la Mayor," *Anthologica Annua,* 37 (1990), 363–379.

190. See Lukács, "De origine," (1960), 230–231.

191. *MI Epp.,* 4:687; *Chron.,* 2:166.

192. See O'Donohoe, *Tridentine Seminary Legislation,* pp. 71–87, and Peter Schmidt, *Das Collegium Germanicum in Rom und die Germaniker: Zur Funktion eines römischen Ausländerseminars (1552–1914)* (Tübingen: Max Niemeyer Verlag, 1984).

193. *MI Epp.,* 4:172–173, 185–186, 349–350.

194. *MI Epp.,* 6:229–233.

195. *M Nadal,* 1:271–272.

196. *M Paed.,* 1:106–129.

197. *FN,* 1:673–674, 690.

198. *P Co.,* 1:569.

199. *Chron.,* 6:15.

200. *M Paed.,* 2:926.

201. See Scaduto, *Laínez,* 2:325–333.

202. *M Paed.,* 2:799–1004.

203. *P Co.,* 2:622.

204. *P Co.,* 1:215, 476–477.

205. *M Paed.,* 2:801.

206. *P Co.,* 1:568–570.

207. *M Paed.,* 2:927.

208. *M Paed.,* 2:935.

209. *M Paed.,* 2:994–1004.

210. See László Lukács, "Die Gründung des wiener päpstlichen Seminars und der Nuntius Giovanni Delfino (1573–1577)," *AHSI,* 23 (1954), 35–75, and "Die nordischen päpstlichen Seminarien und P. Possevino (1577–1587)," ibid., 24 (1955), 33–94.

211. See Schmidt, *Collegium Germanicum,* pp. 1–4.

212. See O'Donohoe, *Tridentine Seminary Legislation,* and "The Seminary Legislation of the Council of Trent," in *Il Concilio di Trento e la riforma tridentina,* 2 vols. (Rome: Herder, 1965), 1:157–172; Mario Scaduto, "Seminari e collegi: In margine al centinario tridentino," *Civiltà Cattolica,* 115/2 (1964), 343–352; 115/3 (1964), 18–28. On the origins and early years of the Seminario, see Pelliccia, *Preparazione ed ammissione,* pp. 257–303, and Pio Paschini, "Le origini del Seminario Romano," in *Cinquecento romano e riforma cattolica: Scritti raccolti in occasione dell'ottantesimo compleanno dell'autore* (Rome: Lateranum, 1958), pp. 1–32.

213. *P Co.,* 2:637; *M Paed.,* 3:356–357. See Scaduto, *Laínez,* 1:435–441.

214. *M Paed.,* 3:16–17, 23–24.

215. *M Paed.,* 2:1011–1028.

216. *Institutum,* 1:491–492; *M Paed.,* 3:9–10.

217. See Scaduto, *Laínez,* 1:442–457, and "Scuola e cultura a Milano nell'età borromaica," in *San Carlo e il suo tempo,* 2 vols. (Rome: Edizioni di Storia e Letteratura, 1986), 2:963–994.

218. *M Paed.,* 3:16–17, n9.

219. *M Paed.,* 3:343.

220. *M Paed.,* 1:436.

221. *MI Epp.,* 3:56.

222. See, for example, Scaduto, "Seminari e collegi," and Arno Seifert, *Weltlicher Staat und Kirchenreform: Die Seminarpolitik Bayerns im 16. Jahrhundert* (Münster: Aschendorffsche Verlagsbuchhandlung, 1978).

223. See Joseph M. O'Keefe, "The Pedagogy of Persuasion: Jesuit Education at Pont-à-Mousson" (S.T.L. thesis, Weston School of Theology, Cambridge, Mass., 1989), p. 61. See also Lukács, "Die nordischen Seminarien."

224. See Hengst, *Jesuiten,* pp. 98–127.

225. See Grendler, *Schooling in Italy,* especially pp. 363–381.

226. Especially notable is Marc Fumaroli, *L'âge de l'éloquence: Rhétorique et "res litteraria" de la Renaissance au seuil de l'époque classique* (Geneva: Droz, 1980). As an example of a specific issue, see Bernabé Bartolomé Martínez, "Las librerías e imprentas de los jesuitas (1540–1767): Una aportación notable a la cultura española," *Hispania Sacra,* 40 (1988), 315–388.

227. *Const.,* #626. See also #82, 92, 304, 308, 603, 605.

228. See A. H. Thomas, *De oudste Constituties van de Dominicanen* (Louvain: Leuvense Universitaire Uitgaven, 1965), p. 361.

229. See Rivka Feldhay, "Knowledge and Salvation in Jesuit Culture," *Science in Context,* 1 (1987), 195–213.

230. See Lawrence J. Flynn, "The *De Arte Rhetorica* of Cyprian Soarez, S.J.," *The Quarterly Journal of Speech,* 42 (1956), 365–374, and "Sources and Influence of Soarez' *De Arte Rhetorica,*" ibid., 43 (1957), 257–265.

231. See, for example, Feldhay, "Knowledge and Salvation"; William A. Wallace, *Galileo and His Sources: The Heritage of the Collegio Romano in Galileo's Science* (Princeton: Princeton University Press, 1984); Steven J. Harris, "Transposing the Merton Thesis: Apostolic Spirituality and the Establishment of the Jesuit Scientific Tradition," *Science in Context,* 3 (1989), 29–65; Joseph MacDonnell, *Jesuit Geometers* (St. Louis: The Institute of Jesuit Sources, 1989).

7. Religious and Theological Culture

1. *M Nadal,* 5:282–285.

2. *FN,* 1:181; 2:198, n35; *M Nadal,* 5:282.

3. *Bhx Pierre Favre, Mémorial,* ed. and trans. Michel de Certeau (Paris: Desclée de Brouwer, 1960), p. 25.

4. *M Nadal,* 1:2; Nadal, *Orat. Obs.,* #464; *Chron.,* 5:419.

5. *Orat. Obs.,* #464.

6. *SpEx.,* #2.

7. *SpEx.,* #363.

8. *FN,* 1:322; *Chron.,* 3:567–568. See also Nadal, *Scholia,* pp. 122–123.

9. *M Nadal,* 5:460–462; *M Paed.,* 2:129–130. See Miguel Nicolau, "Espiritualidad de la Compañía de Jesús en la España del siglo XVI," *Manresa,* 29 (1957), 217–236.

10. *M Paed.,* 2:129–130; *FN,* 1:321–322.

11. See Georg Schurhammer, *Francis Xavier: His Life and Times,* trans. M. Joseph Costelloe, 4 vols. (Rome: The Jesuit Historical Institute, 1973–82), 1:108–147.

12. *M Nadal,* 5:741; Nadal, *Scholia,* p. 382; *P Co.,* 2:604, 606.

13. Nadal, *Scholia,* pp. 126–127, 382; *M Paed.,* 2:255.

14. *MI Epp.,* 1:132–134. See Schurhammer, *Xavier,* 1:247–253.

15. *M Bobad.,* pp. 614–615; Schurhammer, *Xavier,* 1:250–251; James K. Farge, *Biographical Register of Paris Doctors of Theology, 1500–1536* (Toronto: Pontifical Institute of

Mediaeval Studies, 1980), pp. 110–112. See also Farge's *Orthodoxy and Reform in Early Reformation France: The Faculty of Theology of Paris, 1500–1543* (Leiden: E. J. Brill, 1985), and especially, "The University of Paris in the Time of Ignatius of Loyola," in *Ignacio de Loyola y su tiempo,* ed. Juan Plazaola (Bilbao: Ediciones Mensajero, 1992), pp. 221–243.

16. See Farge, *Biographical Register,* pp. 42–43.

17. *FN,* 2:56. See Farge, *Biographical Register,* pp. 262–266.

18. See Farge, *Biographical Register,* pp. 437–441. For the others mentioned in Favre's letter, see ibid., pp. 8–9 (Jean Adam), pp. 39–40 (Jean Benoist, O.P.), pp. 242–243 (Thomas Laurent, O.P.).

19. See Schurhammer, *Xavier,* 1:238–243, and Farge, "University of Paris," pp. 232–233.

20. See Farge, *Biographical Register,* pp. 350–353.

21. See Schurhammer, *Xavier,* 1:238, and Farge, *Biographical Register,* pp. 342–344.

22. See Farge, *Biographical Register,* pp. 318–322; Walter Frederick Bense, "Noel Beda and the Humanist Reformation at Paris, 1540–1534," 3 vols. (Ph.D. diss., The Divinity School, Harvard University, 1967), 2:388–410; and Marc Venard, "La confession entre la réforme humaniste et la réforme catholique," in *Pratiques de la confession, des Pères du désert à Vatican II: quinze études d'histoire,* ed. Groupe de la Bussière (Paris: Editions du Cerf, 1983), pp. 177–183.

23. *FN,* 2:472.

24. *M Nadal,* 5:282–285.

25. See Hugo Rahner, *Ignatius the Theologian,* trans. Michael Barry (New York: Herder and Herder, 1968), pp. 1–31.

26. See Farge, *Biographical Register,* pp. 304–311, and Schurhammer, *Xavier,* 1:109, 113–114, 248, 258.

27. See de Certeau's "Introduction" to the *Mémorial,* pp. 16–18.

28. See Pietro Tacchi Venturi, *Storia della Compagnia di Gesù in Italia,* 2 vols. in 4 (Rome: Edizioni la Civiltà Cattolica, 1938–51), 2/1:102. On Biel, see especially Heiko A. Oberman, *The Harvest of Medieval Theology: Gabriel Biel and Late Medieval Nominalism* (Cambridge: Harvard University Press, 1963).

29. Diego Laínez, "Disputatio de iustitia imputata," in *Disputationes Tridentinae,* ed. Hartmann Grisar, 2 vols. (Innsbruck: F. Rauch, 1886), 2:182–183.

30. *Const.,* #464.

31. *M Salm.,* 2:709–715. See also, however, *M Rib.,* 2:374–384.

32. See Schurhammer, *Xavier,* 1:208; Farge, *Biographical Register,* pp. 39–40, 242–243, 353–356, and "University of Paris," pp. 232–233.

33. See Miguel Nicolau, *Jerónimo Nadal, S.I. (1507–1580): Sus obras y doctrinas espirituales* (Madrid: Consejo Superior de Investigaciones Científicas, 1949), pp. 428–431; *Orat. Obs.,* #472.

34. See James Brodrick, *Saint Peter Canisius* (Chicago: Loyola University Press, 1962), p. 23, and Karlheinz Diez, *Christus und seine Kirche: Zum Kirchenverständnis des Petrus Canisius* (Paderborn: Verlag Bonifatius-Druckerei, 1987), pp. 22–23.

35. See Angelo Martini, "Gli studi teologici di Giovanni de Polanco alle origini della legislazione scolastica della Compagnia di Gesù," *AHSI,* 21 (1952), 238–241, 272–281. For general background, see Paul Oskar Kristeller, "Thomism and the Italian Thought of the Renaissance," in *Medieval Aspects of Renaissance Learning: Three Essays by Paul Oskar Kristeller,* ed. and trans. Edward P. Mahoney (Durham: Duke University Press, 1974), pp. 27–91.

36. *Epist. Mixtae,* 2:125.

37. See John W. O'Malley, "The Feast of Thomas Aquinas in Renaissance Rome: A Neglected Document and Its Import," *Rivista di Storia della Chiesa in Italia,* 35 (1981), 1–27.

38. See Jared Wicks, "Doctrine and Theology," in *Catholicism in Early Modern History: A Guide to Research,* ed. John W. O'Malley (St. Louis: The Center for Reformation Research, 1988), especially pp. 232–241.

39. *MI Epp.,* 12:186.

40. *Const.,* #147–162.

41. *Const.,* #288.

42. *Orat. Obs.,* for instance, #225, 269, 312, 475, 747, 765, 780–781, 850, 888, and especially 729; *Adnotationes et meditationes in Evangelia,* ed. D. Ximénez (Anvers: Martin Nutius, 1594), pp. 19, 376, 410, 449, 486.

43. *Adnotationes et Meditationes,* p. 512.

44. *Const.,* #30, 638, 813–814.

45. Thomas Aquinas, *Summa theologiae,* 1.1.4. On the relationship of the *Summa* to the earlier tradition of "practical" theology in the Dominican order, see Leonard E. Boyle, "The Setting of the *Summa theologiae* of Saint Thomas," The Etienne Gilson Series, 5 (Toronto: Pontifical Institute of Mediaeval Studies, 1982).

46. See my "Introduction," *Collected Works of Erasmus: Spiritualia* (Toronto: University of Toronto Press, 1988), 66:xv–xxi.

47. *FN,* 2:56. See also *M Fabri,* p. 105.

48. *M Nadal,* 1:11–12, 32–33; *M Xav.,* 1:166–167.

49. *M Nadal,* 5:227–231; Nadal, *Pláticas,* pp. 43–45. See Nicolau, *Nadal,* pp. 305–313.

50. *Orat. Obs.,* #506; *Chron.,* 3:557–558.

51. *Orat. Obs.,* #960.

52. Quoted in André Combes, *La théologie mystique de Gerson: Profil de son évolution,* 2 vols. (Rome: Desclée et Socii Editores Pontificii, 1963), 2:354. See Mark Stephen Burrows, *Jean Gerson and De Consolatione Theologiae (1418): The Consolation of a Biblical and Reforming Theology for a Disordered Age* (Tübingen: J. C. B. Mohr [Paul Siebeck], 1991), pp. 135–148, and William J. Courtenay, "Spirituality and Late Scholasticism," in *Christian Spirituality: High Middle Ages and Reformation,* ed. Jill Raitt (New York: Crossroad, 1988), pp. 109–120. See also Nicolau, *Nadal,* pp. 240–254.

53. *M Paed.,* 1:151–152.

54. *MI Epp.,* 6:398–399; 7:65, 99–100; *M Paed.,* 1:554–555. See Paul Dudon, "Le projet de Somme Théologique du Père Jacques Laynez," *Recherches de science religieuse,* 21 (1931), 361–374.

55. *SpEx.,* #363. See Diez, *Christus,* pp. 22–23.

56. *Concilium Tridentinum: Diariorum, actorum, epistolarum, tractatuum nova collectio,* ed. Societas Goerresiana, 13 vols. in 17 (Freiburg: Herder, 1901–67), 9:589.

57. *M Paed.,* 2:499, 775.

58. See especially Albert Rabil, ed., *Renaissance Humanism: Foundations, Forms, and Legacy,* 3 vols. (Philadelphia: The University of Pennsylvania Press, 1988).

59. See Marc Fumaroli, "Définition et description: Scholastique et rhétorique chez les jésuites des XVIe et XVIIe siècles," *Travaux de Linguistique et de Literature,* 18 (1980), 37–48, and John W. O'Malley, "Renaissance Humanism and the Religious Culture of the First Jesuits," *The Heythrop Journal,* 31 (1990), 471–487.

60. See, for example, Erika Rummel, *Erasmus and His Catholic Critics,* 2 vols. (Nieuwkoop: De Graaf Publishers, 1989); Salvatore I. Camporeale, "Giovanmaria dei Tolosani, o.p., 1530–1546: Umanesimo, Riforma e Teologia controversista," *Memorie*

Domenicane, NS 17 (1986), 145–252; *El Erasmismo en España,* ed. Manuel Revuelta Sañudo and Ciriaco Morón Arroyo (Santander: Sociedad Menendez Pelayo, 1986); Silvana Seidel Menchi, *Erasmo in Italia, 1520–1580* (Turin: Bollati Boringhiere, 1987), and *Erasmus als Ketzer: Reformation und Inquisition im Italien des 16. Jahrhunderts* (Leiden: E. J. Brill, 1992).

61. *Chron.,* 3:572–573; *M Nadal,* 4:831–832.

62. *M Nadal,* 5:739–740.

63. *M Nadal,* 4:831–833.

64. *MI Epp.,* 1:522.

65. *M Paed.,* 2:661–663.

66. See John W. O'Malley, *Praise and Blame in Renaissance Rome: Rhetoric, Doctrine, and Reform in the Sacred Orators of the Papal Court, c. 1450–1521* (Durham: Duke University Press, 1979), especially pp. 36–76, 123–194.

67. *Const.,* #414.

68. *MI Epp.,* 1:519–526, or *M Paed.,* 1:367–373.

69. *MI Epp.,* 9:122. See Marc Fumaroli, *L'âge de l'éloquence: Rhétorique et "res literaria" de la Renaissance au seuil de l'époque classique* (Geneva: Droz, 1980).

70. *MI Epp.,* 2:446.

71. *M Nadal,* 5:735.

72. See Jerry H. Bentley, *Humanists and Holy Writ: New Testament Scholarship in the Renaissance* (Princeton: Princeton University Press, 1983), and Guy Bedouelle, "L'humanisme et la Bible," in *Le temps des Réformes et la Bible,* ed. Guy Bedouelle and Bernard Roussel (Bible de tous les temps, 5) (Paris: Beauchesne, 1989), pp. 53–121.

73. Nadal, *Pláticas,* p. 133; *M Nadal,* 5:740.

74. *M Nadal,* 5:829.

75. *M Nadal,* 4:869–870.

76. *M Nadal,* 5:740–741. See also *M Paed.,* 2:118.

77. *MI Const.,* 1:191. See also 1:203, 230; 2:183, and especially 3:xlii–xliv.

78. *MI Const.,* 1:393–394. For the decree, see Norman P. Tanner, ed., *Decrees of the Ecumenical Councils,* 2 vols. (Washington: Georgetown University Press, 1990), 2:663–665. On its formulation, see Hubert Jedin, *A History of the Council of Trent,* trans. Ernest Graf, 2 vols. in English (London: Thomas Nelson and Son, 1957–61), 2:52–98, and Guy Bedouelle, "La Réforme catholique," in Bedouelle, *Les temps des Réformes,* pp. 327–368, especially pp. 342–343.

79. *Const.,* #367. See Ganss's translation, p. 192, n7.

80. On the context, see Peter R. Ackroyd, C. F. Evans, G. W. H. Lampe, and S. L. Greenslade, eds., *The Cambridge History of the Bible: The West from the Reformation to the Present Day,* 3 vols. (Cambridge: Cambridge University Press, 1963–70), 3:91–93, and William Monter, "French Bibles and the Spanish Inquisition, 1552," *Bibliothèque d'Humanisme et Renaissance,* 51 (1989), 147–152.

81. *Chron.,* 6:411.

82. See Ackroyd, *Cambridge History,* 3:61–67; *Dictionnaire de la Bible,* 2:1982–1984.

83. *MI Epp.,* 3:26; 4:651; 5:42, 159, 300–301, 470; 6:259, 687–688; 7:226, 733; 9:422; 10:83, 458. See also *M Broët,* pp. 97–98.

84. *MI Epp.,* 10:83, 458. See also Alfonso Salmerón, *Commentarii in Evangelicam Historiam, et in Acta Apostolorum; Commentarii in omnes Epistolas B. Pauli et canonicas,* 16 vols. (Cologne: A. Hierat and I. Gymnicus, 1612–15), 16:309.

85. *MI Epp.,* 10:461. But see ibid., 5:727–728; 7:400.

86. Gaspar de Loarte, *Exercicio,* fol. 91v. See also Francisco de Borja, "Avisos para leer la Sagrada Escritura," in *Tratados espirituales,* ed. Cándido de Dalmases (Barcelona: Juan Flors, 1964), pp. 415–416.

87. *M Paed.,* 3:108.

88. See Max Huot de Longchamp, "Les mystiques catholiques et la Bible," in Bedouelle, *Les temps des Réformes,* pp. 587–612.

89. See, however, Richard Gawthrop and Gerald Strauss, "Protestantism and Literacy in Early Modern Germany," *Past and Present,* no. 104 (August 1984), 31–55.

90. I have used the third and last edition; see note 84 above.

91. See John D. Willis, " 'Love Your Enemies': Sixteenth-Century Interpretations" (Ph.D. diss., University of Chicago, 1989), pp. 51–65, 174–203, 474–562, 583–586.

92. See Bedouelle, "La Réforme catholique," pp. 361–368.

93. See Diez, *Christus,* pp. 22–26, and W. J. Malley, "The *Contra Julianum* of St. Cyril of Alexandria and St. Peter Canisius," *Theological Studies,* 25 (1964), 70–74.

94. *Beati Petri Canisii Societatis Jesu Epistulae et Acta,* ed. Otto Braunsberger (Freiburg: Herder, 1896), 1:1–68; Jean-François Gilmont, *Les écrits spirituels des premiers jésuites: Inventaire commenté* (Rome: Institutum Historicum Societatis Iesu, 1961), pp. 230–231, 276.

95. See Pedro de Leturia, "Lecturas ascéticas y lecturas místicas entre los jesuítas del siglo XVI," *Estudios Ignacianos,* ed. Ignacio Iparraguirre, 2 vols. (Rome: Institutum Historicum Societatis Iesu, 1957), 2:279.

96. *MI Epp.,* 12:186–187.

97. See Schurhammer, *Xavier,* 1:254–259.

98. *SpEx.,* #363.

99. For a summary of recent interpretations, see Pascual Cebollada, "Loyola y Erasmo: Aportación al estudio de la relación entre ambos," *Manresa,* 62 (1990), 49–60. See also Terence O'Reilly, "The Spiritual Exercises and the Crisis of Medieval Piety," *The Way,* supplement no. 70 (1991), 101–113; Marcella and Paul Grendler, "The Erasmus Holdings of Roman and Vatican Libraries," *Erasmus in English,* 13 (1984), 2–29; Irmgard Bezzel, "Erasmusdrucke des 16. Jahrhunderts in bayerischen Jesuitenbibliotheken," in *Das Verhältnis der Humanisten zum Buch,* ed. Fritz Krafft and Dieter Wuttke (Boppard: Deutsche Forschungsgemeinschaft, 1977), pp. 145–162; Roland Crahay, "Le procès d'Erasme à la fin du XVIe siècle: Position de quelques jésuites," in *Colloque érasmien de Liège,* ed. Jean-Pierre Massaut (Paris: "Les Belles Lettres," 1987), pp. 115–133.

100. See Cebollada, "Loyola y Erasmo," pp. 52–56. See also Mark Rotsaert, "Les premiers contacts de saint Ignace avec l'érasmisme espagnol," *Revue d'histoire de la spiritualité,* 49 (1973), 443–464.

101. *FN,* 2:73.

102. See Seidel Menchi, *Erasmo in Italia,* pp. 308–311.

103. *MI Epp.,* 4:108, 359, 377, 484; 5:421–422; 6:267; 7:706; 8:35; 9:721–722.

104. *MI Epp.,* 6:484–486.

105. See Seidel Menchi, *Erasmo,* pp. 122–123.

106. *MI Epp.,* 5:94–95.

107. *MI Epp.,* 9:721–722.

108. *MI Epp.,* 5:421–422. See also 4:108; 7:706; *M Paed.,* 1:557. See Valentín Moreno Gallego, "Notas historiográficas al encuentro de Loyola y Vives," in *Ignacio y su tiempo,* pp. 901–907.

109. *MI Epp.,* 12:634.

110. *MI Epp.,* 5:94–95.

111. *MI Epp.*, 6:80.

112. See Seidel Menchi, *Erasmo in Italia*, p. 230.

113. *M Paed.*, 1:97, 99, 100, 139.

114. See Josef Wicki, "Der einheimische Klerus in Indien," in *Der einheimische Klerus in Geschichte und Gegenwart: Festschrift P. Dr. Laurenz Kilger OSB*, ed. Johannes Beckmann (Schöneck-Beckenried: Administration der Neuen Zeitschrift für Missionswissenschaft, 1950), p. 25.

115. *M Lain.*, 2:304.

116. *M Paed.*, 3:87, 140. See also ibid., 3:251, 573. See Leturia, "Lecturas ascéticas," in *Estudios*, 2:304; Aldo Scaglione, *The Liberal Arts and the Jesuit College System* (Amsterdam and Philadelphia: John Benjamins Publishing Company, 1986), pp. 78–79.

117. See Jean-Marie Valentin, *Le théâtre des jésuites dans les pays de langue allemande: Répertoire chronologique des pièces représentées et des documents conservés (1555–1773)*, 2 vols. (Stuttgart: A. Hiersemann, 1983–1984), 1:4. See also *M Paed.*, 3:573.

118. *M Paed.*, 3:108.

119. *M Paed.*, 1:608.

120. See Martini, "Studi Polanco," pp. 245–246.

121. *M Paed.*, 3:144.

122. Quoted in Brodrick, *Canisius*, p. 458.

123. See Anton Troll, "Der hl. Petrus Canisius und Erasmus," *Ephemerides Mariologicae*, 24 (1974), 347–367.

124. *Commentarii*, for example, 1:21, 69, 373; 2:17–19; 3:36–37, 63–65, 337; 4:17, 490; 8:417; 11:77; 13:276–279; 14:215; 16:307–310.

125. *Commentarii*, 13:57; 15:14.

126. *Commentarii*, 8:118; 13:57.

127. See Crahay, "Le procès d'Erasme," pp. 116–118.

128. *M Nadal*, 4:549; Nadal, *Orat. Obs.*, #204; *M Paed.*, 3:154. See Leturia, "Lecturas ascéticas," in *Estudios*, 2:269–331; Martini, "Studi Polanco," pp. 250–255; de Certeau, "Introduction" to *Mémorial*, pp. 27–38. On the *Devotio*, see Otto Gründler, "Devotio Moderna," in *Christian Spirituality: High Middle Ages and Reformation*, ed. Jill Raitt (New York: Crossroad, 1988), pp. 176–193, and John Van Engen, "Introduction" in *Devotio Moderna: Basic Writings*, ed. and trans. John Van Engen (New York: Paulist Press, 1988), pp. 5–61.

129. See Leturia, "Lecturas ascéticas," in *Estudios*, 2:297; on the *Meditationes*, see Daniel R. Lesnick, *Preaching in Medieval Florence: The Social World of Franciscan and Dominican Spirituality* (Athens and London: The University of Georgia Press, 1989), pp. 143–171.

130. See Leturia, "La 'Devotio Moderna' en el Montserrat de San Ignacio," in *Estudios*, 2:73–88, and Ewart H. Cousins, "Franciscan Roots of Ignatian Meditation," *Studies in Religion*, supplement no. 15 (1984), 51–64.

131. *SpEx.*, #100.

132. *M Nadal*, 1:19.

133. *Chron.*, 4:451.

134. *M Paed.*, 3:266.

135. *Imitation*, 1:8, 10, 20.

136. *Imitation*, 1:23.

137. *Const.*, #304.

138. *Imitation*, 1:3, 24; 3:26, 43.

139. *Imitation*, 3:54–55.

140. See, for example, Diez on Canisius, *Christus*, pp. 27–28, 366–367.

141. *Imitation*, 4:3, 10.

142. *Imitation*, 1:19; 4:7. See Leturia, "Devotio Moderna," in *Estudios*, 2:73–88.

143. *Imitation*, for example, 3:15.

144. *Imitation*, 3:56.

145. *SpEx.*, #358.

146. *SpEx.*, #63, 109, 147, 247, 299.

147. *SpEx.*, #100, 215.

148. *SpEx.*, #82–89, 130, 229, 319, 210–217.

149. See Peter Burke, "Popular Piety," in O'Malley, *Catholicism*, pp. 113–131.

150. "De oratione," ARSI, cod. Opp. NN 73, fols. 177v, 180v.

151. *Chron.*, 6:305–306.

152. *M Nadal*, 4:390.

153. *Chron.*, 3:130–131.

154. See *Canisii Epistolae*, 4:400–402, 876, 881; *Chron.*, 3:265–266. See also Bernhard Duhr, *Geschichte der Jesuiten in den Ländern deutscher Zunge im XVI. Jahrhundert* (Freiburg: Herdersche Verlagshandlung, 1907), pp. 738–754.

155. *M Nadal*, 1:67–70, 84, 95, 123; *Chron.*, 2:501–502, 534.

156. *P Co.*, 2:613–616. See Brodrick, *Canisius*, pp. 64–66.

157. *Chron.*, 3:114; *M Nadal*, 1:95–96.

158. *Chron.*, 1:269–270; *M Nadal*, 2:27.

159. *Chron.*, 1:269–270; 2:17, 312–313.

160. *Chron.*, 1:487.

161. See Brodrick, *Canisius*, p. 427.

162. *M Paed.*, 3:93.

163. *MI Epp.*, 2:359–362, 365–366, 406.

164. *M Nadal*, 1:56–58. See also Laínez, "De oratione," ARSI, cod. Opp. NN 73, fol. 93v.

165. *Adnotationes et meditationes*, p. 342.

166. Ibid., p. 313.

167. *M Nadal*, 5:594.

168. *M Nadal*, 5:269.

169. *Orat. Obs.*, #878.

170. *M Paed.*, 3:266.

171. Francisco de Borja, "Puntos del Santo Rosario," in *Tratatos espirituales*, pp. 306–317.

172. *Const.*, #342–343.

173. *Adnotationes et Meditationes*, pp. 588–636.

174. Gaspar de Loarte, *Istruttione et avertimenti per meditar i misterii del Rosario della santissima Vergine Madre* (Rome: Justina De' Rossi, 1573); (Venice: De' Franceschi, 1573).

175. *Orat. Obs.*, #41. See John W. O'Malley, "To Travel to Any Part of the World: Jerónimo Nadal and the Jesuit Vocation," *Studies in the Spirituality of Jesuits*, 16/2 (1984), 11–13.

176. *Const.*, #67.

177. See Mario Scaduto, "La strada e i primi gesuiti," *AHSI*, 40 (1971), 323–390; John C. Olin, "The Idea of Pilgrimage in the Experience of Ignatius Loyola," *Church History*, 48 (1979), 387–397.

178. Gaspar de Loarte, *Trattato delle sante peregrinationi, dove s'insegna il modo de farle con molto frutto spirituale, et si tratta ancora delle stationi, & indulgentie che nelle peregrinationi si sogliono guadagnare* (Rome: G. Degli Angeli, 1575).

179. See Brodrick, *Canisius,* pp. 195–196.

180. *M Fabri,* p. 160.

181. See Brodrick, *Canisius;* Diez, *Christus;* Engelbert Maximilian Buxbaum, *Petrus Canisius und die kirchliche Erneuerung des Herzogtums Bayern, 1549–1556* (Rome: Institutum Historicum Societatis Jesu, 1973); Hubert Jedin, "Der heilige Petrus Canisius: Ein Profil und sein Hintergrund," in *Kirche des Glaubens Kirche der Geschichte: Ausgewälte Aufsätze und Vorträge,* 2 vols. (Freiburg: Herder, 1966), 1:381–393. See also Bernhard Duhr, *Geschichte der Jesuiten in den Ländern deutscher Zunge im XVI. Jahrhundert* (Freiburg: Herder, 1907), as well as Alfred Poncelet, *Histoire de la Compagnie de Jésus dans les anciens Pays-Bas: Etablissement de la Compagnie de Jésus en Belgique et ses développements jusqu'a la fin du règne d'Albert et d'Isabelle* (Brussels: Maurice Lamertin, 1926). For more general considerations, see Robert Bireley, "Early Modern Germany," in O'Malley, *Catholicism,* pp. 11–30.

182. See William V. Bangert, *Claude Jay and Alfonso Salmerón: Two Early Jesuits* (Chicago: Loyola University Press, 1985), pp. 42–146.

183. *Chron.,* 1:293–294. See Arthur L. Fisher, "A Study in Early Jesuit Government: The Nature and Origins of the Dissent of Nicolás Bobadilla," *Viator,* 10 (1979), 397–431, especially 424–426.

184. *Chron.,* 1:278; 4:68–79; *MI Epp.,* 6:579; 7:35, 153, 340, 469, 591, 616–618, 632. See F. Whitfield Barton, *Calvin and the Duchess* (Louisville: Westminster/John Knox Press, 1989).

185. *M Nadal,* 1:261; *Chron.,* 4:435, 492–493; 5:556.

186. See Jerzy Kłoczowski, "Catholic Reform in the Polish-Lithuanian Commonwealth (Poland, Lithuania, the Ukraine, and Belorussia)," in O'Malley, *Catholicism,* pp. 83–111, especially pp. 88–89.

187. *MI Epp.,* 3:401–402.

188. See Buxbaum, *Petrus Canisius,* pp. 146–172, and Karl Hengst, *Jesuiten an Universitäten und Jesuitenuniversitäten: Zur Geschichte der Universitäten in der Oberdeutschen und Rheinischen Provinz der Gesellschaft Jesu im Zeitalter der konfessionellen Auseinandersetzung* (Paderborn: Ferdinand Schöningh, 1981), pp. 90–95.

189. *M Nadal,* 1:301, 289–291; 4:214–217; *Orat. Obs.,* #282, 353. See Jos E. Vercruysse, "Nadal et la Contre-Réforme," *Gregorianum,* 72 (1991), 289–315.

190. *M Nadal,* 4:215.

191. See Brodrick, *Canisius,* pp. 451–452.

192. See John W. O'Malley, *Praise and Blame in Renaissance Rome: Rhetoric, Doctrine, and Reform in the Sacred Orators of the Papal Court, c. 1450–1521* (Durham: Duke University Press, 1979), pp. 190–191.

193. *M Nadal,* 1:609; 5:128, 301; *Orat. Obs.,* #227; *Adnotationes et meditationes,* pp. 144, 278.

194. *Orat. Obs.,* #698.

195. "De oratione," ARSI, cod. Opp. NN 73, fol. 202v.

196. "De oratione," ARSI, cod. Opp. NN 73, fol. 145.

197. "De oratione," ARSI, cod. Opp. NN 73, fol. 145.

198. *M Nadal,* 5:315–321.

199. *M Nadal,* 1:298; 4:824; *M. Paed.,* 2:133.

200. *MI Epp.,* 12:259. Compare *M. Paed.,* 3:335.

201. *FN*, 2:5.

202. *M Nadal*, 5:607.

203. *M Nadal*, 5:780.

204. *Chron.*, 1:18.

205. *FN*, 2:331–332.

206. *M Fabri*, pp. 502, 674.

207. *M Fabri*, pp. 107, 507.

208. "De oratione," ARSI, cod. Opp. NN 73, fols. 151–152.

209. See Brodrick, *Canisius*, p. 746.

210. "De oratione," ARSI, cod. Opp. NN 73, fol. 74.

211. *M Nadal*, 4:773; 5:317, 321. See also *M Nadal*, 4:226–229.

212. *M Nadal*, 2:35, 93. See Dennis Edmond Pate, "Jerónimo Nadal and the Early Development of the Society of Jesus, 1545–1573" (Ph.D. diss., University of California, Los Angeles, 1980), pp. 294–295.

213. *M Nadal*, 4:212–214. See also *Chron.*, 1:292; 2:73; 6:394; *M Paed.*, 2:928–929.

214. *M Paed.*, 3:143.

215. See Brodrick, *Canisius*, pp. 709, 717, and Diez, *Christus*, pp. 29–30.

216. *M Bobad.*, p. 623.

217. *M Fabri*, p. 50.

218. *MI Epp.*, 4:115; 6:171; 8:245; 9:57; 10:281, 619. But see 3:169–170.

219. *MI Epp.*, 7:463.

220. See Martini, "Studi Polanco," pp. 255–258.

221. *Chron.*, 2:271.

222. *MI Epp.*, 3:457; 12:383.

223. *M Nadal*, 2:96.

224. See Scaduto, *Laínez*, 2:115–122.

225. See Willis, " 'Love Your Enemies,' " p. 561.

226. *Adnotationes et meditationes*, pp. 240, 299.

227. *Orat. Obs.*, #761.

228. *Orat. Obs.*, #226.

229. *Orat. Obs.*, #1001. See also #217–258. For background, see Alister E. McGrath, *Iustitia Dei: A History of the Christian Doctrine of Justification*, 2 vols. (Cambridge: Cambridge University Press, 1986), especially 2:1–97.

230. *M Paed.*, 2:132.

231. *Orat. Obs.*, #722, 762. See Laínez, "Disputatio de justitia imputata," in *Disputationes Tridentinae*, 2:153–192.

232. *Orat. Obs.*, #730, 762.

233. *Adnotationes et meditationes*, pp. 64–65, 210.

234. *M Nadal*, 4:218–229; *Orat. Obs.*, #729.

235. *M Nadal*, 5:84–85.

236. *Commentarii*, 15:3–72.

237. *MI Epp.*, 1:386–387; 10:690–691; 11:363, 372, 541; *M Paed.*, 1:484.

238. *MI Epp.*, 1:153; 3:545–546; 4:411.

239. *Chron.*, 2:212.

240. *Orat. Obs.*, #749.

241. *M Nadal*, 1:305.

242. See Anita Mancia, "La controversia con i protestanti e i programmi degli studi teologici nella Compagnia di Gesù 1547–1599," *AHSI*, 54 (1985), 3–43, 209–266.

243. *MI Epp.*, 7:398–404. See Dominique Bertrand, "De la décision politique: Lettre de Saint Ignace de Loyola sur la question allemande," *Revue d'Ascétique et de Mystique*, 45 (1969), 47–64.

8. The Jesuits and the Church at Large

1. *MI Epp.*, 12:241; *P Co.*, 2:829–830.
2. See Brian E. Daley, "The Ministry of Disciples: Historical Reflections on the Role of Religious Priests," *Theological Studies*, 48 (1987), 605–629, and John W. O'Malley, "Priesthood, Ministry, and Religious Life: Some Historical and Historiographical Considerations," ibid., 49 (1988), 223–257.
3. See Daley, "Ministry of Disciples."
4. *Chron.*, 1:71.
5. *M Fabri*, p. 695.
6. *M Fabri*, pp. 119–125.
7. *MI Epp.*, 1:447, 458–459.
8. *FN*, 2:491–492.
9. See Henri Fouqueray, *Histoire de la Compagnie de Jésus en France des origines à la suppression (1528–1762)*, 5 vols. (Paris: Alfonse Picard et Fils, 1910–25), 1:195–268; George Huppert, *Public Schools in Renaissance France* (Urbana and Chicago: The University of Illinois Press, 1984), pp. 104–115; A. Lynn Martin, *The Jesuit Mind: The Mentality of an Elite in Early Modern France* (Ithaca: Cornell University Press, 1988).
10. *Chron.*, 1:417–422.
11. See Fouqueray, *Histoire*, 1:210.
12. *MI Epp.*, 8:326. See also 11:448–451.
13. *Chron.*, 5:334–335.
14. *Chron.*, 6:633. See also 6:540–541, 563.
15. *Chron.*, 6:662.
16. *FN*, 1:617–618.
17. *Chron.*, 5:321; *MI Epp.*, 9:450–451, 542.
18. *Chron.*, 5:369–370.
19. *P Co.*, 2:644.
20. *P Co.*, 2:648.
21. See Mario Scaduto, "Le missioni di A. Possevino in Piemonte: Propaganda calvinistica e restaurazione cattolica, 1560–1563," *AHSI*, 28 (1959), 51–191.
22. *MI Epp.*, 12:614–629. See Fouqueray, *Histoire*, 1:216–220.
23. Jerónimo Nadal, "Apologia contra censuram facultatis theologiae parisiensis," in *FN*, 2:38–113.
24. *FN*, 2:98–104.
25. *FN*, 2:52–54.
26. See Antonio Astrain, *Historia de la Compañía de Jesús en la Asistencia de España*, 7 vols. (Madrid: Administración de Razón y Fe, 1912–25), 1:321–384; 2:73–103; Constance Jones Mathers, "Early Spanish Qualms about Loyola and the Society of Jesus," *The Historian*, 53 (1991), 679–690.
27. British Library, cod. Eg. 453, fols. 91–105v, discovered by Terence W. O'Reilly. See O'Reilly, "Melchor Cano and the Spirituality of St. Ignatius Loyola," in *Ignacio de Loyola y su tiempo*, ed. Juan Plazaola (Bilbao: Ediciones Mensajero, 1992), pp. 369–380.
28. See Melquíades Andrés Martín, "Common Denominators of Alumbrados, Erasmians, 'Lutherans,' and Mystics: The Risk of a More 'Intimate' Spirituality," in *The*

Spanish Inquisition and the Inquisitorial Mind, ed. Angel Alcalá (Boulder: Social Science Monographs, 1987), pp. 457–494, and, more generally, Joaquin Tapia, *Iglesia y teologia en Melchor Cano (1509–1560): Un protagonista de la restauración eclesial y teológica en la España del siglo XVI* (Rome: Iglesia Nacional Española, 1989).

29. *M Nadal*, 2:45; *Chron.*, 6:640. See Astrain, *Historia*, 1:561–563.

30. *MI Epp.*, 10:118–119, 217, 410.

31. *Chron.*, 6:563.

32. *Chron.*, 6:690–691.

33. *Chron.*, 5:38–39; *MI Epp.*, 10:118.

34. *Chron.*, 6:247–248, 257–258, 263.

35. *Epist. Mixtae*, 2:608.

36. *Epist. Mixtae*, 2:625–626. See James W. Reites, "St. Ignatius of Loyola and the Jews," *Studies in the Spirituality of Jesuits*, 13/4 (1981), especially 23–29.

37. *Chron.*, 2:645–646.

38. *Chron.*, 4:475.

39. *M Nadal*, 4:820–873.

40. Nadal, *Scholia*, p. 403.

41. *M Nadal*, 4:148–165. See Mario Scaduto, *L'epoca di Giacomo Laínez, 1556–1565*, 2 vols. (Rome: Edizioni la Civiltà Cattolica, 1964–74), 1:595–604.

42. *M Nadal*, 5:649.

43. *M Nadal*, 2:263.

44. *MI Epp.*, 12:244. See also 6:706.

45. *SpEx.*, #170, 353. See Yves Congar, *L'Eglise: De s. Augustin à l'époque moderne* (Paris: Editions du Cerf, 1970), p. 369. For the most broadly conceived study, see Raymund Schwager, *Das dramatische Kirchenverständnis bei Ignatius von Loyola* (Zurich: Benzinger, 1970).

46. *MI Epp.*, 3:234–235; 5:221; 8:464.

47. *MI Epp.*, 12:671.

48. See Congar, *L'Eglise*, pp. 305–338, and Scott M. Hendrix, *Ecclesia in Via* (Leiden: E. J. Brill, 1974), pp. 15–74.

49. Gaspar de Loarte, *Exercicio dela vida christiana* (Cagliari: V. Sembenino, 1567), fols. 150v–151.

50. *M Nadal*, 5:297, 583.

51. *Orat. Obs.*, #259.

52. *Const.*, #527. See Antonio M. de Aldama, *The Constitutions of the Society of Jesus: An Introductory Commentary on the Constitutions*, trans. Aloysius J. Owen (St. Louis: The Institute of Jesuit Sources, 1989), pp. 246–252, and John W. O'Malley, "The Fourth Vow in Its Ignatian Context: A Historical Study," *Studies in the Spirituality of Jesuits*, 15/1 (1983). See also Johannes Günter Gerhartz, *"Insuper Promitto . . .": Die feierlichen Sondergelübde katholischer Orden* (Rome: Pontificia Università Gregoriana, 1966); Burkhart Schneider, "Nuestro principio y principal fundamento: Zum historischen Verständnis des Papstgehorsamsgelübde," *AHSI*, 25 (1956), 488–513.

53. *MI Const.*, 1:162.

54. See Ganss, *Constitutions*, pp. 79–80, n17.

55. *Const.*, #605.

56. *Const.*, #615.

57. *Const.*, #605.

58. *Const.*, #618–632. See de Aldama, *Constitutions*, pp. 252–257.

59. *MI Scripta*, 1:550; *MI Const.*, 1:162, 358, 395.

60. *MI Epp.,* 12:343–344. See also 1:346.

61. See John W. O'Malley, "To Travel to Any Part of the World: Jerónimo Nadal and the Jesuit Vocation," *Studies in the Spirituality of Jesuits,* 16/2 (1984).

62. See Mario Scaduto, "La strada e i primi gesuiti," *AHSI,* 40 (1971), 323–390, and John C. Olin, "The Idea of Pilgrimage in the Experience of Ignatius Loyola," *Church History,* 48 (1979), 387–397.

63. *M Nadal,* 5:195–196, 773–774.

64. Nadal, *Scholia,* p. 175.

65. *M Nadal,* 5:773–774.

66. *M Nadal,* 5:773–774. See also 5:196.

67. See Karlheinz Diez, *Christus und seine Kirche: Zum Kirchenverständnis des Petrus Canisius* (Paderborn: Verlag Bonifatius-Druckerei, 1987), pp. 250–255.

68. See Christoph Moufang, *Katholische Katechismen des sechzehnten Jahrhunderts in deutscher Sprache* (1881; reprint ed., Hildesheim: Georg Olms, 1964), pp. 26, 425.

69. See the full-scale study by Diez, *Christus.*

70. *M Nadal,* 5:49, 653; Nadal, *Pláticas,* p. 58.

71. *M Nadal,* 4:822.

72. *MI Epp.,* 12:623–624.

73. *M Nadal,* 4:165–181.

74. See Brian Tierney, *Origins of Papal Infallibility, 1150–1350: A Study of the Concepts of Infallibility, Sovereignty and Tradition in the Middle Ages* (Leiden: E. J. Brill, 1972).

75. See Diego Laínez, "Disputatio de origine jurisdictionis episcoporum et Romani pontificis primatu," in *Disputationes Tridentinae,* ed. Hartmann Grisar, 2 vols. (Innsbruck: F. Rauch, 1886), 1:1–370. See also Scaduto, *Laínez,* 2:186–190, and Klaus Ganzer, "Gallikanische und römische Primatauffassung im Widerstreit: Zu den ekklesiologischen Auseinandersetzungen auf dem Konzil von Trient," *Historisches Jahrbuch,* 109 (1989), 109–163.

76. *MI Epp.,* 8:460–467 (and another version, 467–476).

77. *M Nadal,* 5:733, 757; *Orat. Obs.,* #582.

78. See Scaduto, *Laínez,* 2:220–222, and Robert Trisco, "Reforming the Roman Curia: Emperor Ferdinand I and the Council of Trent," in *Reform and Authority in the Medieval and Reformation Church,* ed. Guy Fitch Lytle (Washington: The Catholic University of America Press, 1981), pp. 143–337, especially pp. 291–294.

79. See Scaduto, *Laínez,* 2:239–245, and Hubert Jedin, *Geschichte des Konzils von Trient,* 4 vols. in 5 (Freiburg: Herder, 1949–75), 4/2:147–148.

80. See Hermann Josef Sieben, "Option für den Papst: Die Jesuiten auf dem Konzil von Trient, Dritte Sitzungsperiode 1562/63," in *Ignatianische: Eigenart und Methode der Gesellschaft Jesu,* ed. Michael Sievernich and Günter Switek (Freiburg: Herder, 1990), pp. 235–253.

81. *M Lain.,* 8:800–805. See Scaduto, *Laínez,* 2:140–143.

82. See Brian Tierney, *The Foundations of the Conciliar Theory: The Contribution of the Medieval Canonists from Gratian to the Great Schism* (Cambridge: Cambridge University Press, 1955), pp. 57–67, and J. A. Mirus, "On the Deposition of the Pope for Heresy," *Archivum Historiae Pontificiae,* 13 (1975), 231–248.

83. See Sieben, "Option für den Papst," and Alfonso Salmerón, *Commentarii in Evangelicam Historiam et in Acta Apostolorum; Commentarii in omnes Epistolas B. Pauli et canonicas,* 16 vols. (Cologne: A. Hierst and I. Gymnicus, 1612–15), 12:584–586.

84. See Sieben, "Option für den Papst," pp. 245–248.

85. Laínez, *Disputationes Tridentinae,* 2:322–382.

86. Laínez, "Tractatus de simonia," in *Disputationes Tridentinae,* 2:360.

87. Ibid., 2:378–379.

88. English translation in John C. Olin, *Catholic Reform: From Cardinal Ximenes to the Council of Trent, 1495–1563* (New York: Fordham University Press, 1990), pp. 65–79.

89. *MI Epp.,* 9:5. On Cervini, see William V. Hudon, *Marcello Cervini and Ecclesiastical Government in Tridentine Italy* (DeKalb: Northern Illinois University Press, 1992).

90. *Chron.,* 5:14–15.

91. *Chron.,* 1:56; *MI Epp.,* 114–118; Georges Bottereau, "La 'lettre' d'Ignace de Loyola à Gian Pietro Carafa," *AHSI,* 44 (1975), 139–152; Peter A. Quinn, "Ignatius Loyola and Gian Pietro Carafa: Catholic Reformers at Odds," *The Catholic Historical Review,* 67 (1981), 386–400.

92. *FN,* 2:496–497.

93. *MI Epp.,* 8:43–44, 84–85; *Chron.,* 4:17–18; 5:17–18. See José Manuel Aicardo, *Comentario a las Constituciones de la Compañía de Jesús,* 6 vols. (Madrid: Blass y Cia, 1919–32), 2:694–716.

94. *FN,* 1:712; *Chron.,* 5:17–18; *M Nadal,* 2:40.

95. *FN,* 1:581–582. See, however, *P Co.,* 2:580; *FN,* 1:720; Pedro de Leturia, "Los 'recuerdos' presentados por el jesuita Bobadilla al recién elegido Paulo IV," in *Estudios Ignacianos,* ed. Ignacio Iparraguirre, 2 vols. (Rome: Institutum Historicum Societatis Jesu, 1957), 1:447–459.

96. *MI Epp.,* 9:67, 75–76, 293, 313–314, 359–363, 463–468; 12:273.

97. *MI Epp.,* 9:89.

98. *MI Epp.,* 9:162, 185–186, 248–249, 389.

99. *Chron.,* 5:550.

100. *MI Epp.,* 10:288; *Chron.,* 5:47–48.

101. *Orat. Obs.,* #403.

102. See André Ravier, *Ignatius of Loyola and the Founding of the Society of Jesus,* trans. Maura Daly, Joan Daly, and Carson Daly (San Francisco: Ignatius Press, 1987), pp. 275–317.

103. *Chron.,* 6:50–51.

104. *M Nadal,* 2:50–51; 4:732–735; *Chron.,* 6:52–53.

105. *M Nadal,* 2:12–16; *Chron.,* 6:52–53.

106. *P Co.,* 2:602–604.

107. See Scaduto, *Laínez,* 1:3–120, and John W. Padberg, "The General Congregations of the Society of Jesus: A Brief Survey of Their History," *Studies in the Spirituality of Jesuits,* 6/1–2 (1974), 5–9.

108. See Scaduto, *Laínez,* 1:210–215.

109. *MI Epp.,* 1:450–453, 460–467.

110. *Const.,* #817–818; Nadal, *Scholia,* p. 500.

111. See Agostino Borromeo, "The Inquisition and Inquisitorial Censorship," in *Catholicism in Early Modern History: A Guide to Research,* ed. John W. O'Malley (St. Louis: The Center for Reformation Research, 1988), pp. 253–272, and Gustav Henningsen and John Tedeschi, with Charles Amiel, *The Inquisition in Early Modern Europe: Studies on Sources and Methods* (DeKalb: Northern Illinois University Press, 1986).

112. See William Monter, *Frontiers of Heresy: The Spanish Inquisition from the Basque Lands to Sicily* (Cambridge: Cambridge University Press, 1990).

113. See Marcello Del Piazzo and Cándido de Dalmases, "Il processo sull'ortodossia di S. Ignazio e dei suoi compagni svoltosi a Roma nel 1538, Nuovi documenti," *AHSI,* 38 (1969), 431–453.

114. See José Luís Gonzalez Novalin, "La Inquisición y la Compañía de Jesús," *Anthologica Annua*, 37 (1990), 11–56.

115. *Chron.*, 1:127; *FN*, 1:272–273.

116. See Hubert Jedin, *A History of the Council of Trent*, trans. Ernest Graf, 2 vols. in English (London: Thomas Nelson and Sons, 1957–61), 1:466.

117. *MI Epp.*, 1:218–219.

118. *MI Epp.*, 1:214–226, 243–246, 321–325, 346–350. See António Lopes, "Ignace de Loyola, François Xavier et Jean III du Portugal," in *Ignacio y su tiempo*, pp. 636–682, especially pp. 660–661.

119. *FN*, 1:732–733; *MI Epp.*, 9:163, 215, 226–227; *Chron.*, 6:19. See Novalin, "Inquisición," pp. 23–26, and Lopes, "Ignace et Jean III," pp. 661–663.

120. *Chron.*, 2:451.

121. See Novalin, "Inquisición," pp. 26–40.

122. *MI Epp.*, 1:343–344.

123. *P Co.*, 1:545–546.

124. *Orat. Obs.*, #726.

125. *M Nadal*, 4:626.

126. *M Nadal*, 5:430.

127. *M Nadal*, 1:168–169.

128. *Chron.*, 2:35–36; *M Nadal*, 1:76–77, 83. On the vigorous repression of heresy in Messina, see Salvatore Caponetto, "Le città siciliane dinanzi alla Riforma: Messina," in *Città italiane del '500 tra Riforma e Controriforma* (Lucca: Maria Pacini Fazzi, 1988), pp. 103–110.

129. *MI Epp.*, 10:139, 407–408, 579.

130. See Mario Scaduto, "Laínez e l'Indice del 1559: Lullo, Sabunde, Savonarola, Erasmo," *AHSI*, 24 (1955), 3–32, especially 13–16.

131. See Joseph Hilgers, *Der Index der Verbotenen Bücher: In seiner neuen Fassung dargelegt un rechtlich-historisch gewürdigt* (Freiburg: Herder, 1904), pp. 489–490.

132. See Scaduto, "Laínez e l'Indice," p. 22, and *Laínez*, 2:22–35.

133. See Scaduto, "Laínez e l'Indice," p. 23.

134. *M Nadal*, 1:388.

135. *M Nadal*, 1:317, 495; *M Paed.*, 3:145.

136. *Chron.*, 3:22–23; *MI Epp.*, 6:567.

137. *Chron.*, 1:130.

138. See Benedetto da Mantova, *Il Beneficio di Cristo, con le versioni del secolo XVI: Documenti e testimonianze*, ed. Salvatore Caponetto (DeKalb: Northern Illinois University Press, 1972), and Tommaso Bozza, *Nuovi studi sulla Riforma in Italia: I, Il Beneficio di Cristo* (Rome: Edizioni di Storia e Letteratura, 1976).

139. See Scaduto, *Laínez*, 1:82–83, and William V. Bangert, *Claude Jay and Alfonso Salmerón: Two Early Jesuits* (Chicago: Loyola University Press, 1985), pp. 173–174, 239–240.

140. The literature on the subject is abundant. For orientation, see Elizabeth G. Gleason, "On the Nature of Sixteenth-Century Italian Evangelism: Scholarship, 1953–1978," *The Sixteenth Century Journal*, 9/3 (1978), 3–25; Susanna Peyrouel Rambaldi, "Ancora sull'evangelismo italiano: Categoria o invenzione storiografica?" *Società e Storia*, 5 (1982), 935–967; John Martin, "Salvation and Society in Sixteenth-Century Venice: Popular Evangelism in a Renaissance City," *The Journal of Modern History*, 60 (1988), 205–233. See especially Massimo Firpo, "Vittoria Colonna, Giovanni Morone e gli 'spirituali,'" *Rivista di Storia e Letteratura Religiosa*, 24 (1988), 211–261, and Anne Jacobson Schutte,

"Periodization of Sixteenth-Century Italian Religious History: The Post-Cantimori Paradigm Shift," *The Journal of Modern History,* 61 (1989), 269–284.

141. For its importance especially for Colonna, see Firpo, "Colonna, Morone," pp. 235–248.

142. *MI Epp.,* 12:275–276.

143. On the difficult situation there, see Massimo Firpo, "Gli 'Spirituali,' l'Accademia di Modena e il Formulario di fede del 1542: Controllo del dissenso religioso e Nicodemismo," *Rivista di Storia e Letteratura Religiosa,* 20 (1984), 40–111.

144. See Massimo Firpo and Dario Marcatto, eds., *Il processo inquisitoriale del Cardinal Giovanni Morone,* 5 vols. in 6 (Rome: Istituto Storico Italiano per l'Età Moderna e Contemporanea, 1981–89).

145. *M Salm.,* 1:235, with n20; *M Rib.,* 1:266, 270, 283–284.

146. See Firpo, *Processo Morone,* 2/1:36.

147. See Scaduto, *Laínez,* 1:213, with n18.

148. Ibid., 2:250–259. See also Bartolomé Carranza de Miranda, *Comentario sobre el Catechismo cristiano,* ed. José Ignacio Tellechea Idigoras, 2 vols. (Madrid: Biblioteca de Autores Cristianos, 1972), especially 1:48–96, and Tellechea Idigoras, *El proceso romano del Arzobispo Carranza (1567–1576)* (Rome: Iglesia Nacional Española, 1988).

149. See Tapia, *Melchor Cano,* pp. 53–66, 77–80.

150. See Dennis Edmond Pate, "Jerónimo Nadal and the Early Development of the Society of Jesus, 1545–1573" (Ph.D. diss., University of California, Los Angeles, 1980), pp. 270–294; A. Alcalá Galve, "Control de espirituales," in *Historia de la Inquisición en España y America,* ed. Joaquin Perez Villanueva and Bartolome Escandell Bonet (Madrid: Biblioteca de Autores Cristianos, 1984), 1:780–842; Cándido de Dalmases, "San Francisco de Borja y la Inquisición española, 1559–1561," *AHSI,* 41 (1972), 48–135, and *Francis Borgia: Grandee of Spain, Jesuit, Saint,* trans. Cornelius Michael Buckley (St. Louis: The Institute of Jesuit Sources, 1991), pp. 133–147; William V. Bangert, *Jerome Nadal, S.J., 1507–1580: Tracking the First Generation of Jesuits,* ed. Thomas M. McCoog (Chicago: Loyola University Press, 1992), pp. 221–237.

151. *M Nadal,* 2:66–67. See Novalin, "Inquisición," especially pp. 48–53.

152. *M Nadal,* 1:503, 507, 541, 634–635.

153. *M Lain.,* 4:129–132; 8:517–519; *M Borgia,* 3:399; *M Salm.,* 1:274–275.

154. *M Salm.,* 1:252, 256–257, 258, 271; *M Borgia,* 3:434; *M Rib.,* 1:320.

155. *M Salm.,* 1:271, 272, 275–276.

156. *M Lain.,* 7:156.

157. *M Salm.,* 1:272.

158. See Bangert, *Jay and Salmerón,* pp. 283–284.

159. *P Co.,* 2:683.

160. See Ricardo García Villoslada, *Storia del Collegio Romano, dal suo inizio (1551) alla soppressione della Compagnia di Gesù (1773)* (Rome: Pontificia Università Gregoriana, 1954), pp. 64–65. Polanco's report of the event does not mention Carranza, *P Co.,* 2:284. See also 2:683.

161. See José Ignacio Tellechea Idigoras, "Censura inédita del padre Francisco Toledo, S.J., sobre el catecismo del arzobispo Carranza: Cotejo con la de Melchor Cano," *Revista Española de Teologia,* 29 (1969), 3–35.

162. Ibid., p. 15.

163. See John W. O'Malley, "Was Ignatius Loyola a Church Reformer? How to Look at Early Modern Catholicism," *The Catholic Historical Review,* 77 (1991), 177–193.

164. *SpEx.,* #362.

165. See Manuel Ruiz Jurado, "Un caso de profetismo reformista en la Compañía de Jesús: Gandia, 1547–1549," *AHSI*, 43 (1974), 217–266.

166. *MI Epp.*, 12:632–654, especially 635–636.

167. But see *M Nadal*, 2:21–22.

168. See John W. O'Malley, "Historical Thought and the Reform Crisis of the Early Sixteenth Century," *Theological Studies*, 28 (1967), 531–548, and "Developments, Reforms, and Two Great Reformations: Towards a Historical Assessment of Vatican II," ibid., 44 (1983), 373–406, especially 385–389.

169. *MI Epp.*, 8:592–594, 664–665, 673; 9:13–17, 180–181.

170. *FN*, 1:719.

171. *MI Epp.*, 11:245; 10:665.

172. *P Co.*, 2:618.

173. "De oratione," cod. Opp. NN 73, ARSI, fols. 124v–126v; 148v; "De tribulatione," ibid., fol. 73v.

174. "De oratione," fol. 201v; "De tribulatione," fol. 62v.

175. "De tribulatione," fol. 37.

176. See Bangert, *Jay and Salmerón*, pp. 67–103, 177–195.

177. *MI Epp.*, 1:386–389.

178. *Chron.*, 1:180–183; *MI Epp.*, 1:435, 457–460.

179. *M Salm.*, 1:25–28.

180. See Bangert, *Jay and Salmerón*, pp. 100–102.

181. *M Salm.*, 1:100.

182. *M Lain.*, 1:197–198.

183. See Norman P. Tanner, ed., *Decrees of the Ecumenical Councils*, 2 vols. (Washington: Georgetown University Press, 1990), 2:781.

184. Ibid., 2:751.

185. *MI Epp.*, 1:435.

186. *P Co.*, 1:453–454, 462–466.

187. *MI Epp.*, 1:450–453; 4:255–258; *Chron.*, 1:180–181; 4:494–495; 5:34–35.

188. *MI Epp.*, 8:432–436, 675–720. See Ricardo García-Villoslada, *San Ignacio de Loyola: Nueva Biografía* (Madrid: Biblioteca de Autores Cristianos, 1986), pp. 996–1008, and Philip Caraman, *The Lost Empire: The Story of the Jesuits in Ethiopia, 1555–1634* (London: Sidgwick and Jackson, 1985).

189. See Scaduto, *Laínez*, 2:587–603.

190. *M Fabri*, p. 473; *Chron.*, 1:381–382; 2:507; 5:9, 65, 125, 140–141, 197, 355–358. See Scaduto, *Laínez*, 2:603–614. For an instruction from Ignatius on how to proceed in the reform of a convent of nuns, see *MI Epp.*, 8:395–397. For the context in Italy, see Gabriella Zarri, "Monasteri femminili e città (secoli XV–XVIII)," in *Storia d'Italia: Annali 9*, ed. Giorgio Chittolini and Giovanni Miccoli (Turin: Guilio Einaudi, 1986), pp. 359–429.

9. Prescriptions for the Future

1. *MI Scripta*, 1:666–707. See Dennis Edmond Pate, "Jerónimo Nadal and the Early Development of the Society of Jesus, 1545–1573" (Ph.D. diss., University of California, Los Angeles, 1980), pp. 141–164; Francisco Rodrigues, *História da Companhia de Jesus na Assistência de Portugal*, 4 vols. in 7 (Oporto: Apostolado da Impresa, 1931–50), 1/2:33–281; José Carlos Monteiro Pacheco, *Simão Rodrigues: Iniciador da Companhia de Jesus em Portugal* (Braga: Editorial A. O., 1987), pp. 155–183; Ricardo García-Villoslada, *San Ignacio de Loyola: Nueva biografía* (Madrid: Biblioteca de Autores Cristianos, 1986), pp. 642–674.

2. See García-Villoslada, *Ignacio,* pp. 650–652.

3. *MI Epp.,* 1:495–510.

4. *MI Epp.,* 1:687–693.

5. *MI Scripta,* 1:666–667.

6. *M Borgia,* 3:122–124.

7. See García-Villoslada, *Ignacio,* pp. 660–661; Pate, "Nadal," p. 143.

8. *M Nadal,* 2:7.

9. *MI Epp.,* 5:73–74, 189.

10. *MI Epp.,* 5:270–271.

11. *Chron.,* 4:7–8.

12. *Chron.,* 5:164–165; *MI Epp.,* 8:657–658; 9:707–708; *M Nadal,* 1:319–325; 2:10, 35. See also Pacheco, *Rodrigues,* pp. 185–210.

13. *MI Epp.,* 4:669–681.

14. *M Nadal,* 4:98–148. See Pate, "Nadal," pp. 238–258; Mario Scaduto, *L'epoca di Giacomo Laínez, 1556–1565,* 2 vols. (Rome: Edizioni la Civiltà Cattolica, 1964–74), 1:31–47; Arthur L. Fisher, "A Study in Early Jesuit Government: The Nature and Origins of the Dissent of Nicolás Bobadilla," *Viator,* 10 (1979), 397–431; André Ravier, *Ignatius of Loyola and the Founding of the Society of Jesus,* trans. Maura Daly, Joan Daly, and Carson Daly (San Francisco: Ignatius Press, 1987), pp. 275–317; William V. Bangert, *Jerome Nadal, S.J., 1507–1580: Tracking the First Generation of Jesuits* (Chicago: Loyola University Press, 1992), pp. 173–219.

15. *MI Epp.,* 1:277–282.

16. *M Salm.,* 1:20–22.

17. *M Bobad.,* p. 102.

18. *M Nadal,* 2:53.

19. *M Nadal,* 2:51–52.

20. *M Nadal,* 4:101.

21. *M Nadal,* 4:105–106.

22. See Fisher, "Early Jesuit Government," 405–406.

23. *M Nadal,* 4:106–108.

24. See Antonio M. de Aldama, "La composición de las constituciones de la Compañía de Jesús," *AHSI,* 42 (1973), 201–245, and J. H. Amadeo and M. A. Fiorito, "La reunión en Roma de los años 1550–1551 y la elaboración de las Constituciones de la Compañía de Jesús," *Stromata,* 40 (1984), 3–57, 203–260. The most usefully annotated edition is the English translation by George E. Ganss, cited throughout this book: *The Constitutions of the Society of Jesus* (St. Louis: The Institute of Jesuit Sources, 1970). See also Antonio M. de Aldama, *The Constitutions of the Society of Jesus: An Introductory Commentary on the Constitutions,* trans. Aloysius J. Owen (St. Louis: The Institute of Jesuit Sources, 1989).

25. See Ravier, *Ignatius of Loyola,* pp. 151–156.

26. *Const.,* #822. See de Aldama, *Constitutions,* pp. 309–310.

27. *Chron.,* 5:41.

28. *Chron.,* 4:550.

29. See Pate, "Nadal," p. 160.

30. See Cándido de Dalmases, "Le esortazioni del P. Laínez sull' 'Examen Constitutionum,' " *AHSI,* 35 (1966), 132–185.

31. *P Co.,* 2:595–596.

32. See Nadal, *Scholia,* pp. vii–xxv.

33. *Const.,* #134.

34. See de Aldama, *Constitutions*, p. 15.

35. See Howard J. Gray, "What Kind of Document?" *The Way*, supplement no. 61 (1988), 21–34.

36. *Const.*, #557–558.

37. *Const.*, #466.

38. *M Nadal*, 1:133.

39. See Manuel Ruiz Jurado, *Orígenes del noviciado en la Compañía de Jesús* (Rome: Institutum Historicum Societatis Jesu, 1980), pp. 64–65.

40. *Chron.*, 2:208; *M Nadal*, 1:799.

41. *FN*, 1:539–541.

42. *M Nadal*, 1:317.

43. In the *Monumenta Historica* series, see *Monumenta Ignatiana. Regulae Societatis (1540–1556)* (Rome: Institutum Historicum Societatis Jesu, 1948). For their development, see Antonio Astrain, *Historia de la Compañía de Jesús en la Asistencia de España*, 7 vols. (Madrid: Administración de Razón y Fe, 1912–25), 2:419–443.

44. *Chron.*, 1:245; 2:135, 359.

45. See Miguel Nicolau, *Jerónimo Nadal, S.I. (1507–1580): Sus obras y doctrinas espirituales* (Madrid: Consejo Superior de Investigaciones Científicas, 1949), pp. 53–58.

46. *Chron.*, 4:460.

47. *Chron.*, 2:522, 526–527, 554; *MI Epp.*, 4:242.

48. *M Nadal*, 5:73, 368. See also Nicolau, *Nadal*, pp. 305–313.

49. *M Nadal*, 2:70.

50. *Chron.*, 6:666–667.

51. *M Lain.*, 4:649–650.

52. See Alfonso Rodríguez Gutiérrez de Ceballos, "El P. Bartolomé de Bustamante iniciador de la arquitectura jesuítica en España (1501–1570)," *AHSI*, 32 (1963), 3–102.

53. *MI Epp.*, 3:503.

54. *MI Scripta*, 1:416–417, 454–455, 483–490, 502–506.

55. *Autobiography*, "Preface," #5.

56. *Const.*, #582. Nadal, *Scholia*, pp. 159–160.

57. *M Nadal*, 4:619–625; 5:350–356.

58. *M Nadal*, 5:355.

59. *Chron.*, 1:294–295; 3:9; *MI Epp.*, 4:684–690.

60. *M Nadal*, 4:499.

61. *Chron.*, 6:434–435.

62. *Const.*, #577–579.

63. *FN*, 1:609.

64. *Chron.*, 1:435.

65. Nadal, *Scholia*, pp. 6–7, 434–435.

66. *M Nadal*, 4:515–517.

67. See Bernhard Duhr, *Geschichte der Jesuiten in den Ländern deutscher Zunge im XVI. Jahrhundert* (Freiburg: Herdersche Verlagshandlung, 1907), pp. 564–567.

68. *MI Scripta*, 1:489–490; *Chron.*, 5:545; *M Nadal*, 4:408, 515. See Antonio Borràs, "Entorno a la indumentaria de los jesuitas españoles en los siglos XVI y XVII," *AHSI*, 36 (1967), 291–299.

69. *Chron.*, 4:638.

70. I did not have access to the Spanish original but used Pedro de Ribadeneira, *De ratione Instituti Societatis Jesu*, trans. Laurentius Carli (Rome: Typis Civiltatis Catholicae, 1864). On the Chinese mission, see Jonathan D. Spence, *The Memory Palace of Matteo*

Ricci (New York: Viking, 1984), and, for further bibliography, John W. Witek, "From India to Japan: European Missionary Expansion, 1500–1650," in *Catholicism in Early Modern History: A Guide to Research,* ed. John W. O'Malley (St. Louis: Center for Reformation Research, 1988), pp. 193–210, especially pp. 201–204.

71. Ribadeneira, *De ratione Instituti,* p. 55.

72. Nadal, *Scholia,* p. 134.

73. *FN,* 1:549–550.

74. *Institutum Societatis Jesu,* 2 vols. (Prague: Typis Universitatis Carolo-Ferdinandeae, 1757), 1:474.

75. *Chron.,* 2:430; 4:160; *P Co.,* 2:599; Nadal, *Scholia,* p. 158. See A. Lynn Martin, *The Jesuit Mind: The Mentality of an Elite in Early Modern France* (Ithaca: Cornell University Press, 1988), pp. 153–171.

76. *MI Epp.,* 3:249; *Chron.,* 2:34.

77. *FN,* 1:653.

78. See de Dalmases, "Esortazioni Laínez," pp. 149–150; *Chron.,* 1:316–317. On the issue, see also Ribadeneira, *De ratione Instituti,* pp. 62–85.

79. *Const.,* #292–301.

80. *M Paed.,* 1:89.

81. *FN,* 1:633–635.

82. *M Nadál,* 5:408.

83. Thomas Aquinas, *Summa theologiae,* 1–2, 54.

84. *M Nadal,* 4:614.

85. *FN,* 1:612–613, 729; *MI Reg.,* pp. 525–526, 528–529; *M Nadal,* 4:200.

86. See de Aldama, *Constitutions,* p. 15.

87. *FN,* 2:337–338; *MI Scripta,* 1:418, 468–469.

88. *Institutum,* 1:478.

89. See de Dalmases, "Esortazioni Laínez," p. 174.

90. Nadal, *Scholia,* p. 57; *M Nadal,* 4:440, 544; *M Rib.,* 2:399–400.

91. *M Nadal,* 4:497–498.

92. *Chron.,* 1:169–170.

93. *Institutum,* 1:13–14. See de Aldama, *Constitutions,* pp. 189–213. See also Ribadeneira, *De ratione Instituti,* pp. 143–313.

94. *Chron.,* 1:250, 361. See Cándido de Dalmases, *Francis Borgia: Grandee of Spain, Jesuit, Saint,* trans. Cornelius Michael Buckley (St. Louis: The Institute of Jesuit Sources, 1991), pp. 59–62, 70–81, and Manuel Ruiz Jurado, "La entrada del duque de Gandía en la Compañía de Jesús," *Manresa,* 44 (1972), 122–144.

95. See Antonio M. de Aldama, "De coadiutoribus Societatis Iesu in mente et in praxi sancti Ignatii," *AHSI,* 38 (1969), 389–430, especially 424–425.

96. See Ladislaus Lukács, "De graduum diversitate inter sacerdotes in Societate Iesu," *AHSI,* 37 (1968), 237–316, and Ganss's comments in his translation of the *Constitutions,* pp. 349–356.

97. *M Nadal,* 5:752; Nadal, *Pláticas,* pp. 158–160; de Dalmases, "Esortazioni Laínez," pp. 152–155.

98. *Const.,* #553–554, 817–818.

99. See de Aldama, *Constitutions,* pp. 305–307.

100. See de Dalmases, "Esortazioni Laínez," pp. 152–155. See also Giancarlo Angelozzi, "L'insegnamento dei casi di coscienza nella pratica educativa della Compagnia di Gesù," in *La "Ratio Studiorum": Modelli e pratiche educative dei Gesuiti in Italia tra Cinque e*

Seicento, ed. Gian Paolo Brizzi (Rome: Bulzoni Editore, 1981), pp. 121–162, especially pp. 150–151.

101. See Estanislao Olivares, *Los votos de los escolares de la Compañía de Jesús: Su evolución jurídica* (Rome: Institutum Historicum Societatis Jesu, 1961), and Antonio M. de Aldama, *La vida religiosa en la Compañía de Jesús: Comentario a la parte VI de las Constituciones* (Rome: Centrum Ignatianum Spiritualitatis, 1989).

102. See Pate, "Nadal," pp. 149–150.

103. *Const.,* #547.

104. *MI Epp.,* 12:151–152; *M Nadal,* 4:467; 5:415–424.

105. *M Nadal,* 4:556; *MI Reg.,* pp. 290, 561.

106. *P Co.,* 2:745.

107. *Chron.,* 6:761, 832.

108. See de Aldama, *Constitutions,* p. 227.

109. *Const.,* #565.

110. Nadal, *Pláticas,* p. 142; *M Nadal,* 5:197; *Chron.,* 2:247.

111. *M Nadal,* 5:196–199.

112. *M Nadal,* 5:405.

113. *M Nadal,* 4:600, 602–603; 5:794; Nadal, *Scholia,* p. 432; *M Fabri,* pp. 238–239; *Chron.,* 1:231; 5:339.

114. *Institutum,* 1:501.

115. *MI Epp.,* 1:354–356; *M Fabri,* pp. 238–239.

116. Nadal, *Pláticas,* p. 143.

117. *M Nadal,* 5:80.

118. *MI Epp.,* 3:638–639.

119. *Chron.,* 3:68.

120. *Chron.,* 3:40.

121. *M Lain.,* 8:289–290.

122. *Chron.,* 3:19–20; 4:480–481.

123. *M Nadal,* 2:80, 91.

124. *Chron.,* 4:480.

125. *Chron.,* 2:248–249; *MI Epp.,* 3:706.

126. *Chron.,* 2:59.

127. *Const.,* #53–54, 254–256.

128. *Institutum,* 1:477.

129. *Const.,* #554–561.

130. *MI Epp.,* 9:83. Also *Chron.,* 5:539; *M Paed.,* 3:48–49.

131. *Chron.,* 6:202.

132. *Const.,* #557–558.

133. *MI Epp.,* 1:228–229.

134. *MI Epp.,* 1:551–562.

135. *MI Epp.,* 2:54–65.

136. *MI Epp.,* 4:669–681. See also the letter of 14 January 1548 to the college at Coimbra, ibid., 1:687–693.

137. *Const.,* #547.

138. See Ganss, *Constitutions,* p. 249, n8.

139. See Thomas V. Cohen, "Sociologie de la croyance: Jésuites au Portugal et en Espagne (1540–1562)," in *Les jésuites parmi les hommes aux XVIe et XVIIe siècles: Actes du Colloque de Clermont-Ferrand (avril 1985),* ed. G. and G. Demerson, B. Dompnier, and

A. Regond (Clermond-Ferrand: Association des Publications de la Faculté des Lettres et Sciences Humaines, 1987), pp. 24, 31.

140. *M Nadal*, 4:552; *MI Scripta*, 1:485–486.

141. *M Nadal*, 5:508–512.

142. See Ravier, *Ignatius of Loyola*, pp. 369–375.

143. *FN*, 1:684–687.

144. See de Aldama, *Constitutions*, p. 269.

145. *M Lain.*, 4:15–19.

146. *M Nadal*, 4:430, 514–515; 5:727; Nadal, *Pláticas*, p. 177.

147. *M Nadal*, 4:514–515.

148. *M Nadal*, 4:412, 436; 5:438–439, 714; Nadal, *Scholia*, pp. 174–175; Nadal, *Pláticas*, p. 177.

149. *M Nadal*, 4:414–415.

150. *M Nadal*, 5:674, 764–767; Nadal, *Scholia*, p. 247.

151. *Const.*, #766–777, 779, 782–786; Nadal, *Scholia*, pp. 195–196, 198, 242. See de Aldama, *Constitutions*, pp. 278, 288, 291–294.

152. *MI Const.*, 1:218; *MI Epp.*, 8:225.

153. *Chron.*, 5:30.

154. *M Paed.*, 2:954.

155. *Const.*, #91–95, 263, 424, 551. See also Nadal, *Pláticas*, pp. 111–116; de Dalmases, "Esortazioni Laínez," p. 176; de Aldama, *Constitutions*, pp. 58–61.

156. *Const.*, #92.

157. *MI Epp.*, 9:90–92. See de Aldama, *Constitutions*, p. 137.

158. *Chron.*, 6:202–203, 832–833.

159. *Institutum*, 1:478.

160. *MI Epp.*, 7:100, 102–103, 136, 257. See Romeo De Maio, *Michelangelo e la Controriforma* (Rome: Laterza, 1978), pp. 243–249.

161. See Pietro Pirri, "La topografia del Gesù di Roma e le vertenze tra Muzio Muti e S. Ignazio secondo nuovi documenti," *AHSI*, 10 (1941), 177–217, and Thomas M. Lucas, "The Vineyard at the Crossroads: The Urban Vision of Ignatius of Loyola," (Ph.D. diss., The Graduate Theological Union, Berkeley, 1991), pp. 67–86.

162. See Clare Robertson, '*Il Gran Cardinale*': *Alessandro Farnese, Patron of the Arts* (New Haven: Yale University Press, 1992), especially pp. 181–196.

163. Gregory Martin, *Roma Sancta (1581)*, ed. George Bruner Parks (Rome: Edizioni di Storia e Letteratura, 1969), p. 58.

164. See Rodríguez Gutiérrez de Ceballos, "Bustamante," especially pp. 74–77, and *Bartolomé de Bustamante y los orígenes de la arquitectura jesuítica en España* (Rome: Institutum Historicum Societatis Iesu, 1967).

165. See Pietro Pirri, *Giovanni Tristano e i primordi della architettura gesuitica* (Rome: Institutum Historicum Societatis Iesu, 1955). See also *Giuseppe Valeriano S.I.: Architetto e pittore, 1542–1596*, ed. Raineri C. Colombo (Rome: Institutum Historicum Societatis Iesu, 1970), and Rudolf Wittkower, "Problems of the Theme," in *Baroque Art: The Jesuit Contribution*, ed. Rudolf Wittkower and Irma B. Jaffe (New York: Fordham University Press, 1972), pp. 1–14.

166. See, for example, Gian Paolo Brizzi and Anna Maria Matteucci, eds., *Dall'isola alla città: I gesuiti a Bologna* (Bologna: Nuova Alfa Editoriale, 1988).

167. See James S. Ackerman, "The Gesù in the Light of Contemporary Church Design," in Wittkower, *Baroque Art*, pp. 15–28, especially p. 27.

168. *M Nadal*, 4:529.

169. *M Nadal*, 4:199, 604.

170. *M Nadal*, 4:419–420, 604–609.

171. *M Nadal*, 4:448–450.

172. *Chron.*, 2:730.

173. *M Nadal*, 4:201–204, 448–450. See Manuel Ruiz Jurado, "Noticias inéditas sobre la casa profesa de Roma en tiempos de san Ignacio," *AHSI*, 53 (1984), 281–311, especially 293.

174. *Chron.*, 2:540; 4:268; 6:133.

175. *Chron.*, 1:320, 422–423; *M Nadal*, 4:413; *M Paed.*, 3:130; *MI Epp.*, 11:585; *P Co.*, 2:576.

176. See Ribadeneira, *De ratione Instituti*, pp. 498–509.

177. *M Nadal*, 4:513–514, 554–556.

178. *P Co.*, 2:632–633.

179. *M Nadal*, 1:93; 4:552–554, 680.

180. *MI Font. Doc.*, pp. 623–624, 657–658; *M Fabri*, pp. 677–678. See Hubert Jedin, "Das Konzil von Trient und die Reform der liturgischen Bücher," *Ephemerides Liturgicae*, 59 (1945), 5–38, especially 15–24; Guy Bedouelle, "La Réforme catholique," in *Le temps des Réformes et la Bible*, ed. Guy Bedouelle and Bernard Roussel (Bible de tous les temps, 5) (Paris: Beauchesne, 1989), pp. 355–357.

181. See Manuel Ruiz Jurado, "Nadal y Polanco sobre la Formula del Instituto de la Compañía de Jesús," *AHSI*, 47 (1978), 225–239, especially 238.

182. *Const.*, #340–344, 582–583; *M Nadal*, 5:663; Nadal, *Scholia*, p. 159. See Leturia, *Estudios*, 2:189–268.

183. *Institutum*, 1:474, 494.

184. See Joseph de Guibert, *The Jesuits, Their Spiritual Doctrine and Practice: A Historical Study*, trans. William J. Young (Chicago: The Institute of Jesuit Sources, 1964), pp. 221–229.

185. *M Nadal*, 5:26–30.

186. *M Nadal*, 4:576–578, 672–681.

187. *M Nadal*, 5:163. See Nicolau, *Nadal*, pp. 254–258.

188. *Const.*, #250, 288. See Nicolau, *Nadal*, pp. 258–263, and Josef Stierli, *Ignatius von Loyola: Gott suchen in allen Dingen* (Munich: Piper, 1987).

189. *M Nadal*, 4:676; 5:163; Nadal, *Orat. Obs.*, #897, 902.

190. *M Nadal*, 2:59; *P Co.*, 2:604.

191. See Ruiz Jurado, *Orígines del noviciado*, pp. 35–83.

192. *Chron.*, 3:59.

193. *Institutum*, 1:490–491.

194. See Luís Fernández Martín, "San Francisco de Borja y el noviciado de Simancas, 1554–1560," *AHSI*, 55 (1986), 217–260.

195. *Const.*, #64–79.

196. *Chron.*, 5:429–438, 529–531; 6:569–577, 701–702. See Gutiérrez de Caballos, "Bustamante," pp. 54–56.

197. See Ruiz Jurado, *Orígines del noviciado*, pp. 173–221.

198. Nadal, *Scholia*, pp. 163–164; *M Nadal*, 4:175.

199. *M Nadal*, 4:335.

200. See Duhr, *Geschichte der Jesuiten*, p. 529.

201. Ibid., p. 533.

202. *Const.*, #64–79; *M Nadal*, 5:376–388.

203. See de Dalmases, "Esortazioni Laínez," pp. 167–168. See also *M Nadal*, 5:383.

Conclusion

1. *M Xav.*, 1:26.
2. *FN*, 1:580.
3. *P Co.*, 2:510.
4. Nadal, *Orat. Obs.*, #493.
5. *FN*, 1:587–588. See also *Chron.*, 3:61.
6. *Chron.*, 1:10.

Index

Borghese, Marcantonio, 316

Borja, Francisco de, St., 10, 72, 107, 127, 140, 203, 233, 346, 361; and Inquisition, 64, 313, 318–319; on preaching, 99; on prayer, 164; on death, 175–176; on seminaries, 237; on German situation, 275–276; on crisis, 331

Brandolini, Aurelio, 104

Brazil, 53–54, 60, 76–79, 121, 125, 130, 136, 151–152, 157, 159, 181, 187

Brecht, Levin, 225

breviary, 359

Briçonnet, Bishop Guillaume, 246

Broët, Paschase, 9, 32, 129, 145, 170, 274, 289, 308, 333

Bucer, Martin, 279, 280

bullfights, 267

Bustamante, Bartolomé de, 148, 319, 339–340, 357, 361

Cacciaguerra, Bonsignore, 152

Cajetan (Tommaso De Vio), 146–147, 248

Calvin, John, 4, 29, 121, 124, 150, 225, 280, 281

Campion, Edmund, St., 274

Canisius, Peter, St., 30, 201–202, 204, 272–276; on devout conversation, 111; and catechesis, 114, 115, 118, 121, 123–126, 150; on usury, 150; *Notae in lectiones*, 164; on Erasmus, 257–258, 259, 263; on Mary, 270; and Index, 314

Cano, Melchor, 292–293, 317–319, 329, 366–367

Carafa, Cardinal Oliviero, 248

Carafa, Giampietro. *See* Paul IV, Pope

Carlo Borromeo, St., 80, 82, 237

Carneiro, Melchor, 327–328

Carranza, Archbishop Bartolomé, 317–320, 368

cases of conscience. *See* casuistry

Castello, Castellino da, 116

casuistry, 1, 107, 144–147, 218. *See also* accommodation; rhetoric

Catarino, Ambrogio, 50, 173, 280, 314

catechism, 87–90, 115–126, 159; lectures on, 107, 119–120; by Juan de Avila, 116, 118, 126, 166; vow to teach, 117, 347; by Canisius, 123–125, 301–302; by Ledesma, 124, 270; by Auger, 124–125; by Eliano, 189; taught by novices, 362

Catherine, Queen of Portugal, 72, 130, 186

Catherine of Aragon, Queen, 33, 245

Catherine of Siena, St., 264, 358

Cervini, Marcello. *See* Marcellus II, Pope

Cesari, Ottavio, 307

Cesarini, Bishop Ascanio, 236, 295–296, 368

Cetina, Diego de, 140

chaplaincies, military, 168

chapters, 52–53

Charles V, Emperor, 23, 28, 75, 272, 273, 275, 279, 283, 289

chastity, 57–58, 295–296, 348

Chemnitz, Martin, 69, 280, 281

children, involvement in ministries, 60, 101–102, 120–122, 151, 157, 198. *See also* theater

Christianitas, 18, 87–88, 90, 96, 125–126, 133, 166, 212, 254, 297, 327, 365

"Christian Liberty," 154, 338

Cisneros, Abbot García Jiménez de, 24, 46, 138

Cisneros, Cardinal Francisco Jiménez de, 116

classics: justification for, 100, 210, 256–257; use in schools, 215, 221, 241–242. *See also* humanism; rhetoric

Clavius, Cristoph, 234

Claysson, Robert, 224, 288

Clement VIII, Pope, 194

clergy, diocesan: ignorance of, 30, 203–204, 272, 277; Jesuits as different from, 73–74; training of, 202–204, 206, 232–239, 283, 324; marriage of, 309

clothing, Jesuit, 341–342

Cochlaeus, Johann, 272, 280

Codacio, Pietro, 36

Codure, Jean, 9, 32, 71, 132

Coimbra, 53, 94, 202, 217

Colet, John, 105

Collège de Montaigu, 29, 217

Collège de Sainte-Barbe, 29, 245

Collegio Germanico, 130, 234–236, 307, 355

Collegio Romano, 54, 113, 115, 127, 197–199, 205, 216, 233–234; and Aquinas, 228, 253; and Erasmus, 261; financial straits, 307; exemplar, 340–341

Cologne, 55, 202, 205, 238, 248, 273

Colonna, Vittoria, 34

commissaries, 12–13, 52, 63–68, 232, 262–263

common good, 5, 167, 168, 193

Communion: frequent, 50, 152–159, 170, 194–195; feast of Corpus Christi, 156–157; for condemned criminals, 178; in *Imitation of Christ*, 265; under both forms, 309

Compagnia di Gesù (name), 33–34, 69, 194–195. *See also* Jesuita

conciliar theory and conciliarism, 53, 292, 297, 303–305

confessional, 129, 138, 148, 339

confession (sacrament), 20, 83, 87–89, 136–152, 278; general, 24, 39, 137–139; and preaching, 85–86, 89, 96; and women, 140, 147–149, 152; Jesuit privileges, 143–144; and kings, 149; without pay, 149–150; interpreters and, 151–152; and Holy Orders, 157, 158; and confraternities, 194; in *Imitation of Christ*, 265; and pilgrimage, 271; alleged malpractices in, 295–296. *See also* casuistry

confraternities, 88, 116, 126, 167–168, 174, 175, 177–178, 187, 191, 192–199. *See also* Marian Congregations; works of mercy

Congregation, First General, 291–292, 308–309, 333–335; on catechism, 117; on sung masses, 160; on schools, 231; on Vulgate, 257; on *Constitutions*, 326; on prayer, 359; on architecture, 356

Congregation, Second General: on catechism, 117; on sung masses, 160; on schools, 232; on "poor boxes," 349; on architecture, 357; on prayer, 359; on novitiates, 361

congregations, general, 52–53

consolation (and desolation): importance, 19–20, 28, 41–43, 82–84, 365; and confession, 134, 139, 141, 147; and Communion, 153; for the dying, 176–177; for students in schools, 220; in *Imitation of Christ*, 265; in *spirituali*, 315

Constitutions, Jesuit. *See* Ignatius of Loyola

consueta ministeria, 5–6, 71, 84–90, 111, 200, 206, 276, 324–325, 364–365

consultation, 354–356. *See also* obedience

Contarini, Cardinal Gasparo, 34, 35, 315–316

Contarini, Isabella, 187

controversy, theological, 71, 96, 97, 108, 278–279, 281, 282, 302

conversation, devout, 80, 110–114, 140, 359

Cop, Nicholas, 29

Cornibus, Pierre de, 245

correspondence among Jesuits, 2, 9, 62–63, 333, 369

Cortesono, Gioseffo, 220, 227, 235

Coudret, Annibal du, 213–214

Coudret, Louis du, 291

criticism of church, 103–104

Cum infirmitas, 172–173

cursing, 197, 267

devil, 40, 42, 175–176, 225, 267–268

Devotio Moderna, 47, 138, 152, 164, 264–266. *See also Imitation of Christ*

dignity, human, 214, 250, 282. *See also* justification, doctrine of

Dionysius the Carthusian, 264

directories of the *Spiritual Exercises*, 132

director of retreat, 47, 131–132

discernment of spirits, 28, 41–43, 265. *See also* consolation (and desolation)

dismissals and defections, 56–59, 172, 228

distribution of membership, 54–55

doctors, Jesuit, 171–172

Doménech, Jerónimo, 12, 36, 48, 120, 128, 173, 182, 186, 203–204, 288

Dominic, St., 24, 66, 270, 362

Dominican *Constitutions*, 241

Dominican influence, 146–147, 247–251. *See also* Thomas Aquinas

Doria, Andrea, 222

drama. *See* theater

dying, ministry to, 174–178

ecclesiology, 297–306

Eguía, Diego de, 36, 288

Eguía, Esteban de, 36

Eguía, Miguel de, 27

Eliano, Giovanni Battista, 189

elite, relationship to, 21, 71–73, 127, 211–212, 240–241, 374–375

Emerson, Ralph, 274

Emmanuel-Philibert, Duke of Savoy, 291

emotions. *See* consolation (and desolation); rhetoric

England, 28, 274, 316

epikeia and dispensation, 354

Erasmus, 27, 28, 29, 42, 45, 50, 260–264, 314; *De modo orandi Deum*, 47, 163; *Ecclesiastes*, 98, 99, 263; and Bible, 105, 256–257; *Paraphrases*, 257, 263

Este, Duke Ercole d', 34, 238, 274, 325

Estella, Diego de, 98

Estienne, Robert, 258

Estrada, Francisco, 62, 94, 101, 103, 104, 272, 288

Ethiopia, 54, 300, 327–328

Eucharist. *See* Communion

Evangelicals, Italian. *See spirituali*

examination of conscience, 40, 87–88, 137, 145, 150, 151, 265. *See also* confession

exemption. *See* bishops and bishoprics

exorcisms. *See* possession, diabolical

Exponi nobis, 345

Exposcit debitum, 5. *See also* Formula of the Institute

Farnese, Cardinal Alessandro, 36, 171, 191, 357

Farnese, Ottavio, 71, 191

fasting. *See* penances, practice of

Fathers of the Church, 99, 176, 221, 259–260, 263, 358. *See also* Augustine (Augustinianism)

Favre, Pierre, Bl., 9, 29–30, 32, 35, 201, 243, 272, 273; and discernment of spirits, 43; on reform, 82, 286–287; on consolation, 83; on confession, 139, 142; and confraternities,

Japan, 9, 30, 60, 76–78, 195

Jay, Claude, 9, 32, 34, 107, 169, 201, 275; and training of clergy, 202–203, 324; at Trent, 243, 273, 324, 365

Jerusalem, 16, 24, 25–27, 29, 32, 34, 35, 70

Jesuita, 69. *See also* Compagnia di Gesù (name)

Jews (and New Christians), 188–192, 236, 294; Jewish Jesuits, 10, 31, 189–190, 224, 320

John III, King of Portugal, 30, 71, 72, 149, 201, 202, 217, 300, 312, 327, 330, 331, 332, 365

Juana of Austria, Princess, 75, 318

Juan de Avila, St., 99, 116, 118, 120, 121, 126, 166, 293, 318

Julius III, Pope, 5, 144, 191, 192, 202, 234, 275, 306, 366

justification, doctrine of, 108–109, 155, 247, 281–282, 293. *See also* nature and grace

"just war," 277

Kessel, Leonard, 101, 205

Laínez, Diego, 9, 30–31, 293, 308–309, 334; as theologian, 35, 201, 243, 247, 252–253, 277–278, 365; narrates founding, 65; and preaching, 96, 98–99, 103, 104; and sacred lectures, 107, 108, 110; on usury, 150; at Trent, 243, 303–305, 324–326; on papacy, 303–306; and Carranza, 318–319

Landini, Silvestro, 93, 95, 96, 127, 129, 169–170, 195, 312

Lanoy, Nicolaus de, 97

Lara, Don Antonio Marique de, 23

La Storta, vision at, 34

Lateran Councils: Fourth, 35, 74, 135, 156, 172; Fifth, 143, 245, 249

Laurent, Thomas, 248

Laurentano, Michele, 220, 235–236

lay brothers. *See* temporal coadjutors

lectures, sacred, 104–110, 119–120, 145–147

Ledesma, Diego de, 10, 124, 125, 146, 150

Lefèvre d'Etaples, Jacques, 246

Leunis, Jan, 197–198

Lippomano, Andrea, 205, 256

Loarte, Gaspar de, 115, 189, 267, 313, 314, 367; and catechesis, 118, 120; on confession, 139, 141, 150; on Communion, 153; on prayer, 163; on death, 175–176; on reading the Bible, 258; on church, 297–298

Lombard, Peter, 27, 337

Loreto, Holy House at, 270, 271

Louvain, University of, 101, 124, 202, 250, 272, 313

Ludolph of Saxony (the Carthusian), 24, 46, 69, 264

Luther, Martin, 9, 76, 105, 108, 116, 119, 121, 123, 225, 278–279, 373. *See also* justification, doctrine of; Reformation, Protestant

Macropedius, Georgius, 225

Madrid, Alonso de, 46

Madrid, Cristóforo de, 10, 96, 154–155, 312, 314

Mainardi, Agostino, 274

Mainz, University of, 201, 238

Mair (Major), John, 247

Maldonato, Juan de, 259

Manare, Olivier, 288

manifestation of conscience. *See* consultation

Manresa, 4, 25, 41, 65, 101, 128, 152, 249, 264

Marcellus II, Pope, 43, 201, 306, 322–323

Margaret of Austria, 71, 191

Mariana, Juan de, 233–234

Marian Congregations, 196, 197–199, 220, 226, 241

marriage, 79, 180–181, 183–185; of clergy, 309

Martin, Gregory, 97–98, 156, 184, 357

Martínez Guijeño, Juan. *See* Silíceo, Archbishop of Toledo

Mary, veneration of, 197–199, 266, 270. *See also* Hours of Our Lady, Book of; rosary

mass, 162, 164, 340

Mazurier, Martial, 243, 246

meals, 342–343, 358–359

Medici, Duke Cosimo dei, 231

mediocridad, 249, 336, 349–350, 370, 371

Meditationes vitae Christi, 46, 264

Melanchthon, Philipp, 258, 279, 280

Mercurian, Everard, 11, 288, 374

Messina, school at, 201–204

Miani, Gerolamo, St., 186. *See also* Somascans

Michelangelo, 34, 177, 356, 358, 367

military imagery, 34, 45, 69, 352

ministries: list of, 5–6; as self-definition, 18–19, 22; programs of, 84–90. *See also* "help of souls"

miracles, 269

Miró, Diego, 132, 149, 259–260, 288, 312, 331–332

mission. *See* "Fourth Vow"; mobility; pilgrim and pilgrimage

missions to countryside, 126–127

mobility, 15, 73, 239, 265. *See also* "Fourth Vow"; pilgrim and pilgrimage

modus parisiensis, 203, 215–227, 245

monks, Jesuits as different from, 67–68, 299

Monte, Giammaria. *See* Julius III, Pope

Montes pietatis, 168

Montserrat, 24–25, 39, 46, 138, 152

Plautus, 225
Poissy, Colloquy of, 281
Polanco, Juan Alfonso de, 6–7, 9–11, 63, 247, 334–335, 375–376; and *Constitutions*, 7, 335, 352, 360; *Breve directorium* (confession), 114, 141, 142–143, 173; catechism by, 120; directory for *Exercises*, 132; *Methodus* (dying), 176–178
Poland, 207, 274
Pole, Cardinal Reginald, 34, 316, 317
Politi, Ambrogio. *See* Catarino, Ambrogio
Ponce de la Fuente, Constantino, 116, 118
pope, vow to obey. *See* "Fourth Vow"
Porta, Giacomo Della, 357
Portugal, province of, 31–32, 52, 54, 59, 72, 188, 329–333. *See also* John III, King of Portugal
possession, diabolical, 267–268
Possevino, Antonio, 125, 189, 232, 264, 291
Postel, Guillaume, 57
poverty, 32, 44, 66, 149, 219, 240, 348–351, 372. *See also* benefices; professed houses
Prádanos, Juan de, 140, 312
Prague, school at, 61, 207
Prat, Bishop Guillaume du, 288, 290, 291
prayer, 47–48, 68, 162–164, 264, 359–360. *See also Spiritual Exercises*
preaching, 66, 85, 87–88, 91–104, 323; and conversation, 111; by students, 120, 222–223; and confession, 139–140; to prostitutes, 179–180; to Jews, 191; drama as, 224; in Jesuit houses, 358. *See also consueta ministeria;* rhetoric; Word of God
predestination, 50, 84
priesthood. *See* Holy Orders
printing press, 114–115
prisoners, 167–168, 173–174, 177–178
privileges, pastoral. *See* bishops and bishoprics
Probabilism, 145
professed houses, 15, 201, 206, 351, 356. *See also* poverty
professed members. *See* grades of membership
prostitutes, 178–185; daughters of, 187–188
provinces, 52–53
Pseudo-Dionysius the Areopagite, 48–49, 251–252, 269
punishment of students, 230

Quadros, Antonio de, 336
Quarant' ore, 93

Ramírez, Juan, 99, 103, 104, 146, 224
recruitment and admission, 34, 55–56, 60, 80–82. *See also* novices and novitiates
Reformation, Protestant, 16–17, 29, 49, 60, 70–71, 76, 207, 225, 231, 272–283. *See also*

Calvin, John; controversy, theological; Luther, Martin
"reform of the church," 17–18, 284–287, 303–306, 321–327, 369
Regensburg, Diet of, 29, 246, 272, 311, 315
Regimini militantis ecclesiae. See Formula of the Institute
relics, 266, 269
religious life, 66–68
Renée, Duchess of Ferrara, 274
retreat houses, 129–130
rhetoric, 96–100, 145, 253–256, 260. *See also* accommodation; humanism; preaching
Ribadeneira, Pedro de, 25, 36, 288, 342; and Ignatius, 95, 116, 180, 279; and Jews, 189; and schools, 205, 209, 213; and Morone, 316; and *Constitutions*, 336, 341
Ribera, Francisco de, 259
Ricci, Matteo, 342
Rodrigues, Simão, 9, 31–32, 34, 52, 72, 149; and crisis in Portugal, 31–32, 308–309, 329–334
Rodriguez, Cristóbal, 125
Rodriguez, Cristóforo, 312
Rome, 10–12, 16, 35–36, 54, 171; University of, 35, 201, 218, 238, 243, 247; and training of clergy, 54, 236; vice-ridden, 103, 323; opposition in, 295–296; as exemplar, 341. *See also* Collegio Romano
rosary, 270, 278, 360, 361
Rosati, Francesco, 187
rules of the Society, 64, 335, 337–340, 361

Sá, Manuel de, 259
Sá, Mem de, 130
Sadinha, Bishop Pedro Fernandes, 78, 151, 159
saints, veneration of, 246, 266, 268–271, 281
Salamanca, University of, 28, 55, 249
Salmerón, Alfonso, 9, 30–31, 58, 98, 243, 247–248, 274; and New Testament, 107, 108–109, 110, 259, 281; on publishing books, 114, 364; and Trent, 243, 304, 324–326, 365; on Erasmus, 263–264; on Morone and Carranza, 316, 319; and Rodrigues, 332; and Bobadilla, 333–334
Savonarola, Girolamo, 105, 262, 314
scholasticism, 7, 15, 30, 31, 83, 99–100, 109, 110, 145, 146–147, 217, 226, 244–253, 265. *See also* Aristotle; Bonaventure, St.; Nominalism; Thomas Aquinas
schools, 15–16, 80, 90, 115, 197–199, 200–242, 290–291, 374–375. *See also* classics; Collegio Germanico; Collegio Romano; humanism; *modus parisiensis;* punishment of students; Seminario Romano; theater

sciences, 226, 241–242
seminaries, diocesan. *See* clergy, diocesan
Seminario Romano, 161, 236–237, 295
Sens, Council of, 49
Seripando, Girolamo, 173
Silíceo, Archbishop of Toledo, 43, 189, 292, 294–295, 329, 367, 368
simony, 305–306
slave-taking raids, 168
Soares, Cipriano, 241
socioeconomic origins of the Jesuits, 59–61, 209, 296
Sodalities of Our Lady. *See* Marian Congregations
Soldevilla, Antonio, 58
Somascans, 51, 159, 186
Sore, Jacques, 60
Soto, Domingo de, 243, 249
Spain, 52, 53, 54, 59, 72, 188–190, 292–295, 317–319. *See also* Philip II, King of Spain
spiritual coadjutors. *See* grades of membership
spiritual counseling, 47, 140
Spiritual Exercises, 4, 25, 32, 37–50, 87–90, 127–133, 163–164, 255, 266–267, 292–293, 360, 362, 372–374, 376; important individuals who made them, 29, 31, 35, 130, 243, 246, 272; "Contemplation to Obtain Love," 40, 45–46, 48, 68, 84, 165, 250, 360, 370; "Kingdom of Christ" and "Two Standards," 40, 44–45, 69, 266; "Rules for Thinking with the Church," 49–50, 84, 104, 226, 244, 253, 260, 261, 266, 297, 321; Fourteenth "Preliminary Observation," 43–44; Fifteenth "Preliminary Observation," 43, 373; Eighteenth "Preliminary Observation," 85, 87–88, 128; Nineteenth "Preliminary Observation," 129. *See also* consolation (and desolation); discernment of spirits
spirituali, 34, 286, 315–317, 320
Stella, Tommaso, 193
Sturm, Johannes, 217–218
superstitions, 96, 266, 267–268
syphilis, 33, 166, 179, 194

Tauler, Johann, 30, 264
Tellier, Jean, 174
temporal coadjutors, 60–61, 77, 79–80, 101, 357. *See also* grades of membership
Terence, 225, 228, 262
Teresa of Avila, St., 140, 147, 259, 312
Texeda, Juan, 322
theater, 221–225, 242
Theatines, 51, 68–69, 81–82, 152, 306–307
Thomas Aquinas, 13, 28, 146, 153, 155, 158, 228;

theology of, 226, 242, 247–251, 253, 370. *See also* justification, doctrine of; nature and grace
titles, 344
Toledo, Francisco de, 147, 189–190, 233, 249, 259, 320, 368
"tones," 100
Torres, Bartolomé, 171
Torres, Cosme de, 77
Torres, Miguel de, 228, 331
Trent, Council of, 17, 73–74, 321–327, 333–334; on lectures, 104; on confession, 136–137, 140, 142; on religious orders, 143; on Eucharist, 156; on seminaries, 232–233, 234, 237–238; on justification, 246, 250, 282; on Vulgate, 257; on papal reform, 303–305; on confirmation of the Society, 325–326
Trinity, 266, 360
Tristano, Giovanni, 357
Truchsess von Waldburg, Cardinal Otto, 295, 324
Tucci, Stefano, 225

universities, Jesuits teaching at, 201–202, 215–216, 238, 243
usury, 96, 150

Valdés, Archbishop Fernando de, 317
Valencia, University of, 55, 202, 203, 248
Valla, Lorenzo, 256
Valladolid, University of, 31
Vázquez, Dionisio, 140
Vega, Juan de, 72, 122, 125, 173, 180
Velázquez de Cuéllar, Juan, 23
Velliard, Pierre, 29
Venice, 1, 32–33, 148, 158, 161, 166
Vermigli, Peter Martyr, 281, 311, 315
Vignola, Giacomo da, 357
Villanueva, Archbishop Tomás de, St., 196
Villanueva, Francisco de, 194
Viola, Giambattista, 262, 351
Vitoria, Francisco de, 249
Vitoria, Juan Alfonso de, 132
Vives, Juan Luis, 262
vocation, Jesuit, 44–45, 65–68, 157–159. *See also* "apostles" ("apostolic"); "Fourth Vow"; way of proceeding
Vulgate, 257–258, 263

Wauchope, Robert, 246, 251
way of proceeding, 8, 11, 287, 296, 329, 364, 370–375; and prayer, 48; and schools, 207, 227, 242; and accommodation, 255–256; and Inquisitions, 312, 320; and reform, 328; and

poverty, 349; and obedience, 355; and architecture, 357

weapons, students with, 229

Wied, Archbishop Hermann von, 273

Wilhelm IV, Duke of Bavaria, 274

Wischaven, Cornelius, 172, 204, 268, 273, 360

witches, 267

women, 75–76; and "fishing," 113; and *Spiritual Exercises*, 128–129, 132–133; and confession, 140, 147–149, 152; as counselors, 158; and confraternities, 174, 195–197; comforting the dying, 178; helping prostitutes, 180, 185, 187; and Jews, 191; Jesuits too familiar with, 293–294. *See also* prostitutes; daughters of prostitutes

Word of God, 91, 101–104, 110–111, 133, 170. *See also* Bible

works of mercy, 86–89, 95, 119, 121, 150, 165–199, 208

Worms, Diet of (1540), 246, 272

Xavier, Francis, 9, 30, 52, 70, 76–77, 245, 358; and catechesis, 115, 118–119, 120; and confession, 139, 140, 148

Zaccaria, Antonio Maria, St., 152